MAYWOOD PUBLIC LIBRARY

3 12 6 93

W9-BLF-839

CAREER OPPORTUNITIES IN THE ENERGY INDUSTRY

ALLAN TAYLOR AND JAMES ROBERT PARISH

Foreword by
JEFF FULMER

☑Checkmark Books®
An imprint of Infobase Publishing

Maywood Public Library
121 S. 5th Ave.
Maywood, IL 60153

To the Memory of
Charles Woolsey Cole (1906–1978)
Educator, College President, U.S. Ambassador
and
Katharine Bush Salmon Cole (1907–1972)
his lovely and loving wife

Career Opportunities in the Energy Industry

Copyright © 2008 by Allan Taylor and James Robert Parish

All rights reserved. No part of this book may be reproduced or utilized in any form or by any means, electronic or mechanical, including photocopying, recording, or by any information storage or retrieval systems, without permission in writing from the publisher. For information contact:

Checkmark Books
An imprint of Infobase Publishing
132 West 31st Street
New York NY 10001

Library of Congress Cataloging-in-Publication Data

Taylor, T. Allan.
    Career opportunities in the energy industry / by Allan Taylor and James Robert Parish ; foreword by Jeff Fulmer.
        p. cm.
    Includes bibliographical references and index.
    ISBN-13: 978-0-8160-6916-3 (hardcover)
    ISBN-10: 0-8160-6916-6 (hardcover)
    ISBN-13: 978-0-8160-6917-0 (pbk.)
    ISBN-10: 0-8160-6917-4 (pbk.)
    1. Energy industries—Vocational guidance. I. Parish, James Robert. II. Title.
    TJ163.2. T3485 2006
    621.042023—dc22   2007034205

Checkmark Books are available at special discounts when purchased in bulk quantities for businesses, associations, institutions, or sales promotions. Please call our Special Sales Department in New York at (212) 967-8800 or (800) 322-8755.

You can find Ferguson on the World Wide Web at http://www.fergpubco.com

Cover design by Takeshi Takahashi

Printed in the United States of America

VB Hermitage 10 9 8 7 6 5 4 3 2 1

This book is printed on acid-free paper and contains 30 percent post-consumer recycled content.

CONTENTS

FOREWORD

by Jeff Fulmer

The energy industry and its career opportunities are certainly nothing new. Excavations in Britain suggest coal was mined and used during the Stone Age. Natural gas was produced and transported through bamboo pipelines over 2,500 years ago in China. Petroleum was used by the Babylonians in making asphalt for building their walls and towers, and evidence suggests that petroleum wells were drilled during the fourth century in China. It wasn't until the mid-19th century that petroleum wells were drilled in North America, and a few decades later, Thomas Edison developed a practical electric light that kicked off the electric power industry.

* * * *

I remember being 10 years old and traveling into the countryside with my dad to see a construction site. Standing on the lip of a massive hole in the ground full of bulldozers, scrapers, and several workers, I was told it was the early stages of a nuclear power plant. I had no idea what a nuclear power plant was, but the scale of the operation made a lasting impression. A few years later I became increasingly fascinated by geology and exploration. When applying to college I followed Mark Twain's advice by setting out to make my vocation like a vacation, soon landing in the oil and gas industry.

Going quickly into debt as an out-of-state student at the Colorado School of Mines in Golden, I happily accepted summer employment as an oilfield laborer in middle-of-nowhere, western North Dakota. The oil and gas industry boom that had begun in the late 1970s was going full-tilt and finding a place to stay was no easy task. Rents were outrageous! I was quick to sign papers on a 13'×10' windowless concrete room located in the basement of a tavern (below the dance floor). As a roustabout and well pumper, I turned wrenches and valves, measured tank fills, and calculated volumes of produced oil and brine-water. Wells under my responsibility were producing over 4,000 barrels of oil per day and prices were peaking in 1981. Activity was all around, the air (or wind as the case may be in North Dakota) was thick with excitement, people were friendly, the pay was good, and I was irreversibly hooked.

My love affair continued the next summer in San Antonio, Texas, but this time in an office setting. I was exposed to geologists, geophysicists, petroleum engineers, landmen, and other professional and support staff. I knew something about field operations, the associated colorful language, and how to clean the oil off my hands, but I had not a clue on how to deal with office politics, an inescapable aspect of any professional career. Office indoctrination gave me the chance to put some college curriculum to work, engage in intriguing studies, go to fancy lunches with service representatives, and generally grow professionally before completing my undergraduate education and accepting my first permanent position in Bakersfield, California.

The oil and gas industry explores, develops, produces, transports, refines (or processes), markets, and delivers its products globally. The major infrastructure involved includes offshore drilling and production platforms, ocean tankers, pipelines, refineries, natural gas processing plants, storage tanks, pumps, compressors, and marketing centers. Each day the world consumes 85 million barrels of oil and 275 billion cubic feet of natural gas, with an appetite growing every year. As an oil and gas industry professional you're expected to satisfy this thirst while steering clear of attractive drilling sites that are environmentally and/or politically off-limits.

Coming to work in the exploration and production (called the upstream) end of the business, I worked on teams that focused on either maximizing production from existing oil and gas fields or exploring for new ones. At the time, geologists and geophysicists created maps by hand using pencil and paper or contouring with flexible crepe tape on top of sepias or mylar (drafting terms familiar to only us beyond-40 folk). The engineering work in the early 1980s still revolved around manual calculations using handheld calculators, or archaic software programs loaded on corporate mainframes and accessible only through cumbersome dumb terminals that had a habit of keeping you in the office all night.

Lucky for geoscientists and petroleum engineers entering the field today, user-friendly PC programs and workstations pound out 3-D subsurface renderings and pressure transient calculations and make you look smarter than you really are when being reviewed by the boss for bonus consideration. Automation has benefited everyone else involved as well, from the landmen (Note: women working in the land profession have a disdain for being called landwomen) conducting lease title research in the county courthouse, to the administrators ensuring landowner revenue is properly distributed, to geographic information systems (GIS) specialists making eye-popping digital maps.

There are plenty of jokes contrasting geologists with engineers, where engineers are portrayed as uncreative, calculation-centric individuals. Truth be told, petroleum engineering conducted in the upstream industry is highly speculative and requires a good deal of creativity and ingenuity. Whether a petroleum engineer or a geoscientist, you have to enjoy risk-taking. Imagine accurately describing a large Persian rug hidden from your view by a dining room table. The only information you're given are fiber fragments obtained by drilling through the table with a long extension bit attached to a cordless drill. A typical oilfield might be 10 square miles, and each well you locate for your company provides a six-inch diameter sampling of the reservoir. Don't worry, you're only spending several hundred thousand or several million dollars per well. What are a few dry holes anyway? An exploratory wildcat's chance of success is generally 5 to 35 percent, and making drilling recommendations as a new hire can be both exciting and intimidating. Lower-risk opportunities (in-fill drilling, production optimization) are also plentiful, but rewards can be proportionally reduced. In managing your energy career, make sure you span the risk spectrum from low to high, and don't spin your wheels too long on work assignments that are not challenging.

As a green college graduate, I started out working older, existing oilfields in California's San Joaquin Valley. The goal was to increase production by drilling new wells and optimizing those already drilled. Detailed subsurface mapping, reservoir engineering studies, and geophysical surveys all contributed to successful placement of new wells. Many a night I was in the oilfield overseeing logging crews making measurements up and down a well or working with coring crews retrieving intact rock cylinders from the well. (These logs and cores are interpreted to determine reservoir boundaries, rock types, and productive potentials that justify recommendations to management either to double their investment by completing the well or to call it quits and plug and abandon the well.)

Most professions in the oil and gas industry will have you spending appreciable time in the field during your formative years, and, in building your expertise and overall usefulness, you'll be glad you did. Just be leery of taking directions late at night from someone over the phone telling you to drive down the gravel road until you see the drilling rig, finishing with: "You can't miss it."

* * * *

The entire energy industry workforce is aging. Opportunities are ripe for new college graduates and young professionals with just a few years of experience under their belt. In the United States, the baby boomers are starting to enter retirement. Technology-driven industries today are typically populated by workers in their mid-20s to 30s, and the short supply of these folks in most energy fields presents a truly scary scenario. As boardrooms seek to envision their future, their seasoned corporate workforce is being depleted by retirements and no one is around to fill the professional gap. Enter you, a college-educated, motivated individual. They want you and they want you now, and, for at least for the next several years, you'll enjoy negotiating jobs and salaries with a leverage that most new hires in many industries can only dream about. (The world's reliance on oil, gas, coal, and electric power will evolve and, maybe, modify, but it is not going to disappear in the next several decades.)

Nuclear energy has seen dramatic shifts from the building and hiring frenzy of the 1970s, when it was viewed as a solution to the energy crisis, to the severe downturn of the 1980s, due to public fears of perceived dangers and concerns about high construction costs impacting consumer bills. The United States produces approximately 20 percent of its electric power from nuclear reactors, and as price spikes in coal, oil, and gas are felt, renewed support for nuclear power plant construction is rising. Nuclear generation also provides a carbon-free source of power that doesn't contribute to greenhouse gas emissions and is essential in powering naval vessels that need to be at sea for long periods without refueling.

The renewable and alternative energy business is bustling also, partially supported by major energy companies that have diversified their portfolios to embrace non-conventional energy and partially by upstarts being led by forward-thinking entrepreneurs. Energy independence and security sounds like a lofty goal, but technologies and financial incentives are falling into place. Passive solar, geothermal heat pumps, and other energy efficient technologies are reducing energy consumption in retrofitted buildings by 40 to 80 percent. Centralized energy generation and transmission is giving way to electric power micro-grids that continue functioning during any regional blackout. Long-haul transport of crude oil and refined petroleum products is slowly giving way to small-scale oil generation and refining facilities. Consider what Brazil has accomplished since the 1973 oil embargo. With its sugarcane-based fuel, Brazil has created a viable alternative to gasoline that is available at over 29,000 gas stations from Rio to the Amazon. In conjunction with its offshore conventional oil discoveries, Brazil is now claiming true energy independence.

Whether you want to work to maximize the efficiency of thin-film solar panels, design and develop wind farms, harvest landfill natural gas, turn soybean and switchgrass into biodiesel, or convert wastewater into electricity, your technical expertise is needed. Renewable and alternative energy business plans have become more and more appealing in light of elevated commodity prices. These focus fields have the added advantage of moving society away from conventional energy dependencies. Some of these ships will sail and others will take on water as the competitive selection process plays out. Your challenge is to acquire long-term marketable skills in the right fields.

Like the stock market, energy industries ebb and flow, companies come and go, and ultimately your greatest security resides within yourself. So how does the career toolbox that you're building look? Is it stamped from a mold that has widespread applicability? Is it niche focused, or is it a set of atypical credentials? All have their advantages and disadvantages. All are able to provide fulfillment and can take you to the top of your profession. In deciding what's best for you, try thinking of your career as mastering the culinary arts. First master the slicing and dicing, the sauces, and the basic recipes. Learn to do them consistently, efficiently, and in your sleep (similar to a 5:00 A.M. short-order cook). Next, work on specialization to set you apart from your peers. Spend time working beside successful chefs, perfecting such dishes as electric power transmission le foie gras, long-wall mining cannelloni, heavy oil extraction pad thai, or biodiesel falafel. Never stop reading your professional journals and studying pertinent Internet resources, and stay abreast of technical advancements both in and out of your areas of specialization. Advance your project management skills and do everything in your power to understand people and how to effectively interact with and manage them in a work environment. In gaining your professional training, some schools are better known than others and may help you land your first industry job, but ultimately your success will be based on what you can do with your toolbox of knowledge and skills.

* * * *

I benefited from working in both large and small companies. After spending six years working for large companies and receiving the dividends of formal training, multidisciplinary team participation, and exposure to diverse projects and technologies, I jumped off. I was looking to be a bigger fish in a smaller pond, to obtain experience on how to run a company instead of continuing to run well within a company. Some thought I was crazy and accused me of throwing away big company security (there's no such thing) for small

company uncertainty. At the time my professional network didn't extend to the East Coast where I was looking to move and no one admitted that they were hiring over the phone, However, I found that by asking prospective employers for only 20 minutes of their time and paying my own travel to the meeting, a lot could be accomplished. Two of these four 20-minute discussions turned into full-fledged job interviews and, in turn, employment offers.

Into the frying pan I went. I was granted responsibilities that had dramatically more impact on the potential success of my employer than when I was working for a large company. Reporting to an entrepreneur (who liked to say, "Strap on your seatbelt, we're going for a ride"), instead of a corporate manager, allowed me to add yet other tools to my career toolbox. Over the next decade I was fortunate to play key roles in expanding a small natural gas exploration and production company into the largest company of its type in the eastern United States. When the firm was later bought out, the skills I had acquired over the years gave me the foundation I needed to jointly start a company, seek financing, and separately engage in all types of energy industry consulting.

The post 9/11 environment has presented fresh opportunities for energy experts to be of tremendous service in analyzing and protecting infrastructures. A job well done for me today is not measured just by a financial bottom line but a satisfaction that is unlike any other I've enjoyed.

Keep on adding to your toolbox, and wherever your career pursuits take you in the energy industry, I wish you the full extent of professional satisfaction.

Jeff Fulmer holds an M.S. in Petroleum Engineering from the University of Southern California and a B.S. in Geological Engineering from the Colorado School of Mines. He has worked in the oil and gas industry for over 20 years, spending the last few years leading a group of U.S. Department of Defense analysts engaged in critical infrastructure protection. He currently resides in historic Fredericksburg, Virginia, where he enjoys taking long walks with his three children, Rachel, Paul, and Everett.

INDUSTRY OUTLOOK

Energy is what people use to exist, to grow, and to make their lives easier. The energy sector of the United States economy produces, converts, and distributes fuels to produce heat, light, and propulsion. Oil, natural gas, and coal are utilized to make heat and electricity. Wind, flowing water, and sunlight are increasingly being converted into electricity. In addition, oil is refined to propel cars, airplanes, and industrial machines. To achieve all these goals, the companies who are producing, transporting, converting, and distributing these energy sources are supported by a variety of service firms, investors, equipment providers, and government regulators.

By all accounts, the energy sector will be the growth industry of the future. The U.S. Department of Energy estimates that the United States will need 44 percent more electricity by 2020. This country's digitally driven economy is expected to increase electricity demand by 30 to 35 percent by 2010. Today, computer and high-tech peripherals are estimated to account for 13 percent of all electricity usage. By 2020, they are expected to account for 25 percent. The Internet's soaring growth represents a significant energy demand that did not exist before the Internet boom in the mid-1990s. In addition, as the Internet evolves technologically to become eventually the standard telecommunications delivery system for a wide variety of informational, computational, and entertainment services, its energy requirements will only increase.

* * * *

The energy sector is divided between the exploration side (which includes coal, oil and gas, and nuclear in that its main fuel source is mined uranium) and the distribution side, which is the electric distribution business. The electric power business revolves around converting fuel to electricity to power plants and distributing that electricity to consumers. The economics of the two fields, and the regulations that govern them, are different from each other. Generally, individuals make their energy careers in one camp or the other, and there is little crossover between them. Natural gas is the only real bridge between these two sectors, in that it is extracted from the earth together with oil and is also a primary fuel for generating electricity.

Companies in the U.S. energy sector take in nearly $1 trillion in revenue annually, out of the $17 trillion earned by all U.S. businesses. Energy-related businesses employ

nearly 2.5 million people, or about 2 percent of the U.S. workforce, and far more than the banking or telecommunications sectors. Of the 2.5 million energy jobs in the United States, over 85 percent are blue-collar jobs (drivers, laborers, gas station attendants) or technical positions (such as repairpersons, oilrig laborers, plant and research technicians).

Electricity can be generated from a wide variety of fuels: natural gas, coal, uranium (nuclear power), oil, wind, water (hydroelectric power, tidal power), solar radiation (photovoltaic power, solar thermal power), volcanic heat (geothermal power), plant material (biomass power), or hydrogen (fuel cells). The mix of fuel sources for the generation of electricity varies greatly around the world reflecting each country's natural resource base as well as its politics. The United States obtains about half of its electricity from coal and most of the remainder from natural gas and nuclear power. Canada uses hydropower, while exporting its gas to the United States. Norway, also with plentiful water resources and no coal (but plenty of offshore oil), gets all of its power from hydroelectric stations. France has chosen to obtain the vast majority of its electricity generation from nuclear power as a clean alternative to fossil fuels (such as coal or gas), and it has managed to control the costs of nuclear plants in order to enjoy cheap electricity. Saudi Arabia, sitting on top of the largest oil reserves in the world, uses oil to generate most of its electric power, which makes the exploitation of its other major natural resource, the Sun, unattractive financially.

Electricity is most commonly generated by burning a fuel to boil water, and then, using the resultant steam (or, in some cases, hot combustion gas, or falling water) to spin a large magnet by spinning a turbine's protruding blades, creating an electric current. (There are also two types of electricity generation technologies that don't use a turbine at all: fuel cells that use a chemical reaction to produce electricity, and photovoltaic cells using sunlight to induce a chemical reaction.)

The generation of electricity is made more complex by several factors: its demand is extremely inelastic, in that consumers do not vary the amount of electricity they demand based on price (they always need to turn on the lights). In addition, electricity cannot be stored easily and, thus, must be produced as it is consumed. It cannot be routed to a destination as it flows along the path of least resistance regardless, and transmission losses of electricity are substantial, making it best to be produced relatively close to where it will be consumed. Power generation plants produce electric power, and high voltage bulk power transmission systems route the electric power to substations where transformers are used to step down the voltage to a lower voltage for distribution to commercial and residential users. Thus, electricity generated by power plants is fed into what is known as the grid, a 160,000-mile network of insulated copper wires. Within this complex, the jobs are highly varied, from power plant operators to electric line installers and repairers.

* * * *

The three most common industries in the exploration and production side of the energy sector are the coal, oil, and natural gas industries. While oil is the most critical fossil fuel for modern economies, coal is a more plentiful resource. Coal has a number of virtues as a fuel: it can be shipped via boats and railroads, it is easy to store, and it is easy to burn. Its main advantage over other fuel sources is that it is both cheap and plentiful. There are an estimated 1 trillion tons of recoverable coal in the world, by far the largest reserve of fossil fuel left on the planet. The United States, itself, is built upon thick seams of coal. Just as Saudi Arabia dominates the global oil market, the United States has the good luck of having more than 25 percent of the world's recoverable coal reserves— about 270 billion tons—buried within its borders (whereas western Europe has only 36 billion tons, and China has less that half as much as the United States). This means that the United States has a source of fuel to keep its factories running and its cities lit for a long time to come (coal is the major fuel source used in the generation of electricity).

The side effect of this bounty is that, politically, America has a big incentive to drag out any transition to other, cleaner forms of energy generation. In addition, coal is the dirtiest and most carbon-intensive of all fossil fuels—coal plants are responsible for nearly 40 percent of U.S. emissions of carbon dioxide, the main contributor to ozone depletion. To counteract this, there has evolved a technology that gasifies (produces a gas of) the coal before it is burnt, thus avoiding the discharge of carbon dioxide into the atmosphere. This process of gasification breaks down coal into its basic chemical constituents, producing a mixture of carbon monoxide, hydrogen, and other gaseous compounds, a process known as sequestration (separation and removal). This process also separates out sulfur (which can be extracted in a form that can be sold commercially), and nitrogen, which exists as ammonia and can be scrubbed from the coal gas by processes that produce fertilizers or other ammonia-based chemicals. However, the gasification processes presently being utilized are expensive.

The most economical method of coal extraction from coal seams depends on the depth and quality of the seams, and also the geology and environmental factors of the area to be mined. If coal seams are near the surface, the coal is commonly extracted by surface, or strip, mining. Underground mining has several methods (and specific types of jobs related to each one): longwall mining (utilizing a sophisticated machine with a rotating drum that moves mechanically back-and-forth across a wide coal seam, loosening the coal to fall onto a pan line that removes the coal from the work area), continuous mining (which utilizes a machine with a large rotating steel drum equipped with tungsten carbide teeth that scrape the coal from the seam, operating in a room and pillar system where the mine is divided into a series of 20- to 30-foot work areas, or rooms), conventional mining (which uses explosives to break up the coal seam, after which the coal is gathered and loaded onto shuttle cars or conveyors), and shortwall mining (which uses a continuous mining machine with movable roof supports, similar to longwall, and is used to shear coal panels 150–200 feet wide and more than a half-mile long). Modern mining personnel are highly skilled and well trained in the use of the complex instruments and equipment used in today's coal mining operations.

Oil and natural gas furnish about three-fifths of the energy needs of the United States. In addition, they constitute the raw materials for plastics, chemicals, medicines, fertilizers, and synthetic fibers. Formed by a similar geologic process, natural gas often is found in separate deposits and is sometimes mixed with oil. Finding, developing, and extracting oil and gas are the primary functions of the oil and gas mining and drilling industry. While some of this work is done by the large oil companies, more of it is done by independent contractors working within the mining sector of this industry.

Using a variety of methods, on land and at sea, small crews of specialized work personnel search for geologic formations that are likely to contain oil and gas. Sophisticated equipment and advances in computer technology have enhanced this exploration. Seismic prospecting and advanced software analyze areas explored, and new time-lapsed seismic technology tracking the movement of fluids over time has aided in the increased accuracy of present-day exploration. After the possible presence of oil is determined, an oil company selects a well site and installs a derrick—a tower-like steel structure—to support the drilling equipment. A hole is drilled deep into the earth until oil or gas is found (or the company abandons the effort as financially infeasible). Similar techniques are employed in offshore drilling, except that the drilling equipment is part of a steel platform that either sits on the ocean floor, or floats on the surface and is anchored to the ocean floor.

In rotary drilling (the most common kind), a rotating bit that is attached to a length of hollow drill pipes bores a hole in the ground by chipping and cutting rock. A stream of drilling mud (usually a mixture of clay, chemicals, and water) is continuously pumped through the drill pipe and through holes in the drill bit in order to cool the drill bit, plaster the walls of the hole to prevent cave-ins, carry crushed rock to the surface, and prevent blowouts by equalizing pressure inside the hole. More advanced directional or horizontal drilling techniques (used most commonly in offshore drilling operations) allow the drill bit to be turned so that drilling can continue at an angle of up to 90 degrees, enabling it to reach separate pockets of oil or gas. When oil or gas is found, the drill pipe and bit are pulled from the well, and metal pipe (casing) is lowered into the hole and cemented in place. The casing's upper end is fastened to a system of pipes and valves called a wellhead through which natural pressure forces the oil or gas into separation and storage tanks. If natural pressure is not sufficient to force the oil to the surface, pumps may be used. In some cases, water, steam, or gas may be injected into the oil-producing rock formation to improve the recovery process.

Crude oil is transported to refineries by pipeline, ship, barge, truck, or railroad. Crude oil cannot be used as a fuel itself because it contains such a broad spectrum of molecular size. To be practical as a fuel, a material must have known burning characteristics so that it can be matched with, and meet the specifications of, various burner systems. Natural gas usually is transported to processing plants by pipeline. While oil refineries may be many thousands of miles away from the oil producing fields, gas processing plants commonly are near the fields, so that impurities—water, sulfur, and natural gas liquids—can be removed before the gas is piped to customers.

With all its varied processes, the oil and natural gas industry offers a wide range of career choices. As the industry is driven by cutting-edge technology, its personnel need to have the technical expertise to handle its equipment and technology. While starter positions (such as oil rig roustabouts) may require only a high school degree, most jobs in the oil and natural gas industry require a college degree as well as extensive training. The oil and gas extraction industry employed about 316,000 wage and salary workers in 2004. Of these, only four in ten workers were employed directly by oil and gas companies. The rest worked as contractors in the support activities for the mining sector of the industry. Relatively few oil and gas extraction workers are in their teens or early 20s. About 56 percent of the workers in this industry are between 35 and 54 years of age. The industry employs many skilled workers other than those trained specifically for the industry—such as electricians, machinists, pipe fitters, and welders—to install and repair pumps, gauges, pipes, and other equipment. In addition, oil and gas companies need all of the other personnel of any large company—human resource personnel, public relations experts, lawyers, information technologists, administrative assistants, and a range of other occupations. Because of their highly technical and well-paid workforce, oil and gas companies are typically a good career choice for individuals in nearly any discipline.

One overriding problem faces the oil industry and, to a much lesser extent, the gas industry (which is less depleted than oil): When will oil run out, as there is a finite amount of oil and gas in the earth? Figuring out how much oil is left is a problematic exercise, as the oil supply is very difficult to measure. Oil supplies are categorized as (1) undiscovered oil; (2) possible reserves (discovered, with less than a 50 percent chance of being recovered); (3) probable reserves (discovered with greater than a 50 percent chance of being recovered); and (4) proven reserves (all recoverable). Estimates of supply currently hover around 1 trillion barrels of proven reserves and some 2 trillion more ultimately recoverable out of probable, possible, and yet-to-be-found deposits. Contrast that with the annual worldwide consumption (which is climbing) of 30 billion barrels. One element is certain: as oil supplies deplete, oil prices will increase. When oil prices increase, the cost of most everything one can buy increases, which forces consumption down, slows the economy, drives down employment, and lowers standards of living. Discovery of new oil fields peaked back in the 1960s, and oil production peaked for many countries (including the United States) as long ago as the 1970s. All of this raises the issue of making an adjustment in our energy marketplace and a smooth transition into an oil-less future as soon as possible.

* * * *

Nuclear power plants provide about 17 percent of the world's electricity. Some countries depend more on nuclear power for electricity than others do. France, for instance, has about 75 percent of its electricity generated from nuclear power. In the United States, nuclear power supplies about 15 percent of its overall electricity needs, but some states obtain more power from nuclear power plants than others. There are more than 400 nuclear power plants around the world, with more than 100 in the United States. The generation of electrical energy by a nuclear power plant makes use of heat to produce steam or to heat gases to drive turbogenerators. Thus, in its operation the nuclear power plant is similar to the conventional coal-fired power plant, except that the nuclear reactor is substituted for the conventional boiler as the source of the heat.

Nuclear power can come from the fission (splitting of the atom) of uranium, plutonium, or thorium, or the fusion of hydrogen into helium. Today, most fission is done with uranium, which is quite plentiful. The fission of an atom of uranium produces 10 million times the energy produced by the combustion of an atom of carbon from coal. Most nuclear power plants today use enriched uranium. Typically, the uranium is formed into pellets, and then arranged into long rods, and the rods are collected together into bundles. The bundles are then submerged in water inside a pressure vessel, which is the power reactor. An atom of U-235 (the common uranium isotope) fissions when it absorbs a neutron. The fission produces two fission fragments and other particles that fly off at high velocity. When they stop, the kinetic energy is converted to heat. When it is desired for more heat to be produced, the rods are raised out of the uranium bundle. To create less heat, the rods are lowered into the uranium bundle. The rods can also be lowered completely into the uranium bundle to shut the reactor down in the case of an accident or to change the fuel. The heat from the fuel rods is absorbed by the water in which they are immersed that, in turn, generates steam to drive the turbines that produce electricity. After about two years, enough of the U-235 has been converted to fission products and the fission products have built up enough so that the fuel rods must be removed and replaced with new ones. When fuel rods are removed from the reactor, they contain large quantities of highly radioactive fission products and are generating radioactive heat at a high rate. They are put in a large tank of water about the size of a swimming pool. There they become less radioactive as the more highly radioactive isotopes decay and generate less and less heat. The longer the spent fuel is stored like this, the easier it can be handled. However, many reactors have been holding spent fuel so long that their tanks are getting full. Companies must either send the rods off or build more tanks. Ideally, the fuel rods should then be chemically reprocessed. Reprocessing removes any leftover uranium and the plutonium that has been formed. However, the United States shut down its reprocessing plants during the 1970s and has not replaced them. (Britain, France, Belgium and Russia still continue to operate reprocessing plants, and the Japanese are building their own.) The fission products would then be put in a form for long-term storage. Many schemes for long-term storage have been devised, but lawsuits and political pressure have prevented any of them from being implemented in the United States. The decision not to reprocess was made on the grounds that if other countries could be persuaded not to reprocess, the likelihood of nuclear proliferation would be reduced, a forlorn hope because the economic advantages of reprocessing are so great. If reprocessing is not done, the economic benefit of plutonium is lost (plutonium is used instead of uranium in breeder reactors, which are more expensive to build, but produce about 100 times as much energy as do other reactors), and the spent fuel remains radioactive longer and has to be better guarded, because it contains plutonium (which is the material used in making atom bombs and other nuclear weaponry). As there are plenty of uranium reserves for now, it may not be economic to reprocess at present, provided the spent fuel remains available for later reprocessing or until mined uranium gets more expensive.

Compared with coal-fired power plants, nuclear power plants are extremely clean. A coal-fired power plant actually releases more radioactivity into the atmosphere than a properly functioning nuclear power plant. In addition, coal-fired plants release tons of carbon, sulfur, and other elements into the atmosphere. The major problem is the nuclear waste and what to do with it. Additionally, transporting nuclear fuel to and from plants poses some risk, although to date, the safety record in the United States has been exemplary. Nonetheless, these problems have largely derailed the creation of new nuclear power plants in the United States. However, there are strong advocates of nuclear power as an answer to the problems of using coal as a fuel source and the steady depletion of oil and gas reserves. (In the United States there is also the public reaction against being dependent upon foreign sources of oil from the volatile Middle East, tempered only by the public fear of a nuclear accident or theft of nuclear material.)

* * * *

Technology to use the forces of nature for doing work to supply human needs and desires is as old as the first sailing ship. There is a fundamental attractiveness to harnessing such forces at a time when humanity is becoming very conscious of the environmental effects of burning fossil fuels. Sun, wind, waves, rivers, tides, and the heat from radioactive decay in Earth's mantle as well as biomass are all abundant and ongoing, hence the term renewables. Only one, the power of falling water in rivers, has been significantly tapped for electricity so far, although wind may one day catch up. Solar energy's main human application has been in agriculture and forestry, via photosynthesis, and, increasingly, in being harnessed on a personal basis for home heating. Biomass (such as sugar cane residue) is burned where it can be utilized. Other types of renewables are still little used today, often due to the expense involved.

One problem in using renewable energy sources for electricity is the challenge of actually corralling them for that purpose. Apart from photovoltaic (PV) systems, the question arises on how to make them turn dynamos to generate the electricity. If it is heat that is being harnessed, such generating is done via a steam generating system. While the fundamental opportunity of renewables is their abundance and relatively widespread and worldwide occurrence, their basic problem is their variable and diffuse nature (e.g., the Sun is frequently covered by clouds and wind does not always blow), which makes the generation of electricity on a regular basis difficult.

Solar energy is readily harnessed for low temperature heat, and in many homes hot water units routinely utilize it. However, for electricity generation, solar power has a limited potential due to its input being interrupted by night and by cloud cover, which means that the generation inevitably has a low capacity. Also, there is a low intensity of incoming radiation and converting this to high-grade electricity is still relatively inefficient. Two methods commonly used are sunlight acting on photovoltaic cells to produce electricity. These can be readily mounted on buildings, but the cost per unit of electricity—at least ten times that of conventional sources—limits its potential to being applied on buildings where its maximum supply coincides with peak demand for electricity.

The other method is a solar thermal power plant, which has a system of mirrors to concentrate the sunlight onto an absorber, the energy then being used to drive turbines to produce electricity. Again, power costs are two to three times that of conventional sources. A potential main role for solar energy in the future will be that of direct heating where, with adequate insulation, heat pumps using a conventional refrigeration method can be used to warm and cool buildings with very little energy input other than from the Sun.

Many thousands of wind turbines are now operating in various parts of the world. This has been the most rapidly growing means of electricity generation in the last decade and provides a valuable supplement to conventional large-scale power stations. However, in practice, relatively few areas have significant prevailing winds, and, like solar energy, consumers often must depend on alternative power sources to cope with calmer periods. In addition, generation costs are greater than those for coal or nuclear, and allowing for backup capacity and electric grid connection complexities makes it about double. However, government policies in many countries ensure that power from wind turbine farms is able to be sold economically.

Hydroelectric power, using the potential energy of rivers, now supplies 17.5 percent of world electricity (99 percent in Norway as compared to 7 percent in the United States). Apart from those countries with an abundance of rivers, hydro capacity is normally applied to peak-load demand, because it can be so readily stopped and started. However, environmental considerations make such harnessing impossible in some cases. In practice, the utilization of stored water is sometimes complicated by demands for irrigation that may occur in conflict with peak electrical demands.

Hot underground steam (a geothermal power source) can be tapped and brought to the surface, and it may be used to generate electricity. Such geothermal sources are limited to certain areas in the world, such as New Zealand, the Philippines, the United States, and Italy. Another method is pumping water underground to parts of Earth's crust which are very hot and using the hot brine from these regions to create steam to run turbines.

Harnessing tides in a bay or estuary has been used in Europe (France and Belgium primarily), Canada, and Russia. The trapped water is used to turn turbines as it is released through the tidal barrage in either direction (tide coming in, or going out). Worldwide, this technology seems to have little potential, largely due to environmental constraints. However, placing freestanding turbines in major coastal tidal currents is an area of future potential.

An allied type of power source is the harnessing of sea wave motion, which might even provide more power than tides. Generators either coupled to floating devices or turned by air displaced by waves in a hollow concrete structure would produce electricity for delivery to land. However, numerous practical problems have frustrated progress, particularly damage from storms.

Another area is that of biomass sources. Growing crops of wood or using agricultural wastes to burn as fuel for generating electricity has some appeal. However, logistics frequently defeats its large-scale use, in that a lot of energy is required to harvest and move the crops to the power station, and for long-term sustainability, the resultant ash containing mineral nutrients must be returned to the land. In some places, sugar cane pulp is burned as a valuable energy source. It is projected that by 2030, biomass-fuelled electricity production will triple and provide 2 percent of the world's energy.

Unfortunately, at present, sun, wind, tides, and waves cannot be controlled to provide directly either continuous base-load electric power or peak-load electric power when it is needed. In practical terms, they are therefore limited to some 10 to 20 percent of the capacity of an electricity grid, and cannot be applied as economic substitutes for coal or nuclear power, however important they may become in particular areas (or in personal usages, such as home heating). Thus, they are contributors to the world's energy future, even if they are unsuitable (at least at present) for carrying the main burden of supply for generating electricity. As Steve Chu, the Director of the Lawrence Berkeley National Laboratory, stated in a question/answer interview (printed in the *APS-American Physical Society News,* Vol. 15, No. 11, in December 2006): "Both wind and solar are transient in nature. Photovoltaics need to achieve a factor of five or more lower cost before wide-scale deployment. The cost of wind-generated power is competitive with gas, but because it is a transient source, without efficient and cost effective energy storage, the base line will be nuclear power and coal in the near-term future. So you can put your pedal to the floor in sequestration (of carbon emissions from burning coal) and it's not closing the door to renewable sources."

If there were some way that large amounts of electricity from intermittent producers such as solar and wind could be stored efficiently and cost-effectively, the contribution of these technologies would be much greater. Thus, they present a challenge for future engineers, scientists, and technicians interested in these rapidly developing energy industries. Altogether, energy industries and their development and processes present some of the most challenging, diverse, and rewarding potentials for interested job-seeking individuals.

ACKNOWLEDGMENTS

First and foremost, we want to thank our editor, James Chambers, at Facts On File, Inc. Jim has been a concerned, enthusiastic, and unfailingly helpful editor, and his aid is gratefully acknowledged. We also want to thank our agent, Stuart Bernstein, for his help and suggestions on this project. In addition, we, of course, want to thank Jeff Fulmer for the informative and delightful foreword to this book.

Furthermore, we would like to thank the following individuals for their assistance with this project: Christopher Barnes, Virgil Barnes, James Cannon, Jeff Fulmer, Hugh Thompson, and Steven Whitney.

HOW TO USE THIS BOOK

Purpose

The 130 or so careers described in *Career Opportunities in the Energy Industry* make it one of the most inclusive directories of energy jobs available in a single volume. These careers are involved in a critical area of today's technological world. To a certain degree, whether our current society and environment survives may be dependent on the future development and usage of energy resources. The energy sector of the world economy is remarkably diverse, and covers a wide variety of energy sources, from coal to oil and natural gas, from wind to solar power. These energy sources are utilized to provide heat and to generate electricity and, thus, electricity distributors are a major component of the energy sector.

The purpose of *Career Opportunities in the Energy Industry* is to serve as a guide to the most common occupations within the industries that produce, convert, and distribute energy. By consulting this volume, high school and college students interested in a career in an energy industry can learn who does what within the superstructures of these industries. Those who are currently employed within an energy industry will also find the information contained in this book helpful as they expand and/or redefine their career paths.

In *Career Opportunities in the Energy Industry*, jobs are not merely summarized in a few paragraphs but are explained in detail, including duties, alternate titles, salary ranges, employment and advancement prospects (with a Career Ladder detailing typical routes to and from the position), prerequisites (including education and training, experience, and skills requirements), organizations to join, and helpful tips for entering the job arena under discussion. This volume is geared to assist both those seeking to start a career in any of these industries and those experienced members already working within the field who are looking to make career shifts or changes within their profession.

Many of the jobs detailed in this volume are available to individuals with appropriate education credentials (typically at least a high school diploma and often a bachelor's degree, or, for the more technical jobs, a more advanced degree) and from one to five or more years of experience. Job positions discussed in this volume cover entry- and mid-level posts and those that require more training and/or education, as well as more years of experience within their field.

Sources of Information

Research for this book includes the authors' interviews with professionals in various positions within energy industries, and facts, reports, surveys, and other data obtained from job data banks, professional guilds and associations, the federal government, and educational institutions.

The job descriptions provided are based on representative samples of actual job posts, employment documents, research studies, salary surveys, and tables of organization from many sources within the energy sector. Thus, the career descriptions detailed are not theoretical, but represent current job requirements and reflect the actual structure of jobs in all of these industries.

How the Book Is Organized

The job profiles in *Career Opportunities in the Energy Industry* are organized into six main sections: Energy Industry Engineers and Technicians (General), Coal Industry, Electric Power Industry, Nuclear Energy Industry, Oil and Natural Gas Industries, and Renewable Energy Industries. The Energy Industry Engineers and Technicians (General) section covers several job positions that are common to most of the energy industries, such as civil or mechanical engineers. The Coal Industry section has several subsections: Engineers and Scientists, Manual Labor Personnel, Semiskilled Personnel, and Supervisors and Support Personnel. The Electric Power Industry section has three similar subsections: Engineers and Scientists, Manual Labor Personnel, and Support Personnel. The Nuclear Energy Industry section, befitting the field's more complex nature, has five subsections: Engineers, Life and Physical Scientists, Manual Labor Personnel, Nuclear Power Plant Technicians and Operators, and Nuclear Research Technicians and Operators. The Oil and Natural Gas Industries section is subdivided into six subsections: Business Operators, Engineers and Scientists, Refining and Processing, Semiskilled Personnel, Skilled Personnel, and Support Personnel. Finally, the Renewable Energy Industries section, which covers discussion of biomass, geothermal, photovoltaic and solar, hydropower, and wind power industries, has two subsections of jobs endemic to all of these energy industries: Engineers and Scientists, and Manual Labor Personnel. This organization is designed to reflect the different aspects of each of these industries. The introduction, Industry Outlook, provides an overview of these related, but different, industries, and the career opportunities available in each of them.

While the careers discussed in this book are the most frequent job positions found within all these industries, job titles are not universally consistent and their definitions will vary and often overlap from setting to setting. While most of the job positions describe functions specific to each of the industries being discussed, many of the positions may overlap between them. For example, geologists work in the coal industry as well as the oil and natural gas industry and may be employed also by a geothermal exploration company. Each job description notes when there are opportunities for a position in other related areas.

The Job Profile

Each job profile starts with a Career Profile, a brief description of the position's major duties, any alternate job titles for the position, salary ranges, employment prospects, opportunities for promotion, and the job prerequisites insofar as education and training, job experience, special skills, and personality traits are concerned. A Career Ladder graphically illustrates a typical career path to and from the position described, including the positions below and above each job. The rest of the profile is in an extended narrative format with more detailed information on the job that contains the following:

- Position description, including typical major duties and responsibilities, and any optional duties that may or may not be part of the given job
- Salary ranges from entry-level to top earnings, including the factors (such as individual skills or geographic location) that often affect how much a particular position may pay, and indicating any minimum wage levels set by union/guild regulations
- Employment expectations or job forecast, indicating how difficult the post may be to obtain
- Possibilities and suggestions for advancement, and whether such work progression is unusually difficult
- Education required and any special training necessary for the particular job
- Whether any licensing or certification training may be required
- Necessary and/or useful experience, skills, and personal attributes that enhance the potential for success in the job
- Whether there are any union or guild requirements for holding the particular job and/or suggested professional associations related to the job that may be useful
- Tips and practical suggestions for obtaining that initial job in this job category

The Appendixes

Four Appendixes offer further resources for individuals seeking any of the more than 130 job positions described in *Career Opportunities in the Energy Industry*. Appendix I, "Educational Institutions," lists colleges, universities, and educational institutions in every state and the District of Columbia, which offer undergraduate degrees (four-year programs) in biochemistry, biotechnology, chemical engineering, civil engineering, clinical laboratory science, electrical and electromechanical engineering and technology, environmental engineering, geology, industrial engineering, materials engineering, mechanical engineering, mining and mineral engineering and technology, nuclear engineering, nuclear physics, petroleum engineering, physics, soil science, and water resource engineering, as well as other specialties, such as analytical chemistry, applied mathematics, atmospheric science, construction technology, electrical drafting/CAD/CADD, geophysics and seismology, hazardous materials technology, heavy equipment maintenance, hydrology, instrumentation technology, machine shop and machine tool technology, mathematical statistics and probability, pipefitting, power/electrical transmission technology, small engine mechanics, solar energy technology, surveying technology, and welding technology. The listing does *not* include every institution that offers courses or undergraduate degrees in various areas of energy-related subjects. (In addition, not included are such overlapping general majors, such as chemistry or biology, which most colleges/universities offer.) The listings provide each institution's address, telephone number, fax number, e-mail address, and Web site, as well as the major programs relevant to industries.

Appendix II, "Major Trade Periodicals and Other Publications," offers a useful resource list of magazines, newsletters, and directories concerned with energy interests and issues and technologies related to the energy industries in general. (Note that books are not included in this Appendix, but are part of the Bibliography.)

Appendix III, "Professional, Industry, and Trade Associations, Guilds, and Unions" lists professional and trade associations related to the various energy industries. For each entry, the address, telephone number, fax number, e-mail, and Web site are provided.

Appendix IV, "Useful Web Sites" offers a wide range of Internet resources in many categories that are useful for job searching, trade news and information, and networking, as well as a list of general search engines that will help in researching these industries.

A Glossary of terms relevant to all the energy industries includes technical terminology, buzzwords, and names used frequently in the industry. The Glossary is followed by a Bibliography, which includes sources utilized in researching this book. In those instances where online sources are cited, it may be necessary to check the particular Web site to determine whether new updates on the topic are now available. Also included with these sources is an expansive list of current useful books on careers in energy industries.

The Index provides a quick source for locating particular job titles (including cross-references to alternate job names), organizations cited in the text (but not in the Appendixes), and other relevant information appearing in the chapters of this volume.

Lastly, please keep in mind that the Internet is in a constant state of flux and Web sites sometimes change their Web address or, on occasion, cease to exist. If a URL stated in this book—each of which were verified as this volume was written—does not produce the desired Web site, it may be necessary to do a search engine query using the name of the Web Site to locate its new home.

ENERGY INDUSTRY ENGINEERS AND TECHNICIANS (GENERAL)

CIVIL ENGINEER

CAREER PROFILE

Duties: Plan, design, construct, operate and maintain structures utilized in the energy industry

Alternate Title(s): Structural Engineer

Salary Range: $40,000 to $90,000 or more

Employment Prospects: Fair

Advancement Prospects: Fair

Prerequisites:

Education or Training—Bachelor's degree in civil engineering required, with a strong background in mathematics and the physical sciences; master's degree (or higher) in civil engineering is recommended

Experience—Three or more years working with a consulting and/or engineering firm serving as a civil engineer or engineer-in-training; experience should include site testing and performing test data analysis

Special Skills and Personality Traits—Ability to identify, analyze, and solve problems; aptitude at computer-aided design (CAD) techniques and knowledge of other applicable engineering software; capable of being a team player but also functioning without supervision; excellent oral and written communication skills, with special emphasis on technical writing abilities; practical and creative, with a willingness to accept responsibility

Special Requirements—Certification as a licensed Professional Engineer usually required

CAREER LADDER

```
┌─────────────────────────────────────┐
│ Senior Civil Engineer; Engineering   │
│ Manager; Project Manager             │
└─────────────────────────────────────┘

┌─────────────────────────────────────┐
│           Civil Engineer             │
└─────────────────────────────────────┘

┌─────────────────────────────────────┐
│ Entry-level Civil Engineer;          │
│ Engineering Technician               │
└─────────────────────────────────────┘
```

Position Description

Civil engineering is the broadest of engineering fields, partly because it is also the oldest. In the past, engineering was divided into only two fields: military and civil. In fact, within the United States government it is still part of the U.S. Army as the Corps of Engineers.

Civil Engineers usually work in one of the following areas: construction, soil and foundation, town planning, transport, or water resources. They plan, design, construct, operate, and maintain power plants, roads, bridges, dams, water supply projects, sewerage systems, transportation, harbors, canals, dockyards, airports, railways, factories, and large buildings. This field of engineering is broken down into subdisciplines, including general, structural, fire

protection (safety), geotechnical, transportation, hydraulic, water resources, and construction engineering. Those related to the energy industry include the areas of structural, geotechnical, hydraulic, water resources, and construction engineering.

Structural engineering deals with structural design and analysis of structural components of buildings and other structures. This process involves calculating the stresses and forces that affect or arise within a structure. Major design concerns are building structures' resistance to wind and seismic forces and seismically retrofitting existing structures, such as power plants, dams, oil wells, coal mine structures, nuclear reactors, and wind-gathering structures. In addition, elements of a building or a structure must be correctly sized and positioned in relation to each other and to site boundaries and adjacent structures. Structural (and construction) engineers are trained in the methods and procedures of surveying, the science of measuring and mapping relative positions on or under Earth's surface (which includes both power structures above ground and mining structures beneath it).

Geotechnical engineers are primarily concerned with foundations, soil properties, soil mechanics, compression and swelling of soils, seepage, slopes, embankments, retaining walls, ground and rock anchors, the use of synthetic tensile materials in soil structures, soil-structure interaction, and soil dynamics. They work closely with structural and construction civil engineers in the design and planning of most structures used in the production, transmission, and distribution of energy power.

Hydraulic engineering deals with the flow and conveyance of fluids, predominantly water. This area of civil engineering is intimately involved with the design of pipelines, water distribution systems, drainage facilities (including bridges, dams, channels, culverts, levees, and storm sewers), and canals. Hydraulic engineers design these facilities using the concepts of fluid pressure, fluid statics, fluid dynamics, and hydraulics. They focus on designing dams used to generate electric power, as well as the flow of energy liquids, such as oil, working closely with petroleum engineers.

Water resources engineering revolves about the collection and management of water. As a discipline, it combines hydrology, environmental science, meteorology, geology, conservation, and resource management. This area of civil engineering relates to the prediction and management of both the quality and the quantity of water in both underground (aquifers) and above-ground (lakes, rivers, and streams) resources. Water resource engineers analyze and model very small to very large areas of Earth to predict the amount and content of water as it flows into, through, or out of a facility, whereas the actual design of that facility most likely will be handled by other types of civil engineers.

Construction engineering concerns the planning and execution of transportation systems designs; site development; and hydraulic, environmental, structural, and geotechnical engineering projects. As construction firms tend to have higher business risks than other types of civil engineering firms, many construction engineers tend to take on a role that is more businesslike in nature: drafting and reviewing contracts, evaluating logistical operations, and closely monitoring prices of necessary supplies.

In the performance of their occupation, Civil Engineers may execute such tasks as:

- Investigate sites to establish the most suitable foundation for a proposed construction
- Research and advise on the best engineering solutions to meet with a client's needs and budget

- Produce detailed designs and documentation for the construction and implementation of civil engineering projects (such as the building of dams and power plants, the excavation of mines, and the building and placement of power lines, wind turbine structures, or nuclear reactors)
- Organize the delivery of materials, plant, and equipment needed for the construction project and supervise the labor involved
- Develop detailed programs for the coordination of site activities
- Interact with other engineers, architects, landscape architects, and environmental scientists
- Assist governmental bodies in preparing yearly works programs within set budgets, such as the development of new or additional power structures, drainage, roads, or waterways
- Prepare engineering calculations required for the design of projects and draft (or supervise drafting of) the plans and designs, using the latest computer-aided design techniques
- Coordinate and direct research development and testing of materials, processes, or systems related to civil engineering works
- Research, advise on, and plan the control and minimization of air, water, and solid waste pollution and the management of water
- Supervise the testing and commissioning of completed civil engineering works
- Analyze and interpret reports on loading, labor, productivity, quality, materials, and performance
- Analyze risks associated with natural disasters, including wind, earthquake, fire, and floods and design structures and services (such as electric power distribution) to meet appropriate local, state, federal, and professional standards
- Arrange for geological and geophysical investigations on sites designated for construction and carry out feasibility studies
- Interface with local, state, or national regulatory and permitting agencies

Civil Engineers may be headquartered in offices but spend much of their time on project sites. They may have to undertake a lot of traveling, even to the point of relocation as their jobs take them from one major engineering site to another. They usually are required to work long hours and meet strict deadlines while functioning under minimal supervision. They must deal with a wide variety of professional, skilled, and semi-skilled people.

Salaries

According to a 2005 survey by the National Association of Colleges and Employers (NACE), average annual starting salaries for Civil Engineers ranged from $43,679 to $59,625, depending on the level of educational degrees earned (from bachelor's to Ph.D.). In the joint earnings study made by the American Society of Civil Engineers (ASCE) and the National Society of Professional Engineers (NSPE), the *2004 Engineering Income and Salary Survey*, and using April 2004 data, average salaries of Civil Engineers were found to range from $64,750 to $80,000, depending upon the geographic locale. In its 2005 study of engineering salaries, the U.S. Department of Labor's Bureau of Labor Statistics, in their publication *Occupational Outlook Handbook, 2006–07 Edition,* found that salaries of Civil Engineers, as of May 2004, ranged from a low of $42,610 to a high of $94,660. It is not unusual for a senior Civil Engineer with 12 or more years experience to earn a yearly salary of $110,000 or more.

Employment Prospects

According to the U.S. Department of Labor, Civil Engineers are expected to experience average employment growth through 2014. Spurred by general population growth (with its attendant power needs) and an increased emphasis on infrastructure security, more Civil Engineers will be needed to design and construct safe and higher-capacity energy power plants and energy transmission and distribution systems, as well as better transportation infrastructure, water supply systems, pollution control systems, large buildings, and building complexes. They will be needed to repair or replace existing roads, bridges, dams, and other public structures. Because construction and related industries—including those providing design services—employ many Civil Engineers, employment opportunities will vary by geographic area and may decrease during economic slowdowns in which construction is often postponed or curtailed altogether.

Advancement Prospects

There is no one clear typical career path for Civil Engineers. Most engineering graduates start with jobs of low responsibility, and, as they prove their competence, they are given increasingly responsible tasks. However, within each subfield of civil engineering, and even within different segments of the employment market within each branch, the details of a career path can vary. In some subfields and in some firms, entry-level engineers are tasked with primarily monitoring construction in the field, while in other areas they focus on the more routine tasks of analysis or design. More senior engineers can move into doing more complex analysis or design work, or management of more complex design projects. Alternatively, they may gravitate into the management of other engineers or entire projects, or into specialized consulting positions, such as forensic engineering.

Education and Training

The basic educational requirement for a Civil Engineer is a four-year Bachelor of Science (B.S.) or Bachelor of Engineering (B.Eng.) degree in civil engineering from an accredited college program. (Accreditation is handled by the Accreditation Board for Engineering and Technology, Inc., or ABET.)

Many consulting companies and engineering firms require a master's degree as well. Such graduate work may lead either to a Master of Engineering (M.E.), which is a professional master's degree, or to a Master of Science (M.S.) degree, followed by a Ph.D. in civil engineering or a related subdiscipline.

Special Requirements

In order to undertake any civil engineering tasks affecting the public in the United States (or even to represent oneself legally as a civil engineer), Civil Engineers must become licensed Professional Engineers. Licensure requirements vary slightly state by state, but in all cases they entail passing two licensure exams: the Fundamentals of Engineering exam (or FE) and the Principles and Practice exam (or PE). In addition, a state-mandated number of years of working under the supervision of a licensed Professional Engineer must be fulfilled. Information on the Professional Engineer licensure can be gotten from the National Society of Professional Engineers (NSPE) (their Web site is at http://www.nspe.org) or the National Council of Examiners for Engineering and Surveying (NCEES) (their Web site is at http://www.ncees.org).

Experience, Skills, and Personality Traits

Civil Engineers must be able to identify problems, thoroughly analyze them, and find solutions. They must have excellent oral and written communication skills, as they will have to prepare work plans and reports, tabulate laboratory and other site data, and do engineering drawings and permit applications. They should be very familiar with computer-aided design (CAD) and computer-aided manufacturing (CAM) software and proficient with the entire design process, to the extent of being able to coordinate the work of other designers assigned to the project. They should know how to use the computer software employed in their specialty engineering fields, such as STAAD and GTSTUDL programs used by structural Civil Engineers for structural analysis and design.

They will need to have four to 10 years of experience (depending upon the field of civil engineering they are in and the specific requirements of the firms for which they work) as an entry-level Civil Engineer with an engineering or a consulting firm. They should gain some background in a project management role, which would include such tasks as project scheduling, budget preparation, report writing, sampling and data collection, subcontractor supervision, and technical engineering support. They should become knowledgeable in conducting site testing, performing test data analysis, and making design recommendations. In addition, they must become conversant with all applicable state and federal requirements as well as any regional policies that might have a bearing on their projects.

Civil Engineers need to be both creative (in their solutions to design or field problems) and practical (to keep within budget guidelines and client needs). They must be able to work without supervision, but also function as part of a team. They need to be able to accept responsibility and to adhere to the safety requirements of their operation. Above all, they must be able to deliver practical designs, technical calculations, and drawings within the time guidelines assigned to projects and be able to meet the scope requirements of the project.

Unions and Associations

The primary professional association of Civil Engineers is the American Society of Civil Engineers (ASCE). The organization publishes a large amount of information on civil engineering and develops codes and standards that frequently are adapted by federal, state, and local governments, as well as sponsoring conferences and providing continuing education for its members. Other associations dealing with specific sub-disciplines of civil engineering include the National Council of Structural Engineers Association (NCSEA) and the Society of Manufacturing Engineers (SME). Civil Engineers may also find it useful to become members of the larger umbrella engineering organization, the National Society of Professional Engineers (NSPE).

Tips for Entry

1. While earning your civil engineering degree, consider joining a student chapter or club of the American Society of Civil Engineers (ASCE), where you can participate in many activities that allow you to develop professionally outside of the classroom.
2. Look into cooperative education and work-study programs that permit you to earn tuition by attending classes for a portion of the year and work in an engineering-related job for the remainder of the year. In addition, ASCE offers scholarships and fellowships for both undergraduate and graduate students.
3. Take management and business courses to better understand budgetary methods used in the project planning process.

ENGINEERING TECHNICIANS

CAREER PROFILE

Duties: Assist engineers in research and development on energy projects, setting up and maintaining equipment in a research laboratory and drafting plans for new designs on a computer; under supervision, work on quality control, inspect electronic products and processes, conduct tests, and collect data

Alternate Title(s): None

Salary Range: $30,000 to $55,000 or more

Employment Prospects: Fair to Good

Advancement Prospects: Good

Prerequisites:

    Education or Training—Two-year associate's degree in engineering technology at an accredited engineering school is basic requirement; four-year college degree in engineering a plus, but not necessary

    Experience—From two to six years' experience in engineering technology in field of specialization; some entry-level posts may require only minimal job experience

    Special Skills and Personality Traits—Analytical, critical thinking and problem solving capabilities; attention to detail, initiative, and creativity; good communication skills, both verbal and writing, and aptitude to work well with others; high goal orientation towards achievement; dependability; exertion of efforts toward mastering tasks; leadership potential

    Special Requirements—Certification seldom required, but recommended for a competitive advantage when job seeking

CAREER LADDER

```
┌─────────────────────────────────┐
│  Engineer (in area of specialty) │
└─────────────────────────────────┘

┌─────────────────────────────────┐
│     Engineering Technician       │
└─────────────────────────────────┘

┌─────────────────────────────────┐
│       College Graduate           │
└─────────────────────────────────┘
```

Position Description

Engineering Technicians support engineering activities by using the principles and theories of science, engineering, and mathematics to solve technical problems in construction, inspection, maintenance, manufacturing, sales, and research and development. Their work is more limited in scope and more application-oriented than that of scientists and engineers. Those working in quality control may collect data, conduct tests, and inspect products/processes. Those in manufacturing may assist in product design, development, or production. Those involved in research and development assist engineers and/or scientists in building or setting up equipment, preparing and conducting experiments, collecting data, and calculating or recording results. They may make prototype versions of newly designed equipment and assist in other design work, often using design and drafting (CADD) software and equipment.

Most Engineering Technicians specialize, learning their skills by working closely with engineers in their same discipline. Thus, occupational titles of Engineering Technicians tend to reflect their engineering specialties.

Civil Engineering Technicians aid civil engineers in planning and constructing highways, buildings, bridges, dams, wastewater treatment systems, and other structures (such as power plants), as well as undertake related research. They may be assigned to estimate construction costs and specify materials to be used in the construction and even to prepare drawings or perform land-surveying tasks.

Electrical and electronics Engineering Technicians make up over one-third of the labor force of Engineering Technicians. They help design, develop, test, and manufacture electrical and electronic equipment such as communication equipment, radar, industrial (and medical) monitoring or control devices, and computer equipment. They may work in product evaluation and testing, using measuring and diagnostic devices to adjust, test, modify, and repair developmental or operational electrical machinery and electrical control equipment and circuitry in industrial or commercial plants and laboratories. They may be assigned to modify electrical prototypes, parts, assemblies, and systems to correct functional deviations, as well as collaborate with electrical engineers and other personnel to identify, define, and solve developmental problems. They often write procedures for electrical installations and prepare project cost and work-time estimates.

Electromechanical Engineering Technicians combine fundamental principles of mechanical engineering technology with knowledge of electrical and electronic circuits to design, develop, test, and manufacture electric and computer-controlled mechanical systems (such as nuclear-plant controlling devices and electric transmission switching devices).

Environmental Engineering Technicians work closely with environmental engineers and scientists to develop methods and devices used in the prevention, control, or correction of environmental hazards (such as nuclear waste products, or coal-mining by-products). They aid in inspecting and maintaining equipment related to air pollution and recycling. Some inspect water and wastewater treatment systems to ensure that pollution control requirements are met and standards are maintained.

Industrial Engineering Technicians study the efficient use of personnel, materials, and machines in factories, power plants, stores, repair shops, and offices. They prepare layouts of machinery and equipment, plan the flow of work, make statistical studies, and analyze production costs.

Mechanical Engineering Technicians help engineers design, develop, test, and manufacture industrial machinery, consumer products, and other equipment (such as gas turbines, oil-well drilling equipment, or coal-mining machinery). They may assist in product testing, make sketches and rough layouts, and write orders and purchase requests for work furnished by outside contractors. They record and analyze data, comparing test results to design or rated specifications/test objectives, make calculations and estimates, and report their findings to engineers and project managers. When planning production, mechanical Engineering Technicians prepare layouts and drawings of the assembly process and of the parts to be manufactured. They devise, fabricate, and assemble new or modified mechanical components for products such as industrial machinery/equipment or coal-mining drilling equipment and measuring instruments. They estimate labor costs, equipment life spans, and plant space. Some may be assigned to test and inspect machinery and equipment, or work with engineers on quality control and the elimination of any potential production problems.

Salaries

According to the U.S. Bureau of Labor Statistics, median annual earnings in May 2004 of Engineering Technicians ranged from $38,480 to $52,500, depending upon their specialty. Median annual earnings of electrical and electronics Engineering Technicians were $46,310 in May 2004. Their yearly salaries ranged from a low of $29,000 to a high of $67,900. Median annual earnings of civil Engineering Technicians were $38,480 in May 2004. Their yearly income ranged from a low of $24,180 to a high of $57,550. Median annual earnings of mechanical Engineering Technicians in May 2004 were $43,400, and the average annual salary for environmental Engineering Technicians was $36,530.

In their joint annual salary survey of 2006, the American Society of Certified Engineering Technicians (ASCET) and the National Institute for Certification in Engineering Technologies (NICET) found that the largest percentage of Engineering Technicians were earning yearly salaries between $40,000 and $65,000.

Employment Prospects

Job opportunities are best for aspiring Engineering Technicians who have an associate's degree or extensive job training in engineering technology. According to the U.S. Department of Labor, overall employment of Engineering Technicians is expected to increase about as fast as the average for all occupations through 2014. Competitive pressures will force companies (such as those in the electric power and oil and gas industries) to improve and update manufacturing facilities, product designs, and facilities, resulting in more opportunities for Engineering Technicians.

Because Engineering Technicians work closely with engineers, employment of Engineering Technicians is often influenced by the same local and national economic conditions that affect engineers. As a result, the employment outlook tends to vary according to the industry and the particular specialization. Growth in the largest specialty—electrical and electronics Engineering Technicians—is expected to be about as fast as the average, according to the U.S. Department of Labor's *Occupational Outlook Handbook, 2006–07 Edition*, whereas employment of environmental Engineering Technicians is expected to grow faster than average in order to meet the environmental demands of an ever-growing population.

Advancement Prospects

Engineering Technicians can expect to be upgraded to full-fledged engineers within their specialty after sufficient years of training (usually 10 or more) and demonstrated proof of their capabilities. Engineering Technicians usually begin by performing routine tasks under the close supervision of an experienced technician, technologist, or engineer. As the newcomers gain experience, they are given more difficult assignments with only general supervision. (Some of them may even become supervisors.) Becoming engineers in their specialty is a process of gained experience, excellent job recommendations, and, usually, the successful completion of the certification process that most engineers undergo.

Education and Training

Most employers prefer to hire an Engineering Technician who has at least a two-year associate's degree in engineering technology from an accredited school. (Most two-year associate's degree programs are accredited by the Technology Accreditation Commission of the Accreditation Board for Engineering and Technology, or ABET.) Training is available at technical institutes, community colleges, extension divisions of colleges and universities, public and private vocational-training schools, and in the U.S. Armed Forces. Individuals with college courses in science, engineering, and mathematics may qualify for some positions as Engineering Technicians but may need additional specialized training and experience.

Prospective Engineering Technicians should take as many science and mathematics courses as possible. The type of technical courses required depends on the specialty of the aspiring Engineering Technician. For example, mechanical Engineering Technicians need to take courses in fluid mechanics, thermodynamics, and mechanical design, whereas electrical Engineering Technicians may need classes in electrical circuits, microprocessors, and digital electronics.

Experience, Skills, and Personality Traits

On-the-job activities for Engineering Technicians usually include work in a laboratory, traveling to plants or construction sites, and gaining practice working as part of a team. Because they often are part of a team of engineers and other technicians, good communication skills and the aptitude to work well with others is critical. Their laboratory proficiency will include becoming knowledgeable about high-speed oscilloscopes, Multimeters, logic and spectrum analyzers, and becoming proficient in using other standard test equipment. They will need to keep up with new technology and equipment utilized in their specialty, and demonstrate that they can work carefully and accurately.

Because many Engineering Technicians assist in design work, creativity is desirable. They must be able to read schematics and be computer literate. Knowledge of computer-aided design and drafting (CADD) software and techniques is recommended. They must have the ability to perform basic mathematical calculations and be proficient in algebra and trigonometry. They must have solid writing skills, as they will likely be required to prepare (daily) written reports. They will need to be analytical in their thinking, exhibit close attention to detail, and have problem-solving abilities.

Special Requirements

While most employers of Engineering Technicians do not require them to be certified, such certification may provide them with an edge when job seeking. The National Institute for Certification in Engineering Technologies (NICET) has established a voluntary certification program for Engineering Technicians. Certification is available at various levels; each stage combines a written examination in one of about 30 specialties with a specified amount of job-related experience, a supervisory evaluation, and a recommendation. Specialty certifications are also offered by a variety of professional societies and associations in the various disciplines of engineering.

Unions and Associations

The American Society of Certified Engineering Technicians (ASCET) is the only national, professional society created especially for, and administered by, the Engineering Technicians and technologists in all types of engineering disciplines. Engineering Technicians may also find it useful to belong to the primary professional associations devoted to their specialty in engineering.

Tips for Entry

1. While in high school or college, upgrade your computer skills by learning drafting (CAD) methodologies.
2. If your interest resides in electrical engineering or construction, work with the stage crew of college dramatic productions and get experience building sets or working the light board.
3. Join an engineering club and/or get involved in engineering competitions, such as the one offered by the Junior Engineering Technical Society (JETS).

ENVIRONMENTAL ENGINEER

CAREER PROFILE

Duties: Assess the impacts of proposed energy projects on environmental conditions and present recommendations for corrective measurements

Alternate Title(s): Environmental and Safety Engineer; Risk Assessment Engineer

Salary Range: $40,000 to $100,000 or more

Employment Prospects: Good

Advancement Prospects: Fair

Prerequisites:

Education or Training—Undergraduate degree in chemical, civil, environmental, or mechanical engineering required; master's degree in environmental engineering is recommended

Experience—Three to five years or more of practical engineering experience

Special Skills and Personality Traits—Basic knowledge of engineering procedures and techniques; capable of being a team player but also accepting personal responsibility; excellent communication and interpersonal skills, including outstanding presentation skills; good analytical skills and high attention to detail; great love of the outdoors; inquisitiveness and creativity; strong grasp of mathematics; thorough understanding of environmental laws and governmental safety regulations

Special Requirements—Certification as a professional engineer highly recommended

CAREER LADDER

```
┌─────────────────────────────────────┐
│  Director of Environmental Programs; │
│    Senior Environmental Scientist    │
└─────────────────────────────────────┘

┌─────────────────────────────────────┐
│       Environmental Engineer         │
└─────────────────────────────────────┘

┌─────────────────────────────────────┐
│  Engineer; Engineering Technician    │
└─────────────────────────────────────┘
```

Position Description

Environmental Engineers are concerned with assessing and managing the effects of human and other activity on both the natural and the built environment. They are charged primarily with designing and planning prevention, control, and remediation of environmental health hazards. Environmental Engineers apply their knowledge of mathematics, physics, chemistry, biology, and engineering problem-solving skills for the protection of human health and the environment. They design and maintain systems that provide safe drinking water, treat and properly dispose of wastes, maintain or improve air quality, control water pollution in rivers, lakes, and oceans, clean up contaminated land and water resources, and help industry minimize pollution.

Environmental Engineers research and develop new technologies and techniques to improve the environmental acceptability of engineering projects and evaluate the environmental and social impacts of engineering projects. They develop, administer, and implement environmental programs in accordance with governmental standards and monitor pollution prevention activities, compliance, and auditing efforts. Their duties may include collecting soil or groundwater samples and testing them for contamination, conducting hazardous-waste management studies in which they evaluate the significance of the hazard, advising on treatment and containment, and developing possible regulations to prevent mishaps. In addition, their fieldwork may include logging soil borings, groundwater sampling, monitoring of well installations, overseeing remediation system operations/maintenance, administering data collection, and examining the work of contractors.

Environmental Engineers design (and operate) processes to treat commercial and industrial wastes to a standard acceptable for discharge and/or recycling (a process known as wastewater treatment or waste solidification). They conduct research on the environmental impact of proposed construction projects, plant processes, and permit changes, analyzing scientific data and performing quality-control inspections. They may be required to run, maintain, develop, and validate research on atmospheric dispersion models of the physical phenomena associated with the atmospheric transport of pollutants or hazardous chemicals. Environmental Engineers often work with occupational health experts to ensure hazard-free working environments in industrial, manufacturing, and energy producing/distributing settings. They prepare reports/studies on the best approach to environmental management in new and existing engineering projects, taking into account government regulations and legal, environmental, and industrial factors. They may become involved in legal or financial consulting regarding environmental processes or issues, communicating information to other technical staff of businesses, managers, regulatory authorities, and public interest groups.

Many Environmental Engineers work as consultants, helping their clients comply with regulations and cleanup of hazardous waste sites. One emphasis in environmental engineering consulting is on brownfields, land areas that are abandoned because of contamination by hazardous substances. Environmental Engineers help clients clean up the brownfields for reuse, minimizing the liabilities and the costs of building projects. When working as consultants, they may interact with federal, state, and local regulators to resolve compliance issues, establish permit requirements, and assist Environmental Protection Agency (EPA), state, and local regulatory audits. They may represent their client companies in any government and industry rule-making activities.

Most Environmental Engineers involved in the energy industry specialize in particular sectors, such as the minerals industry, the chemical industry, the nuclear power industry, the electric power industry, or civil engineering projects. They may work for chemical companies (helping to reduce wastes in streams, among other tasks), pharmaceutical companies (making container drums that are environmentally safe and not dangerous to plants and animals), pulp and paper mills (reducing wastes and restoring forests), nuclear plants (finding safe means to dispose of nuclear materials), oil companies (discovering ways to enhance energy usage), or government agencies involved with energy conservation and energy usage, such as the EPA or the Department of Energy (DOE). Environmental engineering jobs with consulting companies often require significant travel of their engineers, sometimes including international journeys.

Salaries

According to a 2005 survey by the National Association of Colleges and Employers, the average annual starting salary for Environmental Engineers is $47,384. In their annual analysis of salaries, the U.S. Department of Labor's *Occupational Outlook Handbook, 2006–07 Edition* found that, in May 2004, the median annual earnings of Environmental Engineers ranged from a low of $40,620 to a high of $100,050.

Employment Prospects

According to the U.S. Bureau of Labor Statistics, Environmental Engineers have favorable job opportunities, as their employment is expected to increase much faster than the average for all occupations through 2014. In addition, *Fortune* magazine (March 21, 2005) selected environmental engineering as the fastest growing professional job in the next decade, with a more than 54 percent increase in jobs!

More Environmental Engineers will be needed to comply with environmental regulations and to develop new methods of cleaning up existing hazards. The shift in emphasis to preventing problems rather than just controlling those that already exist and the increasing public health concerns will both enhance demand for Environmental Engineers. Nevertheless, trends in environmental protection and regulation constantly change, so Environmental Engineers must keep abreast of a range of environmental issues to ensure steady employment. Political and economic factors may also have an impact on their employment, in that looser environmental regulations would reduce job opportunities whereas stricter rules would enhance them.

Another factor in their favor is the wide range of employment opportunities open to them. They may work as design engineers in a consulting firm or work for industry. They may work for local, city, or state governments, as well as for the U.S. government's EPA, Department of Transportation, the U.S. Army Corps of Engineers, the U.S. Geological Survey, the U.S. Forest Service, U.S. Department of Interior, or the U.S. Department of Energy. They may even become high school teachers of science or math, or pursue the legal aspects of environmental protection by obtaining a law degree in environmental science.

Advancement Prospects

As consultants, Environmental Engineers might look for full employment within the corporate structure of their client company. If they work for a governmental agency, there are clear-cut paths for advancement. They may enhance their expertise in their own specialty by further education in science and technology and emphasize the research and scientific aspects of their work, even to the extent of eventually teaching at a high school or college level.

They may decide to involve themselves with the larger environmental worldwide issues (and large-scale problems) of acid rain, global warming, and ozone depletion, offering their services and expertise to governments or other international institutions.

Education and Training

A bachelor's degree in engineering is required for almost all entry-level engineering jobs. Such a degree may be in environmental engineering, environmental engineering technology, civil engineering, civil engineering technology, mechanical engineering, chemical engineering, materials engineering, materials engineering technology, or geotechnical, geological, or sanitary engineering. Environmental engineering requires knowledge in many fields of science, including biology, chemistry, geology, hydrology (the study of the movement, distribution, and quality of water), and physics. In addition, engineers need to be very comfortable with mathematical techniques. Those interested in a career in environmental engineering should look for engineering programs that are accredited by the Accreditation Board for Engineering and Technology, Inc. (ABET).

Many Environmental Engineers obtained degrees in some other field of engineering and then pursued a master's degree in environmental engineering, as more and more employers of Environmental Engineers are giving a preference to those who have such accreditation. Some aspiring Environmental Engineers seek internship programs from such places as the Environmental Careers Organization (ECO) while they work at their first engineering jobs.

Experience, Skills, and Personality Traits

Most employers of Environmental Engineers require their candidates to have two to four years of experience in their field of engineering in a staff-level position with a consulting and/or engineering firm, preferably in their engineering specialty. Many of them prefer their Environmental Engineers to have had four or more years in a project management role and to have a knowledge of the most current environmental engineering principles and practices.

Beyond their basic knowledge of engineering procedures and technologies, Environmental Engineers must exhibit a thorough understanding and technical authority in their chosen engineering discipline. They should be computer literate (proficient in MS Access, Excel, and Word programs), as well as be familiar with computer-aided drafting (CAD) and computer-aided manufacturing (CAM) programs. They should have some field experience as an engineering staff member and some experience with Geographic Information System (GIS) techniques and applications. (GIS is a "smart map" tool that allows users to create interactive queries, analyze the spatial information, and edit data.)

Environmental Engineers need a thorough understanding of all environmental laws, both local and national, and all governmental safety regulations. They should be highly detail-oriented, with strong analytical and problem-solving skills. While curious and creative, they also need to be highly practical, as well as team players with a strong work ethic. Finally, since environmental engineering is so intertwined with people, Environmental Engineers must have excellent writing, speaking, and interpersonal skills. Their communication abilities are particularly important, as they often will be interacting with specialists in a wide range of fields outside engineering.

Special Requirements

In many cases, it is recommended that Environmental Engineers possess certification as professional engineers as an additional enhancement for employment. They usually seek licensure by a state government. To become a licensed Professional Engineer, an Environmental Engineer must pass the comprehensive FE (Fundamentals of Engineering) exam, then work a given number of years (usually three to five) as an Engineer in Training (EIT), and then pass the PE (Practicing Engineer) exam.

Unions and Associations

The primary association for Environmental Engineers is the American Academy of Environmental Engineers (AAEE). Other professional organizations of interest to them include the Air and Waste Management Association (A&WMA), the Environmental Division of the American Institute of Chemical Engineers (AIChE), the Environmental and Water Resources Institute (EWRI) of the American Society of Civil Engineers (ASCE), the Environmental Engineering Division (EED) of the American Society of Mechanical Engineers (ASME), and the Water Environment Federation (WEF).

Tips for Entry

1. Include with your engineering and science courses some courses in the humanities as well. It will be important for you to understand how people and societies function, as you will be interacting with a wide range of people outside of your engineering specialty as a part of your duties.
2. While in college, volunteer for field work in your courses to gain an understanding of the techniques and special requirements of gathering data outside of the office or laboratory.
3. Along with your general computer courses, consider technical writing and speech courses to build your abilities in both written and oral communication.

MECHANICAL ENGINEER

CAREER PROFILE

Duties: Perform engineering duties in planning and designing engines, power-producing machines, power-using machines, and other mechanically functioning equipment

Alternate Title(s): Mechanical Design Engineer; Process Engineer; Product Engineer

Salary Range: $40,000 to $95,000 or more

Employment Prospects: Fair to Good

Advancement Prospects: Fair

Prerequisites:

Education or Training—Bachelor's degree in mechanical engineering required; master's degree in mechanical engineering or related technical discipline frequently recommended

Experience—Three to five years or more of mechanical engineering experience in a manufacturing or power plant environment

Special Skills and Personality Traits—Ability to interpret building, mechanical, state, local and federal safety codes; analytical skills; computer literate and particularly proficient with word processing and spreadsheet software; excellent verbal and written communication skills; flexible and self-directed; strong interpersonal capabilities and a team player

Special Requirements—Certification required on all government jobs, and usually required for work in the private sector

CAREER LADDER

```
┌─────────────────────────────────────┐
│  Director of Mechanical Engineering; │
│            Project Manager           │
└─────────────────────────────────────┘

┌─────────────────────────────────────┐
│          Mechanical Engineer         │
└─────────────────────────────────────┘

┌─────────────────────────────────────┐
│         Engineering Technician       │
└─────────────────────────────────────┘
```

Position Description

Mechanical engineering is one of the broadest engineering disciplines. It involves the application of principles of physics for analysis, design, manufacturing, and maintenance of mechanical systems. Mechanical Engineers work on power-producing machines such as electric generators, internal combustion engines, and steam and gas turbines, as well as power-using machines such as refrigeration and air-conditioning equipment, industrial production equipment, machine tools, and material handling systems. They perform engineering analysis and design of existing and new equipment systems (such as pumps, agitators, fans, tanks, vessels, and piping).

The process of mechanical engineering is optimization: Mechanical Engineers strive to optimize the cost of production, as well as the durability, safety, and overall usefulness of objects and systems. Mechanical Engineers research, develop, design, manufacture, and test tools, engines, machines (including power-producing machines), and other mechanical devices. They analyze complex technical problems involving thermal analysis (a branch of materials science where the properties of materials are studied as they change with temperature) and mechanical packaging of systems with moving parts. They research, plan, design, and develop mechanical products and systems, such as instruments, controls, robots, engines, machines, and mechanical, thermal hydraulic, or heat transfer systems for production, transmission, measurement, and use of energy. They may manage power facilities and utilities (high-pressure steam, condensate, chilled water, high voltage electrical, gas, water, and sewer systems), and be involved with utility master plans, cost tracking, and energy conservation requirements. They need to have a solid understanding of such key concepts as mechanics (the study of forces and their effect upon matter and systems), kinematics (the study of the motion of bodies and systems, while ignoring the forces that cause that motion), energy, and thermodynamics (the study of how energy moves through a system). Mechanical Engineers working within the energy industry are particularly involved with thermodynamics.

Thermodynamics deals with the energy interactions in physical systems. Engineering thermodynamics uses the concepts of thermodynamics to solve engineering problems. Typically, engineering thermodynamics is concerned with changing energy from one form to another and with finding ways to make systems more efficient, be they nuclear reactors, oil refineries, or electric power generators and substations. Much of the data used by Mechanical Engineers is empirical (e.g., derived from experience, observation, or experimentation). Engineering thermodynamics develops the theory and techniques required to use empirical thermodynamic data effectively, much of which now can be retrieved from computer databases. There are even software applications that are tailored to specific areas that will give answers for common design situations. Nevertheless, Mechanical Engineers need to have a thorough understanding of the underlying principles of thermodynamics, coupled with the ability to judge the limitations of empirical data when applied to specific design problems.

Additionally, Mechanical Engineers must be adept at drafting, or technical drawing, which is the means by which they create the instructions for manufacturing parts and designing the interweaving elements of an electric power unit or system. This technical drawing can be a computer model or a hand-drawn schematic displaying all the dimensions necessary for manufacturing a part or designing a system. Computer-aided drafting (CAD) software programs allow the designing engineer to create in three dimensions. Combined with computer-aided manufacturing (CAM), or combined CAD/CAM programs, these instructions can be fed into the computer to create the necessary full design, or fed into the necessary machinery to create the required part. Three-dimensional models created with CAD software are commonly used in finite element analysis (FEA), a powerful computational method for simulating the response of structures, structural components or materials to loading. In addition, they are used in computational fluid dynamics (CFD), which is one of the branches of fluid mechanics that employs numerical methods and algorithms to analyze/solve problems that involve fluid flows (such as the transmission and distribution of electric power).

Generally, Mechanical Engineers are responsible for planning and performing design development tasks from concept to implementation. They study, analyze, and evaluate all product or system design concepts and plans, and direct (or conduct) testing necessary to assure adequate performance of designs for all stages and complexities of the development project. They are responsible for documentation of all performed tasks, including the initial descriptions, specifications, testing methodologies, and final implementations. They must have a full understanding of standards and codes, such as those of the Occupational, Safety and Health Administration (OSHA), as applied to both the manufacture of tools and equipment and the design of electric power systems, power plants, and electric distribution systems.

Salaries

In a 2005 survey by the National Association of Colleges and Employers, average starting salaries for Mechanical Engineers ranged from $50,000 to $68,000 yearly, depending upon their level of educational background, from the attainment of a bachelor's degree to the earning of a Ph.D. degree. In their survey of engineering salaries, the U.S. Department of Labor's Bureau of Labor Statistics found that, in May 2004, Mechanical Engineers had annual incomes ranging from a low of $43,000 to a high of $97,000 or more.

Employment Prospects

The U.S. Department of Labor's *Occupational Outlook Handbook, 2006–07 Edition,* projects that Mechanical Engineers will have an average rate of employment growth through 2014. Although total employment in manufacturing industries is expected to decline, employment of Mechanical Engineers, particularly in the electric power industry, should increase as the demand for more efficient, faster, less expensive, and more environmentally friendly technologies increases. The U.S. Department of Energy (DOE) predicts that, during the next five to 20 years, advances in power electronics technologies and their mechanical devices could revolutionize many aspects of power system operations and planning. The place of Mechanical Engineers in the development of new devices for power system operations should provide growing job opportunities in the years to come.

Advancement Prospects

Experienced senior Mechanical Engineers may find professional advancement by accepting further management and supervisory responsibilities as project managers or directors of mechanical engineering within a utility company. In addition, the skills acquired as a Mechanical Engineer can often be applied in other engineering specialties that may provide more responsibility and higher salary possibilities.

Education and Training

Graduation from a college or university that is accredited (by the Accreditation Board for Engineering and Technology, or ABET, Inc.) with a bachelor's degree in mechanical engineering or, in some cases, electrical engineering is a basic requisite for being hired as a Mechanical Engineer. Some Mechanical Engineers may find it important enough to pursue a postgraduate degree such as a master of engineering/master of science, a master of engineering management, or a doctor of philosophy in engineering.

Experience, Skills, and Personality Traits

Mechanical Engineers must possess good verbal and written communication talents and have demonstrable organizational and interpersonal skills. They should be flexible, self-directed, and capable of working in a team environment. They must be computer literate to the extent of being knowledgeable about such software as Lotus Notes, MS Word, Excel, PowerPoint, MS Project, Visio, and Oracle. They need to be proficient with CAD and/or CAD/CAM programming tools as well as other software, such as Pro/Engineer, Solidworks, and Unigraphics. They should be familiar with product design development cycles and have some background in analyzing complex technical problems involving thermal analysis and mechanical packaging of systems with moving parts. They should have a basic knowledge of electrical circuit analysis and the principles of operation of pressure sensors, temperature sensors, speed sensors, solenoids, servos, and pneumatically or hydraulically actuated valves.

Mechanical Engineers must be able to write equipment and material specifications, data sheets, and material requisitions and to interpret specifications furnished by others. Besides their background in design and development, they should have a working knowledge of testing methodologies, production techniques, and maintenance procedures. They should be acquainted with standards relating to mechanical engineering such as those of the American Society of Mechanical Engineers (ASME), the American National Standards Institute (ANSI), and the National Electrical Manufacturing Association (NEMA).

Mechanical Engineers must exhibit careful attention to detail and be highly reliable and responsible in fulfilling their obligations. They need to be creative and attentive thinkers in developing fresh ideas and answers to work-related problems and be willing to take on new responsibilities and challenges.

Special Requirements

In most cases, a certification as a professional engineer is a requirement for employment. Mechanical Engineers may seek licensure by a state government. To become a licensed Professional Engineer, an engineer must pass the comprehensive FE (Fundamentals of Engineering) exam, then work a given number of years (usually three to five) as an Engineer in Training (EIT), and then pass the PE (Practicing Engineer) exam.

Unions and Associations

The major professional association for Mechanical Engineers is the American Society of Mechanical Engineers (ASME). Membership in other organizations, such as the Association of Energy Engineers (AEE) or the National Society of Professional Engineers (NSPE), may also prove useful.

Tips for Entry

1. Along with courses in engineering, be sure to include physics and chemistry, which will provide invaluable background in such topics as thermodynamics.
2. Become computer literate and acquaint yourself with advanced development software, such as C++, as well as analytical and scientific software and computer-aided design (CAD) programs.
3. Take courses in administration and management, as you will need to have a knowledge of business and management principles involved in strategic planning, production methods, and resource allocation and coordination.

COAL INDUSTRY

ENGINEERS AND SCIENTISTS

ANALYTICAL CHEMIST

CAREER PROFILE	CAREER LADDER

Duties: Analyze material (air and soil) samples to gain an understanding of their chemical composition in relation to potential pollution effects from coal-mining procedures

Alternate Title(s): Environmental Chemist; Research Chemist

Salary Range: $35,000 to $90,000 or more

Employment Prospects: Fair

Advancement Prospects: Poor to Fair

Prerequisites:

Education or Training—Bachelor's degree in chemistry or a related discipline is minimum requirement; many research jobs require at least a master's degree, and often a Ph.D.

Experience—Three to five years background as an analytical chemist in both laboratory and field environments

Special Skills and Personality Traits—Ability to utilize sophisticated measurement instruments; accuracy, preciseness, and patience, with a propensity for detail; excellent laboratory and problem-solving skills; good oral and written communication talents; solid computer proficiency

```
┌─────────────────────────────────────┐
│  Consulting Chemist; Senior Researcher │
└─────────────────────────────────────┘

┌─────────────────────────────────────┐
│          Analytical Chemist           │
└─────────────────────────────────────┘

┌─────────────────────────────────────┐
│               Chemist                 │
└─────────────────────────────────────┘
```

Position Description

Chemistry is the study of matter, its composition, structure, properties, and reactions along with the energy changes associated with those reactions. Among the branches (or disciplines) within the field is that of analytical chemistry. Analytical Chemists determine the structure, composition, and nature of substances by examining and identifying their various elements or compounds. They perform qualitative (investigation and identification) and quantitative (determination of the presence of a given element or inorganic compound in a sample) analysis. They use the science of sampling, defining, isolating, concentrating, and preserving samples, setting error limits, and validating results through calibration and standardization procedures. They develop analytical techniques and new ways to make measurements, interpreting data in proper context, and communicating their documented results.

Analytical Chemists analyze organic and inorganic compounds to determine their chemical and physical properties, composition, structure, relationships, and reactions, utilizing chromatography (a method of determining the identity and concentration of molecules within a mixture), and spectroscopy (studying matter by investigating light, sound, or particles that are emitted, absorbed, or scattered by the matter under investigation). They apply their knowledge of chemistry, instrumentation, and statistics to solve problems in almost all areas of chemistry. They use computers and a wide variety of sophisticated laboratory instrumentation for modeling and simulation in their work. For those Analytical Chemists employed by the coal mining industry, they and their measurements are used to assure compliance with environmental and other regulations.

Chemical environmental analysis is involved in monitoring levels of toxic and hazardous substances (at the site of coal-mining operations, for example). The investigation typically consists of analyzing air, water, soil, and other samples using expensive, complex instrumentation in climate-controlled laboratories. This process is both costly and time-consuming, particularly as the analysis of large numbers of samples for the most minute quantities of toxic pollutants must follow strict accountability guidelines to maintain the integrity and homogeneity of the samples investigated, and to meet regulatory requirements.

One advance in the field of chemical environmental analysis is the ongoing development of immunochemical sensors to study and evaluate the release of pollutants into the environment. These sensors are designed to detect and accurately determine the level of specific pollutants, immediately applicable to the coal-mining industry. These sensors can be built into portable and highly automated instruments that can be used at hazardous waste sites, such as mine slag deposits.

Salaries
According to the U.S. Department of Labor's Bureau of Labor Statistics, median annual earnings of chemists, generally, in May 2004 were $56,060. The middle 50 percent earned between $41,900 and $76,080, and the lowest 10 percent earned about $33,170. The highest 10 percent had incomes of more than $98,010. Salaries also depended greatly upon the level of educational degrees that chemists had. The American Chemical Society (ACS) reported in 2004 that the median annual salary of its members with bachelor's degrees was $62,000, whereas those with master's degrees earned a median salary of $72,300, and for those with Ph.D. degrees the median salary was $91,600.

Employment Prospects
According to the U.S. Department of Labor's *Occupational Outlook Handbook, 2006–07 Edition,* employment of chemists in general is expected to grow more slowly than the average rate for all occupations through 2014. Employment in the non-pharmaceutical segments of the chemical industry is expected to decline due to the increased use of automated methodologies. However, there is the ongoing need to monitor and measure air and water pollutants to ensure compliance with local, state, and federal environmental regulations. Thus, Analytical Chemists with experience and training in using a range of instruments for a wide assortment of analyses remain in demand.

Advancement Prospects
Increasingly, analytical methods have been automated, using robots and instrumentation designed to prepare and analyze samples. In addition, powerful personal computers and workstations are enabling the development and use of sophisticated techniques for interpreting instrumental data. As this instrumentation does more analysis, fewer Analyti-

cal Chemists are required to prepare samples and interpret the data. However, the demand for increasingly sophisticated analytical techniques, new generations of instrumentation, automation and computerization, and compliance with regulatory requirements have opened up fresh opportunities for Analytical Chemists in other areas of the field.

Quality assurance specialists are required to validate that analytical laboratories and the chemists working there follow documented and approved procedures. New instrumentation and laboratory information management systems have opened up opportunities for chemists with solid technical and computer skills, and corporate downsizings have provided the impetus for entrepreneurial Analytical Chemists to start their own consulting businesses.

Education and Training
A solid educational background in chemistry and good laboratory, computer, and communication skills are critical in handling a wide variety of chemical measurements. Because analytical chemistry is a service discipline (particularly as applied to the evaluation of mining pollutants), combining the skills of an Analytical Chemist with knowledge of the problems of other chemical disciplines (such as organic, polymer, inorganic, and environmental chemistries) is a valuable asset.

Analytical Chemists looking to work on environmental issues should take courses in ecological studies and become familiar with current legislation and regulations. They should include courses in atmospheric chemistry, water chemistry, soil chemistry, and energy, as well as statistical techniques. In addition, some educational background in customer service, business, and management is becoming increasingly important for Analytical Chemists who must interact with both the public and with members of the industry (in this case, coal mining) for which they work.

Experience, Skills, and Personality Traits
Because Analytical Chemists are increasingly expected to work on interdisciplinary teams, some understanding of other disciplines, such as marketing or economics, is desirable. A background either in academic laboratories or through internships, fellowships, or work-study programs in industry is useful as well.

Good laboratory and mechanical skills and the patience to perform sometimes tedious procedures is necessary for precise and accurate measurements. Analytical Chemists should be proficient in oral and written communication, and should display a degree of leadership ability. Their abilities to learn about and keep up with the latest techniques, instrumentation, and technology are essential. They must have excellent computer know-how and be familiar with development environmental, graphics, and photo-imaging software. Their knowledge of chemical composition, structure, and properties of substances and of the chemical processes and transformations that they undergo must be exemplary. They must be adept at gathering, processing, and analyzing data or information, including evaluating that data to determine compliance with set standards and regulations. They need to be highly organized and be expert at entering, transcribing, recording, and maintaining information in both written and computer storage forms.

Unions and Associations

The primary association for all chemists is the American Chemical Society (ACS).

Tips for Entry

1. Investigate paying or nonpaying internships, fellowships, and co-op industry work experience in the chemical industry as a good way to gain hands-on job experience.
2. Include mathematics (particularly statistics) in your curriculum.
3. Work on your computer skills: practice writing software; setting up functions; entering, transcribing, recording, storing, and maintaining data; and processing information.

COAL GASIFICATION ENGINEER

Duties: Plan, design, construct, operate, and maintain structures and equipment utilized in the process of extracting coal by a coal gasification process

Alternate Title(s): Process Engineer

Salary Range: $40,000 to $95,000 or more

Employment Prospects: Poor

Advancement Prospects: Poor to Fair

Prerequisites:

Education or Training—Bachelor of Science degree in mechanical engineering technology, electrical engineering technology, or mining engineering technology required; a master's degree in one of these three and/or chemical engineering is often also necessary; a Ph.D. in either mining engineering or environment management is recommended

Experience—10 or more years experience in the coal mining and energy business is a necessity

Special Skills and Personality Traits—Basic knowledge of engineering procedures and techniques; capable of being a team player but also accepting personal responsibility; excellent communication and interpersonal abilities, including outstanding presentation skills; fundamental understanding of coal mining, hydrodynamics, geology, and process engineering; good analytical skills and high attention to detail; proven ability in problem solving and project management

Special Requirements—Licensure as a Professional Engineer is a requirement

```
┌─────────────────────────────┐
│      General Manager        │
└─────────────────────────────┘

┌─────────────────────────────┐
│  Coal Gasification Engineer │
└─────────────────────────────┘

┌─────────────────────────────┐
│      Mining Engineer        │
└─────────────────────────────┘
```

Position Description

The traditional means of extracting coal from the earth has been the building of open pits (from which earth is removed and the coal extracted from it) or underground mines. In the latter, the construction of mineshafts and tunnels are necessary, into which miners go with tools, both manual and automated, to extract the coal from the earth. These operations are both costly and problematic, in that both waste and pollution to the environment are inevitable by-products, and the process is dangerous for both the miner's health and safety.

A relatively new process of converting the energy content of coal into electricity, hydrogen, and other energy forms has been introduced that bypasses the traditional methods of extracting coal. It is known as underground coal gasification (UCG). The process was first developed as a large-scale gas production technique in the 1960s (though it had been in use in the Soviet Union since 1928). As a process, it is being tested and accepted in many countries around the globe as well as the United States.

Gasification is the chemical process of converting a solid or liquid fuel into a combustible gas, which can subsequently be used to produce heat or generate power. Underground coal gasification is a gasification process applied to non-mined (or previously difficult to excavate) coal seams, using injection and production wells drilled from the surface, which enables the coal to be converted in situ (on site, instead of being removed to the surface first) into product gas. These product gases are transported to the surface for processing and utilization (and in this process, the coal gas is separated from the carbon dioxide or CO_2). Initially this large-scale method of coal conversion was problematic because transmitting the gases to and from the combustion zone was unreliable and costly. However, improved directional underground drilling—developed for the oil and gas industries in the 1990s—has proven to be directly applicable to the de-gassing of coal seams. Furthermore, methods of using assorted oxidants to convert the coal to gas (according to the type and depth of the coal seam), of controlling the process parameters (of operating pressure and heat dissipation, outlet temperature, and flow of gas through the pipelines to the surface), and of avoiding contamination of the underground environment have all contributed to the growing success of this process.

There are several advantages to UCG, often referred to as an integrated gasification combined cycle (IGCC), over conventional coal extraction techniques. The process is proving to be safer, simpler, cleaner, and more versatile in its extraction methods. It doubles (and may even triple) making available coal resources available to refinement, as much of previously unminable coal (such as coal beds found near earthquake faults or volcanic intrusions, or coal beds too deep for safe conventional mining) are now open to possible extraction. Moreover, there is little to no ash or slag (residue from the mining process) removal or handling needed as most of this inert material remains behind in the underground cavities. Another advantage is that the transport of the gas is done by pipeline, not by railcar. Furthermore, coal gasification power plants cleanse as much as 99 percent of the pollutant-forming impurities from coal-derived gases. In addition, the coal gases, cleaned of their impurities, are fired in a gas turbine to generate one source of electricity. The hot exhaust of the gas turbine is then used to generate steam for a more conventional steam turbine-generator. This dual source of electric power, called a combined cycle, converts much more of coal's inherent energy value into usable electricity, thus boosting the efficiency of coal gasification power plants by 50 percent or more.

The job of a Coal Gasification Engineer is to aid in the design, construction, and operation of an integrated gasification project. During the operation, they oversee the drilling of the injection wells into the identified hydrocarbon (coal) field into which the air or oxygen is forcibly introduced into the targeted coal seam. They also oversee the operation of the production wells and pipelines through which the resultant coal gas is brought to the surface and relayed

to gas cleaning plants, where the impurities inherent in coal are cleansed, and the unwanted carbon dioxide (CO_2) is removed. Then, the resultant coal gas can be sent to processing plants. Thus, one of the major environmental advantages of coal gasification is the opportunity to remove impurities such as sulfur, mercury, and soot before burning the fuel to create energy within electric power generators. (This is unlike traditional coal-burning plants that have to be concerned with the pollutants released by the coal as it burns.)

Salaries
According to the U.S. Department of Labor's U.S. Bureau of Labor Statistics report of 2006–2007, annual earnings in May 2004 for mining engineers (of which Coal Gasification Engineers are a specific discipline) ranged from a low of $39,700 to a high of $103,790, with an average of $64,690.

Employment Prospects
While the U.S. Bureau of Labor Statistics projects a decline in employment of mining engineers generally, the report also indicates that there are still good employment opportunities, as many mining engineers currently employed are expected to approach retirement age during the coming years. As coal gasification is essentially a new and growing industry technology, engineers specializing in this process have many fresh prospects of employment. Favorable job opportunities in the application of this type of mining technology are becoming available worldwide as this technology proves cost effective and safe. Recruiting of graduates from U.S. mining engineering programs has become worldwide. As a result, some graduates may travel frequently or even live outside the United States.

Advancement Prospects
The next career step for an experienced Coal Gasification Engineer is either to become manager of a coal gasification project and, from there, move into the top management levels of the industry, or to become self-employed as a freelance engineer in this field.

Education and Training
A Bachelor of Science degree in mechanical engineering technology, electrical engineering technology, mining engineering technology, or chemical engineering is a basic requirement. In addition, a master's degree in one of these four disciplines is often also demanded. While a Ph.D. in either mining engineering or environment management is not obligatory, it is recommended.

Special Requirements
Like many other engineering disciplines, Coal Gasification Engineers must have a certification as a professional

engineer To become a licensed Professional Engineer, an individual must pass the comprehensive FE (Fundamentals of Engineering) exam, then work a given number of years (usually three to five) as an Engineer in Training (EIT), and then pass the PE (Practicing Engineer) test.

Experience, Skills, and Personality Traits

As the coal gasification process is both a mining and a chemical process, background and experience in both arenas is essential to engineers looking to specialize in this new field. They should be familiar with the various facets of process engineering including piping design, pipeline terminals, and related equipment specifications. They should have some background serving in a project management role within a plant environment and have knowledge of the most current mining and chemical engineering principles and practices.

Beyond their basic knowledge of engineering procedures and technologies, Coal Gasification Engineers should have a thorough understanding of coal mining, hydrodynamics, geology, and process engineering. They must be computer literate (proficient in MS Access, Excel, and Word programs), conversant with product design development cycles, and have experience in analyzing complex technical problems. They need to be heavily detail-oriented and exhibit good communication and interpersonal abilities.

Unions and Associations

The most useful professional associations for Coal Gasification Engineers are the American Chemical Society (ACS) and the Society for Mining, Metallurgy, and Exploration (SME). Other major professional groups might include the American Society of Mechanical Engineers (ASME), the Association of Energy Engineers (AEE) or the National Society of Professional Engineers (NSPE).

Tips for Entry

1. While earning your bachelor's degree in electrical, mechanical, or mining engineering, take courses in chemistry and even consider an advanced degree in chemical engineering.
2. Search for paying or nonpaying internships, fellowships, and co-op industry work in the coal-mining field to gain firsthand experience in the business.
3. Consider working in the hazardous waste treatment industry and/or project engineering in oil or gas refineries and chemical plants to broaden your background in environmental and process engineering.

GEOLOGIST

CAREER PROFILE	CAREER LADDER

CAREER PROFILE

Duties: Applying the principles and practices of geology, locate and identify potential coal beds and aid in their development and the extraction of the coal

Alternate Title(s): Geophysicist; Geoscientist; Geotechnical Mining Engineer; Mine Engineer/Geologist

Salary Range: $37,000 to $95,000 or more

Employment Prospects: Fair to Good

Advancement Prospects: Poor

Prerequisites:

Education or Training—A bachelor's degree in geology, geotechnical engineering, or mining engineering is a basic requirement. In addition, a master's degree in geology, earth science, or environmental engineering is the typical minimum educational requirement for most entry-level research geologists in private industry.

Experience—Two to four or more years in the mining industry with increasing responsibility in geological task management and some field experience

Special Skills and Personality Traits—Ability to multitask, prioritize, and meet deadlines; capable of complex analytical thinking and spatial visualization; excellent interpersonal skills; good written and verbal communication abilities; mathematics and computer proficiency; team player but able to work with little supervision

Special Requirements—Most states require a state license as a practicing geologist

CAREER LADDER

```
┌─────────────────────────────────┐
│  Consultant; Project Manager    │
└─────────────────────────────────┘

┌─────────────────────────────────┐
│          Geologist              │
└─────────────────────────────────┘

┌─────────────────────────────────┐
│      College Graduate;          │
│    Geologist-in-Training        │
└─────────────────────────────────┘
```

Position Description

Geologists study the composition, structure, and other physical aspects of Earth. With the use of sophisticated instruments and by analyzing the composition of the earth and water, they study Earth's geologic past and present to find supplies of natural resources, such as groundwater, metals and other minerals, petroleum, and coal.

Specifically, Geologists read and interpret geologic maps and documents. They collect and interpret data from borehole studies, soil assessments, and fault studies. They research information on the identification of geological formations, foundations, slope stabilization, retaining wall plan development and right-of-way development, and prepare their reports and geologic maps based on their findings. They determine the potential impact of federal, state, and local regulations related to the projected exploration and usage of given geological structures. During this process, they describe and classify soil and rocks and develop soil and geology reports. In a process known as geologic surface mapping, they develop detailed 3-D geologic models using mine-modeling software (such as Arc View, Surfer Oasis Montaj, or Surpac).

On mining projects, they frequently are responsible for mine planning and development, exploration programs, property acquisitions, and resource estimations. In these cases, they develop/coordinate exploration drill plans, and work with federal, state, and local agencies on permits for the drilling plans. Throughout, they develop budgets for and track all associated exploration costs. In the planning for excavation of coal mines, they coordinate and evaluate slope stability studies to determine pit wall design parameters, and coordinate, and analyze pit wall monitoring programs. They assist mining engineers in the mine design, including the scheduling for the expansion of the mine with its associated grade and tonnage reports. They help in designing haul roads used in the extraction and delivery of mined coal, and develop haul simulations. They aid in the preparation of presentation quality maps and documents for federal and state agencies.

Geologists need to be familiar with underground drilling, blasting, rock handling, and ground control methods. In all these processes, they review and apply appropriate geophysical standards in implementing their designed geophysical survey. They interface with mining engineers and other field staff during and following the completion of such geophysical surveys.

Some Geologists may become involved in the issues of air quality in the mining environment, becoming familiar with dust sampling and methane and carbon monoxide detection procedures as outlined in the federal Mine Safety and Health Administration regulations. In this capacity, they may complete the federal Occupational Safety and Health Administration course in Hazardous Waste Operations and Emergency Response.

Salaries

According to the U.S. Department of Labor's *Occupational Outlook Handbook, 2006–07 Edition,* median annual earnings of Geologists (geoscientists) were $68,730 in May 2004. The middle 50 percent earned between $49,260 and $98,380. The lowest 10 percent earned less than $37,700, and the highest 10 percent earned more than $130,750. According to the National Association of Colleges and Employers, beginning salary offers in July 2005 for graduates with bachelor's degrees in geology and related sciences averaged $39,365.

Employment Prospects

According to the U.S. Bureau of Labor Statistics, employment of geoscientists (geologists) is expected to grow more slowly than the average for all occupations through 2014, except for some occupational specialties. Nonetheless, the increasing energy needs of the United States and the abundance of coal fields within the continental United States point to the continued expansion of the coal industry in the future. In addition, due to the relatively low number of qualified geoscience graduates and the large number of expected retirements in the coming years, job opportunities in such areas as oil and natural gas and coal exploration is expected to be good.

Advancement Prospects

One avenue of advancement for experienced Geologists in the coal industry is to assume more managerial responsibilities and become project managers of specific mining operations. Such posts, however, are limited in number and only the most experienced and qualified Geologists are equipped to make such career advancement. Other Geologists may find greater possibilities in joining in, or setting up their own, consulting services. Management, scientific, and technical consulting services increasingly hire geologists and geoscientists due to expanded government contracting and the demand for professionals outside the individual company to provide technical and planning assistance.

Education and Training

A bachelor's degree in geology, geotechnical engineering, or mining engineering is a basic requirement for most geology positions in the coal industry. In addition, a master's degree in geology, geological engineering, geophysics, earth science, or environmental engineering would be recommended. Extensive coursework in chemistry, physics, and mathematics should be a part of the educational background of a Geologist looking for a career in the coal industry.

Special Requirements

Nearly all states require of Geologists certification and licensing as Professional Geologists. In addition, the Energy Minerals Division of the American Association of Petroleum Geologists (AAPG), through its Division of Professional Affairs, offers a peer-reviewed, professional certification program for coal Geologists. Coal Geologist Certification requires eight years experience in coal geology. This experience should be primarily applied and broad-based, although time involved in research is applicable toward certification. Often, graduate education (master's or Ph.D.) can be substituted for experience. Three Certified Coal Geologists sponsors are requested, although any AAPG member can serve as a sponsor if three CCG's are not available.

Experience, Skills, and Personality Traits

Candidates for Geologist positions should have some field experience as an engineering staff member, and some background operating geophysical equipment. They should be familiar with Geographic Information System (GIS) techniques and applications. (GIS is a "smart map" tool that allows users to create interactive queries, analyze the spatial information, and edit data.) Their fieldwork should include the identification of potential rock slide, landslide, and seepage areas as well as mapping strike and dip of bedding and joints of rocks. They need to have a thorough understanding of near surface soil, geologic, and environmental conditions that affect geophysical measurements. Experience with developing conceptual rock slope stability solutions, as well as type, size, and location plan development procedures would be an additional job asset. They should be completely familiar with geophysical data processing methods and geophysical modeling.

Geologists should have good written and verbal communication abilities and display excellent interpersonal skills. They need to have computer proficiency, particularly in Microsoft Word, Excel, PowerPoint, and Outlook, as well as have basic skills in macro automation and the use of mine modeling and design software (such as Surpac). In addition, they must be skilled in the use of computer-aided design (CAD) and gridding/contouring programs for the preparation of geologic maps and sections. They may be required to move heavy geophysical equipment in sometimes harsh field conditions. They should be self-starters, capable of multi-tasking, prioritizing, and meeting deadlines. Above all, they must be able to function well within a team environment.

Unions and Associations

The primary associations for Geologists are the American Geological Institute (AGI) and the American Association of Petroleum Geologists (AAPG). Other professional societies include the American Society for Surface Mining and Reclamation (ASSMR), the Association of Engineering Geologists (AEG), the Institute of Shaft Drilling Technology (ISDT), the International Erosion Control Association (IECA), and the Society for Mining, Metallurgy, and Exploration (SME).

Tips for Entry

1. As a geology student, spend your summers living/working under field conditions with faculty members to gain practical experience, as well as gain extra college credits.
2. Internships with geological consulting firms are another good source for hands-on involvement with geologic and geoscientific practices/procedures.
3. Perfect your computer skills, as those students who have proficiency with computer modeling, data analysis and integration, digital mapping, remote sensing, and geographic information systems will be best prepared for entering the job market for Geologists.

MINE SAFETY ENGINEER

CAREER PROFILE

Duties: Implement and coordinate coal mine safety programs, and ensure proper working conditions for mineworkers in compliance with state and federal regulations

Alternate Title(s): Mine Safety Inspector; Safety Director

Salary Range: $39,000 to $95,000 or more

Employment Prospects: Good

Advancement Prospects: Fair

Prerequisites:

Education or Training—Bachelor's degree in mining engineering or a related engineering field is a basic requirement; master's degree in specialized engineering field, such as environmental or geological, is recommended; specialized instruction in mine safety and rescue procedures also advisable

Experience—Three to five years or more in mine planning and development, as well as fieldwork in an assortment of mining environments

Special Skills and Personality Traits—Ability to visualize three-dimensional objects from two-dimensional drawings; aptitude for mathematics and science (especially chemistry and physics); excellent communication (both oral and written) and interpersonal skills; good instructional, investigative, leadership, and supervisory capabilities

Special Requirements—Certification as a Professional Engineer (PEng) is a requirement

CAREER LADDER

```
┌─────────────────────────────────────┐
│ Business Mining Analyst; Mining      │
│ Consultant; Safety Inspector in      │
│ Related Engineering Field            │
└─────────────────────────────────────┘

┌─────────────────────────────────────┐
│      Mine Safety Engineer            │
└─────────────────────────────────────┘

┌─────────────────────────────────────┐
│        Mining Engineer               │
└─────────────────────────────────────┘
```

Position Description

Coal mining can be a dangerous career, involving many health and safety hazards. Coal mines, in either open pits or deep underground, are filled with heavy dust, poor ventilation, and toxic fumes. In open pit mines, there can be slope failures with falling rock or debris. In underground mines, there are the potentials of mining roof collapses and gas explosions. Most of these risks can be greatly reduced in modern mines, and multiple fatality incidents are relatively rare nowadays in the developed world. In less technically advanced countries, however, thousands of mineworkers still die annually in coal mines.

The goal of a Mine Safety Engineer is to eliminate all safety and health risks in coal mines, not an easy task. They promote and enforce mine safety standards and regulations. They use their extensive knowledge of mine design and practices to ensure the well-being of workers on the job. They inspect underground (or open-pit) mining areas and train mine personnel to guarantee compliance with state and federal laws and accepted mining practices designed to prevent mine accidents. They inspect mine workings to detect unsafe timbers (used to support the ceilings and walls of the mine shafts), cribbing, roof bolts, electric wiring, elevators, explosives storage, equipment, and general working conditions. They check for coal gas fumes and that the air is safe to breathe. They advise on procedures for examining walls and roof surfaces for evidence of strata faults (which might indicate cave-in or rockslide hazards).

Mine Safety Engineers teach all mining personnel safe working procedures, such as how to avoid back injury and the proper entry and exit procedures to and from the mine. They see to it that all workers wear/carry protective clothing and equipment, such as hard hats, goggles, gloves, safety lamps, steel-toed boots, safety belts, harnesses, and earmuffs or plugs for ear drum protection (particularly from blastings set off in the tunnels). They counsel mine employees on how to deal with heat stress, fatigue, cramps, and hygiene issues related to heat, such as rashes or prickly heat. They recommend drinking water and wearing of oxygen and gas masks when working in areas that contain toxic gases. In addition, Mine Safety Engineers educate and try to prevent common illnesses, such as pneumonoultramicroscopicsilicovolcanoconiosis (a chronic lung disease caused from inhaling dust particles).

Mine Safety Engineers must perform atmospheric tests continually and monitor the airflow, oxygen content, flammability rates, and toxic contaminants in the air of mines. They recommend alteration or installation of ventilation shafts, partitions, or equipment to remedy inadequate air circulation. As many accidents and deaths occur because of unsafe electrical wiring, unsteady ladders, and faulty vehicles, they must inspect and monitor areas such as brake systems on moving vehicles, faulty ladders, and unsafe elevated walkways. They study the aftermath of explosions, fires, electrocutions, and other such accidents, identifying causes and recommending remedial action. They may administer first aid in case of accidents and lead rescue activities during emergencies, as well as maintain rescue equipment.

Mine Safety Engineers usually divide their working time between an office, a laboratory, and at mines. At mine sites, they are required to wear protective equipment, and may need to work in enclosed or high spaces while conducting experiments, which can often be hot, tiring, and dirty. In their office and laboratory, they use traditional and computer-aided design (CAD) systems to aid in their analysis and design tasks.

Salaries

According to the U.S. Department of Labor's *Occupational Outlook Handbook, 2006–07 Edition,* median annual earnings in May 2004 of mining engineers (which include Mine Safety Engineers) ranged from a low of $39,000 to a high of $103,000, with an average salary being $64,700.

Employment Prospects

According the U.S. Department of Labor's Bureau of Labor Statistics, Mine Safety Engineers (along with mining and

geological engineers) are expected to have good employment opportunities, despite a projected decline in employment in the industries in which mining (and mine safety) engineers are concentrated. Many mining engineers (and safety engineers) currently employed are approaching retirement age which should create job openings in the coming years. In addition, there are a much smaller annual number of graduates in mining engineering than in other engineering fields, and the volume is not anticipated to increase substantially.

Favorable job opportunities also may be available worldwide as mining operations from abroad recruit graduates of U.S. mining engineering programs.

Advancement Prospects

Experienced Mine Safety Engineers may decide to set up their own consulting businesses or pair up with geological and metallurgical engineers to open up a larger consulting firm that specializes in mining, safety, and other related areas. As an alternative, Mine Safety Engineers may want to become construction contractors, safety inspectors in other disciplines, or freelance business mining analysts.

Education and Training

A bachelor's degree in mining engineering, or possibly in a related engineering field (such as engineering technology), is a basic requirement for any candidate for the post of Mine Safety Engineer. A solid background in mathematics and science, with some concentration in English, social studies, and humanities are the usual admission requirements for undergraduate engineering schools. In addition, candidates need to be computer literate, and to have some training in basic health protective measures and procedures.

Some Mine Safety Engineers also choose to earn a master's degree in a specific area, such as geological engineering. Mine Safety Engineers are required to update their skills and knowledge constantly to keep up with rapid technological advancements in the mining field and in safety methods. They must be familiar with all the latest improvements in mining procedures, in the monitoring of hazardous gases, and innovative procedures used for gas drainage and ventilation. In addition, they need to keep current with all state and federal regulations regarding mine safety.

Special Requirements

In the United States, all states and the District of Columbia require licensure for engineers who offer their services directly to the public. All engineers who are licensed are called professional engineers (PE). This licensure usually requires a degree from an accredited engineering program, four years of relevant work experience, and the successful completion of a state examination. Most states recognize licensure from other such jurisdictions, if the manner in which the initial license was obtained meets or exceeds their own licensure requirements.

Experience, Skills, and Personality Traits

Mine Safety Engineers should have three to five or more years background in mine design, planning, and development. They need hands-on experience in using both traditional and computer-aided design (CAD) systems in designing mining safety operations and in analyzing the effects and potential problems of specific safety procedures.

As Mine Safety Engineers must be devoted to the health and safety of miners, they should be unusually sympathetic to people's well-being. Their communication and interpersonal skills must be solid, as they must deal constantly with miners, technicians, scientists, and management. They need to be heavily detail-oriented and analytical in their research. They should have a natural aptitude for mathematics and science (particularly chemistry and physics) and be able to visualize what three-dimensional objects (such as mining equipment and mine shafts) would look like from just two-dimensional drawings.

They need to make quick but logical decisions and act speedily in times of emergency. They have to be flexible to adapt quickly from an office environment to a laboratory or mine site and be equipped to supervise and lead others. Since most mines are located in remote locations, Mine Safety Engineers must be prepared to travel to and from work sites, and to labor for long hours, even weekend shifts when required.

Unions and Associations

Professional organizations and associations of interest for Mine Safety Engineers include the American Institute of Mining, Metallurgical and Petroleum Engineers (AIME); the Mining and Metallurgical Society of America (MMSA); the National Mining Association (NMA); and the Society for Mining, Metallurgy, and Exploration (SME). Mine Safety Engineers also may find it useful to be members of the larger umbrella engineering group, the National Society of Professional Engineers (NSPE).

Tips for Entry

1. During high school, gain a solid background in mathematics (algebra, geometry, trigonometry, and calculus) and science (biology, chemistry, and physics), as they are basic requirements for admission into most engineering schools.
2. Include some additional course work in English (for your writing communication skills), and sociology or psychology (to understand interpersonal relations and to learn how to teach and lead people).
3. Consider taking basic health and safety courses at a local Red Cross organization or a hospital.

MINING ENGINEER

CAREER PROFILE

Duties: Find, extract, and prepare coal for use by manufacturing industries and power utilities

Alternate Title(s): Mine Design Engineer; Mine Development Engineer; Mine Geotechnical Engineer; Mine Layout Engineer; Mine Maintenance Engineer; Mine Planning Engineer; Mine Production Engineer; Mine Systems Engineer; Mine Ventilation Engineer

Salary Range: $40,000 to $100,000 or more

Employment Prospects: Fair

Advancement Prospects: Poor to Fair

Prerequisites:

Education or Training—Bachelor's degree in mining engineering or in a related engineering discipline is required; a master's degree in an allied engineering discipline is recommended

Experience—Entry-level engineer's work for three to five years under the supervision of seasoned engineers before becoming full-fledged Mining Engineers

Special Skills and Personality Traits—Analytical and detail-oriented; creative and inquisitive; capable of critical thinking and operations analysis; excellent communication (both oral and writing) and interpersonal abilities; solid mathematics and computer skills

Special Requirements—Licensing as a Professional Engineer (PE) is required

CAREER LADDER

```
┌─────────────────────────────────┐
│  Engineering Staff Supervisor;   │
│  Manager of Mine Operations      │
└─────────────────────────────────┘

┌─────────────────────────────────┐
│        Mining Engineer           │
└─────────────────────────────────┘

┌─────────────────────────────────┐
│ College Graduate; Mining Technician │
└─────────────────────────────────┘
```

Position Description

Coal mining is the extraction of coal from the earth for use as fuel. A coal mine and its accompanying structures are collectively known as a colliery. The most economical method of coal extraction from coal seams in the earth depends on the depth and quality of the seams, as well as the geology and environmental factors of the area to be mined. Coal mining is characterized generally by whether it is a surface or an underground operation.

If the coal seams are near the surface, the coal is extracted by strip mining, which exposes the coal by the continuous digging of an open pit or strip. As the coal is extracted, the waste earth (called overburden) from the still covered coal fills the former pit, and the strip progresses. Another form of surface mining is called mountaintop removal mining. This process involves removing the highest part of a mountain with explosives and earth-moving machinery to uncover the coal seams contained within. Mountaintop removal creates an immense quantity of excess overburden, which is typically placed in valley fills on the side of the former mountains. One consequence is that any streams flowing through these valleys are usually buried.

Most coal seams have to be mined by digging underground. In deep mining, pillars of timber are set up to support the coal mine roof as the mining of the coal vein progresses. Several processes are used to extract the coal, including the traditional method of explosives to break up the coal seam as well as by different types of machinery (many of which are computer-controlled).

In general, coal Mining Engineers find, extract, and prepare coal for use by power utilities and manufacturing industries. They conduct preliminary surveys/studies of coal deposits to assess the economic and environmental feasibility of potential mining operations. They determine the appropriate means of mining the deposits safely and efficiently, designing open pit and underground mines. They plan and advise on appropriate drilling and blasting methods for mining, construction, and/or demolition. They supervise the construction of mine shafts/tunnels in underground operations and design shafts, ventilation systems, power supply equipment, mine services, and haulage and conveying methods to transport the coal to the surface (or from the open pit mine) and on to processing plants.

The primary responsibility of Mining Engineers is the safe, economical, and environmentally sound operation of the mines. As such, they plan, organize, and supervise the development of mines and mine structures, as well as the operation/maintenance of mines. They work with geologists and metallurgical engineers to locate and appraise new ore deposits and, in conjunction with mechanical and electrical engineers, plan and design new (or select appropriate) mining equipment and machinery for mining operations, as well as that equipment used to prepare coal for processing by power or manufacturing industries.

One of the most dramatic changes in the mining industry is due to the effect of sophisticated three-dimensional mine-planning software. Once a mine operation has been decided on, Mining Engineers create detailed designs that take into account the topography, infrastructure, and physical parameters of the targeted coal seam. With the new 3-D computer technology, tasks such as rendering graphic images of drill holes have become much easier as the data can now be manipulated and visualized. Today's range of integrated mine-planning tools allow for massively complex models to be built to optimize extracting/processing coal.

Thus, Mining Engineers design, develop, and implement computer applications in mine design, mine modeling, mapping, and the ongoing monitoring of mine conditions. They prepare operations and project estimates, schedules, and reports. Working with mine safety engineers, they implement and coordinate mine safety programs, and, generally, supervise/coordinate the work of mining technicians, machine operators, technologists, survey personnel, and other engineers and scientists involved in the mining process. With the increased emphasis on protecting the environment, many Mining Engineers work to solve (or specialize in solving) problems related to land reclamation and water and air pollution control.

Most Mining Engineers work in office buildings, laboratories, or industrial plants. Others may spend most of their time at construction sites and mines where they monitor or direct operations, resolving on-site problems as they occur. Some of them may travel extensively to work sites or processing plants. Mining Engineers usually report directly to senior management.

Salaries

Median annual earnings of Mining Engineers in May 2004, according to the U.S. Department of Labor's Bureau of Labor Statistics, were $60,370. The lowest 10 percent had annual incomes of approximately $39,700, and the highest 10 percent earned over $103,000. According to a 2005 survey by the National Association of Colleges and Employers, starting salary offers for Mining Engineers with bachelor's degrees were $48,643.

Employment Prospects

Although the U.S. Department of Labor estimates a projected decline in employment of Mining Engineers in the coming years, their *Occupational Outlook Handbook, 2006–07 Edition* indicates that Mining Engineers should have good employment opportunities, in that many Mining Engineers currently employed are approaching retirement age. Furthermore, the *Handbook* states that relatively few schools offer mining engineering programs, and the small number of yearly graduates with mining engineering degrees is not expected to increase substantially.

In addition, favorable job opportunities may become increasingly available as mining operations around the world recruit graduates from American mining engineering programs. As a result, some Mining Engineers may travel frequently or live abroad. While many of the mining industries, such as coal, metal, and copper, are expected to have declines in employment, there is a resurgence of interest in coal (plentiful throughout North America) as an alternative energy source to oil and natural gas. This increased interest in coal may well offset the projected industry decline in the next several years.

Advancement Prospects

New engineering graduates hired as entry-level Mining Engineers usually work under the supervision of veteran Mining Engineers and, in some of the larger mining outfits, may even receive formal classroom or seminar-type training. As these beginning Mining Engineers gain knowledge and experience, they are assigned to more difficult projects and gain greater independence in developing mining equipment and mine construction designs.

Some Mining Engineers may become technical specialists, or they may supervise a staff or team of engineers and technicians. Some eventually become project managers or other higher management (or sales) personnel within the coal industry.

Education and Training

A bachelor's degree in mining engineering (or, in some cases, a related engineering discipline, such as electrical or mechanical engineering) is an absolute requirement. In addition to the standard engineering degree, many colleges offer degrees in engineering technology (in either two- or four-year programs). These programs concentrate on practical design and production work, rather than on more theoretical and scientific knowledge. Graduates of four-year technology programs may obtain entry-level engineering positions similar to those obtained by graduates with a bachelor's degree in engineering, but some employers may regard them as having skills somewhere between those of a technician and a full-blown engineer.

A master's degree or doctorate in a related engineering discipline may be demanded for some mining engineering posts. Some Mining Engineers obtain graduate degrees in other engineering disciplines to learn about new technology, or in business administration to enhance their chances of moving into higher management levels.

Special Requirements

All states require that practicing Mining Engineers must have a license as a Professional Engineer (PE). This licensure requires a bachelor's degree from an accredited engineering program, four years of relevant work experience, and the successful completion of a state examination.

Experience, Skills, and Personality Traits

For most entry-level Mining Engineers, experience is gained on the job, under the tutelage of a seasoned engineer. They can put to use their knowledge of the practical applications of engineering science/technology to specific coal mining problems. In addition, they can apply their knowledge of design techniques, tools, and principles involved in the production of precision technical blueprints and models.

Mining Engineers need to be highly computer literate. They should be creative, inquisitive, analytical, and quite detail-oriented. They need to have solid time-management and decision-making talents, along with the ability to organize, plan, and prioritize work. They must have excellent interpersonal and communication skills (both oral and written) and be team workers. Moreover, they must be dependable and persistent even in the face of obstacles.

Unions and Associations

The two relevant associations for Mining Engineers are the American Institute of Mining, Metallurgical, and Petroleum Engineers, Inc. (AIME), and the Society for Mining, Metallurgy, and Exploration (SME). Other organizations that might prove useful to Mining Engineers are the American Society for Mining and Reclamation (ASMR) and the Institute of Shaft Drilling Technology (ISDT), as well as the general association for engineers, the National Society of Professional Engineers (NSPE).

Tips for Entry

1. Along with your mining engineering program, include courses in speech and technical writing to augment your verbal and writing proficiency.
2. Add one or more languages other than English to enhance your job potential.
3. Expand your computer knowledge to include familiarity with applications and programming, as well as computer-aided design (CAD) techniques, as you will need such know-how as a Mining Engineer.

MANUAL LABOR
PERSONNEL

MACHINE OPERATORS

CAREER PROFILE

Duties: Continuous Mining Machine Operator: operate a self-propelled mining machine that mines ore from the coal face and loads it onto conveyors in a continuous operation; Cutter Operator: operate a coal-cutting machine; Dragline Operator: operate an overburden stripping machine that scoops the earth away in surface mines to expose coal; Drilling Machine Operator: operate a mobile drilling machine to drill blastholes in underground mine or in face of strip coal mine; Loading Machine Operator: operate loading machines to load coal into shuttle or mine cars or onto conveyors; Longwall Machine Operator: operate equipment to shear coal from the long-wall face in an underground mine; Rock Dusting Machine Operator: operate a machine that distributes rock dust over the interior surfaces of a coal mine to prevent coal dust explosions; Shortwall Coal Cutter Operator: control a machine to undercut coal in small areas

Alternate Title(s): Continuous Mining Machine Operator: None; Cutter Operator: Cutting Machine Operator, Holer, Machineman, Undercutter; Dragline Operator: Overburden Stripping Operator; Drilling Machine Operator: Coal Driller, Driller Operator, Horizontal-Drill Operator, Rotary-Drill Operator; Loading Machine Operator: Machine Loader, Mechanical-Shovel Operator, Mucking-Machine Operator; Longwall Machine Operator: Longwall Miner, Longwall Shear Operator, Longwall Mining Machine Tender; Rock Dusting Machine Operator: Rock-Dust Man, Rock-Dust Sprayer, Rock Duster

Salary Range: $30,000 to $65,000 or more

Employment Prospects: Poor to Fair

Advancement Prospects: Poor to Fair

Prerequisites:

Education or Training—High school diploma required; some training in mine procedures and safety necessary, as well as specialized training in specific machine operations

Experience—One to three years as an apprentice helper to a seasoned machine operator

Special Skills and Personality Traits—Excellent communication and interpersonal skills; good vision and manual dexterity; mechanical abilities; physically fit; precision in movements and work; some technical experience and aptitude with machinery

Special Requirements—Certificate of competency from a Miners' Examining Board usually required

CAREER LADDER

```
┌─────────────────────────────────┐
│  Mine Health and Safety Inspectors; │
│  Mine Supervisory Positions     │
└─────────────────────────────────┘

┌─────────────────────────────────┐
│       Machine Operators         │
└─────────────────────────────────┘

┌─────────────────────────────────┐
│     Mine Helper-Apprentice      │
└─────────────────────────────────┘
```

Position Description

For most underground coal mines, above the mine and surrounding the shaft(s) leading down to it are the operational buildings: the mine office, the engine house, the machine and repair shops, sheds and other outbuildings, and, towering above all of them the tipple-tower, a tall skeleton of structural iron work that covers the mouth of the main mine shaft. All workers and all materials used in the mine (including timber, tools, machinery, powder, coal cars, and mine locomotives,) move up and down the same way. The mine itself is a vast system of tunnels, some of them so low that workers must work in a stooping posture. The tunnels lead to rooms at the end of which are the headings and the blank, black face of the coal seam where the actual mining is undertaken. Through the system of tunnels run underground electric railways, with switching stations, sidings, and a main belt-line. All day long large locomotives, some weighing as much as 13 tons, gather the trains of cars filled with coal and drag them to the weigh station where they are checked for weight so each miner is given credit for coal mined. The ore is then dropped into waiting bins, which are lifted upward to the open air and onward to the top of the tipple-tower where the coal is then dumped into railroad cars stationed below it.

Underground mining primarily includes three methods: conventional, continuous, and longwall (or shortwall) mining. Conventional mining, which, at some mines, is being slowly phased out, is the oldest process, requiring the most workers and procedures. A strip, or kerf, is drill cut underneath the coal seam to control the direction in which coal falls after it has been blasted. A Cutter Operator uses a huge electric chain saw with a cutter bar from six to 15 feet long (the cutting machine) to slice the kerf. Then, a Drilling Machine Operator, using a mobile drilling machine, drills holes (known as blasting holes) in the coal seam. Shot firers (or blasters) then place the explosives in the hole. Extreme caution has to be taken throughout this procedure and all workers must be clear of the area before the explosives are detonated. After the blast, Loading Machine Operators, using a mechanical power shovel, load the coal into small rubber-tired cars (run by shuttle-car operators) which bring the coal to a central location for weighing and transportation to the surface.

The continuous mining method eliminates the drilling and blasting procedures of conventional mining with a machine called a continuous miner, which both mines the coal and loads it onto conveyors or into shuttle cars in one continuous operation. Until recently, the Continuous Mining Machine Operator had to sit or lie in the machine's cab and operate the levers that cut or ripped out the coal from the coal bed and loaded it onto the conveyor or the shuttle car. However, the introduction of remote-controlled continuous mining machines (which also aid in guaranteeing safety) now allows an operator to control the machine from a distance.

In longwall mining, which is similar to continuous mining, Longwall Machine Operators run large machines with rotating drums that automatically shear the ore and load it onto the conveyor. At the same time, hydraulic jacks continually reinforce the tunnel roof. As the coal is cut, these jacks hydraulically winch forward, supporting the roof as they progress along the tunnel. One advantage is that all the roadways behind the cutting are in worked-out areas in which no further mining is necessary.

The opposite of longwall mining is a process called shortwall mining, in which comparatively small areas of the coal face are worked separately. This process is commonly known also as room and pillar mining, and is frequently employed when the coal seam is four feet or under in thickness. The coal seams are mined by a machine manned by a Shortwall Coal Cutter Operator. It cuts a network of rooms into the coal seam. As the rooms are carved out, pillars composed of coal are left behind in each room to support the roof of the mine, often reinforced by timber beams.

One significant problem in underground mining is the buildup of rock dust produced in the mine by blasting, drilling, shoveling, and handling both the coal and the rock surrounding the ore. Rock dust in suspension varies in particle size and composition, but it always represents a health hazard when inhaled, and can be a contributing factor in coal dust explosions. A machine, known as a rock duster and operated by a Rock Dusting Machine Operator, sprays inert dust (dry or wet) on the roof, floor, and ribs in all working places and all the hauling tunnels (called haulageways) to settle the coal dust. The machine has a flexible hose fed by a powerful blower, and typically employs powdered limestone to dilute the coal dust, thereby reducing explosion hazards and lessening the health hazard of breathing untreated coal dust.

In surface coal mining (sometimes known as open pit mining), earth usually has to be removed before the coal deposit can be tapped. This earthen layer is called the overburden. In many surface mines, the overburden is first drilled and blasted. Then, Dragline Operators (also called overburden stripping operators) scoop the earth away to expose the coal. Some of these dragline machines are the largest land machines on Earth. Next, Loading Machine Operators rip the exposed coal from the seam and dump it into trucks to be driven to the preparation plant where the coal is refined for use by utility companies and other industries.

Salaries

According to the U.S. Department of Labor's *Occupational Outlook Handbook, 2006–07 Edition,* average wage and salary earnings in mining in general were significantly higher than the average for all industries in 2004. Average weekly earnings of nonsupervisory workers in coal mining in 2004 came to $1,030. In May 2004, about 27.5 percent of workers in coal mining were members of the United Mine Workers of American (UMWA), receiving guaranteed paid holidays per contract and other benefits from the union's welfare and retirement funds.

The *Handbook* details the median hourly earnings in May 2004 of the different types of coal workers. Continuous Mining Machine Operators' hourly wages averaged $18.35, whereas excavating and Loading Machine and Dragline Operators earned an average of $15.20. In contract, mechanics and operators of mobile heavy equipment earned hourly average wages of $19.15.

Employment Prospects

According to the U.S. Bureau of Labor Statistics (of the U.S. Department of Labor), employment in mining is expected to decline by 13 percent through the year 2014. This continuing long-term decline is due to increased productivity resulting from technological advances in mining operations and larger mining equipment, consolidation, international competition, and stringent environmental regulations. New mining machines that operate remotely by computer and that self-diagnose mechanical problems require fewer workers for operation/maintenance. Advances in longwall and surface mining, which are less labor intensive, also have increased productivity. In addition, such innovations as roof bolting, self-advancing roof supports and continuous mining machinery have led to safer, more efficient operations that also necessitate fewer workers.

Despite these trends of declining employment, job opportunities for construction, extraction, and production workers in coal mining should be somewhat favorable. Many present mine workers are approaching retirement age, and younger miners and equipment operators will be needed to replace the retirees.

Advancement Prospects

As mine production workers gain more experience, they can advance to higher paying jobs requiring greater skill. For example, a mining machine operator's helper might become an operator. When vacancies occur, announcements are posted, and all qualified workers can bid for the job, as per union contracts. Positions are filled based on seniority and ability. Miners who have gained skill and experience operating one or more of the mining machines may choose to take special training and become mine safety, health, and compliance officers, whose primary duties include mine safety inspection. Usually promotions into supervisory positions take at least five years' experience as a miner, or a degree in mining engineering. For most professional and managerial positions in coal mining, a master's degree in engineering, one of the physical sciences, or business administration is preferred. Environmental management posts require thorough knowledge of local, state, and federal regulations and a strong natural science background, or a background in a technical field such as environmental engineering or hydrology.

Education and Training

While a high school diploma may not be demanded for some apprentice (helper) positions in the mining industry, it would be helpful for any future career advancement. Most mine workers start as helpers to experienced workers and learn skills on the job. Nonetheless, with the introduction of more technologically advanced machinery and mining methods, some formal training may be required. Some employers even prefer to hire recent graduates of high school vocational programs in mining or graduates of junior college or technical school programs in mine technology.

By law, mining companies must offer formal training in either classrooms or training mines for the first few weeks of a new miner's employment. The Federal Mine Safety and Health Act of 1977 mandates that mines operating in the United States have an approved worker training program in health and safety issues. Each plan must include at least 40 hours of basic safety training for new miners who have no experience in underground mines, and 24 hours for new miners working in surface mines. In addition, each miner must receive at least eight hours of refresher safety training a year, and any job changes require new safety training appropriate to the new job.

Many mines are now employing more high-tech teaching tools for miner training, such as machinery simulators and virtual reality simulators. By replicating actual mine conditions and emergencies, mine workers can become better prepared and companies can instantly assess a mine worker's progress and skills.

Special Requirements

In most states and at most mines, every individual employed in both surface and underground mining must have a certificate of competency from the Miners' Examining Board. Mine machinery operators need to complete a course of instruction in first aid and mine rescue methods. Those looking for advancement into supervisory, or possibly management, positions, will need to obtain certificates in mine technology (usually gained from at least one year's enrollment in specialized mine technology programs offered by a few colleges).

Experience, Skills, and Personality Traits

Apprenticeship as a helper (or laborer) to experienced miners and mining machinery operators typically takes at least one year, and usually from two to three years. Most states require miners or mining machinery operators to obtain a certificate of competency from the state's Miners' Examining Board and to have completed instruction in first aid, prescribed mine rescue methods, and uses of appliances. Many states insist that no person be employed as an apprentice miner for a period longer than 12 months after becoming eligible to obtain a certificate of competency.

Coal mine workers in general, and particularly operators of coal mining machinery, must be very mechanically inclined. They should be physically fit and able to work in confined spaces. They must be very precise in all their work and should have excellent motor coordination and manual dexterity. They should have excellent communication and interpersonal skills, as they will be working in close quarters with fellow mine workers. They need to be able to react quickly to any type of mine emergency and be well prepared to take all necessary precautions for themselves and their coworkers.

Unions and Associations

The major union representing mine workers is the United Mine Workers of America (UMWA), though there are other unions, such as the International Union of Operating Engineers (IUOE), that also represent miners. Associations of interest to miners, particularly those working with machinery, include the National Mining Association (NMA) and the Society for Mining, Metallurgy, and Exploration, Inc. (SME).

Tips for Entry

1. In high school, add courses in first aid, as well as health and safety, as you will need this basic knowledge to understand better the health and safety requirements of the coal mining industry.
2. Investigate vocational programs offered at your high school that might be useful to you in your future mining career, and consider junior college or technical school programs in mine technology.
3. Explore possible summer jobs or internships in industry or factories where you can expand your mechanical interests and abilities and/or gain some experience in working with machinery.

ROTARY AUGER OPERATOR

CAREER PROFILE

Duties: Operate coal auger drill machinery and monitor/maintain controls and equipment

Alternate Title(s): Boring Machine Operator; Core Drill Operator; Drill Rig Operator; Earth Auger Operator; Earth Boring Machine Operator; Earth Driller; Exploratory Drill Operator; Test Borer

Salary Range: $22,000 to $55,000 or more

Employment Prospects: Poor to Fair

Advancement Prospects: Poor

Prerequisites:

   Education or Training—High school diploma or an equivalent General Education Diploma (GED) required, with a strong emphasis on math and science; two-year graduate degree in drilling, mechanics, or construction recommended

   Experience—Most skills learned on the job

   Special Skills and Personality Traits—Excellent perception and visualization abilities; good communication (oral and written) and interpersonal know-how; mechanical ability; problem solver; reliable computer skills

   Special Requirements—Other than a valid driver's license, a surface mining certification may be required

CAREER LADDER

```
┌─────────────────────────────────┐
│   Advanced Drill Operator;       │
│ Drill Operation Lead Operator;   │
│       Drill Supervisor           │
└─────────────────────────────────┘

┌─────────────────────────────────┐
│     Rotary Auger Operator        │
└─────────────────────────────────┘

┌─────────────────────────────────┐
│  High-School Graduate; Mechanical│
│           Technician             │
└─────────────────────────────────┘
```

Position Description

A rotary auger is a type of drilling equipment that uses a screw device to penetrate (or bore), break up, and then transport the drilled material to the earth's surface. It is used in soils or poorly consolidated materials to remove cuttings (or drilled material) from the borehole (the penetration of the surface created by the drilling equipment) by mechanical means without the use of drilling fluids. (For deeper drillings, fluids may be required to cool the drilling devices.) These cuttings are used to help determine coal bed thicknesses, the type/depth of the depositions or earth or rock (called the overburden) above the coal bed, and any geologic changes that further drilling would encounter. This data assists mining engineers in choosing the appropriate method for, and in estimating the cost of, sinking shafts or driving tunnels for the development and exploitation of the coal deposit.

Rotary Auger Operators (frequently called core drill operators or earth drillers) run simple power auger drill rigs (designed primarily for shallow-depth drilling up to about 100 feet), or more complex core boring drill rigs (designed for deeper drilling up to about 400 feet), both of which are mounted on heavy mobile equipment such as trucks and trailers. Operators may be required to drive trucks with this equipment to drilling sites. It is their job to get the auger (or other drill) placed, aligned, and stabilized. They check with mining engineering supervisors on how deep to dig and if the drill is positioned at the right angle. During the drilling, they control the drill's speed. They monitor the tone of the drill to determine through which layer of earth they are digging. (They use the sound of the drill to know when it has reached a different, tougher layer, and decide whether or not to change the drill bit.) As they remove core samples, they ensure that the sample accurately reflects the area/depth of the location they are drilling. During this process, they must observe all appropriate safety procedures against possible contaminants or toxins. They record where they drilled and what they believe the samples contain (which will accompany the samples to laboratories for analysis).

Power auger rigs designed for shallow-depth drilling have relatively simple operating controls and ordinarily do not necessitate auxiliary equipment. Drill operators handle these controls to rotate, press, auger (drill), withdraw, and empty the auger buckets containing the samples. In completing each cycle (of drilling, withdrawing, and dumping), they must be skilled at maneuvering auger tools in and out of the hole as rapidly as the drilling is accomplished. Because samples may be disturbed in the drilling, operators must be skilled at rigging up a reflecting light with a mirror to provide a clear view of the sides of the borehole, or even provide rigging to lower an individual safely into the hole for a direct view of the geologic strata.

The controls for the more complex core boring rigs (designed for deeper drilling) contain a greater number of levers and must be manipulated at more frequent intervals, due to increased care needed in driving the various types of drill bits and core barrels (containing the core samples). They need to maintain the proper balance of engine power, hydraulic pressure, winching, and auxiliary water pump system (to cool the drilling bits) to offset unpredictable formation changes in the layers being drilled, as well as cope with subsurface conditions, and overcome any core recovery problems. As this operation is more complex, operators needed to be guided by geological specifications, equipment blueprints, and maintenance manuals.

For drillings that must be made to even greater depths, more skilled operators are need to operate the larger auxiliary equipment, diameter drill bits, core barrels, and longer sections of drill rods to extend the reach of drilling tools to extreme depths (from 3,000 to 5,000 feet). This type of work requires precise bit speed, pressure control, and drilling mud technology to recover substantial cores for analysis.

Operators of auger drills and other similar types of drilling devices must be skilled at changing equipment and technique as the drilling progresses and different subsurface materials and conditions are encountered. They must be capable of offsetting subsurface resistances to the auger tools by improvising additional weights in the form of heavy rocks or steel bars, and stave off caving conditions caused by loose subsurface materials by using casings to prevent the entire borehole from collapsing. In addition, they need to be proficient at performing field maintenance of auger drill rig equipment, replacing any obviously worn or damaged parts.

More advanced drill operators using drill equipment that can dig deeper must be able to adjust and control the big speed, pressure, water volume, and velocity precisely so core samples are protected from breaking up or washing away, as well as use the bits and equipment components safely to their maximum limit. They need to respond to unusual machinery sounds and vibrations, sudden variances in water pressure, or any erratic drill rig action. They must recognize poor core recovery results, which may be indications of formation changes, and bring them to the attention of the mining geologist or supervisor. Throughout, they must be able to distinguish features of most underlying formations by the action of the drill, color of the return water, and rate of coring, knowing and using the proper drilling procedures to insure maximum recovery of samples and accurate recording of depths.

Salaries

In a November 2005 salary study, the Minnesota Department of Employment and Economic Development, in conjunction with the U.S. Bureau of Labor Statistics, found that the average annual wages in the United States of earth drillers (of which Rotary Auger Operators are one type) were $36,733. The lowest 10 percent earned approximately $22,700 annually, and the top 10 percent earned $53,955.

Employment Prospects

According to the November 2005 study by the U.S. Department of Labor's Bureau of Labor Statistics, earth drillers (including Rotary Augur Operators) will experience slower than average job opportunity growth than other occupations through 2014. However, with the renewed interest in coal as an alternative energy source to oil and natural gas, this growth pattern may shift in the coming years.

Advancement Prospects

Some Rotary Auger Operators obtain further training (in such areas as the use of water pumps and wire cable hoists, as well as the preparation and use of drilling fluids) and progress into more advanced earth drilling jobs. Alternatively, they may move up into supervisory positions. Many drillers become self-employed, adding to their technical skills to enhance their job opportunities.

Education and Training

A high school diploma is an absolute requirement for any drilling position. In addition, most employers look for candidates who have also taken courses (and, preferably, earned a degree) at a professional technical or two-year school. An emphasis on math, mechanics, science, basic computer skills, and technical/mechanical drafting (including blueprint reading) is recommended. Most earth drillers receive on-the-job training.

Special Requirements

Typically, the only requirement for drill operators is to have a valid state driver's license. In some instances, though rarely, a surface mining certification may be required.

Experience, Skills, and Personality Traits

Many drill operators come to their job with little or no training. They acquire their skills informally on the job, starting as a helper and learning their trade from a veteran worker. They will learn how to operate drilling equipment, watching gauges, dials, and output to ensure the machine is working properly. They should have basic mechanical skills to maintain the equipment on a routine basis.

Specifically, they should understand geological drilling policies, procedures, regulations, and safety requirements. They should have excellent manual dexterity. They must be able to react quickly, exhibit good body coordination, and make quick, precise adjustments to machine controls. They should be able to lift and carry heavy objects, to do repetitive movements repeatedly, and to stand for long periods of time. They need to be able to make out details of objects that are near and far away, and have excellent peripheral vision. They should have good communication skills (as they need to understand their instructions and to record their findings precisely) and interpersonal skills in their interactions with their supervisors.

Unions and Associations

The major association for drilling operators is the Society for Mining, Metallurgy, and Exploration (SME), though they may also find it useful to belong to the American Institute of Mining, Metallurgical, and Petroleum Engineers, Inc. (AIME).

Tips for Entry

1. Add health and safety education courses to your curriculum, as you may need this background in cases of emergencies on the job, and include fitness activities to enhance your physical well-being.
2. Since many drillers eventually are attracted to self-employment, consider taking business and accounting courses as well.
3. During high school, investigate internship programs (or summer work programs) that will put you in business situations handling machines/equipment to increase your know-how and dexterity.

SEMISKILLED PERSONNEL

MACHINERY MAINTENANCE AND REPAIR PERSONNEL

CAREER PROFILE

Duties: Lubricate, adjust, repair, and inspect machinery used in coal mining

Alternate Title(s): Machine Maintenance Mechanic; Repairer

Salary Range: $20,000 to $50,000 or more

Employment Prospects: Poor to Fair

Advancement Prospects: Poor

Prerequisites:

Education or Training—High school diploma is required; technical training in mechanics at trade school or two-year associate's degree in mechanics recommended

Experience—Two to five years as a maintenance and repair apprentice to an experienced mine mechanic

Special Skills and Personality Traits—Ability to follow blueprints, schematic drawings and diagrams, and service manuals; capable of setting up and operating metalworking machinery/tools used in repair; good physical condition; mechanical aptitude and manual dexterity

Special Requirements—Certification of competency from the individual state's Miners' Examining Boards is usually required

CAREER LADDER

```
┌─────────────────────────────────────┐
│  Senior Maintenance Mechanics or     │
│     Engineers; Mine Supervisors      │
└─────────────────────────────────────┘

┌─────────────────────────────────────┐
│     Machinery Maintenance and        │
│         Repair Personnel             │
└─────────────────────────────────────┘

┌─────────────────────────────────────┐
│   Apprentice Repair Personnel;       │
│      High School Graduate            │
└─────────────────────────────────────┘
```

Position Description

While many operators of coal-mining machinery lubricate and assist in the maintenance of their equipment on a daily basis, most maintenance and repair of coal-mining machinery, equipment, and superstructure is within the province of Machinery Maintenance and Repair Personnel. They confer with machine operators and observe, test, and evaluate the operation of machines. In order to maintain and repair machinery effectively, they must be able to detect minor problems and correct them before they become major difficulties. Machinery Maintenance and Repair Personnel use their understanding of the equipment, technical manuals, and careful observation to uncover causes of problems. As an example, when they hear a vibration from a machine,

they must decide whether it is due to worn belts, weak motor bearings, or something else. Computerized diagnostic systems and vibration analysis techniques greatly aid them in determining the problem, but they still need years of training and experience to function effectively.

On an ongoing basis, they inspect, adjust, lubricate, and repair machinery used within coal mines as well as elements of its superstructure (such as parts of the mine shaft) when necessary. They diagnose any malfunction, such as with the mechanical or hydraulic components, and execute repairs in accordance with blueprints, schematic drawings, operating manuals, and manufacturers' specifications. They employ hand tools, power tools, and precision measuring instruments to accomplish repairs. If necessary, they disassemble machinery and equipment to gain access to problem areas, remove parts (examining them for defects, such as breakage or excessive wear), and make the necessary repairs or replacement of such items. When repairing electronically controlled machinery, Maintenance and Repair Personnel may work closely with electronic repairers or electricians employed by the mine company. Increasingly, maintenance and repair mechanics need electronic and computer skills to repair sophisticated equipment on their own. Once repairs are completed, they perform tests and do test-runs to verify the adequacy of the repairs and ensure that the machine or equipment is now running smoothly.

Maintenance and Repair mechanics must be able to use brazing, soldering, and welding equipment in their repairs. They may have to set up and operate metalworking tools, such as lathes, drill presses, or grinders, to make or repair parts. When replacements for broken or defective parts are not readily available or readily manufactured on the spot, they use catalogs to order replacement parts. When such items become available, they will need to follow blueprints, engineering specifications, and technical manuals to fix the equipment. They may have to rely on their electronic and computer skills to repair computer-controlled mine equipment by entering codes/instructions to reprogram this equipment. They must document repairs done and maintenance performed. By keeping complete and up-to-date records, Maintenance and Repair mechanics try to anticipate trouble and service equipment quickly to avoid interrupting coal mine activities and production.

In large mining operations, there may be several Maintenance and Repair Personnel assigned to daily maintenance and repairs. They may specialize in specific areas of the coal mine production processes. For instance, some may concentrate on repairs and maintenance of mine shaft parts, such as timbers, cage guides, guardrails, cable, and compressed-air, steam, and water pipes in the shaft, as well as doors and brattices of canvas or wood. Others may concentrate on the upkeep of underground mine cars and conveyors, using welds, bolts, rivets, and refits parts, such as axles, wheels, bodies, and couplings. Still others may focus on stripping and loading shovels, drilling and cutting machines, or continuous mining machines. This last group are often referred to as mine-machinery mechanics.

Most Maintenance and Repair Personnel report directly to mechanical engineers or to mine supervisors, regardless of whether they work in underground coal mines or in above ground open mines.

Salaries

According to the U.S. Department of Labor's *Occupational Outlook Handbook, 2006–07 Edition,* median hourly earnings of Machinery Maintenance and Repair Personnel were $15.70 in May 2004. The middle 50 percent earned between $12.21 and $20.18. The lowest 10 percent earned about $9.60, and the highest 10 percent earned more than $24.59. These hourly wages translate into annual salaries that range from a low of about $20,000 to a high of $50,000 or more. Some repair personnel may be union members, with their wages determined by union contracts.

Employment Prospects

According to the U.S. Bureau of Labor Statistics, employment of machinery mechanics and maintenance workers is projected to grow more slowly than the average for all occupations through 2014. Nevertheless, applicants with skills and experience in machine repair and maintenance should have somewhat favorable job prospects, as many mechanics are expected to retire in the coming years. One other encouraging fact is that even with any downturn in coal mine production, maintenance and repair mechanics are frequently retained to do overhauling of machinery and equipment and to keep expensive machinery operating regardless of the level of ongoing production.

Advancement Prospects

Advancement for Maintenance and Repair Personnel may come, initially, by gaining additional skills to make repairs that are more complex or perform maintenance on more intricate mining machinery/equipment. They may also become supervisors of specific areas of the mine production process. They may decide to further their education and become mechanical engineers, opening up a variety of possible job opportunities within the coal industry, or in other commercial fields that utilize mechanical engineers.

Education and Training

Coal mine owners prefer to hire Maintenance and Repair Personnel who have completed high school or technical school and have taken courses in mechanical drawing, mathematics, blueprint reading, computers, and electronics. Most newly hired Maintenance and Repair workers receive short-term on-the-job training from more experienced mechanics. They start out performing routine tasks, such as cleaning, lubricating, and testing machinery and equipment. In some cases, Maintenance and Repair Personnel may learn their trade through four-year apprenticeship programs that combine classroom instruction with on-the-job training. They may take courses offered by machinery manufacturers and community colleges and then learn from experienced repairers how to operate, disassemble, repair, and reassemble machinery and equipment.

Special Requirements

Most states require that all persons employed or engaged in coal mines must obtain a certificate of competency from the state's Miners' Examining Board, as well as completing a course of instruction in first aid to potentially injured mine workers and in mine rescue methods and appliances as prescribed by the federal Mine Safety and Health Administration (MSHA).

Experience, Skills, and Personality Traits

Most initial experience is gained by on-the-job training with experienced maintenance and repair mechanics. Mechanical aptitude is paramount, and Maintenance and Repair Personnel must have excellent finger and manual dexterity. They need to have good communication and interpersonal skills, with reading comprehension being particularly important, as they will have to understand the technical manuals and manufacturer specifications dealing with a variety of coal-mining machinery and equipment.

They should be agile and in good physical condition, as they often will have to work in awkward positions, including on top of ladders or in cramped conditions under or beside large machinery, which may expose them to additional hazards. They may have to wear protective equipment, such as hard hats, safety glasses, steel-tipped shoes, hearing protectors, and belts. They need to have excellent vision and hearing sensitivity. They must be precise and steady in their movements and work and must exhibit muscular endurance and resistance to muscle fatigue.

Unions and Associations

About 25 percent of industrial machinery mechanics and maintenance workers are union members. Labor unions that represent these workers in the coal industry may include the United Steelworkers of America (USWA), the International Association of Machinists and Aerospace Workers (IAMAW), or the International Union of Electronic, Electrical, Salaried, Machine, and Furniture Workers-Communications Workers of America (IUE-CWA). Mechanics looking to become mechanical engineers may find it useful to belong to the American Society of Mechanical Engineers (ASME).

Tips for Entry

1. During high school, investigate summer jobs or internships in manufacturing environments where you can gain practical experience working with and learning how to maintain/repair machinery and equipment.
2. Besides your mechanical abilities, develop your computer skills, as much present-day coal-mining equipment is automated to some extent, which will affect your maintenance and repair tasks.
3. Consider initial employment in a manufacturing environment to become (better) acquainted with machine maintenance and repair techniques and technologies.

OTHER SEMISKILLED PERSONNEL

CAREER PROFILE

Duties: <u>Roof Bolter</u>: operate self-propelled machine to install roof-support bolts in underground coal mine; <u>Shot Firer</u>: handle procedures and safe detonation of explosives in underground coal mine; <u>Stopping Builder</u>: build doors or brattices in underground coal mine passageways to control proper air circulation throughout

Alternate Title(s): <u>Roof Bolter</u>: Bolting-Machine Operator, Raise Driller, Stoper; <u>Shot Firer</u>: Blaster, Explosive Worker, Ordnance Handling Expert, Shooter, Underground Shot Firer; <u>Stopping Builder</u>: Airman, Bratticeman, Ventilation Mason, Ventilation Worker

Salary Range: $30,000 to $55,000 or more

Employment Prospects: Poor to Fair

Advancement Prospects: Fair

Prerequisites:

Education or Training—High school graduate; new miners required to have 40 training hours plus pass a written exam; specialized training (particularly in mine safety procedures and regulations) usually required as well

Experience—One to three years as a mineworker apprentice

Special Skills and Personality Traits—Construction and mechanical skills; familiarity with appropriate mining equipment; good vision and manual dexterity; physically fit; precision in movements and work

Special Requirements—Roof Bolters and Shot Firers need certifications

CAREER LADDER

```
┌─────────────────────────────┐
│  Mining Machine Operators;  │
│      Mining Supervisor      │
└─────────────────────────────┘

┌─────────────────────────────┐
│    Semiskilled Personnel    │
└─────────────────────────────┘

┌─────────────────────────────┐
│  Apprentice Mine Worker;    │
│       Miner Helper          │
└─────────────────────────────┘
```

Position Description

Underground mining of coal is accomplished in several ways. In what is called a drift mine, a shaft is dug horizontally into the side of a hill and the coal is mined from within the hill. Slope mines usually begin in a valley bottom and a tunnel slopes down to the coal to be mined within the hill (or mountain). Shaft mines are the deepest mines: a vertical shaft with an elevator is made from the surface down to the coal.

There are two main methods of mining the coal. In room and pillar mining (the most common type), the coal ore is mined by a machine that cuts a network of rooms into the coal seam. As the rooms are carved out, pillars composed of coal are left in each room to support the roof of the mine, often reinforced by timber beams. This immediate roof above the coal seam consists of rock, commonly shale, softer and weaker than the rock strata above it. This roof needs to be supported as the coal is extracted, as the main roof above this immediate top may vary from a few feet to several hundred or even thousands of feet in thickness. The other mining method is longwall mining. As the coal is removed by mechanized shearers, temporary hydraulic-powered roof supports are used to hold up the roof. This method is more efficient in that more coal can be removed. However, the equipment is more expensive and cannot always be used due to geological circumstances.

In both types of coal extraction, roof control is of paramount importance. The extent to which a roof can be controlled (i.e., supported) determines the size of the working areas at the coal face (the solid surface of the unbroken portion of the coal bed), as well as in the haulageways (the tunnel floors through which the mined coal is hauled to the main shaft and conveyed to the surface) and other passages. As coal is excavated from a working face, mine stresses accumulate in the roof. Unless the roof is properly supported, stress pressures may cause the roof to fracture and/or collapse. This is where the job of the Roof Bolter comes into play.

A Roof Bolter uses timber or metal to reinforce the roofs of the haulageways, side drifts (tunnels), and working places. In addition, strengthening pins, known as roof bolts, are employed to anchor a weak immediate roof to a stronger firm roof structure above it or to bind several layers of weak rock strata into a beam or bridge strong enough to support its own weight across a working place. Thus, roof bolts provide roof control without the drawback of posts and bars that hinder movement of workers, equipment, and material. Roof Bolters operate the machine that installs these bolts. They position safety jacks to support the roof until the bolts can be installed. They position the machine, drill into the rock face, advance into the roof at a specified distance, and then replace the drill hole with a bolt. The Roof Bolter than starts a rotation that turns the bolt, opening its expansion head to exert the required pressure upon the rock formation. They test the bolt for the correct tension and tighten the ends of the anchored truss bolts. The bolts are placed in a definite pattern, designed to clamp together the several roof beds to form a strong composite beam.

When mining engineers determine that blasting must be done in the underground mine, Shot Firers (also known as blasters) are utilized. These mine workers are directly responsible for the use of explosives in either surface mine blasting (where the mine is being dug from the surface downward) or underground coal mine operations. They determine the strength and pattern of blast that is required to fracture/separate the material, from solid rock formations. They study these formations to determine the amount, type, and location of explosive charge required. They mark the pattern and depth of drill holes needed (and may be responsible for the drilling of the blast holes). They insert, pack, or pour explosives into the blast holes and compact the charges with a tamping rod. They connect the electric wires, fill the blast hole with clay, drill chips, or other material and tamp the material to secure the charge and prevent the force of the blast from escaping through the blast hole. They inspect the blasting area to ensure that all safety laws are observed and signal workers to clear the area. They connect the wires to the electrical firing device, and then use a blasting galvanometer to test the electric blasting circuits to locate any faulty connections. They then push the plunger (or turn the dial) and press buttons to set off single or multiple blasts. In underground coal mines, a steel chain mat, called a shot-firing (or blasting) curtain, often is suspended from the roof a distance from the face of an advancing tunnel being blasted to limit any damage to equipment from flying debris when the shot is set off.

In addition to their blasting duties, Shot Firers handle, store, and transport explosives and accessories in accordance with safety regulations. They keep an inventory of blasting agents on hand and frequently transport the blasting material from area to area, using light trucks. They also repair the blasting equipment and electrical tools they use on the job. Above all, they keep a complete written record (known as a blasting log) of all blasts done and their results.

Another critical element in underground coal mining is the ventilation system, an arrangement of connecting airways together with the pressure sources and control devices that produce and govern the airflow. Through the airshaft an enormous fan pumps air into the mine, and the air is circulated through connected thin tubes of steel, fiberglass, or coated fabric (called ventubes). It moves through every mile of tunneling, never crossing its own path and never stopping, until it again reaches the main entry point, but now at the foot of the hoisting shaft through which (now fouled by the gases, dust, and impurities of the mine) it pours out. Mine workings are usually subdivided to form a number of separate ventilating districts. Each district is given a specified supply of fresh air and is free from contamination by the air of other districts. Thus, the main intake air coming down the mine shaft is split into the different districts, and the return air from the districts is reunited into a single main air return.

Stopping Builders (also known as brattice builders) build doors or brattices (ventilation walls or partitions) in the underground passageways to control the proper circulation of air through the passageways and to the working places of the mine and to remove gas and dust. The brattices may be canvas, wood, brick, concrete, or concrete blocks as specified in the ventilation plans for the mine. These doors are opened to allow the passage of coal cars and then closed again. As a precautionary measure, inspectors pass constantly from place to place, testing for pressure of gas with safety-lamps and measure the volume/flow of air current. Stopping Builders make requested adjustments to brattices, or build new ones when necessary.

In addition, Stopping Builders may also erect partitions to support the roof in areas unsuited for timbering or bolting, and may install the rigid or flexible air ducts that transport air into the work areas. They may assist in the drilling/blasting of obstructing boulders to reopen ventilation shafts. Brattices can be used to isolate old workrooms or working areas containing water or hazardous gases. Additionally, they can be used to confine the ventilating current of air to only certain passages, and, even, in some cases, to smother a mine fire.

Salaries

According to the U.S. Bureau of Labor Statistics, in their *Career Guide to Industries, 2006–07 Edition*, coal mine production workers in general earned $21.57 an hour in 2004. The study found that the median hourly wages of maintenance and repair workers in coal mining was $18.04, which translates roughly to an annual median salary of $40,000.

Employment Prospects

According to this *Career Guide to Industries, 2006–07 Edition*, employment in coal mining is expected to decline substantially through the year 2014. This continuing decline is due to increased productivity resulting from technological advances in mining operations and larger mining equipment, consolidation of coal-mining businesses, international competition, and more stringent environmental regulations.

While the demand for coal (the cheapest and most abundant fossil fuel) to produce electricity and to aid in the production of steel products should remain high, employment is expected to decline by about 23 percent through 2014, primarily due to more efficient and automated production operations. However, some job opportunities may become available as mine employees reach retirement age and need to be replaced by younger workers.

Advancement Prospects

Career advancement for experienced coal-mine semiskilled workers, such as Roof Bolters, Shot Firers, and Stopping Builders, is usually to positions as machine operators of one kind or another. Further training is needed, but experienced and ambitious workers may be able to make the transition. With further years of seasoning, they may even look forward to supervisory positions, with the resultant increase in responsibility and wage earnings. Some may decide, with special training, to become mine safety, health, and compliance officers (which may require a degree in mining engineering).

Education and Training

Generally, workers in mining production occupations must be at least 18 years old, in good physical condition, and able to work in confined spaces. While a high school diploma may not be necessary, it is recommended for beginning mine helpers to have one. Most workers start as helpers to veteran workers and learn skills on the job. However, formal training is becoming more crucial as more high-tech machinery and mining methods are being introduced. Some employers are now insisting upon a high school education, with some formal training in mine technology.

Special Requirements

In addition to the required worker training programs that mines must provide, Roof Bolters and Shot Firers must obtain a certificate of competency from the Miners' Examining Board of the state in which they work. In most states, the worker must be recertified every five years.

Experience, Skills, and Personality Traits

While many of the tasks required for these semiskilled positions are learned on the job, mining companies must offer formal training in classrooms and/or training mines for a few weeks before new mine production workers actually begin work. The Federal Mine Safety and Health Act of 1977 mandates that each U.S. mine have an approved worker training program in health and safety issues. Each plan must include at least 40 hours of basic safety training for new miners with no experience in underground mines, and 24 hours for new miners involved in surface mines. By training in simulated actual mine conditions and emergencies, mine workers are better prepared and companies can instantly assess a mineworker's progress and skills.

Semiskilled coal-mine workers in general, and particularly the three job positions described, require applicants to be mechanically inclined. They should be physically fit and able to work in confined spaces. They need excellent motor coordination and manual dexterity, and should have solid interpersonal abilities, as they will be toiling in close quarters with fellow mine workers. They need to be able to react quickly to any type of mine emergency and be well prepared to take all necessary precautions for themselves and their fellow workers.

Unions and Associations

About 27.5 percent of workers in coal mining are members of the United Mine Workers of America (UMWA), which helps to guarantee wages, paid holidays, and sick leave days. While the National Mining Association (NMA) represents the industry as a whole, many states and areas of the United States have local and regional associations in which membership may prove beneficial to coal-mine workers.

Tips for Entry

1. While a high school diploma is frequently not required for beginning mine workers, it is a good idea, particularly as new mining technology requires some solid science and technical background.
2. Explore possible summer jobs or internships in industry or factories where you can expand your mechanical interests and abilities and/or gain some experience in basic construction procedures.
3. Take health and safety courses in school as you will need to rely upon this basic knowledge in your coal mining occupation.

SUPERVISORS AND SUPPORT PERSONNEL

GEOSCIENCE TECHNICIAN

CAREER PROFILE

Duties: Assist mining engineers and geophysicists in determining depth, range, and accessibility of coal deposits

Alternate Title(s): Geological Technician; Geophysical Prospecting Surveyor; Geophysical Technician; GIS Specialist; GIS/CADD Mapping Specialist; Surveying Technician

Salary Range: $25,000 to $60,000 or more

Employment Prospects: Poor to Fair

Advancement Prospects: Poor to Fair

Prerequisites:

Education or Training—Bachelor of Science degree in computer science, earth science, geography, geology, or related field; in some cases, associate's degree in one of these or a related field may suffice

Experience—Two to four years' experience in geographic and geologic field surveying utilizing Global Positioning Systems (GPS) and geographic information systems (GIS) technologies

Special Skills and Personality Traits—Capable of complex analytical thinking, including spatial visualization; excellent communication and interpersonal skills; mechanical aptitude with good attention to detail; solid background in basic chemistry, physics, and mathematics; strong computer skills, especially in computer modeling

CAREER LADDER

```
┌─────────────────────────────────────┐
│ Geologist; Geophysicist; Geoscientist │
└─────────────────────────────────────┘

┌─────────────────────────────────────┐
│       Geoscience Technician          │
└─────────────────────────────────────┘

┌─────────────────────────────────────┐
│ Assistant Technician; College Graduate│
└─────────────────────────────────────┘
```

Position Description

Science technicians, in general, use the principles and theories of science and mathematics to solve problems in research and development. Their jobs tend to be more practically oriented than those of scientists. They set up, operate, and maintain laboratory instruments, make observations, calculate and record results, and usually are required to develop conclusions based upon their observations and calculations. They must keep detailed logs of their work-related activities, and they make extensive use of computers, computer-interfaced equipment, and high-technology industrial applications.

Geoscience Technicians assist earth scientists, such as geologists, engineers, and geophysicists, as well as geo-scientists, to find/develop mineral and fuel resources. They search for locations likely to yield coal (or mineral) deposits in sufficient quantity to justify extraction costs. In addition, they analyze proposed mining activity with collected natural resource data. They make observations, analyze proposed mining activity, collect and analyze samples, and record information useful in the exploration for potential coal (or mineral) deposits.

Most Geoscience Technicians work in both the field and in laboratories. However, they may spend long periods working on remote sites before returning to their laboratory activities. They usually are tasked with ordering, checking, packing, and shipping of equipment/supplies utilized for such field surveys. In the field, they collect, record, and transport back to laboratories samples of rock, soil, drill cuttings, and water. They undertake geophysical surveys, involving the measurement of such factors as magnetism and gravity and using Global Positioning Systems (GPS) technology (a technical system that locates points on Earth using radio signals transmitted by satellites) to establish locations of coal deposits. In addition, they operate various remote sensing and imagery geophysical instruments to survey hidden rock features. In the process, they may mark the outlines of potential coal deposit areas and indicate the positioning of drill cuttings to be employed in the initial exploration of these areas by mining engineers.

In the laboratory, they collate this data with other information collected from such sources as geochemical sampling surveys, seismic studies, and meteorological observations. With all this geographic and geologic information, they utilize geographic information systems (GIS) computer programs to analyze the data. Next, they use Computer Aided Design (CAD) software to translate this technical data into understandable maps, graphs, and tables. As GIS specialists, Geoscience Technicians are responsible for the standardizing and digitizing of the geospatial and tabular data (dataset) and for maintaining the accuracy of the resultant GIS database and related documentation.

Geoscience Technicians typically begin work as trainees in routine positions under the direct supervision of a scientist or a more seasoned technician. Job candidates whose training or educational background encompasses extensive hands-on experience with a variety of laboratory equipment, including computers, usually require only a short period of on-the-job training.

Geoscience Technicians are utilized in other industries as well, particularly in the exploration for petroleum and natural gas deposits. Their GIS skills are also applicable to many industrial engineering projects, commercial land use companies, and even wastewater treatment and/or water reclamation agencies. Many Geoscience Technicians work freelance, hiring on for specific projects, mining or otherwise.

Salaries

According to the U.S. Bureau of Labor Statistics, in their *Career Guide to Industries, 2006–07 Edition*, median hourly earnings of Geoscience Technicians was $19.35, which translates into a median annual wage of approximately $40,200. Salaries for graduates who start as technician helpers or assistants start around $20,000, while seasoned Geoscience Technicians may earn in excess of $60,000 annually.

Employment Prospects

According the U.S. Department of Labor, slower-than-average employment growth is expected for Geoscience Technicians (which include both geological and petroleum technicians), because employment in both the oil and gas extraction and coal-mining industries is expected to decline through the year 2014. However, the department's study also projects that, due to a lack of qualified candidates, prospective job seekers should experience little competition for posts, especially in such energy-related fields as coal mining. In addition, according to this study, job opportunities also will be favorable in professional, scientific, and technical service firms (who contract with mining, oil, and natural gas companies). Continued reliance in the United States on coal as a cheaper alternative to imported natural gas and petroleum should also boost both jobs within that area and allied service jobs, such as Geoscience Technicians, who aid the scientists and engineers in the industry.

Advancement Prospects

One path of career advancement for Geoscience Technicians is to pursue further scientific and technical education and obtain a bachelor's degree (if they have only an associate's degree) and then, in addition, earn a master's degree in general geology or earth science. Most geoscientists need at least a master's degree for employment.

Education and Training

Many employers of Geoscience Technicians prefer applicants to have at least two years of specialized training or an associate's degree in applied science or science-related technology. However, because employers' preferences vary, some Geoscience Technicians pursue a bachelor's degree in geology, geography, engineering science, or, at the very least, take several geology, earth science, and mathematics courses at a four-year college. A solid educational background in applied basic chemistry, physics, and mathematics is vital. Additionally, a strong background in computer technology is paramount (even to the extent of gaining a degree in computer science).

Experience, Skills, and Personality Traits

Geoscience Technicians must be proficient at data research and collection, as well as the conversion of spatial data between software/hardware platforms, and data documentation (frequently known as metadata). They will need experience in translating, manipulating, and working with assorted GIS formats and datasets to the point of becoming proficient in GIS application development utilizing systematic development processes. They must be proficient in the use of computer-assisted design (CAD) and be familiar with such GIS programs as ArcGIS, PETRA, and other similar software packages. They will need to gain experience with various computer languages such as object-oriented programming, UNIX scripting, JavaScript, XML, ASP, and .NET. Some experience with databases such as SQL, Oracle, or JDBC would also be helpful.

Geoscience Technicians need to have a good sense of two-dimensional and three-dimensional relationships. They must be highly organized, analytical in their work, and have excellent visual skills. They should be physically fit and be able to function well in remote locations. They should be able to work as part of a team, and able to interface effectively with coworkers, geoscientists, and mining engineers. They should have excellent verbal and written communication abilities, as they must prepare reports and proposals.

Unions and Associations

Groups of interest for Geoscience Technicians include the American Institute of Professional Geologists (AIPG), the Geological Society of America (GSA), and the Society of Exploration Geophysicists (SEG). In addition, they may find it beneficial to belong to the American Congress on Surveying and Mapping (ASCM) or the Association of American Geographers (AAG).

Tips for Entry

1. As computer skills are essential, take advanced courses in such subjects as computer modeling, data analysis and integration, digital mapping, and geographic information systems.
2. Investigate summer internships for geographic or geologic programs to gain practical field experience.
3. Alternatively, investigate summer openings in laboratories, as some employers prefer such a background in the science technicians they hire.

MINE INSPECTORS AND SENIOR SUPERVISORS

CAREER PROFILE

Duties: <u>Fire Boss</u>: responsible for monitoring the mine for dangers; <u>First-Line Supervisor</u>: direct and coordinate activities of mechanics, repairers, coal extractive workers and their helpers; <u>Mine Inspector</u>: inspect mines for compliance with contractual agreements and with health/safety laws; <u>Mine Superintendent</u>: oversee all activities of personnel engaged in extracting coal from underground or surface mines; <u>Mine Supervisor</u>: direct and coordinate the activities of mid-level mine supervisors

Alternate Title(s): <u>Fire Boss</u>: Assistant Mine Foreman, Mine Examiner; <u>First-Line Supervisor</u>: Mid-Level Supervisor/Manager; <u>Mine Inspector</u>: Check Viewer, Coal-Mine Inspector, Safety Inspector; <u>Mine Superintendent</u>: Colliery Superintendent; <u>Mine Supervisor</u>: General Supervisor

Salary Range: $30,000 to $90,000 or more

Employment Prospects: Fair

Advancement Prospects: Poor to Fair

Prerequisites:

Education or Training—Bachelor of Science degree in one of the physical sciences required for most mid-level supervisory positions; a master's degree in engineering, preferably mining, or business administration (if a bachelor's degree in engineering is already earned) desirable for higher level management positions

Experience—Four to eight years or more of experience in supervision of mining activities; knowledge of environmental regulatory laws and procedures and a strong natural science background

Special Skills and Personality Traits—<u>Fire Boss and Mine Inspector</u>: attention to detail, good instructional and investigative skills; <u>Supervisors and Superintendent</u>: excellent leadership and supervisory talents, problem-solving and good communication skills, skillful negotiator and mediator

Special Requirements—State licensing and certification necessary in all positions; professional engineer certification required for top-level supervisory posts

CAREER LADDER

Mine Safety Engineer; Mine Supervisor, Mine Superintendent; Vice President of Mining Operations

Fire Boss, Mine Inspector; First-Line Supervisor; Mine Superintendent, Mine Supervisor

Other Mine Supervisor Positions

Position Description

The individual designated to inspect a coal mine for explosive, poisonous, or suffocating gases and other dangers is called a Fire Boss (sometimes also known as a mine examiner). Usually the Fire Boss is the first person to enter a mine, to verify its safety before a shift crew of mine workers enters. Fire Bosses need to be state certified and are regarded as supervisory mine officials. They typically make a second examination of the mine during the shift. They must be highly knowledgeable of the nature/properties of poisonous, noxious, and explosive gases and the methods for their detection and control. They also need to understand the practical aspects of coal mining, especially regarding ventilation and mine roof control. (In some instances, this post may loosely refer to a mine foreman or shift manager.)

First-Line Supervisors are mid-level supervisors responsible for the direct management of mine workers. There frequently are two types of First-Line Supervisors: those who supervise and coordinate the activities of extractive workers (the coal miners) and their helpers, and those who supervise and coordinate the activities of mechanics, repairers, and installers of machinery and their helpers. In supervising the activities of the coal miners, First-Line Supervisors assign work to mine employees, using material and worker requirements data/plans established by mine supervisors. They confer with staff and workers to ensure production personnel problems are resolved, as well as analyze worker difficulties and recommend motivational plans to higher management. They train workers in construction methods and the operation of equipment. They examine and inspect equipment (as well as work sites and materials) to verify that specifications have been met, and order necessary materials, supplies, or repairs of existing tools, gear, and machinery. They recommend measures to improve production and to increase efficiency and safety. They record daily information, such as personnel, production, and operational data, on specified forms, evaluate worker production and attitude, and, in turn, recommend promotions, transfers, and any needs for new hires. By using measuring and marking equipment, they locate, measure, and mark site locations for drilling, blasting, and mining.

First-Line Supervisors of mechanics, installers, and repairers assign them to service appliances, repair and maintain vehicles, and install machinery and equipment. They direct, coordinate, and assist in such work activities as engine tune-ups and circuit breaker installations. They monitor repair and installation operations and inspect, test, and measure finished work. They complete and maintain reports, such as time and production records, inventories, and test results. In addition, they requisition needed materials/supplies and train repair mechanics in the use of specialized equipment and work aids, such as blueprints, hand tools, and test gear. They establish and/or adjust work methods and procedures to maintain equipment/machinery

to sustain production schedules for the mine. They confer with management and workers' representatives to coordinate work activities and resolve any problems. They recommend or initiate personnel actions, such as employment, performance evaluations, promotions, transfers, discharges, and disciplinary measures. First-Line Supervisors usually report directly to mine supervisors.

The individual charged with inspecting underground or open-pit surface mines to ascertain compliance with contractual agreements and with health/safety laws is the Mine Inspector. In fulfilling their duties, Mine Inspectors check for rotted or incorrectly positioned support timbers, dangerously placed or defective electrical and mechanical equipment, improperly stored explosives, and other (potentially) hazardous conditions. They test the air quality to detect toxic or explosive gas or dust, using portable gas-analysis equipment. They observe mine activities to spot any violations of federal and state health and safety standards. In addition, they scrutinize the mine workings to verify compliance with contractual stipulations concerning production rates or mining done within specified limits. They may instruct mine workers in safety and first aid procedures. When employed by a governmental agency (instead of by a mine operator or mining company), they are usually known as Mine Inspectors and they conduct periodic mine checkups specifically to enforce federal and/or state mining laws.

Mine Supervisors coordinate and supervise the activities of mining mid-level supervisors, such as pit supervisors and section supervisors. They direct the opening of any new cuts or pits in surface mines and any underground rooms and passageways in underground operations. They designate mining personnel regarding the construction and installation of equipment as directed by Mine Superintendents. They coordinate their activities with mine safety engineers and report any safety violations to Mine Superintendents. They inspect mines continually and instruct supervisory personnel when and how to take necessary measures to improve production and working conditions.

Mine Superintendents are the senior management individuals with the overall responsibility for the activities and production of a coal mine. Under federal coal mining law, a Mine Superintendent is usually considered the "Principle Officer for Health and Safety." As such, the welfare for the entire workforce in a mining operation is a Mine Superintendent's legal responsibility. Similarly, they are tasked with ensuring compliance with applicable environmental regulations.

They plan and coordinate activities of all personnel engaged in the extraction of coal from underground or surface mines or pits. Their overall management of the coal mine includes planning, budgeting, staffing, cost management and containment, and monitoring profitability. They review data (such as maps, survey reports, and geological records) and confer with engineering, maintenance, and supervisory personnel to plan and direct mine development. They calculate mining or quarrying operational costs, estimate potential income, and instruct pit supervisors to abandon or to open mine sections, pits, or other working areas. They study maps/blueprints to determine the digging of and location for haulageways (tunnels through which the coal will be brought to the main shaft for transport to the surface), access roads, ventilation shafts, rail tracks, and conveyor systems. They study land contours and rock formations, and specify the places for installation of pillars, timbers, and roof bolts within the mine, as well as the use of equipment for cutting, drilling, blasting, and loading the coal. They must be knowledgeable of mining laws and safety regulations, and they issue directives to mine workers to ensure adherence to applicable regulations. They review and consolidate records pertaining to the grade of coal being mined, air quality, safety reports, and production documentation. They tour and inspect the mine to detect/resolve problems regarding production, equipment maintenance, safety, and personnel.

Mine Superintendents are the senior mine company officials that negotiate with workers, union personnel, and other parties to settle any grievances. Mine managers, mining engineers, safety managers, maintenance managers, plant managers, and purchasing managers report directly to the Mine Superintendent. In most instances, Mine Superintendents also represent the mining company within the community. They are expected to meet with landowners, public officials, and other parties to resolve property issues and community concerns related to mining activities.

Salaries

Annual salaries for Fire Bosses, Mine Inspectors, and First-Line Supervisors range from $35,000 to $60,000 or more. The U.S. Department of Labor's Bureau of Labor Statistics found that in May 2004, the median hourly earnings of First-Line Supervisors was $27.66 (or approximately $57,500 a year).

Mine Supervisors typically earn yearly salaries ranging from $40,000 to $75,000 or more. As expected, Mine Superintendents have much higher incomes due to their overall responsibilities. Their annual earnings may range from $65,000 to $100,000 or more depending on the size and profitability of their mining operation. At this level, yearly bonuses for high production and successful compliance with safety and environmental regulations are common.

Employment Prospects

While employment in the coal mining industry is expected to decline by about 23 percent through 2014 with the continued implementation of more efficient and automated production operations, as per the U.S. Department of Labor's *Occupational Outlook Handbook, 2006–07 Edition*, the demand

for effective and professional supervisors will not lessen. They will need to be well-acquainted with technological changes in mine production and with new equipment being utilized. With the increased dependence in the United States on coal as a source of energy, and with the improvements in clean coal technologies (which help the industry cope with increasingly restrictive environmental regulations), the field as a whole will continue to grow, albeit at a slower pace.

Advancement Prospects

Fire Bosses and Mine Inspectors have the potential to advance to positions as mine safety engineers by adding the necessary educational requirements and earning degrees in mining engineering, if they have not already done so before taking these lower-level supervisory positions. Mid-level First-Line Supervisors who supervise specific groups of mine workers may look to move up to the job of Mine Supervisor as the next step in their career advancement. In turn, Mine Supervisors, with years of experience and some additional training in business management, may aim to become Mine Superintendents. Mine Superintendents may aspire to higher levels within the upper echelons of management in the mining company, such as the vice president of operations.

Education and Training

A bachelor's degree in one of the physical sciences (if not in mining engineering, which is preferred by most employers) is the usual requirement for all mid-level and lower supervisors in coal mining. For Fire Bosses, an associate's degree in applied science in coal mining technology may be sufficient educational background, along with a state certificate of competency. For Mine Supervisors and Mine Superintendents, a Bachelor of Science degree in geology, civil or mining engineering, or a related field is the basic requirement, as well as additional training in mine health, safety, and training standards. Mine Superintendents usually are also required to have a master's degree in mine engineering or business administration.

Special Requirements

Most states require that all persons employed or engaged in coal mines obtain a certificate of competency from the state's Miners' Examining Board, as well as complete a course of instruction in first aid to potentially injured mine workers and in mine rescue methods and appliances as prescribed by the federal Mine Safety and Health Administration (MSHA). For mid-level mining supervising posts and mine safety positions (as well as higher management positions), they are usually required to have a certificate of competency in such areas as the theory and practice of coal mining; the nature and properties of poisonous, noxious, and explosive gases and methods for their detection and control; the practical aspects of coal mining pertaining especially to ventilation and roof control; and the requirement of coal mining laws of the state in which they are working, as well as federal laws governing the coal mining industry.

All Mine Supervisors (including the Mine Superintendent) who have engineering degrees should be certified as professional engineers.

Experience, Skills, and Personality Traits

Applicants for mid-level supervisory posts in coal mining are typically required to have two to four years of practical experience underground in coal mines. For higher levels of management, including Mine Supervisors and Superintendents, five to eight years of related work experience in mining technology are usually expected. They should have background in managing senior staff and have some business management training.

As both Fire Bosses and Mine Inspectors are—by the nature of their job—devoted to the health and safety of miners, they should be unusually sympathetic, socially oriented people. Their communication and interpersonal abilities must be exemplary, as they must deal constantly with miners, technicians, and other mine supervisors. They need to be heavily detail-oriented and analytical in their inspection techniques. In addition, they need to make quick but logical decisions and be able to act speedily in emergency situations.

Mid-level mine supervisors, as well Mine Supervisors, must possess good communicative and interpersonal skills and be adept in management techniques. They need to have excellent vision and physical stamina, be mechanically inclined, and have superior manual dexterity. Mine Superintendents need to have all those abilities as well as be computer literate and well versed in reading and interpreting all types of mine documentation, studies, and reports. They will need to deal with financial and business matters concerning the mine operation and should be familiar with spreadsheets and word processing techniques. They must be able to organize, direct, and motivate people and be good negotiators with mine personnel, labor representatives, government officials, and the general public.

Unions and Associations

The two most relevant associations for both mid-level mine supervisors and Mine Supervisors and Mine Superintendents are the American Institute of Mining, Metallurgical, and Petroleum Engineers, Inc. (AIME) and the Society for Mining, Metallurgy, and Exploration (SME). Among other organizations that might prove useful to mine supervisors are the American Society for Mining and Reclamation (ASMR) and the National Mining Association (NMA), as well as the general association for engineers, the National Society of Professional Engineers (NSPE).

Tips for Entry

1. While obtaining your science or engineering degree (bachelor or associate), take business management courses as they will provide you with skills you will need as you advance your career into the management side of the coal mining industry.
2. Take psychology and/or sociology courses as well, to give you insights into how to persuade and supervise other individuals.
3. While working in mines, keep current with technological advances in mine safety and techniques and keep your computer skills up to date, as this knowledge will be a key part of your duties as a mine supervisor.

OTHER SUPERVISORY POSITIONS

CAREER PROFILE

Duties: <u>Bank Boss</u>: supervise and coordinate workers operating machinery; <u>Dispatcher</u>: coordinate and schedule movements of haulage trains in underground mining; <u>Loader Boss</u>: supervise the loading of coal onto conveyors or cars in a mine; <u>Maintenance Supervisor, Mobile-Battery Equipment</u>: coordinate activities of workers engaged in maintenance/repair of mobile battery-powered mining equipment; <u>Pit Supervisor</u>: supervise and coordinate workers engaged in strip or pit mining; <u>Preparation Plant Supervisor</u>: oversee and coordinate workers engaged in the preparation of coal after mining; <u>Section Supervisor</u>: manage workers engaged in underground, surface, or pit mining in specific sections of the mine; <u>Surface Supervisor</u>: control and coordinate activities of workers operating equipment used to move personnel, machinery, and supplies

Alternate Title(s): <u>Bank Boss</u>: Machine Boss; <u>Dispatcher</u>: Car Distributor, Haulage Boss, Motor Boss; <u>Loader Boss</u>: Loading Boss, Loading-Unit Boss; <u>Maintenance Supervisor, Mobile-Battery Equipment</u>: Repair Supervisor; <u>Pit Supervisor</u>: Dimension-Quarry Supervisor, Strip-Mine Supervisor; <u>Preparation Plant Supervisor</u>: Breaker Boss, Tipple Supervisor, Washery Boss; <u>Section Supervisor</u>: Mine Captain, Muck Boss, Mucker Boss, Room Boss, Shift Boss; <u>Surface Supervisor</u>: First-Line Manager, Transportation and Material-Moving Machine and Vehicle Supervisors

Salary Range: $30,000 to $55,000 or more

Employment Prospects: Poor to Fair

Advancement Prospects: Fair to Good

Prerequisites:

Education or Training—Bachelor of Science degree in a physical science, mining technology, or a related field required; an associate's degree in mine technology with mining experience may suffice for a supervisory post

Experience—Three to five years of experience in underground or surface coal mining

Special Skills and Personality Traits—Excellent leadership and supervisory skills; good communication and interpersonal talents; problem-solving abilities and thorough technical knowledge of coal mining equipment and techniques

Special Requirements—Certificate of competency from a state Miners' Examining Board almost always required

CAREER LADDER

First-Line Supervisor; Mine Supervisor

Other Supervisory Positions

Mine Worker

Position Description

A person who supervises and coordinates activities for workers operating coal mine machinery is typically termed a Bank Boss (or sometimes called a machine boss). Mine workers they supervise include those who undercut the working face of a coal seam prior to blasting and machine loaders who pack the blasted coal into conveyor or railway cars. They may also work as surface mine managers, supervising workers operating front-end loaders, bulldozers, and trucks conveying mined coal to processing plants. They may assist mine repair personnel with faulty equipment.

Mine Dispatchers coordinate the movements of haulage trains (of cars or conveyors) in an underground coal mine to or from the working site or dump areas. They schedule the movements of trains hauling coal refuse, personnel, or supplies—focusing on the capacity of the hauling system, the interval between trains, and the length and direction of the train tracks. They direct movements of special vehicles, such as emergency or repair railcars, to minimize impact and interference with scheduled hauling operations, using phone, radio, or track signals. They reroute trains in event of emergencies (such as power failures, explosions, fires, or accidents), using controls to throw track switches to regulate the movement of trains when necessary. They investigate the cause of train delays and reschedule subsequent hauling operations. They transmit reports of accidents or system malfunctions to mine safety engineers and their repair crews. They keep records on train movements, frequently monitoring movements on lighted panelboards showing the location of each train within the underground mine.

Loader Bosses supervise crews of loader mine workers moving coal onto a conveyor or onto train cars that will carry the coal from mine work stations to a central site to be transported to the surface. When automated loading machines are utilized, Loader Bosses will supervise the operators of these machines.

Special Maintenance Supervisors supervise/coordinate the activities of mine workers who maintain and repair mobile battery-powered mining equipment. They review the list of mobile battery-powered equipment needing repairs, examining (by the use of electrical and hydraulic schematics) the defective equipment and its batteries to determine malfunctions. They assign personnel to perform the repairs and inspect the fixed equipment to ensure it conforms to company and federal safety standards. They notify mine supervisors when the equipment is ready to be put back into service. They inspect work areas for any defective apparatus or hazardous electrical conditions as determined by federal and/or state regulations. They complete accident reports, and, frequently, train new employees.

Pit Supervisors coordinate the activities of workers engaged in strip or pit mining or in quarrying in surface mines. They study contour maps and aerial photographs to determine locations for access roads in and out of surface mines and specific areas for cuts. They supervise road construction crews and lay out any needed blast patterns for them to use. They supervise the drilling and shooting crews during the creation of blast holes and the detonation of blast charges. They plan the site of the spoil pile (dump area) for refuse from the mining so as not to interfere with the actual mining. They coordinate the stripping of coal ore, drilling, blasting, quarrying, and loading activities in the operation and frequently assist workers with any faulty equipment. Under the guidance of the mine superintendent, they determine property lines and legal limits of the mining operations in order to comply with the rights of adjoining property owners and mining laws. They schedule the time needed for repair work on drilling machines and stripping and loading shovels. They requisition needed supplies, such as explosives, lubricants, bits, and machine parts. At all times, they scrutinize the mining operation to detect any violation of safety regulations and, in the process, compile safety and production records. They may train new workers.

Preparation Plant Supervisors coordinate the activities of workers engaged in the crushing, sizing, cleaning, testing, and loading of coal at the preparation plant at the mine, called a tipple. They receive daily reports of quantity of coal produced and the grade of the materials to be loaded onto railroad cars or trucks for transport away from the mining area. They transmit loading orders to equipment operators and loading crews. They monitor the activities of workers to ensure that impurities and materials of unspecified size are extracted from the coal ore before transport. They direct the operation of crushers, pumps, and furnaces, often assisting workers with any faulty equipment. They inspect the processing and loading equipment and prepare all necessary maintenance scheduling. From the weight of the loaded train cars or trucks, they compute and report on the daily production to the mine superintendent.

Section Supervisors coordinate activities of mine workers engaged in underground, surface, or pit mining in specified sections of the operation. They oversee such activities as timbering, roof bolting, track-laying, undercutting (of the mine ore prior to blasting), drilling, blasting, loading, and conveying the coal for their section of the mine. They examine all malfunctioning equipment and order the transfer of the faulty units to surface shops for repair or order repairs to be done at the work site. They constantly inspect their section for any hazards (such as gas, falling rock, or poor ventilation), using such devices as safety lamps, anemometers, and crowbars. They maintain records of the production of their section, the area mined, and the location of both personnel and equipment. They order and distribute supplies, such as drill bits, wire, machine parts, bulbs, and chalk (used in marking areas for drilling).

Surface Supervisors coordinate the activities of workers engaged in operating equipment to move personnel, machinery, and supplies to various levels of an underground coal mine. They consult with mine supervisors to establish daily work schedules for such activities. They coordinate the use of hoisting devices to raise or lower equipment that transports personnel, machinery, and supplies to and from the various mine levels. They direct mine workers who load/ unload materials from trucks or railroad cars ready for transport back and forth to the surface. They inspect equipment to detect any malfunctions and schedule repairs as needed. In addition, they are in charge of resolving any grievances and frequently conduct safety meetings with workers under their supervision.

Salaries

As supervisors of specific areas of underground and surface coal mining, these various supervisory personnel, according to industry sources, have annual salaries ranging from $30,000 to $55,000 or higher, depending upon the extent of their responsibilities, their technical background and expertise, and their years of service in their position.

Employment Prospects

According to the U.S. Department of Labor's *Occupational Outlook Handbook, 2006–07 Edition*, employment in the coal mining industry is expected to decline by about 23 percent through 2014 with the continued implementation of more efficient and automated production operations. Nonetheless, the need for effective and professional supervisors within coal mines will not lessen. They will need to be constantly aware of technological changes in mine production and any new equipment and techniques that can ease their tasks and those of their workers. With the increased dependence in the United States on coal as a source of energy, and with the improvements in clean coal technologies (which help the industry deal with increasingly restrictive environmental regulations), the coal industry as a whole should be able to continue growing, albeit at a slower pace.

Advancement Prospects

All supervisory personnel handling specific areas of supervision over mine workers and procedures have potential career advancement in applying for positions as first-line supervisors or mining supervisors in charge of all (or most) mining activities. To accomplish such career advances, they must obtain mining engineering degrees if they have not already done so.

Education and Training

For most mine supervisory posts, a Bachelor of Science degree in a physical science, mining technology (the preferred degree), or a related field is a basic educational necessity. In some cases, an associate's degree in mine tech-

nology and two to four years of experience in coal mining may be sufficient for promotion from a mine worker job to a specific second-level supervisory position.

All mine supervisory personnel must be trained in mine health and safety procedures and be familiar with company, state, and federal regulations pertaining to mine environmental issues, health, and safety.

Special Requirements

Most states require that all persons employed or engaged in coal mines must obtain a certificate of competency from the state's Miners' Examining Board, as well as completing a course of instruction in first aid, mine rescue methods, and equipment as prescribed by the federal Mine Safety and Health Administration (MSHA). In addition, they are usually required to have a certificate of competency in such areas as the theory and practice of coal mining; the nature and properties of poisonous, noxious, and explosive gases and methods for their detection and control; the practical aspects of coal mining pertaining especially to ventilation and roof control; and the requirements of coal mining laws of the state in which they are working, as well as federal laws governing the coal mining industry. They may also be required to have a certificate applying to their specific area of supervision (such as a certificate for running mine machinery).

All mine supervisors who have engineering degrees should be certified as professional engineers.

Experience, Skills, and Personality Traits

Regardless of their special areas of mining production, all supervisors should have three to five years' experience in underground coal mining and some familiarity with the supervisory duties of the position to which they aspire (frequently gained as a helper or aide to such supervisors). Further training gained in technical training courses or on-the-job training is usually necessary, as well as instruction in methods of directing, motivating, and supervising workers.

Mine supervisory personnel must have exemplary communication and interpersonal skills, as they must deal constantly with mine workers, technicians, and other mine supervisors. They need to be detail-oriented individuals, analytical in their inspection techniques, and persistent in their duties. In addition, they need to be able to make quick but logical decisions and be able to act speedily in times of emergency.

Unions and Associations

For most mine supervisory personnel, memberships in the two most relevant associations for mine supervisors are the American Institute of Mining, Metallurgical, and Petroleum Engineers, Inc. (AIME) and the Society for Mining, Metallurgy, and Exploration (SME). Other groups of interest include the National Mining Association (NMA) and, for those who have engineering degrees, the National Society of Professional Engineers (NSPE).

Tips for Entry

1. While obtaining your bachelor's degree, investigate internship programs or summer jobs working in a coal mine operation to gain first-hand experience in the actual working procedures of the industry.

2. If you are mechanically inclined, find options to apply your abilities to actual machine environments through summer jobs or internship programs.

3. Take courses in business management and/or sociology to better understand how to motivate/direct others in the execution of their jobs.

ELECTRIC POWER
INDUSTRY

ENGINEERS AND SCIENTISTS

ELECTRICAL ENGINEER

Duties: Develop, test, and supervise the generation, transmission, and distribution of electricity

Alternate Title(s): Electrical Systems Engineer; Power Supply Design Engineer

Salary Range: $45,000 to $95,000 or more

Employment Prospects: Good

Advancement Prospects: Fair

Prerequisites:

Education or Training—Bachelor's degree (B.S.) in applied science, engineering, science, or technology required, with strong emphasis on mathematics, physics, and computer science; in some cases a postgraduate master's degree is recommended

Experience—Five to nine years of experience with electrical power systems, practices, and philosophies; three to five years' field engineering experience; some background in electric utility technical and support work

Special Skills and Personality Traits—Ability to work independently, accepting full responsibility for assigned tasks, and labor cooperatively in a team environment; excellent technical training, speaking, and writing skills; good computer proficiency and working knowledge of electrical systems software

Special Requirements—Certification as a professional engineer usually required

```
┌─────────────────────────────────────┐
│  Project Manager; Senior Electrical  │
│              Engineer                │
└─────────────────────────────────────┘

┌─────────────────────────────────────┐
│         Electrical Engineer          │
└─────────────────────────────────────┘

┌─────────────────────────────────────┐
│  Electrical or Electronics Technician │
└─────────────────────────────────────┘
```

Position Description

Electrical engineering, as a professional discipline, deals with the study and application of electricity, electronics, and electromagnetism. Electrical Engineers design, develop, test, and supervise the manufacture of electrical equipment. While the terms "electrical" and "electronics" engineering often are used interchangeably, Electrical Engineers traditionally focus on the generation and supply of electrical power, whereas electronics engineers work on applications of electricity to control systems or signal processing. Electrical Engineers primarily specialize in the areas of power systems engineering and electrical equipment manufacturing.

Power systems engineering deals with the generation, transmission, and distribution of electric power as well as the design of a range of related devices, such as transformers, electric generators, electric motors, and other power electronic devices. As do many other countries, the United States maintains an electrical network that connects assorted electric generators together with users of the electric power coming from them. Users purchase electricity from this power grid and thus avoid the costly expense of having to generate their own electric power. Electrical Engineers may work on the design and maintenance of the power grid as well as the power systems that connect to it. Such systems are called on-grid power systems and may supply the grid with additional power, may draw power from the grid, or do both.

Electrical Engineers may also work on systems that do *not* connect to the grid. These systems are called off-grid power systems and are used by companies for several reasons. It may be cheaper for a user, say a mine, to generate its own power rather than pay for the connection to the grid, or, in the case of most mobile electric power applications, connection to the grid is not practical.

Grids adopt three-phase electric power with an alternating current. Transformers allow electric power to be converted to and from higher voltages. (Many larger industries and organizations receive this three-phase electric power directly because it can be used to drive highly efficient electric motors, whereas most residential customers with their low-power appliances must receive the single-phase electric power.) Higher voltages suffer less power loss during transmission but must be dropped to lower voltages before the electricity reaches the users' appliances. For these reasons, electrical substations exist throughout power grids to convert power to higher voltages before transmission and to lower voltages after transmission and before distribution to individual users.

Electrical Engineers may work at any step in this process of generation, transmission, and distribution. They are responsible for maintaining power plant electrical switchgear, uninterruptible power supply (UPS) systems, electrical distribution systems, and the grounding, bonding, and shielding (GBS) of all electrical transmission lines and equipment. They supervise routine preventive and corrective maintenance, as well as develop and/or revise procedures for operations and maintenance of power plants, transformers, and electrical substations. They may develop and/or revise training plans for electrical operators and maintainers. As engineers working in the field, they frequently are responsible for troubleshooting, testing, and inspecting complex electrical systems, relay calibration, and power metering.

Electrical Engineers may work with project teams to create all design documents and drawings for electric equipment, including creating written diagrams from schematics, generating bills of materials, and applying field mark-ups of project as-built drawings. They often apply engineering application software to complete such engineering tasks as ground grid design, relay coordination, transformer sizing, and load size and short circuit studies. They may recommend new infrastructure equipment installations and modification to facilities to accommodate new equipment needs and technology. In all cases, they evaluate programs and projects to assure compliance with all environmental, energy use, safety, and security standards as set by both government and the electric power industry.

Electrical Engineers may also work in engineering services firms, providing technical expertise to other types of companies on specific electric projects or programs.

Salaries

Generally, engineers earn some of the highest average starting salaries among individuals holding bachelor's degrees.

According to a 2005 survey of the engineering profession by the National Association of Colleges and Employers, average annual starting salaries for Electrical Engineers ranged from $50,000 to $80,000, depending upon the level of education they have, from a bachelor's degree to a Ph.D. The *Occupational Outlook Handbook, 2006–07 Edition,* of the U.S. Bureau of Labor Statistics states that the median earnings in May 2004 for Electrical Engineers ranged from a low of $47,000 to a high of $108,000.

Employment Prospects

With the increasing electrical needs of the American economy and the strong demand for such electrical devices as giant electric power generators, job prospects for qualified and certified Electrical Engineers are good, in all phases of the electric power industry. The U.S. Department of Labor anticipates the employment of Electrical Engineers is expected to increase about as fast as the average for all occupations through 2014.

Advancement Prospects

Beginning Electrical Engineers can look for advancement, after at least five or more years' experience, to posts as senior Electrical Engineer or engineering project manager within their company, or by transferring to another electric utility company. They may also find career elevation by moving to an engineering service firm that provides technical engineering expertise to other companies nationally or internationally.

Education and Training

A bachelor's degree in electrical engineering is a basic requirement for being hired as an Electrical Engineer. In some cases, a candidate for an entry-level position may be required only to be a graduate of an electrical technical school (or have obtained the necessary training and degree while in the military) and have three to five years' minimum experience as an electrical engineer. In other instances, a master's or more advanced degree in electrical engineering may also be necessary. In all cases, three to five years' (or more) background as an electrical technician or engineer is also recommended.

Special Requirements

A bachelor's degree from a credible electrical engineering program represents the first step toward professional certification, as the degree itself is certified by the Accreditation Board of Engineering and Technology (ABET). Becoming a licensed Electrical Engineer usually requires the degree from an ABET-certified engineering program, four years of relevant work experience, and the successful completion of a state examination. (Certification programs from such professional associations as IEEE greatly aid engineer applicants.) With the completion of the licensing program, Electrical Engineers are designated with the title of professional engineer.

Experience, Skills, and Personality Traits

Electrical Engineers must have knowledge of and experience in the operation of electric power systems and their components, generators, transmission lines, and electric substations. They should have experience in the maintenance and operation of power plant electrical switchgear, distribution systems, and equipment, including methods of recovery from system or equipment failure. They should be proficient in the use of electronic test and diagnostic equipment and testing operational procedures. They should have some experience with electrical control design, ac/dc schematics, and transmission line design. They need to be familiar with engineering standards, including those set by the National Electric Code (NEC), the National Electric Safety Code (NESC), the National Electric Manufacturers Association (NEMA), the Institute of Electrical and Electronics Engineers (IEEE), and the American National Standards Institute (ANSI), as well as any applicable construction standards, methods, practices, techniques, materials, and equipment essential to comply with national regulations and standards.

Electrical Engineers must have excellent computer abilities and be proficient with the use of word processing, spreadsheet, and graphics application software. Besides a working knowledge of such Windows programs as Power-Tools (from SKY Systems Analysis, Inc.), Electrical Engineers may need to become familiar with assembly language programming and such higher order computer languages as BASIC, or C. They will need a working knowledge of CADD (computer-aided design and drafting) systems used to develop engineering drawings. They must possess strong project management talents, excellent communication abilities, and proven teamwork and leadership skills. Some background in quality control and quality assurance may be required.

Unions and Associations

The major professional association for Electrical Engineers is the Institute of Electrical and Electronic Engineers (IEEE). Membership in other associations, such as the Association of Energy Engineers (AEE), the Electrical Generating Systems Association (EGSA), the National Association of Power Engineers (NAPE), or the National Society of Professional Engineers (NSPE), may also prove to be useful.

Tips for Entry

1. Along with your studies for your bachelor's degree, be sure to include extensive course work in both basic and advanced computer software programs.
2. Additional courses in technical writing would be helpful, as excellent writing skills are a requirement for most Electrical Engineer jobs.
3. As an electrical or electronics technician, expand your knowledge beyond whatever specialty you have to encompass other areas of electrical engineering to enhance your chances for promotion.

PERFORMANCE ENGINEER

CAREER PROFILE

Duties: Supervise and conduct tests and inspections to determine the efficiency of power plant/substation equipment and transmission/distribution power lines

Alternate Title(s): Asset Performance Engineer

Salary Range: $50,000 to $95,000 or more

Employment Prospects: Poor to Fair

Advancement Prospects: Poor

Prerequisites:

    Education or Training—Bachelor of Science (B.S.) degree in electrical engineering or mechanical engineering minimum requirement; master's degree in chemical, electrical, industrial, or mechanical engineering may be required; superior computer skills are essential

    Experience—Five to 15 years (or more) of operations and maintenance background in power plant environment

    Special Skills and Personality Traits—Excellent oral and written communication capabilities; familiarity with performance and measurement methodologies and benchmarking tools; good interpersonal skills; proven ability in problem solving and project management

    Special Requirements—Licensing as a professional engineer, or a state professional engineer-in-training certificate typically required

CAREER LADDER

```
┌─────────────────────────────────────┐
│  Power Plant Management Positions;   │
│   Power Plant System Operator        │
└─────────────────────────────────────┘

┌─────────────────────────────────────┐
│       Performance Engineer           │
└─────────────────────────────────────┘

┌─────────────────────────────────────┐
│  Electrical Engineer; Engineering    │
│            Technician                │
└─────────────────────────────────────┘
```

Position Description

Among the fuel sources used for the generation of electric power in the United States are coal, nuclear, natural gas, fuel oil, hydro (water power), and various forms of renewable energy. Within any of these fuel sources, the technology employed to generate electricity can be equally diverse. For example, gas technology includes steam turbines, combined-cycle turbines, and single-cycle combustion turbines. Each type of generation has unique operating and cost characteristics that make it more or less suitable to a specific electronic power supply need. Utilities or generating companies usually build generation portfolios comprised of various generation types in order to match the needs of their customers as well as the specific requirements of their geographic location.

Electric transmission from the generating plant is the movement of large amounts of electricity over long distances. In this process electricity is moved from a central generating unit (the plant) to inter-connections (the power station transformer/switchyard, distribution substations, and neighboring utility transmissions) with an electrical distribution system (via transmission lines) to the ultimate customer. This transmission system that connects the generating unit to the supply and demand across the electric network is commonly called an electric grid. During this process, electricity is boosted up in voltage (for transmission over lines to substations) and then stepped down in voltage (at switchyards and local light pole transformers) for distribution to customers.

During this process and in every step, there is one common requirement: securing the best performance obtainable from the electronic equipment utilized. That is where the job of Performance Engineer enters the picture. These engineers participate in the design and development of a framework and process to determine electrical utility asset (equipment) health and performance.

Performance Engineers are responsible for supervising/conducting tests and inspections to determine the efficiency of power plant equipment (from turbines to generators, from transmission lines and the superstructure that carries them to the switches, breakers, bus bars, and other protective equipment that configure the flow of electric power and provide protection to both the generation units and the transmission grid). Performance Engineers conduct analyses of system data, equipment data, and process data in order to recommend actions required to measure the performance of electronic systems and to identify opportunities for improvement.

They test and inspect equipment (including boilers, turbines, heat exchangers, air compressors, generators, pumps, fans, and air heaters) and analyze data to ensure that the systems and associated equipment are working as intended. They diagnose faults in the operation of instruments and control machinery to determine if performance problems are due to operations, maintenance, or equipment deficiencies. They develop performance data models and other performance systems for effective monitoring and optimization of the electronic units, systems, and equipment performance.

Performance Engineers assist in planning, scheduling, supervising, coordinating, and reporting on the testing of the components that go into the operation and maintenance of the power plant, substations, and transmission lines. They develop and manage unit performance efficiency tools and recommend unit performance tests, as well as establish performance standards and goals and recommend equipment and operational enhancements. They may be asked to train plant employees in safety regulations and procedures involved in their work. They prepare reports, analyses, and studies from their work for supervising engineers and other operational management personnel. In addition, they may assist with the preparation and review of the final business plans for recommended equipment modifications or replacements.

Performance Engineers also work in other energy industries, such as coal, nuclear energy, and oil and natural gas.

Salaries

Performance Engineers are either electrical or mechanical engineers by education and training. According to the U.S. Department of Labor's Bureau of Labor Statistics, annual earnings in May 2004 for mechanical engineers ranged from a low of $43,900 to a high of $97,850, whereas annual salaries in May 2004 for electrical engineers ranged from a low of $47,310 to a high of $109,070.

Employment Prospects

The *Occupational Outlook Handbook, 2006–07 Edition* of the Bureau of Labor Statistics estimates that mechanical engineers are projected to have an average rate of employment growth through 2014, and electrical engineers may have even a faster rate of employment growth through 2014. However, Performance Engineers are a very specific type of electric and/or mechanical technician in the electric energy industry. They are needed at every power generating plant and within every power distribution system, but there is minimal job attrition. Therefore, job opportunities are only poor to fair.

Advancement Prospects

The usual path of career progression for Performance Engineers is to become administrators or managers within power generation plants and distribution systems (utility companies). Sufficient training in administrative and management duties, procedures, and practices are required. Nonetheless, an extensive knowledge of the specific equipment and control systems of electric power generation and distribution are valuable assets needed by system operators and managers.

Education and Training

A Bachelor of Science degree in electrical engineering or mechanical engineering is an absolute requirement for this position. Usually, as a basic training for this position, Performance Engineers should have a minimum of five to 10 years of experience in operations and maintenance procedures. In addition, experience with thermodynamics and a familiarity with computer modeling practices is a necessity.

The computer skills that Performance Engineers need include an expert working knowledge of Microsoft Windows Operating System and the Microsoft Office programs, such as Word, Excel, PowerPoint, and Access. Other programming skills that would be useful include those of an intermediate data analyst, such as experience with Visual Basic for Applications, Structured Query Language, and ActiveX Data Objects.

In addition, their training should include familiarity with standard energy maintenance policies and processes and industry standards, such as those set by the Electric Power Research Institute (EPRI).

Special Requirements

Performance Engineers need a certification as a practicing professional engineer in order to gain employment. Whether their training is as a mechanical engineer or an electrical engineer, they usually seek licensing by a state government. To become a licensed Professional Engineer, an engineer must pass the comprehensive Fundamentals of Engineering (FE) exam, then work a given number of years (usually three to five) as an Engineer in Training (EIT), and then pass the Practicing Engineer (PE) exam. Some employers will hire engineers who have secured a state professional engineer-in-training certificate.

Experience, Skills, and Personality Traits

Besides their operations and maintenance experience, Performance Engineers need to understand asset or information analysis, which includes knowledge of business processes and functions, as well as maintenance planning and budgeting, preferably in a power utility environment. With this knowledge, they will be able to analyze and interpret maintenance data in order to devise proper testing procedures.

Performance Engineers must be able to plan, organize, and establish priority to meet goals set for the production processes in a power plant environment. They should demonstrate a proven ability in problem solving and project management. They need to be able to communicate clearly and effectively, both orally and in writing, and have excellent interpersonal and relationship-building talents. In addition, they need to have good meeting facilitation and presentation skills to be able to support their written conclusions.

Unions and Associations

For mechanical engineers, the major professional association is the American Society of Mechanical Engineers (ASME). For electrical engineers, it is the Institute of Electrical and Electronic Engineers (IEEE). Membership in other groups, such as the Association of Energy Engineers (AEE), the Electrical Generating Systems Association (EGSA), the National Association of Power Engineers (NAPE), or the National Society of Professional Engineers (NSPE), may also be useful.

Tips for Entry

1. Along with getting your engineering degree, take extensive computer courses, particularly those concentrating on Microsoft Windows programs dealing with Access and Excel design and development applications.
2. Include in your curriculum classes in administration and management, so you will become familiar with business and management principles involved in strategic planning, resource allocation, production methods, and coordination of people and resources.
3. In addition, course work in technical writing should prove useful, as excellent technical writing skills are necessary for Performance Engineers to write clear and concise (but detailed) reports on their testing of equipment and their resultant recommendations to utility management.

POWER DISTRIBUTOR AND DISPATCHER

CAREER PROFILE

Duties: Control the flow of electricity through transmission lines to industrial plants and substations that, in turn, supply residential and commercial electricity through distribution lines

Alternate Title(s): Distribution Systems Operator; Load Dispatcher; Substation Operator; Switchboard Operator

Salary Range: $38,000 to $80,000 or more

Employment Prospects: Poor

Advancement Prospects: Fair

Prerequisites:

Education or Training—High school degree minimum requirement; in many cases, college-level courses and, possibly, a Bachelor of Science (B.S.) degree are also required for applicants to be competitive

Experience—Prior background in a technical job, preferably with electronic equipment, a necessity, as well as computer proficiency; years of training and experience as an apprentice required before becoming a fully qualified Power Distributor and Dispatcher

Special Skills and Personality Traits—Capable of accepting responsibility and making appropriate decisions; excellent manual and finger dexterity; good knowledge of mathematics and excellent computer skills; outstanding mechanical abilities, with a thorough knowledge of electric and electronic equipment; patience and persistence, with close attention to detail; sensitivity to potential problems and excellent use of deductive reasoning in solving them

Special Requirements—Certification as a systems operator is usually required

CAREER LADDER

```
┌─────────────────────────────────────┐
│      Power Plant Supervisor;         │
│         Shift Supervisor             │
└─────────────────────────────────────┘

┌─────────────────────────────────────┐
│   Power Distributor and Dispatcher   │
└─────────────────────────────────────┘

┌─────────────────────────────────────┐
│   Electric Power System Apprentice;  │
│        Mechanical Technician         │
└─────────────────────────────────────┘
```

Position Description

Typically, electric power transmission is the process of transmitting electricity between a power-generating plant and a substation near a populated area. This process is distinct from that of electricity distribution (the delivery of electric power from the substation to the consumer). Due to the large amount of power involved, transmission normally takes place at high voltage and is usually transmitted over long distances through overhead power transmission lines.

Underground power transmission is used only in densely populated areas (such as large cities) mainly due to the increased costs of installation and maintenance.

A power transmission system (network) is sometimes referred to as a grid; however, for reasons of economy, the network is rarely a true grid. Redundant paths and electric lines are provided so that power can be routed from any power plant to any load center (usually substations) through a variety of routes, based on the economics of the transmission path and the cost of power. Thus, a grid is simply the interconnection of facilities (power stations, transmission circuits, and substations) that provides whatever electric power redundancy is available. Engineers design transmission networks to transport the electrical energy as efficiently as possible, while taking into account economic factors, network safety, and redundancy. These networks use such components as power lines, cables, circuit breakers, switches, and transformers.

At the generating plants, the energy is produced at a relatively low voltage and then stepped up by the power station transformer to a higher voltage (which is more efficient) for transmission over long distances to grid exit points (substations). At the substations, transformers are again used to step the voltage down to a lower voltage for distribution to commercial and residential users. In addition, these substations can split the distribution power in multiple directions, and they often have circuit breakers and switches so that they can be disconnected from the transmission grid or so that separate distribution lines can be disconnected from the substation when necessary. Finally, at the point of use, the energy is converted once again, by transformers attached to the power poles carrying the power lines, to the low voltage that commercial and residential buildings and products can use.

The electric power personnel who control this distribution and dispatching of electric power are called Power Distributors and Dispatchers. They control the flow of electricity through transmission lines. They monitor and operate current converters, voltage transformers, and circuit breakers. They calculate and determine electric load estimates or equipment requirements, so they can choose the required control settings. They check all the distribution equipment and record these readings onto a pilot board, which is a map of the transmission grid (network) system displaying the status of transmission circuits and connections between power generating plants and substations.

Power Distributors and Dispatchers distribute and regulate the flow of power between the various entities in the network (the generating stations, substations, distribution lines, and end users), keeping track of the status of all circuits and connections. They anticipate power needs, such as those caused by changes in the weather, and communicate with power plant operators in their control rooms to start or stop boilers and generators in order to bring electric power production into balance with those requirements. They handle emergencies, such as transformer or transmission line failures, and route electric current around affected areas. They coordinate with engineers, planners, field personnel, and other utility workers to provide information such as clearances, switching orders, and distribution process changes. In substations, they also operate and monitor equipment that increases or decreases voltage, and they operate switchboard levers to control the flow of electricity in and out of the substations.

They inspect machinery or equipment to determine adjustments or repairs needed, as well as monitor them to detect problems. They compute production, construction, or installation specifications and prepare safety reports, as well as maintain all equipment service records and production work records. They may direct and coordinate activities of workers or staff in this process and in the repair, maintenance, and cleaning of equipment and machinery. Power Distributors and Dispatchers usually report to senior supervisors of utility companies.

Salaries

According to the U.S. Department of Labor's *Occupational Outlook Handbook, 2006–07 Edition*, median annual salaries of Power Distributors and Dispatchers were $57,330 in May 2004. The middle 50 percent earned between $48,010 and $69,100. The lowest 10 percent earned less than $38,220, and the highest 10 percent received more than $83,030.

Employment Prospects

There is keen competition for the relatively high-paying positions of Power Distributors and Dispatchers. While electricity demands are always increasing, the slow pace of construction of new generating plants and the resultant need for expansion of distribution lines and substations will limit opportunities. In addition, the rising use of automatic controls and more computerized equipment may boost productivity but lessen the demand for distributors and dispatchers. As a result, individuals with training in computers and automated equipment may have the best chance at such jobs. Some job opportunities will arise from the need to replace workers who retire or leave the occupation, but cost constraints may limit the number of workers hired to replace them.

The U.S. Bureau of Labor Statistics forecasts a decline in employment of Power Distributors and Dispatchers through the year 2014, as the utilities industry continues to restructure in response to demands of deregulation and increasing competition. While most of this restructuring has been accomplished by 2007, the focus still is on reducing costs.

Advancement Prospects

A good number of years of training and experience, as well as certification, are necessary for an individual to become a fully qualified Power Distributor and Dispatcher. With further training and experience, a Power Distributor and Dispatcher may be able to advance to a position as senior distributor. If they display management potential, they may advance to become shift supervisors and from there move to higher levels of senior management within the utility company. Utilities tend to promote from within, so opportunities to advance by moving from one employer to another are very limited. Generally, individuals hired by electric power companies have relatively secure jobs. Even during economic downturns, these companies rarely lay off employees.

Education and Training

Utility employers usually hire high school graduates for entry-level distributor and dispatcher positions. Those with strong math and science skills are preferred. In addition, college-level courses and some prior experience in a mechanical or technical job should be useful in this very competitive job market. As computers are now used to keep records, generate reports, monitor line performance, and track maintenance, utilities look for computer proficiency in candidates for this position. Most entry-level workers start as helpers or laborers in power plants or in other areas of the utility field such as power line construction. Those that are selected for training as Power Distributors and Dispatchers undergo extensive on-the-job and classroom instruction. Several years of training and experience are compulsory before becoming a fully qualified Power Distributor and Dispatcher.

Special Requirements

Many utility employers ask their experienced Power Distributors and Dispatchers to seek certification as system operators by the North American Electric Reliability Council (NERC). Their system operator certification program includes the examinations required to obtain initial certification. A system operator credential is a personal certification issued to an individual for successfully passing a NERC system operator certification exam. The credential is maintained by accumulating a specified number of continuing education hours within a specified time period. Thus, this program allows system operators to maintain their credentials through continuing education rather than to recertify by retaking an examination.

Experience, Skills, and Personality Traits

Power Distributors and Dispatchers are expected to be knowledgeable about the principles, methods, procedures, and practices used in the safe and efficient distribution of electric power through the network grid to end users. They should be familiar with the machinery and equipment used in electrical power transmission and be knowledgeable about control center procedures. Additionally, they must be mindful of all safety rules as stated in the substation's safety manual and be practiced in the application of safety practices and procedures.

They must be skilled in the monitoring of the operation (e.g., watching gauges, dials, and other indicators to make sure substation equipment and transmission lines are working properly). They should be able to perform routine maintenance on substation equipment and be able to determine when and what kind of maintenance is needed. As troubleshooters, they should be able to determine causes of operating errors, and be able to decide what to do about the situation. They must have the know-how to tell when something is wrong or is likely to go wrong. They need to be able to recognize an emergency condition when it occurs and to react quickly.

They must have excellent manual dexterity and good wrist-finger speed (the ability to make fast, simple, repeated movements of the fingers, hands, and wrists). Their reading comprehension must be exemplary for them to be able to read technical drawings and understand technical operating, service, or repair manuals and blueprints. They need to have good writing skills as well, as they will have to maintain production and work records, as well as safety reports. Their math skills will help them to compute production, construction, or installation specifications, and their interpersonal skills will aid them in their conferring with engineering, technical, or manufacturing personnel.

Unions and Associations

Some Power Distributors and Dispatchers may belong to one of the electrical unions, the International Brotherhood of Electrical Workers (IBEW) of AFL-CIO, or the Utility Workers Union of America (UWUA). Membership in other professional associations that might prove useful to them would include the Electric Power Supply Association (EPSA), the Electrical Generating Systems Association (EGSA), the Energy Providers Coalition for Education (EPCE), and the Institute of Electrical and Electronics Engineers (IEEE).

Tips for Entry

1. In school, develop your mathematics skills (including algebra, calculus, and geometry) and become computer literate.
2. Seek an apprentice position (or a summer job) in a tool shop, preferably one dealing with electronic or electrical equipment, so you become familiar with them, their uses, repair, and maintenance.
3. Practice inspecting electronic and electrical equipment to identify the cause of errors or defects, and use your hands and arms in handling, installing, positioning, and moving materials and manipulating objects, as these are abilities that will be useful for you in this job.

POWER PLANT OPERATOR

Duties: Control and operate a range of machinery and instruments used for electric power generation, often through the use of panel boards, control boards, or semi-automatic equipment

Alternate Title(s): Control Room Operator; Generating Station Operator; Power Generation Plant Operator; Power Station Operator; Power System Operator

Salary Range: $30,000 to $70,000 or more

Employment Prospects: Poor

Advancement Prospects: Poor to Fair

Prerequisites:

Education or Training—High school degree minimum requirement; often college-level courses, if not a bachelor's degree, have become necessary in a competitive market

Experience—Prior experience in a mechanical or technical job a necessity, as well as computer proficiency; several years of training and experience are required before becoming a fully qualified power plant operator

Special Skills and Personality Traits—Able to accept responsibility, make appropriate decisions, and prioritize and handle multiple tasks and projects concurrently; effective oral and written communication skills; excellent mechanical abilities and manual dexterity; good analytical and problem-solving skills; logical and thorough approach to work; perceptual speed (the ability to quickly and accurately compare similarities and differences between things) and near vision (the ability to see details at close range); physically fit

```
┌─────────────────────────────┐
│   Power Plant Supervisor;   │
│       Shift Supervisor      │
└─────────────────────────────┘

┌─────────────────────────────┐
│    Power Plant Operator     │
└─────────────────────────────┘

┌─────────────────────────────┐
│ High School or College Graduate; │
│     Mechanical Technician   │
└─────────────────────────────┘
```

Position Description

Electricity is probably the most vital underpinning for most everyday activities. From the moment the first electric light is switched on in the morning, a connection is made to a huge network of people, electric lines, and generating machinery. Power Plant Operators control the equipment that generates electricity that will be distributed over a network of transmission lines to industrial plants and electric power substations and, finally, over distribution lines to commercial and residential users.

By the use of control boards, Power Plant Operators operate, control, and monitor boilers, turbines, generators, and auxiliary equipment in power-generating plants. They distribute power demands among generators, combining the current from several generators, and monitoring instruments to maintain voltage and regulate electricity flows from the plant. When power requirements change, they must start and stop generators and connect or disconnect them from circuits. They often use computers to keep records of switching operations and the loads on generators, lines, and transformers.

Power Plant Operators in facilities with automated control systems work mainly in a control room and often are called control room operators or, if they are in training, control room operator trainees or assistants. In older plants, the controls for the equipment are often not centralized, and operators (called switchboard operators) control the flow of electricity from a central point in the plant. Operators called auxiliary equipment operators work throughout the plant, operating and monitoring valves, switches, and gauges.

The tasks of Power Plant Operators, be they control room operators or auxiliary equipment operators, usually include:

- Adjusting controls to generate specified electrical power, or to regulate the flow of power between generating stations and substations
- Taking readings from charts, meters, and gauges at established intervals, and undertaking corrective steps as necessary
- Controlling generator output to match the phase, frequency, and voltage of electricity supplied to panels
- Placing standby emergency electrical generators on line in emergencies and monitoring the temperature, output, and lubrication of the system
- Receiving outage calls and summoning needed personnel during power outages and emergencies
- Starting or stopping generators, auxiliary pumping equipment, turbines, and other power plant equipment, and connecting or disconnecting equipment from circuits
- Regulating equipment operations and conditions such as water levels, based on data from the recording and indicating instruments or from computers
- Cleaning, lubricating, and maintaining equipment to prevent failure or deterioration
- Collecting oil, water, and electrolyte samples for laboratory analysis
- Controlling and maintaining auxiliary equipment, such as pumps, fans, compressors, condensers, feedwater heaters, filters, and chlorinators
- Testing electrical power distribution machinery and equipment, using standard testing devices
- Inspecting records and log book entries, and communicating with other plant personnel in order to assess equipment operating status
- Monitoring and inspecting power plant equipment and indicators to detect evidence of operating problems
- Recording and compiling operational data, completing and maintaining forms, logs, and reports

Because electricity is provided around the clock, Power Plant Operators often work nights and weekends, usually on rotating shifts. Shifts are usually eight hours long, with three shifts per day, and are often rotated so that duty on less desirable shifts is shared by all Operators. Power Plant Operators generally report to a shift supervisor or to senior system operational personnel.

Salaries

According to the U.S. Department of Labor's Bureau of Labor Statistics, median annual earnings of Power Plant Operators were $52,530 in May 2004. The middle 50 percent earned between $43,310 and $62,030. The lowest 10 percent had incomes of less than $34,550, and the highest 10 percent earned more than $70,330.

Employment Prospects

There is very strong competition for jobs as Power Plant Operators. While demand for electricity is constantly increasing, the slow pace of construction of new plants will limit job possibilities. In addition, the accelerating use of automatic controls and more computerized equipment should boost productivity but also decrease the demand for Operators. As a result, individuals with training in computers and automated equipment will have the best job prospects. Most entry-level workers start as helpers or laborers in order to get their training under the guidance of experienced operators.

The U.S. Department of Labor's *Occupational Outlook Handbook, 2006–07 Edition* indicates an anticipated decline in employment of Power Plant Operators through 2014, as the utilities industry continues to restructure in response to deregulation and increasing competition. Independent power producers are now allowed to sell power directly to industrial and other wholesale customers. Consequently, some utilities that, historically, operated as regulated local monopolies have restructured their operations to reduce costs and to compete effectively. This focus on reducing overhead affects both regulated utilities and those that have been deregulated. Hence, the number of job openings for Power Plant Operators is expected to decline.

Advancement Prospects

Several years of training and experience are necessary for an individual to become a fully qualified Power Plant Operator. With further training and experience, they may be able to advance to posts as shift supervisors and from there to higher levels of senior management at the power plant. Utilities tend to promote from within, so opportunities to advance by moving from one employer to another are very limited. It should be noted that, generally, individuals hired by electric power companies have relatively secure jobs. Even during economic downturns, these operations seldom lay off employees.

Education and Training

Employers generally seek high school graduates for entry-level operator positions. Those with strong math and science skills are preferred. College or vocational level courses in steam and mechanical fundamentals of power plants and in electrical and electronic technology or prior experience in a mechanical or technical job may be beneficial. Power Plant Operators are required typically to complete a three- to five-year power system operator apprenticeship program, or to have sufficient work experience in the trade. In addition to their preliminary training as Power Plant Operators, most workers are given periodic refresher training.

Experience, Skills, and Personality Traits

Power Plant Operators are expected to be knowledgeable about the principles, methods, procedures, and practices employed in the safe operation of an electrical power generating plant. They should be familiar with the machinery and equipment used in electrical power generation and have an understanding of water chemistry and testing as it applies to an electrical power generation plant. Additionally, they must be cognizant of all safety rules as stated in the plant's safety manual, and be practiced in the application of safety practices and procedures.

They need to be skilled in the use of common hand and power tools and be able to make minor repairs to power plant equipment. They should know how to maintain records, be able to understand and follow oral instructions, and be able to interpret an extensive variety of technical instructions in mathematical or diagram form, dealing with both abstract and concrete variables. They must be able to recognize an emergency condition when it occurs and to react quickly. They should have good interpersonal skills, be physically fit, and be able to work safely with and around mechanical equipment.

Unions and Associations

Some Power Plant Operators, particularly those who work with auxiliary equipment, may belong to one of the electrical unions, the International Brotherhood of Electrical Workers (IBEW) of AFL-CIO, or the Utility Workers Union of America (UWUA).

Tips for Entry

1. In school, study mathematics, including arithmetic, algebra, calculus, and geometry, as well as statistics, and their applications.
2. Take an apprentice position (or a summer job) in a tool shop, preferably one dealing with electronic equipment, so you become familiar with machines and tools, including their uses, maintenance, and repair.
3. Practice inspecting equipment, materials, and structures to identify the cause of errors or defects, and use your hands and arms in handling, installing, positioning, moving materials, and manipulating objects, as these are abilities you must have for this position.

MANUAL LABOR
PERSONNEL

ELECTRICAL AND ELECTRONICS INSTALLER AND REPAIRER

CAREER PROFILE

Duties: Inspect, test, maintain, and/or repair existing electrical systems and electrical equipment used in electric power systems

Alternate Title(s): Maintenance Electrician; Power Transformers Repairer; Powerhouse Electrician; Relay Technician

Salary Range: $35,000 to $70,000 or more

Employment Prospects: Poor to Fair

Advancement Prospects: Fair

Prerequisites:

Education or Training—High school degree basic requirement; further training at vocational schools, community colleges recommended

Experience—From two to four years of apprentice work background with electrical testing, maintenance, and repair work usually required

Special Skills and Personality Traits—Excellent communication skills; good eyesight and color perception; manual and finger dexterity, reliable eye-hand coordination, and good balance; problem sensitivity and good deductive reasoning; thorough knowledge of electrical equipment, wiring, and electronics

Special Requirements—Certification usually is not necessary, but may be highly recommended

CAREER LADDER

```
┌─────────────────────────────────┐
│     Electronics Supervisor;      │
│       Electrical Engineer        │
└─────────────────────────────────┘

┌─────────────────────────────────┐
│ Electrical and Electronics Installer │
│          and Repairer            │
└─────────────────────────────────┘

┌─────────────────────────────────┐
│ Apprentice Electrical and Electronics │
│           Technician             │
└─────────────────────────────────┘
```

Position Description

Businesses and other organizations depend on complex electronic equipment for many functions. For example, electric power companies use electronic equipment to operate and control generating plants, substations, in-service relays, and electronic monitoring equipment. Such complex pieces of electronic apparatus are installed, maintained, and repaired by Electrical and Electronics Installers and Repairers.

Electrical equipment and electronic equipment are two distinct types of industrial gear, although much equipment contains both electrical and electronic components. Usually, the electrical portions provide the power for the equipment or device, whereas the electronic components control the apparatus, although many types of equipment still are controlled with electrical devices. Electronic sensors monitor the equipment and the manufacturing process (such as the production of electric power), providing feedback to the programmable logic control (PLC), which controls the equipment. The PLC processes the data provided by the sensors and makes adjustments to optimize output. To adjust the output, the PLC sends signals to the electrical, hydraulic, and pneumatic devices that power the equipment in order to change feed rates, pressures, and other variables in the processes that the equipment is handling.

When equipment breaks down (and some electronic equipment is self-monitoring and able to alert repairers about malfunctions), Electrical and Electronics Installers and Repairers check for common causes of trouble (loose connections or defective components). They analyze test data to diagnose malfunctions, as well as to determine the performance characteristics of the equipment and the system in which it operates to aid in their evaluation of how changes to the system might have modified the performance of the equipment. If the problem(s) are not found easily, they consult manuals, schematics, wiring diagrams, manufacturers' specifications (that detail connections and provide instructions on how to locate problems), and engineering personnel. They may open and close switches to isolate defective relays and then perform any necessary adjustments or repairs. Automated electronic control systems are increasingly complex, making diagnosis more challenging. With such systems, repairers use software programs and testing equipment to find the malfunctions.

Because power plants cannot allow production equipment to stand idle, there are backup systems designed to take over when the primary system fails. In such instances, repairers usually remove and replace defective units (such as circuit boards), instead of fixing them. Defective units are discarded or returned to the manufacturer or to a specialized shop for repair. Repair technicians there, often called bench technicians, have the training, tools, and parts needed to diagnose and repair such complex components or common circuit defects such as poorly soldered joints, blown fuses, or malfunctioning transistors.

In some cases, Electrical and Electronics Installers may fit older electronics equipment with new automated control devices. Older devices may still be in good working order but limited by inefficient control systems for which replacement parts may no longer be available. Installers replace old electronic control units with new PLCs. Setting up and installing a new PLC entails connecting it to different sensors and electrically powered units (such as electric motors, switches, and pumps) and writing a computer program to operate the new PLC.

As Electrical and Electronics Installers and Repairers not only must solve equipment problems but also determine the optimum functioning of the equipment, they run signal quality and connectivity tests for individual cables and record the results. They disconnect voltage regulators, bolts, and screws and connect replacement regulators to high-voltage lines. In addition, they fix, replace, and clean equipment and components (such as circuit breakers, brushes, and commutators). They maintain inventories of spare parts of all equipment, requisitioning new parts when necessary.

During their analysis, testing, and repair procedures, electricians or Electrical and Electronics Installers and Repairers work closely with (and may report to) electrical engineers and electric power systems operators, as well as communicate with other workers who are installing and maintaining equipment.

Salaries

According to the U.S. Department of Labor's *Occupational Outlook Handbook, 2006–07 Edition*, median hourly earnings of Electrical and Electronics Installers and Repairers within the electric power industry were $25.86 in May 2004. The middle 50 percent earned between $22.47 and $29.73 per hour. The lowest 10 percent earned less than $18.01, and the highest 10 percent earned more than $33.82. This translates into annual yearly salaries that range from $37,000 to $70,000 or more.

Employment Prospects

Job opportunities for Electrical and Electronics Installers and Repairers should be best for applicants who have a thorough knowledge of electrical equipment and electronics as well as have significant repair experience. Overall employment of Electrical and Electronics Installers and Repairers is expected to grow more slowly than the average for all occupations during the period from 2004 to 2014 (according to the U.S. Department of Labor), and employment of these workers in the electric power industry is expected to decline slightly. The Department attributes this decline to the consolidation and privatization in the electric utilities industry, which should improve overall productivity, thus reducing employment. Newer equipment is expected to be more reliable and easier to repair, further limiting employment of installers and repairers.

Nonetheless, there should be job openings as employers (power stations, power facilities, utility companies, and their like) must constantly replace workers who leave the industry, move to different jobs, or exit altogether from the labor force.

Advancement Prospects

Experienced Electrical and Electronics Installers and Repairers with advanced training may become specialists or troubleshooters who help other repairers diagnose difficult problems. Installers or repairers with leadership ability may become supervisors of other installation and repair personnel.

Some experienced installers and repairers may decide to open up their own repair shops. On the other hand, with further extended college engineering course work, they may earn college (and, possibly, graduate) degrees and become electrical engineers.

Education and Training

To be employed in this area of the electric power industry, applicants must have the appropriate knowledge of electrical equipment and electronics. This comprehension can be obtained by attending vocational schools or community colleges, which provide one- to two-year programs. Some less skilled installers and repairers, however, may enter the industry at the bottom having received only a high school diploma. Such entry-level installers and repairers will likely work closely with seasoned technicians who will provide direction and technical guidance.

Specifically, Electrical and Electronics Installers and Repairers should exhibit knowledge of circuit boards, processors, chips, electronic equipment, and computer hardware and software, including applications and programming. They should have working experience with appropriate machines and tools, including their design, uses, repair, and maintenance. Their mathematics skills should include proficiency in algebra, geometry, calculus, and statistics (with its applications).

Special Requirements

While certification may not be required in this field, it is highly recommended. It can be achieved through organizations such as the Association of Communications and Electronics Schools International, Inc. (ACES Int'l), the Consumer Electronics Association (CEA), the Electronics Technicians Association International (ETAI), and the International Society of Certified Electronics Technicians (ISCET). In seeking certification, applicants need to pass certain exams related to their degree of training and experience.

Experience, Skills, and Personality Traits

Electrical and Electronics Installers and Repairers must have excellent eyesight and color perception to be able to work successfully with the complex (color-coded) parts of an electronic system. They should have excellent manual dexterity, as well as the ability to make precisely coordinated movements of the fingers of one or both hands to grasp, manipulate, or assemble very small objects. They must be able to adjust the controls of machinery quickly (and repeatedly) to exact positions. They need good perceptual speed, which is the ability to compare quickly and accurately similarities and differences among sets of letters, numbers, objects, pictures, or patterns. Along with this ability, they must be capable of identifying information by categorizing, estimating, recognizing differences or similarities, and detecting changes in circumstances or events related to the equipment they are testing. Similarly, they need to be able to arrange things or actions into a certain order or pattern according to a specific rule or set of rules. They should be able to tell when something is wrong, or is likely to go wrong, and use deductive reasoning (applying general rules to specific problems to produce answers that make sense).

They should be proficient in gathering information—observing, receiving, and otherwise obtaining information from all relevant sources. Finally, they should have above average communication skills and a professional appearance to deal effectively with customers, as well as with their supervisors, peers, or subordinates.

Unions and Associations

For Electrical and Electronics Installers and Repairers, membership in such associations as the Electronics Technicians Association International (ETAI) or the International Society of Certified Electronics Technicians (ISCET) might prove beneficial. Some Electrical Installers and Repairers may belong to the International Brotherhood of Electrical Workers (IBEW) Union of the AFL-CIO.

Tips for Entry

1. Along with your vocational training in electrical and electronic equipment, take the extensive mathematics courses that your career will demand. In addition, be sure to be fully computer literate.
2. Undertake some technical writing and communication course work, as you will need these skills.
3. Spend time using your hands to handle, control, or feel objects, tools, or equipment controls, as these abilities will be essential in your work.

LINE INSTALLER AND REPAIRER

CAREER PROFILE

Duties: Install, test, and repair cables or wires used in electrical power of distribution systems, and erect poles and light- or heavy-duty transmission towers

Alternate Title(s): Electrical Line Worker; Line Erector; Lineman; Line Mechanic; Power Line Worker; Power Lineman

Salary Range: $27,000 to $65,000 or more

Employment Prospects: Poor

Advancement Prospects: Poor to Fair

Prerequisites:

Education or Training—High school diploma minimum requirement; technical knowledge of electricity or electronics obtained through vocational/technical programs usually a must

Experience—Some hands-on power line field work in vocational programs necessary, though most Line Installers and Repairers train on the job

Special Skills and Personality Traits—Ability to lift heavy objects and to climb; unafraid of heights; basic knowledge of algebra and trigonometry; capable of near vision and being able to distinguish colors; excellent mechanical ability; exemplary customer service and interpersonal skills; good oral comprehension and communication; manual dexterity and multi-limb coordination; satisfactory driving record

CAREER LADDER

```
┌─────────────────────────────────┐
│     Manual Labor Supervisor      │
└─────────────────────────────────┘

┌─────────────────────────────────┐
│    Line Installer and Repairer   │
└─────────────────────────────────┘

┌─────────────────────────────────┐
│      High School Graduate        │
└─────────────────────────────────┘
```

Position Description

Vast networks of wires and cables provide customers throughout the United States with electrical power and communication services. Networks of electric power lines deliver electricity from generating plants to commercial and residential customers. Communications networks of telephone and cable television lines provide voice, video, Internet, and other communication services. These line networks are installed, maintained, and repaired by electrical power Line Installers and Repairers and telecommunications Line Installers and Repairers.

While the tasks performed by electrical power line and telecommunications Line Installers and Repairers are quite similar, they are two distinct occupations. Working with power lines requires specialized knowledge of transformers, electrical power distribution systems, and substations; working with telecommunications lines requires specialized knowledge of fiber optics and telecommunications switches and routers. Nonetheless, the procedures for installing both these kinds of lines are quite similar.

Line Installers position new power lines by constructing utility poles, towers, and underground trenches to carry the wires and cables. Before installing poles, they attach cross-arms, insulators, and other auxiliary equipment. They employ a variety of construction equipment, including digger derricks, trenchers, cable plows, and borers. Digger derricks are trucks equipped with augers (used to dig holes in the ground) and cranes (used to set utility poles in place).

Trenchers and cable plows are used to cut openings in the earth for the laying of underground cables. Borers, which tunnel under the land surface, are used to install tubes for the wires and cables instead of opening a trench in the soil.

Once the construction is completed, Line Installers string cable along the poles, towers, tunnels, or trenches. While working on poles and towers, Line Installers first use truck-mounted buckets to reach the top of the structure or manually climb the pole or tower. They pull up cable from large reels mounted on trucks, set the line in place and pull it tight (using winches) so that it has the correct amount of tension. They attach the cable to the already-attached insulators and to the structure using hand and hydraulic tools. Underground cable is laid directly in a trench, pulled through a tunnel, or strung through a conduit running through a trench.

Other installation duties may include setting up service to customers by stringing cable between the customers' premises and the lines running on poles or towers or in trenches. While installing the wiring to customers, installers check the connection for proper voltage readings and may install or replace transformers, circuit breakers, switches, fuses, and other equipment to control and direct the electrical current. They may set up watt-hour meters and connect service drops between power lines and consumers' facilities. Installers may also splice or solder cables together or to overhead transmission lines, customer service lines, or street light lines, using hand tools, epoxies, or specialized equipment. They test each conductor to be installed, according to electrical diagrams and specifications, to identify corresponding conductors and to prevent incorrect connections. They may be required to trim trees that could be hazardous to the functioning of cables or wires.

In addition to installation, Line Installers and Repairers are also responsible for maintenance and any necessary repairs. They periodically travel in trucks, helicopters, and airplanes to inspect visually the wires and cables. They use sensitive monitoring and testing equipment that can detect malfunctions in the electric power network (such as loss of current flow), and then they travel to the site of the malfunction. Using wiring diagrams and schematics, they repair or replace defective cables and/or equipment.

Installation and repair work may also require splicing, or joining, separate pieces of cable. Each cable contains numerous individual wires. Thus, splicing the cables together requires that each wire in one piece of cable be joined to another wire in the matching piece. Line Installers splice cables using small hand tools, epoxy, or mechanical equipment. At each splice, they place insulation over the conductor and seal the splice with moisture-proof covering.

Besides the physical work, Line Installers and Repairers provide information to supervisors, coworkers, and subordinates by telephone, in written form, by e-mail, or in person. They usually report to the systems manager or to other senior engineering staff.

Salaries

According to the U.S. Bureau of Labor Statistics, earnings for Line Installers and Repairers tend to be higher than those in most other occupations that do not require postsecondary (college) education. Median hourly earnings for electrical power Line Installers and Repairers were $23.61 (or about $49,000 a year) in May 2004. The middle 50 percent were paid between $18.00 and $27.64 an hour. The lowest 10 percent earned less than $13.31 an hour, and the highest 10 percent earned more than $32.54 an hour. Annual salaries for Line Installers and Repairers in May 2004 ranged from a low of approximately $27,500 to a high of about $67,680.

Employment Prospects

According to the U.S. Department of Labor, overall employment of Line Installers and Repairers is expected to grow more slowly than the average for all occupations through 2014. Nonetheless, because many Line Installers and Repairers are nearing retirement, job opportunities for newcomers should be very good, particularly for electrical power line installers. However, despite consistently rising demand for electricity, power industry deregulation is pushing companies to cut costs and maintenance, which tends to reduce employment. According to the department's *Occupational Outlook Handbook, 2006–07 Edition*, most new jobs are expected to arise in the construction side of power line installation.

Advancement Prospects

Entry-level Line Installers and Repairers are usually hired as ground workers, helpers, or tree trimmers (who clear branches from telephone and power lines). These employees may advance to positions of stringing cable or wires and performing service installations after an adequate amount of hands-on work with seasoned crews of installers and repairers. With additional experience, they may advance to more sophisticated maintenance and repair posts, and become responsible for increasingly larger portions of the network.

For Line Installers and Repairers who demonstrate both initiative and leadership potential, promotion to supervisory or training positions also is possible. However, most advanced supervisory positions require a college degree.

Education and Training

The usual basic requirement for this position is a high school diploma. In addition, most employers of Line Installers and Repairers strongly suggest applicants acquire a technical knowledge of electricity or electronics or job experience that can be obtained through vocational/technical programs, community colleges, or the Armed Forces. Many of these programs are operated with assistance from local employers and/or unions. Some schools, working with local companies, offer one-year certificate programs that emphasize hands-on fieldwork. More advanced two-year associate's degree programs provide students with a broader knowledge of electrical utilities technology (and telecommunications) through their courses. Graduates from such programs often get preferential treatment in the hiring process.

Electrical Line Installers and Repairers frequently must complete formal apprenticeships or other employer training programs. These programs, which can last up to five years, combine on-the-job training with formal classroom courses. Government safety regulations strictly define the training and education requirements for such apprenticeship programs.

Experience, Skills, and Personality Traits

Electrical Line Installers and Repairers need a basic understanding of algebra and trigonometry, along with basic mechanical ability. They need good eyesight, particularly the ability to see details at close range, otherwise known as near vision. They should exhibit multi-limb coordination (coordinating two or more limbs while sitting, standing, or lying down), excellent manual dexterity (using their hand or hands to grasp, manipulate, or assemble objects), and good finger dexterity (using the fingers of one or both hands to grasp, manipulate, or assemble very small objects).

Because their work demands lifting heavy objects (many employers insist that applicants be able to lift at least 50 pounds) as well as climbing and other physical activity, applicants for this position should have stamina, strength, and coordination and must be unafraid of heights. They need to have good visualization abilities (to imagine how something will look after it is moved around or when its parts are moved or rearranged) and must be able to distinguish colors, as wires and cables are often color-coded.

Electrical Line Installers and Repairers need to have good reading comprehension (to be able to read blueprints, schematics, technical drawings, and other work-related documents) and oral comprehension (to be able to understand spoken information, ideas, and instructions). They should be able to tell when something is wrong or is likely to go wrong, as well as being natural problem solvers. Finally, as they may have to deal with customers, their interpersonal skills are important.

Unions and Associations

Most Line Installers and Repairers belong to unions, principally the Communications Workers of America (CWA), the International Brotherhood of Electrical Workers (IBEW), and the Utility Workers Union of America (UWUA). Membership in these unions helps to guarantee wage rates and wage increases (as set by union contract) and the time needed to advance from one job level to another. These unions also sponsor and administer jointly with employers many on-the-job training programs.

Tips for Entry

1. During high school (and any further vocational studies), be sure to include basic courses in algebra and trigonometry, as these skills will be essential to your job.
2. Spend time using your hands to handle, control, or feel objects (both large and small), tools, or controls to test your manual dexterity and improve it if necessary.
3. Be sure you have a good driving record and are experienced in driving vans or light trucks, as electrical Line Installers and Repairers are frequently required to hold commercial driver's licenses and operate company-owned vehicles.

MAINTENANCE SUPERVISOR

CAREER PROFILE

Duties: Direct and supervise mechanics and technicians in the installation, alternation, overhaul, maintenance, and repair of electrical and mechanical equipment and instruments of an electric power plant or station

Alternate Title(s): Electrical Substation Maintenance Supervisor; Electrical/Technical Maintenance Foreman; Maintenance Foreman; Mechanical Maintenance Supervisor; Power Plant Engineering Maintenance Supervisor

Salary Range: $50,000 to $90,000 or more

Employment Prospects: Fair

Advancement Prospects: Poor to Fair

Prerequisites:

Education or Training—Bachelor of Science degree in electrical engineering or mechanical engineering

Experience—Between five and 10 years of power plant experience, preferably in maintenance of electrical and instrument control (E&IC) systems; two to five years' supervisory experience helpful

Special Skills and Personality Traits—Ability to read and interpret wiring and schematic diagrams; effective communication and organizational skills; excellent computer capabilities; familiarity with performance equipment testing and analyzing data; good leadership abilities; knowledgeable of labor bargaining procedures and union contracts; possess a valid driver's license with an acceptable driving record

Special Requirements—Certification as a professional engineer helpful; other certifications may be required

CAREER LADDER

```
┌─────────────────────────────────────┐
│        Power Plant Operator          │
└─────────────────────────────────────┘

┌─────────────────────────────────────┐
│       Maintenance Supervisor         │
└─────────────────────────────────────┘

┌─────────────────────────────────────┐
│   Plant Installer and Repairer;      │
│       Engineering Technician         │
└─────────────────────────────────────┘
```

Position Description

Maintenance Supervisors are responsible for supervising the activities of plant engineers, engineering technicians, installers and repairers, and other support staff. They direct and supervise mechanics, engineers, and technicians in the installation, alteration, overhaul, maintenance, and repair of electrical and mechanical equipment, instruments, and controls in electrical generation power plants, substations, and electric power transmission systems.

They assist top management in the planning, organizing, coordinating, directing, and controlling of maintenance to maximize the safe, efficient, and economical generation and transmission of electrical power. They establish programs to make certain that maintenance is performed according to applicable plant policies/procedures, plant licenses requirements, applicable manufacturer's recommendations, industry codes/standards, and all relevant federal, state, and local regulatory requirements. They develop, maintain, and enforce safe working conditions by making sure the facility uses proper and adequate tools, equipment, protective clothing, devices, and training. They participate in the setting of safety goals for an accident-free work environment and communicate to employees the importance of a safe work environment. They investigate, report, and track incidents and/or accidents, including analyzing root causes and detailing corrective action taken. They report these findings to top management and then communicate these findings to employees.

Maintenance Supervisors plan and direct benchmarking efforts to identify best practices, highlight performance gaps, and indicate areas of improvement and plans to implement same. In so doing, they also provide effective maintenance schedules and supply expertise to support periods of plant refueling and any forced outages. They supervise the use, care, and upkeep of all tools, equipment, and materials. They work with top plant and substation management in planning, prioritizing, and scheduling regular maintenance work, and they conduct planning meetings as required. In addition, they assist in developing long- and short-range plans for maintenance and formulate and recommend policies, procedures, and programs designed to achieve these goals in line with corporate objectives. They work at controlling costs and increasing work efficiency by coordinating plant work force analyses and improvement suggestions through employee attitude surveys.

They administer the plant's human resources policies and programs, including employment, salary actions, promotions, demotions, discipline, termination, and transfer. Usually, Maintenance Supervisors participate in the development, control, and monitoring of Operations and Maintenance (O&M) and capital budgets. In addition, they are typically responsible for developing and administering mechanical and electrical training programs for plant maintenance personnel.

Salaries

Depending on the scope of their duties and years of experience, Maintenance Supervisors can anticipate annual salaries to range from a low of $50,000 to a high of $90,000 or more. Talented candidates that lack direct experience with power plant procedures may expect a lower starting salary, with increases as they complete the requisite training programs. Most such position opportunities include full benefits, a bonus program, and, in some instances, a relocation package.

Employment Prospects

Employment opportunities for electrical and mechanical engineers will remain average with other occupations through 2014. Entry-level engineers to the electric power industry need to gain years of hands-on experience with the equipment, control systems, and procedures before advancing to the administrative level of a Maintenance Supervisor. In addition, they must demonstrate leadership and supervisory talents.

Advancement Prospects

Job advancement for Maintenance Supervisors is usually into the higher levels of power plant or utility company management. By broadening their specific expertise in equipment and control systems to an overall understanding of plant operations, they may be able to capitalize on their technical expertise to advance to operational control of the system as power plant operators.

Education and Training

A Bachelor of Science degree in engineering, preferably electrical or mechanical, is the customary requirement for employment in this job. In a few cases, a Maintenance Supervisor trainee may be required only to be a high school graduate or have an associate's degree in power systems or electrical engineering but must also have three to five years of experience in the maintenance of electric generation equipment. In most instances, candidates will be asked to pass a standardized First Line Supervisor's Test, which will evaluate their supervisory competency.

Special Requirements

Certification as a professional engineer is a usual requirement for Maintenance Supervisors. In some cases, they may also have to be certified in such matters as supervising asbestos handling.

Experience, Skills, and Personality Traits

Most power companies and utilities require their Maintenance Supervisors to have from five to 10 or more years of power plant maintenance background in electrical and instrument control systems, usually as an install-and-repair technician, a mechanic, or an electrical engineer. They need to be knowledgeable in electrical theory, cable splicing procedures, and wire termination, as well as the equipment utilized for the production of electric power (such as steam turbines and valves, seal oil systems, safety valves, boiler feed pumps, rotating equipment, and other mechanical and electrical systems). They must be able to read and understand wiring and schematic diagrams, and must have excellent computer skills.

Maintenance Supervisors' experience should encompass developing and implementing maintenance policies and procedures. They need experience at performing equipment testing and then analyzing the data. The post also requires supervisory experience working with maintenance, engineering and instrumental control (E&IC) workers, and contracted personnel. They will be required to train employees, provide feedback to workers and management, and review employee performance. In addition, they will develop, monitor, and control the maintenance budget. They need exceptionally effective communication, both verbal and written, and organizational skills. They must be team players, efficient problem solvers, and good at conflict management (including being knowledgeable about bargaining unit agreements and union contracts).

At power substations (where the electric power generated at the power plant is converted and transmitted over power lines to customers), Maintenance Supervisors need to have a thorough understanding of the fundamentals of protective relaying as it applies to transmission, subtransmission, and electric distribution systems. This includes a working knowledge of the equipment and methods used in installing, calibrating, functionally testing, and troubleshooting typical protective relay schemes in a substation environment.

Unions and Associations

As electrical engineers, Maintenance Supervisors should belong to the Institute of Electrical and Electronic Engineers (IEEE), their major professional association. On the other hand, if their training (and degree) is in mechanical engineering, they should belong to the American Society of Mechanical Engineers (ASME). In addition, membership in other associations, such as the Association of Energy Engineers (AEE), the Electrical Generating Systems Association (EGSA), the National Association of Power Engineers (NAPE), or the National Society of Professional Engineers (NSPE), may prove to be useful.

Tips for Entry

1. While obtaining your engineering degree, take courses in psychology and business administration and management to understand how to control and supervise people and to understand the budgetary process.
2. During college, search out summer jobs or internship programs to work in manufacturing plant environments to gain experience working with tools and equipment.
3. Take technical writing courses and speech courses, as your communication skills will be critical as you add on supervisory duties.

SUPPORT PERSONNEL

CLERICAL AND ADMINISTRATIVE ASSOCIATE POSITIONS

CAREER PROFILE

Duties: Under general supervision, perform difficult and complex clerical and administrative support duties related to power plant operation

Alternate Title(s): Administrative Assistant; Customer Service Clerk; Production Clerk; Senior Clerk

Salary Range: $23,000 to $50,000 or more

Employment Prospects: Fair

Advancement Prospects: Fair

Prerequisites:

Education or Training—High school diploma required; computer proficiency a necessity; for some positions, an associate's (two-year) degree in information technology and/or secretarial and administrative science may be required

Experience—Two to five years of clerical-related experience, or administrative work in a technical field; work experience on electric utility projects preferable

Special Skills and Personality Traits—Ability to prioritize and handle multiple tasks, as well as prepare and process documents and spreadsheets; capable of maintaining organized and accurate filing/record keeping systems; detail-oriented and able to work with numerical data and process requests in a timely manner; effective oral and written communication talents; self-starter and team player; strong customer service and interpersonal skills

Special Requirements—Certification as a Certified Administrative Professional (CAP) is recommended

CAREER LADDER

Power Plant Supervisory Positions

Clerical and Administrative Positions

High School Graduation; Technical Clerk

Position Description

The various Clerical and Administrative Associate positions are responsible for performing administrative support duties within an electric power system. They carry out such functions as compiling account reviews; handling billing inquiries and adjustments; activities related to credit checks; processing of customer requests, resolving customer complaints, and answering customer inquiries; scheduling maintenance outage and project schedules, as well as construction timeframes; and assembling records and reports on various aspects of production, including work schedules, materials and parts used in construction and maintenance, and machine/instrument readings.

They review and process the more complex documents relating to generation and transmission of electrical power, which requires them to have considerable procedural knowledge of power plant and transmission systems. In so doing, they must ensure completeness, accuracy, and compliance with company requirements on all such documents. They may be asked to review reports and data supplied by other plant or system personnel, verifying their accuracy and adherence to standard procedures and practices. They maintain appropriate records and files of these documents and reports. They compile special reports at the behest of plant and system operators from available records and request necessary information for other areas.

They process the required paperwork when a plant or system hires contract personnel. They keep track of time for contract personnel as needed. They prepare cost-tracking reports as requested, and run reports from contractor systems for wanted information. They maintain confidentiality in all such matters. In addition, they prepare all invoices that come into their specific plant or system operating area for distribution or processing per standard accounting rules.

They answer customer or public inquiries, complete applications for service, and process customer complaints, referring them to the proper personnel. They initiate and/ or answer routine correspondence in response to written or telephone inquiries and answer and follow up routine complaints upon request by senior management. They may be required to take and transcribe shorthand (and/ or machine) dictation, review the work of lower classified administrative personnel, and perform other assigned administrative tasks.

Two specific types of administrative associates are the data technician and the project scheduler. Using software applications tools, data technicians process transactions and messages to validate and process the hourly/daily workload of personnel. They prioritize hourly/daily transaction processing to ensure that all regulatory deadlines are met. They monitor and detect, whenever possible, any processing failures during the various stages of electric generation and transmission using computer-based diagnostic tools and take corrective actions to make sure that all electronic messages and transactions are processed within deadlines. In addition, they typically receive, investigate, answer, or transfer (to a higher management level) all helpdesk phone calls and/or e-mails from the public, external companies, or internal personnel related to the electronic transaction processing of the plant and the system. This type of administrative position usually requires an associate's degree in information technology.

Project schedulers assist in the development/analysis of maintenance outage (when there is a temporary suspension of operation for maintenance or repair) and project schedules. They take part in the planning processes for such outage, verify progress, and procure needed information as required. They use sophisticated software application tools (such as the Primavera project planner and resource management software, known as P3e) to provide scheduled maintenance, to collect progress data, to develop and implement off-line schedule/status reports, and make

available consistent, accurate information to the outage execution teams. They develop "work-around" schedules to alleviate forecasted impacts on the production or transmission outputs and then update daily the active schedule, providing status, percentage completed, and additional personnel requirements. They prepare and analyze metrics reports, and provide weekly summary level status reports as directed. A background and experience in scheduling and cost engineering is usually necessary for this administrative post.

Salaries

According to the U.S. Department of Labor's *Occupational Outlook Handbook, 2006–07 Edition*, median annual earnings of administrative assistants (associates and administrative clerks) were $34,970 in May 2004. The middle 50 percent earned between $28,500 and $43,430. The lowest 10 percent earned less than $23,810, and the highest 10 percent earned more than $53,460 a year.

Employment Prospects

While the overall employment of administrative assistants is expected to grow more slowly than the average for all occupations through 2014 (as per the U.S. Bureau of Labor Statistics), jobs available for well-qualified (computer literate) applicants for lower administrative positions in the electric power industry should be about average in growth, partly due to the continued expansion and sophistication of the industry. Job openings often will result from the need to replace administrative personnel who, with the benefit of experience and further training, have moved into higher levels of plant and system management, or who have transferred to other occupations altogether. Again, applicants with extensive software applications knowledge will have the best opportunity for employment.

Advancement Prospects

Clerical and Administrative Associates generally progress by being promoted to other administrative positions with more responsibilities, which, within the electric power industry, usually means more training. Senior Clerical and Administrative Associates must perform acceptably on the appropriate AEP (Advanced Educational Placement) System Placement Exercises, and must have demonstrated their ability to treat company business as confidential and display detailed knowledge of power plant practices and procedures.

Some administrative personnel may aim at higher management levels in an electric power utility company. However, for such positions, they may have to expand their educational background toward obtaining a four-year engineering degree, and be willing to gain three to five years of practical engineering experience in the power industry.

Education and Training

While high school graduates who have basic office skills may qualify for entry-level administrative or clerical positions in the electric power industry, the more technical aspects and needs of the field also require any applicants for Clerical or Administrative Associate to have an extensive knowledge and familiarity with appropriate software applications. Proficiency in the use of Microsoft Office products, such as Word, Passport, PowerPoint, and Excel are a basic requirement. Working knowledge of such software packages as Smallworld, MACSS, and Lotus Notes may also be required. Some employers may also insist on formal post-high school training in the secretarial science field or equivalent education and/or work experience.

Special Requirements

Testing and certification for proficiency in administrative and office skills is available through such organizations as the International Association of Administrative Professionals (IAAP). Success in taking the appropriate Advanced Educational Placement (AEP) System Exercises can lead to the designation of a Certified Administrative Professional (CAP).

Experience, Skills, and Personality Traits

The minimum experience necessary for this position usually is two to three years of clerical experience, preferably in a technical field. Knowledge or experience in dealing with a constantly varying number of people and its effect on human resources and payroll in a power plant or system setting is an additional prerequisite. These associates must be proficient in utilizing secretarial and administrative office procedures and practices (such as keying, business English, letter writing, telephone techniques, and file organization).

Beyond a proficiency in the use of personal computers and Microsoft Office software, applicants should be thoroughly knowledgeable in the use of various kinds of office equipment. They need to be self-starters and team players with exceptional customer-service and interpersonal skills with both in-house personnel and with external customers and contractors. They must possess good multi-tasking capabilities and have above average written and verbal communication talents. They must be highly organized and be able to resolve complex order inquiries in a timely manner. As many of their tasks require some independent analysis and arithmetic calculation, they should be able to work with large quantities of numerical data, have good mathematical skills, and demonstrate an appreciation for detail.

Unions and Associations

While there are no unions representing Clerical or Administrative Associates, it may be useful for them to belong to such umbrella associations as the International Association of Administrative Professionals (IAAP) or the National Management Association (NMA).

Tips for Entry

1. As an in-depth computer knowledge is a basic requirement for work in the electric power industry, take as many computer courses as you can during your high school years and search for practical experience in the use of the basic Microsoft Office software applications.

2. Investigate summer job or internship positions in scientific or technical companies to become familiar with office procedures and practices in a technical environment.

3. Explore ways to gain customer service experience by volunteering for charity and public events in your community.

NUCLEAR ENERGY
INDUSTRY

ENGINEERS

MATERIALS ENGINEER

CAREER PROFILE

Duties: Analyze the properties of the materials used in the construction of a nuclear plant and its equipment to ensure their integrity during operation

Alternate Title(s): Corrosion Engineer; Failure Analyst; Materials and Processes Manager; Materials Scientist; Physical Metallurgist

Salary Range: $45,000 to $100,000 or more

Employment Prospects: Fair

Advancement Prospects: Poor

Prerequisites:

Education or Training—Bachelor of Science degree in material science, metallurgy, or chemistry is preferred; postgraduate study that focuses on metallurgy and minerals processing and engineering is recommended

Experience—One to two years' background in nuclear power plant processes and environment; two to four years of experience in the testing of metals and other materials used in construction

Special Skills and Personality Traits—Capable of critical thinking and complex problem solving; excellent computer skills; good oral and written communication skills; persistence and thoroughness

Special Requirements—Certification as a professional engineer usually required; nuclear power plant security clearance necessary

CAREER LADDER

```
┌─────────────────────────────────┐
│    Senior Technical Manager;     │
│      Independent Consultant      │
└─────────────────────────────────┘

┌─────────────────────────────────┐
│        Materials Engineer        │
└─────────────────────────────────┘

┌─────────────────────────────────┐
│    College Graduate; Chemist;    │
│           Metallurgist           │
└─────────────────────────────────┘
```

Position Description

Materials science encompasses the study of the structure and properties of a wide number of materials, from metals and ceramics to polymers (plastics), semiconductors, and combinations of materials called composites (such as fiberglass, which is a mixture of glass and a polymer). Materials science and engineering heavily rely on physics, chemistry, and other engineering disciplines, including mechanical and electrical. Physical properties of materials are usually the deciding factor in choosing which items will be used for any particular application. Many elements have to be examined, such as material composition and structure (chemistry), fracture and stress analysis (mechanical engineering), conductivity (electrical engineering), and optical and thermal properties (physics). Generally, Materials Engineers evaluate materials and develop machinery and processes to manufacture materials for use in products that must meet specialized design and performance specifications. Most Materials Engineers specialize in a particular material.

As a branch of materials science, metallurgy is concerned with the technology and science of metallic materials, the production of metals and alloys, their adaptation and performance in service. As such, it is attentive to the chemical reactions involved in the processes by which metals are produced, as well as the chemical, physical, and mechanical behavior of metallic materials. The field of metallurgy may be divided into process metallurgy and physical metallurgy.

Physical metallurgy investigates the effects of composition and treatment on the structure of metals and the relations of the structure to the properties of metals. Physical metallurgists study the behavior of metals under stress, temperature, and pressure by using various techniques and equipment to assess both their physical structure and behavior. They test metals for tolerance under tension, compression, and shear, using instruments to determine the hardness of metals and to scrutinize their crystalline structures. They devise testing methods to evaluate the effects of various conditions and use and to investigate metal corrosion and fatigue of metals.

In the nuclear energy industry, Materials Engineers use their training as physical metallurgists to analyze the properties of the materials out of which nuclear plants and their various equipment are constructed. Their responsibility is to ensure that these materials will maintain their integrity during the processes of nuclear energy production and under the dynamic loads that are produced by the plant in operation. They conduct nondestructive examination testing—both failure analysis and structural analysis testing—using sophisticated computer software, to make certain that the nuclear plant equipment and structure will withstand the temperatures, pressures, and neutron flux generated by the plant's operation. They work closely with metallurgical technicians, nuclear engineers, chemical engineers, and mechanical engineers on materials specifications and periodic testing of materials through nondestructive examination and evaluation. They generate reports on their findings and analyses for senior management.

Along with nuclear plant service engineers, Materials Engineers identify and specify the purchasing requirements of the plant's operations. They may meet with vendors, solicit bids, and evaluate needed products and services. They can be responsible for managing supply room facilities to ensure that the right materials and parts of the proper quality and quantity are maintained and purchased at the best price. Much of this purchasing side of their job is accomplished by utilizing the e-commerce techniques of the Internet. Materials Engineers generally report directly to nuclear plant operational managers.

Salaries

According to the U.S. Department of Labor's Bureau of Labor Statistics, median annual salaries in May 2004 for Materials Engineers ranged from a low of $44,130 to a high of $101,120. According to a 2005 survey by the National Association of Colleges and Employers, the average starting salary for a Materials Engineer with a bachelor's degree was $50,982.

Employment Prospects

According to the U.S. Department of Labor's *Occupational Outlook Handbook, 2006–07 Edition,* Materials Engineers generally are expected to have employment growth about as fast as the average for all occupations through 2014. However, within the nuclear energy industry, employment of engineers generally is always dependent upon the potential for the construction of new nuclear plants. In Europe, nuclear plant construction has increased over the last several years, but such corresponding growth has *not* yet occurred in the United States. Decisions on new facilities have both a political and a cultural element that, at times, has hindered expansion. With increased efforts to counteract the U.S. dependence on oil and natural gas from abroad, there may be renewed interest in nuclear power plant expansion, with a resultant higher employment rate for engineers, such as Materials Engineers.

Advancement Prospects

As there is an increasing demand for metallurgists in various industries, Materials Engineers working in the nuclear energy field may search out research opportunities in private industry firms, academic research, and government laboratories. Staying within the nuclear industry, they may progress to posts of senior technical management where a high level of technical competence is expected. They may also choose to work as independent consultants (on their own or as a member of a consulting firm), contracting their services to larger organizations.

Education and Training

A Bachelor of Science degree in metallurgy (or metallurgical engineering), material science, or chemical engineering is a basic requirement. While graduate training is usually not required for the majority of entry-level engineering jobs, a master's degree in a related engineering discipline may be expected. Most Materials Engineers receive on-the-job training, but they may also be mandated to attend classes or seminars sponsored by the American Society of Metallurgists (ASM).

Special Requirements

Certification and licensing as a professional engineer is usually a necessity for employment as a Materials Engineer within the nuclear energy industry. Following graduation from an accredited educational program, metallurgical engineers must undergo three to four years of supervised work experience in metallurgical or materials engineering. Thereafter, after passing a professional practice examination, they may seek licensure by a state government. Information about professional engineer certification and licensure can be obtained from the National Society of Professional Engineers (NSPE).

In addition, the United States Nuclear Regulatory Commission (NRC) requires all nuclear plant employees and contractor employees to pass drug and alcohol screening tests, psychological evaluations, and background checks into such areas as former employment, education records, criminal records, and credit histories.

Experience, Skills, and Personality Traits

As metallurgists, Materials Engineers must have a solid understanding of chemistry, applied physics, and complex math. They need to be familiar with the processes of welding and joining of metals, as they will need to test such processes in the equipment and structure of nuclear plant materials. Likewise, they should have a detailed understanding of product design and manufacturing of the materials employed in the construction of a nuclear plant and the manufacturing of its equipment.

Their skills need to include an ability to analyze problems, design tests to evaluate materials and equipment performance, evaluate information, and communicate results both individually and as part of the engineering team of the plant. As such, they must be able to communicate well orally, in writing, and graphically. They must be (or become) familiar with technical specifications on equipment, parts, and other materials so they will be able to make recommendations for materials to be used (based on design objectives, such as strength, weight, heat resistance, electrical conductivity, and cost). They must enjoy problem solving and be practical and creative in their analytical thinking. Persistence, perseverance, curiosity, and the ability to concentrate on detail are also essential. Above all, they should be highly computer literate.

Unions and Associations

Major associations that may prove useful to Materials Engineers within the nuclear energy industry include the ASM International (formerly the American Society for Metals), the Minerals, Metals, and Materials Society (TMS), and the Society for Mining, Metallurgy, and Exploration (SME).

Tips for Entry

1. During high school, along with your heavy load of math and science curriculum, undertake business and communications classes, as these skills will be necessary for your career as a metallurgical engineer.
2. Throughout your college years, explore options to work with your hands building scientific apparatus, performing laboratory experiments, and learning about (and practicing) computer modeling techniques.
3. Read nuclear industry journals and subscribe to useful e-mail newsletters about the industry, as the more you know about nuclear energy and the industry that produces it, the easier it will be to talk to people who are working in the field and those who will be interviewing you for employment.

MECHANICAL, STRUCTURAL, AND ELECTRICAL ENGINEERS

CAREER PROFILE

Duties: <u>Mechanical Engineer</u>: monitor and supervise areas involving heat transfer and fluid flow in a nuclear reactor facility; <u>Structural Engineer</u>: ensure the physical integrity of the nuclear plant structures; <u>Electrical Engineer</u>: oversee the routing of electric power in a nuclear plant to all of its components and supervise the conversion of energy to electric power

Alternate Title(s): None

Salary Range: $40,000 to $95,000 or more

Employment Prospects: Fair

Advancement Prospects: Fair

Prerequisites:

Education or Training—Bachelor of Science degree in mechanical, civil, or electrical engineering; master's degree in nuclear engineering recommended

Experience—Four to seven years background in electric power industry and two to three years work experience with nuclear power plants

Special Skills and Personality Traits—<u>Mechanical Engineer</u>: ability to interpret building, mechanical, state, and local safety codes; analytical talent; computer literate and particularly proficient with word processing and spreadsheet software; excellent verbal and written communication skills; flexible and self-directed; strong interpersonal aptitude and capacity to function well as a team member; <u>Structural Engineer</u>: Ability to identify, analyze, and solve problems; proficiency with computer-aided design (CAD) techniques and knowledgeable about other applicable engineering software; capable of being a group player but also of operating without supervision; excellent oral and written communication talents, with special emphasis on technical writing abilities; practical and creative; <u>Electrical Engineer</u>: Ability to work independently, but also work cooperatively in a team environment; excellent technical training, speaking, and writing skills; good computer know-how and working knowledge of electrical systems testing and analysis software

Special Requirements—Certification as a licensed Professional Engineer is required of all engineers working in a nuclear power plant; nuclear power plant security clearance necessary

CAREER LADDER

> **Senior Plant Operations Manager; Independent Consultant**

> **Nuclear Mechanical, Structural, and Electrical Engineers**

> **Engineering Technician**

Position Description

Mechanical Engineers working in a nuclear power plant monitor/supervise those operations involving heat transfer and fluid flow: diffusing the heat generated by the nuclear reactor core; directing the energy from the core to spin the turbine to generate electricity; providing emergency heat removal in case of any accident; and circulating the water that cools the nuclear reactor and regulates its temperature. In addition, they usually supervise all machinery design. They match the right machine component to the desired function, procure the appropriate replacement parts, and provide innovative designs to improve plant performance. Piping, valves, pumps, turbines, and diesel machines are the main overall responsibility of Mechanical Engineers, as well as the layout and structural integrity of switchgear, cables, and other instrumentation.

With their civil engineering training and background, Structural Engineers in nuclear power plants ensure the physical integrity of the facility's structures, including the containment building and radiation shielding for the interior nuclear reactor. They ascertain whether the structure will safely handle the loads produced by the ordinary operation of the plant, that in any kind of accident the reactor core will remain intact and safely cooled, and that the buildings will safely withstand extreme-magnitude natural events, such as hurricanes or earthquakes. Structural Engineers make sure plant equipment is installed properly so that the plant can generate the projected electricity under normal conditions. In addition, they are tasked with reviewing any additions of plant equipment loads and any drilling in the walls to make certain that an adequate design margin of safety remains.

Electrical Engineers working in nuclear power facilities oversee the routing of electric power in the plant to all of its components, which may vary in their power requirements anywhere from 12 volts DC (direct current) to 765,000 volts AC (alternating current). They also oversee the conversion of energy by the turbines to electric power that will be transmitted elsewhere to customers. Finally, Electrical Engineers monitor the integration of all plant functions through process controls and protection electric circuitry. In most recent nuclear plant new design configurations, computer/software expertise has become increasingly key for Electrical Engineers involved in the design and function of fresh digital instrumentation and control systems. These engineers may be responsible for replacing analog circuitry with more efficient automated microprocessor-based systems.

There are at least two specific types of Electrical Engineers who function under the supervision of the plant's chief Electrical Engineer. High-voltage Electrical Engineers are specifically responsible for the electrical output of the turbine (which is turned by the high-pressure steam coming from the nuclear reactor). They prepare procedures and tests for the high-voltage monitoring, switching, and transmission equipment, as well the relaying support and instrumentation apparatus. They constantly review performance data and formulate potential design modifications, which they provide to their Electrical Engineer supervisor.

DC Electrical Engineers oversee the design and operation of the direct-current normal and emergency power supplies, such as batteries, battery chargers, inverters, alarms panels, and connecting circuitry. They are responsible for emergency lighting, emergency oil pump power supplies, and the emergency reactor core cooling system DC circuits. Additionally, they monitor the alarm systems, ground detention equipment, and all direct current load centers.

Salaries

In a 2005 survey by the National Association of Colleges and Employers, average starting salaries for Mechanical Engineers ranged from $50,000 to $68,000, depending on their level of educational background. In their review of engineering salaries, the U.S. Department of Labor's Bureau of Labor Statistics found that, in May 2004, Mechanical Engineers had yearly salaries ranging from a low of $43,000 to a high of $97,000 or more.

According to a 2005 survey by the National Association of Colleges and Employers, average annual starting salaries for Civil/Structural Engineers ranged from $43,679 to $59,625, depending on the level of educational degrees earned. In the joint earnings study made by the American Society of Civil Engineers (ASCE) and the National Society of Professional Engineers (NSPE), the *2004 Engineering Income and Salary Survey*, average salaries in April 2004 of Civil Engineers were found to range from $64,750 to $80,000, depending on the geographic locale within the United States. In its 2005 study of engineering salaries, the U.S. Department of Labor's Bureau of Labor Statistics in their publication *Occupational Outlook Handbook, 2006–07 Edition* found that salaries of Civil Engineers, as of May 2004, ranged from a low of $42,610 to a high of $94,660.

According to their 2005 review of the engineering profession, the National Association of Colleges and Employers determined that the average annual starting salaries for Electrical Engineers ranged from $50,000 to $80,000, depending on the individual's level of education. *The Occupational Outlook Handbook, 2006–07 Edition* of the U.S. Bureau of Labor Statistics states that the average annual earnings (as of May 2004) for Electrical Engineers spanned from $47,000 to $108,000.

Employment Prospects

According to the U.S. Department of Labor's Bureau of Labor Statistics, employment of nuclear engineers is expected to grow more slowly than the average for all occupations through 2014. This holds true also for the Mechanical, Structural, and Electrical Engineers operating within the nuclear industry. Nonetheless, nuclear engineers are anticipated to have fair career opportunities because the small number of nuclear engineering graduates is likely to be in rough balance with the number of job openings.

Although no commercial nuclear power plants have been built in the United States for many years, nuclear engineers, as well as their supporting engineering staff (including Mechanical, Structural, and Electrical Engineers) will be required to operate existing facilities. In addition, the threat of global warming has resulted in an increased interest in nuclear power as an alternative to oil, natural gas, and coal power sources (as those sources produce a high level of atmospheric pollution). The world's increasing energy needs (and decision-makers' commitment to lessen carbon emissions) may help to overcome public concerns about the inherent dangers of nuclear technology and open the potential of building new nuclear reactor plants in the near future.

Advancement Prospects

Experienced Mechanical Engineers, Structural Engineers, and Electrical Engineers may find professional advancement by accepting further management and supervisory duties within the nuclear plant management structure as operational managers. Alternatively, they may become specialized independent consultants to the industry.

Education and Training

Basic educational requirements for Mechanical, Structural, or Electrical Engineers working in the nuclear power industry include a Bachelor of Science degree in their own special branch of engineering, and, in most instances, a master's degree in nuclear engineering. Some may opt to obtain also a postgraduate degree (Ph.D.) in nuclear engineering or an allied field.

Newly hired Mechanical, Structural, or Electrical Engineers function under the guidance of veteran nuclear engineers. Extensive computer skills and knowledge of computer simulation techniques are essential background for all three engineering posts. Special safety precautions must be taken by all Engineers who work within nuclear plants, and particularly by those who work with fissionable matter such as reactor fuels. They must wear thermoluminescent dosimeters, film badges, or other devices used for recording cumulative radiation exposure time and, in some areas, must wear protective clothing.

Special Requirements

All engineers in nuclear power plants must be licensed Professional Engineers. Licensure requirements vary slightly state by state, but in all cases, they entail passing two licensure exams: the Fundamentals of Engineering exam (or FE) and the Principles and Practice exam (or PE). In addition, a state-mandated number of years of work under the supervision of a licensed Professional Engineer must be completed. Information on the Professional Engineer licensure can be obtained from the National Society of Professional Engineers (NSPE) or the National Council of Examiners for Engineering and Surveying (NCEES).

In addition, the United States Nuclear Regulatory Commission (NRC) requires all nuclear plant employees and contractor employees to pass drug and alcohol screening tests, psychological evaluations, and background checks into such areas as former employment, education records, criminal records, and credit histories.

Experience, Skills, and Personality Traits

Mechanical Engineers must exhibit careful attention to detail and be highly creative in developing new ideas for, and answers to, work-related problems. They must have solid verbal and written communication skills and have demonstrable organizational and interpersonal talents. They should be flexible, self-directed, and capable of working in a team environment. They must be highly computer literate and proficient with CAD and/or CAD/CAM programming tools. They should be conversant with product design development cycles and have background in analyzing complex technical problems involving thermal analysis and mechanical packaging of systems with moving parts. They should have a basic knowledge of electrical circuit analysis and the principles of operation of pressure sensors, temperature sensors, speed sensors, solenoids, servos, and pneumatically or hydraulically actuated valves.

Mechanical Engineers must be able to write equipment and material specifications, data sheets, and material requisitions, and interpret specifications furnished by others. Besides their background in design and development, they should have a working knowledge of testing methodologies, production techniques, and maintenance procedures. They should be acquainted with such standards relating to mechanical engineering as those of the American Society of Mechanical Engineers (ASME), the American National Standards Institute (ANSI), and the National Electrical Manufacturing Association (NEMA).

As civil engineers, Structural Engineers must be able to identify problems, analyze them, and find practical solutions. They must have excellent oral and written communication skills, as they will have to create work plans and reports, tabulate laboratory and other site data, and prepare engineering drawings and permit applications. They should be completely conversant with computer-aided design (CAD) and computer-aided manufacturing (CAM) software and proficient with the entire design process. They should be familiar with the computer software used for structural analysis and testing, such as the STAAD and GTSTUDL programs. They should have four to 10 years of experience as an entry-level civil engineer with an engineering firm or a consulting firm, gaining experience in project scheduling, report writing, sampling and data collection, conducting site testing, and performing test data analysis. In addition, they must become conversant with all applicable state and federal requirements as far as the design of nuclear plants and equipment are concerned.

Electrical Engineers must have knowledge of and experience in the operation of electric power systems and its components, generators, transmission lines, and electric substations. They should have experience in the maintenance and operation of power plant electrical switchgear, distribution systems, and equipment, including methods of recovery from system or equipment failure. They should be proficient in the use of electronic test and diagnostic equipment.and testing operational procedures. They should have some experience with electrical control design, AC/DC schematics, high-voltage line monitoring and testing of switching and transmission equipment. They need to be familiar with engineering standards, including those set by the National Electric Code (NEC), the National Electric Safety Code (NESC), the National Electric Manufacturers Association (NEMA), the Institute of Electrical and Electronics Engineers (IEEE), and the American National Standards Institute (ANSI), as well as all applicable construction standards, methods, practices, techniques, materials, and equipment necessary to comply with national regulations and standards as regarding nuclear power plant operations. They must possess strong project management skills, and excellent communication abilities, as well as proven teamwork and leadership talents.

Unions and Associations

For Mechanical Engineers, membership in the American Society of Mechanical Engineers (ASME) is highly beneficial. For Structural Engineers, the American Society of Civil Engineers (ASCE) is the most essential professional association they may have. (This organization publishes a large amount of information on civil engineering and develops codes and standards that frequently are adapted by federal, state, and local governments, as well as sponsors conferences and provides continuing education for its members.) In addition, joining the National Council of Structural Engineers Association (NCSEA) is recommended. The key professional association for Electrical Engineers is the Institute of Electrical and Electronics Engineers (IEEE). Membership in other groups, such as the Electrical Generating Systems Association (EGSA) or the National Association of Power Engineers (NAPE) is suggested.

In addition, all engineers who work within the nuclear power industry may find participation in the American Nuclear Society (ANC), as well as such umbrella groups as the Association of Energy Engineers (AEE) or the National Society of Professional Engineers (NSPE), to be valuable.

Tips for Entry

1. As a Mechanical Engineer, in your computer work become familiar with advanced development software, such as C++, as well as analytical and scientific software and computer-aided design (CAD) programs.
2. Civil engineers earning a civil engineering degree should consider joining a student chapter or club of the American Society of Civil Engineers (ASCE), where they can participate in many activities that allow them to develop professionally outside of the classroom. They should also look into cooperative education and work-study programs that allow them to earn tuition by attending classes for a portion of the year and working in an engineering-related job for the remainder of the year. ASCE offers scholarships and fellowships for both undergraduate and graduate students.
3. For students working on their degree in electrical engineering, participation in an engineering internship at an electric power plant while in college is a great way to apply classroom learning to an actual work situation. It also allows them to build skills and make contacts with people working in the field of electrical engineering as applied to the energy industry.

NUCLEAR ENGINEER

CAREER PROFILE

Duties: Design, develop, monitor, and operate nuclear plants that generate power

Alternate Title(s): Nuclear Reactor Engineer

Salary Range: $50,000 to $115,000 or more

Employment Prospects: Poor to Fair

Advancement Prospects: Fair

Prerequisites:

    Education or Training—Bachelor of Science degree in nuclear engineering required; master's degree in mathematics, physics, or engineering design usually necessary as well; a doctoral (Ph.D.) degree in nuclear engineering often compulsory for private and government research jobs

    Experience—On-the-job training usually accomplished under the guidance of experienced engineers; engineering internship during college is highly recommended

    Special Skills and Personality Traits—Capable of working in a team environment; creativity and curiosity; detail-oriented; effective interpersonal talents; excellent oral and written communication skills; exemplary computer skills; good time management and multi-tasking abilities; solid technical abilities; strong analytical proficiency

    Special Requirements—Certification as a licensed Professional Engineer is required of all engineers working in a nuclear power plant; nuclear power plant security clearance required

CAREER LADDER

```
Nuclear Plant Supervisor; Nuclear
Research Positions; Government or
Higher Management Posts
```

```
Nuclear Engineer
```

```
Nuclear Technician; College Graduate
```

Position Description

Nuclear engineering is the branch of engineering that deals with the production and use of nuclear energy and nuclear radiation. It involves the conception, development, design, construction, operation, and decommissioning of facilities in which nuclear energy or nuclear radiation is generated or used. Such operations include nuclear power plants, nuclear propulsion reactors used for the propulsion of ships and submarines, nuclear reactors employed to power space satellites/vehicles, nuclear production reactors which produce fissile or fusile materials used in nuclear weapons, nuclear research reactors which generate neutrons and gamma rays for scientific research for medical and industrial applica-

tions, particle accelerators which produce nuclear radiation utilized in medical and industrial applications, and nuclear waste repositories.

Nuclear power plants provide about 17 percent of the world's electricity. Some countries depend more upon nuclear power for generating electricity than others do. France produces about 75 percent of its electricity from nuclear power, whereas, in the United States, about 15 percent of the electricity comes from nuclear power (but some states generate more power from such plants than others do).

The basis of the nuclear reaction process is uranium, a common element on the planet incorporated during the Earth's formation. U-238 uranium is the most common form of the element. However, the U-235 form is the one used in all nuclear radiation and creation of nuclear energy because it can easily be induced into a state of fission, producing an incredible amount of energy (in the form of heat and gamma radiation). The fission of a single atom of uranium produces 10 million times the energy produced by the combustion of a single atom of carbon from coal.

Nuclear plants are composed of a relatively compact heat source (the nuclear reactor) and its control rods, which power a conventional steam turbine-based power plant. Within the nuclear reactor, the enriched uranium is formed into small pellets that are arranged into long rods. These rods are collected together into bundles, and the bundles are then submerged in water inside a pressure vessel in the reactor. (The water acts as a coolant on the uranium, which, on its own, would eventually overheat and melt.) The uranium bundles heat the water and turn it into steam. This process takes place within a containment structure. The steam is vented to a turbine, which, in turn, spins a generator to produce electric power.

Nuclear Engineers working in nuclear energy plants are responsible for the overall operation of the nuclear installation. They are trained to design, estimate the cost of assembling, and oversee the construction and operation of nuclear reactors, power plants, and nuclear fuel reprocessing and reclamation systems. They design and develop nuclear equipment such as reactor cores, radiation shielding, and associated mechanisms. They monitor nuclear facility operations to identify any design, construction, or operation practices that violate safety regulations and laws or that could jeopardize the safety of the operation and the people involved. They carefully study any accidents that occur to obtain sufficient data that can be used to design preventive measures.

Nuclear Engineers are responsible for initiating corrective actions or ordering plant shutdowns in emergency situations. They conduct tests of nuclear fuel behavior and cycles, as well as the performance of nuclear machinery/equipment, to optimize the performance of the nuclear plant. They recommend preventive measures in the handling of nuclear material and technology, based on data they have obtained from monitoring plant operations and their evaluation of test results. They write the operational instructions to be employed in nuclear plant operation and keep abreast of developments/changes in the nuclear field by reading technical journals and through independent study/research. They use mathematics, economics, and engineering principles to help resolve problems and often employ computers and simulation techniques in problem analysis. In some instances, they may perform administrative duties: directing projects, supervising other workers, and preparing budgets. Most importantly, they apply nuclear safety regulations in all phases of their work.

Another area of power generation with which many Nuclear Engineers are becoming involved is fusion. Unlike fission (where the massive nucleus splits into smaller nuclei with the simultaneous release of energy), fusion is a nuclear reaction in which nuclei combine to form more massive nuclei with the simultaneous release or absorption of energy, depending upon the masses of the nuclei involved. The combination by fusion of nuclei, such as hydrogen or helium, will release tremendous amounts of energy. (Nuclear fusion of such light elements releases the energy that causes stars to shine and hydrogen bombs to explode.) Nuclear fusion of heavy elements (absorbing, not releasing energy) occurs in the extremely high-energy conditions that produce supernova star explosions. Nuclear fusion in stars and supernovae is the primary process by which new natural elements are created. It is this process that is planned to generate power in future fusion power plants.

Nuclear Engineers involved in the research and development of such fusion power plants face many challenging engineering problems, including the development of technologies for heating the fusion fuel to hundreds of millions of degrees (necessary to create the fusion mechanism), methods to confine/contain this ultrahot fuel, and the means to compress this fusion fuel to many thousand times its natural solid density for actual use as a power source.

Salaries

Salaries for Nuclear Engineers are commensurate with their heavy responsibilities. According to a 2005 survey by the National Association of Colleges and Employers, an average starting annual salary for a Nuclear Engineer with a bachelor's degree is $51,182, and for a Nuclear Engineer with a master's degree it is $58,814. In its *Occupational Outlook Handbook, 2006–07 Edition,* the U.S. Department of Labor indicates that, in May 2004, annual average salaries for Nuclear Engineers ranged from a low of $61,790 to a high of $118,870. The national median annual wage for Nuclear Engineers is $6,940 a month (or $83,280 a year). Wages will vary by employer and area of the country, as well as the engineer's level of education and job responsibilities.

Employment Prospects

According to the U.S. Department of Labor's Bureau of Labor Statistics, employment of Nuclear Engineers is expected to grow more slowly than the average for all occupations through 2014. Nonetheless, Nuclear Engineers are expected to have fair opportunities because the small number of nuclear engineering graduates is likely to be in rough balance with the number of job openings. Most openings will result from the need to replace Nuclear Engineers who transfer to other occupations (or go into research or become employed by the federal government) or leave the labor force altogether.

Although no commercial nuclear power plants have been built in the United States for several years, Nuclear Engineers will be needed to operate, repair, or decommission existing plants (let alone work on the reactors utilized in nuclear submarines and at government installations). There also is a need for Nuclear Engineers to research and develop future nuclear power sources. In addition, the threat of global warming has resulted in an increased interest in nuclear power as an alternative to oil, natural gas, and coal power sources (as those sources produce a high level of carbon dioxide). The increasing energy needs of the world (and the commitment to lessen carbon emissions) may help to overcome public concerns about the inherent dangers of nuclear technology and open the possibilities of construction of new reactor plants in the coming years.

Advancement Prospects

Recently graduated Nuclear Engineers usually begin their careers as assistant engineers under the tutelage of seasoned engineers. As assistant engineers gain experience, they may progress to associate and senior-level positions. From their senior level, Nuclear Engineers may make career advancements into production supervision or project management. Some companies offer work-study programs for employees wishing to upgrade their skills, particularly in management.

Advancement to senior positions (such as a senior research engineer) can be facilitated by the pursuit of postgraduate study in nuclear science. In turn, Nuclear Engineers working within the nuclear power plant environment may decide to shift their career paths to research in such areas as nuclear medical technology or defense-related areas. Military and civilian nuclear power engineers have similar skills, and the federal government frequently hires Nuclear Engineers with experience in the various nuclear fields it regulates.

Education and Training

Basic educational requirements for Nuclear Engineers include a Bachelor of Science degree in one of the engineering disciplines, preferably nuclear engineering, and, in most cases, a master's degree as well. For most research jobs in nuclear engineering, a postgraduate degree (Ph.D.) in nuclear engineering is an additional necessity.

Newly hired Nuclear Engineers work under the guidance of experienced engineers. Both mathematical and mechanical aptitudes are essential, and knowledge of computer simulation techniques is valuable. Special precautions must be taken by Nuclear Engineers who work with fissionable matter such as reactor fuels. They must wear thermoluminescent dosimeters, film badges, or other devices used for recording cumulative radiation exposure time and, in some work areas, must wear protective clothing.

Special Requirements

Nuclear Engineers need to be certified as professional engineers. This licensure usually requires a degree from an accredited engineering program, as well as four years of relevant work experience, followed by the successful completion of a Fundamentals of Engineering Exam. For Nuclear Engineers with postgraduate degrees, the four-year work requirement may be waived.

In addition, the U.S. Nuclear Regulatory Commission (NRC) requires all nuclear plant employees and contractor employees to pass drug and alcohol screening tests, psychological evaluations, and background checks into such areas as former employment, education records, criminal records, and credit histories.

Experience, Skills, and Personality Traits

Nuclear Engineers work in extended teams, and caution and risk control are standard for the industry—appropriately so, given the dangers of nuclear radiation. Work in nuclear power stations is usually indoors, often on a seven-day shift system, and conditions can be both hot and cramped.

Nuclear Engineers working in nuclear power plants need to have extensive knowledge of reactor physics and of fuel and core reactor design analysis methods. They must be able to comprehend complex reactor physics/design problems and provide solutions to them. They must have a high level of written and verbal communications abilities, along with strong interpersonal skills. They should be able to handle multiple tasks with sometimes conflicting requirements. They should be manually adept, persistent and accurate in their work, and have an analytical mind with a logical approach to problem solving. They should demonstrate leadership abilities, and be comfortable with a teamwork approach to their labor. They must have good planning and organizational abilities and be extremely safety conscious.

Unions and Associations

The primary association for Nuclear Engineers is the American Nuclear Society (ANC). Another association of potential interest to Nuclear Engineers is the Nuclear Energy Institute (NEI).

Tips for Entry

1. Participating in an engineering internship while in college is a great way to apply what you are learning in the classroom to a work situation. It also allows you to build skills and make contacts with people working in the field of engineering of your choice.
2. Some two-year colleges have agreements with the engineering departments of four-year schools, which allow you to move to the university for the last two years to earn your bachelor's degree in engineering.
3. Along with your science, engineering, and math curriculum, take courses in technical writing and business administration, as these skills will help you in advancing your career into higher management levels within the nuclear power industry.

OTHER NUCLEAR ENGINEERS

CAREER PROFILE

Duties: <u>Equipment Reliability Engineer</u>: analyze equipment performance and devise maintenance schedules; <u>Fire Protection Engineer</u>: safeguard the nuclear reactor and nuclear plant equipment from damage by accidental fires; <u>Instrumentation and Control Engineer</u>: responsible for operational functions of control systems and sensing devices in a nuclear power plant; <u>Nuclear-Criticality Safety Engineer</u>: research, analyze, and evaluate proposed and existing methods of transportation, handling, and storage of nuclear fuel; <u>Nuclear-Fuels Research Engineer</u>: study behavior of nuclear fuels in different reactor environments to determine their safest and most efficient usage; <u>Nuclear Maintenance Engineer</u>: keep nuclear plant equipment in optimal condition; <u>Nuclear Reclamation (Reprocessing) Engineer</u>: plan, design, and oversee construction and operation of nuclear fuels reprocessing systems; <u>Process/Project Engineering Manager</u>: using business management and industrial engineering tools, improve the efficiency of the business and operational functions of a nuclear power plant; <u>Radiation-Protection Engineer</u>: supervise and coordinate monitoring of radiation levels and condition of the facility's nuclear equipment; <u>Reactor Equipment Engineer</u>: verify the equipment functions within the nuclear reactor

Alternate Title(s): None

Salary Range: $50,000 to $95,000 or more

Employment Prospects: Fair

Advancement Prospects: Fair

Prerequisites:

Education or Training—Bachelor of Science degree in nuclear engineering recommended, or an engineering degree with emphasis on mathematics, physics, or engineering design; in some cases, a master's degree in nuclear engineering is recommended as well

Experience—On-the-job training usually done under the guidance of veteran engineers; engineering internship during college is highly advisable

Special Skills and Personality Traits—Work well in a team environment; creativity; detail-oriented; effective interpersonal, oral, and written communication skills; efficient time management and multi-tasking abilities; strong technical and analytical skills

Special Requirements—Certification as a professional engineer required; nuclear power plant security clearance necessary

CAREER LADDER

Senior Nuclear Engineer;
Nuclear Power Plant Manager;
Independent Consultant

Other Nuclear Engineers

College Graduate; Nuclear Technician

Position Description

Equipment Reliability Engineers spend half their workday in their offices studying equipment performance reports and specifications to evaluate systems and devise equipment maintenance schedules. They devote the balance of their on-duty time in the plant to testing equipment, such as attaching a probe on a pump to measure vibration, taking oil samples to analyze for the presence of certain metallic compounds as evidence of bearing deterioration, or using thermographic instruments to detect worn parts.

Fire Protection Engineers are responsible for protecting the nuclear reactor and nuclear plant equipment from any fire, avoiding forced shutdowns of the fuel-making process and minimizing property loss by preventing fires from occurring or putting out a fire that does get started as soon as possible, or detecting and suppressing the fire until help arrives to put it out. In addition, Fire Protection Engineers are involved in developing and/or improving interior plant designs and work procedures to protect safety-related equipment from the effects of any fire accident.

Instrumentation and Control Engineers have an overall responsibility for the good working condition of switches, wiring, relaying equipment, terminal boards, control systems, and sensing devices (both analog and digital) used at a nuclear power facility. They are usually involved with setting the designs and functions of circuits and are responsible for creating detailed engineering documentation for the plant. Their reports and recommendations go directly to the plant's nuclear engineers.

Nuclear-Criticality Safety Engineers analyze and evaluate proposed/existing methods of transportation, handling, and storage of nuclear fuel to preclude accidents at nuclear facilities. They study reports of nuclear fuel characteristics to determine potential or inherent problems. They read blueprints of proposed storage facilities and visit storage sites to determine their adequacy. They determine potential hazards and accident conditions that may exist in fuel handling and storage and recommend any necessary preventive measures. They summarize their findings and communicate directly with senior nuclear engineers. In addition, they prepare the final proposal reports for handling/storage of fuels to be submitted to the Nuclear Regulatory Commission and other federal government agencies.

Nuclear-Fuels Research Engineers study the behavior of fuels and fuel configurations in nuclear reactor environments to establish the safest and most efficient usage of nuclear fuels. In so doing, they apply their theoretical and experiential knowledge of reactor physics and the thermal and metallurgical characteristics of nuclear fuels and fuel cell claddings (the outer layer of the fuel rods protecting the nuclear fuel from the coolant). They design fuel behavior tests and coordinate activities of experimental research teams in their test operations. They monitor test reactor indicators of given factors, such as neutron power level, coolant level, and vital pressure, temperature, and humidity readings, modifying test procedures when necessary to meet test goals. They synthesize the analyses of test results, prepare technical reports on their findings, and offer recommendations.

Nuclear Maintenance Engineers keep the nuclear plant machinery in optimal condition to ensure the reliability of plant operations. Their task is to keep the plant producing electricity as long as possible, and to avoid any unscheduled plant shutdowns. They oversee and advise on routine maintenance procedures and practices, including the scheduled replacement of worn parts. They conduct equipment failure analysis and recommend corrective actions to improve reliability.

Nuclear Reclamation (Reprocessing) Engineers plan, design, and supervise the construction and operation of nuclear fuels reprocessing systems. They research and perform experiments to determine acceptable methods of reclaiming various types of nuclear fuels. They design nuclear fuel reclamation systems and equipment for pilot plants. In so doing, they communicate with vendors and contractors and compute cost estimates of reclamation systems. They write project proposals and submit them to both company review boards and federal agencies (such as the Nuclear Regulatory Commission). They study safety procedures, guidelines, and controls and confer with safety officials to ensure that safety limits are not violated in design, construction, or operation of such systems and equipment. They test system equipment and approve equipment needed for pilot operations. They monitor these operations to detect any potential or inherent problems, initiating corrective actions and even ordering reclamation operation shutdowns in emergencies. In their reports, they identify operational and processing problems and recommend solutions. In the preparation of their regular review reports, they maintain detailed logs of plant operations.

Process/Project Managers are engineers involved in the business end of plant operations. They use their knowledge of and skills in operations research, industrial engineering, and business management to improve the efficiency of the business and operational functions of a nuclear power facility. Specifically, they devise the timetable for all of the work to be performed during the regularly scheduled refueling and maintenance operations, keeping the outage time and power downtime as short as possible. They are in their offices 60 percent of the time, and the rest of their work time is allocated to meeting with maintenance personnel and inspecting the plant to verify that maintenance was completed correctly.

Radiation-Protection Engineers supervise/coordinate the activities of all plant personnel engaged in monitoring radiation levels and the condition of the equipment used to generate nuclear energy to ensure the safe operation of the plant's facilities. They evaluate water chemical analysis data in both primary and supportive plant systems to determine compliance with radiation content and corrosion control regulations (as set by federal statute and monitored by the Nuclear Regulatory Commission). They investigate any problems, such as radioactive leaks in reactors and auxiliary systems or excessive radiation or corrosion of equipment, applying their knowledge of radiation protection techniques and principles of chemistry and engineering to correct such conditions. They confer with departmental supervisors, manufacturing representatives, and state and federal regulatory agency staff to discuss problems, to develop tests to detect radioactive leaks, and to design plans to monitor equipment and safety programs. They direct reactor personnel in the testing/analyzing of water samples and in the monitoring of processing systems. They prepare reports on environmental monitoring operations, radioactive waste releases, and waste shipping documentation for review by senior administrative personnel before final submission to regulatory agencies.

Reactor Equipment Engineers verify the equipment functions with the nuclear reactor and take receipt of the fuel to be utilized in the plant's nuclear processing cycle. Specifically, they are responsible for the reactor's control rod drive system, reactor instrumentation, and the control rod sequence changes during the processing cycle.

Salaries

According to a 2005 survey by the National Association of Colleges and Employers, an average starting annual salary for a Nuclear Engineer with a bachelor's degree is $51,182, and for a Nuclear Engineer with a master's degree it is $58,814. In its *Occupational Outlook Handbook, 2006–07 Edition,* the U.S. Department of Labor indicates that, in May 2004, annual median salaries for Nuclear Engineers generally ranged from a low of $61,790 to a high of $118,870. Wages will vary by employer and area of the country, as well as the engineer's level of education and job responsibilities.

Employment Prospects

According to the U.S. Department of Labor's Bureau of Labor Statistics, employment of Nuclear Engineers is expected to grow more slowly than the average for all occupations through 2014. Nonetheless, most Nuclear Engineers are expected to have fair job opportunities because the small number of nuclear engineering graduates is likely to be in rough balance with the number of job openings. Most vacancies will result from the need to replace Nuclear Engineers who transfer to other occupations (or go into research or become employed by the federal government) or leave the labor force altogether.

Although no commercial nuclear power plants have been built in the United States for many years, Nuclear Engineers of all types will be needed to operate existing plants. There also is a need for Nuclear Engineers to research and develop future nuclear power sources. In addition, the threat of global warming has resulted in an escalating interest in nuclear power as an alternative to oil, natural gas, and coal power sources. New advanced-design nuclear reactors are being developed that are faster and less expensive to build. In addition, there are projects to restart shut down nuclear plants, which may open the prospect of more jobs for Nuclear Engineers in the near future.

Advancement Prospects

Extensive training programs at nuclear power plants enable Nuclear Engineers to broaden and deepen their skills and knowledge in their own particular specialties and disciplines. In addition, cross-disciplinary learning is encouraged, and opportunity is provided to train in other fields. Lateral career moves are not uncommon, and engineers have been transferred, for instance, to the business management side of the industry. Alternatively, Nuclear Engineers may decide to leave the commercial sector for governmental or military work. Some Nuclear Engineers may choose to become independent consultants to the industry as a whole or to organizations in countries other than the United States.

Education and Training

A Bachelor of Science degree in one of the engineering sciences, preferably nuclear engineering, is the basic educational requirement for Nuclear Engineers. In many cases, a master's degree in a specific engineering discipline or nuclear engineering is recommended as well. For most research jobs in nuclear engineering, a postgraduate degree (Ph.D.) in nuclear engineering is a frequent requirement.

Newly hired Nuclear Engineers work under the guidance of experienced engineers. Both mathematical and mechanical aptitudes are essential, and knowledge of computer simulation techniques is valuable. Special precautions must be taken by Nuclear Engineers who work with fissionable matter such as reactor fuels. They must wear thermoluminescent dosimeters, film badges, or other devices used for recording cumulative radiation exposure time and, in some work areas, must wear protective clothing.

Special Requirements

Nuclear Engineers must be certified as professional engineers. This licensure usually requires a degree from an accredited engineering program, as well as four years of relevant work experience, followed by the successful completion of a Fundamentals of Engineering Exam. For Nuclear Engineers with postgraduate degrees, the four-year work requirement may be waived.

In addition, the United States Nuclear Regulatory Commission (NRC) requires all nuclear plant employees and contractor employees to pass drug and alcohol screening tests, psychological evaluations, and background checks into such areas as former employment, education records, criminal records, and credit histories.

Experience, Skills, and Personality Traits

Nuclear Engineers work within a team environment, and caution and risk control are standard for the industry—appropriately so, given the dangers of nuclear radiation. Work in nuclear power stations is usually indoors, either in an office or within the plant itself.

Regardless of their special discipline, Nuclear Engineers working in nuclear power plants need to have extensive knowledge of reactor physics and of fuel and core reactor design analysis methods. They must be able to comprehend complex reactor physics/design problems and provide solutions to them. They must have strong interpersonal skills and a high level of written and verbal ability, particularly in technical writing. They should be able to handle multiple tasks with sometimes conflicting requirements. They should be manually adept, be persistent and accurate in their work, and have an analytical mind with a logical approach to problem solving. They must have good planning and organizational skills and be extremely safety conscious.

Unions and Associations

The primary association for Nuclear Engineers is the American Nuclear Society (ANC). Another association of potential interest to Nuclear Engineers is the Nuclear Energy Institute (NEI).

Tips for Entry

1. While in college earning your nuclear engineering degree, participation in an engineering internship is a great way to apply what you have learned in the classroom to a work situation. It also allows you to build skills and make contacts with people working in the engineering specialty field of your choice.

2. Besides your concentrated science, engineering, and math curriculum, take courses in technical writing and business administration, as these skills will help you in advancing your career into higher management levels within the nuclear power industry.

3. Read nuclear industry journals and subscribe to useful e-mail newsletters about the field, as the more you know about the technology behind the production of nuclear energy and the industry that produces it, the easier it will be to talk to people who are working in it and to those supervisors who will be interviewing you for employment.

LIFE AND PHYSICAL SCIENTISTS

CHEMIST

CAREER PROFILE

Duties: Obtain, test, and analyze materials, including water, oil, and particulate samples in support of nuclear power plant operations

Alternate Title(s): Chemical-Radiation Scientist; Radiation Chemist; Radiochemist

Salary Range: $35,000 to $95,000 or more

Employment Prospects: Poor to Fair

Advancement Prospects: Fair

Prerequisites:

Education or Training—Bachelor's degree in chemistry, nuclear chemistry, or a related discipline required; master's degree in nuclear chemistry usually preferred; Ph.D. degree necessary for most research and teaching positions

Experience—Two to five years' experience in nuclear power plant environment assisting senior chemists

Special Skills and Personality Traits—Ability to think logically and creatively; aptitude for detailed and accurate work; comfortable with laboratory analysis and research; demonstrated capacity for writing clear technical and analytical reports; excellent computer skills; good manual dexterity; patience, perseverance, and an enquiring mind

Special Requirements—Certification as a professional chemist required; nuclear power plant security clearance usually necessary

CAREER LADDER

```
┌─────────────────────────────────┐
│  Independent Consultant;         │
│  Nuclear Research Chemist;       │
│  Senior Technical Manager        │
└─────────────────────────────────┘

┌─────────────────────────────────┐
│            Chemist               │
└─────────────────────────────────┘

┌─────────────────────────────────┐
│  College Graduate;               │
│  Chemical Technician             │
└─────────────────────────────────┘
```

Position Description

Chemists study the properties of matter, preparing test materials to study how chemicals combine. They analyze compounds to learn their physical and chemical makeup. They observe how substances react to heat, light, other chemicals, or chemical processes. One such process is radiation.

Radiation, or nuclear, chemistry (sometimes known as nucleonics) is that branch of chemistry that is concerned with the chemical effects, including decomposition, of energetic radiation or particles on matter. It is the study of chemical changes resulting from the absorption of high-energy, ionizing radiation, particularly in absorbing materials of low and intermediate atomic weight, like most liquids and most biological systems (such as humans). Nuclear chemistry also involves the study of nuclear reactions: the use of nuclear species as projectiles to convert the nuclei of one element into another. Neutron reactions are studied by placing samples in a high neutron flux (a large number of neutrons per unit area) produced by a nuclear reactor. Nuclei can also react with each other, but being positively charged, they repel each other with great force. The projectile nuclei must have a high-energy quotient to overcome the repulsion and to react with the target nuclei. High-energy nuclei are produced in cyclotrons and various types of electronuclear accelerators.

Nuclear-chemical techniques frequently are used to analyze materials for trace elements (elements that occur in minute amounts) by irradiating them with nuclear species as projectiles to convert stable nuclides into radioactive ones, which are then measured with nuclear-radiation detectors. This process, known as activation analysis, can quantify elements in such materials as soil, rocks, meteorites, and lunar samples. Other important applications of nuclear chemistry include the development of methods for the production of radioactive species employed in medical diagnoses and treatments, as well as for radioactive isotopic tracers, which are used in studying the chemical behavior of elements.

Nuclear chemistry is integral to a nuclear power plant's safety, major component reliability, radiation field management, nuclear fuel integrity, and the overall economic viability of plant operation. Chemists test materials (water, oil, and particulate samples) and monitor the operations of the nuclear-powered electric generation process, using specialized laboratory equipment including chemical and radiation-detection equipment. They collect samples of water, gases, and solids at specified intervals, using automatic sampling equipment. They analyze these materials, according to specified procedures, to determine if chemical components and radiation levels are within established limits. They monitor and modify the chemical and water chemistry balances throughout the power generating process to reduce corrosion damage and to minimize the input of corrosion products into the plant's coolant systems.

Chemists direct the setting up and maintenance of the monitoring equipment that automatically detects deviations from standard operations. They routinely adjust the pace of the nuclear reaction within the reactor (and are usually authorized to shut the reactor down in any emergency) by controlling the level of boron added to the cooling water. (The boron absorbs the neutrons that sustain the nuclear reaction between fuel rods in the reactor.) They adjust this process when test results and monitoring of the nuclear equipment indicate that radiation levels, chemical balance, and discharge of radionuclides (frequently called radioisotopes) exceed standards. Chemists supervise any necessary decontamination procedures to ensure the safety of the workers in the plant and the continued operation of the processing equipment in the power plant. They direct the continuous calibration and maintenance of chemical instrumentation sensing elements and sample system equipment. Throughout the testing process, Chemists record all tests results and prepare reports for review by plant management. They advise the facility's management and personnel of methods of protection from excessive exposure to radiation. They may have a staff of chemical technicians to aid them in the process of collecting and testing, and they typically report to senior nuclear operations managers.

Salaries

According to the U.S. Department of Labor's *Occupational Outlook Handbook, 2006–07 Edition,* median annual earn-
ings of Chemists (in general) during 2004 were $56,060. The middle 50 percent earned between $41,900 and $76,080. The lowest 10 percent earned less than $33,170, and the highest 10 percent earned more than $98,010 a year.

The American Chemical Society (ACS) reported that, in 2004, the median yearly salary of all of its members with only a bachelor's degree was $62,000; for those with only a master's degree, it was $72,300; and for those with a Ph.D., it was $91,600. According to the society's survey of recent graduates, inexperienced chemistry graduates with a bachelor's degree earned a median annual starting salary of $32,500 in October 2004; those with a master's degree earned a median beginning salary of $43,600; and those with a Ph.D. had median starting income of $65,000.

Employment Prospects

Employment of Chemists, generally, is expected to grow more slowly than the average rate for all occupations through 2014, according to the U.S. Department of Labor's Bureau of Labor Statistics. Job growth will be concentrated in pharmaceutical and medicine manufacturing and in professional, scientific, and technical service firms. Employment in the nonpharmaceutical segments of the chemical industry is actually expected to decline. With the current hold on new (or restarting old) nuclear power plant construction in the United States, the demand for Chemists is also somewhat limited in this area. Some job openings will result from the need to replace Chemists who retire or otherwise leave the labor force.

Advancement Prospects

Some Chemists working in nuclear power plants may decide to advance their careers into the supervisory and management ranks of plant personnel. For this, they should gain basic understanding of business administration, marketing, and economics, as well as risk management (the latter is important in the present deregulated and privatized electricity marketplace). Others may become independent consultants to the nuclear power industry or work for one of the national or state regulatory bodies. Alternatively, some Chemists may choose to make a lateral career move into other industries, such as the pharmaceutical field, for which they must have some background in medicinal or synthetic organic chemistry.

Those Chemists who decide to concentrate their careers in research and development (R&D) will need to have advanced degrees, a master's degree at the very least, and most likely a Ph.D. In basic research, they will investigate properties, composition, and structure of matter and the laws that govern the combination of elements and reactions of substances. In applied R&D, they may create new products and processes or improve existing ones, often using knowledge gained from basic research.

Education and Training

A bachelor's degree in chemistry or a related discipline is usually the minimum educational requirement for entry-level Chemist jobs within the nuclear power industry, as it is in most other fields. Many jobs, particularly those in research, also require a master's degree, and, in most cases, a Ph.D. as well.

Chemists need to be knowledgeable in arithmetic, algebra, geometry, calculus, and statistics and their applications. They should have a solid background in computers, as most employers prefer job applicants who are able to apply computer skills to modeling and simulation tasks, as well as operate computerized laboratory equipment. Nuclear Chemists must be familiar with the various testing and analysis equipment utilized in the nuclear industry, as well as national and local standards and regulations as applied to the industry.

Special Requirements

Certification as a professional Chemist, usually from the American Chemical Society (ACS), is an absolute requirement. Individuals with advanced degrees (master's or Ph.D.) may be granted certification on the strength of their educational background.

In addition, the U.S. Nuclear Regulatory Commission (NRC) requires all nuclear plant employees and contractor employees to pass drug and alcohol testing, psychological evaluations, and background checks.

Experience, Skills, and Personality Traits

Nuclear power plant employers look for Chemists who have several years of experience in the application of radiation processing and testing techniques and have some expertise in the application of nuclear analytical techniques. Chemists should have good verbal and written communication skills, particularly a demonstrable ability in preparing analytical technical reports. Experience, either in academic laboratories or through internships or work-study programs in industry, is beneficial. Knowledge of how to operate scanning probe microscopes and spectrometers is a distinct advantage.

Chemists must have a solid background in computer technology, including software involved in database user interface and querying (such as Microsoft Access and structured query language, or SQL), and analytical or scientific software (such as statistical analysis software and Wavefunction Spartan). They must be able to think logically and creatively and have an aptitude for careful and accurate work. They need to have good manual dexterity and enjoy laboratory and research work. They should exhibit patience, perseverance, and intellectual curiosity. They should have good interpersonal talents and leadership abilities.

Unions and Associations

The major professional association for Chemists is the American Chemical Society (ACS). Chemists working in the nuclear power industry may find it useful to belong to the Electric Power Research Institute (EPRI) for its various nuclear power programs and research facilities.

Tips for Entry

1. While completing your undergraduate and graduate education, investigate work in academic laboratories, or industry-based internships, fellowships, or work-study programs to gain practical experience.
2. Consider *not* specializing in any subfield of chemistry, which may give you more flexibility when job hunting or changing jobs. Many employers also seek applicants with a broad scientific and mathematical background, as they often provide new graduates with additional training or education.
3. As part of your undergraduate studies, take courses in business administration and basic first aid and health techniques, as the former will be useful later in your career, and the latter will provide necessary background in health issues, which are directly applicable to your position as a nuclear power plant Chemist.

GEOPHYSICIST

CAREER PROFILE

Duties: Analyze and interpret geological, geochemical, and geophysical information useful to the construction and ongoing production processes of a nuclear power plant

Alternate Title(s): Engineering Geophysicist; Geoscientist; Nuclear Geophysicist

Salary Range: $37,000 to $110,000 or more

Employment Prospects: Fair

Advancement Prospects: Fair to Good

Prerequisites:

Education or Training—Bachelor of Science degree and a master's degree in general geology or earth science minimum educational requirement; Ph.D degree necessary for high-level research and college teaching positions

Experience—Three to five years' work experience under supervision of professional Geophysicist

Special Skills and Personality Traits—Ability to think logically and capacity for complex analytical thinking; computer proficiency essential; excellent interpersonal skills; good spatial visualization capabilities; solid skills in advanced mathematical modeling and statistical analysis applications; strong oral and written communication abilities

Special Requirements—State licensing usually required; nuclear power plant security clearance necessary

CAREER LADDER

```
┌─────────────────────────────────────┐
│   Government Position; Owner of      │
│   Independent Consulting Firm;       │
│   Teacher (university level)         │
└─────────────────────────────────────┘

┌─────────────────────────────────────┐
│            Geophysicist              │
└─────────────────────────────────────┘

┌─────────────────────────────────────┐
│          Graduate Student            │
└─────────────────────────────────────┘
```

Position Description

Geophysicists and geologists are both considered geoscientists. Whereas geology studies the composition, processes, and history of Earth, geophysics involves the application of physical theories and measurements to discover and study the structure, composition, and dynamic changes of Earth, its atmosphere, hydrosphere (the water of Earth's surface), and magnetosphere (that area of space, around Earth, that is controlled by Earth's magnetic field). The distinguishing characteristic of geophysics is its use of instruments to make direct or indirect measurements of the parts of Earth being studied, in contrast to the more direct observations that are typical of geology. Whereas geologists typically analyze fairly static systems, Geophysicists usually examine systems in flux.

Major areas of focus in geophysics include seismology, geomagnetism, and meteorology, as well as the study of large-scale processes of heat and mass transfer in Earth and variations in Earth's gravitation field. Geophysical surveys measure local variations in magnetic and gravitational field to determine distinctions in the structure and composition of rocks (which is useful in the prospecting for oil and mineral reserves and in recommendations to civil engineers in the development of building sites for new construction).

Geophysicists generally assess, examine, and explore the physical properties of Earth and apply physical measurements to investigate specific geologic problems. Among several subdisciplines, engineering geophysicists apply geologic and physical principals to the field of civil and environmental engineering to advise on major construction projects (such as hydroelectric and nuclear power plants) and assist in environmental remediation hazard-reduction of the disposal of their waste products (including nuclear waste material).

Geophysicists analyze/interpret geological, geochemical, and geophysical information from sources such as survey data, well logs, boreholes, and aerial photographs. They also plan and conduct field studies to collect data for advising on safety requirements for construction (or deconstruction) of nuclear power plants or disposition of nuclear wastes from those facilities.

Geophysicists prepare geological maps, cross-sectional diagrams, charts, and reports concerning land use and resource management based on results of their fieldwork and laboratory research. They assess ground and surface water movement to advise on waste management and on safe and secure areas for waste storage. They also identify potential risks at such locations for mudslides, earthquakes, and other natural disasters, as well as other earth processes that would affect the integrity of such waste storage areas. They assess potential construction projects to identify any engineering problems, applying their geological knowledge and using test equipment. They advise on foundation design for nuclear power plant construction, as well as appropriate land use and resource management. Throughout these processes, they may design, develop, and operate software for processing and interpreting geophysical data sets. They may adjust or develop appropriate instrumentation for taking physical measurements in surveys. In addition, they develop mathematical models as an aid in interpreting the results from their geophysical surveys.

Most Geophysicists advising the nuclear power industry are part of outside consulting firms or are independent consultants. Most use computer-generated models of what they are studying. That way, they can take the same situation and vary the factors one at a time. They then can apply those findings to similar leakage flow of pollutants (such as nuclear waste products) to determine the optimal underground storage for such waste material.

Salaries

According to the U.S. Department of Labor's *Occupational Outlook Handbook, 2006–07 Edition,* median annual earnings of geoscientists in general were $68,730 in May 2004. The middle 50 percent earned between $49,260 and $98,380. The lowest 10 percent had incomes of less than $37,700, whereas the highest 10 percent earned more than $130,750. According to the National Association of Colleges and Employers (NACE), beginning salary offers in July 2005 for graduates with bachelor's degrees in geology and related sciences average $39,365 per year.

Employment Prospects

According to the U.S. Department of Labor's Bureau of Labor Statistics, overall employment of geoscientists is expected to grow more slowly than average for all occupations through 2014. However, due to the relatively low number of qualified geoscience graduates and the large number of expected retirements during this period, opportunities are expected to be fair to good in many areas of geoscience. In addition, job growth is anticipated within management, scientific, and technical consulting services. Demand will be spurred by a continuing emphasis on the need for energy, environmental protection, and responsible land management. However, consultants are especially vulnerable to layoff during periods of economic recession.

Advancement Prospects

Most Geophysicists reach the limits of their current specialization (but not necessarily the limits of knowledge in their profession) at the end of the first five years as professional scientists. Some may begin to branch out into new areas of study, and many begin to write articles and circulate them among colleagues. Most successful Geophysicists move through several areas of specialization and are generally able to encompass the complexities of their profession. Some who have had proven successes in fieldwork and in lab analysis may be given supervisory responsibilities over newer entrants to the profession. Others may decide to teach at local universities, and some shift into government service. After 10 years of active field research, laboratory analysis, and report writing, a large number of geophysicists return to academic circles. Teaching, particularly at research institutions, allows for greater leeway in project investigation.

Education and Training

A bachelor's degree in geology or geophysics may be adequate for a few entry-level posts, but most Geophysicists (as well as most other geoscientists) need at least a master's degree in general geology, earth science, physics, mathematics, or engineering. A master's degree also is the minimum educational requirement for most entry-level research positions in private industry. A Ph.D. degree is necessary for most high-level research and college teaching positions.

Course work should include a basic geological core syllabus and a basic physics curriculum (including quantum mechanics, electromagnetism, and gravity). Mathematics, logic, and ecological science are other important areas of study, as well as computer science. Nuclear power plants that employ Geophysicists will put new hires through an intense, two-day to two-week training course in mission, internal protocols, security measures, and responsibilities.

Special Requirements

Most states require a state license of professional geologists and geophysicists, which usually demands a bachelor's degree in geology, three to five years of approved supervised work experience, and the passing of a fundamentals exam and, later, a professional geologist or geophysicist exam.

In addition, for those Geophysicists working within nuclear power plants, the U.S. Nuclear Regulatory Commission (NRC) requires all nuclear plant employees and contractor employees to pass drug and alcohol screening tests, psychological evaluations, and background checks into such areas as former employment, education records, criminal records, and credit histories.

Experience, Skills, and Personality Traits

Computer skills are essential for prospective Geophysicists. Students who have had experience with computer modeling, data analysis and integration, digital mapping, remote sensing, and geographic information systems will be the most prepared entering the job market. Knowledge of geographic information systems (GIS) and the Global Positioning System (GPS), which is a locator system that relies on satellites, is becoming more essential. Familiarity with map creation software, such as ESRI ArcView, Geomechanical design analysis (GDA), or Terrain surface mapping, is also extremely useful. Most Geophysicists begin their careers in field exploration or as research assistants/technicians in laboratories or offices.

Geophysicists should have good interpersonal skills, as they often work as part of a team with other geoscientists or environmental scientists, engineers, and technicians. They also must be able to function independently and, thus, must have good personal time management abilities. They need strong oral and written communication skills as their writing of technical reports and research (as well as their communication of the research results) will be extensive. They need to be inquisitive, be able to think logically, and be capable of complex analytical thinking, including spatial visualization and the ability to develop comprehensive conclusions, often from sparse data. They will need to be strong physically to be able to move their equipment during field research. Beyond their strong science background, Geophysicists must have a curious mind and a fascination with natural phenomena in order to succeed.

Unions and Associations

The primary association of interest for Geophysicists is the Geological Society of America (GSA). Membership in such other institutions as the American Geological Institute (AGI) and the American Geophysical Union (AGU) should prove beneficial for information, research results, and contact with peers.

Tips for Entry

1. As with many other scientific and technical professions, a summer internship in geology or geophysics while you are in high school will give you a sense of the career you have chosen.
2. As your job may later require foreign travel, or even consulting outside of the United States, knowledge of a second language is beneficial.
3. Settle on your area of specialization early to aid in applying for jobs, but beware that successful Geophysicists and geologists—no matter their career focus—need to be open-minded and willing to challenge previously held assumptions when their data proves those hypotheses might not be true.

HEALTH PHYSICIST

Duties: Responsible for all phases of radiation protection at a nuclear reactor plant

Alternate Title(s): Power Reactor Health Physicist; Radiation Safety Specialist; Reactor Health Physicist

Salary Range: $35,000 to $95,000 or more

Employment Prospects: Fair

Advancement Prospects: Good

Prerequisites:

Education or Training—Bachelor of Science degree in physics, chemistry, engineering, biology, or health science (with specialized courses in physics, nuclear engineering, radiation biology, radiological health, and occupational health) is required; graduate degree (either a master's or a Ph.D.) in health physics, radiologic hygiene, or nuclear engineering is recommended

Experience—Two to four years of practical experience with radiation safety programs in a nuclear plant environment, usually under supervision of a trained professional health physicist

Special Skills and Personality Traits—Ability to utilize sophisticated measurement instruments; capacity for accuracy, preciseness, and patience; excellent laboratory and problem-solving skills; good management and interpersonal talents; detail-oriented; solid oral and written communication abilities; strong computer proficiency

Special Requirements—Certification as a Health Physicist required; nuclear power plant security clearance necessary

> **Other Health Physicist Positions (Medical, Educational, Environmental); Research or Education Positions; Independent Consultant**

> **Health Physicist**

> **College Graduate; Nuclear Power Plant Technician**

Position Description

Health Physicists are interdisciplinary radiation protection and safety specialists whose expertise draws from chemistry, environmental science, mathematics, medicine, physics, radiation biology, and radiological health. This career specialty requires a thorough understanding of the generation, measurement, and characteristics of radiation; the environmental transport of radionuclides; dosimetry (the measurement of doses in matter and tissue from ionizing radiation, also known as radioactivity); effects of radiation in biological systems; and the governmental, medical, and industry regulations/recommendations governing the use of radiation. Health Physicists work in nuclear power facilities, regulatory agencies, hospitals, research centers, universities, government agencies, and medical centers that utilize radiation for testing or treatment. Health Physicists are trained to work in three areas of activity: research, consulting, and education/training.

Health Physicists working at a nuclear power plant are responsible for all phases of radiation protection at the reactor site. Additionally, they are in charge of the selection, purchase, and maintenance of all radiation protection, laboratory, and detection equipment. Nuclear power plant workers require extensive safety training from Health Physicists. They must study the plant's process systems in detail so that they can respond quickly and with expertise in the unlikely event of a radiation accident. They are trained to assess the potential environmental impact that the nuclear power plant represents and to ensure that the facility complies with federal and state safety and health regulations.

Power reactor Health Physicists usually are assigned multiple responsibilities, such as administering the plant's chemistry and radiation safety programs, evaluating the potential radiation exposure to the plant's personnel, determining contamination levels, designing/analyzing the plant's radiation shielding, and applying for the necessary federal and state safety licenses and keeping them up to date. Utilizing national and industry regulations, Health Physicists may research and develop radiation standards and guidelines for the nuclear plant in which they work. They may take part in any needed decontamination operations.

Personnel requirements for each nuclear reactor site differ and depend on the specific needs of each facility. It is common for a power reactor Health Physicist to supervise as many as 70 to 80 technicians and professionals, such as chemists and radiological chemists. The daily work of a Health Physicist may involve reviewing all radiological monitoring data for as many as 2,000 permanent reactor site employees. In addition, area radiological surveys, radiation records, and internal and external dosimetry information must be reviewed. Survey and laboratory results must be analyzed to ensure that the reactor is operating within prescribed limits. In all this work, Health Physicists will administer and supervise all individuals involved in these activities.

Health Physicists draw upon their technical knowledge and varied experience to advise and make recommendations to nuclear plant management regarding methods and equipment for use during plant operations. They assist nuclear engineers and scientists in designing facilities and radiation-control programs. As the primary individual of responsibility during any radiation emergency, a Health Physicist commonly has total control of the involved area.

Salaries

Earnings for Health Physicists are comparable to those for engineers and scientists. According to a 2005 salary survey made by the Health Physics Society (HPS), starting annual salaries for beginning jobs ranged from $19,000 to $45,000 depending on the level of educational background (bachelor's degree as opposed to master's degree or Ph.D.) and geographic location. For experienced Health Physicists, salaries ranged from a low of about $40,000 yearly to a high of $150,000 or more (and an average annual salary of $89,000), depending on level of educational background, years of experience, and geographic location. For example, Health Physicists with a master's degree and six to 15 years

of background had an average annual salary of $88,454, with a maximum annual salary of $185,000 being reported to the survey. For Health Physicists with a Ph.D. and six to 15 years of experience, their average annual salary was $127,941, and the maximum salary being reported for this position was $250,000.

Employment Prospects

The job outlook for Health Physicists in general is favorable, particularly as their training and skills qualify them for a variety of jobs. However, as no commercial nuclear power plants have been built in the United States for many years and most nuclear plants only hire one Health Physicist to oversee the radiation protection of all employees, employment opportunities for Health Physicists in the nuclear power industry are somewhat limited. If (and when) the nuclear power industry begins to expand once more, there should be ample employment opportunities, as their job skills are essential to the industry.

Advancement Prospects

With an advanced graduate degree and ample experience, Health Physicists may progress to research and teaching positions or act as consultants to biologists, biochemists, biophysicists, chemists, ecologists, geneticists, mining and petroleum drillers, physicists, and physicians. In some cases, there may be possibilities of promotion for Health Physicists to supervisory jobs or to posts directing research.

Education and Training

A Bachelor of Science degree in biology, chemistry, engineering, physics, or health science with specialized courses in physics, mathematics, chemistry, nuclear engineering, radiation biology, radiological health, and occupational health is a basic requirement. Most employers require advanced degrees as well. For Health Physicists employed in the nuclear power industry, a master's degree in health science or health physics with an emphasis on nuclear engineering is recommended. Studies should cover courses in biochemistry, environmental radioactivity, genetics, hazards evaluation, radiation biophysics, nuclear physics and engineering, and radiation dosimetry.

Academic training alone will not make a Health Physicist good at his or her job. Practical experience in applying radiation protection principles is essential. To provide hands-on, real-life experience, many universities offer cooperative programs in collaboration with national laboratories and with power utilities.

Special Requirements

Certification as a Certified Health Physicist (CHP) indicates that the recipient has completed certain requirements of study and professional experience, which the American Board of Health Physics (ABHP) considers to constitute an adequate foundation in health physics, and that the recipient has passed an examination designed to test competence in this field. An applicant for certification must possess at least a bachelor's degree from an accredited college or university and at least six years of responsible professional experience in health physics (less if the applicant has an advanced graduate degree).

Certification is a requirement at most nuclear power plants and for any teaching or training in health physics at an educational institution. In addition, the U.S. Nuclear Regulatory Commission (NRC) requires all nuclear plant employees and contractor employees to pass drug and alcohol screening tests, psychological evaluations, and background checks into such areas as former employment, education records, criminal records, and credit histories.

Experience, Skills, and Personality Traits

Health Physicists must be knowledgeable about air and water sampling techniques and methods of analysis, which are essential in detecting and determining concentrations of radionuclides in air and water. Training in electronics is required in order to have an operational understanding of radiation detection instruments. Health Physicists should have good analytical skills and be very detail-oriented. They must be able to adjust well to changes and to incorporate new devices and methods into their work, as radiation safety procedures are constantly improving. They need to be capable of planning and directing programs, as well as be able to supervise training activities.

Health Physicists must be capable of precision, patience, and accuracy in their work. They must be able to express their views well, both orally and in writing. Much of their work entails persuading higher management to take certain safety precautions, as well as writing and maintaining technical reports and directives. They often are asked to speak before groups and to contribute to publications. In addition, Health Physicists need to be competent in their computer skills. They should be able to manage computer data and transfer of data between different formats and platforms, and experience using health physics–related computer software (Microschield, RESRAD, or D&D) is an advantage.

Unions and Associations

The major association that advances the profession of health physics is the American Academy of Health Physicists (AAHP). Health Physicists working in the nuclear power industry may also find it useful to belong to the Health Physics Society (HPS), as well as the American Nuclear Society (ANS).

Tips for Entry

1. While in college, explore potential internship programs in health science that are offered as part of a cooperative program with national laboratories and utility companies as a practical way to apply your academic work in radiation protection principles with a real-life experience.

2. Include courses in business administration and sociology to understand how to manage individuals under your supervision and how to work with nuclear power plant management by understanding how they view their plant operations as a business.

3. In seeking financial aid for your college studies in health science, contact the U.S. Department of Energy's (DOE) Applied Health Physics Fellowship Program. Qualified fellows, who are selected through national competition, receive an annual fellowship and payment of all tuition and fees by the DOE.

NUCLEAR PHYSICIST

CAREER PROFILE

Duties: Apply knowledge of the structure of the nuclei of atoms and the particles that make up those nuclei to research concerning nuclear energy and to techniques used in the generation of electric power from nuclear reactors

Alternate Title(s): Applied Physicist

Salary Range: $50,000 to $110,000 or more

Employment Prospects: Poor to Fair

Advancement Prospects: Fair

Prerequisites:

Education or Training—Bachelor's degree in physics required; master's degree recommended for most jobs within industry; doctoral degree mandatory for most jobs in basic research and development and teaching

Experience—Two to four years as a postdoctoral researcher recommended for research and teaching positions; some professional experience in power generation industry

Special Skills and Personality Traits—Analytical, mathematical, and problem-solving abilities; excellent computer skills; good oral and written communication talents; imagination, initiative, and an inquisitive mind; knowledge of the practical application of engineering science and technology to principles of nuclear physics

Special Requirements—State certification necessary for most teaching positions

CAREER LADDER

```
┌─────────────────────────────┐
│      Nuclear Engineer       │
└─────────────────────────────┘

┌─────────────────────────────┐
│      Nuclear Physicist      │
└─────────────────────────────┘

┌─────────────────────────────┐
│      Nuclear Technician     │
└─────────────────────────────┘
```

Position Description

Physicists, in general, explore and identify basic principles and laws governing motion and gravitation, the macroscopic and microscopic behavior of gases, the structure and behavior of matter, the generation and transfer of energy, and the interaction of matter and energy. A number of physicists use these principles in theoretical areas, while others apply their knowledge of physics to practical concerns. Some physicists also find ways to apply physical laws and theories to problems in nuclear energy.

Nuclear physics is the study of the nuclei, which lie at the core of every atom. Over 99.9 percent of the mass of all the ordinary matter in the universe is found in nuclei. Protons and neutrons are the building blocks of the structure of the nucleus, so a large part of nuclear physics is trying to understand the force that holds protons and neutrons together and the forces that create unstable nuclei resulting in the release of radiation energy.

A principle research tool of nuclear physics is a high-energy beam of particles, such as protons or electrons, directed as projectiles against nuclear targets. By analyzing the directions and energies of the recoiling particles and any resulting nuclear fragments, Nuclear Physicists can gather data about nuclear structure, the strong force that bind nuclear components together, and the release of energy from the nucleus. This research has had direct applications in how nuclear reactors are built and are operated by nuclear engineers. However, with the cessation of all building of new nuclear power plants in the United States since the 1980s, research has concentrated on developing methods of quality control and monitoring of the process of generating electric power from the radiation energy released within nuclear reactors.

Besides such testing, Nuclear Physicists design computer simulations to model physical data so that it can be better comprehended and interpreted. They develop theories and laws based on observation and experiments and apply them to problems in such arenas as nuclear energy. They observe the structure and properties of matter and the transformation and propagation of energy, using equipment such as masers and lasers, to explore/identify principles governing these processes. They may then employ the knowledge and/or technology gained from their work to develop new techniques useful to the design/production of energy generated by nuclear reactions. They may be involved in the development of new reactor core design concepts, based on their research into nuclear reactions, or may be consulted in the development of new procedures in nuclear testing, or shipping and storage of nuclear waste product.

Most Nuclear Physicists work in academic posts, such as being on university faculties, or in large research laboratories, usually funded or operated by the federal government. Others may be hired by commercial companies, such as nuclear power plants, to labor in a variety of research areas and environments.

Salaries

According to the U.S. Department of Labor's *Occupational Outlook Handbook, 2006–07 Edition,* median annual earnings of physicists (including Nuclear Physicists) in May 2004 were $87,450. The middle 50 percent earned between $66,590 and $109,420. The lowest 10 percent earned less than $49,450, and the highest 10 percent earned more than $132,780.

The American Institute of Physics reported a median annual salary of $104,000 in 2004 for its full-time members with Ph.D.'s (excluding those in postdoctoral positions); the median was $94,000 for those with master's degrees and $72,000 for bachelor's degree holders.

Employment Prospects

Employment of physicists, according to the U.S. Department of Labor's Bureau of Labor Statistics, is expected to grow more slowly than the average for all occupations through 2014. This situation is particularly true for basic research in federal laboratories, which may increase to a degree through this period, but will still result in high competition for basic research jobs. Although research and development

expenditures in private industry should continue to expand, the emphasis is being placed increasingly on manufacturing research and product and software development other than basic research. Ongoing research by Nuclear Physicists that is directly applicable to the nuclear power industry is unlikely given, the moratorium on building of nuclear power plants in the United States, at least until there is a change in the political and social climate that might result in the building of new nuclear power plants and an expansion of the use of nuclear energy as a power source for the electrical needs of the country.

Opportunities may be more plentiful for individuals with a master's degree, particularly graduates from programs preparing students for applied research and development and manufacturing positions in private industry. Individuals with only a bachelor's degree in physics are usually *not* qualified to enter most physicist research jobs, but may qualify for posts such as nuclear technicians.

Advancement Prospects

Nuclear Physicists, like other types of physicists, who have only a bachelor's degree are rarely eligible to fill posts in research or in teaching at the college level. However, they usually are qualified to work as nuclear technicians or research assistants in nuclear engineering-related areas. Getting a master's degree qualifies them for other positions in applied research and development that require a physics background. To work fully as a Nuclear Physicist, individuals must complete a Ph.D. in physics with a strong concentration in mathematics. To labor in research areas related to nuclear power, many Nuclear Physicists may decide to broaden their background by becoming a nuclear engineer as well as a physicist. With years of training and successful work within a nuclear power plant environment, further career advancement typically means a concentration on management rather than research, applied or otherwise.

Education and Training

A Bachelor of Science degree in physics is just the first goal of an applied Nuclear Physicist in an educational career that, in most cases, extends to eight or more years of college. As undergraduates, they usually must take courses in mathematics, all of the physical sciences, and, in addition, may find laboratory classes in metalworking useful. To obtain work as a Nuclear Physicist, most individuals must obtain both a master's degree and a Ph.D. After completing a Ph.D., they typically work two to four years as a postdoctoral researcher. This is a low paying (usually $25,000 to $40,000 per year) position, but it is designed to allow them to continue to study and develop their careers under the tutelage of experienced physicists, without some of the other pressures of being a working scientist. Initial work may be under the close supervision of senior scientists, but after some experience, physicists may perform increasingly complex tasks and work more independently.

Special Requirements

Nuclear Physicists who wish to teach at either a high school level or a college are usually required to gain a state educational certification. Otherwise, there is no specific certification or license required for research Nuclear Physicists, unless they decide to further advance their career by becoming a nuclear engineer, for which they usually need an industry (or government) certification.

Experience, Skills, and Personality Traits

Strong mathematical abilities and problem-solving and analytical skills are necessary requirements of Nuclear Physicists. They must have good oral and written communication talents as they often work as part of a team, both in postdoctoral activities and in applying their research to the practical problems of nuclear power generation. In addition, they will have to write research papers or proposals and may have direct contact with clients or customers who do not have physics backgrounds. They need inquisitive minds and imagination as well as initiative and perseverance.

Unions and Associations

For physicists, the major association for their career is the American Institute of Physics (AIP). For Nuclear Physicists, membership in the American Nuclear Society (ANS) is highly recommended.

Tips for Entry

1. While obtaining your high school diploma, a summer job in a physics research laboratory is an excellent way of gaining hands-on experience in laboratory research procedures.

2. While in college, explore research programs open for research assistants to work at nuclear research laboratories to add practical experience to your theoretical course work in nuclear physics.

3. Additional work experience, either in academic laboratories or through internships, fellowships, or work-study programs in industry, may also prove beneficial.

MANUAL LABOR PERSONNEL

OTHER MANUAL LABOR PERSONNEL

CAREER PROFILE

Duties: Boilermaker: Inspect, maintain, and repair boilers, pressure vessels, and tanks utilized in a nuclear power plant to heat or boil the water that runs steam generators to produce electricity; Bricklayer: Lay firebrick and refractory tile to build, rebuild, reline, or patch the high-temperature and heating equipment used in nuclear power plants; Carpenter: Build wooden structures and scaffolds used in and around nuclear power plants; Electrician: Install, test, and maintain electrical equipment and systems used in a nuclear power facility; Millwright: Install, repair, replace, and dismantle turbines used in nuclear power plants; Sheet Metal Worker: Plan, lay out, fabricate, assemble, install, and repair sheet metal parts and equipment used in a nuclear power plant; Welder: Join together, by welding, metal components of products, such as pipelines, utilized in a nuclear power facility

Alternate Title(s): Boilermaker: Boilermaker Mechanic; Bricklayer: Brickmason, Firebrick and Refractory Tile Bricklayer; Carpenter: Bracer, Form Builder, Rough Carpenter, Wood-form Builder; Electrician: Electronics Technician, Maintenance Electrician, Nuclear Maintenance Electrician; Millwright: None; Sheet Metal Worker: Sheet Metal Mechanic; Welder: Welding-Assembler, Welder-Fitter

Salary Range: Boilermaker: $14.00 to $32.00 or more per hour; Bricklayer: $15.00 to $30.00 or more per hour; Carpenter: $11.00 to $28.00 or more per hour; Electrician: $12.00 to $33.00 or more per hour; Millwright: $13.00 to $32.00 or more per hour; Sheet Metal Worker: $10.00 to $30.00 or more per hour; Welder: $10.00 to $22.00 or more per hour

Employment Prospects: Fair to Good

Advancement Prospects: Fair

Prerequisites:

Education or Training—High school degree and vocational school training recommended; formal apprenticeship in trade usually required

Experience—Usually four to five years on-the-job training under professional guidance with supplemental technical course work in classroom environment

Special Skills and Personality Traits—Ability to read blueprints and layout plans; basic mathematics and mechanical drawing skills; detailed-oriented and able to bend, stoop, and work in awkward positions; good physical condition and sense of balance; manual dexterity and good eye-hand coordination

Special Requirements—Certification may be required; nuclear power plant security clearance usually necessary

CAREER LADDER

> **Supervisory Position; Independent Contractor**

> **Boilermaker; Bricklayer; Carpenter; Electrician; Millwright; Sheet Metal Worker; Welder**

> **Apprentice Position**

Position Description

Boilermakers assemble, install, maintain, and repair boilers, pressure vessels, tanks, and vats that hold liquids and gases. Boilers and pressure vessels supply steam (in the case of nuclear power plants, created by heating water from the nuclear chain reaction within the reactor) to drive huge turbines in electric power plants. Tanks, vats, and other containers are used to process and store chemicals, waste products, and hundreds of other products. Boilers and other high-pressure vessels usually are made in sections, by casting each piece out of molten iron or steel. Boiler sections are then welded together, often using automated orbital welding machines, which make more consistent welds than are possible by hand. The large boilers employed in nuclear power plants are typically assembled on site.

Following blueprints, Boilermakers locate and mark reference points for the boiler foundation, attach rigging and signal crane operators to lift heavy frame and plate sections and other parts into place, and then align the sections. They use hammers, files, grinders, and cutting torches to remove irregular edges, so that all edges fit properly before bolting or welding the edges together. They align and attach liquid or gas tubes, stacks, valves, gauges, and other parts and test the assembled vessels by pumping water or gas under specified pressure into the vessel and monitoring instruments for evidence of leakage. Boilermakers regularly maintain boiler vessels and repair them when necessary. They inspect tubes, fittings, valves, controls, and auxiliary machinery and clean (or supervise the cleaning of) boilers using scrapers, wire brushes, and special cleaning solvents. In nuclear power plants, such repair work is accomplished under special conditions, due to residual radioactivity that may be present, with great care given to necessary safety regulations.

Some Bricklayers specialize in laying firebrick and refractory tile to build, rebuild, reline, or patch high-temperature or heating equipment, such as boilers, ovens, furnaces, condensers, converters, and soaking pits. They lay out the work, using chalklines, plumb bobs, tapes, squares, and levels. They remove burned or damaged brick and clean surfaces using brick hammers or powered abrasive saws. They cut bricks to size, spreading fire-clay mortar over them and then laying them in place. They spread or spray a silica coating (known as a refractory) over exposed bricks to protect them against deterioration by heat. They may replace bolts, brackets, and heating elements, weld cracks or holes in vessel shells, or perform other repair work. They may be required to pack insulation into shells and frames to insulate heating equipment, such as boilers and condensers. Besides nuclear power plants, most firebrick and refractory tile Bricklayers are employed in steel mills.

Carpenters assemble, erect, install, and repair structures and fixtures made from wood and other materials. Some Carpenters, known as rough carpenters, build rough wood structures, such as concrete forms, scaffolds, tunnel and sewer supports, and temporary frame shelters, according to drawings, blueprints, or oral instructions. Others, known as form builders, construct built-in-place or prefabricated wooden forms, according to specifications, for molding concrete structures, or for erecting scaffolding (say, to effect repair work on machinery in a nuclear power plant). Working from blueprints or instructions from supervisors, they first do a layout—measuring, marking, and arranging materials—in accordance with existing building codes. They measure boards, timbers, or plywood, saw them to required sizes, and join them with nails, screws, or adhesive materials. Finally, Carpenters check the accuracy of their work with levels, rules, plumb bobs, framing squares, or electronic versions of these tools, making any necessary adjustments.

Electricians install, test, and maintain electrical systems. They may work either in construction (assembling and installing electrical systems) or in maintenance (maintaining, repairing and upgrading existing electrical systems and equipment), or in both areas. Since no new nuclear power plants have been built in the United States for years, electricians employed at such facilities are primarily maintenance electricians. They inspect the plant's electrical equipment, control panels, transformers, and generators to identify hazards, defects, and any needs for adjustment or repair and to ensure compliance with codes. In testing electrical systems and continuity of circuits in electrical wiring, equipment, and fixtures, they use equipment such as ammeters, voltmeters, and oscilloscopes to diagnose problems and ensure compatibility and safety throughout the system. They may change items such as circuit breakers, fuses, switches, electrical and electronic components, or wires. When working on the complex electronic devices utilized in a nuclear power plant, they work closely with nuclear engineers, technicians, and other maintenance workers. Electricians attempt to locate and correct problems before breakdowns occur, and they advise management whether continued operation of any of the equipment could be hazardous.

Millwrights install, repair, replace, and dismantle machinery and heavy equipment utilized in the nuclear power industry. When new machinery arrives at a plant, Millwrights oversee its unloading, inspection, and movement into position. To lift and move light machinery, millwrights employ rigging and hoisting devices, such as pulleys and cables. With heavier equipment, they may need the assistance of hydraulic lift-truck or crane operators to position the machinery. Because Millwrights often must decide which device to use for moving machinery, they must know the load-bearing properties of rope, cables, hoists, and cranes. They work with plant supervisors and managers to determine the optimal placement of machines in the plant. If such placement requires building a new foundation, Millwrights either prepare the foundation themselves or supervise its construction. Thus, they must know how to read blueprints and work with an assortment of building materials.

To assemble machinery, Millwrights fit bearings, align gears and wheels, attach motors, and connect belts, according to the manufacturer's blueprints/drawings. Precision leveling and alignment are important, so devices such as lasers and ultrasonic measuring and alignment tools frequently are used. In addition, Millwrights must be knowledgeable about cutting torches, welding machines, hydraulic torque wrenches, hydraulic stud tensioners, soldering guns, and other metalworking devices. Millwrights are usually in charge of installing and maintaining the turbines in power plants. These turbines can weigh hundreds of tons and contain thousands of parts, which necessitates specialized training for Millwrights and, usually, a job certification by the manufacturer. In addition to installing and dismantling machinery, many Millwrights work with mechanics and maintenance workers to repair and maintain plant equipment. This includes preventive maintenance, such as lubrication and fixing or replacing worn parts.

Sheet Metal Workers plan, lay out, fabricate, assemble, install, maintain, and repair sheet metal parts, equipment and products, such as the heating, ventilation, and air-conditioning duct systems used in nuclear power plants. They read and interpret blueprints, sketches, or product specifications to determine sequence and methods of fabricating, assembling, and installing the needed sheet metal products. In many instances, Sheet Metal Workers use computerized metalworking equipment when they cut, drill, and form parts with computer-controlled saws, lasers, shears, and presses. Before assembling the pieces, they check each part for accuracy using measuring instruments such as calipers and micrometers. After inspection and approval, they fasten seams and joints together with welds, bolts, cement, rivets, solder, or other connecting devices. They then take the parts to the plant site, where they further assemble the pieces as they install them. Some jobs are done completely at the jobsite. In addition to installation, some Sheet Metal Workers specialize in testing, balancing, adjusting, and servicing existing air-conditioning and ventilation systems to guarantee they are functioning properly and to improve their energy efficiency. Properly installed duct systems are important in a nuclear power plant and Sheet Metal Workers who specialize in this work are sometimes referred to as HVAC (heating, ventilation and air-conditioning) technicians.

Welding is the most common way of permanently joining metal parts. In this process, heat is applied to metal pieces, melting and fusing them to form a bond. Among other uses, welding is employed to join beams when constructing buildings or other structures and to join pipes in pipelines, power plants, and refineries. Welding is accomplished both by hand and by machinery controlled by the welder, such as a wire feeder. Arc welding is the most common type of welding. It uses two large metal alligator clips that carry a strong electrical current. One clip is attached to any part of the piece being welded, and the second clip is connected to a thin welding rod that will create a powerful electrical circuit when it touches the piece. In the process, the rod and piece melt together, cooling

quickly to form a solid bond. During welding, the flux that surrounds the rod's core vaporizes, forming an inert gas that serves to protect the weld from atmospheric elements that might weaken it.

Like arc welding, soldering uses molten metal to join two pieces of metal. Only the added metal is melted. Because soldering does not melt the workpiece, it normally does not create the common distortions or weaknesses in the workpieces that can occur with welding. Soldering commonly is used to join electrical, electronic, and other small metal parts used throughout power plants. Welding and soldering workers often are exposed to the hazard of the intense light created by the welding arc, as well as poisonous fumes and extremely hot materials. Safety clothing and protective lenses for their eyes are critical.

Salaries

According to the U.S. Department of Labor's Bureau of Labor Statistics in its *Occupational Outlook Handbook, 2006–07 Edition,* Boilermakers in May 2004 had hourly wage earnings from a low of $14.00 to a high of more than $32.00, and a median hourly earning of $21.68. Apprentices generally start at about half of journey-level (full-time certified workers) wages, with income gradually increasing as progress in made in the apprenticeship.

According to the Bureau, in May 2004, hourly wage earnings of Bricklayers ranged from a low of $11.68 to a high of $30.43, with a median hourly wage of $20.07. Apprentices usually start at about 50 percent of the wage rate paid to experienced workers.

In May 2004, hourly wages of Carpenters ranged from a low of less than $10.36 to a high of $28.65, according to the U.S. Department of Labor. Median hourly earnings were $16.78. (Apprenticeship programs are usually limited and are mostly for those Carpenters working for commercial and industrial building contractors.)

According to the U.S. Department of Labor, in May 2004, median hourly earnings of Electricians were $20.33. Salaries for Electricians ranged from a low of $12.00 to a high of $33.00 or more. Apprentices usually start at between 40 and 50 percent of the rate paid to fully trained Electricians, receiving periodic pay increases throughout the course of their training.

Median hourly earnings of Millwrights were $21.02 in May 2004 according to the U.S. Department of Labor. The lowest 10 percent earned less than $13.02, the middle 50 percent earned between $16.53 and $27.07 an hour, and the highest 10 percent earned more than $32.17 an hour.

According to the U.S. Department of Labor, in May 2004, median hourly earnings of Sheet Metal Workers were $17.09, with a salary range from $9.80 to $30.78. As with electrician apprentices, apprentice Sheet Metal Workers normally start at about 40 to 50 percent of the rate paid to experienced workers.

The U.S. Department of Labor indicates that median hourly earnings of Welders and solderers were $14.72 in May 2004. The middle 50 percent earned between $11.90 and $18.05. The lowest 10 percent had hourly income of less than $9.79, while the top 10 percent earned over $22.20.

Employment Prospects

The U.S. Department of Labor's *Occupational Outlook Handbook, 2006–07 Edition* finds that employment of Boilermakers is expected to have an average growth through the year 2014. Within the nuclear power industry, most of the Boilermaker work is devoted to maintenance and repair (or deconstruction if the plant is being closed down). However, many boilers are getting older and will need replacing, which will create some demand for more Boilermakers. In addition, nuclear power plants, like other utilities, will need to upgrade many of their boiler systems in the next few years to meet the Federal Clean Air Act.

A large number of Bricklayers are expected to retire over the next decade, and in some areas, there are not enough applicants for the skilled jobs to replace those that are leaving. Thus, job opportunities for Bricklayers are projected to be good and will increase about as fast as the average for all occupations through 2014.

Generally, job opportunities for Carpenters are forecast to be excellent over the next several years, according to the U.S. Department of Labor. Employment will increase about as fast as average for all occupations through 2014. However, with the limited number of Carpentry jobs required by the nuclear power industry, work within that industry will grow no faster than the average for all occupations during this period.

The *Occupational Outlook Handbook, 2006–07 Edition* projects that employment of Electricians is expected to increase as fast as the average for all occupations through the year 2014. As with many other skilled professions over the next decade, a large number of Electricians are expected to retire, creating many vacancies. Opportunities for maintenance Electricians may be somewhat limited by the increased contracting out for electrical services in an effort to reduce operating costs. Alternatively, however, there may be increased job positions for maintenance Electricians in electrical contracting firms.

According to the U.S. Department of Labor, employment of Millwrights is anticipated to grow more slowly than the average for all occupations through 2014. As Millwrights always will be needed to maintain, repair, or dismantle machinery, skilled applicants should have good job opportunities, particularly those trained in installing newer production technologies. Nonetheless, the demand for Millwrights may be adversely affected as lower paid workers, such as electronics technicians and industrial machinery mechanics and maintenance workers, assume some installation and maintenance duties.

Job opportunities for Sheet Metal Workers are expected to be good, according to the Bureau of Labor Statistics, particularly in the construction industry. Work options should be particularly good for individuals who acquire apprenticeship training or who are certified welders. While some workers in construction may experience periods of unemployment when economic conditions dampen construction activity, maintenance of existing equipment—which is less affected by economic fluctuations than is new construction—comprises a large part of the work done by Sheet Metal Workers. Thus, employment prospects for them should remain good.

Employment of welding and soldering workers is expected to expand more slowly than the average for all occupations in the next several years, as per the U.S. Department of Labor. Despite this, job prospects should be good, as many employers are reporting difficulty finding enough qualified people. Within the nuclear power industry, most welding work is maintenance or repair work, not construction. Thus, the demand for welding work is lower than in many other industries. Generally, however, technology is creating more uses for welding and, thus, expanding employment likelihood. New methods are being developed to bond dissimilar materials and nonmetallic materials, such as plastics, composites, and new alloys. In addition, laser beam and electron beam welding and other new techniques are improving the end results, making welding more competitive with other methods of joining materials.

Advancement Prospects

For all of these manual labor positions, the most common job advance (beyond higher wages due to work experience and seniority) is to upgrade into a supervisory post, after additional training and experience. Carpenters, in particular, have greater opportunities than most other construction/repair workers do to become general construction supervisors, because carpenters are exposed to the entire construction and repair process. Because of their broader work training, apprentices in any of these manual labor positions have an advantage in promotion over those who have not undergone the full program. Some of them may become independent contractors and even owners of businesses employing many workers. They may spend most of their time as managers rather than as bricklayers, electricians, carpenters, and so forth.

Electricians who have sufficient capital and management skills may start their own contracting business, although this job move may require an electrical contractor's license. Many electricians also become electrical inspectors. While Welders can advance to more skilled welding jobs, they may prefer to become welding technicians, supervisors, inspectors, or instructors. Some of them may decide to open their own repair shops.

Education and Training

One constant in all these jobs is the necessity of having a high school education, which provides a good background in mathematics and basic science, as well as in writing and communicating with others. Generally, high school courses in English, mathematics, physics, mechanical drawing, and blueprint reading are recommended.

The most common way for individuals in these jobs to pick up their skills is by observing and learning from experienced workers. Others may receive training in vocational education schools or from industry-based programs offered by public and private vocational-technical schools and training academies in affiliation with local unions and/or contractor organizations. The armed forces are another way to gain technical training, particularly in welding and electrical work. Another option is to obtain a job directly with a contractor who will then provide on-the-job training. Entry-level workers generally start as helpers, advancing as experience is accrued.

The other common method of learning necessary skills is through apprenticeship programs. While some employers provide basic training, they usually prefer to hire workers with experience or more formal training. Thus, apprenticeship courses can supply the necessary skills and can lead to certification as professionals. Some employers with union membership offer formal apprenticeships. Unions themselves frequently provide financial backing for apprenticeship programs for future union members. The number of available apprenticeship programs may be limited, but such courses give an employment edge to those individuals who take part. Applicants must have a high school degree and, usually, must be 18 years of age and meet any special requirements of the type of position they are seeking.

Special Requirements

Electricians usually need to be licensed. Although licensing requirements vary from area to area, electricians typically must pass an examination that tests their knowledge of electrical theory, the National Electrical Code, and local electric and building codes.

Welders generally become certified, a process whereby the employer sends the worker to an institution, such as an independent testing laboratory, equipment manufacturer, or technical school, to weld a specimen according to specific codes and standards required by the employer. Testing procedures are based on the standards and codes set by industry associations with which the employer may be affiliated. If the worker is successful in the test, the inspector will then certify that the Welder is able to work with a particular welding procedure.

For most other manual labor positions, certifications may not be required, but, of course, they are always useful as a part of the work background. Successful completion of apprenticeship programs may provide a certification as well as the needed professional status.

In addition, the U.S. Nuclear Regulatory Commission (NRC) requires all nuclear plant employees and contractor employees to pass drug and alcohol screening tests, psychological evaluations, and background checks into such areas as former employment, education records, criminal records, and credit histories.

Experience, Skills, and Personality Traits

For all these manual labor positions, individuals will gain needed experience in apprenticeship programs or other on-the-job training. For these jobs, applicants need to be in good physical shape, have a good sense of balance, exhibit solid manual dexterity, and have excellent eyesight and eye-hand coordination. Mechanical aptitude is particularly important for Millwrights, Sheet Metal Workers, and Welders but a useful attribute for all these positions. Good color vision is important for Electricians, as they frequently must identify electrical wires coded by color. Computer skills and the ability to solve arithmetic problems quickly and accurately are additional requirements for most of these work positions.

Unions and Associations

There are unions for all these positions. For Boilermakers, membership in the International Brotherhood of Boilermakers, Iron Ship Builders, Blacksmiths, Forgers, and Helpers (IBB) is highly recommended, as about half of all boilermakers belong to labor organizations.

For Bricklayers, there is the International Union of Bricklayers and Allied Craftworkers, International Masonry Institute (IMI), as well as the Associated Builders and Contractors (ABC), the Associated General Contractors of America, Inc. (AGC), the Brick Industry Association (BIA), and the National Concrete Masonry Association (NCMA).

For Carpenters, there is the United Brotherhood of Carpenters and Joiners of America (UBCJA). Other groups of interest include the National Association of Home Builders' Home Builders Institute (HBI), the National Center for Construction Education and Research (NCCER), and the Associated General Contractors of America, Inc. (AGC).

For Electricians, the primary union is the International Brotherhood of Electrical Workers (IBEW). Other associations of interest (particularly for information about apprenticeship programs) include the Associated Builders and Contractors, Workforce Development Department (ABC), the Independent Electrical Contractors, Inc. (IECI), the National Electrical Contractors Association (NECA), and the National Joint Apprenticeship Training Committee (NJATC).

For Millwrights, the National Tooling and Machining Association (NTMA) is the primary association. Information about apprenticeship programs can be gained from the United Brotherhood of Carpenters and Joiners of America

(UBCJA), the Associated General Contractors of America (AGC), or the Associated Builders and Contractors, Workforce Development Department (ABC).

Many Sheet Metal Workers belong to a union, primarily the Sheet Metal Workers International Association (SMWIA) or the Sheet Metal and Air-Conditioning Contractors' National Association (SMACNA). It should be noted that in some locales union workers receive supplemental wages from their union when they are on layoff or shortened workweeks. Information about apprenticeship programs can be obtained from the unions.

Many Welders belong to unions. Among these are the International Association of Machinists and Aerospace Workers (IAMAW); the International Brotherhood of Boilermakers, Iron Ship Builders, Blacksmiths, Forgers and Helpers (IBB); the International Union, United Automobile, Aerospace and Agricultural Implement Workers of America (IU); the United Association of Journeymen and Apprentices of the Plumbing, and Pipefitting Industry of the United States and Canada (UAJAP); and the United Electrical, Radio, and Machine Workers of America (UERMWA).

Information about apprenticeship programs can be gotten from the American Welding Society (AWS).

Tips for Entry

1. During high school, in addition to your regular curriculum, include courses in computer science (as you will need these skills) and in business management (as you may want to become an independent contractor some day, and will need business expertise).

2. Learning how to communicate in *both* English and Spanish is an additional useful skill. It is increasingly important to be able to relay instructions and safety precautions to workers with limited understanding of English, and Spanish-speaking workers make up a large part of the construction workforce in most areas of the country.

3. While in high school, explore possible summer jobs with contractors in the area of your interest to gain hands-on experience as well as make potential useful contacts for your future career.

PIPE FITTER

CAREER PROFILE

Duties: Install, repair, and maintain process piping systems that carry liquid, steam, or gas in nuclear power plants

Alternate Title(s): Pipe Welder; Steamfitter

Salary Range: $19,000 to $70,000 or more

Employment Prospects: Fair to Good

Advancement Prospects: Fair

Prerequisites:

Education or Training—High school degree required; apprenticeship program completion required

Experience—Completion of apprenticeship program, usually consisting of four to five years of on-the-job training along with classroom instruction; experience working in power plants, refineries, or industrial plants; some background with mechanical drawing and blueprint reading helpful

Special Skills and Personality Traits—Communication skills, both verbal and written; dependability and attention to detail; math proficiency; good manual dexterity and mechanical abilities; physically strong with good eyesight; reliable time-management and problem-solving talents

Special Requirements—Professional licensing certification required; union membership recommended; nuclear power plant security clearance usually necessary

CAREER LADDER

Contractor Supervisory Positions; Self-Employed, or Owner of Consulting Contractor Business

Pipe Fitter

High School Graduate; Apprentice Pipe Fitter

Position Description

Professionals in the pipe trades build and repair all of the complex systems that rely on the circulation of liquids, steam, or gas. They assemble and maintain industrial refrigeration and climate control systems and the sophisticated sprinkler systems that extinguish fires in buildings and factories. Pipe trade professionals include Pipe Fitters, steamfitters, and plumbers, all of whom are considered to be in a single professional trade. However, workers usually specialize in one area. Plumbers install and repair water, waste, and gas systems in homes and commercial buildings, whereas Pipe Fitters and steamfitters lay out, assemble, fabricate, maintain, troubleshoot, and repair piping systems that carry hot (or cold) water, steam, chemicals and fuel (used in heating, cooling, or lubricating), air, or other liquids or gases

needed for manufacturing, industrial establishments, and power-generating systems.

They also install automatic controls that are sometimes used to regulate these systems. While Pipe Fitters are sometimes known as steamfitters, steamfitters actually do *not* work with pipes that carry water (either potable, or drinkable, water or industrial water) or natural gas. They install pipe systems that move other liquids or gases under high pressure.

Pipe Fitters are required to interpret plans, drawings, and blueprints, measure and cut sections of piping to exact specifications, and install the system of pipes, valves, pumps, and backflow prevention equipment that is required. They may have to cut or drill holes in walls or floors to accommodate the passage of pipes. It may be necessary for them to mount brackets or special hangers on walls and ceilings to hold pipes and set sleeves or inserts to provide support for pipes. They fit valves, couplings, or assemblies to tanks, pumps, or systems, using hand tools. They connect sections of pipe by welding, soldering, or brazing them together. They often must cut sections of pipe using a variety of techniques—from simple manual pipe cutters to heavy saws or oxyacetylene blowtorches for the thickest and largest materials. To cut and bend lengths of pipe, they use saws, pipe cutters, and pipe-bending machines.

However, the trade involves more than simply connecting pipes and valves. Pipe Fitters must understand the physics of how liquids, gases, and steam flow, and they often use computer-assisted design (CAD) software to create intricate systems. When the project is completed (or pipes repaired or replaced), Pipe Fitters must ensure that each section is leak free (using pressure gauges and other like equipment), particularly important for systems that carry toxic or radioactive materials.

Pipe Fitters within a nuclear power plant install, repair, and replace the pipes connecting the nuclear reactor to the steam generator, the steam line pipes going to the steam turbine (which runs the generator that produces the electricity output), and those back and forth between the cooling water (or gas) condenser (in which the turbine sits) and the cooling tower. (In fast nuclear reactors, as opposed to the more traditional thermal slow reactors, the coolant that is used is usually a liquid metal like molten sodium, which creates different requirements for the piping that carries it.) The piping connecting the various parts of a nuclear reactor vary greatly in size and have special requirements, all of which nuclear Pipe Fitters must take into account. They need to be knowledgeable about the various types of pipe fittings and riggings, as well as all types of valves, and have some experience with hydraulic bolt torque wrenches, stud tensioners, and pumping units. At all times during their work, they must wear the same protective clothing/devices as the engineers and technicians in the plant.

Salaries

Pipe Fitters (along with pipe layers, plumbers, and steamfitters) are among the highest paid construction occupations. According to the U.S. Department of Labor's *Occupational Outlook Handbook, 2006–07 Edition*, in May 2004, median hourly earnings of Pipe Fitters were $19.85 (or about $41,300 annually). The middle 50 percent earned hourly wages between $15.01 ($31,220 annually) and $26.67 ($55,474 annually). The lowest 10 percent earned less than $11.62 ($24,170 per year), and the highest 10 percent earned more than $33.72 ($70,140 yearly).

In an October 2006 survey of Pipe Fitter salaries (made by PayScale, Inc.), median hourly salary rates ranged from $10.60 (for those with less than a year's experience) to $24.85 (for those with 20 or more years experience), and,

for experienced Pipe Fitters, from a low of $14.00 to a high of $36.80 depending on geographic location.

Employment Prospects

According to the U.S. Department of Labor, job opportunities, generally, for skilled Pipe Fitters are expected to be excellent, as demand is anticipated to outpace the supply of workers training in this craft. Many employers report difficulty finding potential workers with the right qualifications. In addition, many individuals currently working in this trade are expected to retire over the next 10 years, creating additional job vacancies.

Although no commercial nuclear power plants have been built in the United States for many years, Pipe Fitters will be needed to repair and replace pipe equipment in existing facilities. Traditionally, some nuclear power plant operations, with their extensive pipe systems, have employed their own Pipe Fitters to maintain/repair the equipment. However, nowadays, to reduce labor costs, many companies no longer employ full-time, in-house Pipe Fitters. Instead, they rely on workers provided under service contracts with plumbing and pipe fitting contractors to maintain/repair piping equipment on a regular basis.

According to the U.S. Department of Labor, in 2004 more than one in 10 pipelayers, plumbers, Pipe Fitters, and steamfitters were self-employed. Almost one in three pipelayers, plumbers, Pipe Fitters, and steamfitters belonged to a union.

Advancement Prospects

With additional training, Pipe Fitters may become supervisors for plumbing and pipe fitting contractors. Others may go into business for themselves, often starting as a self-employed Pipe Fitter working from home. Some then may expand their work to become owners of contractor businesses employing many workers and may spend most of their time as managers rather than as Pipe Fitters. Others may choose to move into closely related areas such as construction management or building inspection.

Education and Training

The basic educational requirement for Pipe Fitters is a high school degree. Besides the usual academic curriculum, concentration on mathematics, drafting, and industrial technology is recommended. Pipe Fitters (as well as plumbers and steamfitters) are typically trained through formal apprenticeship programs under the supervision of professionals. Apprenticeship programs usually are administered by either union locals and their affiliated companies or by nonunion contractor organizations (such as the Mechanical Contractors Association of America, the National Association of Plumbing-Heating-Cooling Contractors, or the National Association of Home Builders). Apprenticeships—both union and nonunion—consist of four to five years of on-the-job training, in addition to a minimum of 144 to 216 hours per year of related classroom instruction.

Applicants for union or nonunion apprentice jobs must be at least 18 years old and in good physical condition. Pipe fitting skills gained while serving in the U.S. Armed Forces are considered very good training, and individuals with this background may be given credit for previous experience, shortening their apprenticeship tenure. At the successful conclusion of apprenticeship programs, Pipe Fitters can apply for certification as a professional journeyman in their area of specialty. They usually also must fulfill a one-year probationary period following the completion of their apprenticeship.

Special Requirements

Although there are no uniform national licensing qualifications for Pipe Fitters, most states and municipalities require them to be licensed. Licensing requirements vary from area to area, but most localities expect workers to pass an examination that tests their knowledge of the trade and of local plumbing and pipe fitting codes. Union or nonunion certification in their area of specialization is usually an additional requirement.

In addition, the U.S. Nuclear Regulatory Commission (NRC) requires all nuclear plant employees and contractor employees to pass drug and alcohol screening tests, psychological evaluations, and background checks into such areas as former employment, education records, criminal records, and credit histories.

Experience, Skills, and Personality Traits

With most apprenticeship programs, Pipe Fitters learn from on-the-job training from experienced workers while earning a wage (usually some percentage of the journeyman standard pay rate, which increases each year throughout the program).

Pipe Fitters need both to be mechanically inclined and to have excellent manual dexterity to operate their equipment. They must have good communication skills and be adept with computers. They should be able to work as part of a team, but also be adept at functioning independently, utilizing their own work ethic, integrity, and time-management abilities. They should be very detail-oriented, able to understand in-depth written and verbal instructions, and used to repetitive physical and mental activities. They need to have strong mathematics and problem-solving talents.

Unions and Associations

Over two-thirds of Pipe Fitters employed are members of the one union that represents their craft: the United Association of Journeymen and Apprentices of the Plumbing and Pipefitting Industry of the United States and Canada (UA). The union sponsors apprenticeship programs and award certifications in an assortment of areas for Pipe Fitters.

Tips for Entry

1. During high school, consider summer apprenticeship programs in the building or plumbing trades to gain practical experience in preparation for your apprenticeship studies after graduation.
2. Take writing courses along with your English and computer courses, as you will need to keep records of all your work done as a Pipe Fitter.
3. As many plumbers and Pipe Fitters eventually become self-employed and have to prepare cost estimates for their clients (as well as manage their business), you may find it useful to take accounting and business management courses while in high school.

NUCLEAR POWER PLANT TECHNICIANS AND OPERATORS

HAZARDOUS MATERIALS REMOVAL WORKER

CAREER PROFILE

Duties: Identify, remove, pack, transport, or dispose of hazardous radioactive materials from nuclear power plants

Alternate Title(s): Decontamination Worker; Nuclear Decommissioning Worker; Nuclear Waste Treatment Operator

Salary Range: $21,000 to $56,000 or more

Employment Prospects: Fair

Advancement Prospects: Poor to Fair

Prerequisites:

Education or Training—High school diploma required, with good foundation in mathematics and chemistry; additional training necessary for licensing as a Hazardous Material Removal Worker required by federal regulation

Experience—Training programs provide initial experience; on-the-job employment provides further additional expertise

Special Skills and Personality Traits—Able to deal with loud noises and unpleasant odors; attentive to detail; capable of good record keeping; excellent judgment, self control, and ability to follow procedures explicitly even under extreme stress; good manual dexterity; physically fit

Special Requirements—Federal regulations require licensing; nuclear power plant security clearance necessary

CAREER LADDER

```
┌─────────────────────────────────────┐
│  Hazardous Waste Removal Supervisor; │
│  Independent Removal Contractor      │
└─────────────────────────────────────┘

┌─────────────────────────────────────┐
│  Hazardous Materials Removal Worker  │
└─────────────────────────────────────┘

┌─────────────────────────────────────┐
│  High School Graduate; Hazardous     │
│  Waste Removal Trainee               │
└─────────────────────────────────────┘
```

Position Description

The removal of hazardous materials (or hazmats) from public places, private businesses, and the environment is often called abatement, remediation, or decontamination. Hazardous Materials Removal Workers identify, remove, package, transport, and dispose of assorted hazardous materials, including asbestos, lead, and radioactive materials. Radioactive materials are classified as either high- or low-level wastes. High-level wastes are primarily nuclear reactor fuels used in the production of electricity. Low-level wastes encompass any radioactively contaminated protective clothing, tools, filters, medical equipment, or other items used in or around nuclear reactors.

There are three levels of Hazardous Materials (hazmat) Removal Workers who deal with radioactive materials. The lowest level is decontamination technicians. These laborers use brooms, mops, and other tools to cleanse contaminated areas and remove exposed items for decontamination or disposal. Some of these jobs are now being accomplished by robots controlled by decontamination technicians outside the contamination site.

The next level is that of radiation protection technicians. These workers use radiation survey meters to locate and evaluate contaminated materials. They employ high-pressure cleaning equipment to wash contaminated areas, and they also package radioactive materials for transportation and disposal.

The third level is that of decommissioning and decontamination (D&D) workers, who remove radioactive materials from nuclear facilities and power plants. With a variety of handtools, they break down contaminated items such as gloveboxes, which are used to process radioactive materials. They build concrete storage boxes for the nuclear waste and may be required to transfer materials from the nuclear site to these cement boxes or other storage containers. At decommissioning nuclear sites (such as nuclear power plants being shut down), these employees clean and decontaminate the facilities, as well as remove any radioactive or contaminated materials.

After a nuclear reactor's operating cycle, the reactor is shut down for refueling. The fuel discharged at that time (spent fuel) is stored either at the reactor site or in a common facility away from the reactor site. If the capacity of on-site water pool storage (in which spent fuel rods, containing the radioactive pellets used in the generation of nuclear energy, are kept) is exceeded, the now cooled aged fuel may have to be stored in modular dry storage facilities known as Independent Spent Fuel Storage Installations (ISFSI) at the reactor site or at an off-site facility. The spent fuel rods are stored in water, which provides both cooling (as the spent fuel continues to generate decay heat resulting from residual radioactive decay) and shielding to protect the environment from residual ionizing radiation. After several years of cooling, these spent fuel rods may be able to be moved to dry cask storage. All the handling of this waste material is done by Hazardous Materials Removal Workers.

At nuclear waste treatment plants, waste-treatment operators (also called nuclear-waste-process operators) control the heat exchange unit, pumps, compressors, and related equipment to decontaminate, neutralize, and dispose of radioactive waste liquids collected from chemical processing operations. They test the radioactive residue left after baking a sample of the liquid under heat lamps to evaporate the water, comparing the Geiger reading with charts to determine whether the radioactivity level is now within prescribed safety limits. If so, they start pumps to admit the waste liquid into the sewer system or into storage tanks for evaporation (to reduce the volume of liquid) and into lead containers for permanent storage. They record all data, such as the number of gallons of waste pumped into the sewer system or into storage tanks, and all radioactivity levels. They also monitor the panel board, which controls the operation of recovery systems that store radioactive waste materials or dispose of the now-treated and safe waste.

All Hazardous Waste Removal Workers wear some type of protective gear, but the level of safety gear varies with the job. Those who need the most protection, particularly most nuclear waste workers, wear full body suits and respirators (which filter the air they breathe), as well as film and radiation detectors.

Salaries

According to the U.S. Bureau of Labor Statistics, median hourly earnings of Hazardous Materials Removal Workers in May 2004 were $16.02 (or annual incomes of $33,322). The middle 50 percent of workers earned between $12.52 and $22.27 an hour (or annual earnings from $26,042 to $46,322). The lowest 10 percent earned less than $10.48 per hour (annual: $21,798), and the highest 10 percent earned more than $27.25 per hour (annual: $56,680).

In an updated survey of national estimates of salaries of Hazardous Materials Removal Workers, the U.S. Bureau of Labor Statistics found that median annual wages for the middle 50 percent of workers in May 2005 had risen to $33,690. In addition, the yearly income earned from bottom to top ranged from $21,470 to $59,120.

Employment Prospects

According to the U.S. Department of Labor, employment of Hazardous Materials Removal Workers (in general) is expected to grow much faster than the average for all occupations through the year 2014. In particular, employment of nuclear Hazardous Materials Removal Workers is expected to grow in response to the accelerating public pressure for safer and cleaner nuclear and electric generator facilities. Renewed interest in nuclear power production (as an alternative to coal, oil, and gas energy production) could lead to the construction of additional nuclear facilities in the near future. However, the number of older closed facilities that need decommissioning may continue to grow due to federal legislation. These workers are not much affected by economic fluctuations because the facilities in which they work must operate, regardless of the state of the economy.

Advancement Prospects

Nuclear Hazardous Materials Removal Workers may choose to widen the type of materials for which they are certified so they can work with a variety of substances. With additional experience, they can become supervisors, and some may open their own businesses or become trade contractors specializing in removal of hazardous substances. Some become consultants to businesses and contractors who need help with hazardous materials. They may even branch further out by becoming environmental technicians, environmental safety managers, or industrial hygienists.

Education and Training

A high school diploma is a basic requirement for a person to become a Hazardous Materials Removal Worker. A solid foundation in mathematics and chemistry is necessary, along with courses in biology and physics. Some understanding of industrial technology, building construction, and industrial safety processes is helpful, and a basic familiarity with first aid procedures is important. In addition, hazmat workers must be computer literate. They need to be fully conversant with all federal and state regulations pertaining to nuclear materials. Agencies that maintain regulations applicable to radioactive waste are the Department of Transportation (DOT), the Nuclear Regulatory Commission (NRC), and the Environmental Protection Agency (EPA).

Special Requirements
Federal regulations require a license to work in the occupation, and most states require a state certification as well. A formal 32- to 40-hour training program in dealing with asbestos, lead, and hazardous waste must be completed to obtain the basic license as a removal worker. For decommissioning, decontamination, and other hazmat workers employed at nuclear facilities, training is more extensive. In addition to the standard 40-hour training course, workers must take courses in regulations governing nuclear materials and radiation safety. Many agencies, organizations, and companies throughout the country provide training programs that are approved by the U.S. Environmental Protection Agency (EPA), the U.S. Department of Energy (DOE), and other federal and state regulatory bodies. Workers are required to take refresher courses every year to maintain their licenses.

In addition, the U.S. Nuclear Regulatory Commission (NRC) requires all nuclear plant employees and contractor employees to pass drug and alcohol screening tests, psychological evaluations, and background checks.

Experience, Skills, and Personality Traits
Hazardous Waste Removal Workers of all types must be able to use hand tools and power equipment and should be familiar with construction tools, techniques, and principles. They must have excellent manual dexterity and be physically fit, as they often must perform their jobs in cramped conditions, standing, stooping, and kneeling for long periods. In these confined conditions, they may need to use sharp tools to dismantle contaminated objects. In addition, they need to have both physical strength and agility, as they will most likely need to lift heavy objects. They should be able to work under pressure and in dangerous conditions.

Hazmat removal workers need to be detail-oriented, able to do basic math conversions and calculations, and capable of keeping thorough records of all their work. Because of the inherent danger in removing hazardous materials, particularly those that are radioactive, hazmat workers must work together as a team and are closely supervised. They must follow all rules and regulations exactly and check on each other's progress. Hazardous Materials Removal Workers need great self-control and a level head to cope with the daily stress associated with handling hazardous materials.

Unions and Associations
Besides the American Nuclear Society (ANC), organizations of specific interest to hazmat removal workers include the Air and Waste Management Association (A&WMA) and the Dangerous Goods Advisory Council (DGAC). For up-to-date information on waste management, they should consult Waste Management News, an online newsletter (http://www.topix.net/business/waste-management).

Tips for Entry
1. Besides your foundation in mathematics and chemistry during high school, learn communication skills in English as well. You will be reading blueprints and safety warnings and following detailed written instructions and regulations as a hazmat removal worker.
2. Consider working for a local construction company in the summers, as much hazardous materials (including radioactive components) removal work is done in buildings.
3. Alternatively, consider summertime employment in a machine tool shop to become adept at handling tools of all sorts and sizes.

INSTRUMENT TECHNICIAN

CAREER PROFILE

Duties: Inspect, test, adjust, and repair equipment, instruments, and control systems used in a nuclear power generating plant

Alternate Title(s): Electrical Technician; Electrical Engineering Technician (Power Plant); Electronics Technician; Instrument and Controls Technician; Nuclear Equipment Engineering Technician; Power Plant Technician (Electrical)

Salary Range: $45,000 to $65,000 or more

Employment Prospects: Fair to Good

Advancement Prospects: Fair

Prerequisites:

Education or Training—High school degree required; an Associate of Applied Science (two-year) college degree in electrical engineering technology, electronics, and/or mechanics usually required as well; four-year college degree not necessary, but recommended

Experience—Successful completion of an electrical, electronics, or mechanical technician training curriculum is the typical requirement, but experience from a government naval nuclear training program may be an acceptable substitute

Special Skills and Personality Traits—Detail-oriented and comfortable with deadlines; excellent interpersonal and communication skills; good hand-eye coordination and good physical stamina; mechanical ability; patience and persistence; solid computer skills

Special Requirements—Certification as an electrical/mechanical technician and as a nuclear power plant technician required; nuclear power plant security clearance necessary

CAREER LADDER

```
┌─────────────────────────────────┐
│  Electrical Engineer; Mechanical │
│            Engineer              │
└─────────────────────────────────┘

┌─────────────────────────────────┐
│      Instrument Technician       │
└─────────────────────────────────┘

┌─────────────────────────────────┐
│  Instrument Technician Trainee   │
└─────────────────────────────────┘
```

Position Description

A nuclear power generating plant depends on complex electrical and electronic equipment for the operation and control of its nuclear reactor, steam generator, pumps, turbines, and related equipment. Electrical equipment and electronic equipment are two distinct types of industrial tools, although much equipment contains both electrical and electronic components. In general, the electrical portions provide the power for the equipment, while electronic parts control the devices (though many types of apparatus still are run with electrical devices). Electronic sensors monitor the equipment, providing feedback to the programmable logic control (PLC), which guides the equipment. The PLC processes the information provided by the sensors and makes any necessary adjustments to modify or to optimize power output. To adjust this output, the PLC sends signals to the electrical, hydraulic, and pneumatic devices that power the various components in the nuclear power generation process. Utilizing technical specifications and nuclear program directives, Instrument Technicians develop, review, and perform preventive, predictive, and corrective maintenance on electrical (motors and sequential control), electronic (inverters and radio-controlled cranes), electro-mechanical (circuit breakers and motor operated valves, or MOVs), and recording equipment employed in the power plant.

Instrument Technicians are responsible for the inspection, testing, adjusting, and repairing of electrical, electronic, mechanical, and pneumatic instruments, equipment, and systems used to indicate, record, and control the power generating operations of nuclear power electric generating plants. They inspect meters, indicators, and gauges to detect abnormal fluctuations. They test the accuracy of flowmeters, pressure gauges, temperature indicators, controllers, radiation counters or detectors, and other recording, indicating, or controlling equipment to locate defective components in the system. In doing this, they use test equipment, such as pressure gauges, mercury manometers, potentiometers, pulse and signal generators, oscilloscopes, transistor curve tracers, ammeters, voltmeters, and wattmeters. In addition, they trace and test electronic solid state and vacuum tube circuitry and components to locate defective parts in analog and digital protection or radiation monitoring systems, using test equipment, schematics, and maintenance manuals.

Following power plant maintenance procedures, they remove defective instruments from the systems, decontaminate, disassemble and clean apparatus, and replace defective parts, and then replace repaired instruments into the system, using handtools. They lubricate instruments and replace defective wiring and tubing. They may also replace reactor plant motors, circuit breakers, controllers, and switchboards during plant downtime or outage periods. In preparation for planned downtime, Instrument Technicians interface with other plant technicians and engineers in preparing documentation (which includes performance and troubleshooting plans for analyzing malfunctions) to be used during these maintenance periods.

They calibrate readings on instruments according to industry standards, adjust phasing, and align stages to ensure accuracy in the recording and indicating functions of the instruments and equipment. Throughout this process, they record the calibrations they make and the parts and components used, as well as keep an accurate inventory of parts on hand in the plant. They prepare schematic drawings, sketches, and reports to reflect changes or alterations made in instruments, circuits, equipment, and systems.

Instrument Technicians provide technical support for the plant's electrical and mechanical engineers, including the diagnosis and repair of faulty equipment and the selection and installation of replacement and/or new equipment.

They give technical assistance and resolution when electrical problems are encountered and assemble electrical and electronic systems and prototypes according to engineering data and their knowledge of electrical and mechanical principles. They undertake complex electrical workshop functions, such as assembling protection relays. They modify electrical prototypes, parts, assemblies, and systems to correct any functional deviations. They set up and operate test equipment under both simulated and live operating conditions, recording the results and preparing reports. They may build, calibrate, maintain, troubleshoot, and repair electrical instruments or testing equipment. Most important, they ensure that all assembling, installing, testing, and calibrating of electrical, electronic, and mechanical instruments and equipment conform to industry and governmental regulations and safety requirements.

Instrument Technicians usually work under the direct supervision of the nuclear power plant's electrical engineers, mechanical engineers, or operations manager in all stages of planning, design, maintenance, and production.

Salaries

According to Salary.com's December 2006 analysis of survey data processed by their certified compensation professional staff, median national annual salaries for Instrument Technicians ranged from a low of $47,700 to a high of $63,223, but, in some cases, may range lower or higher depending on geographic location and amount of experience.

Employment Prospects

Nuclear power plants, like all other types of electric power generating plants, must have Instrument Technicians to maintain and guarantee continuous and accurate production. This job is a necessity for the industry and, thus, job opportunities are fair to good, depending upon the availability of positions. Most Instrument Technicians start as trainee apprentices to an experienced Instrument Technician to gain an understanding of the specifics of taking measurements from and maintaining instruments and equipment utilized by a nuclear power plant.

Advancement Prospects

With additional education, training, and certification, Instrument Technicians may choose to advance their career by becoming either electrical or mechanical engineers. They may decide to remain within the nuclear power plant field or to transfer to other energy industries, as their skills as engineers are easily applicable. Alternatively, they may branch out into other industries. In California alone, according to the state's Labor Market Information Division, there were 23,000 job openings projected for Instrument Technicians (all industries) in 2005.

Education and Training

The minimum requirement for this position is a two-year associate's degree in science, chemistry, physics, or other science-related area or, instead, four years equivalent experience within the nuclear power industry. Usually a four-year college degree is not necessary. However, specialized training through apprenticeship programs and/or on-the-job training is a basic requirement. Most apprenticeship programs consist of three to five years of on-the-job training along with classroom studies.

Special Requirements

As well as being certified as an electrical and/or mechanical technician (required by most states), Instrument Technicians need to be certified for work within a nuclear power plant. Certification training programs for electrical technicians are available from the Institute of Electrical and Electronics Engineers (IEEE) among other professional associations, and for mechanical technicians from the American Society of Mechanical Engineers (ASME). Certification as a nuclear Instrument Technician usually requires two years of documented experience in the operation and maintenance of a nuclear facility, as well as course work. Information can be obtained from the National Institute for the Certification of Engineering Technologies (NICET), the Radiochemistry Society, and other professional associations affiliated with the nuclear energy industry.

In addition, the U.S. Nuclear Regulatory Commission (NRC) requires all nuclear plant employees and contractor employees to pass drug and alcohol screening tests, psychological evaluations, and background checks.

Experience, Skills, and Personality Traits

Most Instrument Technicians gain seasoning and learn the specific responsibilities of their position as trainees under the direct supervision of an experienced technician or engineer. (Typically, training periods last from four to seven years.) In addition to their proficiency in handling the plant's instrument/controls systems, they will need to be well versed in the use of (and capable of data input to) the plant's computerized maintenance management system (CMMS), which assigns/monitors work schedules pertaining to the instruments and control systems. Thus, Instrument Technicians must have a solid proficiency in computer applications. They need not only electrical and electronic skills, but also mechanical abilities.

Instrument Technicians must have excellent manual dexterity and good eye-hand coordination. They need to be physically fit (capable of bending, twisting, kneeling, stooping, crouching or crawling), and be able to climb ladders and scaffolds, work at heights, and inspect hard to reach areas. As part of the nuclear operations team, Instrument Technicians must have good interpersonal and communication skills. They must have excellent eyesight and have good written communication skills, as they must keep accurate records of all their work. In addition, they have to be thoroughly trained in all radiation safety protocols, as well as industry and governmental standards as set by the American National Standards Institute (ANSI) and the Institute of Nuclear Power Operations (INPO).

Unions and Associations

While there are no specific professional associations organized for nuclear technicians, Instrument Technicians may find it useful to belong to such generic industry associations as the American Nuclear Society (ANC) or the Instrument Society of America (ISA).

Tips for Entry

1. During high school, include courses in mathematics, drafting (blueprint reading), and technical writing, as these skills will be important to you as an Instrument Technician.
2. While in high school or while pursuing an associate's degree, consider summer internship programs at electric (or nuclear) power plants to gain an understanding of the instrument and control systems needed for power generation.
3. After gaining your degree, consider an authorized training program at a nuclear facility, such as the program given by the Tennessee Valley Authority, to help you gain needed certification as a nuclear technician.

NUCLEAR MONITORING TECHNICIAN

CAREER PROFILE

Duties: Collect and test samples to monitor amounts of radiation present during nuclear power production to determine potential contamination of humans, facilities, and environment

Alternate Title(s): Chemical-Radiation Technician; Health Physics Technician; Radiation Monitor; Radiation Protection Technician (RPT); Radiation Safety Officer; Radiochemical Technician; Radiological Control Technician (RadCon Technician)

Salary Range: $35,000 to $70,000 or more

Employment Prospects: Fair

Advancement Prospects: Fair

Prerequisites:

> **Education or Training**—High school graduate, with heavy concentration on mathematics and science; training in vocational schools, related on-the-job experience, or an associate's science degree (preferably in nuclear health or nuclear technology) recommended; in some cases a bachelor's degree may be required
>
> **Experience**—Three to five years' apprenticeship (or vocational) training usually required, consisting of both on-the-job experience and informal training with experienced technicians
>
> **Special Skills and Personality Traits**—Ability to sustain a long span of concentration; attention to detail, capacity for following instructions exactly, and dependability; excellent communication and organizational skills; good manual and finger dexterity; solid computer proficiency
>
> **Special Requirements**—Most nuclear technicians require a security clearance and should be certified as nuclear technicians before working within a nuclear power plant.

CAREER LADDER

```
┌─────────────────────────────────────┐
│   Health Physicist; Nuclear Engineer; │
│       Nuclear Plant Supervisor        │
└─────────────────────────────────────┘

┌─────────────────────────────────────┐
│    Nuclear Monitoring Technician      │
└─────────────────────────────────────┘

┌─────────────────────────────────────┐
│      Nuclear Technician Trainee       │
└─────────────────────────────────────┘
```

Position Description

Nuclear Monitoring Technicians calculate the limits of safe radiation exposure times for nuclear power plant personnel, using plant contamination readings (registered on dosimeter equipment worn by facility personnel) and prescribed safe levels of radiation as set forth by industry and governmental standards for nuclear power plants. (Dosimetry is the measurement of absorbed radiation dose in matter and tissue resulting from the exposure to ionizing radiation.)

Nuclear Monitoring Technicians check personnel to determine the amounts and intensities of radiation exposure. They provide the initial response to any abnormal events and to any alarms generated by their radiation monitoring equipment. They instruct nuclear plant personnel in radiation safety procedures and demonstrate the use of protective clothing and equipment. They monitor the time/intensity of exposure of personnel working in such higher risk sections as nuclear waste disposal areas. They may make periodic urinalyses of personnel and notify the supervisor when overexposure to radiation is indicated from such tests. They inform plant supervisors when individual exposures or specific radiation levels approach maximum permissible limits.

Throughout both production times and downtimes, they determine the intensities and types of radiation present in work areas, on equipment, and in materials by employing various radiation detectors (such as beta-gamma survey meters, gamma-background monitors, and alphabeta-gamma counters) and other monitoring equipment. They collect air samples to determine airborne concentration of radioactivity, as well as samples of water, gases, and solids to determine radioactivity levels, and document any excessive contamination. In addition, they collect and analyze monitoring equipment worn by plant personnel, such as film badges and pocket detection chambers, or measure individual exposure to radiation.

Nuclear Monitoring Technicians set up equipment throughout nuclear power plants that, automatically, will detect area radiation deviations, and they check all types of detection equipment used to ensure its accuracy. They calibrate and maintain chemical instrumentation sensing elements and sampling system equipment, using calibration instruments and hand tools. They take smear tests of suspected contaminated areas by wiping the floor with filter paper and placing the paper into a radiation scaler to obtain a contamination count. From the results of this testing, they may recommend work stoppage in unsafe areas, post warning signs, and even rope off contaminated areas. They log into computers all their collected data, such as status of areas being decontaminated, the rate of radiation exposure to personnel, and location and intensity of radioactivity in infected areas.

Nuclear Monitoring Technicians determine or recommend to plant supervisory personnel specific radioactive decontamination procedures, according to the size and nature of the equipment involved and the degree of contamination. In addition, they themselves will decontaminate objects by cleaning them with special soap or solvents or by abrading them with wire brushes, buffing wheels, or sandblasting machines. They may weigh and mix decontamination chemical solutions in a tank and, using hoist equipment, immerse objects into these solutions for specified periods.

Nuclear Monitoring Technicians prepare reports on contamination tests, material and equipment decontaminated, and methods used in the decontamination process. They work closely with the plant's health physicist and nuclear engineers involved directly with nuclear fuels, the nuclear reactor, and other highly radioactive areas of the plant and usually report directly to top-level nuclear plant supervisory personnel,

Salaries

Annual earnings for Nuclear Monitoring Technicians range from lows of about $35,000 to highs of $70,000 or more, according to industry sources. Wages will vary according to geographic location (to a degree) and to experience (the primary determinant).

Employment Prospects

The position of Nuclear Monitoring Technician is a crucial one for nuclear power plants. Each plant needs a staff of radiation monitoring technicians to work closely with plant supervisors and health personnel in monitoring radiation exposure and potential contaminations. However, with the uncertainty surrounding the future of nuclear power throughout the United States, the overall job market for most nuclear technicians, including Nuclear Monitoring Technicians, has slowed and is projected to decline through 2012, at least until nuclear power's future is clarified. Most hiring will be to replace present workers who leave the labor market or change careers. Still, the specialized nature of the job of Nuclear Monitoring Technician may enhance employment prospects because of the lack of qualified technicians for this position.

Advancement Prospects

Nuclear Monitoring Technicians may decide to concentrate more on health issues and, with additional training and education, transfer to posts as health physicists or move directly into areas of medical uses of radioactive material, working in hospital or clinic environments or at government installations. Other experienced Nuclear Monitoring Technicians with a Bachelor of Science degree can become nuclear engineers. Some nuclear plant employers may pay job-related educational costs or even offer work-study plans. Other technicians may decide to concentrate on management as a career move and, with more training, move into plant supervisory positions.

Education and Training

The minimum requirement is high school graduation with heavy emphasis on mathematics and the sciences, supplemented by some amount of relevant experience (such as U.S. Navy service involving nuclear training). Most nuclear power plant employers prefer nuclear technician trainees to have two to four years of college. Specifically, personnel involved in direct exposure to radiation and responsible for the health of others are usually required to have an associate's science degree in nuclear health or nuclear technology.

Special Requirements

Nuclear Monitoring Technicians need to be certified for their position by a certification institution, such as the National Registry of Radiation Protecting Technologists (NRRPT) or the Board of Certified Safety Professionals (CSP). Some states may insist on state certification as well. In addition, the U.S. Nuclear Regulatory Commission (NRC) requires all nuclear plant employees and contractor employees to pass drug and alcohol screening tests, psychological evaluations, and background checks.

Experience, Skills, and Personality Traits

Nuclear Monitoring Technicians have to be fully trained in the use of radiation-testing equipment and well versed in all industry/government safety regulations and measures. They must be able to pay strict attention at all times to their detection equipment and their readings. They must have excellent manual and finger dexterity to utilize their monitoring equipment properly. Their dependability and reliability must be superior. They must be able to communicate their full understanding of all nuclear safety regulations and protocols to their fellow workers and plant supervisory personnel and be able to instruct them about potential health hazards and necessary radiation safety measures.

Besides skillful verbal abilities, they need good writing skills to keep thorough and concise logs of their work and from this data generate reports directed to their nuclear power plant supervisors. To maintain these logs, they must be detail-oriented and have good computer skills. They need to be extremely patient, organized, precise, and thorough in executing their work

Unions and Associations

Many, but not all, technicians working in nuclear power plants are members of the Utility Workers Union of American (UWUA) of the AFL-CIO Division of Oil, Chemical, and Atomic Workers.

In addition, Nuclear Monitoring Technicians may find it useful to belong to the Health Physics Society (HPS), a scientific and professional organization whose members specialize in occupational and environmental radiation safety. For those technicians looking to become nuclear engineers, membership in the American Nuclear Society (ANS) may be beneficial.

Tips for Entry

1. During high school, seek summer jobs or internships (which are usually non-paying) with nuclear power plants or medical institutions that are involved with radiation treatments to gain a firsthand understanding of the health and safety issues involved with the use of nuclear power.
2. During your computer course work, practice creating forms for reports, transcribing, entering, recording, and storing detailed information, as these are skills necessary for your future work as a Nuclear Monitoring Technician.
3. Besides your science and math classes, take a writing course and one in speech, both of which will aid you in your communication skills that you can apply to work in your career choice.

NUCLEAR REACTOR OPERATORS

CAREER PROFILE

Duties: <u>Auxiliary Nuclear Reactor Operator</u>: Operate equipment outside the nuclear control room that is used for the release, control, and utilization of nuclear energy; <u>Nuclear Reactor Operator</u>: From the nuclear control room, controls nuclear reactor that produces steam for generation of electric power and coordinates operation of auxiliary equipment; <u>Senior Reactor Operator</u>: Responsible for the direction and supervision of the daily (and nightly) operations of a nuclear reactor in the generation of electric power

Alternate Title(s): <u>Auxiliary Nuclear Reactor Operator</u>: Non-Licensed Nuclear Equipment Operator (NLO), Nuclear Equipment Operator, Nuclear Plant Equipment Operator; <u>Nuclear Reactor Operator</u>: Nuclear Control Operator; Nuclear Control Room Operator, Nuclear Plant Operator (NPO), Nuclear Power Reactor Operator, Nuclear Station Operator; <u>Senior Reactor Operator</u>: Nuclear Plant Shift Supervisor, Nuclear Reactor Supervisor

Salary Range: <u>Auxiliary Nuclear Reactor Operator</u>: $25,000 to $40,000 or more; <u>Nuclear Reactor Operator</u>: $50,000 to $80,000 or more; <u>Senior Reactor Operator</u>: $85,000 to $150,000 or more

Employment Prospects: Fair

Advancement Prospects: Fair to Good

Prerequisites:

Education or Training—High school diploma with heavy emphasis on the sciences and mathematics minimum requirement, supplemented with some relevant experience working with nuclear reactors (such as in the U.S. Navy); two to four years of college preferred

Experience—Two to four years' training within a nuclear power plant environment

Special Skills and Personality Traits—Ability to read diagrams; good oral, written, and interpersonal skills; manual dexterity; mechanical abilities; sense of responsibility and personal initiative; solid computer expertise

Special Requirements—The Nuclear Regulatory Commission requires licensing of, and a security clearance for, all individuals who supervise or operate the controls of a nuclear reactor

CAREER LADDER

Licensed Nuclear Reactor Operator; Senior Reactor Operator; Senior Supervisor, Nuclear Plant Operations

Auxiliary (non-licensed) Nuclear Reactor Operator; Nuclear Reactor Operator; Senior Reactor Operator

Nuclear Reactor Operator Trainee

Position Description

The nuclear chain reaction in the reactor core produces energy in the form of heat. The heat generated in the reactor is removed by a primary coolant (usually water) flowing through it. This heat must be removed efficiently—and at the same rate it is being generated—in order to prevent overheating the core and to transport the energy outside the core (where it can be converted to produce steam or to heat gases to drive turbogenerators, which, themselves, generate electrical energy).

A nuclear power plant is staffed around the clock. Each unit has a supervisor (a Senior Nuclear Reactor Operator), control room nuclear reactor operators, and auxiliary operators who run the equipment. At multi-unit stations, there may be a shift manager (senior operator) responsible for the entire site. While the nuclear unit is in service, some of the activities that operators perform include testing safety-significant emergency equipment, conducting support maintenance, performing minor maintenance, and processing radioactive liquids and gases. During a refueling outage, usually conducted every one to two years, the operators transfer new nuclear fuel into the reactor, removing old fuel from the reactor.

Auxiliary Nuclear Reactor Operators usually are not required to have a license. Their formal training program is primarily concerned with the four non-licensed watch stations at the nuclear plant: outside equipment, the turbine building, auxiliary building, and fire/safety equipment. Under the direction of the control room supervisor (a senior operator), they run all plant auxiliary equipment that is not normally operated from the control room. They perform routine tests, incidental maintenance, electrical switching assignments, or other duties specified as necessary to assure continuity of power generation. They carry out periodic inspections of all assigned equipment spaces. They report to a control room Nuclear Reactor Operator any abnormal plant or equipment conditions and take additional (established) steps to initiate corrective action. To do so, they must be thoroughly familiar with the conditions/limitations of equipment operation and be able to denote any variances—and reasons for such—on all reports, logs, and surveillance forms. Under the guidance of licensed Senior Reactor Operators, they may assist in handling new and spent nuclear fuel. Auxiliary Nuclear Reactor Operators must be familiar with and observe plant operating procedures, proper radiological control practices, industrial safety practices, and fire protection/prevention requirements. They are members of the reactor's fire and safety watch (FASW), or fire brigade. As such, they must be thoroughly familiar with all required emergency medical and first aid procedures, confined space rescue processes, and the handling of hazardous material spills. Throughout all their duties, they are tasked with accurate documentation of all their work.

Nuclear Reactor Operators control the equipment that affects the power of the reactor. Usually reporting to Senior Reactor Operators, Nuclear Reactor Operators are licensed operators who are responsible for working the reactor's controls and for the safe and competent operation of the nuclear reactor. They check radiation-monitoring devices to assure proper operation, read and record meters/gauges, and maintain the reactor operations log. Under supervision, they adjust controls to start and shut down the reactor, to position the fuel rods in the reactor, and to regulate flux levels, coolant temperatures, and rate of power flow, as well as other control elements that affect the power level within the reactor. In so doing, they follow standard instructions and prescribed practices. They dispatch orders and instructions to plant and auxiliary personnel through radiotelephones or intercommunications systems to coordinate the operation of such auxiliary equipment as pumps, compressors, switchgears, and water-treatment systems. Under the guidance of Senior Reactor Operators, they assist in preparing, transferring, loading, and unloading nuclear fuel elements.

Nuclear Reactor Operators monitor all systems for normal running conditions, performing activities such as checking gauges to assess output and the effects of power generator loading on other equipment. They note malfunctions of equipment, instruments, or controls and report them immediately to Senior Reactor Operators. They supervise the monitoring and operation of boilers, turbines, wells, and auxiliary power plant equipment. They implement control room operational procedures, such as those governing start-up and shutdown activities. They respond to system or unit abnormalities, diagnosing the cause, and recommend, or take, corrective action depending on the problem. They direct all other reactor personnel in crises in accordance with emergency operating procedures. Throughout, they record all operating data, such as the results of surveillance tests and inspections.

Senior Reactor Operators have the overall responsibility for the power plant and are often called shift managers or shift supervisors. There may be several Senior Reactor Operators working on each operating shift in order to cover all operations that are ongoing. They supervise and coordinate the activities of all workers engaged in the operation and control of the reactor, turbine generator, and auxiliary equipment utilized in the generation of electric power. They devise/write the operating procedures for all plant operations, based on review and interpretation of government regulations, technical manuals, and conferences with manufacturers' representatives and senior plant management. They review status reports of all operations and monitor and analyze readings of instrumentation systems to ensure that reactor and auxiliary equipment are operated safely and in accordance with Nuclear Regulatory Commission (NRC) parameters. They confer with supervisory Nuclear Reactor Operator personnel to coordinate activities of operations and maintenance workers engaged in performance of routine and emergency shutdowns, as well as standard maintenance of equipment and machinery. They prepare training manuals and outlines and instruct workers in such subjects as chemistry, health physics, mathematics, reactor physics, and electrical theory as they apply to nuclear power plant operations, according to federal regulatory requirements.

Salaries

According to the U.S. Department of Labor's Bureau of Labor Statistics, as of May 2005, Auxiliary Nuclear Reactor Operators have annual salaries that range from $25,000 to $40,000 or more. Nuclear Reactor Operators have a median annual wage of $66,230. Their yearly salaries range from $51,370 for the lowest 10 percent to $87,100 for the highest 90 percent. Senior Reactor Operators can earn annually from $85,000 to $150,000 or more depending on their years of experience.

Employment Prospects

According to Nuclear Energy Institute (NEI) surveys conducted in 2004 and 2005, the nuclear industry is facing a critical shortage of workers over the next five years (from 2006–11). The survey found that nuclear energy companies might lose an estimated 23,000 workers during this period, representing 40 percent of all jobs in the sector. Nearly half of industry employees were found to be over 47 years old and only 8 percent were younger than 32.

However, as of the present there is no growth in the industry as there has been no new nuclear reactor plant construction for years (due to public fears over the dangers inherent in nuclear energy and mirrored in government regulations). Therefore, the number of jobs nationally for nuclear power plant operators is expected to decline through the year 2012. Power utilities generally are restructuring operations to cut costs and compete effectively. As a result, they are reducing the number of jobs at all levels. In addition, the increasing use of automatic controls to handle many of the nuclear power control room operations should diminish the necessity for Nuclear Reactor Operators. Yet, despite the decline, job openings will occur as workers retire or leave their current employment at nuclear power facilities.

Advancement Prospects

Career advancement to positions as Nuclear Reactor Operators for Auxiliary Nuclear Reactor Operators can come only with the acquisition of a nuclear operating license from the Nuclear Regulatory Commission (NRC). In turn, Nuclear Reactor Operators must have four or more years' on-the-job experience before even applying for a certification as a Senior Reactor Operator. Individuals who meet the experience and education requirements enroll in a 12- to 16-month licensed operator training program at the company. Training programs typically include instruction and testing in generic fundamentals (such as reactor physics, heat transfer, thermodynamics, and fluid flow) and instruction on plant systems, integrated operations, transient and accident analysis, and procedures.

Each candidate for either license or certification must take a rigorous examination, which includes a five-hour written test, an in-plant walk through, and demonstration of expertise on a simulator. Upon passing these tests, the candidate receives a license from the NRC that allows the individual to operate (or to supervise those who operate) the controls of the nuclear plant facility.

Senior Reactor Operators with nine to 12 years of experience may decide to advance to higher management levels within the power plant company or to the business management of the plant when, and if, vacancies occur. The positive aspect is that nearly all advancement within the nuclear power industry comes from within, rather than hiring from without.

Education and Training

The minimum requirement for Auxiliary Nuclear Reactor Operators is a high school diploma, with a heavy concentration on mathematics and physics, and a minimum of two years experience in the operation of power plant equipment. Many nuclear power plant owners prefer candidates to have a four-year college degree as well. College courses or experience in mechanical or technical jobs is usually beneficial for employment.

Training as a nuclear technician (gained while serving in the U.S. Navy or while working as a technician in a nuclear power plant) can provide the experience necessary for nuclear reactor operational work. In addition, nuclear power plant employers increasingly require solid computer expertise. Nuclear power plant operators must also meet the requirements of Nuclear Regulatory Commission (NRC) psychological, drug, alcohol, and medical testing policies and/or regulations.

Special Requirements

American nuclear power plants require Nuclear Reactor Operators to be fully trained and examined on all aspects of their position before they can do any part of their duties. Usually all tasks of the work area must be mastered and demonstrated to a supervisor in order to achieve certification for an operator's post. The nuclear power plant also certifies equipment operators and shift technical advisers. Shift supervisors are licensed Senior Reactor Operators who are certified to perform the higher-level duties of shift supervisor. Usually, it is the nuclear power plant's vice president for nuclear operations who approves shift supervisor certification.

Furthermore, Nuclear Reactor Operators and Senior Reactor Operators (but usually not Auxiliary Reactor Operators) must be licensed by the federal government through the United States Nuclear Regulatory Commission (NRC) before operating reactor or nuclear safety systems. Licenses from the NRC expire six years after the date of issuance or upon termination of employment with the nuclear facility. The renewal process requires applicants to provide written evidence of their experience under the existing license, a certification from the facility that the applicant is a safe and competent performer who has satisfactorily completed the re-qualification program for the facility, and certification that the applicant's medical condition and general health are satisfactory.

Finally, the NRC requires all nuclear plant employees and contractor employees to pass drug and alcohol screening tests, psychological evaluations, and background checks into such areas as former employment, education records, criminal records, and credit histories.

Experience, Skills, and Personality Traits

Nuclear Reactor Operators must have a strong sense of responsibility and a high personal initiative. They need good oral, written, and interpersonal skills, and their computer abilities must be strong. They should have good mechanical talents, have good hand-eye coordination, and be able to read piping and instrument diagrams. They must be knowledgeable of federal and state rules and regulations governing the operation, maintenance, and licensing of nuclear reactors. In addition, Nuclear Reactor Operators will have to gain supervisory skills and the ability to organize/schedule the labor of other workers to advance to positions as Senior Reactor Operators.

Unions and Associations

Associations of interest for Nuclear Reactor Operators include the American Nuclear Society (ANS), the North American Young Generation in Nuclear (NA-YGN), and the Professional Reactor Operator Society (NUCPROS).

Tips for Entry

1. During high school look into summer work programs or internships (which are usually non-paying) in power plant environments to gain experience in handling power plant equipment and to understand their complex control systems.
2. After high school (or college), consider enlisting in the U.S. Navy, which has excellent training programs for nuclear professionals. What you learn can be translated directly into work within nuclear reactor power plant environments.
3. Along with your concentrated studies in science and math, take a technical writing course and a speech class, both of which will aid you in your communication skills that you will apply to your duties as a Nuclear Reactor Operator.

NUCLEAR RESEARCH TECHNICIANS AND OPERATORS

ACCELERATOR OPERATOR

CAREER PROFILE

Duties: Working with nuclear physicists, control the operation of the particle accelerator used in research experiments involving properties of subatomic particles and in the study of the nucleus of the atom

Alternate Title(s): None

Salary Range: $25,000 to $70,000 or more

Employment Prospects: Fair to Good

Advancement Prospects: Good

Prerequisites:

Education or Training—High school degree minimum requirement, with heavy concentration on physics and mathematics; Bachelor of Science degree in physics or nuclear engineering recommended

Experience—Two to three years of related work experience (in nuclear industry) usually required

Special Skills and Personality Traits—Effective communication skills, both verbal and written; highly motivated with excellent interpersonal and leadership abilities; mechanical proficiency and ability to understand complex operation systems; solid computer skills

Special Requirements—Licensing as an Accelerator Operator fully trained in radiation safety is required

CAREER LADDER

```
┌─────────────────────────────────┐
│ Accelerator Supervisory Crew Chief; │
│   Nuclear Laboratory Positions;    │
│        Nuclear Engineer            │
└─────────────────────────────────┘

┌─────────────────────────────────┐
│       Accelerator Operator        │
└─────────────────────────────────┘

┌─────────────────────────────────┐
│   Accelerator Operator Trainee;   │
│       Nuclear Technician          │
└─────────────────────────────────┘
```

Position Description

Particle accelerators are large pieces of equipment used to accelerate and study subatomic particles. An accelerator usually consists of a vacuum chamber surrounded by a long sequence of vacuum pumps, magnets, radio-frequency cavities, high voltage instruments, and electronic circuits. The vacuum chamber is a metal pipe where air is pumped out to make the residual pressure as low as possible. Inside the large pipe, particles are accelerated by electric fields. Powerful amplifiers provide intense radio waves that are fed into resonating structures. Each time the particles traverse these structures in the pipe, some of the energy of the radio wave is transferred to them, and they are accelerated. Thus, accelerators give high energy to the subatomic particles when they collide with targets. Out of this interaction come many other subatomic particles that pass into detectors. From the information gathered in the detectors, nuclear physicists and their assistants can determine properties of the particles and their interactions. The higher the energy of the accelerated particles, the more closely the structure of matter can be probed. For this reason, a major goal of accelerator researchers is to produce higher and higher particle energies.

Particle accelerators come in two basic designs, linear (linac) and circular (synchrotron). The longer a linac is, the higher the energy of the particles it can produce. A synchrotron achieves high energy by circulating particles many times before they hit their targets. Accelerators are used in medical research as well as in physics research. The study of how high-energy particles interact with their targets and the resultant energy produced has a direct applicability to the design of nuclear reactors and higher energy output.

Accelerator operators are responsible for the operation of the accelerator. They review the schedule for experiments being done on the accelerator to ascertain the particle beam parameters specified by the physicist experimenters, such as energy, intensity, and repetition rate. They supervise accelerator maintenance personnel to ensure the readiness of support systems, such as vacuum, water-cooling, and radiofrequency power sources. They set the control panel switches—according to strict standard procedures—to route electric power from the source and direct the particle beam through the injector unit. They turn panel controls and watch meters and panel lights to adjust the beam steering units and direct the beam to the accelerator. They are responsible for pushing the console buttons in a prescribed sequence to control the beam path in the accelerator. They adjust controls to increase the beam pulse rate, energy, and intensity according to the specified levels for the particular experiment.

When the beam parameters meet those specifications, Accelerator Operators notify the physicist experimenter in the target control room, and then push the control levers that steer the beam to the experimenter's target, as directed. They monitor readings at their console during the experiment to ensure that the accelerator systems meet specifications, notifying the experimenter of any change in conditions. They may alter the beam parameters during the experiment based on the experimenter's instructions. They log in all data relative to beam specifications, equipment settings used, and beam conditions for future reference.

During this process, they identify any equipment malfunctions, and assist in the diagnosis/correction of such malfunctions. They ensure that maintenance workers have vacated any hazardous locations before operations are begun. As a member of the team of nuclear research operators, they participate in maintenance and modification of systems, and are a source of information on the operation of the accelerator equipment. In addition, those operators with programming skills frequently are asked to develop control applications and create software designed to enhance machine operations due to their expertise in the day-to-day operation of the accelerator. Finally, safety conditions during all accelerator operations rest with the senior or primary Accelerator Operator (sometimes called the accelerator operations manager), who is also usually in charge of all operator training. The safe functioning of the accelerator facility is achieved by strict adherence to a combination of engineering and administrative controls derived from standards set by the industry, Department of Energy (DOE) directives, and federal safety and health laws.

Salaries

According to a salary study made by PayScale, Inc., median annual salaries for nuclear technicians (including Accelerator Operators) in November 2006 ranged from $42,000 to $70,000 or more, dependent on geographic locale and on longevity in the position. Beginning salaries for trainees in this post ranged from $25,000 to $30,000, and the highest median yearly salaries of $80,000 or more were for those with 10 to 19 years experience.

Employment Prospects

According to the U.S. Bureau of Labor Statistics, overall employment of science technicians is expected to increase about as fast as average for all occupations through the year 2014. There is a need for trained and experienced Accelerator Operators at every nuclear research laboratory that uses an accelerator. The position can be approached as a full career, but frequently it is used as a stepping-stone to other vocations in the nuclear industry, so vacancies occur on a regular basis.

Advancement Prospects

As Accelerator Operators gain experience and move from trainee status to more difficult tasks, they may decide to aim at becoming supervisors of other technicians and operators. (The position of crew chief at some installations is a respected supervisory position, particularly as they are usually responsible for any safety issues that might happen on site during their shift.) Instead, some may decide to use their post to advance to other positions within the nuclear laboratory in which they work, or outside it in other nuclear facilities. Others may choose to pursue additional education and training and become nuclear engineers. In any of these situations, training and experience as an Accelerator Operator provides an excellent background for a variety of careers within the nuclear industry.

Education and Training

The minimum educational requirement is a high school degree with a heavy concentration on science courses (particularly physics) and mathematics. Recommended course work includes basic engineering, mathematics, and related scientific subject matter comparable to the technical content of a four-year post-secondary school curriculum. A Bachelor of Science degree in physics or engineering is a viable alternative. Training in U.S. Navy nuclear installations may be considered sufficient experience to substitute for a college degree.

Accelerator Operators usually start as trainees in routine jobs and learn how to operate the accelerator under the guidance of an experienced technician or a nuclear scientist. Training will include learning how to monitor accelerator and accelerator beamline performance and document the system data as required. As they gain expertise (usually over a period of one to two years), they typically take on more difficult tasks (such as identifying potential accelerator problems) and, in time, carry out their duties under only general supervision.

Special Requirements

Most states require Accelerator Operators to be licensed and trained in all relevant radiation safety regulations. They usually also require periodic refresher training for all Accelerator Operators regardless of seniority.

Experience, Skills, and Personality Traits

Besides their educational background in physics, engineering, and math, Accelerator Operators need to have excellent computer skills. They should have a working knowledge of Microsoft Windows and basic Windows applications. At times, operators with outstanding programming skills may be qualified to develop some control applications and create software that enhances accelerator operations. Some laboratories have utilized programs written by such operator-programmers to improve machine efficiency and beam availability, as well as develop applications for information distribution throughout the facility.

Accelerator Operators also must possess leadership talents and have solid communication capabilities in order to interact effectively with operations support staff and the nuclear physicists who are conducting experiments using the accelerator. Operators need strong written communication skills to provide accurate and concise documentation of operations activities. They should be able to use hand and machine tools and be mechanically inclined, in order to perform the necessary tasks related to operation and maintenance of accelerators and accelerator beamlines. They need to have a basic familiarity with the physics theories that underlie the performance of the accelerator and develop an understanding of the complex operating systems involved. They have to develop an instinct for anticipating difficulties and an ability to identify standard hardware failures.

Accelerator Operators must pay close attention to detail and exhibit an extreme amount of patience and persistence in their duties. In addition, they must be aware of all safety protocols and regulations set by the nuclear industry and the federal government.

Unions and Associations

The primary national association of interest for Accelerator Operators is the American Nuclear Society (ANS).

Tips for Entry

1. While in high school and concentrating on basic science courses (particularly physics) and mathematics, also take some technical writing and speech classes to develop and enhance your communication skills.

2. Expand your computer proficiency beyond Microsoft Word to scripting languages and development tools such as Perl and VBScript to enhance your job application potential.

3. Search for summer work programs or internship assignments with manufacturing companies to gain mechanical experience in handling tools and working with the controls of operational equipment.

HOT-CELL TECHNICIAN

CAREER PROFILE

Duties: Operate remote-controlled equipment in a hot cell to conduct metallurgical and chemical tests on radioactive materials to obtain data relating to the effects of radiation to aid nuclear scientists and researchers

Alternate Title(s): Irradiation Technician

Salary Range: $25,000 to $55,000 or more

Employment Prospects: Poor to Fair

Advancement Prospects: Fair

Prerequisites:

Education or Training—High school graduate with concentration on the sciences and mathematics; two to four years of college recommended

Experience—Some relevant experience in jobs involving radiation (such as U.S. Navy service); other technical training done on the job

Special Skills and Personality Traits—Ability to sustain a long span of attention and follow instructions precisely; excellent scientific and mathematical aptitude; good hand-to-eye coordination and manual dexterity; mechanical ability; physical strength; computer proficiency

Special Requirements—Certification or licensing seldom required; government security clearance usually required

CAREER LADDER

Laboratory Lead Technician; Nuclear Engineer

Hot-Cell Technician

Nuclear Technician Trainee

Position Description

A hot cell is a heavily shielded room (usually with walls of concrete or metal that are a meter or more in thickness) in which radioactive materials can be handled remotely using robotic or otherwise remote manipulators and viewed through specially shielded windows. Hot cells are employed to inspect spent nuclear fuel rods and to work with other items that are high-energy gamma ray emitters. Hot cells are used to test methods of treating radioactive waste by removing the most toxic elements to reduce overall toxicity, fissile content, and volume before being placed into permanent disposal containers for an underground repository. Hot cells are also used to provide a simple, efficient, and safe way for the transfer of radioactive waste from a transfer cask to the

large shipping containers used for shipment to the waste's final repository off site.

Hot-Cell Technicians operate the remote-controlled equipment employed in the hot cell. They control the slave (or robotic) manipulators from outside the cell to remove metal or chemical material from shielded containers inside the hot cell, placing the material on a bench or equipment work station within the hot cell. They test the chemical or metallurgical properties of materials according to standardized procedures, and observe the reactions to the testing through the protective cell window. They set up and operate machines to cut, lap, and polish test pieces, following blueprints, X-ray negatives, and sketches.

Hot-Cell Technicians test physical properties of irradiated materials, using equipment, such as tensile testers, hardness testers, metallographic units, micrometers, and gauges. They immerse test samples in chemical compounds to prepare them for testing. They place irradiated nuclear fuel materials in environmental chambers within the hot cell to check reactions to temperature changes. They perform mechanical (using lathe, cutters, drills, and other equipment within the hot cell), metallurgical, and chemical processing of radioactive materials. Throughout all their testing, they record results for further analysis by nuclear engineers and scientists.

They place specimens used in shielded containers for removal from the hot cell by using manipulators controlled by them from outside the hot cell. They participate in the cleaning and decontamination of the hot cell during periods of maintenance shutdown. They may devise (or modify existing) adapters and fixtures used in the hot cell operations, and may supply technical support to engineering and scientific personnel relative to work done within the hot cell. They normally interface with facility supervisors, work associates, and others requesting support services at the facility. They usually labor with minimum supervision, exercising independent judgment relative to the techniques and methods employed in hot cell processes and experiments.

Salaries
According to industry sources, median earnings for Hot-Cell Technicians range from beginning salaries for technicians with one to four years' experience of $14 an hour (or about $29,000 annually) to over $29 an hour (or $60,000 or more annually) for technicians with 15 or more years of experience.

Employment Prospects
Hot-Cell Technicians are employed mainly by government agencies, academic and industrial research centers, military installations, and nuclear power plants. With the uncertainty about the future of nuclear power in the United States, the employment situation is poor to fair. There is a slow overall job market for nuclear technicians in general. Hiring will be mostly to replace present workers who leave the labor force or change careers. Still, some positions require specific types of specialized experience, such as Hot-Cell Technicians, and are difficult to fill because qualified technicians are scarce.

Advancement Prospects
Hot-Cell Technicians with some college background and years of experience in their post can be promoted to senior and lead technician status at their facilities. Seasoned technicians with a Bachelor of Science (B.S.) degree may decide to become nuclear engineers, with a number of career

options thus opening up for them. Some employers may pay job-related educational costs, while a few others may even offer work-study plans.

Education and Training
The minimum requirement is high school graduation with a very heavy emphasis on courses in the sciences and mathematics, supplemented by some amount of relevant experience. U.S. Navy service in nuclear submarines, with their extensive training programs, usually proves to be a very adequate substitute for advanced education. Nonetheless, many employers and facilities prefer nuclear technician trainees to have had two to four years of college as well. In addition, technical training is accomplished on the job, and is supplemented with classroom teaching.

Special Requirements
Hot-Cell Technicians usually are required to pass a security background investigation, with security screening and drug testing.

Experience, Skills, and Personality Traits
At the very least, some vocational and demonstrable experience (at least two to four years) as a mechanical technician is usually required. Direct experience with nuclear facilities is a plus. Hot-Cell Technicians need to have a facility with general machine tool usage, and forklift and crane experience would be directly transferable to their work as technicians manipulating equipment within hot cells.

They should have scientific and mathematical aptitude as well as mechanical abilities, and their computer skills should be exemplary. Their manual and finger dexterity must be excellent. They should be physically fit and used to prolonged periods of standing while working. They need to have a long span of attention, be highly detail-oriented, and be able to follow instructions exactly.

Hot-Cell Technicians should be qualified, or be able to be qualified, in the use of normal radiological protective clothing and respiratory protective equipment and thus be able to work in a radioactive environment using this necessary protective equipment.

Unions and Associations
The primary association of interest for all nuclear technicians, including Hot-Cell Technicians, is the American Nuclear Society (ANS). Some technicians may also affiliate with one or more craft unions.

Tips for Entry
1. A summer job in a laboratory is an excellent experience for working later as a nuclear research technician.

2. Consider joining the U.S. Armed Forces, as many branches train and employ nuclear technicians and provide excellent experience for individuals seeking nuclear research jobs.
3. While completing a science technology program in high school, take advantage of any chance to work as an intern, preferably within the nuclear industry or at a research laboratory. This experience will be very helpful for gaining a job as a nuclear research technician.

OTHER NUCLEAR RESEARCH OPERATORS

CAREER PROFILE

Duties: <u>Gamma-Facilities Operator</u>: Controls gamma radiation equipment to irradiate materials for scientific research; <u>Radioisotope-Production Operator</u>: Controls laboratory compounding equipment enclosed in protective hot cell to prepare radioisotopes and other radioactive materials for use as tracers for biological, biomedical, physiological, and industrial purposes; <u>Test-and-Research Reactor Operator</u>: Controls operation of nuclear reactor to create fissionable materials used for research purposes

Alternate Title(s): <u>Gamma-Facilities Operator</u>: Pile Operator; <u>Radioisotope-Production Operator</u>: Isotope-Production Technician; <u>Test-and-Research Reactor Operator</u>: Nuclear Equipment Operation Technician

Salary Range: $30,000 to $80,000 or more

Employment Prospects: Fair to Good

Advancement Prospects: Fair

Prerequisites:

Education or Training—High school diploma required, with strong emphasis on science and mathematics; two-year associate's degree in applied science or science-applied technology recommended; specialized nuclear training may be substituted for associate's degree

Experience—Laboratory experience necessary, preferably at a nuclear facility; demonstrable experience as a mechanical technician usually required

Special Skills and Personality Traits—Able to work under pressure and to make fast and accurate decisions; detail-oriented; good communication and computer skills; mechanically adept; physically fit and able to sustain prolonged periods of standing or sitting while working

Special Requirements—Licensing by the Nuclear Regulatory Commission (NRC) not usually required, except at government laboratories and facilities

CAREER LADDER

| Senior Technician; Nuclear Engineer |

| Other Nuclear Research Operators |

| Nuclear Technician Trainee |

Position Description

Nuclear technicians are members of project teams that assist nuclear engineers and scientists in the servicing and maintenance of various types of existing nuclear facilities and in the research and development of new facilities. They may be involved with defense or medical applications, or function as reactor or accelerator systems operators at existing power, defense, or medical facilities.

Working under the general direction of nuclear engineers, nuclear technicians set up tests, install instruments, operate reactors, and assist crafts workers in the construction of monitoring equipment for fissionable materials and experimental models of nuclear devices and facilities. They use remote-controlled hand tools as well as oscilloscopes, ammeters, voltmeters, and electronic counters in their work and follow extremely rigid safety precautions at all times.

Gamma-Facilities Operators are responsible for testing materials for scientific research by using irradiation. They insert capsules of materials to be irradiated into tubes leading to the core of a nuclear reactor by the use of an extension tool that they control remotely from outside the facility. They compute radiation time and dosage for each experiment, and the gamma intensities required at various distances from the grid, using standard formulas, conversion tables, and a slide rule. They submit this data to their supervisor and the science experimenter for review.

During the experiment, they tend to the cutoff saw, mounted on the water-filled canal floor (as a radiation shield). This saw cuts the fuel elements to size to be fitted into the shielding boxes by extension tools. They place the fuel elements in geometric configurations around the tube in the gamma facility, according to radiation intensity specifications. They then lower the experimental materials, such as foods, plastics, or metal, into the tube to subject the material to irradiation for the specified and approved amount of time. Upon completion, they lower the extension tool into the floor of the canal and transfer materials, as well as the spent nuclear fuel elements discharged from the reactor, to storage areas on the canal floor or into casks for subsequent shipment. They write summaries of the irradiation activities performed to be submitted to their supervisor and to the experiment clients. During the process, the operators monitor the instruments/gauges that control the heating, ventilating, seam, and water systems, as well as the instruments that record the gamma intensity, temperatures of the experiments, and the state of the fuel elements in the canal.

Radioisotope-Production Operators are responsible for controlling laboratory-compounding equipment, enclosed in protective hot cells that prepare radioisotopes and other radioactive materials for use as tracers in biological, biomedical, physiological, and industrial standardized procedures. They place specified amounts of chemicals into a special container to be irradiated within a nuclear reactor or by other irradiation equipment. They secure vacuum pump heads to the outlet valve on the container to replace the air with inert gas, and they route the container to the irradiation facility.

Once the chemicals are irradiated and placed into their shielded cell, Radioisotope-Production Operators move manipulating devices to open the container and transfer the irradiated contents into a glass vessel. They open pneumatic valves or use the manipulators to add specified types and quantities of chemical reagents into the glass vessel (according to the specified instructions for the experiment) to produce the radioactive product. They control the manipulators to pour the irradiated liquids required to perform standard chemical analyses. They then withdraw the radioactive sample, filling the shipping container inside the cell with the prescribed quantity of radioisotope material for transportation to a chemical laboratory for analysis once the sample is approved by the supervisor and the experiment client.

Test-and-Research Reactor Operators control the operation of a nuclear reactor in the creation of fissionable materials employed for research purposes, for studying the structure of atoms, or to determine the properties of specific materials. They position field elements (usually uranium) and the object to be irradiated into place in the reactor core by the use of slave manipulating devices attached to the reactor. From mockups, blueprints, and wiring and instrumentation diagrams, they install instrumentation leads in the core to measure the operating temperature and pressure in the reactor. They activate the reactor and insert the object to be irradiated into a pneumatic tube (called a rabbit tube), a beam hole, or an irradiation tunnel according to the size of the object and the nature of the experiment.

During the process, they monitor instruments at the console and reactor panels to control the nuclear chain reaction, following the directions of the nuclear experimenters. They calculate applicable limits of operating factors, such as temperature and pressure, using standard formulas, and adjust controls to maintain operating conditions, such as power level, airflow and waterflow, temperature, and radiation and neutron levels within the reactor. They record the experimental data, such as type of material irradiated, exposure time, the reactor pile atmospheric conditions, and the position of the control rods in the nuclear core. At the end, they disassemble reactor parts, such as the core plug (shield) and the control rods, using both a crane and handtools. They lift spent fuel elements and irradiated objects from the core, using extension tools, and drop them through a chute into the reactor's canal for possible recovery of fissionable material or disposal. They often work as a member of a team, alternating between operating the reactor controls and monitoring the instruments, gauges, and other recording devices in the facility's control room.

Salaries

According to a salary study of nuclear technicians conducted by PayScale, Inc., median annual salaries in 2006 ranged from $55,000 for technicians with one to four years' experience to over $80,000 for those with 10 to 19 years experience. The U.S. Bureau of Labor Statistics compiled wage data for the third quarter of the 2006 employment cost index for science technicians (which includes nuclear technicians). The study indicated that the average annual salary for science technicians was $62,317. The annual wage earnings ranged from a low of $30,472 to a high of $90,522, with the median annual salary being $63,648.

Employment Prospects

According to the U.S. Bureau of Labor Statistics, overall employment of science technicians is expected to increase about as fast as average for all occupations through the year 2014. Job opportunities are expected to be best for graduates of applied science technology programs who are well trained on nuclear research equipment used in industrial and government laboratories and production facilities. As the instrumentation and techniques utilized in industrial research and development become increasingly more complex, employers are seeking individuals with highly developed technical and communication skills.

Applicants interested in civil service positions should apply at Federal Job Information Centers, located in most major metropolitan areas. Other job seekers should apply directly to private employers engaged in research, design, and operation of nuclear facilities or to firms in nuclear medicine.

Advancement Prospects

Nuclear technicians usually begin work at laboratories or other research facilities in routine posts, under the direct supervision of a nuclear scientist or a more experienced technician. As technicians gain more experience, they typically take on more responsibilities under general supervision and may eventually become supervisors themselves. However, technicians employed at university research facilities often have their career advancement tied to those of particular professors. When that professors retire or leave, these technicians may face uncertain employment prospects.

Education and Training

Many employers of nuclear technicians prefer applicants who have at least two years of specialized training or an associate's degree in applied science or science-applied technology, preferably nuclear. Some technical and community colleges offer associate's degrees in the specific technology of nuclear science or a more general education in science and mathematics. Technical institutes usually offer technician training but include less theory and general education than do technical or community colleges. The length of programs at technical institutes varies, although one-year certificate programs and two-year associate's degree programs are common.

An applicant's educational background should emphasize science and math. Science courses taken beyond high school, in an associate's or bachelor's degree program, should be laboratory-oriented, with an emphasis on bench skills. A solid background in applied basic chemistry, phys-

ics, and math is vital. Technicians can acquire good career preparation through two-year formal training programs that combine the teaching of scientific principles and theory with practical hands-on application in a laboratory setting with up-to-date equipment. Training experience can also be gained by service in the Navy or other branches of the U.S. Armed Forces by enrolling in their nuclear technician training programs.

Special Requirements

While licensing by the Nuclear Regulatory Commission (NRC) is not usually required (except at United States government facilities), many nuclear technicians must be able to pass security background investigation/security screening and drug testing. Some employers may require a current Department of Defense (DOD) security clearance.

Experience, Skills, and Personality Traits

Nuclear technicians must be highly organized and detail-oriented, have good communication skills, and be able to work well as a team member. They will need to write accurate summaries of their activities and methodically record experimental data. Their physical activities may range from sedentary gauge monitoring to mechanical facility of handling equipment in awkward or cumbersome circumstances. They must have good vision, depth perception, and color discrimination. They need to be mechanically adept at using their hands or fingers to grasp, move, or assemble small objects, as well as to make quick, precise adjustments to machine controls. They must be able to work under great pressure and be conditioned to make fast, accurate decisions and adapt to rapidly changing situations where there is no room for error.

Nuclear technicians will need to monitor instruments, gauges, and recording devices during the operation of nuclear equipment, under the direction of nuclear experimenters. They must calculate equipment-operating factors, such as radiation times, dosages, temperatures, gamma intensities, and pressure, using standard formulas and conversion tables. Because computers are employed so extensively in all types of research and development laboratories, technicians should have strong computer skills, especially in computer modeling.

Unions and Associations

Some nuclear technicians may be members of the Utility Workers Union of America, or the AFL-CIO Division of Oil, Chemical, and Atomic Workers, while others may affiliate with other craft unions.

Major professional associations of interest to nuclear technicians include the American Nuclear Society (ANS) and the North American Young Generation in Nuclear (NA-YGN) Association.

Tips for Entry

1. While in high school, or while obtaining your associate's degree, a summer job in a laboratory is an excellent background experience for a nuclear laboratory research technician.
2. While completing your science technology program, you may have a chance to work as an intern, which likely will prove to be valuable experience for getting a job as a nuclear technician.
3. For scholarships, fellowships, and research grants available from the U.S. government, consult the Department of Energy (DOE) Office of Nuclear Energy, Science and Technology, available online at http://www.ne.doe.gov.

OIL AND NATURAL GAS INDUSTRIES

BUSINESS OPERATIONS

ACCOUNTANT

CAREER PROFILE

Duties: Apply principles of accounting to analyze financial data, prepare financial reports, estimate future revenues and expenditures for preparation of budgets, provide detailed cost information on business activity, and maintain record of company-owned or leased equipment, buildings, and other property

Alternate Title(s): Budget Accountant; Cost Accountant; Management Accountant; Property Accountant

Salary Range: $30,000 to $80,000 or more

Employment Prospects: Good

Advancement Prospects: Fair

Prerequisites:

Education or Training—Bachelor's degree in accounting or a related field is a requirement; a master's degree in accounting or a master's degree in business administration with a concentration in accounting may be necessary as well

Experience—Previous background in accounting or auditing, usually through summer or part-time internship programs is helpful

Special Skills and Personality Traits—Capacity for deductive reasoning and meticulous presentation of information; excellent math talents; exceptional written and oral communication abilities; outstanding computer skills; understanding of business operations, trends, revenues, record keeping, and costs

Special Requirements—Licensing and certification required

CAREER LADDER

Corporate Financial Officer (CFO); Financial Manager; Independent Certified Public Accountant

Accountant

Accounting Clerk; Auditing Clerk; Bookkeeper

Position Description

Accountants apply principles of the accounting trade to analyze financial data and prepare reports. They compile and analyze fiscal information detailing assets, liabilities, and capital and prepare balance sheets, profit and loss statements, and other documentation to summarize the current and projected financial position of companies. They audit contracts, orders, and vouchers, preparing reports to substantiate individual transactions prior to settlement. They frequently are responsible for creating budgets by analyzing past and present financial operations, as well as estimates of

future revenues and expenditures. To do this, they scrutinize records of present and past operations, trends and costs, estimated and realized revenues, administrative commitments, and future project development and expansions to develop realistic budgets for top management to review. They may maintain budgeting systems which provide a control over expenditures made to carry out such business activities as advertising and marketing, production, maintenance, or specific project activities (such as construction). They advise management on budget matters, such as effective use of resources and assumptions underlying budget forecasts.

Accountants are responsible for cost projections and reports analyzing changes in product design, raw materials, manufacturing methods, or services provided to determine their effect on costs. They analyze actual costs and prepare periodic reports comparing standard industry expenditures to the actual costs entailed by the company. They provide upper management with presentations specifying and comparing factors affecting prices and profitability of products or services.

Accountants may also keep records of company-owned or leased equipment, buildings, and other property, documenting their description, value, location, and other pertinent information. They conduct periodic inventories to keep records current, ensure that equipment is properly maintained, and distribute cost of maintenance to appropriate accounts. They examine all pertinent records to determine that acquisition, sale, retirement, and other entries have been made properly and prepare statements reflecting monthly appreciated and depreciated values. They prepare annual statements for income tax purposes and may specialize in appraisal and evaluation of real property or equipment for sale, acquisition, or tax purposes.

Today's oil and gas companies usually are involved in four different types of functions or segments: exploration and production (E&P), transportation, refining and gas processing, and marketing/distribution. Financing and accounting in the oil and gas industry is challenged by the constant changes from within the business, coupled with the industry's extremely high levels of speculative investment in which there is no guarantee of a successful return on expenditures. It is also characterized by lengthy periods between the initial investment and any returns, which in and of itself attracts many regulatory accounting rules/standards. In addition, many oil and gas wells are operated in a joint venture, with multiple owners, operators, and interests. Companies can have wells in different counties and states, on private land, or land owned by state or federal agencies. All of this means that tax rates can be different for wells just a few miles apart.

Accountants for the industry must take into account the financial management implications of exploring/producing oil and gas, the financing of energy projects, and the strategic/enterprise risk management decision-making processes of the industry. They need to understand how the results of financial prospects in an oil and gas company are measured/reported through special accounting procedures. Commonly, four different types of accounting books are maintained to more easily identify and classify costs: pre-drilling, drilling, development, and production and other costs. Accountants must be familiar with various accounting processes: calculating different methods of depreciation for assets; differentiating capital versus operating leases; the criteria used for capitalization and expense in the industry; consolidating subsidiaries of less than 100 percent ownership; the accounting for joint ventures and joint operating agreements (JOA); the use of contractual accounting records such as

production sharing agreements (PSA); various inventory valuation methods; and the disposition of long-term assets.

Accountants must be knowledgeable of the legal requirements governing the content/style of annual reports, stock market expectations on financial disclosures made within them, and such other relevant issues as the reporting of forward sales, areas of interest, cash flows, borrowing and repayment schedules, contingent liabilities, environmental expenditures, and auditor comments. Accountants are usually involved in the development of other reports, such as those to shareholders, to lenders and financial institutions, and to the stock exchange.

Oil and gas industry Accountants need to be familiar with the generally accepted accounting principles of different countries. They will have to know how to classify oil and gas reserves for financial purposes, know how intangible drilling costs are treated, and understand the role of International Financial Reporting Standards (IFRS) and International Accounting Standards (IAS) in today's energy environment. They must be conversant with the specifics of the accounting procedural reforms legislated by the U.S. Congress in the Sarbanes-Oxley Act of 2002, governing procedures for auditor independence, corporate administration, and enhanced financial disclosure, as well as what effect compliance with the regulations will have on all personnel and internal accounting and auditing controls within the company. In addition, they must be thoroughly knowledgeable about the specific types of taxes relating to the oil and gas industry and the timing of payments to different taxing authorities.

Salaries

According to a 2005 salary survey conducted by Robert Half International, a staffing services firm specializing in accounting and finance, accountants with up to one year of experience earned between $28,250 and $45,000 annually. Those with one to three years of experience earned between $33,000 and $52,000. Senior accountants had incomes between $40,750 and $69,750, financial managers between $48,000 and $90,000, and directors of accounting between $64,750 and $200,750. The large variation in salaries reflects differences in size of the firm, location, level of education, and the accountant's professional credentials.

Furthermore, according to a salary survey conducted by the National Association of Colleges and Employers, bachelor's degree candidates in accounting received starting offers averaging $43,269 a year in 2005, and master's degree candidates in accounting were offered $46,251 initially. Jeff Bush, president of Denver-based CSI Recruiting, a recruiter company for the oil and gas industry, points out that salaries for accountants have risen 10 to 20 percent in the last five years to reflect the lack of qualified accountants. He states that those with a minimum of five years' experience can command a base salary of between $55,000 and $75,000 a year.

Employment Prospects

According to the U.S. Bureau of Labor Statistics' *Occupational Outlook Handbook, 2006–07 Edition*, employment of accountants (and auditors) is expected to grow faster than average for all occupations through the year 2014. This is particularly true for the booming oil and gas industry.

According to a 2004 survey conducted by the American Petroleum Institute (API), the average employee in the oil and gas industry is 49, among the oldest of any industry. Trade sources estimate that 42 percent of the industry's workforce (which includes Accountants) will reach retirement age within the next five years. As the industry has both its own jargon and its own accounting and financial complexities, it is not easy for Accountants from other fields to transition into this industry.

Advancement Prospects

Some Accountants may decide to advance further into the management of the companies for which they work, attaining jobs as financial directors or, even, becoming the chief financial officer (CFO). Others may choose to become independent accounting contractors by becoming Certified Public Accountants (CPAs), who provide their services both within and without the oil and natural gas industry.

Education and Training

Accountant positions require at least a bachelor's degree in accounting or a related field, and may require a master's degree in accounting or a master's degree in business administration with a concentration in accounting. In addition, professional recognition through certification or licensure provides a distinct advantage in the job market. The vast majority of states in the U.S. require certified public accountant (CPA) candidates to be college graduates.

Special Requirements

Accountants working in the oil and natural gas industry usually must be at least accredited in accountancy. Information on the Accredited in Accountancy, Accredited Business Accountant, Accredited Tax Advisor, or Accredited Tax Preparer designations may be obtained from the Accreditation Council for Accountancy and Taxation (http://www.acatcredentials.org).

Certifications include the Certified Public Accountant (CPA), the Certified Management Accountant (CMA), and the Certified Internal Auditor (CIA). Data about these certifications can be obtained from the American Institute of Certified Public Accountants (http://www.aicpa.org), the Institute of Management Accountants (http://www.imanet.org), the Institute of Internal Auditors (http://www.theiia.org), and the National Association of State Boards of Accountancy (http://www.nasba.org).

Experience, Skills, and Personality Traits

Previous experience in accounting can help an applicant gain a job. Such seasoning can be gained through summer or part-time internship programs conducted by public accounting or business firms. In addition, practical knowledge of computers is a great asset. Accountants in the oil and natural gas industry should be aware of standard accounting software (such as billing software, Intuit QuickBooks, and Sage CPA Client Checkbook and Practice Manager), as well as specialized tax and property tax compliance software, enterprise resource planning (ERP) software, financial analysis software, and tax preparation programs.

Accountants need to have a thorough knowledge of mathematics, have a facility of dealing with numbers, and understand standard economic and accounting principles/practices. They must understand the financial markets, banking, and the analysis/reporting of financial data. They must be able to solve complex problems and have excellent decision-making abilities. Both their written and verbal communication skills must be exemplary. They should be able to work independently, perform well under pressure, and be able to interpret and explain complex data. They should have good deductive reasoning (ability to apply general rules to specific problems to produce answers that make sense) and information ordering (ability to arrange things in a certain order or pattern according to a specific set of rules). Their job requires immense concentration, attention to detail, and patience and persistence in gathering the necessary information to be provided in their reports. They will need excellent interpersonal skills to work with both upper management and department managers.

Unions and Associations

Associations of particular interest to Accountants in the oil and natural gas industry include the American Petroleum Institute (API), the Council of Petroleum Accountants Societies (COPAS), the Independent Petroleum Association of America (IPAA), and the Institute of Petroleum Accounting (IPA).

Tips for Entry

1. During college, search for specific accounting experience through summer or part-time internship programs offered by public accounting or business firms.
2. Consider obtaining a Certified Public Accountant (CPA) certificate as a boost to your professional career as an Accountant.
3. During college, take both writing and speech courses, as these skills will be necessary to your career as an Accountant.

COMPLIANCE MANAGER

CAREER PROFILE

Duties: Analyze and implement state, federal, and/or local requirements (including health, safety, and environmental) as necessary to maintain approved oil and natural gas exploration, extraction, production, and transportation

Alternate Title(s): Compliance Officer and Inspector; Environmental Compliance Manager; Health, Safety, and Environment Compliance Coordinator; Regulatory Compliance Officer

Salary Range: $35,000 to $60,000 or more

Employment Prospects: Fair to Good

Advancement Prospects: Fair

Prerequisites:

　Education or Training—High school degree mandatory; four-year college degree in a science or technology-related area required; usually long-term on-the-job training will be necessary

　Experience—Familiarity with, or part-time work in, the oil and natural gas industry

　Special Skills and Personality Traits—Able to work independently, as well as cooperatively with others; computer proficiency; exemplary record-keeping skills; good communication and time-management abilities;

　Special Requirements—State certification may be required

CAREER LADDER

```
┌─────────────────────────────────────┐
│ Consultant; Government Inspector;    │
│ Plant Manager or Other Supervisory   │
│ Position                             │
└─────────────────────────────────────┘

┌─────────────────────────────────────┐
│ Compliance Manager                   │
└─────────────────────────────────────┘

┌─────────────────────────────────────┐
│ Equipment Operator; Trainee,         │
│ Compliance Programs                  │
└─────────────────────────────────────┘
```

Position Description

There are four basic business strategies that most organizations in the energy industry follow: implement effective asset management procedures, ensure continued availability of resources, create strong investor confidence, and comply with extensive industry and regulatory requirements. For organizations that provide or distribute energy-related products (such as crude oil, refined petroleum, or natural gas), the cost of compliance is high, requires significant investments to meet requirements, and affects all points of these organizations. They face a growing burden of financial regulation as well as the need to comply with increasingly complex industry measures, from emissions trading schemes to benchmarks on the performance of networks and billing accuracy. The impact of meeting industry and legislative compliance requirements is as broad as it is deep.

For example, the guidelines from the U.S. Department of Labor's Occupational Health and Safety Administration (OSHA) have a significant impact on how oil and natural gas organizations deal with hazardous materials and how they ensure the safety of their employees. OSHA regulations require the implementation of a Process Safety Management (PSM) program, which requires immediate and accurate information delivered to employees pertaining to their job function or task. Changing regulations have an impact on corporate governance, placing responsibility on the employer to maintain up-to-date information. The same requirements apply to different layers of the organization, particularly safety for the production environment and governance for executive management. The relationship between employees and executives is linked through policy and procedures and is affected by business process, risk management, and document and record management, while effectiveness is measured by responsiveness to exceptions or problems.

Compliance Managers deal with a diverse set of matters, ranging from the environment to licensing to workers' rights. They examine, evaluate, and investigate their company's conformity with laws and regulations governing contract compliance of licenses and permits and other compliance and enforcement inspection activities, particularly those pertaining to health, safety, and environmental concerns. Most oil and natural gas companies' safety plans correspond to three easily identified risk areas: office, shop (machining and maintenance), and field (drilling, borehole, and exploration). While safety plans for office and shop environments are fairly standard, safety procedures related to oil and gas fieldwork are more specialized.

Compliance Managers examine all permits, licenses, applications and records of the company for which they work to ensure full compliance with all industry and governmental licensing requirements. They may interview employees to determine the nature of any suspected violations of regulations and to obtain evidence of any breach. They monitor follow-up actions in cases where violations were found and review all compliance monitoring reports. Working with environmental technicians and specialists, they perform laboratory and field tests to monitor a company's environment and investigate sources of pollution that may affect health and are clearly against regulations. Relying on their training and experience, they educate employees on safety and health requirements, regulations, rules, practices, and proper safety procedures specific to their job requirements to ensure compliance.

Compliance Managers undertake internal audits, walk-throughs, and reviews, keeping careful records. Some records are about their inspection results, while others document information, such as test or survey results. They prepare written, oral, tabular, and graphic reports summarizing requirements and regulations, including enforcement and chain of responsibility documentation. They enforce the use of safety equipment, identify potential causes for accidents, watch for noncompliance on the part of employees, and recommend changes in policies and procedures to prevent accidents and illness. They usually assist top management in preparation of safety and health budgets. Throughout, they must be adept at using software specifically designed to maintain records and the tracking of the disparate regulations, compliance permits, and policies, which makes their jobs of gathering and checking data or tracking multiple compliance reporting deadlines that much easier.

Salaries

Salary studies conducted by PayScale, Inc. (last updated as of December, 2006) found that the median annual salaries for environmental, health, and safety Compliance Managers ranged from $35,339 (starting salary) to over $60,000 for managers with 20 or more years of experience. Those managers with one to four years of experience had a median yearly income of $36,400, whereas those with five to nine years of experience earned $45,000 or more.

Employment Prospects

As the position of Compliance Manager is essential to the operation of all oil and natural gas companies (whether they are involved with exploration, production, or distribution), the prospects of employment are fair to good, dependent on the number of jobs available at any one instance. With the increased production of oil and gas for the energy needs of the United States (as well as the rest of the world), demand for trained and experienced Compliance Managers as part of the business operation of oil and gas companies is guaranteed.

Advancement Prospects

Experienced and successful Compliance Managers may be promoted to higher management posts within the company, such as a plant manager, or they may decide to become independent consultants to the industry. Some Compliance Managers may choose to take advantage of their background to work within any one of various government agencies, such as the Environmental Protection Agency (EPA) or the Department of Energy (DOE).

Education and Training

Both a high school diploma and a bachelor's degree (in biology, chemistry, physics, engineering, or a related technology field) from a four-year college or university is the usual requirement for this position. A higher degree, such as a master's degree in environmental science, is often suggested. While some training within the oil and gas industry is preferred, it may not always be necessary, as many employers provide formal training in areas such as safety and inspection procedures.

Special Requirements

In some states, Compliance Managers who are responsible for the environmental health of their company may be required to be registered and certified.

Experience, Skills, and Personality Traits

For most Compliance Managers, experience is gained by training on the job under the supervision of experienced compliance personnel. They must have excellent communication skills, both oral and written, and be very detail-oriented. They must have the ability to read, analyze, and interpret general business periodicals, professional journals, technical procedures, and governmental regulations, as well as write reports, business correspondence, and procedure manuals. They should be knowledgeable about basic word processing and spreadsheet software, and be able to learn programs that are specifically designed for record keeping, compiling compliance performance statistics, and streamlining the tracking of regulations, permits, and policies. They must be able to present information effectively and respond to questions from groups of managers, clients, customers, and the general public.

Unions and Associations

Associations of interest for Compliance Managers in the oil and gas industry include the American Petroleum Institute (API), the Independent Petroleum Association of America (IPAA), and the American Gas Association (AGA).

Tips for Entry

1. Mathematics and computer skills are important, as well as science and technology, but also include courses in business management and accounting, as well as drafting and blueprint reading.

2. Investigate summer programs or intern programs with oil and gas companies to gain firsthand experience in the processes/procedures of the industry.

3. Take health and safety education courses, as your knowledge and experience in this area will be crucial to one aspect of your job as a Compliance Manager.

CUSTOMER SERVICE REPRESENTATIVE

CAREER PROFILE

Duties: Interact with customers to provide information in response to inquiries about oil or gas company's products and services, as well as handle and resolve complaints

Alternate Title(s): Account Manager; Account Service Representative; Claims Service Representative; Client Services Representative; Customer Service Specialist; Member Services Representative

Salary Range: $18,000 to $45,000 or more

Employment Prospects: Excellent

Advancement Prospects: Fair to Good

Prerequisites:

Education or Training—Bachelor's degree usually required, though an associate's degree may be sufficient; some training in business administration and basic chemistry and physics helpful; bilingual skills useful

Experience—Business experience (one to five years) in oil and gas industry or related energy field may be necessary

Special Skills and Personality Traits—Ability to follow established guidelines, policies and procedures, and work closely with other departments or business units as necessary; excellent written and oral communication skills; good analytical, organizational, and problem-solving capabilities; interpersonal talents, including marketing and negotiation abilities; reliable computer skills

CAREER LADDER

```
┌─────────────────────────────────────┐
│  Supervisory or Managerial Positions;│
│  Product Development Director         │
└─────────────────────────────────────┘

┌─────────────────────────────────────┐
│  Customer Service Representative      │
└─────────────────────────────────────┘

┌─────────────────────────────────────┐
│  Sales or Marketing Assistant;        │
│  College Graduate                     │
└─────────────────────────────────────┘
```

Position Description

Customer Service Representatives are a company's direct point of contact with its customers. They are responsible for ensuring that these customers—who may be individual consumers or other companies—receive an adequate level of service or help with their questions and concerns. They interact with customers to provide information in response to inquiries about products/services and to handle and resolve complaints. They communicate with customers through a variety of means: by telephone, e-mail, fax, regular mail correspondence, or in person.

Many customer inquiries involve routine questions and requests. Obtaining the answers to such questions usually requires simply looking up data on a computer. Other queries, however, may be more involved, and may require additional research and further explanation on the part of the Customer Service Representative. In handling customers' complaints, Customer Service Representatives must attempt to resolve the problem according to the guidelines established by their company. These procedures may involve asking questions to determine the validity of a complaint, offering possible solutions, or providing customers with refunds, exchanges, or other offers (such as discounts or coupons).

In some cases, Customer Service Representatives are responsible for helping customers decide what types of products or services would best suit their needs. They may even aid customers in completing purchases or transactions. While their primary function is not sales, Customer Service Representatives may spend a part of their time with customers encouraging them to purchase additional products or services. They may also make changes or updates to a customer's profile or account information. They may process orders and inquiries and provide a communication link between customers and other company departments to ensure order completion. They may even handle order entry information, packaging and shipping instructions, and negotiate and execute returns and any warranty issues. They are usually required to keep records of transactions and may be responsible for updating and maintaining databases of customer information. Their records of their contacts with customers become the basis of their reports to their managers.

Customer Service Representatives within the oil and gas industry use their computers and telephones extensively. They frequently enter information into a computer as they are speaking to customers, accessing information so that they can answer specific queries relating to the customer's account or their other questions. The representative may also have to consult company guidelines for dealing with queries or complaints. Should they encounter a situation to which they do not know how to respond, they must consult their supervisor to determine the best course of action, and, if warranted, transfer the call to other personnel who may be better able to respond to the customer's needs.

Customer Service Representatives of the oil and gas industry need to be fully aware of the technical aspects of the business, the equipment used, and the methods of production, refining, and distribution. They must be conversant with all aspects of the particular area of the industry in which their company operates to be able to satisfy the needs/queries of their firm's customers.

Salaries

According to the U.S. Department of Labor's Bureau of Labor Statistics in their *Occupational Outlook Handbook, 2006–07 Edition*, the median annual earnings in May 2004 for Customer Service Representatives were $27,020. The middle 50 percent earned between $21,510 and $34,560. The lowest 10 percent received less that $17,680, while the highest 10 percent had incomes of more than $44,160.

In salary survey reports compiled by PayScale, Inc., in 2007 median yearly salaries of Customer Service Representatives ranged from $28,900 to $37,550. Senior Customer Service Representatives had annual salaries ranging from $32,000 to $50,000, depending on geographic location and years of experience.

Employment Prospects

According to the U.S. Department of Labor, prospects for obtaining a job as a Customer Service Representative are expected to be excellent and to increase faster than the average for all occupations through the year 2014. In addition to potential new openings occurring as companies in the oil and gas industry expand, numerous job availabilities should result from the need to replace experienced Customer Service Representatives who transfer to other industries or occupations or leave the labor force altogether. Replacement needs may be significant in this occupation, because many young people work as Customer Service Representatives before switching to other jobs.

Technology, however, might temper this job growth, as the Internet and automated systems have provided customers with means of obtaining information and conducting transactions that do *not* entail interacting with another person. The use of computer software to filter e-mails, generating automatic responses or directing messages to the appropriate representative, and the use of similar systems to answer or route telephone inquiries may also affect this job market. Despite such developments, it still is expected that the need for Customer Service Representatives will remain strong, as technology cannot completely replace human skills. As more sophisticated technologies are able to resolve many customers' questions and concerns, the nature of the inquiries to be handled by Customer Service Representatives is likely to become increasingly complex.

Advancement Prospects

While many customer service jobs are entry-level and are often good introductory positions into a company or an industry, this does not apply so well with the technological needs of an industry such as the oil and gas industry. Most Customer Service Representative positions in this industry require some experience working within the industry, usually in some marketing, sales, or promotion post. With seasoning, some representatives can move up within their company into supervisory or managerial positions, or they may transfer into areas such as product development, where they can use their knowledge gained as a Customer Service Representative to improve the company's products/services.

Education and Training

Most companies in the oil and gas industry require applicants for Customer Service Representative positions to have an associate's or a bachelor's degree (unlike other industries that may demand only a high school diploma). Course work in one or more sciences, as well as in business administration, is highly recommended.

Customer Service Representatives are typically provided with training prior to beginning work, and instruction continues once on the job. This training generally covers customer service and phone skills, common problems that customers have with the firm's products or services, the use or operation of the telephone and/or computer systems, and a thorough introduction to company policies. Because of a constant need to update skills and knowledge, most Customer Service Representatives continue to receive training throughout their career.

Experience, Skills, and Personality Traits

Because of their constant interaction with the public, Customer Service Representatives must have excellent communication and problem-solving skills. Verbal communication and listening abilities are especially key. They need to be competent in the use of e-mail, and exhibit good typing, spelling, and written communication skills. They need to have great interpersonal talent and a professional manner. The ability to deal effectively with problems and complaints and to remain courteous in the most trying of circumstances is crucial. They should have a clear and pleasant speaking voice, and be fluent in English. Bilingual skills are becoming increasingly important, particularly in an industry (oil and gas) which conducts as much of its business in other countries as it does nationally.

Computer skills are essential, particularly in Excel and Word. Prior marketing experience is highly valuable, as well as relevant business experience, preferably in the oil and gas industry or an allied energy field. Customer Service Repre-sentatives need to be objective, consistent in their work, and highly organized. They need to be able to follow established policies, but also to initiate and adapt to change.

Unions and Associations

There are no professional associations specifically organized for Customer Service Representatives. They may find it useful to belong to such broad associations as the American Marketing Association (AMA) and the American Tele-services Association (ATA), or such gas and oil industry associations as the American Gas Association (AGA) and the American Petroleum Institute (API).

Tips for Entry

1. During high school and college, volunteer to help with meetings, fairs, or phone-line fund-raisers where you can practice your helpful and courteous interaction with other people.
2. Investigate internship programs in the oil and gas industry to gain experience and learn about the technology, procedures, and processes of this business.
3. Take both writing and speech courses to enhance your communication skills.

MARKETING MANAGER AND MARKET RESEARCH ANALYST

CAREER PROFILE

Duties: <u>Marketing Manager</u>: Develop detailed marketing strategy and supervise other marketing personnel; <u>Market Research Analyst</u>: Analyze and evaluate marketing and promotional statistical data, making recommendations based upon their findings

Alternate Title(s): <u>Marketing Manager</u>: Business Development Manager; Marketing Director; <u>Market Research Analyst</u>: Business Development Specialist; Market Analyst; Product Line Manager; Project Manager

Salary Range: <u>Marketing Manager</u>: $60,000 to $120,000 or more; <u>Market Research Analyst</u>: $40,000 to $95,000 or more

Employment Prospects: Fair to Good

Advancement Prospects: Poor to Fair

Prerequisites:

Education or Training—<u>Marketing Manager</u>: Bachelor's degree in business administration preferable, but liberal arts background frequently acceptable; master's degree in business administration with emphasis on marketing may be required; <u>Market Research Analyst</u>: Bachelor's and master's degree in economics or marketing usually preferred; for top positions a Ph.D. may be necessary

Experience—<u>Marketing Manager</u>: Extensive experience in sales, advertising and promotion, and purchasing usually necessary, including background in supervising; <u>Market Research Analyst</u>: Solid background in gathering/analyzing data, conducting interviews/surveys, and writing statistical reports on findings necessary

Special Skills and Personality Traits—<u>Marketing Manager</u>: Excellent communication (oral and written) skills; good management and supervisory talents; tactful in dealing with personnel and customers, but also decisive; highly motivated and creative; resistant to stress; <u>Market Research Analyst</u>: Excellent communication/interpersonal abilities; computer proficiency, particularly in statistical data analysis; heavily detail-oriented; patience and persistence

Special Requirements—While available, certifications seldom required for either post

CAREER LADDER

Senior Management Positions, Owner of Market Consulting Business; Independent Market Research Consultant; Marketing Manager

Marketing Manager; Market Research Analyst

Marketing Assistant; Sales or Promotion Assistant

Position Description

Marketing is more than just advertising or sales. As the *Encyclopedia of Business* states, "marketing pertains to the interactive process that requires developing, pricing, placing, and promoting goods, ideas, or services in order to facilitate exchanges between customers and sellers to satisfy the needs and wants of consumers." The ultimate goal of marketing is to match a company's products/services to the people who need and want them, thus ensuring profitability for that company.

Marketing Managers develop the firm's detailed marketing strategy. With the help of such subordinates as product development managers and market research analysts, they determine the demand for products and services that the firm offers (along with their competitors), and identify potential customers. Marketing Managers create pricing strategy to help their firm maximize its profits and market share, as well as ensure that customers are satisfied. Working with other departments, they monitor trends indicating need for new products/services and oversee product development, as well as create budgets, evaluate expenditures, and direct research on development appropriations and profit-loss projections. Further, Marketing Managers work with advertising and promotion managers to support the firm's products/services in the marketplace. They usually are tasked with negotiating contracts with vendors and distributors (to manage product distribution), establishing distribution networks and strategies.

In addition, Marketing Managers within the oil and gas industries must have a broad knowledge of the dynamics and contractual practices of the international crude, product, and oil freight markets. They are responsible for the strategic, business, and operational planning, project appraisal and performance analysis relating to the refining, supply and distribution, and marketing of petroleum products. As such, they must be conversant with methods of domestic product distribution and marketing to both wholesale and retail accounts and outlets. Their company's market may be both the upstream part of the business (oil and gas exploration, drilling, and production) and the downstream component (the refining of oil and/or gas). They may be required to help establish local marketing operations as well as evaluate personnel and implement performance-monitoring processes.

Marketing Managers with oil and gas companies who deal internationally may also be accountable for the coordination of all the marketing activities with the global divisions of their company. As such, they will have to evaluate energy markets, infrastructure, the regulatory environment, competitors, and potential new business opportunities as governed by the laws, practices, regulations and restrictions (such as tariffs, quotas, embargoes, and exchange controls), and the economic and industrial environments of each country involved.

Market Research Analysts research market conditions in local, regional, national, or international areas to determine potential sales of their company's products/services. They establish the research methodology used, and design the format for data gathering. (Moreover, they often train interviewers to conduct the surveys.) They analyze statistical data to predict future sales and marketing trends. They gather data on competitors' methods of doing business. They collect information on customer needs, preferences, and buying habits. From all their statistical data, they prepare reports and graphic illustrations that will be used to aid the company's management in guaranteeing their firm's success.

Salaries

According to wage information provided by the Occupational Employment Statistics (OES) program in cooperation with the U.S. Department of Labor's Bureau of Labor Statistics, the median annual salary during 2006 for Marketing Managers was $85,200. Half of all Marketing Managers earn annually between $60,120 and $119,320. Many Marketing Managers earn bonuses equal to 10 percent or more of their salaries.

According to the U.S. Department of Labor's Bureau of Labor Statistics in their *Occupational Outlook Handbook, 2006–07 Edition*, median annual earnings of Market Research Analysts in May 2004 were $56,140. The middle 50 percent earned between $40,510 and $79,990. The lowest 10 percent had incomes of less than $30,890, while the highest 10 percent were paid more than $105,870.

Employment Prospects

The position of Marketing Manager is a highly coveted one, resulting in keen competition. College graduates with higher degrees in business and related experience, a significant level of creativity, and strong communication and computer skills should have the best job opportunities. According to the Bureau of Labor Statistics, employment of Marketing Managers is expected to increase faster than the average for all occupations through 2014, particularly in industries related to energy production.

Similarly, employment of market researchers is expected to grow faster than average for all occupations through 2014. Many job openings will result from the need to replace experienced researchers who transfer to other occupations or who retire. Job posts should be best for those applicants with a master's or Ph.D. degree in marketing (or a related field) and strong quantitative skills. Bachelor's degree holders may face competition, but those with good quantitative capabilities, including a strong background in mathematics, statistics, survey design, and computer science, will have the strongest prospects.

Advancement Prospects

For most Marketing Managers, career advancement means moving into higher management positions within their company. Competition for such openings is extremely keen. Nonetheless, successful Marketing Managers may be promoted to such positions in their own or another firm. Managers with extensive experience and sufficient capital may become owners of their own market-consulting firms.

With management training, Market Research Analysts can look to become Marketing Managers, promotion managers, or sales managers. Alternatively, they may decide to start their own market research consulting business.

Education and Training

Companies in the gas and oil industry usually prefer their Marketing Managers to have both a bachelor's and a master's degree in business administration, or have a bachelor's degree in a scientific or engineering field and a master's degree in business administration, with an emphasis on marketing. In addition, they usually require from five to 10 years seasoning in the oil and gas industry in advertising, marketing, promotion, or sales positions with steady increases in responsibilities. Many marketing posts are filled by promoting experienced staff or related professional personnel (such as sales representatives, promotion and advertising personnel, or public relations specialists).

For Market Research Analysts, a bachelor's degree is the minimum educational requirement, and, usually, a master's degree is required. Continuing education is also important to keep current with the latest methods of developing, conducting, and analyzing surveys and other data. Market researchers may earn advanced degrees in business administration, marketing, statistics, communications, or some related discipline. Because of the importance of quantitative skills to market researchers, courses in mathematics, statistics, sampling theory, and survey design, as well as computer science are recommended.

Special Requirements

While certification for Marketing Managers is seldom required, some associations do offer certification programs for these managers, which may add to their qualifications in this competitive job market. Similarly, certification is usually not required for Market Research Analysts. However, the Marketing Research Association (MRA) does offer a certification program for professional researchers. Such certification is based on education and experience requirements, as well as on continuing education.

Experience, Skills, and Personality Traits

Marketing personnel applying for positions as Marketing Managers should participate in management training programs conducted either in-house or at local colleges. In addition, taking active part in seminars and conferences, often held by professional societies, is helpful. Marketing Managers must be mature, creative, highly motivated, flexible (but also decisive), and resistant to stress. They must have excellent communication abilities and solid computer skills. They need good judgment and exceptional ability to establish and maintain effective personal relationships with supervisory and staff members (both those under their supervision and those in other areas of the industry with whom they interact) and with client firms.

Much of a Market Research Analyst's time is spent on precise data analysis, so those considering such careers must be very detail-oriented. Patience and persistence are necessary, because they must spend long hours on independent study and problem solving. At the same time, they must work well with others (often interviewing a wide variety of individuals) and have excellent communication skills. They must be able to present their findings both orally and in writing in a concise manner. Their computer skills, particularly in statistical data analysis, must be exemplary.

Unions and Associations

For both Marketing Managers and Market Research Analysts, membership in the American Marketing Association (AMA) is very important. In addition, participation in such professional societies as the American Gas Association (AGA), the American Petroleum Institute (API), the Gas Processors Association (GPA), or the Independent Petroleum Association of America (IPAA) should be useful.

Tips for Entry

1. For students pursuing a marketing career, courses in management and the completion of a business administration internship while in school is highly recommended.
2. The ability to communicate in a language other than English may open up employment opportunities, both in rapidly growing areas around the United States and in potential positions abroad.
3. While in college, as an aspiring market researcher, it is recommended that you gain experience gathering and analyzing data, conducting interviews or surveys, and writing reports on their findings. This experience may prove invaluable as most of your initial work will most likely center on these duties.

PUBLIC RELATIONS REPRESENTATIVE

CAREER PROFILE

Duties: Plan and conduct public relations program designed to create and maintain favorable public image for an oil or gas company

Alternate Title(s): Communications Specialist; Corporate Communications Director; Information and Communications Specialist; Media Outreach Coordinator; Media Specialist; Public Affairs Officer; Public Information Officer; Public Relations Account Executive; Public Relations Specialist

Salary Range: $26,000 to $80,000 or more

Employment Prospects: Good

Advancement Prospects: Fair to Good

Prerequisites:

Education or Training—Bachelor's degree in public relations, journalism, advertising, or communications required; additional course work in business administration, finance, creative writing, and psychology helpful

Experience—Public relations background gained from internship program desirable

Special Skills and Personality Traits—Creativity and initiative; decision-making, problem-solving, and research skills; excellent communication and interpersonal abilities; good judgment; outgoing personality and self-confidence, with an understanding of human psychology

Special Requirements—Accreditation as a public relations specialist may not be required, but is desirable

CAREER LADDER

```
┌─────────────────────────────────────┐
│   Public Relations Manager; Other    │
│       Supervisory Positions          │
└─────────────────────────────────────┘

┌─────────────────────────────────────┐
│   Public Relations Representative    │
└─────────────────────────────────────┘

┌─────────────────────────────────────┐
│ Marketing Assistant; Research Assistant │
└─────────────────────────────────────┘
```

Position Description

Public Relations Representatives are responsible for such organizational functions in a company as media, community, consumer, industry, and governmental relations. They also are involved in any political work (such as campaign fund-raisers) on behalf of their company, any special interest-group representation, and, sometimes, conflict mediation and employee and investor relations. They must be fully cognizant of the attitudes/concerns of community, consumer, employee, and public interest groups, and they must maintain cooperative relationships with them and with representatives from print and broadcast journalism and electronic media.

Public Relations Representatives draft fact sheets and press releases, prepare photographs, scripts, motion pictures, or tape recordings, and contact people in the media who might print, display, or broadcast their material. They purchase advertising space and time on broadcasts as required. They confer with production and support personnel to coordinate the production of any radio/television advertisements, on-air promotions, or Internet advertising. They may also prepare or edit organizational publications for internal and external audiences, such as employee newsletters, stockholders' reports, and Internet announcements.

Public Relations Representatives also arrange and conduct programs to keep up contact between their organization's representatives and the public. For this purpose, they set up speaking engagements and may prepare speeches to be given by their company's officials. They frequently represent their employer at community meetings and at public, social, and business gatherings. They make film, slide, or other visual presentations at meetings and school assemblies and plan their company's participation at conventions and other professional meetings. In addition, they are responsible for preparing annual reports and writing proposals for various projects. Under the direction of higher management, Public Relations Representatives may study the objectives, promotional policies, and needs of their company to develop public relations strategies that will influence public opinion or promote the company's philosophies, products, and services. In so doing, they confer with other managers to identify trends and key group interests/concerns or to provide advice on business decisions. They may also coach customer service representatives and other client representatives in effective means of communication with the public and with employees or a client company's personnel.

Salaries

According to the U.S. Department of Labor's Bureau of Labor Statistics in their *Occupational Outlook Handbook, 2006–07 Edition*, the median annual earnings in May 2004 for Public Relations Representatives were $43,830. The middle 50 percent earned between $32,970 and $59,360. The lowest 10 percent received less than $25,750, and the top 10 percent had incomes of over $81,120.

Employment Prospects

Competition for entry-level public relations jobs is keen, as many people are attracted to this profession because of the high profile nature of the work, with the result that there usually are more qualified applicants than there are job openings. Opportunities should be best for college graduates who combine a degree in journalism, public relations, advertising, or a related communications field with a public relations internship or other related work experience.

Nonetheless, the U.S. Department of Labor expects that employment of Public Relations Representatives will grow faster than the average for all occupations through 2014, particularly as there is a continued and growing need for good public relations in an increasingly competitive business environment nationally and internationally. The value of a firm is measured not just by its balance sheet, but also by the strength of its relationships with those on whom it depends for its success. Due to the increased demand for corporate accountability, the emphasis is placed squarely on improving the image of the company and its management, as well as on building public confidence in its products and services.

Advancement Prospects

Public Relations Representatives with excellent skills and a record of accomplishment may advance their career by becoming the public relations manager. From there they may progress to becoming public relations director or other higher management posts. Alternatively, they may join public relations consulting firms or, with sufficient capital, launch their own businesses. A doctoral degree (Ph.D.) is a tremendous asset for any teaching, writing, or consulting work.

Education and Training

A bachelor's degree in public relations, journalism, advertising, or communication, coupled with public relations experience that can be gained through an internship, is considered excellent preparation for a career in public relations. A typical public relations education at many colleges and universities includes courses in public relations principles and techniques, public relations management and administration, including organizational development; writing, emphasizing news releases, proposals, annual reports, scripts, speeches, and related items; visual communications, encompassing desktop publishing and computer graphics; and research, emphasizing social science and survey design/implementation. Additional courses in advertising, business administration, finance, psychology, and sociology are helpful.

Special Requirements

The Universal Accreditation Board accredits Public Relations Representatives who are members of the Public Relations Society of America (PRSA) and who participate in the Examination for Accreditation in Public Relations process. This process includes both a readiness review and an examination, which are designed for candidates with a bachelor's degree who have at least five years of full-time work in public relations. By passing the examination, candidates earn the Accredited in Public Relations (APR) designation. In addition, the International Association of Business Communicators (IABC) has an accreditation program for professionals in the communications field, who can earn the designation of Accredited Business Communicator (ABC).

Employers frequently consider professional recognition through accreditation as a sign of competence in this field, which can be especially helpful in this competitive job market.

Experience, Skills, and Personality Traits

Most companies in the gas and oil industry prefer to hire college graduates who have had job experience. Some firms may seek graduates who have worked in electronic or print journalism. Other employers want applicants with demonstrable communication skills and training or experience in a field related to the gas and oil industry. Many colleges help students gain part-time internships in public relations that provide valuable experience and training. A portfolio of published (print or online) articles, television or radio scripts, slide presentations, and other work is an asset in finding a public relations job.

Public Relations Representatives must be creative and have good judgment and the ability to communicate their ideas clearly. They must have excellent decision-making, problem-solving, and research skills. They need to be able to take the initiative and be competitive, yet able to function as part of a management team and be open to new ideas. They need to have a sociable personality, exhibiting self-confidence, a solid understanding of human psychology, and an enthusiasm for motivating people. In addition, they should be highly computer literate and have an eye for effective graphic art presentation of material.

Unions and Associations

Membership in local chapters of the Public Relations Student Society of America (PRSSA), which is affiliated with the Public Relations Society of America (PRSA), or in student chapters of the International Association of Business Communicators (IABC) provides an opportunity for students to exchange views with public relations specialists and to make professional contacts. Joining the Public Relations Society of America is especially helpful for Public Relations Representatives in their career and ongoing professional training.

Tips for Entry

1. During college, write for a school publication, Web site, or television or radio station which will provide valuable experience and material for your portfolio.
2. Look for internship programs in the oil and gas industry, or a related energy field, to gain practical experience in the techniques and processes of that industry.
3. Consider becoming bilingual (Spanish or Arabic are good choices), as this ability will prove useful in your public relations work for the oil and gas industries (particularly as they deal as much with international clients as domestic ones).

ENGINEERS AND SCIENTISTS

CHEMICAL ENGINEER

CAREER PROFILE	CAREER LADDER

Duties: Design chemical plant equipment and devise processes for manufacturing chemicals and products from petroleum derivatives, utilizing principles and technology of chemistry, physics, mathematics, engineering, and related physical and natural sciences

Alternate Title(s): Development Engineer; Process Control Engineer; Process Engineer; Refinery Process Engineer

Salary Range: $49,000 to $115,000 or more

Employment Prospects: Fair to Good

Advancement Prospects: Fair

Prerequisites:

Education or Training—Bachelor of Science degree in chemical engineering required; master's degree or higher is required for some research, teaching, consulting, and managerial posts

Experience—Five to seven years' experience as a process engineer in a chemical manufacturing plant

Special Skills and Personality Traits—Ability to think analytically and to visualize complex processes and equipment; aptitude for chemistry, mathematics, and physics; capable of working effectively in teams with people from various disciplines and educational backgrounds; enjoy being innovative, doing precise work, making decisions, and problem solving; good oral and written communication skills

Special Requirements—Licensing as a Professional Engineer and certification as a Chemical Engineer usually required

---

Team Supervisor; Operations Management Positions; Owner, Consulting Firm

Chemical Engineer

Chemical-Engineering Technician; Junior Process Engineer

Position Description

Chemical Engineers are considered engineering generalists because of their unique ability (among engineers) to understand and exploit chemical change. They draw on the principles of chemistry, mathematics, and physics and their familiarity with all forms of matter and energy and their manipulation to develop and produce a diverse range of products. Examples include ultra-strong fibers, fabrics, adhesives and composites for vehicles, and optical or spectroscopic properties for opto-electronic devices. Chemical Engineers develop processes, design equipment, and pro-

vide technical and management services for plants that convert raw materials into a wide range of end products. They trouble-shoot problems in industrial processing plants and ensure efficient, safe, and environmentally responsible plant operations.

They conduct research to develop new and improved chemical manufacturing processes. They design and oversee the construction, control, and improvement of equipment to carry out these chemical processes on a commercial scale. They analyze operating procedures, equipment, and machinery functions to reduce processing time and cost. They design equipment to control movement, storage, and packaging of solids, liquids, and gases. They design and plan measurement and control systems for chemical plants and determine the most effective arrangement of unit operations such as mixing, grinding, crushing, heat transfer, size reduction, hydrogenation, distillation, purification, oxidation, polymerization, evaporation, and fermentation. They exercise their judgment to compromise between process requirements, economic evaluation, operator effectiveness, and physical and health hazards. They perform tests throughout all stages of production to determine the degree of control needed over such variables as temperature, density, specific gravity, and pressure.

Chemical Engineers often direct the activities of workers who operate/control such equipment as condensers, absorption and evaporation towers, kilns, pumps, valves, boilers, compressors, grinders, pipelines, electro-magnets, and centrifuges to effect required chemical or physical change.

Thus, Chemical Engineers work wherever there is a process of conversion (e.g., petroleum refining, oil sands extraction, energy conversion, polymer processing, metal extraction and refining, and power generation).

One of these processes is the refining of petroleum or natural gas. For example, during the refining process, two of the 42 gallons in each barrel of oil are chemicals used to manufacture other products. These chemicals, known as petrochemicals, are primarily composed of hydrogen, carbon, nitrogen, and sulfur. When the molecules of these ingredients are changed and shifted in various combinations, hundreds of chemical products are produced for utilization in commonly used items. These products include ammonia, polyethylene, and polypropylene, which are employed to make such items as appliance and automotive parts, luggage, plastic toys, and containers. Other products made from petrochemicals are fibers to make clothes, paints, and even surfboards. Chemical Engineers work in nearly all phases of the production of these petrochemicals and their chemical products.

Salaries

According to a 2005 survey by the National Association of Colleges and Employers, the average starting annual salary for a Chemical Engineer with a bachelor's degree was $53,813. For one with a master's degree the average starting pay was $57,260, and for one with a Ph.D., the starting salary was $79,591.

In their salary study of engineering salaries, the U.S. Department of Labor's Bureau of Labor Statistics in their *Occupational Outlook Handbook, 2006–07 Edition* found that yearly salaries in May 2004 for Chemical Engineers ranged from a low of $49,030 to a high of $107,530. For experienced Chemical Engineers it is not uncommon to have incomes ranging from $90,000 to $130,000 or more.

Employment Prospects

The U.S. Department of Labor, in their *Occupational Outlook Handbook, 2006–07 Edition*, estimates that employment growth for Chemical Engineers will be about as fast as the average for all occupations through 2014. Continued emphasis on the ongoing need to solve pollution and environmental protection problems will create the need for more Chemical Engineers. While the pharmaceutical industry will continue to provide excellent opportunities for Chemical Engineers, as will the developing fields of biotechnology and nanotechnology, the oil and gas industry, particularly in its refining processing, will also continue to offer excellent career posts for Chemical Engineers. In addition to job openings created by increased demand, many Chemical Engineers will be needed to replace those who leave the labor force or change occupations.

Advancement Prospects

Chemical Engineers usually begin their professional careers as junior or assistant engineers. As they gain experience, they are assigned projects that are more difficult and the independence to develop their own designs. They may move from product manufacturing to project or production engineer positions. As a project engineer, they usually supervise other engineers and technicians. The next career steps are to supervising engineer, chief engineer, or, if within a manufacturing environment, plant manager. Those Chemical Engineers primarily engaged in research may progress to such positions as supervisor, project engineer, or director of research. Many Chemical Engineers who seek top executive positions in administration or management may find it best to complete additional graduate study in both chemical engineering and business administration to improve their advancement opportunities. Chemical Engineers with promotional skills may decide to move into sales. Some engineers with experience and professional contacts may open their own consulting firms.

Education and Training

A Bachelor of Science degree in chemical engineering is the most common entry-level requirement for Chemical Engineers. A master's degree or higher is required for some research, teaching, consulting, and managerial positions. Passing a state board exam given by the Department of Consumer Affairs of the state is usually required of Chemical Engineers to do consulting work.

Chemical processes are becoming more complex and automated, and recent developments in computer-aided design (CAD) have enabled engineers to create designs more intricate and accurate than were ever possible before. To keep up with such rapid changes and advances in their field, most Chemical Engineers further their education throughout their careers by attending continuing education courses.

Special Requirements

All 50 states and the District of Columbia require licensure for Chemical Engineers (as well as all other engineers) who offer their services directly to the public. Engineers who are licensed are called Professional Engineers (PE). This licensure generally requires a degree from an accredited engineering program, four years of relevant work experience, and successful completion of a state examination. Information about licensure can be obtained from the National Society of Professional Engineers (NSPE). Most states recognize licensure from other states. Independent of licensure, various certification programs are offered by professional organizations to demonstrate competency in specific fields of engineering.

Experience, Skills, and Personality Traits

As their field is a multidisciplinary one, Chemical Engineers must have an aptitude for chemistry, mathematics, and physics. They need to be able to think analytically and to visualize complex processes and equipment involved in such processes. As they interact with other people much of the time, they have excellent oral/writing skills so as to communicate their ideas to managers, technicians, craftworkers, other engineers, production personnel, and customers. Written reports and oral presentations are an important part of their duties. They must be able to work effectively in teams with people from assorted disciplines and educational backgrounds.

Chemical Engineers must be adept at solving problems, enjoy being innovative, have initiative, and be precise in their work. They must be proficient with basic computer tools, such as Windows, Excel, Word, and Access. They should enjoy making decisions and directing the work of others, as well as be willing to improve their knowledge and skills on an ongoing basis.

Unions and Associations

Professional associations of direct interest for Chemical Engineers are the American Institute of Chemical Engineers (AIChE) and the Society of Petroleum Engineers (SPE). Both these organizations offer voluntary certification programs to their members. Membership in the American Chemical Society (ACS) may also prove to be beneficial.

Tips for Entry

1. While in college, take every opportunity to enhance your computer skills, as this is a basic requirement, beyond your scientific training, for your future job as a Chemical Engineer.
2. Taking both technical writing and speech courses may aid you in increasing your communication skills.
3. Consider participating in an internship with an engineering firm while in college. Most internships are part of a four-year degree program. It will offer you a chance to apply what you have learned in the classroom in an actual work situation and will give you the opportunity to network with people in the field.

CHEMIST

CAREER PROFILE

Duties: Research the properties, composition, and principles of elements and compounds, and apply chemical principles to develop a wide range of products and processes, such as new fuels, polymers, pharmaceutical products or foods, or work in the oil and gas industry

Alternate Title(s): Analytical Chemist; Environmental Chemist; Physical and Theoretical Chemist; Research Chemist; Research and Development Chemist

Salary Range: $32,000 to $95,000 or more

Employment Prospects: Fair

Advancement Prospects: Fair

Prerequisites:

Education or Training—Bachelor of Science degree in chemistry required; master's (M.Sc.) and/or doctoral (Ph.D.) recommended

Experience—Two to four years of work-related experience, usually as a chemical technician

Special Skills and Personality Traits—Able to work in a highly competitive environment and meet strict deadlines; capable of working independently as well as in a team environment; detail-oriented in performance of job; excellent computer skills; exhibits patience and persistence; good speaking, reading, and writing skills; mathematical ability and problem-solving skills; self-starter

Special Requirements—Certification as Chemistry Major available

CAREER LADDER

Senior Management Positions; Owner, Consulting and Service Firm

Chemist

College Graduate; Chemical Technician

Position Description

Chemists study the composition, structure, and properties of substances and the interactions between them. They search for new information about materials and look for ways to put this knowledge to practical use. They analyze organic and inorganic compounds to determine chemical and physical properties, utilizing such techniques as chromatography, spectroscopy, and spectrophotometry. They apply scientific principles/techniques using specialized instruments (such as lasers, spectrometers, benchtop centrifuges, X-ray diffraction equipment) and technical computer software (such as graphics or photo-imaging software, computer-aided design, or CAD, software, and database user interface and query

software like Microsoft Access and Structured Query Language or SQL) to measure, identify, and evaluate changes in matter. Chemists have developed a wide variety of new and improved synthetic fibers, paints, adhesives, drugs, cosmetics, electronic components, lubricants, and thousands of other products. They also develop processes that save energy and reduce pollution, such as improved oil refining and petrochemical processing methods.

There are four main specialties of Chemists: organic (working with carbon and its compounds), inorganic (working with compounds of non-carbon structure, such as metals and minerals), physical (concentrating on the study of quantitative relationships between the chemical and physical properties of substances), and analytical (examining the content of substances and measuring the amount of each component present, such as pollutants in air, water, and soil). The oil and gas industry employs primarily physical Chemists and analytical Chemists.

Most Chemists are involved in either research and development (R&D) or production. In basic research, Chemists investigate the properties, composition, and structure of matter and the laws that govern the combination of elements and reactions of substances, seeking new scientific knowledge of chemical processes or theories. In applied research, Chemists create new products and processes or improve existing ones, typically using knowledge gained from basic research. For instance, synthetic rubber and plastics resulted from research on small molecules united to form large ones (a process called polymerization). In production, they prepare compounds in the form and amount required for commercial use. They prepare instructions that specify ingredients, mixing times, and temperatures for each step of the process. They monitor automated processes to ensure correct product yield and test samples to be sure they meet industry/government standards.

Chemists frequently work with chemical engineers, biologists, geologists, and other scientific personnel on multidisciplinary research and development projects. In addition, they direct/advise other staff in test procedures, and supervise the work of chemical technologists and technicians working on their projects.

Salaries

According to the U.S. Department of Labor's Bureau of Labor Statistics in their *Occupational Outlook Handbook, 2006–07 Edition*, the median annual earnings in May 2004 for Chemists were $56,060. The middle 50 percent had yearly incomes between $41,900 and $76,080. The lowest 10 percent received less than $33,170, and the highest 10 percent earned more than $98,010.

In the American Chemical Society's 2005 Starting Salary Survey, the median yearly salary of inexperienced Bachelor of Science 2005 graduates was $35,000. For graduates with master's degrees the median starting annual salary was $45,000, and for new Ph.D.'s the starting income was $72,400. In addition, the 2005 census of all Society members in the workforce revealed that Chemists with bachelor's degrees had median annual salaries of $64,000. For Chemists with master's degrees, the median salary was $75,000, and for Ph.D.s, the median salary was $93,800.

Employment Prospects

The Bureau of Labor Statistics forecasts that employment of Chemists, generally, is expected to grow more slowly than the average rate for all occupations through 2014. The report projects that job growth for Chemists will be concentrated in pharmaceutical and medicine manufacturing and in professional, scientific, and technical service firms, such as those that constitute part of the oil and gas industries. Nonetheless, new Chemists at all levels may experience competition for jobs. Graduates with master's degrees, and particularly those with a Ph.D., will enjoy better job opportunities than those with only a bachelor's degree.

Advancement Prospects

Private industry employs about two-thirds of all Chemists, and most industrial Chemists are involved in research and development (R&D). Entry-level bachelor's degree Chemists may work in quality control, performing analytical testing, in research, plant, or company laboratories. They may also operate with senior researchers in R&D labs. As they gain experience, they work more independently and can advance to team leaders and other supervisory positions or change career path to chemical sales or other business functions. Those with sufficient capital and contacts may decide to start their own consulting and service firm.

Education and Training

A Bachelor of Science degree in chemistry is the usual minimum educational requirement for entry-level Chemist jobs. However, many research jobs require a master's degree, or, more often, a Ph.D. degree as well. Because R&D Chemists are increasingly expected to work on interdisciplinary teams, some understanding of other disciplines is important, including business and marketing or economics.

Special Requirements

The American Chemical Society (ACS) certifies chemistry programs offered at colleges and universities. Students taking such a curriculum can be certified as American Chemical Society Chemistry Majors. Such certification may be included in their credentials when applying for employment or graduate school and allows them to join the American Chemical Society without the usual annual probationary period of membership.

Experience, Skills, and Personality Traits

Most employers in the oil and gas industries prefer candidates for Chemist positions to have at least three to five years' industrial experience. Many schools and companies offer undergraduate and graduate cooperative chemistry programs that combine industrial work experience, internships in research labs, and study or work abroad programs with the academic program.

Chemists must be very exact in their work, as errors could cause serious consequences, such as dangerous chemical reactions. They must be able to work in a highly competitive environment and meet strict deadlines. They need to make decisions or set tasks without consulting supervisors, but also be clearly able to work within a team environment. They must have good communication skills, mathematical ability, and be well versed in computer techniques/technologies. They should enjoy synthesizing information and finding innovative solutions to problems, working with instruments at tasks requiring both patience and precision. In addition, they should be comfortable directing the work of other scientists and technicians.

Unions and Associations

The American Chemical Society (ACS) is the primary professional association for Chemists. The ACS has a Department of Career Services that maintains a database of employers who are looking for candidates, especially in the fields of chemistry and chemical engineering. Members and student affiliates can post their résumé on the department's database, found at http://www.cen-chemjobs.org. At the society's national and regional meetings, there are always ChemJobs Career Centers and other job-hunting related activities of tremendous value to society members.

Tips for Entry

1. Note that computer courses have become essential for Chemists, as employers prefer job applicants who are able to apply computer skills to modeling and simulation tasks, as well as operate computerized laboratory equipment.

2. Take classes in statistics, because Chemists need the ability to apply basic statistical techniques to their research findings.

3. Opportunities to gain experience while in college, as in co-ops, internships, summer work, and study abroad have become key in adding value to your education and career development. These work-integrated learning programs help you to apply classroom theory, advance your technical skills, familiarize you with diverse work cultures, explore career options, and provide useful industry contacts.

GEOLOGIST

Duties: In studying the nature and history of the Earth's crust, apply this knowledge to exploring for minerals and hydrocarbons (oil and gas), developing resources for production, building engineering foundations and stable slopes, and conducting environmental investigations

Alternate Title(s): Development Geologist; Exploration Geologist; Geoscientist; Petroleum Geologist

Salary Range: $38,000 to $125,000 or more

Employment Prospects: Fair to Good

Advancement Prospects: Fair

Prerequisites:

Education or Training—Bachelor's degree in geology or geophysics minimum requirement; master's degree usually necessary; in some cases, doctoral degree (Ph.D.) recommended

Experience—Two to five years' field experience as a geological apprentice or an entry-level geologist usually mandatory

Special Skills and Personality Traits—Aptitude for mathematics and science; capable of visualizing three-dimensional objects from two-dimensional drawings; high computer proficiency; interpersonal skills and ability to work well in a team environment; open, inquiring, analytical mind with excellent decision-making talents; strong oral and written communication skills

Special Requirements—Certification not always required, but recommended; state licensure may be demanded

```
┌─────────────────────────────────┐
│   Geologic Project Leader;       │
│   Independent Consultant         │
└─────────────────────────────────┘

┌─────────────────────────────────┐
│          Geologist               │
└─────────────────────────────────┘

┌─────────────────────────────────┐
│   Geological Technician;         │
│   Research Assistant             │
└─────────────────────────────────┘
```

Position Description

Geologists (and geophysicists) are often called geoscientists. While these two occupations are closely related, they are distinctly different. Geologists study how rocks were formed and how they have altered since they were created. In addition, they track the evolution of life by studying plant and animal fossils. Geophysicists study not only Earth's surface, but also its interior. Additionally, they examine forces that affect the Earth, such as magnetism and gravity. Regardless, geologists and geophysicists have some duties in common. Those who do research gather and analyze information and then interpret their results.

Petroleum Geologists explore the stratigraphic structure of earth, using information gathered from boreholes, geophysical and geochemical data, geological maps, rock samples, and remote sensing imagery to determine where to drill for oil and gas. They study well logs, analyze cores and cuttings from well drillings, and interpret data obtained by electrical or radioactive well logging and other subsurface surveys to identify earth strata. They examine aerial photographs, evaluate results of geophysical prospecting, and prepare surface and subsurface maps/diagrams of both the ocean and land depicting the stratigraphic arrangement and composition of earth to estimate probable gas and oil deposits.

To interpret the geological information, they use sophisticated geophysical instrumentation such as sonars, geological compasses, paramagenetic susceptibility analyzers, various soil sampling apparatus (such as sediment piston corers and soil augers), and a variety of electromagnetic geophysical instruments (including degaussing wands and impulse magnetizers). Their computer programs encompass map creation software, graphics or photo-imaging software, and a variety of analytical and scientific software (such as well logging software, the Clover Technology Galena software package, and the Waterloo Hydrogeologic FlowPath II software).

Petroleum Geologists recommend to their employers the acquisition, retention, or release of property leases or contracts, based on their research. In addition, they estimate oil reserves in proven or prospective fields and consult with and help petroleum engineers to optimize the extraction process by determining the geological characteristics of an underground gas or oil reservoir and the fluids in it. Typically, petroleum geologists learn to locate three different types of target locales: exploration drill sites (big scale and high risk), field-development drill sites (medium scale and medium risk), and producing-field drill sites (small scale and lowest risk).

Geologists who work in the field can expect to spend five to 15 hours a day outdoors, conducting geological surveys and sample/measurement studies. Once they have completed their fieldwork, most return to laboratories and test their samples for content and composition.

Salaries

According to the U.S. Department of Labor's Bureau of Labor Statistics in their *Occupational Outlook Handbook, 2006–07 Edition*, the median annual salaries in May 2004 for Geologists were $68,730. The middle 50 percent earned yearly between $49,260 and $98,380, whereas the lowest 10 percent earned less than $37,700 and the highest 10 percent had incomes of more than $130,750. PayScale, Inc.'s salary survey report on 2006 earnings of petroleum Geologists reflected that the median annual salaries for those with less than one year's experience was $50,000. Those with one to four years' experience had median earnings of $67,250, and those with five to nine years' experience had a median income of $71,000. Finally, those petroleum Geologists who had 10 to 19 years experience received median salaries of $97,484, and those with twenty years' or more experience got median annual earnings of $115,000.

The oil and gas industry tends to offer the highest industry salaries at each degree level. For instance, the average yearly salary for all entry-level Geologists with a master's degree is about $31,500, and the average in the petroleum industry is about $59,700, according to industry sources.

Employment Prospects

Historically, employment of petroleum Geologists (and geophysicists) has been cyclical and greatly affected by the price of oil and gas. When prices were low, oil and gas producers curtailed exploration activities and cut back on their staff of Geologists. When prices were higher, companies had the funds and incentive to renew exploration efforts and hire Geologists (and other geoscientists) in larger numbers. In recent years, the growing worldwide demand for oil and gas and the development of new exploration and recovery techniques, particularly in deep water and in previously inaccessible sites (such as in Alaska and the Gulf of Mexico), has returned some stability to the petroleum industry. Most likely, employment in the industry will always be subject to these fluctuations, and job growth may be further limited due to increasing efficiencies in finding oil and gas.

Nonetheless, the employment outlook for new graduates with a geology degree seeking work in the oil and gas industries appears to be bright. Many firms plan to grow slowly regardless of the price of oil, and they have strategies that include hiring new talent into the now rapidly maturing workforces. Companies will likely prefer students fluent in more than one language who are globally mobile and willing to work in international locations.

Job openings also are available for petroleum geologists with three to 15 years of professional experience, as many smaller operations are willing to pay a premium in salary/bonuses to people trained by larger companies. Job-hopping has always been a part of the petroleum landscape, so it is important for petroleum Geologists to develop and maintain a personal network of contacts and be active in the industry's professional societies.

Advancement Prospects

Geologists often begin their careers in field exploration or as research assistants or technicians in laboratories/offices. As they gain experience, they are given more challenging assignments. Eventually, they may be promoted to project leader, program manager, or other higher management or research posts. Fewer and fewer Geologists remain with the same company for their entire careers. Many of them become independent, or freelance, consultants. Most consultants have knowledge and experience in a particular regional area or specialty and are available to work on an hourly, daily, or job basis. Some Geologists function both as consultant and independently, working on maps and drilling proposals on their own time, but being available for consulting assignments when the opportunity arises. Few Geologists (about 10 percent) leave the profession (as opposed to retiring), and when they do, they tend to migrate to other related sciences or to government work.

Education and Training

While a bachelor's degree is adequate for a few entry-level positions, most Geologists (including petroleum Geologists) need at least a master's degree in geology or earth science. In some cases, a Ph.D. may be mandatory. Computer skills are essential: Students experienced with computer modeling, data analysis and integration, digital mapping, remote sensing, geographic information systems, and the Global Positioning System, or GPS (a locator system that uses satellites), will be best positioned for the job market.

Special Requirements

Certification as a petroleum Geologist is available from the American Association of Petroleum Geologists (AAPG) and their Division of Professional Affairs (DPA). Such certification does not come automatically with membership in AAPG, but requires a special application. Such certification may be extremely helpful in applying for jobs. Many states also require a state license (information usually available from the state's Department of Consumer Affairs) for Geologists who do research within the state.

Experience, Skills, and Personality Traits

Geologists must have excellent interpersonal skills, as they usually work as part of a team with other geoscientists and with environmental scientists, engineers, and technicians. Strong communication capabilities are key, as writing of technical reports and research proposals and communicating research results to others are important aspects of the work. (One geologist has said, "You'll be asked simple questions, and you've got to come up with ways of answering them when no one method is foolproof. Is there oil under here? If so, how much? How long will it take to get it out? These questions can only be answered with probabilities, not certainties.") Geologists must be inquisitive, logical, and capable of complex analytical thinking (including spatial visualization and the ability to

develop comprehensive conclusions), often from sparse data. They need to be highly focused and self-motivated. They must be familiar with the fundamentals of science, from chemistry to physics and biology, and be adept mathematically.

Unions and Associations

The primary associations for Geologists are the American Geological Institute (AGI) and the Geological Society of America (GSA). For petroleum Engineers, there is the American Association of Petroleum Geologists (AAPG) and the Society of Petroleum Engineers (SPE).

Tips for Entry

1. During college and graduate work, seek work as an intern within the oil and gas industries. Many employers choose new employees from the pool of candidates they have utilized as interns.
2. Learn about the fundamentals of finance and accounting so that, if you choose to be an independent or consultant Geologist, you can manage your business or practice.
3. Become a member of such organizations as AAPG, GSA, or SPE and other groups that provide for student affiliations. Attend meetings/conventions and volunteer for jobs that will enable you to meet and work with established Geologists.
4. The most active oil companies are those most likely to need the services of petroleum Geologists. Drilling and activity reports are available from the Petroleum Information Corporation and can greatly aid you in deciding what companies to contact.

GEOPHYSICIST

CAREER PROFILE	CAREER LADDER

Duties: Use knowledge of physics, chemistry, and mathematics to study the Earth's interior forces and exterior characteristics by quantitative physical means, using gravity, magnetic, electrical, and seismic methods

Alternate Title(s): Exploration Geophysicist; Geophysical Prospector; Geoscientist; Physical Geoscientist; Project Geophysicist

Salary Range: $36,000 to $120,000 or more

Employment Prospects: Poor to Fair

Advancement Prospects: Fair

Prerequisites:

Education or Training—Bachelor of Science degree in geophysics or a related science minimum requirement; master's degree often preferred, and Ph.D. degree essential for research

Experience—Three to five years' or more experience in natural gas or petroleum industry

Special Skills and Personality Traits—Capable of complex analytical thinking; exhibit a fascination with natural phenomena; good interpersonal/communication skills; knowledge of a second language useful; strong science background; excellent computer abilities

Special Requirements—Some states may require licensing

CAREER LADDER

> Geophysical Project Leader; Other Management Positions; Government Service; Teaching

> Geophysicist

> Engineering Technician; Geophysical Technologist

Position Description

Geologists and Geophysicists are sometimes termed geoscientists. While these two occupations are closely related, they have significant differences. Geologists study how rocks were formed over the ages and how they have since changed. They also research the evolution of life by studying plant and animal fossils. Geophysicists study not only Earth's surface, but also its interior. In addition, they study the forces that affect Earth, such as magnetism and gravity. Thus, geologists analyze fairly static systems, while Geophysicists examine systems in flux.

Geophysicists employ the principles of chemistry, mathematics, and physics to research not only Earth's surface, but also its internal composition, its ground and surface waters, its atmosphere, oceans, and magnetic, electrical, and gravitational forces. They analyze data obtained to compute the shape of the Earth, estimate the composition and structure of its interior, determine flow pattern of ocean tides and currents, study physical properties of Earth's atmosphere, and help locate petroleum/mineral deposits.

In petroleum exploration, Geophysicists examine and interpret information on sediments, mineral and rock compositions, and geologic structure to determine where oil and gas deposits are most likely to occur. They conduct (and supervise) research, using geophysical instruments such as the seismograph, gravimeter, magnetometer, and electrical-resistivity apparatus to measure characteristics of Earth at potential sites. They compute variations in physical forces existing at different locations and interpret data to reveal subsurface structures likely to contain petroleum or gas deposits. They prepare charts, profiles, subsurface contour maps, and determine desirable locations for drilling operations. During this exploration process, they often direct the field crews drilling boreholes and collecting samples of rock and soil for chemical analysis of hydrocarbon content. Some Geophysicists may specialize in particular instrumentation and be specifically designated electrical prospectors, gravity prospectors, magnetic prospectors, or seismic prospectors.

Geophysicists usually head exploration operations. Other geological specialists may be involved in exploration activities, including paleontologists (who study fossil remains to locate oil), mineralogists (who study physical and chemical properties of mineral and rock samples), stratigraphers (who determine the rock layers most like to contain oil and natural gas), and photogeologists (who examine and interpret aerial photographs of land surfaces). Other workers involved in exploration crews include gravity or seismic prospecting observers (who operate and maintain electronic seismic equipment), scouts (who investigate the exploration, drilling, and leasing activities of other companies to identify promising areas to explore and lease), and lease buyers (who make the business arrangements to obtain use of the land or mineral rights from its owners).

While some exploration Geophysicists work several months in the field, most other Geophysicists function in an office environment, compiling and interpreting data collected from the field. In addition, they design, develop, and operate the computer systems and software used for processing/interpreting the geophysical data sets. They develop the instrumentation for taking physical measurements in surveys, including gravity meters, electrical, electromagnetic, and radar transmitters and receivers, seismic recorders, and radiometric systems. They are constantly researching new methods and instrumentation. They also develop the mathematical models utilized in interpreting the geophysical survey results.

Salaries

In their 2006 salary survey report on Geophysicists, Pay-Scale, Inc. found that the median annual income for Geophysicists with less than one year of experience was $60,000, but yearly salaries might dip as low as $36,000 depending on geographic location. For those Geophysicists with five to nine years in the profession, their median annual salary was $75,000. For those with 10 to 19 years experience, their median annual salary was $90,000, and for those with 20 years or more experience, it was in excess of $120,000.

Employment Prospects

Historically, employment of petroleum geologists, Geophysicists, and other geoscientists has been cyclical and affected considerably by the price of oil and gas. When prices were

low, oil and gas producers curtailed exploration activities and laid off personnel. When prices were higher, companies had the funds and incentive to renew exploration efforts and hire geoscientists in larger numbers.

Although worldwide demand for oil and gas is expected to grow, overall U.S. wage and salary employment in the oil and gas extraction industry is expected to decline by 6 percent through the year 2014, compared to an employment increase of 14 percent in all industries combined, according to the U.S. Department of Labor's *Occupational Outlook Handbook, 2006–07 Edition.*

In general, the level of future crude petroleum and national gas exploration and development and, therefore, employment opportunities in this industry, remains contingent upon the size of accessible reserves available and the going prices for oil and gas. Rising worldwide demand for oil and gas is likely to cause higher long-term prices and generate the needed incentive to continue exploring and developing oil and gas resources in the United States, at least in the short run. Increasingly, many companies are targeting lucrative foreign locations for oil/gas resources. Thus, Geophysicists with language abilities may have a better chance for employment.

In addition, the need to replace Geophysicists who transfer to other industries (or the government) or leave the workforce will be the major source of job openings.

Advancement Prospects

Geophysicists often begin their careers in field exploration or as research assistants or technicians in laboratories/offices. As they gain experience, they are given more difficult assignments. Some find advancement by moving into a government service, or by branching out into new areas of study. Many begin to write articles and circulate them among colleagues. Those who have been successful as field researchers and lab analysts are rewarded with supervisory responsibilities over new entrants to the profession. Experienced Geophysicists may also move into private consulting or advance into management posts.

Geophysicists tend to leave the profession only when they retire, die, or find a scientific challenge more interesting. Some venture into more obscure branches of physics, led by their initial interaction with geophysics. Others transfer into teaching at university settings.

Education and Training

While the minimum education requirement for Geophysicists is a Bachelor of Science degree in geophysics or a related science (with courses in geophysics, electronics, physics, chemistry, geology, mathematics, and computer science), most companies prefer a master's degree as well. A doctoral (Ph.D.) degree is considered essential for extensive research. Many employers in the gas and oil industries provide additional training in the specialized techniques of oil and gas exploration.

A strong background in sciences, with emphasis on math, physics, and geology is crucial. Students with a physics major often have an easier time in graduate school than those with only a geology major. As computer proficiency is essential, expertise should be gained in working with various computer platforms and software programs. Additionally, a knowledge of geographic information systems (GIS) and the Global Positioning System (GPS)—both locator systems using satellites—is key.

Special Requirements
Some states may require a certification as a petroleum Geophysicist or a specialty Geophysicist. Applications are usually made to the state's Department of Consumer Affairs.

Experience, Skills, and Personality Traits
Geophysicists should enjoy applying physics and mathematics in practical ways and take pleasure in technical and engineering work. They should have analytical minds and the capacity to analyze and synthesize data. They need excellent spatial reasoning abilities and decision-making skills. They must be precise but also allow for the development of innovative approaches. They should be able to work well in a team environment and be comfortable functioning in remote locales.

Those who succeed in geophysics seem to have the ability to be flexible and the willingness to challenge previously held assumptions. Many Geophysicists move through a number of specializations in five-year blocks. Initial specialization is important because it leads to five years of learning that particular aspect of the profession. They tend to enjoy learning how geological systems interrelate, and they are interested in learning about the systems that interact with the ones they already know. This continuous challenge and the perpetual education this occupation encourages seem to be two of the major reasons Geophysicists are so satisfied with their work.

Unions and Associations
The four main associations of interest for Geophysicists in the oil and natural gas industries are the American Association of Petroleum Geologists (AAPG), the American Geophysical Union (AGU), the Geological Society of America (GSA), and the Society of Exploration Geophysicists (SEG).

Tips for Entry
1. Become adept in one or more languages other than English to better position yourself for employment in the global economy of the oil and gas industries.
2. Obtain critical field experience during college through summer internships.
3. As many Geophysicists eventually either work as consultants for private companies or obtain jobs through grants from the government, polish your writing skills so that you will be able to market yourself in a professional manner.

PETROLEUM ENGINEER

CAREER PROFILE

Duties: Apply the principles of geology, physics, chemistry, and the engineering sciences to the recovery, development, and processing of petroleum and natural gas.

Alternate Title(s): Completion Engineer; Drilling Engineer; Drilling Manager; Operations Engineer; Operations Manager; Production Engineer; Project Production Engineer; Project Reservoir Engineer; Reservoir Engineer; Subsurface Engineer

Salary Range: $48,000 to $140,000 or more

Employment Prospects: Fair

Advancement Prospects: Fair to Good

Prerequisites:

Education or Training—Bachelor of Science degree in petroleum engineering minimum requirement; master's and/or doctoral (Ph.D.) degree usually preferred

Experience—Three to five years' seasoning in petroleum (and/or gas) exploration and production

Special Skills and Personality Traits—Able to accept responsibility and work without supervision; ability to identify, analyze, and solve problems; aptitude for mathematics and science, computing and design; capable of working independently and also in a team environment; decisive, creative, and practical; good communication skills; high energy to deal with demanding workloads and changing priorities

Special Requirements—All states require registration, and many states require licensing.

CAREER LADDER

```
┌─────────────────────────────────────┐
│  Engineering Team Leader; Other      │
│  Management Positions; Owner,        │
│  Consulting Firm; Sales or Marketing │
│  Management Positions                │
└─────────────────────────────────────┘

┌─────────────────────────────────────┐
│        Petroleum Engineer            │
└─────────────────────────────────────┘

┌─────────────────────────────────────┐
│  Assistant Petroleum Engineer;       │
│  Engineering Technician              │
└─────────────────────────────────────┘
```

Position Description

Petroleum Engineers plan and supervise the drilling of new oil wells. They also supervise well operation/maintenance. Actually, petroleum engineering has many specialties. Drilling engineers work with geologists and contractors in designing and supervising drilling operations, while production engineers develop processes/equipment to optimize oil and gas production. Reservoir engineers help determine ideal recovery processes, estimate the number of wells that can be drilled economically, and simulate future performance using sophisticated computer models.

Initially, Petroleum Engineers (often known by their specialty as reservoir engineers) receive information on where underground pools of oil or gas may be located from petrophysicists, who have estimated the porosity, permeability, and oil content of the reservoir rock that has been sampled at the drill site. The Petroleum Engineers' task is to determine how to extract the most oil most economically. They begin by analyzing data about the oil: its depth, the type of surrounding rock, and the surface of the land above the oil. Then they decide where the wells should go and what processes will be needed to force the oil to the surface. With this data, Petroleum Engineers estimate how much it will cost to obtain the oil or gas. They also consider how much money the fuels will sell for. If there will be an adequate profit, they set about finalizing the removal plans.

In this process, Petroleum Engineers may recommend supplementary processes to enhance the recovery and stimulation of the flow through such processes as pressurizing or heating the subsurface areas. They develop the well-drilling plan for management approval, specifying factors including drilling time, the number of special activities required (such as directional drilling), and costs related to testing and material requirements (such as well casing and drilling muds). They may consult with scientific, engineering, and technical personnel to solve any design problems.

At the drill site(s), Petroleum Engineers supervise the drilling operations. Those who specialize in this task are known as drilling engineers. They coordinate the activities of all workers at the site and assign all tasks. They supervise the construction of the drilling platform and inspect it at completion. They also test drilling machinery/equipment for efficiency and safety. When drilling begins, they determine the drill rate, monitor how much oil (or gas) is produced, and resolve on-site drilling problems. They advise when to substitute drilling mud compounds or different tool bits to improve the drilling conditions. They inspect the well bore to determine that final casing and tubing installations are completed and will work properly and safely.

Petroleum Engineers (who are production or completion engineers) prepare the completion procedure for the well. They plan the oil and gas field recovery containers, piping, and treatment vessels to receive, remove contaminants from, and separate the oil (or gas) products flowing from the well. For this purpose, they will choose the surface collection, dehydration, and storage facilities to be used. They monitor the production rate of the oil (or gas) from the working wells and plan any rework process to correct well production.

Throughout this process, Petroleum Engineers design and implement appropriate production, processing, and transportation options, as well as design and implement health, safety, and environmental controls. They must coordinate these high technology plans with the use of laborers, often in dangerous conditions. The drilling rig crew and machines they employ become the remote partners of the Petroleum Engineer in implementing every drilling operation. Understanding and accounting for the issues and communication challenges of building these teams is a vital part of a Petroleum Engineer's job.

Salaries
Petroleum Engineers historically have been one of the highest paid engineering disciplines. According to the U.S. Department of Labor's Bureau of Labor Statistics in their *Occupational Outlook Handbook, 2006–07 Edition*, annual salaries for Petroleum Engineers in May 2004 ranged from a low of $48,260 (the lower 10 percent of engineers) to a high of $140,800 (for the top 10 percent of engineers). The median yearly salary was $88,500.

In the salary survey report conducted by PayScale, Inc. in 2006, median annual salaries for Petroleum Engineers ranged from $62,800 to $115,000, depending on geographic location. Median annual salaries according to years of experience ranged from $62,352 (for those engineers with less than a year's experience) to $140,292 (for Petroleum Engineers with 20 years' or more seasoning).

Employment Prospects
Employment opportunities for Petroleum Engineers are expected to decline through 2014, according to the U.S. Department of Labor's Bureau of Labor Statistics, as most of the potential petroleum-producing areas in the United States already have been explored. Nonetheless, jobs are still expected to occur because the number of openings is likely to exceed the relatively small number of new graduates. Most job possibilities should result from the need to replace Petroleum Engineers who transfer to other occupations or leave the labor force. Petroleum Engineers work around the world and, in fact, the best employment opportunities may be abroad. Many foreign employers seek U.S.-trained Petroleum Engineers, and many U.S. employers maintain overseas branches.

Advancement Prospects
Beginning petroleum engineering graduates usually do routine work under the supervision of experienced engineers. As they gain knowledge and expertise, they are assigned more difficult tasks, where they have greater independence to develop their own designs, solve problems, and make decisions on their own. Those with leadership skills may move up to become team leaders of engineers and technicians. Others who want to gravitate into company management may advance by getting a master's degree in petroleum engineering or in business administration. Engineers with promotional talents may move into sales or marketing in the oil or gas industries, while those with experience and professional contacts may select to open their own consulting firms. Many Petroleum Engineers who leave the profession are hired by environmental companies, work for the government (such as the Environmental Protection Agency or EPA), teach, or become consultants to professional oil and gas organizations or investment banks and other financial service firms.

Education and Training
A Bachelor of Science degree in petroleum engineering is a basic requirement for this position. Many Petroleum

Engineers also have master's or doctoral (Ph.D.) degrees. While bachelor's degree programs in engineering typically are designed to last four years, many students find that it requires between four and five years to complete their studies. High school preparation should include a solid background in mathematics and science, as well as courses in English, social studies, humanities, and computer and information technology.

Newly hired graduates usually work under the direction of experienced engineers (which may include some formal classroom training) for up to a year before being assigned more complicated projects.

Special Requirements

All states require registration of engineers whose work may affect life, health, or property, which would include all engineers employed by companies in the oil and gas industries. Many states also require licensing of engineers working within their jurisdiction.

Experience, Skills, and Personality Traits

Petroleum Engineers must have the ability to identify, analyze, and solve problems. While they need to be capable of working independently, they typically work on a team with geoscientists, contractors, or technicians. They have constant interaction with coworkers. Whether they are functioning in a team situation or just asking for advice, they have to be able to communicate and work well with a variety of technicians, technical workers, and specialists in many fields outside engineering. In addition, they need to communicate (orally and in writing) all the findings, reports, and plans to upper management. They should be creative and

heavily detail-oriented. They need computer proficiency, and they need an aptitude for mathematics and design. Self-confidence is also crucial, as on-site decisions have to be made quickly and surely. Above all, Petroleum Engineers must have high energy levels to deal with the demanding workloads and changing priorities of their profession.

Unions and Associations

The principle professional organization for Petroleum Engineers is the Society of Petroleum Engineers (SPE). Other major professional associations for Petroleum Engineers are the American Association of Petroleum Geologists (AAPG); the American Gas Association (AGA); the American Institute of Mining, Metallurgical, and Petroleum Engineers (AIME); the American Petroleum Institute (API); the Gas Processors Association (GPA); and the Society for Mining, Metallurgy, and Exploration (SME).

Tips for Entry

1. Participate in an engineering internship or co-op while you are in college. Many universities and colleges offer co-op and internship programs, where firsthand experience in the field can be gained and industry contacts can be made.
2. Become fluent in one or more languages other than English, as many of your best job opportunities as a Petroleum Engineer may be outside the United States.
3. Be prepared for a continual learning process throughout your career. Technology is always shifting. Such professional associations as the Society of Petroleum Engineers offer compact courses to update skills and to continue your professional development.

PETROPHYSICIST

CAREER PROFILE

Duties: Once a drill site for oil or natural gas is established, estimate the porosity, permeability, and oil (or gas) content of the reservoir rock that has been sampled at the location

Alternate Title(s): Deepwater Petrophysicist; Petroleum Engineering Specialist; Petrophysical Engineer; Rock Properties Petrophysicist

Salary Range: $75,000 to $120,000 or more

Employment Prospects: Fair

Advancement Prospects: Fair

Prerequisites:

Education or Training—Bachelor of Science degree in a geoscience or engineering discipline required; master's degree usually preferred as well

Experience—Five to eight years' background within the oil or natural gas industries, preferably with a service company or producer

Special Skills and Personality Traits—Ability to interact effectively with geoscientists and other petroleum engineers; capacity to think independently and challenge answers not supported by facts; detail-oriented; excellent computer skills; good communication and organizational capabilities; patience and persistence; self-starter and able to work under deadline pressure

Special Requirements—All states require registration, and many states require licensing

CAREER LADDER

```
┌─────────────────────────────────────┐
│   Engineering Team Leader; Other     │
│   Management Positions; Owner,       │
│         Consulting Firm              │
└─────────────────────────────────────┘

┌─────────────────────────────────────┐
│          Petrophysicist              │
└─────────────────────────────────────┘

┌─────────────────────────────────────┐
│   Assistant Petroleum Engineer;      │
│      Engineering Technician;         │
│         Project Geologist            │
└─────────────────────────────────────┘
```

Position Description

Petrophysics is the study of the physical and chemical properties that describe the occurrence and behavior of rocks, soils, and fluids. Petrophysics mainly studies reservoirs of resources (such as oil and natural gas) found under Earth's surface. It concerns itself with the measurement of field data from a well or wells, the processing of that data, its incorporation into physical models that describe the rock, the calculation/interpretation of reservoir properties, and the integration of these calculations with other data from test/actual production to describe the reservoir completely from a geologic and engineering perspective.

Petrophysicists (often called petrophysical engineers) are primarily involved in the exploration phase of the discovery of an accumulation of gas or oil resource in a reservoir. Most Petrophysicists are employed to compute what are commonly called reservoir (or conventional) petrophysical properties. These properties include porosity (the measure of the amount of space between individual grains in a rock). This space can be filled with water or hydrocarbons. Water saturation, another property, is a measure of the amount of pore space that is filled with water. Additional properties include permeability (fluid), which is the quantity of fluid (usually hydrocarbon) that can flow from the rock as a function of time and pressure, and net reservoir rock, which is the thickness of rock with enough permeability to deliver fluids to a well bore. Another quantity, net pay, is computed to determine the thickness of rock that can deliver hydrocarbons to the well bore at a profitable rate. These measurements and computed properties are used by Petrophysicists to determine the amount of oil or gas in a well bore and the rate at which that hydrocarbon can be extracted.

Well logging is the technique used for recording the rock and fluid properties to find the subsurface hydrocarbon zones. In the logging procedure, a logging tool is lowered on the end of a wireline into an oil well (or hole) to measure the rock and fluid properties of the rock formation. The Petrophysicists interpret these measurements to locate and quantify potential depth zones containing the oil and gas (hydrocarbons). This process can also be accomplished with a new technique, Logging While Drilling (LWD), where the sensors are integrated into the drill string and the petrophysical measurements are made while the well is being drilled.

A key tool is a computer program, GeoFrame, which is a processing/interpretation software that allows Petrophysicists to develop/implement interpretation models and to evaluate rock formations of interest. Another recent development consists of a CMR (Combinable Magnetic Resonance) tool, using nuclear magnetic resonance technology, to provide essential data about rock texture. Throughout the evaluation process, the Petrophysicist follows the logging operations closely to make changes dictated by rock properties or bore hole conditions.

As Tom Neville, Senior Petrophysicist in Melbourne, Australia, states, "Whether it be providing estimates of porosity and water saturation for a back of the envelope estimate of hydrocarbon in place, or providing input to a full field reservoir simulation model to be used in evaluating economic viability of a potential development, petrophysics lies at the center of the petroleum resource evaluation and development process." Thus, Petrophysicists are a basic link between the static earth models of the geologist and geophysicist and the dynamic production models of a reservoir petroleum engineer.

Salaries

Petroleum engineers historically have been one of the highest paid engineering disciplines. Petrophysicists, as specialty petroleum employees have incomes on the high end of the pay scale of petroleum engineers. According to industry sources, those Petrophysicists with five or more years' experience can expect annual salaries ranging from $95,000 to $125,000. Starting yearly salaries for qualified applicants (with appropriate educational background and experience in the gas or oil industries) can range from $75,000 to $90,000.

Employment Prospects

Employment opportunities for Petrophysicists, like petroleum engineers, are expected to decline through 2014, according to the U.S. Department of Labor's Bureau of Labor Statistics, as most of the potential petroleum-producing areas in the United States already have been explored. Nonetheless, favorable opportunities are expected to occur because the number of job openings is likely to exceed the relatively small number of graduates with the requisite qualifications and the necessary experience in the industry. Most job possibilities should result from the need to replace Petrophysicists who transfer to other occupations or leave the labor force. Petrophysicists work around the world and many of the best employment opportunities may be in other countries. Many foreign employers seek U.S.-trained petroleum engineers and Petrophysicists, and many U.S. employers maintain overseas branches.

Advancement Prospects

Applicants for Petrophysicist positions usually start their careers in the oil and/or gas industries as petroleum engineering technicians under the supervision of seasoned geologists, geoscientists, petroleum engineers, and, eventually, Petrophysicists. As they gain knowledge and experience, they are assigned to specific projects, where they have greater independence to develop their skills, solve problems, and make decisions on their own.

Many Petrophysicists stay within their high-paid posts, moving from one company to another. Some may eventually decide to advance to higher management levels within the oil or gas industries. Other veteran Petrophysicists, who have made the appropriate professional contacts, may choose to open their own consulting firms.

Education and Training

A Bachelor of Science degree in a geoscience (such as geology) or engineering discipline (such as petroleum engineering) is a basic requirement. Most Petrophysicists also obtain a master's degree in a science or engineering-related discipline. Additionally, they usually expect applicants to have had from five to seven years' experience working for an operating company in the oil or gas industries.

Special Requirements

All states require registration of engineers whose work may affect life, health, or property, which would include all engineers employed by companies in the oil and gas industries. Many states also require licensing of engineers working within the jurisdiction.

Experience, Skills, and Personality Traits

Petrophysicists are specialized technicians who must be capable of working within cross-functional integrated teams, sharing their knowledge of petrophysical applications and evaluation processes with geoscientists and various petroleum engineers. They need to be skilled in all core petrophysical areas, including operations, well and reservoir management, and the delivery of field development plans, and be familiar with drilling operations, understanding the impact of formation evaluation programs on those undertakings. Their strong understanding of rock properties, formation evaluation technology, and data acquisition methods, needs to be tempered by a comprehensive appreciation of cost/benefit tradeoffs.

They need to be knowledgeable of major petrophysical software packages applied in the industry for well and reservoir interpretation and be current with the latest industry tools and petrophysical interpretation techniques, working with both clastic (sedimentary rocks) and carbonate reservoir systems. They have to accept personal responsibility for their project and recommendations and have a willingness to work through others. They should have the ability to think independently and the courage to reject ideas/proposals that do not meet hard scrutiny.

Petrophysicists should be self-starters and possess excellent organizational abilities. They must have superior inter-personal and communication skills and be able to work under pressure. In addition, they should be willing to coach and train less experienced personnel.

Unions and Associations

Groups of interest for Petrophysicists include the American Association of Petroleum Geologists (AAPG), the American Gas Association (AGA), the American Geological Institute (AGI), the American Petroleum Institute (API), the Geological Society of America (GSA), and the Society of Petroleum Engineers (SPE).

Tips for Entry

1. Perfect your computer skills, as they will be essential to your career as a geoscientist, petroleum engineer, and Petrophysicist.
2. Be prepared to labor five to seven years as an engineering technician or as a working project geologist assistant to gain experience in the techniques/processes of well drilling and evaluation.
3. Familiarity with one or more languages other than English may prove to be a useful career advancement tool.

REFINING AND PROCESSING

NATURAL GAS PROCESSING PLANT OPERATOR

CAREER PROFILE

Duties: Distribute or process gas for utility companies and for industrial use by controlling equipment, such as compressors, evaporators, heat exchangers, and refrigeration equipment to maintain specified pressures on main pipelines

Alternate Title(s): Gas Compressor Operator; Gas Pipeline Operator; Gas Pumping Station Operator; Liquefaction-and-Regasification Plant Operator; Natural Gas Treating Unit Operator

Salary Range: $35,000 to $90,000 or more

Employment Prospects: Fair

Advancement Prospects: Fair

Prerequisites:

Education or Training—High school diploma required, and some vocational training or job-related course work may also be needed; in some cases, an Associate's Degree in an Industrial Process Operator program is recommended

Experience—Usually two to four years in a processing plant environment working with experienced employees

Special Skills and Personality Traits—Able to work with little supervision; comfortable around large, noisy equipment; conscientious and safety-minded; excellent decision-making skills; good communication and organizational abilities; mechanically inclined and knowledgeable about/handy with machines and tools; precise and responsible

Special Requirements—Some states may require a state certification or license

CAREER LADDER

Control Operators in Other Industries; Gas Processing Plant Manager

Natural Gas Processing Plant Operator

Engineering Technician; Utility Worker

Position Description

Processing natural gas is, generally, less complicated than the processing and refining of crude oil. The natural gas used by consumers is composed almost entirely of methane. However, natural gas found at the wellhead is by no means as pure. Raw natural gas comes from three types of wells: oil, gas, and condensate. Natural gas that comes from oil wells can exist separate from oil in the formation (from which they both are extracted) or dissolved in the crude oil. Gas wells typically produce raw natural gas by itself, while condensate wells produce free natural gas along with a semi-liquid hydrocarbon condensate. However, whatever the source of the natural gas, it commonly exists in mixtures with other hydrocarbons along with water vapor, hydrogen sulfide, carbon dioxide, helium, nitrogen, and other compounds.

Natural gas processing consists of separating the hydrocarbons and fluids from the pure natural gas. Most transportation pipelines (that carry the gas to commercial and public dispensing plants) usually impose restrictions on the composition of the natural gas that is allowed into the pipeline. Thus, before the natural gas can be transported it must be purified. The products removed are known as "natural gas liquids" (or NGLs), and they are valuable by-products. These NGLs (such as ethane, propane, and natural gasoline) are sold separately and for a variety of different uses (including enhancing oil recovery in oil wells, providing raw materials for oil refineries or petrochemical plants, and as energy sources).

While some of the natural gas processing steps can be accomplished at or near the wellhead, much of the purification occurs at a processing plant, usually located in a natural gas producing region. The extracted natural gas is transported to these processing plants through a network of pipelines. In addition, some final processing is sometimes accomplished by straddle extraction plants to remove remaining small quantities of NGLs to make an even purer product.

Natural Gas Processing Plant Operators control the equipment used to process gas. From computerized control panels, they monitor, adjust, and maintain the processing units and other equipment. Their primary objective is to ensure that the gas produced is free of impurities. They open valves to admit gas and specified chemicals into treating vessels to remove impurities. They adjust the controls of auxiliary equipment, such as pumps, heating coils, and cooling towers. They modify temperature and pressure gauges to keep heat and pressure at maximum efficiency and safety.

Natural Gas Processing Plant Operators perform routine tests (or deliver test samples to a laboratory) to determine the qualities of gas being processed. They drain samples of boiler water from the treating unit for lab analysis.

They control the operation of compressors, scrubbers, evaporators, and refrigeration equipment to liquefy, compress, or regasify natural gas. They start the pumps and adjust the controls of auxiliary equipment to transfer the liquid gas from the storage tanks and to regulate the temperature and pressure of units that regasify liquid gas into the distribution pipelines. They may adjust and repair gas meters, and regulators (called governors), using hand tools, or may advise and assist maintenance workers repairing these and other control instruments. They monitor the functioning of equipment, observe temperature, level, and flow gauges, and perform regular unit checks to ensure that all equipment is operating properly. They test gas, chemicals, and air to assess factors such as purity and moisture content, to detect quality problems, and to find any gas or chemical leaks. They usually must post meter and gauge readings in a daily logbook and submit daily reports to plant management on facility operations.

Salaries

According to a January 2007 salary survey report on gas plant operators made by PayScale, Inc., median annual salaries of operators with one to four years' experience was $40,000, and those with five to nine years' experience had incomes approaching $44,000. Operators with 10 to 19 years' experience earned median yearly salaries of $57,000, and those with 20 years or more experience had incomes of $58,000. Industry sources indicate that salaries for gas processing plant operators can range from beginning salaries of approximately $35,000 to $90,000 or more for experienced operators.

Employment Prospects

Although worldwide demand for oil and gas is expected to grow, overall U.S. employment in the oil and gas extraction and processing industries is expected to decline by 6 percent through the year 2014, compared to an employment increase of 14 percent in all industries combined, according to the U.S. Department of Labor's Bureau of Labor Statistics in their *Occupational Outlook Handbook, 2006–07 Edition*. In general, the level of future natural gas exploration and development and, therefore, employment opportunities in this industry, remains contingent upon the size of accessible reserves available and the going prices for gas. Environmental concerns in the United States and restrictions on drilling in environmentally sensitive areas have meant a decline in domestic production.

In addition, employment in the natural gas exploration and production industry normally would grow with the increasing demand for such a cleaner-burning fuel as natural gas. However, recent high natural gas prices have limited demand and have caused some planned future power plants to return to coal as a power source. These trends, of course, may be reversed with advances in technology that increase the proportion of exploratory wells that yield both oil and gas and extend the production of existing wells.

Despite an overall decline in employment in the gas extraction industry, and, as a result, in the gas processing industry, job opportunities still should be fair. The need to replace workers who transfer to other industries, retire, or leave the workforce will be the major source of job openings.

Advancement Prospects

Natural Gas Processing Plant Operators who show an affinity for management and take courses in business management and economics may aim at joining their company's management as plant manager or an operations manager. Others may select to leave the gas industry for more stable manufacturing companies as machine setters, operators, or tenders. Alternatively, after achieving a college degree in mechanics or mechanical engineering, they may seek jobs as operators of stationary engines and mechanical equipment in industrial processes.

Education and Training

Most gas processing plant employers prefer to hire high school graduates who have experience or post-secondary education in electronics, electrical systems, mechanics, or instrumentation. A familiarity with computers and a background in chemistry, mathematics, and physics will be good assets in their work in the industry.

In larger processing companies, new employees are typically hired as utility workers. Initially, they may do many of the physical jobs, such as cleaning, painting, and maintaining the pipeline stations. As they gain experience, they may be given additional responsibilities in other areas of compressor or meter stations. It often takes several years before utility workers can officially be classified as Natural Gas Processing Plant Operators. During the training period, utility workers may take in-house and technical school courses on compressor, metering, and control room operations.

Special Requirements

Some states may require Natural Gas Processing Plant Operators to have a state license or to have earned a power engineering certificate.

Experience, Skills, and Personality Traits

A Natural Gas Processing Plant Operator's job is not normally too demanding physically, as much of the individual's workday is spent in a control room, monitoring the processes involved in gas production and processing. Operators may also spend time outdoors, performing routine checks on equipment and even driving to stations to check and repair equipment. Processing operators, as well as pipeline operators and maintenance workers, must be aware of potential hazards and know how to handle emergency situations. Hazards include fluids under high pressure and deadly hydrogen sulfide, which is often a component of gas that comes directly from the well.

Natural Gas Processing Plant Operators should be mechanically inclined and have good decision-making and organizational skills. They have to be extremely conscientious, safety-minded, and precise in executing their duties. They should have good communication skills as they will deal with many people, from co-workers to management personnel. Operators should be comfortable working around large, noisy equipment and be able to work on their own with little supervision.

Unions and Associations

The principle association of interest for Natural Gas Processing Plant Operators is the Gas Processors Association (GPA). They may find it useful also to join the Interstate Natural Gas Association of America (INGAA), a trade organization of Natural Gas Companies.

Tips for Entry

1. Take an apprentice position (or a summer job) in a tool or industrial shop where equipment and operations are managed by control boards so you become familiar with the automatic control process.
2. After high school, consider pursuing an associate's degree in an Industrial Process Operator program to give you an advantage in your job search.
3. Besides a concentration in chemistry, physics, and math courses, take classes in sociology, writing, and public speaking, to expand your communication skills.

REFINERY OPERATORS

CAREER PROFILE

Duties: <u>Refinery Operator</u>: Responsible for day-to-day operations of oil refineries and upgrading facilities; <u>Refinery Operator Helper</u>: Assist Refinery Operator in distillation and processing of crude and refined oil; <u>Furnace Operator</u>: Control operation of burners to maintain temperature in furnaces of petroleum-processing units; <u>Gauger</u>: Test oil in refinery storage tanks and regulate the flow of oil into pipelines

Alternate Title(s): <u>Refinery Operator</u>: Oil Refiner, Refiner, Refining Process Operator, Upgrader Process Operator; <u>Refinery Operator Helper</u>: Absorption Plant Operator Helper, Purification Operator Helper; <u>Gauger:</u> Field Gauger, Oil Gauger, Tank Terminal Gauger, Terminal Gauger

Salary Range: $30,000 to $75,000 or more

Employment Prospects: Fair

Advancement Prospects: Fair

Prerequisites:

Education or Training—High school degree and one or more years of post-secondary education training needed; in some cases associate's degree in chemical or petroleum engineering may be required

Experience—In-house training courses while working with veteran operators

Special Skills and Personality Traits—Ability to work in a team environment and give clear directions in emergency situations; physical agility; capability of working changing shifts and remaining alert; capacity for thinking/learning quickly; enjoyment in controlling equipment, instruments and machinery; excellent problem-solving and decision-making skills; good communication talents

Special Requirements—Certification as a petroleum process operator may be required

CAREER LADDER

```
┌─────────────────────────────────────┐
│  Refinery Management or Supervisory  │
│  Positions; Refinery Positions in    │
│  Other Industries                    │
└─────────────────────────────────────┘

┌─────────────────────────────────────┐
│         Refinery Operators           │
└─────────────────────────────────────┘

┌─────────────────────────────────────┐
│        Petroleum Technician          │
└─────────────────────────────────────┘
```

Position Description

Oil refinery is the process that converts petroleum crude oil into automotive fuels (gasoline/petrol and diesel oil), liquefied petroleum gases, jet aircraft fuel, heating fuel, asphalt, bulk tar, and petroleum coke. Raw oil or unprocessed (crude) oil is not very useful in its natural state. To be usable, it must undergo a number of processes in the field and at the refinery. In the field, raw oil (or oilsand) is treated so it can move through major pipelines. At upgrading facilities, it is treated to the point that it can be used by a refinery.

At the refinery, it undergoes several additional distillation steps (such as cracking, blending, reforming) that separate it into useable products. First, it is heated to turn the oil into gas. (The components of crude oil turn to gas at different temperatures, so the gasoline, kerosene, and other oils can be separated from each other.) Next, the gases are cooled so they return to their liquid state. The different oils are then blended, separated, or purified for use in fuels and lubricants and to create by-products that can be used in petrochemical processes (to form such materials as plastics and waxes). The final step in gasoline production is the blending of fuels with different octane ratings, vapor pressures, and other properties to meet product specifications.

Refinery Operators' job titles and duties vary from one refinery/upgrading facility to another. There are often different categories of process operators and various refineries have diverse combinations of categories. Operators may be known by the process in which they are involved (e.g., treater, blender, bitumen extractor, or upgrader operator) or by the department unit in which they work (e.g., catalytic cranking unit operator or pumping unit operator).

In general, however, Refinery Operators control the continuous operation of petroleum refining and processing units to generate products by various methods. They analyze specifications, schedules, operating logs, test results of oil samples, and laboratory recommendations to determine any changes in equipment controls needed to turn out specified quantities/qualities of products. They plan the movement of products through pipelines to processing, storage, and shipping units, utilizing their knowledge of system interconnections and capacities. They conduct ongoing routine checks on equipment, noting any possible problems, recording their readings (manually or on a computer), and scheduling any maintenance work. They may lubricate equipment and clean the interiors of processing units by circulating chemicals and solvents through them.

Some Refinery Operators are control room operators who monitor process indicators and observe control instruments and automatic warning signals, which provide data about the operation of each unit in their section. When signals indicate problems, they inspect equipment to determine the location and nature of malfunction. They move and set controls to make necessary adjustments to ensure safe and efficient plant operation.

Refinery Operator Helpers assist by patrolling areas and inspecting equipment to detect malfunctions. They read flowmeters and temperature and pressure gauges, recording data. They report the operation conditions of units to Refinery Operators. They turn controls as instructed to direct flow of product to other units, to maintain specified levels of oil in tanks and towers, and to start, stop, and regulate equipment.

Furnace Operators are a specific type of Refinery Operator. They handle the operation of burners to maintain the temperature in furnaces of petroleum-processing units according to specifications. They start the furnace and turn valves/switches to regulate the flow of fuel oil or gas to burners. They verify the operating condition of units and record their findings. They examine the furnace to detect overheating of walls and tubes and any leakage. They observe flame distribution and combustion conditions in the furnace, the color of burner flame, and gas issuing from the stack and move air damper controls to correct combustion conditions.

Gaugers take samples of products and test them for quality and grade level, using centrifugal testers and comparing the samples against standards. They record test data, the amount of crude oil or gas used, and the volume produced and report to senior Refinery Operators.

Salaries

According to wage information provided by the *Occupational Employment Statistics (OES)* program in cooperation with the U.S. Department of Labor's Bureau of Labor Statistics and taken from the Fourth Quarter 2006 Employment Cost Index, average annual salaries for Refinery Operators ranged from a low of $33,150 to a high of $71,331. In its Salary Survey Report, updated January 12, 2007, PayScale, Inc. found that Refinery Operators with one to four years' experience had a median yearly salary of $30,700. Those with five to nine years had median salaries of $50,000, and those with 20 years' or more seasoning had median salaries of $71,500.

Employment Prospects

According to the U.S. Department of Labor's Bureau of Labor Statistics, employment possibilities for Refinery Operators will decline through the year 2014, mirroring that of the petroleum industry in general. In the United States, there is strong pressure to prevent the development of new refineries due to the public's environmental concerns. (No major refinery has been built in the country since 1976.) However, many existing refineries have been expanded and many operations have installed the equipment needed to comply with environmental protection regulations. The greatest demand will be for replacements of operators who have transferred to another industry or have retired. Nonetheless, considering the increasing energy needs of the country, the demand for continued oil supplies (and their refinery byproducts) will only persist, thus guaranteeing, to some degree, job openings for Refinery Operators.

Advancement Prospects

There is a considerable mobility among jobs within most refineries, often as part of a formal development or training program. Experience as a Refinery Operator in all the operating units controlled by the central control room is a major prerequisite for chief operators. Experienced Refinery Operators may advance to supervisory and other management posts. Experienced operators also may move into related positions in other industries, such as petrochemical plants, water treatment plants, or power generation facilities. Others pursue further education and gain appropriate engineering degrees to advance into engineering positions in the oil or gas industry.

Education and Training

The minimum education requirement for Refinery Operators is a high school diploma accompanied by training in power engineering or process operations. For some posts, employers may prefer applicants to have a two-year diploma in chemical or petroleum engineering technology.

Larger oil refining companies have in-house training programs. Smaller operations usually send new employees to training workshops. Many Refinery Operators learn their skills on the job from veteran workers. Trainees labor to become journeymen (workers who have completed training and/or certification in a particular field of the refinery operation and are now regarded as qualified and experienced).

Special Requirements

Some refinery companies may require a company certification as a petroleum process/refinery operator or technician.

Experience, Skills, and Personality Traits

Experience for beginning Refinery Operators is typically gained on the job by working with more experienced operators. Since refineries operate 24 hours a day, year-round, Refinery Operators usually work eight- or 12-hour shifts.

Routine checks inside/outside the refinery are undertaken regardless of weather conditions. Lifting heavy items is routinely required. Where refinery units are spread over a wide area, Refinery Operators may do a lot of walking.

Refinery Operators must be interested in working with massive systems and complex machines and enjoy controlling equipment, instruments and machinery. They have to analyze information to solve problems and must have the ability to think and learn quickly. They need to be precise in their job. They must like working in a team environment and be able to work different shifts while remaining alert. They should have good communication skills and be able to comprehend work-related specifications and other materials.

Unions and Associations

Membership in the American Petroleum Institute may be of particular interest for petroleum Refinery Operators.

Tips for Entry

1. During high school, take an apprentice job in a machine or an electrical repair shop to gain practical experience working with machines/electrical equipment.

2. Consider finding a part-time (or summer) job as a journeyman working for a construction company contracted by an oil refinery for construction or repair work to gain first-hand knowledge of oil refinery equipment/processes.

3. Look at pursuing a two-year associate's degree in chemical or petroleum engineering to enhance your job possibilities with oil refining and processing companies.

SEMISKILLED PERSONNEL

LABORERS

CAREER PROFILE

Duties: <u>Roughneck</u>: Responsible for the operation of equipment and machines in the drilling operation as required by the driller; <u>Roustabout</u>: Responsible for general labor tasks, maintenance, and construction work at oil fields and on offshore oil rigs

Alternate Title(s): <u>Roughneck</u>: Connection Worker, Floor Hand, Gang Worker, Rotary-Drill Helper; <u>Roustabout</u>: Lease Hand, Oil Field Roustabout, Roustabout Crew Leader, Roustabout Hand, Roustabout Pusher

Salary Range: <u>Roughneck</u>: $40,000 to $50,000 or more; <u>Roustabout</u>: $26,000 to $35,000 or more

Employment Prospects: Fair to Good

Advancement Prospects: Good

Prerequisites:

Education or Training—Formal academic qualifications frequently not needed, but high school diploma highly recommended

Experience—Work experience in shipbuilding, construction, or engineering useful

Special Skills and Personality Traits—Ability to work well in a team environment; adept with good practical hand skills; enjoy working outdoors; mechanical aptitude; strong and physically fit; solid interpersonal skills

CAREER LADDER

```
┌─────────────────────────────────────┐
│  Oil Well Driller; Other Skilled Well│
│             Personnel                │
└─────────────────────────────────────┘

┌─────────────────────────────────────┐
│             Roughneck                │
└─────────────────────────────────────┘

┌─────────────────────────────────────┐
│            Roustabout                │
└─────────────────────────────────────┘

┌─────────────────────────────────────┐
│  High School Graduate; Entry-level   │
│             Worker                   │
└─────────────────────────────────────┘
```

Position Description

While also utilized in general maintenance and construction work at drilling rigs on land-based oil fields, Roustabouts and Roughnecks are primarily based on offshore facilities such as oil or gas rigs or drilling platforms. Oil and gas drilling rigs are small, mobile structures on land or water, whereas production platforms on water are much larger, accommodating 50 to 100 workers, with living facilities as well as the well production equipment and structures.

Roustabouts are entry-level positions in the oil and gas industries. As general laborers, they do maintenance and construction work at oilfields and offshore facilities. They use various vehicles to move equipment, piping, and waste materials and may drive extensively to pick up/transport assorted supplies and materials as needed. They fell trees to make clearings at drill sites and to create roads. They remove trees and underlying brush to reduce fire hazards. Once the site is clear, they dig trenches for foundations. Next, they erect forms, mix concrete, and pour it into forms. They bolt or nail together the framework for derricks (which are the superstructure of the drilling rigs). They unload the framework, piping, and other materials from trucks by hand, truck winches, or motorized lifts. In addition, Roustabouts connect piping to create pipelines between holding tanks and loading areas. They walk along pipelines to locate leaks, making visual inspections and using electronic detectors. They clean up any spilled oil by bailing it into containers. They may clean and service trucks and auxiliary equipment.

On offshore facilities, Roustabouts usually work as part of a team of up to 20 people. They help to keep the drilling area in good working order, including cleaning, scraping, and painting the platform deck, equipment, and work areas. They offload supplies from boats and move them to storage areas. They use lifting gear and winches to load and stack equipment and guide cranes to move larger loads about the platform's decks. They supply equipment to rig floors on demand and usually work under the supervision of a lead Roustabout.

Roughnecks carry out duties that are more skilled as part of the actual drilling operation. They are responsible for the operation of equipment and machines as required by the driller (supervisor of the drilling crew). They unscrew or tighten pipes, casing, tubing, and pump rods, using hand and power wrenches and tongs. They collect core and cutting samples. They add fresh lengths of drill pipe as the drill moves deeper into rock. They insert and extract the entire drill, clean, maintain, and repair the drilling equipment. They use lifting gear, ropes, and winches to perform these duties. Additionally, they are typically present in the mud process room at all times. They help to repair mud pumps and aid in the mixing and conditioning of the lubricants (drilling mud) for the drill bit. Their responsibilities include ensuring shakers and machines are working properly. They often must dismantle and repair oil field machinery, boilers, or steam engine parts. They usually work under the supervision of the driller or an assistant driller.

Roustabouts and Roughnecks work up to 12 hours a day on a 24-hour shift rotation. They normally work on an offshore rig or platform for two or three weeks, followed by two or three weeks of rest ashore. Offshore workers must wear protective clothing, which includes eye protection, harnesses, hard hats, gloves, ear mufflers, and thermal boiler suits.

Salaries

As entry-level workers in the oil and gas industries, Roustabouts can expect annual salaries to start at about $26,000 and range as high as $35,000 or more, according to industry sources. In turn, Roughnecks (many of them former Roustabouts) may expect annual salaries to range from $40,000 to $50,000 or more, depending on the size of the drilling company for which they work and on the extent of their responsibilities. Workers in both positions can expect their airfares to be paid by the oil rig company, and their benefits include medical insurance, meals, room, and board.

Employment Prospects

Despite the overall decline in employment in the oil and gas extraction industries, job opportunities for these two positions remain fair to good as the turnover rate for these two laborer jobs is quite high. Roustabouts often become Roughnecks, and Roughnecks frequently move on to other drilling posts. Thus, the need to replace workers is constant. Those applicants who have had experience in the construc-

tion, shipbuilding, or other engineering businesses have an edge in employment possibilities.

Advancement Prospects

Roustabouts who show ability can become Roughnecks after sufficient training, usually six months to two years. Alternatively, they may move up to become switchers, gaugers, or pumpers. In turn, those Roughnecks who have shown skill and have gained sufficient experience can advance to derrick operators and, after several years, to assistant drillers and drillers.

Experience gained in these gas and oil extraction jobs also has application in other industries. For example, Roustabouts can move directly to construction jobs. Roughnecks, in turn, may become marine engineering technicians.

Education and Training

While no formal academic qualifications are needed to work as a Roustabout, most employers want applicants to have a high school diploma or a General Educational Development credential (GED) and be 18 years of age or over. Applicants usually have to pass a medical examination as part of their recruitment process. Some companies may administer aptitude tests and screen prospective employees for drug use.

Basic skills are learned through on-the-job training. Oil and gas industry employers put employees through extensive operations and safety training to prevent accidents and environmental damage. This training is an ongoing operation, and routine emergency drills are continuous. Offshore workers usually must complete offshore survival and firefighting training.

Experience, Skills, and Personality Traits

While no previous experience is necessary for either of these positions, those with some relevant work experience, for example in shipbuilding, construction, or engineering have an advantage. In addition, know-how driving various types of trucks and operating forklifts can be helpful.

Both of these positions are all weather, outdoor jobs and require heavy lifting. Roustabouts and Roughnecks must be physically fit and have good practical skills. They should be adept at handling hand tools and power tools and have basic computer proficiency for recording information. They must be able to live/work as a member of a team and be able to get along with other workers. While assertive, they must be able to follow instructions and be very aware of health and safety issues.

Unions and Associations

There are no specific professional associations organized for Roustabouts or Roughnecks. For general information about training and career opportunities, they should contact the American Petroleum Institute (API).

Tips for Entry

1. During high school, investigate job training programs (or take a summer job) with a construction firm, as you will need these skills.
2. In addition to basic math and science courses, take classes in industrial safety and first aid and in equipment maintenance and repair. Summer work in a machine or equipment repair business would be valuable background experience.
3. Be willing to work as a Roustabout—cleaning, loading supplies, and helping move equipment—as it will give you insight into what work on an offshore oil rig is like and how you can advance to higher positions.

PUMPER

CAREER PROFILE

Duties: Operate power pumps and auxiliary equipment to produce flow of oil or gas from wells at extraction sites

Alternate Title(s): Oil Field Pumper; Oil Pumper; Oil Well Pumper; Oilfield Plant and Field Operator; Well Tender; Wellhead Pumper; Wellpumper

Salary Range: $25,000 to $45,000 or more

Employment Prospects: Fair

Advancement Prospects: Fair

Prerequisites:

    Education or Training—High school diploma or a General Educational Development credential (GED) required

    Experience—Familiarity with operating equipment recommended; previous work in petroleum technology a bonus

    Special Skills and Personality Traits—Good writing skills; good eye-hand coordination; mechanical ability; physically fit; solid mathematics background

CAREER LADDER

```
┌─────────────────────────────────────────┐
│ Gas or Oil Plant Operator; Pumping       │
│ Station Operator; Refinery Operator;     │
│ First-Line Supervisor/Manager            │
└─────────────────────────────────────────┘

┌─────────────────────────────────────────┐
│             Wellhead Pumper              │
└─────────────────────────────────────────┘

┌─────────────────────────────────────────┐
│ Pumper Helper; Roughneck;                │
│ Roustabout                               │
└─────────────────────────────────────────┘
```

Position Description

Pumpers work both at oil and gas wells in the field and in oil refineries and gas processing plants. In the field, they operate the pumps and auxiliary equipment to produce the flow of oil or gas from the wells. They start the pumps and open the valves to pump the oil into storage tanks or into pipelines. They start the compressor engines to divert oil from storage tanks into compressor units and auxiliary equipment to recover the natural gas from the oil. They open valves to return the compressed gas to the bottom of specified wells to repressurize them and force oil to the surface. They operate engines and pumps in order to shut off wells according to production schedules established by petroleum engineers and production supervisors, and to switch the flow of oil into unfilled storage tanks. In oil fields where oil flows under natural pressure and does not require pumping, Pumpers (known as switchers) open and close valves to regulate the flow.

Pumpers monitor control panels throughout pumping operations to ensure that materials are being pumped at the correct pressure, density, rate, and concentration. They read flowmeters, gauge the oil in tanks with a calibrated steel tape, and prepare reports on the amount/quality of oil pumped and in storage. They collect and bottle samples of oil for laboratory analysis. They control pumping and blending equipment used to acidize, cement, or fracture gas or oil wells and permeable rock formations around the wells.

Other Pumpers, known as treaters (or crude-oil treaters) operate the chemical, electrical, and centrifugal oil-treatment units to remove sediment and water from crude oil before transporting the resource by pipeline to refineries. First, they open valves and start the pumps to draw the oil from storage tanks to treating units. They open valves to mix specified chemicals with the oil and adjust controls to heat the mixture to particular temperatures. They start the centrifugal machines that break up oil and water emulsions and drain off the water. They open the valves and start pumps to transfer oil into settling tanks where sediment is precipitated from oil. They test samples to determine the content of oil specified for pipeline transportation and record all pertinent data on the process. Other treaters tend treating-plant equipment to remove impurities from natural gas.

In refineries, Pumpers control the pumps and manifold systems that circulate crude, semi-processed, and finished petroleum products, water, and chemical solutions through the processing, storage, and shipping departments of the refinery, according to established schedules. They plan the movement of products through pipelines to processing, storage, and shipping units, utilizing their knowledge of interconnections and capacities of pipelines, valve manifolds, pumps, and tankage. They synchronize their activities with other pumphouses to ensure a continuous flow of oil products and a minimum of contamination between products. They peruse pressure meters and flowmeters and turn valves to regulate pumping speeds according to schedules. They signal still-pump operators, pumper helpers, and gaugers by telephone or radio to operate pumps in designated units, to open and close pipeline and tank valves, and to gauge, sample, and determine the temperature of tank contents. They record all operating data, such as the products and quantities pumped, gauging results, and operating times.

All Pumpers perform routine maintenance on their equipment, repairing gas and oil meters and gauges. They often drive trucks to transport high-pressure pumping equipment, chemicals, fluids, or gases to be pumped into wells. They unload and assemble pipes and pumping equipment and may attach pumps and hoses to wellheads. They lubricate and repair pumps, using grease guns, oilcans, and hand tools. They examine pipelines for leaks, reporting any major breakdowns and well difficulties. In all these duties, they are aided by pumper helpers who are usually assigned many of the menial tasks of maintaining the pumps and auxiliary equipment.

Salaries

According to the U.S. Department of Labor's Bureau of Labor Statistics, in May 2004 entry-level pumper employees had yearly incomes of $26,270, whereas the mean employee annual earnings totaled $34,960. Experienced Pumpers received a mean annual salary of $43,700, with some as high as $52,000.

Employment Prospects

Although worldwide demand for oil and gas is expected to grow, overall U.S. wage and salary employment in the oil and gas extraction and refining industries is expected to decline by 6 percent through the year 2014, according the U.S. Department of Labor. Furthermore, the number of positions for Pumpers is expected to decrease by as much as 11 percent. Despite this overall decline in employment, job opportunities will still be present. The need to replace Pumpers who transfer to other industries, retire, or leave the workforce will be the major source of job openings as more workers in the oil and gas industries approach retirement age and others seek more stable employment in other industries.

Advancement Prospects

Promotion opportunities may be somewhat limited due to the general decline of the domestic petroleum industry (particularly in the refinery side). Advancement prospects remain best for those with skill and experience. Veteran Pumpers may advance to other occupations within the industry. They may become gas or oil plant operators or natural gas pumping station or oil refinery operators. Eventually, they may progress to becoming supervisors or managers at well sites or at refinery or processing plants.

Education and Training

To work as Pumpers, candidates must have a high school diploma or General Educational Development credential (GED). Some Pumpers train through apprenticeship programs, which may extend as long as three years. They receive both classroom and hands-on training. Some employers may require that applicants pass a physical exam, as well as drug testing and/or background checks before employment.

Experience, Skills, and Personality Traits

While know-how will be gained from on-the-job training under the supervision of seasoned Pumpers, applicants for Pumper positions with background in operating equipment in a safe manner can greatly bolster their potential of being hired.

Pumpers need to be physically fit, have a good sense of balance, the ability to judge distances, and excellent eye-hand-foot coordination. Pumpers need to be good at mathematics (algebra, geometry, calculus, statistics, and their applications) and be able to enter, transcribe, record, and maintain data in written and/or computer form. They will need to be able to read procedural manuals, billing documents, and other instructional material. They should be mechanically inclined, with a working knowledge of machines and tools, including their designs, uses, repair, and maintenance. A familiarity with the oil and gas production processes, quality control, costs, and other techniques will aid them in maximizing their production.

Unions and Associations

Professional associations related to Pumpers include the Drilling Engineering Association (DEA), the Petroleum Equipment Suppliers Association (PESA), and the Petroleum Technology Transfer Council (PTTC). In addition, membership in the American Petroleum Institute (API) will assist them in keeping up to date on the latest developments in their field.

Tips for Entry

1. During high school, consider a summer job (or part-time work) in a machine shop to get familiar with

handling machinery, related equipment, and machine tools, as well as working within a business environment.

2. Investigate potential internship programs in the oil and gas industry to become knowledgeable about the production processes and technologies with which you will have to work.

3. Any experience you can gain in repairing machinery, such as cars, will be valuable as performing routine maintenance on vehicles and equipment will be an important part of your job as a Pumper.

WELL SERVICE EQUIPMENT OPERATORS

CAREER PROFILE

Duties: Hoist Operator: Operate hoist to lower and raise instruments and tools into and out of oil or gas wells; Oil Well Pumping Service Operator: Control pumping and blending equipment to acidize, cement, or fracture gas or oil wells and permeable rock formations; Power Tong Operator: Operate hydraulic power tongs that are used to connect casing as it is lowered into an oil or gas well

Alternate Title(s): Hoist Operator: Winch Operator; Oil Well Pumping Service Operator: Acidizer, Cementer, Formation-Fracturing Operator; Power Tong Operator: Casing Tong Operator

Salary Range: $23,000 to $75,000 or more

Employment Prospects: Fair

Advancement Prospects: Fair

Prerequisites:

Education or Training—High school diploma required; related post-secondary technical education in petroleum engineering recommended

Experience—Previous experience on a drilling rig crew or a service rig crew recommended

Special Skills and Personality Traits—Ability to work efficiently and effectively under pressure; detail-oriented; excellent communication and interpersonal skills; good analytical and decision- making abilities; initiative; physical strength and stamina

Special Requirements—Certifications in first aid and safety, blowout prevention, and hazardous waste materials may be required

CAREER LADDER

```
┌─────────────────────────────────────┐
│        Supervisory Positions         │
└─────────────────────────────────────┘

┌─────────────────────────────────────┐
│   Well Service Equipment Operators   │
└─────────────────────────────────────┘

┌─────────────────────────────────────┐
│              Roughneck               │
└─────────────────────────────────────┘
```

Position Description

Hoist Operators control the truck-mounted hoist employed to lower and raise instruments and tools on an electric conductor cable into and out of oil or gas wells. These instruments are used to perform various well services and surveys, such as directional drilling, electric well logging, perforating, and sidewall sample taking. Hoist Operators also assist other workers in loading and unloading equipment from trucks and in connecting instruments and tools to conductor cables. They aid in attaching the cable pulley to the hoist block of the drilling rig or to the special pulley-mount placed in position over the borehole (a process known as rigging up). They load the log recorder with film to prepare for logging of oil or gas well boreholes and observe the indicator to verify the depth of instruments in the borehole. They may repair cables and hoisting equipment and may load explosive charges in such tools as gun or jet perforators.

Oil Well Service Operators control the pumping and blending equipment used to acidize, cement, or fracture gas or oil wells and permeable rock formations. When the initial drilling well shows commercial potential, a string of casing is run into the drill hole. Casing strings consist of multiple joints of large-diameter steel pipe that are screwed together as the pipe is run in the hole. These casing strings are permanently set in the wells with space between the casing and the hole filled with cement, poured by the Oil Well Service Operator (who has mixed the dry cement according to specifications). The casing and its cement sheath protect the mud used in lubricating the drilling process from being demoisturized by surrounding shale formations and protect near-surface potable water zones from contamination by any deeper saltwater zones. The casing also provides a smooth conduit for tools being run in and out of the hole.

Some wells may produce freely without any stimulation once the oil or gas field is breached. Most wells, however, are stimulated either by pumping acid into the formation or by hydraulic fracturing. Oil Well Service Operators, known as acidizer operators and formation-fracturing operators, mix the acids and the fracturing chemicals to be used, after consulting with drilling superintendents on well conditions, pipe sizes, and the amounts to be used. These stimulating operations consist of pumping the treating liquids out of a surface tank, down the well through tubing anchored on the surface, and then out into the formation to break up the impediments to the flow of oil or gas. In onshore operations, the pumps and tanks are truck-mounted, whereas, offshore, they are skid-mounted on the platform. Another type of fracturing, typically utilized in sandstone formations, is hydraulic fracturing, where the zone is broken open to allow for the oil fluids to move to the wellbore.

Power Tong Operators manipulate the hydraulic power tongs used to connect casing sections as they are lowered into a well. The operators manage the hydraulic controls that provide power and operational control to the tongs. They monitor pressure gauges to make sure the correct amount of pressure is applied so casing joints are connected properly.

Much of the work of Well Service Equipment Operators is performed outdoors, where they are exposed to all types of weather conditions and the dirt, dust, noise, and fumes common to oil rigs. Because the work is potentially hazardous, safety is a primary concern for everyone on the rig. Hazards include working on wet, slippery rig floors and ocean platforms, working near or with heavy tools and moving machinery, and exposure to chemical substances.

Salaries

According to the U.S. Department of Labor's Bureau of Labor Statistics in their *Occupational Outlook Handbook, 2006–07 Edition*, median annual salaries for service unit operators in the oil and gas industries in May 2004 were $32,984. Other industry sources indicate that today yearly income for Well Service Equipment Operators can range from a low of $23,000 to a high of $75,000 or more, with average salaries in the mid-$50,000 range.

Employment Prospects

Like that of most jobs in the oil and gas industries, employment of Well Service Equipment Operators remains contingent upon the amount of crude petroleum and natural gas exploration and development that may occur in the future. Stable and favorable prices for oil and gas are needed to allow companies sufficient revenue to expand exploration and production projects to keep pace with growing global energy demands. In addition, fewer reserves of oil and gas in the United States will cause a decline in domestic production, unless new oil and gas fields are found and developed.

Despite the overall decline in employment within the oil and gas extraction industry, job opportunities will remain fair, based on the need to replace workers who transfer to other industries, retire, or leave the workforce altogether. This will be the major source of job openings as more workers in the industry approach retirement age and others seek more stable employment opportunities in other industries, such as construction. Employment opportunities will be best for those with previous experience and technically skilled personnel who can work with the new technologies used by the industries.

Advancement Prospects

Well Service Equipment Operators are employed by contractors who hire out their personnel to oil and natural gas companies. Operators usually start as roustabouts, then roughnecks, gaining experience in the techniques and technologies of the industry. After their on-the-job experience, and, in some cases, in-house courses given by their companies, they specialize and move into operator positions.

Well Service Equipment Operators may expand their skills to include pumping equipment and, then, may advance to the post of field supervisor. Some may go on to become field station managers.

Education and Training

Well Service Equipment Operators must have at least a high school diploma, combined with the ability and desire to learn quickly and put into daily practice what they have learned. Related post-secondary education and experience on a drilling rig crew or a service rig crew are definite assets. Most firms provide company training programs with courses and on-the-job training. In some cases, such as with acidizer oil well service operators, employers may require a two-year diploma, or even a four-year degree in petroleum engineering.

Special Requirements

Well Service Equipment Operators who handle corrosive and poisonous materials may have to be certified in first aid, safety procedures, blowout prevention processes, and the handling of hazardous waste materials.

Experience, Skills, and Personality Traits

Well Service Equipment Operators need to be able to work efficiently and effectively under considerable pressure. They must be careful and thorough in their work, and be able to pay close attention to detail. While capable of working well alone and exhibiting initiative, they also have to be team members and relate well with other members of the drill or rig crews and their supervisors. They must have good communication skills and good analytical and decision-making abilities. They should enjoy operating machinery and other complex equipment, be comfortable with clear rules and guidelines for their work, and take pleasure in solving problems. Above all, they must have physical strength and stamina.

Unions and Associations

For Well Service Equipment Operators, membership in the American Gas Association (AGA) or the American Petro-leum Institute (API) will aid them in keeping up to date on the latest developments in their respective fields.

Tips for Entry

1. During high school, consider a summer job (or part-time work) in a machine shop to become familiar with handling machinery, related equipment, and machine tools, as well as working within a business environment.
2. Investigate potential internship programs in the oil and gas industry to become knowledgeable about the production processes and technologies with which you will have to work.
3. Consider continuing your education with technical courses in petroleum and natural gas engineering, even getting an associate's degree, to enhance your employment potential.

SKILLED PERSONNEL

OIL WELL DRILLERS

CAREER PROFILE

Duties: <u>Driller</u>: Supervise the oil rig crew and operate and control the rig's machinery during drilling; <u>Driller's Assistant</u>: Help move, set up, and operate drilling rigs and related equipment; <u>Rig Manager</u>: Responsible for every aspect of the oil rig and its operations

Alternate Title(s): <u>Driller</u>: Core Driller, Drill Foreman, Drill Operator, Oil Well Driller, Rotary Driller, Well Driller; <u>Driller's Assistant</u>: Assistant Driller, Blast Hole Driller, Driller's Offsider; <u>Rig Manager</u>: Tool Pusher

Salary Range: <u>Driller</u>: $30,000 to $80,000 or more; <u>Driller's Assistant</u>: $25,000 to $30,000; <u>Rig Manager</u>: $70,000 to $150,000 or more

Employment Prospects: Fair to Good

Advancement Prospects: Fair to Good

Prerequisites:

Education or Training—High school diploma required; in some cases, an associate's or a bachelor's degree recommended; vocational training or job-related course work usually mandatory

Experience—<u>Driller</u>: Several years' work in other drilling personnel positions; <u>Driller's Assistant</u>: Background in roughneck or other oil technician positions; <u>Rig Manager</u>: Experience in other well drilling posts, including supervisory positions

Special Skills and Personality Traits—<u>Driller</u>: Ability to judge distances and spatial relationships; emotional stability and capacity for getting along well with co-workers; good communication and organizational talents; leadership and management skills; mechanical ability and good manual dexterity; physical strength and stamina; <u>Driller's Assistant</u>: Ability to work as a team member; aptitude for mechanics and ability to handle machinery; enjoy practical and manual activities; willing to work in remote areas under difficult conditions; good organizational skills, including an ability to record details accurately; physically fit; <u>Rig Manager</u>: Ability to work quickly and anticipate the next procedure; capacity for planning and directing the work of other personnel; excellent physical health; good communication and organizational skills; mechanical ability; problem solver

Special Requirements—<u>Drillers</u> may be required to have a certification as a journeyman, and a state license; <u>Rig Managers</u> need various professional certifications

CAREER LADDER

Oil Company Management Positions

Rig Manager

Driller

Driller's Assistant; Other Skilled Well Personnel

Roughneck; Roustabout

Position Description

Drillers are responsible for the oil rigs (land or offshore) and rig personnel, supervising rig crews and overseeing the operation of drilling equipment. They operate the draw-works (the rotating drum that spools in drilling line that raises or lowers the drilling devices), rotary drill equipment, and pumps and supervise the assembly of the drillstring (the tube of steel pipe sections extending from the surface down to the drill itself, called a drill bit). They count sections of the drill rod to determine depths of the boreholes. They observe pressure gauges and move the throttles/levers that control the speed of rotary tables and regulate the pressure of drill bits. They oversee the operation of slush pumps that ensure correct circulation and consistency of drilling fluid (or mud) in the well. They recover any lost or broken bits, casings, or drill pipes from wells, using special tools. They maintain/adjust machinery and train crews to make drill work safe and effective. They monitor and keep a record of drilling progress, and communicate with well-site supervisors. (Drillers usually report to Rig Managers.)

As a trainee for the position of Driller, Driller Assistants help move drilling rigs and equipment from site to site, setting up the rigs, and connecting power cables and hoses for water and air supply. They help obtain drilling core samples, mixing and testing drilling fluids and chemicals and operating equipment. They may assist in slotting, welding, and inserting casing screens and assist with well development and pumping tests. They may use equipment and tools to correct problems in drilled holes caused by mechanical breakdowns or by harmful natural conditions. They dig and clean mud pits and drains, and clean and maintain equipment and the drill and camp sites. They carry out minor maintenance and repairs.

Drilling Rig Managers supervise all oil rig activity, and are responsible for safety on site. They are the senior on-site company representatives for oil rig contractors. They coordinate the work of the rig crews. (Most drilling rigs have two or three crews for the rig to be in operation continuously.) They organize the setting up and dismantling of rigs. They make all the necessary arrangements to prepare the area for drilling. They ensure that the entire drilling operation runs efficiently and safely, and that all operations comply with company policies and government regulations. In addition, they make certain that emergency evacuation and medical procedures are posted and understood by the oil rig crews.

Salaries

According to the state of California's Occupational Guide entry for oil and gas drill operators, in the first quarter of 2006 they had a mean average annual salary of $50,089. Driller's Assistants have roughly the same salary range as that of roustabouts: about $25,000 to $30,000. In its December 2006 salary survey report on Oil Well Drillers, PayScale, Inc. listed that Drillers' median annual earnings range from $65,000 to $80,000. Oil and gas industry sources indicate that annual salaries for Rig Managers are much higher, ranging from $70,000 to $150,000 or higher.

Employment Prospects

Although worldwide demand for oil and gas is expected to grow, overall employment in the U.S. oil and gas extraction industries is anticipated to decline by 6 percent through the year 2014, according to the U.S. Department of Labor's Bureau of Labor Statistics. The level of future crude petroleum and natural gas exploration and development and, therefore, employment opportunities in these industries, remains contingent upon the size of accessible reserves available and the current prices for oil and gas. Another factor is concern over environmental impact.

Despite the overall decline in employment, job opportunities should remain fair to good, due to the need to replace workers who transfer to other industries, retire, or leave the workforce altogether.

Advancement Prospects

Drillers, their assistants, and Rig Managers start out as roustabouts (known also as lease hands), or roughnecks (also known as floor hands). They then work as motor hands and derrick hands (derrick operators), before advancing to Drillers and, then, to Rig Managers.

Experienced drillers usually move upward to become Rig Managers. In turn, Rig Managers frequently advance into other drilling industry management posts. Alternatively, Drillers and Rig Managers may decide to transfer to companies involved in other types of drilling projects, such as mineral mining or water reclamation projects. They may be hired by specialist companies as mud technicians or directional drillers or move into drilling-related equipment sales or rig training, regulatory, or safety positions within the industry or with governmental agencies.

Education and Training

A high school diploma or a General Educational Development credential (GED) is a basic requirement for any oil drilling job. Additional relevant courses (such as shop, math, and drafting) at a professional technical or two-year college are recommended. A few community colleges offer programs in drilling and petroleum technology. Additionally, some firms offer apprenticeship programs, usually for a term of three or four years, that include on-the-job training and technical course work.

Most oil and gas drillers learn their skills informally on the job. During training (which may take several years), they start out as a roustabout, learning from an experienced worker, advance to being a roughneck, and then become a Driller's Assistant or move to another skilled post in the rig crew. It takes several years of training to gain the experience needed to be a driller. Rig Managers need to work in many positions on the rig crew to be familiar with all aspects of the operation. In addition, they usually have some formal management and supervisory training.

Special Requirements

Some states may require a license for oil field work specialty contractors and their Drillers. In addition, Drillers may be required to be certified as journeymen in their trade. In turn, Rig Managers may need formal training, leading to certification, in such areas as first aid, hydrogen sulfide awareness, blowout prevention, well control, workplace hazardous materials information, and transportation of dangerous goods.

Experience, Skills, and Personality Traits

Some previous work within the oil and gas extraction industries is helpful, but most rig Drillers gain know-how by working on the rig as apprentices, and then become Rig Managers only after many years' experience.

Rig Drillers and Driller's Assistants need the ability to work well as part of a dedicated team. They should have good communication and organizational skills and be able to keep detailed records. They must have an aptitude for mechanics and handling machinery. They need excellent manual dexterity and the ability to judge distances and spatial relationships. They need to exhibit leadership and have physical strength and stamina, as they will be working in remote areas, frequently under difficult conditions. Drillers need to make quick decisions during drilling operations and handle emergencies calmly and effectively. They are the oil

rig crew's morale booster; they may assist management with personnel recruitment.

In addition to all these characteristics, Rig Managers need to be able to work quickly, respond fast to all types of situations, and think ahead to the next procedure while solving the present problem. They must have the ability to plan and direct the work of all other personnel on the oil rig. In addition, they must be knowledgeable about pertinent environmental issues.

Unions and Associations

The primary professional association of interest to Drillers and other drilling personnel is the American Petroleum Institute (API). In addition, Drillers and Rig Managers should consider the Petroleum Equipment Suppliers Association (PESA), which comprises equipment manufacturers and well site service and supply companies.

Tips for Entry

1. During high school, look into potential internship programs offered by oil companies to become familiar with the processes and technologies of the oil and gas industries.
2. Investigate summer jobs in machine shops to become adept in handling machinery and to enhance your mechanical abilities.
3. Becoming knowledgeable in one or more languages other than English may prove to be useful in your career as a Driller, as you may find lucrative job opportunities with U.S. or foreign companies operating abroad.

OIL WELL OPERATORS

CAREER PROFILE

Duties: <u>Bottom-Hole Pressure Recording Operator</u>: Chart pressure temperature and other characteristics of oil and gas wells using special instruments; <u>Derrickhand</u>: Run pipe in and out of well holes and operate the pumps that circulate mud (lubricant) through the pipe; <u>Mud Analysis Well Logging Operator</u>: Evaluate mud and drill cuttings during drilling operations; <u>Mud-Plant Operator</u>: Operate machine that mixes mud used during drilling; <u>Perforator Operator</u>: Operate equipment to explode charges in oil or gas wells; <u>Service Unit Operator</u>: Operate equipment to increase oil flow or remove obstructions from wells; <u>Well Puller</u>: Control power hoisting equipment to pull rods and to lower tools into well

Alternate Title(s): <u>Derrickhand</u>: Derrick Operator, Derrick Worker, Derrickman; <u>Mud Analysis Well Logging Operator</u>: Mudlogger; <u>Perforator Operator</u>: Gun-Perforator Operator; <u>Service Unit Operator</u>: Oil Well Sounding Device Operator; <u>Well Puller</u>: Hydraulic Oil-Tool Operator, Pulling-Machine Operator, Rig Operator, Tube Puller

Salary Range: $30,000 to $70,000 or more

Employment Prospects: Fair

Advancement Prospects: Fair

Prerequisites:

Education or Training—High school diploma required; related post-secondary technical education in petroleum technology or engineering often necessary

Experience—Previous work on a drilling rig crew or a service rig crew recommended

Special Skills and Personality Traits—Ability to labor efficiently under pressure; detail- and safety-oriented; excellent decision-making talents; good communication and interpersonal skills; initiative; physical strength and stamina

Special Requirements—Licenses and certifications may be required

CAREER LADDER

> **Supervisory Positions**

> **Oil Well Operators**

> **Rig Technicians; Roughnecks**

Position Description

Bottom-Hole Pressure Recording Operators chart the pressure, temperature, and other characteristics of oil and gas well boreholes (for exploratory wells) or producing wells, using special subsurface instruments. They give directions to hoist operators to lower instruments (such as thermometers and clinographs, which record the deviation of boreholes and wells from the vertical) into the well to establish, among other things, the pressure at various depths to determine rate of natural flow of oil from the well and the depth of the well. They interpret the findings for the use of engineering personnel and management to determine further drilling or producing procedures.

Derrickhands work in the oil rig's derrick, about ninety feet above the drill floor, to guide the drill pipe (called the drill string) in and out of the well hole. They steady the pipe from the top while it is connected or disconnected at the bottom. They are also responsible for maintaining the fluid pumps and circulation system, which direct the flow of the mud lubricant through the well. They work under the direction of the driller and assist the driller with crew supervision and safety measures.

Mud is a vital part of the drilling operation. It lubricates the drill bit and carries the drill cuttings up the well. Mud-Plant Operators tend the machine that mixes the mud used in drilling oil and gas wells. They operate the water valves and hopper gates that admit specified quantities of water and dry mix into the mixing chamber. They test mud samples for viscosity and weight, and, when the mud is approved for use, they start the pumps that force the mud into drilling wells. Mud Analysis Well Logging Operators analyze mud and drill cutting samples during drilling operations and inspect these samples to determine the nature of the earth formations encountered and the presence of oil or gas in the formations. They use ultraviolet light, microscopes, and other special testing equipment. They keep records of the readings and tests made, and calculate the depth of formations found to contain gas or oil. Both operators report to mud engineers who are outside contractors whose purpose is to determine the correct mud to be used and to supervise the operation.

Perforator Operators control truck-mounted hoisting equipment and associated electrical control panels to position and explode charges (torpedoes) in oil or gas wells to pierce drill pipes, casings, tubings, and fracture earth formations to start or renew the flow of oil in wells. They move controls at the panelboard to detonate the charge in the gun that propels bullets through the wall of the bore to pierce or fracture oil- or gas-bearing formations or to ignite chemical charges which burn fissures in rock formations for passage of oil or processing fluids (such as mud or cement). They are assisted by gun-perforator loaders who pack the explosive power or chemicals into the gun perforators and maintain and inventory the equipment.

Service Unit Operators operate specialized equipment to increase oil flow from producing wells or to remove stuck pipe, casing, tools or other obstructions from drilling wells by using specialized subsurface tools and instruments. They assemble and lower detection instruments into wells that have obstructions and ascertain the depth of the obstructions. They lower specialized equipment to the point of obstruction and push switches or pull levers to back off pipe by chemical or explosive action, or to sever the pipe at the point of obstruction, permitting recovery of the pipestring and the resumption of drilling operations.

Well Pullers control the power hoisting equipment that pull casing, tubing, and pumping rods from oil and gas wells for repair and that lower repaired equipment, testing devices, and servicing tools into the well. They lower swabbing equipment into the well to clear mud from screens at the bottom of the well and to establish flow of oil. They lower pressure-recording devices and special tools to fish for broken rods or tubing and to scrape paraffin and incrustations from casing and tubing. They test pipe for leaks, using hydraulic-testing equipment.

Salaries

According to the U.S. Department of Labor's Bureau of Labor Statistics in their *Occupational Outlook Handbook, 2006–07 Edition*, in May 2004, median annual earnings of oil and gas operators ranged from $32,716 to $48,884. According to other industry sources, yearly earnings for oil and gas well and field operators in 2006 ranged from $30,000 to $70,000 or more. Most operators have the option to work overtime at time and a half, yielding from 400 to 600 hours more work per year.

Employment Prospects

Like that of most workers in the oil and gas industries, employment of Oil Well Operators depends on the amount of crude petroleum and natural gas exploration and development that is occurring. Stable and favorable prices for oil and gas are needed to allow companies sufficient revenue to expand exploration and production projects to keep pace with growing global energy demands and guarantee employment to operators. In addition, fewer reserves of oil and gas in the United States will cause a decline in domestic production, unless new oil and gas fields are found and developed.

Despite the overall decline in employment in the oil and gas extraction industry, job opportunities will remain fair, as there will be the need to replace workers who transfer to other industries, retire, or leave the workforce. Job openings will be best for those with previous experience and technically skilled personnel who can work with the new technologies used by the industries.

Advancement Prospects

Most Oil Well Operators start out in the industry as roust-abouts (known also as lease hands), and then advance to roughnecks (also known as floor hands), general laborers who learn the techniques and technology on the job. They may then work as well service operators before deciding upon their specialty as an Oil Well Operator.

With sufficient experience (and some management training), some Oil Well Operators may advance to supervisory positions in their specialty fields, or move into general management posts within their companies. Others may find lucrative positions in other industries, such as construction.

Education and Training

Oil Well Operators must have at least a high school diploma. Related post-secondary education and experience on a drilling rig crew or a service rig crew are definite assets. For some posts, employers may require an associate's degree, or even a bachelor's degree, in petroleum technology or engineering. Trainees for specific operator positions often learn on the job under the tutelage of experienced operators.

Special Requirements

Oil Well Operators who handle corrosive and poisonous materials may have to be certified in first aid and in the handling of hazardous waste materials. Some employers may require additional training and certification of their Oil Well Operators in such areas as safety procedures or blowout prevention processes. Perforator Operators usually need to be licensed to handle explosives.

Experience, Skills, and Personality Traits

Oil Well Operators must be able to work effectively on their own while under pressure, but must also function as a part of a tightly knit crew team in which members are dependent upon each other for safe and successful well production. They need to be detail-oriented and take initiative. They must have good communication skills in order to understand and give clear, concise directions. They should have excellent analytical and decision-making abilities and good organizational skills and display leadership and potential management talents. They need to have manual dexterity, be physically strong, and have great stamina.

Unions and Associations

The primary professional associations of interest for Oil Well Operators are the American Petroleum Institute (API) and the Society of Petroleum Engineers (SPE).

Tips for Entry

1. During high school, consider a summer job (or part-time work) in a machine shop to become familiar with handling machinery, related equipment, and machine tools.
2. Investigate potential internship programs in the oil and gas industries as a way of becoming knowledgeable about the production processes and technologies with which you will work.
3. Consider continuing your education and gaining an associate's degree (or even a bachelor's) in petroleum technology or engineering to enhance your employment potential.

SUPPORT PERSONNEL

LANDMAN

CAREER PROFILE

Duties: Responsible for the acquisition, maintenance, development, and negotiations of property rights to land (including offshore underground deposits) to be used in the search for, and extraction of, natural resources

Alternate Title(s): Petroleum Landman, Right-of-Way Agent

Salary Range: $65,000 to $100,000 or more

Employment Prospects: Fair

Advancement Prospects: Fair

Prerequisites:

Education or Training—High school degree required; bachelor's degree in business or petroleum land management preferred

Experience—One to three years of experience in the petroleum industry, preferably in training for in-house corporate Landman position

Special Skills and Personality Traits—Ability to work well with other departments and handle many projects simultaneously; business background recommended; excellent communication and interpersonal talents; good computer, math, and researching abilities; legal knowledge; skilled in negotiation

Special Requirements—Certification as Professional Landman often necessary

CAREER LADDER

```
┌─────────────────────────────────────────┐
│  Self-Employed Independent Landman;       │
│  Senior Landmen Positions; Real Estate    │
│  Industry Management Positions            │
└─────────────────────────────────────────┘

┌─────────────────────────────────────────┐
│               Landman                     │
└─────────────────────────────────────────┘

┌─────────────────────────────────────────┐
│  College Graduate; Petroleum Technician   │
└─────────────────────────────────────────┘
```

Position Description

Landmen constitute the business side of the oil and gas exploration and production business. A job that is unique to North America, the Landman is responsible for obtaining permission to drill a well. Before a well may be drilled on private property in the United States or Canada, the land must be leased from the landowner who owns the subsurface oil and gas rights. The rights may be acquired in the form of leases, outright purchases of real property, some form of partnering arrangement, or through other contractual agreements. Landmen deal directly with farmers, ranchers, and other landowners and usually need to research ownership records maintained in county, state, or governmental offices. They review abstracts and title opin-

ions, secure title remedial rights, and request title approval for drilling and division order purposes. Landmen then obtain a detailed title analysis of the sought-after land and are responsible for ensuring that all pertinent data is obtained and defined. (This involves developing, revising, and maintaining a record system that allows the drilling company to track its obligations, such as the payment of rentals, taxes, and royalties.)

In addition, they need to acquire permits from various government agencies before a well can be drilled. The permit sets forth the requirements for the drilling company to restore the land after the well is drilled and properly plug and abandon nonproductive wells. They negotiate, draft, prepare, and manage the resultant contracts and agreements and handle any lease acquisitions of private, state, or government land, as well as the leasing of surface rights from private landowners and companies. They maintain accurate oil and gas contract records to assure the continued validity of leases and compliance with all contract terms. They coordinate the payment of lease rentals and royalties to assure that they are made in an accurate and timely manner.

Landmen are also involved in securing environmental clearances and pipeline right-of-way agreements and settling any damages with the surface owner prior to drilling. They proactively seek out leasing and/or partnering opportunities in areas of interest to the drilling company. They build rapport with lessors (people who grant leases), government officials, and industry counterparts. Additionally, Landmen are involved in the environmental sector in environmental compliance and in conducting environmental site assessments.

Salaries

Due to the variety of skills necessary for this post, Landmen's salaries tend to be high. According to industry sources, starting annual income ranges between $60,000 and $75,000 and can run as high as $100,000 or more for experienced Landmen.

Employment Prospects

While there is a projected decline in employment prospects for the oil and gas industry as a whole in the United States, the position of Landmen is essential to all oil and gas exploration. Best prospects for employment will result from the need to replace experienced Landmen who have moved into senior positions, retired, become independent consultants, or moved to another industry.

Advancement Prospects

Experienced Landmen may decide to become independent consultants. They serve clients on a contractual basis. They are frequently hired to research courthouse records to determine ownership and prepare the necessary reports. They may also be employed to conduct surface inspections of the acquired land before drilling. Other Landmen may choose to retire from the industry and, trading on their expertise, move into the realtor business, making way for the advancement of less senior Landmen and the hiring of new graduates for beginning positions.

Education and Training

Beyond a high school education, most employers of Landmen require a bachelor's degree from an accredited school in petroleum land management, energy management, business administration, law, or a related discipline. The majority of members of the American Association of Professional Landmen (AAPL) have business degrees, and many of them have obtained law degrees as well. Several universities offer petroleum and minerals land management degree programs.

Training is usually done on the job under the supervision of seasoned Landmen, and may last one or two years. AAPL awards student scholarships, and offers continuing education programs for its members.

Special Requirements

Some companies and some states may require Landmen to be certified. The American Association of Professional Landmen (AAPL) provides certificate training through its Certified Professional Landman and Certified Professional Landman/ESA programs.

Experience, Skills, and Personality Traits

Landmen who have prior experience in the oil, gas, or mineral exploration industry have an additional asset to offer their potential employers. All Landmen need to have excellent interpersonal skills, as they will have to work with other departments and act as a liaison with internal/external customers to resolve ownership problems, royalty/rental inquiries, and release demands. They must have good communication, negotiation, and research talents, along with some legal knowledge, particularly a clear understanding of contract law. Their computer proficiency should include using Word and Excel and a familiarity with Dwights P2000, the data management system designed to store well production, seismic, and lease data.

They should have some knowledge in global information systems (GIS) mapping techniques and be skilled in basic math. They need to be detail-oriented and very precise in their work. They should be agreeable to traveling, be adept at dealing with other firms, and be comfortable with testifying at regulatory hearings when required.

Unions and Associations

The primary association for Landmen is the American Association of Professional Landmen (AAPL). This group provides its members with professional development opportunities through seminars, workshops, home study programs, conferences, and annual meetings, as well as a bimonthly magazine and other written materials. Another professional organization of interest for Landmen working in the oil and gas industry is the American Petroleum Institute (API).

Tips for Entry

1. As you look at colleges that offer a land management program, investigate a possibility of a scholarship, if

you need it, from the American Association of Professional Landmen.

2. Be sure to include courses in communications, basic research techniques, and basic law (in particular contract law), as these are skills you will need as a Landman.

3. Seek internship programs, summer jobs, or other part-time job opportunities in the oil or gas industries to gain firsthand knowledge of their workplace and to begin to make contacts. The ability to network will also be a key facet of your future career.

MECHANICAL ENGINEER AND MAINTENANCE TECHNICIAN

CAREER PROFILE

Duties: <u>Mechanical Engineer</u>: Research, develop, design, and test tools, machines, and other mechanical devices used in the industry; <u>Maintenance Technician</u>: Help keep equipment/machines working properly at oil and natural gas facilities

Alternate Title(s): <u>Mechanical Engineer</u>: None; <u>Maintenance Technician</u>: Engineering Technician, Field Mechanic, Maintenance Machinist, Mechanic, Motorman

Salary Range: <u>Mechanical Engineer</u>: $45,000 to $95,000 or more; <u>Maintenance Technician</u>: $25,000 to $50,000 or more

Employment Prospects: Fair

Advancement Prospects: Fair

Prerequisites:

Education or Training—<u>Mechanical Engineer</u>: Bachelor's degree in mechanical engineering minimum requirement; <u>Maintenance Technician</u>: High school diploma necessary; two-year associate's degree in engineering technology and mechanics may be required, or, if a union member, completion of a four-year apprenticeship program in machinery maintenance may be substituted

Experience—Some background in oil and gas industries helpful; on-the-job training by veteran engineers and workers or product representatives usual

Special Skills and Personality Traits—Able to work as part of a team; capable of following blueprints, schematic drawings, diagrams, and service manuals; creative, analytical, detail-oriented, and inquisitive; good communication skills; mechanical ability and manual dexterity; physically fit

Special Requirements—Licenses usually required for Mechanical Engineers

CAREER LADDER

Industrial Engineering Positions; Independent Engineering Consultant; Maintenance Supervisor; Millwright

Mechanical Engineer; Maintenance Technician

College Graduate, Engineer-in-Training; High School or Technical School Graduate

Position Description

Mechanical engineering is one of the broadest engineering disciplines. Because Mechanical Engineers have a wide knowledge of technical theory, they are able to understand the "larger picture" of the technology and technical processes of their industry.

Mechanical Engineers research, develop, design, manufacture, and test tools, engines, machines, and other mechanical devices utilized at drilling well sites, offshore oil rigs, oil refineries and gas processing plants, and other oil and natural gas industries facilities. They work on power-producing machines such as electric generators and steam and gas turbines. They also develop machine tools and industrial production equipment. They utilize computer-aided design (CAD) and computer-aided manufacturing (CAM) technologies for design data processing.

In the oil and gas industries, Mechanical Engineers work on the design and operation of permanent drilling platforms for offshore production, gas processing plants, oil and gas pipelines, refineries, oil and gas tankers, and terminals. They may work on large machinery, tanks, and furnaces, or the valves and tools utilized to maintain production and processing equipment. They develop the control systems to monitor/operate these operations. They work closely with engineering and Maintenance Technicians to keep equipment running as efficiently as possible and explore new ways to make the technical processes of the industries safer and more efficient.

Maintenance Technicians (sometimes called mechanics) repair and maintain machines, mechanical equipment, plumbing, and electrical, air-conditioning, and heating systems. They clean and lubricate machinery, perform basic diagnostic tests, check performance, and test machine parts. They use their understanding of the equipment, technical manuals, and careful observation to discover the cause of any breakdowns.

After diagnosing the problem, they may disassemble the equipment to repair or replace necessary parts and then, once the repair is made, perform tests to ensure that the machine or equipment is now running smoothly. Today, Maintenance Technicians need electronic and computer skills to repair sophisticated equipment (such as that used in the oil and gas industries) on their own. They also conduct preventive maintenance and may be involved in the installation of new equipment. Maintenance Technicians employ a variety of tools to perform their duties, from screwdrivers and wrenches to hoist lifts. They use catalogs to order replacement parts and often must follow blueprints, technical manuals, and engineering specifications to maintain/fix equipment.

Salaries

According to a 2005 survey by the National Association of Colleges and Employers, Mechanical Engineers with a bachelor's degree earned an average annual starting salary of $50,236, and those with a master's degree received an average starting income of $59,880. In May 2004, according to the U.S. Department of Labor's Bureau of Labor Statistics in their *Occupational Outlook Handbook, 2006–07 Edition*, yearly salaries for Mechanical Engineers ranged from $43,900 to $97,850.

According to the *Occupational Outlook Handbook, 2006–07 Edition*, median annual earnings for Maintenance Technicians (mechanics) in May 2004 were $39,032. Yearly wages ranged from lows of $25,232 to highs of $57,343.

Employment Prospects

The U.S. Department of Labor projects that Mechanical Engineers will have an average rate of employment growth through 2014. Employment of Mechanical Engineers in the oil and gas industries will depend greatly on the economic well-being of those businesses. Nevertheless, employment opportunities will occur with the expected retirement of experienced Mechanical Engineers over the next decade. In addition, there are usually additional openings because some engineers are promoted, change employers or careers, or leave the profession, in some cases to start their own firms.

Employment of Maintenance Technicians in general is expected to grow more slowly than other occupations through 2014, according to the U.S. Department of Labor. Nevertheless, many Maintenance Technicians are expected to retire in coming years, and employers have reported difficulty in recruiting young workers with the necessary skills to fill their posts. Many job openings will stem from the need to replace these mechanics or others who transfer to other occupations or industries. Additionally, while production at drilling sites or refineries may slacken, Maintenance Technicians often are retained to tend to the equipment or do major overhaul to keep the expensive machinery operational.

Advancement Prospects

Mechanical Engineers have skills gained by their earning a degree in mechanical engineering that often can be applied in other engineering specialties, making them more flexible in their career paths. Some may also decide to join engineering consulting firms (or start their own) as opposed to working for a specific oil or gas company. They may take supervisory positions with larger companies within the industry or enter other managerial or sales jobs.

Maintenance Technicians may gain additional skills to make repairs to more complex machinery or work as supervisors. The most highly trained Maintenance Technicians may decide to capitalize on their equipment/machine repairing skills to be promoted to master mechanics or become millwrights in charge of the installation of all new equipment or the dismantling of old machinery. In addition, Maintenance Technicians frequently find it easy to transfer to other industries with similar machinery to that they have worked on in the oil and gas business.

Education and Training

A bachelor's degree in mechanical engineering is required for almost all entry-level Mechanical Engineers. In addition to the standard engineering degree, many colleges offer two- or four-year degree programs in engineering technology, which are aimed at preparing students for practical design and production work, rather than for jobs that require more theoretical and scientific knowledge.

Beyond a high school diploma, many graduates looking to become Maintenance Technicians in industries like oil and gas may decide to earn a two-year associate's degree in engineering technology as well. In contrast, Maintenance Technicians, as industrial machinery mechanics, can often learn their trade through four-year apprenticeship programs, which are usually sponsored by a local trade union.

Special Requirements

In many cases, employers require engineers to be licensed as Professional Engineers (PE). This licensure generally requires an engineering degree from an accredited program, four years of relevant work experience, and the successful completion of a state examination. Independent of licensure, a certification program for Mechanical Engineers is offered by the American Society of Mechanical Engineers (ASME) to demonstrate their competency.

Experience, Skills, and Personality Traits

Mechanical Engineers should be creative, inquisitive, analytical, and heavily detail-oriented. They need excellent communication skills, as they often must interact with spe-cialists in a wide range of fields outside engineering. They must to be able to work as part of a team.

Mechanical aptitude and manual dexterity are important characteristics of Maintenance Technicians. They must possess solid communication skills, particularly good reading comprehension, as they have to understand blueprints, schematic drawings/diagrams/technical manuals for a wide range of machines. In addition, they need to be physically fit and agile, as they may sometimes have to lift heavy objects or climb to reach equipment.

Unions and Associations

The primary professional association of Mechanical Engineers is the American Society of Mechanical Engineers (ASME). Some Maintenance Technicians may be union members. Labor unions that represent these workers include the United Steelworkers of America (USWA), the International Association of Machinists and Aerospace Workers (IAMAW), and the International Union of Electronic, Electrical, Salaried, Machine, and Furniture Workers-Communications Workers of America (IUE-CWA).

Tips for Entry

1. Instead of a four-year engineering major investigate alternative programs offered by some engineering schools and two-year colleges whereby the two-year college provides the initial engineering education, and the engineering school will automatically admit you for your last two years.
2. Investigate summer internships or other programs that will allow you to work within the oil or gas industries to gain first-hand knowledge of the machinery and equipment used.
3. In addition, consider working in a machine shop to enhance your mechanical abilities and to test your manual dexterity with equipment and machines.

RENEWABLE ENERGY INDUSTRIES (INCLUDING BIOMASS, GEOTHERMAL, HYDROPOWER, PHOTOVOLTAIC, SOLAR, AND WIND)

ENGINEERS AND SCIENTISTS

CHEMICAL ENGINEER

CAREER PROFILE

Duties: Use chemistry, physics, and math—along with engineering tools—to solve problems relating to the development of new and improved chemical manufacturing processes in the production/use of biomass renewable alternatives to oil and natural gas

Alternate Title(s): Development Engineer; Process Control Engineer; Process Development Engineer; Process Engineer; Project Engineer

Salary Range: $45,000 to $115,000 or more

Employment Prospects: Good

Advancement Prospects: Fair

Prerequisites:

Education or Training—Bachelor's degree in engineering, preferably chemical engineering, required; master's degree or higher may also be necessary

Experience—Previous laboratory work desirable

Special Skills and Personality Traits—Aptitude at being a team player; creative, inquisitive, analytical, and detail-oriented; good communication and interpersonal abilities; problem-solver

Special Requirements—Licensing as a Professional Engineer (PE) may be required, as well as a professional certification as a Chemical Engineer

CAREER LADDER

```
┌─────────────────────────────────────┐
│   Independent Consultant; Project     │
│   Management Positions; Teacher       │
└─────────────────────────────────────┘

┌─────────────────────────────────────┐
│         Chemical Engineer             │
└─────────────────────────────────────┘

┌─────────────────────────────────────┐
│   Chemical Technician; Junior or      │
│        Assistant Engineer             │
└─────────────────────────────────────┘
```

Position Description

Renewable energy is an energy force that can be replenished at the same rate as it is used. Renewable energy derives from the Sun or from processes set in motion by the Sun and includes direct use of solar power along with windmills, hydroelectric dams, ocean thermal energy systems, and biomass (solid wood, methane gas, or liquid fuels). Biofuels were barely a factor in the energy marketplace during much of the 20th century, as long as petroleum and natural gas energy sources were plentiful and, relatively, inexpensive. As oil prices have risen, fuels derived from renewable sources (such as corn, soybeans, and other crops, as well as wood) have gained attention. In addition, as concerns escalate over energy security and, longer-term, over dwindling hydrocarbon resources and environmental pollution, energy derived from biofuels (such as biodiesel, ethanol,

and biobutanol) has taken high priority in research facilities in the United States and abroad.

Biomass energy involves a wide range of low and high technologies, from wood burning to the use of manure, sea kelp, and various farm crops to make gas and liquid biofuels. Brazil leads the world in the utilization of pure ethyl alcohol derived from sugarcane as a replacement for petroleum. A common fuel in the United States is corn-derived ethyl alcohol, which is employed as a low-pollution octane booster in a 10 percent blend with gasoline called gasohol. Another form of renewable energy used in rural areas of the world is the gas-producing biogas digester.

Chemical Engineers use chemistry, physics, and math along with engineering tools to solve problems relating to the production and use of new, cleaner-burning biofuels that are not carbon-based. Some Chemical Engineers work solely in research and development. They conduct research to develop new and improved chemical manufacturing procedures. Chemical Engineers working in design and construction are often called project engineers. They design equipment and processes for large-scale chemical manufacturing, plan and test methods of manufacturing products and treating by-products, and supervise such production. They analyze operating procedures and equipment and machinery functions to reduce processing time and cost. They design equipment to control movement, storage, and packaging of solids, liquids, and gases. They design and plan measurement and control systems for chemical plants based on data collected in laboratory experiments and pilot plant operations. They determine the most effective arrangement of production unit operations, such as mixing, grinding, crushing, heat transfer, size reduction, hydrogenation, distillation, purification, oxidation, polymerization, evaporation, and fermentation. They prepare estimates of production costs and production progress reports for management. As they elaborate on their recommendations, they must exercise their judgment to compromise between process requirements, economic evaluation, operator effectiveness, and physical/health hazards.

When overseeing actual production, Chemical Engineers direct activities of workers who operate/control such equipment as condensers, absorption and evaporation towers, kilns, pumps, boilers, compressors, grinders, pipelines, electro-magnets, and centrifuges to effect the required chemical or physical changes. They perform tests and take measurements throughout all stages of production to determine the degree of control possible over variables, such as temperature, density, specific gravity, and pressure.

Salaries

According to a 2005 survey by the National Association of Colleges and Employers, Chemical Engineers with a bachelor's degree may expect an average annual starting salary of $53,813, whereas those with a master's degree have an average annual starting income of $57,260, and those with a Ph.D. degree, $79,591. In May 2004, the U.S. Department of Labor's Bureau of Labor Statistics found that median annual salaries for Chemical Engineers ranged from $49,030 to $115,180, with an average median being $76,770.

Employment Prospects

The U.S. Department of Labor's Bureau of Labor Statistics in their *Occupational Outlook Handbook, 2006–2007 Edition*, projected that employment of Chemical Engineers is expected to grow about as fast as the average for all occupations through 2014. While overall employment in the chemical manufacturing industry is expected to decline, it is anticipated that most employment growth for Chemical Engineers will be in service industries such as scientific research and development services, particularly in energy. In addition to job openings created by increased demand, many Chemical Engineers will be required to replace those who leave the labor force through retirement or change their occupation.

Advancement Prospects

Some Chemical Engineers with a business background may decide to become independent consultants to the energy industry or to national government agencies as a means of expanding their career options. Others, who have displayed leadership talents, may choose to progress in their career (and boost their salary potential) by joining the management ranks of their company, first as a project manager, and then in higher management positions. Chemical Engineers primarily engaged in research and development may be given increasingly responsible assignments (and escalations in salary) and may eventually progress to such posts as supervisor, project engineer, or director of research. Some Chemical Engineers pursue a Ph.D. in their field so they can teach chemical engineering.

Education and Training

A bachelor's degree in engineering is required for almost all entry-level engineering jobs. Some engineering schools and two-year colleges have agreements whereby the college provides the initial engineering education, and the engineering institution automatically admits students for their last two years. In addition, a few engineering schools have arrangements that allow students who spend three years in a liberal arts college studying pre-engineering subjects and two years in an engineering school studying core subjects to receive a bachelor's degree from each school. Some colleges and universities offer five-year master's degree programs. Additionally, some five-year or even six-year cooperative program plans combine classroom study with practical work, permitting students to gain valuable on-the-job experience and a means of financing part of their education.

Many Chemical Engineers attend graduate school to specialize in a particular area of chemical engineering. In addition, some jobs require a master's or a doctoral degree (Ph. D.), and all teaching positions have a Ph.D. requisite.

Special Requirements

Many states require licensure for engineers. Engineers who are licensed are called professional engineers (PE). This licensure generally requires a degree from an accredited engineering program, four years of relevant work experience, and successful completion of a state examination. Independent of licensure, there are certification programs for Chemical Engineers offered by their professional organization to demonstrate competency in their specific field of engineering.

Experience, Skills, and Personality Traits

Many employers prefer their candidates to have had some previous experience with an engineering firm. In large companies, many newly hired graduates may receive formal classroom training as well as work under the guidance of veteran Chemical Engineers.

Chemical processes are continuously becoming more complex and automated, and recent developments in computer-aided design (CAD) have enabled engineers to create designs more intricate and accurate than were before possible. Thus, computer skills are important for Chemical Engineers.

Employers look for Chemical Engineers who are creative and curious. They also seek individuals who are detail-oriented and analytical. Oral and written communication abilities are also crucial. As Chemical Engineers work with a wide variety of individuals, they must have good interpersonal skills and be a team player. They will need to be able to communicate their ideas to managers, technicians, craftworkers, production workers, and, in some cases, even customers. Above all, Chemical Engineers must be adept at problem solving, have initiative, and be able to make sound, timely decisions.

Unions and Associations

The primary professional association for Chemical Engineers is the American Institute of Chemical Engineers (AIChE). In addition, they will find value in belonging to the American Chemical Society (ACS).

Tips for Entry

1. You might consider participating in an internship with an engineering firm while in college. Such internships are usually part of a four-year degree program. It offers you a chance to apply what you have learned in the classroom to a work situation. In addition, you can build your skills and make contacts with people in the field.

2. In high school, you should take all the advanced classes in math and science available to you. This includes Advanced Placement (AP) and International Baccalaureate (IB) courses if they are offered at your school.

3. When considering job offers in the field of Chemical Engineering, look beyond the salary to consider how well your employer will be able to meet your needs in such other important areas as commuting time, perks, travel requirements, and special expenses like relocation or commuting fares.

DESIGN ENGINEER

CAREER PROFILE

Duties: Responsible for the design and development of new products, equipment, or facilities

Alternate Title(s): Process Design Engineer; Product Design Engineer; Project Engineer

Salary Range: $55,000 to $100,000 or more

Employment Prospects: Good

Advancement Prospects: Fair

Prerequisites:

Education or Training—Bachelor of Science degree in engineering required; master's degree may be essential in some cases

Experience—Some work in/or knowledge of manufacturing and fabrication methods

Special Skills and Personality Traits—Ability to read, interpret, and comprehend technical drawings; capacity for analytical reporting; creative problem-solving ability; excellent computer skills; knowledgeable of materials, manufacturing processes, and achievable tolerance levels; strong quantitative and analytical skills; understanding of the product development process

Special Requirements—Licensing as a Professional Engineer (PE) usually required

CAREER LADDER

```
┌─────────────────────────────────────┐
│  Independent Consultant; Project     │
│       Management Positions           │
└─────────────────────────────────────┘

┌─────────────────────────────────────┐
│          Design Engineer             │
└─────────────────────────────────────┘

┌─────────────────────────────────────┐
│  College Graduate; Engineering       │
│            Technician                │
└─────────────────────────────────────┘
```

Position Description

Design engineering covers multiple engineering disciplines, primarily electrical, mechanical, and civil. Design Engineers differ from designer/drafters in that they set the direction of the design effort. Designer/drafters usually report to Design Engineers, who lead the project. Design Engineers work with industrial designers and marketing personnel to develop the product's concept and its specifications. They then oversee the design process.

Design Engineers conduct analytical studies on the original engineering proposals to develop designs for products, such as engines, equipment, machines, associated and subsystems components, and other structures, utilizing and applying engineering principles, research data, and the proposed product specifications. They analyze the data to determine the feasibility of the proposal. They confer with

research personnel to clarify or resolve problems in preparation for developing the design.

They usually direct a team of designers in creating the computer-aided design (CAD) files necessary for prototype and production. (However, with the introduction of solid modeling software, such as Autodesk Inventor, SolidWorks, Pro-Engineer, or Catia, Design Engineers often create the files themselves.) The next step in the process is prototyping. A model of the product is created and reviewed. Design Engineers plan/develop the experimental test programs to be used. Prototypes are either functional (where they are employed for testing) or non-functional (where they are utilized for form and fit checking). It is at this stage that, hopefully, design flaws are found and corrected. In addition, tooling, manufacturing fixtures, and packaging, if appropriate, are usually developed. Design Engineers are responsible for analyzing test data and reports to determine if the design meets functional and performance specifications, conferring with research and other engineering personnel in handling any needed design modifications. They must evaluate the design's overall effectiveness, cost, reliability, and safety.

Once the design is finalized, the next step is pre-production. Design Engineers, working with manufacturing engineers and quality engineers, review an initial run of components and assemblies for design compliance. These are often determined through a process called statistical process control (SPC). Variations in the product are correlated with aspects of the process and eliminated. Design Engineers may follow the product and make requested changes and corrections throughout its life. This process is often referred to as cradle to grave engineering.

Design Engineers work in assorted renewable energy industries. They may be laboring on better designs for windmills, wind machines, or wind turbines. They may be involved in designing parabolic collectors for collecting the sun's energy or designing the panels that hold photovoltaic cells used to collect and translate the Sun's energy directly into electric current. Alternatively, Design Engineers are part of the engineering teams behind the design of hydroelectric dams and their auxiliary power-generating facilities. In the field of bioenergy (tapping the energy stored in biomass, or organic matter), Design Engineers are needed to aid in the planning and building of bioenergy plants that process agricultural and other waste products to create energy.

Salaries

In their 2007 salary survey report on 2006 salaries for Design Engineers, PayScale, Inc. found that median annual salaries ranged from $58,760 to $90,000 (tied to geographic location). According to the U.S. Department of Labor's Bureau of Labor Statistics in their *Occupational Outlook Handbook, 2006–2007 Edition*, the median yearly wage in May 2004 for Design Engineers was $67,220. Annual salaries for Design Engineers can extend from $50,000 to $100,000 or more, depending on the engineer's experience and the complexity of the design engineering required.

Employment Prospects

Overall engineering employment is expected to grow about as fast as the average for all occupations over the 2004–14 period, according to the U.S. Department of Labor's Bureau of Labor Statistics. Compared with most other workers, a smaller proportion of engineers leave their field each year. Nevertheless, many job openings occur from such replacement needs. Some employment openings will be created by engineers who transfer to management, sales, or other professional occupations. With the increasing interest in renewable energy projects, the demand for experienced Design Engineers will increase, both for commercial projects and

for private home design of such equipment as solar heating systems.

Advancement Prospects

Experienced Design Engineers may look to become project managers in their firm and then move into higher management or sales positions within their company. Others, with some business background, may decide to set up their own consulting firms. Design Engineers are also utilized in many manufacturing and electric power facilities.

Education and Training

A Bachelor of Science degree in engineering from an accredited college or university is a basic requirement for all Design Engineers. Some employers may also require a master's degree. Additional training or experience in the specific areas of mechanical and electrical engineering is highly recommended. Most engineering programs involve a concentration of study in an engineering specialty, along with courses in both mathematics and the physical and life sciences. Many programs include design courses, sometimes accompanied by a computer or laboratory class or both. Bachelor's degree programs in engineering typically are designed to last four years, but many students find that it takes up to five years to complete their studies.

It is important for Design Engineers, as it is for those working in other technical and scientific occupations, to continue their education throughout their careers because much of their value to their employer depends on their knowledge of the latest technology.

Special Requirements

Most companies require Design Engineers to be licensed as Professional Engineers (PE), as a recognition of their professional status. Professional certification programs are also available from most engineering professional associations.

Experience, Skills, and Personality Traits

Design Engineers need to have experience in or knowledge of manufacturing and fabrication methods. Many employers require at least two to three years prior related work experience. Design Engineers need to have a thorough comprehension of statistical quality control processes and an understanding of marketing and project management. They should have a proven high level of creative problem-solving abilities and strong quantitative and analytical skills. They must have a working knowledge of materials, manufacturing processes, and achievable tolerances of materials. They should have experience in analytical reporting, including data analysis, retrieval, and formatting. They need a basic proficiency in such computer programs as Microsoft Office, Outlook, Project, Access, Adobe Acrobat, and Visio. Prior experience or training in computer-aided design (CAD) techniques are an additional prerequisite.

Design Engineers must be well organized, accurate, and have a strong attention to detail. They should have excellent communication and interpersonal skills, as they will deal with a wide diversity of technical and non-technical personnel. In addition, they will have to be able to read, comprehend, and interpret technical drawings and specification charts. They should have leadership talent and be able to supervise/guide technicians and other workers they oversee.

Unions and Associations

As many Design Engineers are mechanical engineers by training, their primary professional association is the American Society of Mechanical Engineers (ASME). For those Design Engineers whose major training has been in electrical engineering, membership in the Institute of Electrical and Electronics Engineers (IEEE) should prove useful. Another association of interest for Design Engineers is the International Sustainable Energy Organization (ISEO), which provides a worldwide information exchange of various sources of energy, news items, and implementation tools.

Tips for Entry

1. If you are interested in pursuing a career in design engineering, during high school you should include as many mathematics and physical science courses as you can.

2. In choosing an engineering college program, it might be worthwhile investigating five-year or even six-year cooperative plans that combine classroom study and practical work through internship programs, permitting you to gain valuable experience, make contacts, and finance part of your education.

3. Of additional value would be time spent within a manufacturing environment, possibly through a summer job, to gain an overview of manufacturing processes and cost benefit analysis as applied to the manufacture of products.

ELECTRICAL ENGINEER

CAREER PROFILE

Duties: Design, develop, test, and supervise the manufacture and installation of electrical equipment related to such renewable energy fields as solar power, wind power, and water power.

Alternate Title(s): Control Engineer; Power Engineer; Production Engineer

Salary Range: $45,000 to $105,000 or more

Employment Prospects: Fair to Good

Advancement Prospects: Fair

Prerequisites:

Education or Training—Bachelor's degree in electrical engineering required; master's degree in some specialty of electrical engineering usually also necessary

Experience—Some background working in an engineering firm recommended

Special Skills and Personality Traits—Ability to work as a team member; analytical and detail-oriented; computer proficiency, including familiarity with computer-aided design programs; creative and inquisitive; excellent numerical skills; strong interpersonal and communication talents

Special Requirements—Licensing as a Professional Engineer (PE) usually required

CAREER LADDER

```
┌─────────────────────────────────────┐
│   Project Staff Supervisor; Other    │
│   Project Management Positions;      │
│   Sales Management Positions         │
└─────────────────────────────────────┘

┌─────────────────────────────────────┐
│        Electrical Engineer           │
└─────────────────────────────────────┘

┌─────────────────────────────────────┐
│   College Graduate; Electrical       │
│   Engineering Technician             │
└─────────────────────────────────────┘
```

Position Description

Electrical Engineers design, develop, test, and supervise the deployment of electrical systems and electronic devices. They design electrical equipment, facilities, components, products, and systems for commercial, industrial, and domestic purposes. They design and direct engineering personnel in the fabrication of test control apparatus, and determine the methods, procedures and conditions for testing products. They direct activities to ensure that the manufacturing, construction, installation, and operational testing conform to the project's specifications and meet customer requirements. They often guide and coordinate the operation, maintenance, and repair of equipment/systems in field installations. In all their work, they typically use computer-assisted engineering and design software and equipment to perform their engineering tasks.

While the terms "electrical" and "electronics" engineering often are used interchangeably, Electrical Engineers have traditionally focused on the problems associated with large-scale electrical systems, such as power transmission and motor control, whereas electronics engineers tend to work on applications of electricity to small-scale electronic systems (such as computers and integrated circuits) and on applications of electricity to control systems or signal processing.

In their supervision of the manufacturing and installation of electrical equipment, components, or systems, Electrical Engineers perform detailed calculations to establish standards and specifications. In this process, they also prepare specifications for purchase of materials and equipment. They usually inspect completed installations and observe operations to ensure conformance to design and equipment specifications and compliance with operational and safety standards.

Electrical Engineers work in several areas of renewable and sustainable energy systems, such as wind power farms (where they may be employed as electrical technicians, called windsmiths, operating and maintaining the wind turbines), solar power industry projects (where they handle research and development on solar products to lower their costs and improve their reliability), or hydropower plants (where they work on the development of turbines connected to dams or to run of the river projects where a portion of a river's water is diverted into a canal or pipe to spin turbines).

Salaries

In a 2005 survey conducted by the National Association of Colleges and Employers, it was found that average starting annual salaries for Electrical Engineers started at $51,888 for those with bachelor's degrees. For those with master's degrees, average beginning yearly income was $64,416, and for those with Ph.D. degrees, starting salaries averaged $80,206. According to the U.S. Department of Labor's Bureau of Labor Statistics in their *Occupational Outlook Handbook, 2006–07 Edition*, annual salaries for Electrical Engineers in May 2004 ranged from $47,310 to $108,070.

Employment Prospects

While overall engineering employment is expected to grow about as fast as the average for all occupations through 2014, according to the U.S. Department of Labor, employment opportunities for Electrical Engineers should be particularly favorable. The Department of Labor estimates that the number of job openings resulting from employment growth and from the need to replace Electrical Engineers who transfer to other occupations or leave the labor force will be in rough balance with the supply of graduates. Although international competition and the use of engineering services performed in other countries may limit employment growth to a certain extent, the strong public demand for electrical devices, such as giant electric power generators used to maintain the electrical grids in the country or wireless phone transmitters now utilized by many people should boost growth. In addition, with the burgeoning public concern over environmental issues coupled with the public demand for alternative sources of energy that are not carbon-based and the development of new technologies, such as solar power and photovoltaic cells and the expansion of wind farms wherever possible, the need for Electrical Engineers who specialize in these areas will only accelerate. Prospects should be particularly good for Electrical Engineers working in service firms providing technical expertise to other companies on specific projects.

Advancement Prospects

Some Electrical Engineers move into engineering management or into sales. In sales, an engineering background enables them to discuss technical aspects and assist in product planning, installation, and use. Electrical Engineers may advance to become technical specialists or to supervise a staff or team of engineers and technicians. Supervisory engineers usually are responsible for major components or entire projects. They may eventually become engineering managers. Alternatively, Electrical Engineers with some business background may choose to become independent consultants.

Education and Training

Most students prepare for this field by earning a bachelor's degree, either in electrical engineering or applied science, and they may need between four and five years to complete their studies. Furthermore, they usually need a bachelor's degree in some specialty of electrical engineering for entry-level work in this occupation. Since this field of engineering is so broad, Electrical Engineers, along with electronics engineers, often pursue a master's degree in their specialty.

Special Requirements

All 50 states and the District of Columbia require certification and licensure for engineers to work for either public or private clients. Engineers who are licensed are called Professional Engineers (PE). This licensure generally requires a degree from an accredited engineering program, four years of relevant work experience, and the successful completion of a state examination. Information about the Professional Engineer licensure can be obtained from the National Society of Professional Engineers (NSPE) in Alexandria, Virginia, (http://www.nspe.org) or the National Council of Examiners for Engineering and Surveying (NCEES) in Clemson, South Carolina (http://www.ncees.org).

Experience, Skills, and Personality Traits

Entry-level Electrical Engineers usually work under the guidance of experienced engineers and, in many large companies, also may receive formal classroom or seminar-type training. As new engineers gain seasoning, they are assigned projects that are more difficult with greater independence to develop designs, solve problems, and make decisions.

Among the most important technical skills that Electrical Engineers must exhibit are strong numerical skills, computer literacy, and the ability to understand the technical language and concepts that relate to electrical engineering. While most Electrical Engineers will understand basic circuit theory (that is, the interactions of elements such as resistors, capacitors, diodes, transistors, and inductors in a circuit), the theories they employ generally depend upon the type of work they do. Today, most engineering work involves the use of computers and it is commonplace to use computer-aided design and computer-aided engineering tools (CAD/CAE) to draw up plans for efficient production. Electrical Engineers who take part in the actual production—guiding products through all stages of the manufacturing process—may also determine performance standards for new products and write maintenance schedules to ensure that these standards will be met. Some engineers also write technical manuals, instructional pamphlets, and installation instructions.

Electrical Engineers frequently present the findings of their work in oral presentations, as well as in technical reports. This requires keeping of accurate records and the ability to communicate findings clearly. Much of their time may be spent consulting with specialists in other engineering disciplines and business occupations. Most Electrical Engineers work as part of a team, requiring them to have interpersonal as well as technical skills. Many senior engineers manage a team of technicians or other engineers, and, for this reason, project management skills are important. Above all, Electrical Engineers should be creative, inquisitive, analytical, and detail-oriented.

Unions and Associations

The primary professional association for Electrical Engineers is the Institute of Electrical and Electronics Engineers (IEEE). Obsolescence of technical skills is a serious concern for Electrical Engineers. Membership and participation in this technical societies—with its extensive annual conferences and publications—is therefore essential to maintaining proficiency in their field.

Tips for Entry

1. In preparation for engineering school, take all the advanced math and science courses you can while in high school.
2. While in college, consider participating in an internship with an engineering firm. This will allow you to build skills and apply what you have learned in the classroom, as well as network within your chosen field.
3. Along with your technical training, enroll in business management courses to gain project-management skills.

GEOTECHNICAL ENGINEER

CAREER PROFILE

Duties: Investigate the soil and bedrock on and below a site to determine their engineering properties and how they will interact with, on, or in a proposed construction on the site

Alternate Title(s): Civil Engineer; Project Engineer; Project Manager; Structural Engineer

Salary Range: $40,000 to $95,000 or more

Employment Prospects: Fair

Advancement Prospects: Fair

Prerequisites:

Education or Training—Bachelor's degree in Civil Engineering required; master's or a doctoral degree (Ph.D.) may be mandatory

Experience—Some previous work in an engineering firm recommended

Special Skills and Personality Traits—Creative and analytical; excellent organization and communication skills; problem-solver who is comfortable with abstract ideas; proficient in math; strong computer skills

Special Requirements—License as a Professional Engineer (PE) usually required

CAREER LADDER

```
┌─────────────────────────────────────────┐
│   Civil Engineering Manager; Other       │
│   Project Management Positions;          │
│   Independent Engineering Consultant      │
└─────────────────────────────────────────┘

┌─────────────────────────────────────────┐
│         Geotechnical Engineer            │
└─────────────────────────────────────────┘

┌─────────────────────────────────────────┐
│   College Graduate; Geotechnical         │
│   Technician                             │
└─────────────────────────────────────────┘
```

Position Description

Geotechnical engineering is the branch of civil engineering concerned with the engineering behavior of earth materials. Geotechnical Engineers perform geotechnical investigations to obtain data on the physical properties of soil and rock underlying (and sometimes adjacent to) a site to design earthworks and foundations for proposed structures and for repair of distress to earthworks and structures caused by subsurface conditions. A geotechnical investigation will encompass both surface and subsurface exploration of the site. Surface exploration can include geologic mapping, geophysical methods, and photogrammetry, or it can be as simple as an engineer walking around the site to observe its physical condition. To obtain data about the soil conditions below the surface, some form of subsurface exploration is required. Subsurface exploration typically involves soil sampling and laboratory testing of the retrieved soil samples. Methods of observing the soil below the surface and deter-

mining physical properties of the soils and rock include test pits, trenching, borings, and cone penetration tests (where instrumental probes with conical tips are pushed into the soil hydraulically).

The purpose of this investigation of soil and bedrock is to determine their engineering properties, including how they will interact with, on, or in a proposed construction. By analyzing reports, maps, drawings, blueprints, hydrological characteristics and other topographical and geologic data, Geotechnical Engineers can plan and design projects. They design the type of foundations, earthworks, and/or pavement subgrades required for the intended man-made structures. In their design work, they usually use computer-assisted design (CAD) and computer-assisted engineering (CAE) software to prepare the engineering and design documents. They calculate costs and determine the feasibility of projects, based on their analysis and by applying their knowledge and techniques of engineering and advanced mathematics.

They prepare, or direct the preparation and modification of, reports, specifications, plans, construction schedules, environmental impact studies, and designs for projects. They inspect the construction site to monitor progress and ensure conformance to the engineering plans, specifications, and construction and safety standards.

Geotechnical Engineers can be found working with utility companies and communities in siting and designing wind turbine farms. They are consulted in the construction of dams for hydroelectric power and the construction of water systems (such as canals), of electric power stations for the distribution of electricity, of bioenergy plants, and of the development of hot water reservoirs to tap into geothermal energy for direct use or for the production of electricity.

Salaries

According to a 2005 survey by the National Association of Colleges and Employers, the average starting annual salary for civil engineers with a bachelor's degree was $43,679. For those with a master's degree, it was $48,050, and for those with Ph.D. degrees, it was $59,625. In their salary survey of engineers, the U.S. Department of Labor's Bureau of Labor Statistics in their *Occupational Outlook Handbook, 2006–07 Edition* found that median yearly pay for civil engineers (including Geotechnical Engineers) ranged from $42,610 to $94,660, with the median income being $64,230.

Employment Prospects

According to the U.S. Department of Labor, civil engineers are expected to see average employment growth through 2014. While the supply of new graduates is generally adequate for the number of entry-level positions, there are shortages of highly qualified engineers with particular skills and experience. The strongest demand will most likely be in construction, transportation, energy production and distribution, environmental protection, and seismic engineering. Due to the great reliance on computer technology in this field, opportunities will be especially good for civil and Geotechnical Engineers with training or experience in computer science and with specific computer applications in design work. However, employment in this profession is heavily influenced by fluctuations in construction activity and government hiring. Thus, job openings will tend to vary by geographic area.

Advancement Prospects

Geotechnical Engineers working in government usually begin their careers as junior engineers. As they gain seasoning, they may advance to assistant, associate, and senior-level posts. To attain higher salaries, qualified engineers working in civil service can move into management and administrative positions.

Geotechnical Engineers working in private industry can be promoted to more responsible jobs such as staff engineer, project engineer, or principal engineer. Some qualified Geotechnical Engineers may decide to work as consultants in a private firm or enter administrative work where they can advance to the upper management level. A Master of Science degree is becoming increasingly key for advancement in all fields of civil engineering.

Education and Training

A Bachelor of Science degree in civil engineering is the minimum requirement for most entry-level positions. A master's degree in this field is recommended. Some bachelor's programs are combined with a master's program into one five-year sequence. Another route is to get a bachelor's degree in another engineering field or geology, then a master's degree in geotechnical engineering. By itself, this type of program usually takes one or two years beyond the bachelor's. However, not many universities in the United States offer a master's degree in this subject.

Special Requirements

All 50 states and the District of Columbia require licensure for engineers to work for either public or private clients. Engineers who are licensed are called Professional Engineers (PE). This licensure generally requires a degree from an accredited engineering program, four years of relevant work experience, and the successful completion of a state examination. Information about the Professional Engineer licensure can be obtained from the National Society of Professional Engineers (NSPE) in Alexandria, Virginia, (http://www.nspe.org) or the National Council of Examiners for Engineering and Surveying (NCEES) in Clemson, South Carolina (http://www.ncees.org).

Experience, Skills, and Personality Traits

Newly hired graduates usually work under the guidance of veteran engineers. In large companies, they may also receive formal classroom training. As they gain knowledge and experience, they receive greater independence and are assigned to more difficult tasks.

Employers prefer to hire Geotechnical Engineers who are creative and analytical. They look for individuals who can solve problems and work well with abstract ideas. Oral and written communication skills are very important, as well as being able to function as part of a team of engineers. Geotechnical Engineers must combine mathematical and mechanical aptitude with an ability to organize, analyze, and evaluate technical data to solve detailed problems. In addition, strong computer proficiency is required by most employers of Geotechnical Engineers.

Unions and Associations

The primary professional association for Geotechnical Engineers is the American Society of Civil Engineers (ASCE). As they work on renewable energy projects, they may also want to consult such groups as the American Wind Energy Association (AWEA), the Geothermal Resources Council (GRC), or the National Hydropower Association (NHA).

Tips for Entry

1. A solid high school background in mathematics (algebra, geometry, trigonometry, and calculus) and science (biology, chemistry, and physics) will greatly aid you in seeking a college for a bachelor's degree program in engineering.

2. Consider participating in an internship with an engineering firm while you are in college, as it will allow you to apply what you have learned in the classroom in a work situation, and you will be able to make contacts with people in your field.

3. As you are likely to do much more writing on the job than you expect, take a writing class, plus other humanities courses that require you to develop your communication skills. Some course work in business subjects may help you later to make a smooth career shift into the business world.

HYDROLOGIST AND HYDRAULIC ENGINEER

Duties: <u>Hydrologist</u>: Study the quantity, distribution, circulation, and physical properties of underground and surface waters to locate water and energy resources, predict water-related geologic hazards, and offer environmental site assessments; <u>Hydraulic Engineer</u>: Design and direct construction of power and other hydraulic engineering projects for control/use of water

Alternate Title(s): <u>Hydrologist</u>: Environmental Consultant, Groundwater Consultant, Hydrogeologist; <u>Hydraulic Engineer</u>: Environmental Engineer, Hydrologic Engineer;

Salary Range: <u>Hydrologist</u>: $38,000 to $95,000 or more; <u>Hydraulic Engineer</u>: $42,000 to $95,000 or more

Employment Prospects: Fair to Good

Advancement Prospects: Fair

Prerequisites:

Education or Training—Bachelor's degree in civil engineering usually required; master's degree required for research positions; doctoral degree necessary for college teaching and most high-level research posts

Experience—Some field research experience as an assistant or intern is recommended

Special Skills and Personality Traits—Excellent computer proficiency; good interpersonal and communication skills; knowledgeable of federal environmental laws, regulations, and programs; physical stamina; problem solver; program management abilities; well organized

Special Requirements—Certification is recommended for both positions and may be required

> **Senior Civil Engineer; Project Leader or Manager; Program Manager; Independent Consultant**

> **Hydraulic Engineer; Hydrologist**

> **Research Assistant; Research Technician**

Position Description

Hydrology is the study of the waters of the Earth: their occurrence, circulation, and distribution; their chemical and physical properties; and their reaction with the environment, including their relationship to living things. The hydrologic cycle consists of the passage of water from the oceans into the atmosphere by evaporation and transpiration, onto the lands by precipitation, over and under lands as runoff and

infiltration, and back to the oceans. Hydrology is primarily concerned with the part of the cycle after the precipitation of water onto the land and before its return to the oceans. Hydrologists study the cycle by measuring such variables as the amount and intensity of precipitation, the sum of water stored as snow or in glaciers, the movement of glaciers, the rate of flow in streams, and the soil-water balance (which also includes the study of the amount of flow of groundwater). They can deduce the flow underground by characteristics, including permeability, of the soil and bedrock; by how water behaves near other sources of water, such as rivers and oceans; and through fluid flow models based on water movements on the Earth's surface. Hydrologists also study water pollution. They use their skills to determine the movement/extent of contamination from landfills, mine runoff, and other potentially contaminated sites to surface and subsurface water. Hydrologists employ sophisticated techniques and instruments, such as remote sensing technology, and numerical modeling to monitor the change in regional and global water cycles. Surface-water Hydrologists use sensitive stream-measuring devices to assess flow rates and the quality of water.

Hydrologists utilize their observations of hydrologic processes to make predictions of the future behavior of hydrologic systems (i.e., water flow and water quality). These estimates are important for engineers and economists so that proper risk analysis can be performed to influence investment decisions in future infrastructure projects and to determine the yield reliability characteristics of water supply systems. These estimates also are key in designing dams for water supply or hydroelectric power generation and formulating operating rules for large dams that are part of systems that include agricultural, industrial, and residential demands.

Hydrologists also aid in the search for, assessment of, and development of geothermal energy that heats water seeping into underground reservoirs, which can then be tapped for a variety of uses. Low to medium temperature (70 to 225 degrees Fahrenheit) water reservoirs can be used directly to heat buildings, to grow and dry crops, and for fish farms. The energy produced from high temperature reservoirs (225 to 600 degrees Fahrenheit) can spin a turbine to generate electricity.

Hydrologists frequently work with environmental engineers in consulting firms that advise and help businesses and government agencies to comply with environmental policy, particularly with regard to groundwater decontamination and flood control. They also conduct research on sources of pollutants and make recommendations on how best to clean and preserve the environment. The federal government also hires both Hydrologists and Hydraulic Engineers for many of its agencies.

Hydraulic engineering is a subdiscipline of civil engineering and is concerned with the flow and conveyance of fluids, primarily water. Hydraulic Engineers design and direct the construction of power and other hydraulic engineering projects for control/use of water. They compute and estimate rates of water flow. They specify the type and size of equipment (including conduits, pressure valves, and surge tanks) to be used in transporting water and converting waterpower into electricity. They may direct, through subordinate supervisors, the activities of workers engaged in

dredging, digging cutoffs, placing jetties, and constructing levees to stabilize streams or open waterways. Hydraulic Engineers design and coordinate the construction of artificial canals, conduits, and mains to transport and distribute water and plan reservoirs, pressure valves, and booster stations to guarantee the proper water pressure at all levels. They frequently build laboratory models to study construction and water flow problems.

Salaries

According to the U.S. Department of Labor's Bureau of Labor Statistics in their *Occupational Outlook Handbook, 2006–07 Edition*, median annual salaries of Hydrologists in May 2004 were $61,510, with the middle 50 percent earning between $47,080 and $77,910. The lowest 10 percent had incomes of less than $38,580, and the highest 10 percent earned more than $94,460. Yearly salaries for Hydraulic Engineers were similar, ranging from lows of $42,000 to highs of $95,000 or more.

Employment Prospects

According to the U.S. Department of Labor, employment of Hydrologists is expected to grow much faster than the average for all occupations, with job growth being strongest at private-sector consulting firms. Demand for Hydrologists will be spurred partly by public policy, which will oblige companies and organizations to comply with complex environmental laws and regulations, particularly those regarding groundwater decontamination and flood control. Job opportunities will also increase with the public's escalating awareness regarding the need to monitor the quality of the environment, to interpret the impact of human actions on terrestrial and aquatic ecosystems, and to develop more environmentally favorable energy sources, such as geothermal and hydropower resources.

While civil engineers generally are anticipated to have average employment growth through 2014, Hydraulic Engineers should expect additional employment possibilities with the mounting public demand to find energy sources to replace the reliance of the United States on foreign oil and gas resources. With increased climate changes manifesting themselves, the demand for better coastal protection with levees and better flood control will ensure employment potentials for Hydraulic Engineers.

Advancement Prospects

Hydrologists often begin their careers in field exploration or, occasionally, as research assistants or technicians in laboratories or offices. As they gain experience, they are given more difficult assignments. Eventually, they may be promoted to project leader, program manager, or another management and/or research post. Beginning Hydraulic Engineers usually work under the supervision of seasoned engineers. As they gain knowledge and practical experience, they are assigned to specific projects to work on their own, to develop their own designs, solve problems, and make decisions. They may advance to supervision of a staff or a team of engineers and technicians. Some may eventually become engineering managers or enter other managerial jobs.

Education and Training

While a bachelor's degree may be adequate for a few entry-level positions as Hydrologists, usually a master's degree is necessary. It is also the minimum educational requirement for most entry-level applied research positions in private industry and in state and federal agencies. A doctoral degree is necessary for college teaching and most high-level research posts. In addition, an understanding of environmental regulations and government permit issues is valuable for those Hydrologists planning to work in the geothermal industry.

For Hydraulic Engineers, a bachelor's degree in engineering, preferably civil or chemical, is mandatory for almost all entry-level jobs. Graduate training is essential for engineering faculty positions and for many research and development programs.

Special Requirements

Many employers and most states require Hydrologists to be certified in their field. The American Institute of Hydrology (AIH) offers certification programs in professional hydrology. Certification is highly recommended for those seeking advancement in their field. Hydraulic Engineers, like other types of engineers, should be certified as Professional Engineers (PE), as most employers will require it.

Experience, Skills, and Personality Traits

Hydrologists and Hydraulic Engineers must have excellent interpersonal skills, as they usually work as part of a team with other scientists, engineers, and technicians. Strong oral and written communication skills also are essential, because writing technical reports and research proposals and then communicating technical and research results to company managers, regulators, and the public are important aspects of their work. Computer proficiency is key, especially familiarity with spreadsheets, databases, and research tools (including map creation software, modeling techniques, and graphics or photo imaging software). A knowledge of geographic information systems (GIS) and the Global Positioning System (GPS)—a locator system that uses satellites—is critical.

Hydrologists and Hydraulic Engineers need to be skilled in independently planning/organizing data and should have a basic knowledge of the principles/practices of project management. They must have strong mathematics skills, as well as a solid background in chemistry, geography, and physics. Those involved in fieldwork must have physical stamina.

Unions and Associations

Professional associations of interest for Hydrologists and Hydraulic Engineers include the American Institute of Hydrology (AIH), the International Association for Environmental Hydrology (IAEH), and the Environmental and Water Resources Institute (EWRI) of the American Society of Civil Engineers (ASCE).

Tips for Entry

1. While in college, investigate internships or cooperative programs with engineering firms or consulting companies to gain practical experience.
2. If you want information on obtaining a position as a Hydrologist or Hydraulic Engineer with the federal government, consult the Office of Personnel Management through USAJOBS, the federal government's official employment information system, at http://www.usajobs.opm.gov.
3. For Hydrologists and Hydraulic Engineers who enter the field of consulting, courses in business, finance, marketing, or economics will be useful.

METEOROLOGIST

CAREER PROFILE

Duties: Interpret atmospheric phenomena and meteorological data gathered by surface and atmosphere stations, satellites, and radar to prepare reports/forecasts for public and other uses

Alternate Title(s): Atmospheric Scientist; Environmental Meteorologist; Hydrometeorological Technician; Hydrometeorologist; Research Meteorologist

Salary Range: $20,000 to $100,000 or more

Employment Prospects: Fair to Good

Advancement Prospects: Fair

Prerequisites:

Education or Training—Bachelor's degree in meteorology or atmospheric science minimal requirement; master's degree recommended

Experience—On-the-job training under the guidance of seasoned Meteorologists

Special Skills and Personality Traits—Able to analyze and communicate technical information; creativity; exceptional oral and written communication skills; expertise in the use of computer modeling tools; good eye for detail; highly self-motivated; thorough understanding of mathematics, physics, geography, and computer science

Special Requirements—Certification as a consulting Meteorologist usually required

CAREER LADDER

```
┌─────────────────────────────────┐
│   Supervisory or Administrative  │
│   Positions; Private Consultant  │
└─────────────────────────────────┘

┌─────────────────────────────────┐
│          Meteorologist           │
└─────────────────────────────────┘

┌─────────────────────────────────┐
│   College Graduate; Intern       │
│   Position as Trainee            │
└─────────────────────────────────┘
```

Position Description

Meteorology is the scientific study of global atmospheric processes and their related phenomena: the receipt of solar radiation, evaporation, precipitation; and the determination of, and changes in, atmospheric pressure (and, therefore, wind). It is generally concerned with short-term processes (i.e., hours and days rather than months and seasons) operating in the troposphere and mesosphere, which are the atmospheric layers of Earth's weather systems. Individual fields within Meteorology include aerology (the study of free air not adjacent to Earth's surface), aeronomy (the study of the physics of the upper atmosphere), applied meteorology (the application of weather data for specific practical problems), dynamic meteorology (the study of atmospheric motions, using the principles of fluid dynamics), and physical meteorology (the study of the physical properties of the atmosphere). Prediction is a unifying theme throughout meteorology and its various disciplines, and it sets the direction for research and technological development.

Meteorologists analyze and interpret meteorological data, reports, maps, photographs, and prognostic charts to predict long- and short-range weather conditions, using computer models and their knowledge of climate theory, physics, and mathematics. They gather their data from such sources as surface and upper air stations, satellites, and radar and prepare reports and forecasts. They conduct basic or applied meteorological research into the processes and determinants of atmospheric phenomena, weather, and climate. They measure wind, temperature, and humidity in the troposphere, using weather balloons.

Frequently referred to as atmospheric scientists, they apply their meteorological knowledge to problems in areas including agriculture, pollution control, and water management and to issues such as global warning or ozone depletion. They operate computer graphic equipment to produce weather reports and maps for analysis, distribution, or use in weather broadcasts. They may establish, staff, and direct forecasting services at weather stations or at radio or television broadcasting facilities. They prepare forecasts and briefings to meet the needs of industry, business, government, and other groups.

Meteorologists help engineers employed by companies in the wind power industry to identify appropriate sites with suitable wind conditions to build wind turbines. Other Meteorologists may specialize in the study of the occurrence, movement, and changes in the state of water in the atmosphere. This discipline, known as hydrometeorology, a combined branch of meteorology and hydrology, is concerned with specific hydrologic problems, such as flood control, hydroelectric power, irrigation, and water resources.

The National Oceanic and Atmospheric Administration (NOAA) has the major governmental responsibility in the United States for monitoring and forecasting the weather and conducting meteorological research. The Air Force Weather Agency (AFWA) and the Fleet Numerical Weather Central (FNWC) have similar responsibilities within the U.S. Air Force and U.S. Navy, respectively; space applications to meteorology are researched by the National Aeronautics and Space Administration (NASA) as well as by the National Environmental Satellite Service (NESS), which is under the auspices of NOAA. In addition to a host of universities conducting meteorological research, there is the National Center for Atmospheric Research (NCAR), which is operated by an affiliation of universities and sponsored by the U.S. National Science Foundation (NSF). In addition, the World Weather Watch (WWW), organized by the World Meteorological Organization (WMO), collects and disseminates information on a global basis. A number of private companies also engage in operational and research meteorological activities.

Salaries

According to the U.S. Department of Labor's Bureau of Labor Statistics in their *Occupational Outlook Handbook, 2006–07 Edition*, median annual income for Meteorologists in May 2004 was $70,100. The middle 50 percent had yearly salaries between $48,880 and $86,610. The lowest 10 percent earned less than $34,590, and the highest 10 percent earned more than $106,020.

The average annual salary for Meteorologists in nonsupervisory, supervisory, and managerial positions employed by the federal government in 2005 was about $80,499. Those with a bachelor's degree and no experience received a starting salary of $27,955 or $34,544, depending on their college grades. Those with a master's degree could start at $42,090

to $54,393, and those with a Ph.D. could begin at $70,280. Initial salaries for Meteorologists employed in private industry are slightly higher in most areas of the country.

Employment Prospects

The U.S. Department of Labor projects that the employment of Meteorologists will increase about as fast as the average for all occupations through 2014. In private industry, job opportunities for Meteorologists are expected to be better than in the Federal Government over the same period. As research leads to continuing improvements in weather forecasting, demand is expected to grow for private weather consulting firms to provide more detailed data than has formerly been available, especially to climate-sensitive industries. As wind power becomes even more cost competitive, there will be a rising demand for the establishment of more wind power plants, and the need for Meteorologists as consultants will increase.

Advancement Prospects

Advancement for most Meteorologists means taking on more managerial responsibilities. Those with many years of experience may become private consultants. Some Meteorologists establish their own consulting firms.

Education and Training

A bachelor's degree in meteorology or atmospheric science, or in mathematics or the physical sciences with courses in meteorology, is the usual minimum educational requirement for an entry-level position as a Meteorologist. Obtaining a master's degree enhances employment opportunities, pay, and advancement potential. A master's degree usually is necessary for conducting applied research and development, and a Ph.D. is demanded for most basic research positions. Because Meteorology is a small field, relatively few colleges and universities offer degrees in meteorology or atmospheric science. In 2005, the American Meteorological Society (AMS) approved approximately 100 undergraduate and graduate atmospheric science programs. Many of these curricula combine the study of meteorology with another field, such as agriculture, hydrology, oceanography, engineering, or physics.

Special Requirements

The title Certified Consulting Meteorologist is granted by the American Meteorological Society (AMS). This certification is generally considered by prospective employers to be recognition that the Meteorologist is particularly qualified as a consultant.

Experience, Skills, and Personality Traits

Meteorologists need to be able to gather/analyze information on atmospheric conditions. They must be able to spot and interpret trends and then be able to communicate technical information clearly, both orally and in writing. They must have a good eye for detail and have a thorough understanding of geography, mathematics, meteorology, physics, and computer science. They should have an expertise in the use of computer modeling tools and some experience with such software as Microsoft Excel Spreadsheets. They should be highly motivated and be capable of judging the costs/benefits of their recommendations. If they are in supervisory posts, they need to motivate, develop, and direct their staff.

Unions and Associations

The major professional association for Meteorologists is the American Meteorological Society (AMS). As consultants, they may find that membership in such other international institutions as the International Association of Meteorology and Atmospheric Science (IAMAS) or the World Meteorological Organization (WMO) to be useful.

Tips for Entry

1. Include courses in business, statistics, and economics in your educational program, as an increasing emphasis in the field of meteorology is being placed on long-range seasonal forecasting to assist businesses.
2. Become thoroughly adept in mathematics (including algebra, trigonometry, geometry, calculus, and probability and statistics), as mathematical modeling of the atmosphere is a key part of present-day meteorology.
3. Consider obtaining an additional bachelor's degree in basic engineering to complement your degree in meteorology, or earn a master's degree in the field to enhance your employment opportunities.

SOLAR ENGINEER

CAREER PROFILE

Duties: Design and develop solar energy systems

Alternate Title(s): Embedded Systems Engineer-Solar Energy; Photovoltaic Engineer; Solar Energy System Design Engineer; Solar Field Engineer; Solar Photovoltaic Design Engineer

Salary Range: $30,000 to $105,000 or more

Employment Prospects: Fair to Good

Advancement Prospects: Fair

Prerequisites:

    Education or Training—Bachelor's degree in chemical, electrical, environmental, materials, or mechanical engineering required; master's degree recommended by some employers

    Experience—Previous hands-on experience in a construction-related field

    Special Skills and Personality Traits—Analytical and detail-oriented; creative and inquisitive; superior computer proficiency; solid communication and interpersonal abilities; leadership talent; project management and time-management skills

    Special Requirements—Certification as a Professional Engineer (PE) usually required

CAREER LADDER

```
┌─────────────────────────────────────┐
│  Project Management or Sales Positions;│
│        Independent Consultant         │
└─────────────────────────────────────┘

┌─────────────────────────────────────┐
│            Solar Engineer             │
└─────────────────────────────────────┘

┌─────────────────────────────────────┐
│     College Graduate; Engineering     │
│              Technician               │
└─────────────────────────────────────┘
```

Position Description

Humanity's growing knowledge of the Sun's ability to produce both heat and electricity has led to the invention of numerous technologies for capturing the Sun's energy. One of the most common of these technologies is the photovoltaic (PV) cell, also known as a solar cell, which can produce electricity directly from sunlight. PV cells perform this conversion without any moving parts, noise, pollution, radiation, or maintenance. They are made of a semiconductor material, typically silicon (usually from beach sand), which is treated chemically to create a positive charge layer and a negative charge layer. When sunlight strikes a PV cell, the cell absorbs a portion of the light that strikes it. When the energy from the absorbed light strikes electrons in the outer shell of an atom, these electrons are freed from their parent atoms and can then travel into a circuit in the form of electricity. These loose electrons are gathered by wires attached to the cell. PV cells can be hooked together into modules and then into an array to meet many different types of electricity requirements, from pumping water to operating calculators and watches to lighting homes and communities.

Another technology using sunlight is known as a concentrating solar power system (also called solar thermal electric system), where mirrors are employed to focus incoming sunlight onto a receiver. The receiver collects the Sun's energy in the form of heat, which can then be used directly or converted into electricity utilizing a generator. This technology is still in development and tends to carry a high cost. In addition to these two methodologies, energy from the Sun can be used to heat water for buildings and swimming pools. Solar water heating systems for buildings typically include a solar collector, in which fluid is heated by the Sun, and a storage tank, which holds the hot fluid after it has been heated. Systems using fluids other than water require the additional step of passing water through a heat exchanger to heat the water from the hot fluid.

Solar Engineers design and develop solar energy systems, working with product development and marketing personnel to specify, design, and transfer to manufacturing new and novel photovoltaic module designs, or innovative types of parabolic troughs, power towers, or parabolic dishes to be used in solar power systems. They design and conduct research and development (R&D) experiments that lead to improved efficiencies. They analyze their data and discern trends, presenting development updates and action plans to upper management. Most Solar Engineers have a solid background in electrical and/or mechanical engineering. Some Solar Engineers with experience in electrical or electronics engineering may help to design (or enhance the given design) of parabolic collectors, which focus sunlight into a fiber optic system that illuminates building interiors with sunlight.

In some cases, solar energy developing companies hire Solar Engineers, who are made responsible for the installation of solar electric systems for homes or businesses. These Solar Engineers manage the engineering plans for rooftop and ground mounted photovoltaic system, and ensure that field installations match the engineering designs and construction plans. They calculate the wind, weight, and solar radiation projections and requirements that will affect the performance of the solar electric system design. They may interface with architects and clients in resolving technical issues and with suppliers and manufacturers regarding equipment. They may oversee the evaluation (monitoring) of the performance of installed systems, and may train technicians for product installation and maintenance. In this process, they may assess the integrity of the installation in terms of civil engineering aspects and compliance with manufacturer specifications and safety codes required for utility approval. In addition, they often assist marketing and sales personnel in developing product promotional materials.

Salaries

Starting annual income for Solar Engineers with a bachelor's degree typically ranges from $30,000 to $60,000, depending on the organization and the specific duties and responsibilities. Yearly salaries for experienced Solar Engineers span from $40,000 to $105,000 or more.

Employment Prospects

Overall engineering employment is projected by the U.S. Department of Labor's Bureau of Labor Statistics to grow about as fast as the average for all occupations to 2014. Non-traditional Engineers have customarily been concentrated in slow-growing manufacturing industries, in which they design, build, test, and improve manufactured products. However, increasing employment of engineers in faster growing service industries, such as the solar energy industry, should generate more employment growth during the coming years. It is important for engineers to continue their education throughout their careers because much of their value to their employer depends on their solid knowledge of the latest technology. By keeping current in their field, Solar Engineers can deliver the best solutions and greatest value to their employers. As solar energy continues to develop as a renewable source of energy and is used more widely, the need for trained and experienced Solar Engineers is going to accelerate.

Advancement Prospects

Some Solar Engineers may decide to advance into higher levels of management in the firms who employ them, usually into product or project management posts. Others may choose to expand professionally into the sales/marketing of solar energy products, or become independent consultants in the field.

Education and Training

Most Solar Engineers have a bachelor's degree in Engineering (chemical, civil, electrical, environmental, materials, or mechanical). Some may have a bachelor's degree in physics or materials science with a specialization in solar energy and engineering. In some instances, employers may require a master's degree as well.

Special Requirements

Certification as a Professional Engineer (PE) may be required by employers. In addition, solar energy companies that sell their products to the public may demand their Solar Engineers have a certification from the North American Board of Certified Energy Practitioners (NABCEP).

Experience, Skills, and Personality Traits

Many companies that design and manufacture solar energy systems demand that their Solar Engineers have some previous practical, field experience in a construction-related area.

Solar Engineers need to have excellent computer skills and be adept at computer-aided design (CAD) techniques. If they work with photovoltaic cell development, they may need experience in C or C++ programming, as well as other advanced software tools. Solar Engineers must be self-motivated with excellent time-management and project-management talents. They should have great communication skills and leadership abilities, and be equipped to work as part of a team.

Unions and Associations

Beyond belonging to professional associations devoted to their background specialty (such as the Institute of Electrical and Electronics Engineers, or IEEE, for electrical engineers, or the American Society of Mechanical Engineers, or ASME, for mechanical engineers), Solar Engineers will find it useful to have a membership in the American Solar Energy Society (ASES) or in the Solar Energy Industries Association (SEIA).

Tips for Entry

1. During college, take a summer job, or an intern assignment, with a construction company to gain practical experience in the construction of buildings and to enhance your employment possibilities.

2. Consider obtaining a bachelor's degree in more than one field of engineering, or obtaining a master's degree in a field of engineering other than your bachelor's degree to enhance your career possibilities in solar energy.

3. Besides taking writing and public speaking classes (to enhance your communication skills), enroll in business management courses, as they should prove beneficial in handling your project management responsibilities.

MANUAL LABOR PERSONNEL

ELECTRICIAN

CAREER PROFILE

Duties: Install, maintain, and repair electrical wiring, equipment, fixtures, and systems

Alternate Title(s): Electrical Contractor; Electrical Repairer; Electrical Technician; Inside Wireman; Journeyman Electrician; Maintenance Electrician

Salary Range: $25,000 to $70,000 or more

Employment Prospects: Good

Advancement Prospects: Fair to Good

Prerequisites:

Education or Training—High school degree required; vocational-technical school degree optional

Experience—Apprenticeship programs sponsored by joint training committees recommended

Special Skills and Personality Traits—Ability to read blueprints and wiring schematics; careful eye for details; excellent interpersonal abilities; good manual dexterity and physical stamina; sound judgment and patience

Special Requirements—Licensing as a journeyman Electrician required

CAREER LADDER

Project Supervisor; Project Manager;
Construction Superintendent;
Independent Contractor;
Electrical Engineer

Electrician

Apprentice Electrician; Electrician's
Helper

Position Description

Electricians install and repair electrical systems, apparatus, and wiring, as well as electrical and electronic components of industrial machinery and equipment. There are two general types of electrical work: construction work, which is concerned with the assembling, installation and testing of electrical systems, and maintenance work, which is focused on maintenance/repair of already installed but non-functioning electrical systems. Traditionally, construction electricians are employed by contractors during the secondary phases of building, whereas maintenance electricians work as freelancers or for large factories, office buildings, hospitals, installations, or other institutional structures. Today, many electricians work in both construction and maintenance.

Electricians rely on manuals, schematic diagrams, and blueprints when installing electrical systems. (These guides indicate the locations of circuits, outlets, load centers, panel boards, and other equipment.) Electricians must follow the National Electric Code and comply with state and local building codes when they set up these systems. When Elec-

tricians install wiring systems in factories and other commercial settings, they first place conduit (pipe or tubing) inside partitions, walls, or other concealed areas as designated by the blueprints. They also fasten to the walls small metal or plastic boxes that will house electrical switches and outlets. They pull insulated wires or cables through the conduit to complete the circuit between these boxes. The gauge and number of wires installed depends upon the load and end use of that portion of the electrical system. The greater the diameter of the wire is, the higher the voltage and amperage that can flow through it.

Electricians connect all types of wire to circuit breakers, transformers, outlets, or other electric/electronic components. They join the wires in boxes with assorted specially designed connectors. During installation, electricians use both hand and power tools. After they install the wiring, they use testing equipment (such as ammeters, ohmmeters, voltmeters, and oscilloscopes) to check the circuits for proper connections, ensuring electrical compatibility and the safety of the components installed.

In maintenance work, Electricians diagnose malfunctioning systems, apparatus, and components, using test equipment and hand tools to locate the cause of a breakdown and correct the problem. They inspect electrical systems, equipment and components to identify hazards, defects, and the need for adjustment or repair and to ensure compliance with codes. They advise management on whether continued operation of equipment could be hazardous. When laboring with complex electronic devices, Electricians often work with electrical engineers, engineering technicians, line installers and repairers, or industrial machinery installation, repair, and maintenance workers. In their repair activities, Electricians may replace faulty electrical components of machines (such as relays, switches, and position-sensing devices), faulty electronic components (such as printed circuit boards), and electric motor bearings (and then rewire the motors). They may plan the layout/installation of electrical wiring, equipment, and fixtures, based on job specifications and relevant codes. They may direct/train workers to install, maintain, or repair electrical wiring, equipment, and fixtures.

Electricians employed in the wind power industry usually are required to operate/maintain the wind turbine machines, and often are called windsmiths. The photovoltaic cell and solar hot water industries employ many professional and skilled workers, including Electricians, whose duties may include wiring solar panels to mounting systems, as well as installing solar electric systems. The geothermal industry also hires Electricians to work in its electricity production processes and in the designing/construction of power plants. Similarly, the design, construction, and maintenance of hydropower plants require both electrical engineers and Electricians.

Salaries

According to the U.S. Department of Labor's Bureau of Labor Statistics in their *Occupational Outlook Handbook, 2006–07 Edition*, median annual salaries for Electricians in May 2004 were $42,254. The middle 50 percent earned between $32,070 and $55,909. The lowest 10 percent had incomes of less than $25,315, and the highest 10 percent earned more than $69,897. Apprentice Electricians usually start at between 40 and 50 percent of the rate paid to fully trained Electricians, depending on experience. As apprentices become more accomplished, they receive periodic pay increases throughout their training.

Employment Prospects

Employment of Electricians is expected to increase as fast as average for all occupations through 2014, according to the U.S. Department of Labor. In addition to jobs created by the increased demand for electrical work, many openings are anticipated to occur over the next decade as a large number of electricians are expected to retire. This will create good career opportunities for the most qualified jobseekers.

Advancement Prospects

Experienced Electricians can advance to jobs as supervisors. In construction, they may become project managers or construction superintendents. Those with sufficient capital and management abilities may launch their own contracting business, although this may require an electrical contractor's license. In maintenance, they may become system supervisors. Some Electricians may decide to work as trade or vocational school instructors or join a sales force as a building supply sales representative. Many Electricians also become electrical inspectors or estimators. Some may choose further education to gain a college degree as electrical engineers.

Education and Training

Most Electricians learn their trade through apprenticeship programs. These combine on-the-job training with related classroom instruction. Apprenticeship courses may be sponsored by joint training committees made up of local unions of the International Brotherhood of Electrical Workers (IBEW) and local chapters of the National Electrical Contractors Association (NECA), company management committees of individual electrical contracting companies, or local chapters of the Associated Builders and Contractors (ABC) and the Independent Electrical Contractors Association (IECA). Because of the comprehensive training received, those who complete apprenticeship programs qualify to do both maintenance and construction electrical work. A high school diploma or a General Educational Development credential (GED) is required, as well as good mathematics and English skills. Programs usually last between four and five years, and each year typically includes at least 144 hours of classroom instruction and 2,000 hours of hands-on training.

Some individuals may choose to obtain their classroom training outside an apprenticeship program. Some public and private vocational-technical schools offer such programs, as do training academies in affiliation with local unions and contractor organizations. Employers often hire students who complete these programs and usually start them at a more advanced level than those without the training. A few persons become Electricians by first working as helpers, assisting Electricians setting up job sites, gathering materials, and doing other non-electrical work, before entering an apprenticeship program. In addition, Electricians must continue to take courses to keep up with changes in codes, materials, and installation methods.

Special Requirements

All states require licensing of Electricians, and many such jurisdictions have their own licensing exams that test knowledge of local regulations as well as information contained in the National Electric Code (which is the national register of electrical regulations).

Experience, Skills, and Personality Traits

Electricians need the basic skills to handle tools and materials accurately, efficiently, and safely. Good manual dexterity, eye-hand coordination, physical fitness and stamina, patience, and a sense of balance are also important. They must be able to read and interpret blueprints and wiring schematics for installation and diagnostic purposes. They should have good interpersonal skills so that they can interact well with customers. They need to have strong mathematical skills, good vision, and be able to distinguish colors, as all electric wiring is color-coded to avoid mistakes and injuries. In addition, Electricians must have good mechanical ability, a thorough knowledge of the principles of electricity, circuitry, and power distribution within a structure, and familiarity with the materials/techniques of construction.

Unions and Associations

Many Electricians are members of the International Brotherhood of Electrical Workers (IBEW). Other organizations that represent Electricians are the International Union of Electronic, Electrical, Salaried, Machine, and Furniture Workers (the Industrial Division of the Communications Workers of America) (IUE-CWA), the International Association of Machinists and Aerospace Workers (IAMAW), and the United Steelworkers of America (USA). Other groups of interest for Electricians include the Independent Electrical Contractors Association (IECA), and the National Electrical Contractors Association (NECA).

Tips for Entry

1. As knowledge of construction materials and techniques are essential for Electricians, while in high school, consider a summer job with a construction firm.
2. After high school, as an alternative to applying for an apprenticeship program (which may have limited openings available), consider taking courses at a professional vocational/technical school or a two-year college to better position yourself for an apprenticeship program.
3. It is recommended that you become fluent in both English and Spanish in order to relay instructions and safety precautions to workers with limited understanding of English. (Spanish-speaking workers make up a large part of the construction workforce in many areas.) In turn, Spanish-speaking workers need very good English skills to understand instructions presented in classes and installation instructions, which are usually written in English and are highly technical.

IRON AND SHEET METAL WORKER

CAREER PROFILE

Duties: Make, install, and maintain heating, ventilation, and air-conditioning duct systems and other building parts/products made from metal sheets

Alternate Title(s): Heating, Ventilation, and Air Conditioning (HVAC) Technician; HVAC Sheet Metal Specialist; Ironworker; Sheet Metal Installer; Sheet Metal Layout Mechanic; Sheet Metal Mechanic; Sheet Metal Worker

Salary Range: $20,000 to $70,000 or more

Employment Prospects: Good

Advancement Prospects: Fair to Good

Prerequisites:

Education or Training—High school diploma required; apprenticeship program recommended

Experience—Apprenticeship program experience suggested; on-the-job training is an alternative

Special Skills and Personality Traits—Ability to work on narrow beams and girders at heights and not suffer from dizziness; excellent physical condition; good agility, balance, eyesight, and depth perception; manual dexterity and the capability to carry out complex, repetitive tasks quickly and methodically

Special Requirements—Certification usually required

CAREER LADDER

```
┌──────────────────────────────────────┐
│  Supervisory or Management Positions;  │
│        Independent Contractor          │
└──────────────────────────────────────┘

┌──────────────────────────────────────┐
│      Iron and Sheet Metal Worker       │
└──────────────────────────────────────┘

┌──────────────────────────────────────┐
│              Apprentice                │
└──────────────────────────────────────┘
```

Position Description

Iron and Sheet Metal Workers make, install, maintain, and repair a wide variety of products made from metal sheets, such as roofs, siding, rain gutters, skylights, restaurant equipment, and outdoor signs. They may also work with fiberglass and plastic materials. Although some workers specialize in fabrication, installation, or maintenance, most Iron and Sheet Metal Workers handle all three jobs. They do both construction-related sheet metal work and mass production of sheet metal products in manufacturing.

Iron and Sheet Metal Workers first study plans/specifications to determine the kind and quantity of materials needed. They then measure, cut, bend, shape, and fashion the flat pieces of sheet metal into three-dimensional forms to make ductwork, roofing, siding for houses, traffic and warning signs, car bumpers, and other custom products. Frequently today, Iron and Sheet Metal Workers use computerized metalworking equipment, allowing them to experiment easily with different layouts and to work more quickly. In shops without computerized equipment, and for products that cannot be made on such equipment, they make the required calculations and use tapes, rulers, and other measuring devices for layout work. They then cut or stamp the parts on machine tools.

Before assembling pieces, Iron and Sheet Metal Workers check each part for accuracy, using such measuring instruments as calipers and micrometers, and, if necessary, finish the product by using hand, rotary, or squaring shears and hacksaws. After the parts have been inspected, they fasten seams and joints together with welds, bolts, solder, or other connecting devices, smoothing and polishing the surface. Then, they take the parts to the construction site, where they further assemble the pieces as they install them. (Some jobs may be done completely at the jobsite.)

Iron and Sheet Metal Workers are also involved in the installation and anchoring of piping or ductwork. In this process, they use many tools (including heavy scissors, power and hand drills, and punches) either for assembly at the jobsite or to attach prefabricated pieces. Some Iron and Sheet Metal Workers specialize in testing, balancing, adjusting, and servicing existing heating, ventilation, and air-conditioning (HVAC) systems to ensure they are functioning properly and to improve their energy efficiency. Those specializing in this area are often called HVAC (heating, ventilation, and air-conditioning) technicians.

Many Iron and Sheet Metal Workers work in manufacturing facilities, producing sheet metal for use in the automotive, aircraft, and other industries. They also make sheet metal parts for manufacturing equipment or machinery. This work is usually done on a much larger scale and requires heavier equipment and more automated machinery than that in smaller sheet metal shops.

A related occupation within the construction industry is that of structural and reinforcing iron and metal workers, who place/install iron or steel girders, columns, and other construction materials to form buildings, bridges, and other structures. They are frequently called ironworkers and may fabricate structural metal in fabricating shops located away from construction sites. Ironworkers also set the reinforcing bars (often called rebars) in the forms that hold the concrete pillars found in parking garages and arenas.

Construction sheet metal workers create the sheet metal sidings and turbines utilized in the construction of wind plants. In addition, their work is critical in the construction of solar, geothermal, and bioenergy power plants.

Salaries

According to the U.S. Department of Labor's Bureau of Labor Statistics in their *Occupational Outlook Handbook, 2006–07 Edition*, median annual salaries for Sheet Metal Workers in May 2004 were $35,520. The middle 50 percent earned between $25,960 and $49,650. The lowest 10 percent of all Sheet Metal Workers earned less than $20,370, and the highest 10 percent earned more than $63,970.

Apprentices normally start at about 40 to 50 percent of the rate paid to experienced workers. In some locales, union workers receive supplemental wages from the union when they are on layoff or shortened workweeks.

Employment Prospects

Employment of Iron and Sheet Metal Workers in the construction industry is projected by the U.S. Department of Labor to increase as fast as the average for all occupations, reflecting both employment growth and openings arising each year as experienced Iron and Sheet Metal Workers leave the occupation. Opportunities should be particularly good for individuals who acquire apprenticeship training or who are certified welders. Job prospects in manufacturing will not be as good, as many plants that employ Iron and Sheet Metal Workers are moving to lower wage parts of the country or abroad.

Iron and Sheet Metal Workers in construction may experience periods of unemployment, particularly when construction projects end and economic conditions dampen construction activity. Nevertheless, employment of these workers is less sensitive to declines in new construction than is the employment of some other construction personnel, as maintenance of existing equipment makes up a large part of the work done by Iron and Sheet Metal Workers. In addition, a large proportion of sheet metal installation/maintenance is accomplished indoors, so they usually lose less work time due to inclement weather than other construction workers do.

Advancement Prospects

Iron and Sheet Metal Workers in construction may advance to supervisory jobs. Some of these workers take additional training in welding and do more specialized tasks. Workers who perform building and system testing are able to become instructors in the construction and building fields. Others may start their own contracting businesses, despite this type of contracting business tends to be more expensive to start than other types. In addition, they usually must earn a sheet metal contractor's license from the state in which they work. Iron and Sheet Metal Workers in manufacturing may advance to posts as supervisors, estimators, quality inspectors, and other management positions.

Education and Training

A high school diploma is a basic requirement for any apprenticeship program. Most employers recommend a three- to five-year apprenticeship consisting of on-the-job training and evening classroom instruction as the best option to learn this trade. (Generally, the more formalized the training received by individuals, the more thoroughly skilled they become, and the more likely that they will be in demand by employers.)

Entry-level workers typically start as helpers, carrying metal and cleaning up debris in a metal shop, while they learn about uses of materials/tools from veteran workers. Later, they learn to operate machines that bend or cut metal. In time, helpers go out on a jobsite to learn installation techniques. Some employers may send helpers to courses at a trade or vocational school or community college to receive further formal training. Helpers are promoted to the journey level when they show the requisite knowledge and skills. The training needed to become proficient in manufacturing usually takes less time than that required for construction work.

Some employers, particularly large nonresidential construction contractors with union membership, offer formal apprenticeships. These programs combine on-the-job training with classroom instruction. Such programs usually last four to five years and provide instruction in both sheet metal fabrication and installation. They may be administered by local joint committees composed of the Sheet Metal Workers' International Association (SMWIA) and local chapters of the Sheet Metal and Air-Conditioning Contractors' National Association (SMACNA).

Apprentices learn the basics of pattern layout and how to cut, bend, fabricate, and install sheet metal. Gradually, they advance to more difficult jobs. Some workers may focus on exterior or architectural sheet metal installation. In the classroom, apprentices are taught drafting, plan and specification reading, trigonometry and geometry applications to layout work, the use of computerized equipment, welding, and the principles of heating, air-conditioning, and ventilating systems. Safety is stressed at all times throughout the program.

It is important for experienced Iron and Sheet Metal Workers to keep abreast of new technological developments, such as the use of computerized layout and laser-cutting machines. They often take additional training, provided by their union or by their employer, to improve existing skills or to acquire new ones.

Special Requirements

Most states require that Iron and Sheet Metal Workers be certified in their field. Most certifications are gained through apprenticeship programs.

Experience, Skills, and Personality Traits

Iron and Sheet Metal Workers need to be in good physical condition and have mechanical and mathematical aptitude as well as solid reading skills. They also need to have good eye-hand coordination, spatial and form perception, and manual dexterity. They should be agile and have good balance in order to work at great heights on narrow beams and girders. They must be adept at reading blueprints and schematic drawings. They must be highly motivated, exhibit exemplary problem-solving talents, and be able to get along with fellow workers.

Unions and Associations

Most Iron and Sheet Metal Workers are union members and belong to the International Association of Bridge, Structural, Ornamental and Reinforcing Iron Workers (also known as the Ironworkers Association, or IWA), the Sheet Metal and Air-Conditioning Contractors' National Association (SMACNA), or the Sheet Metal Workers' International Association (SMWIA).

Tips for Entry

1. High school courses in general mathematics, mechanical drawing, English, and welding are considered helpful in preparing for a career in sheet metal work.
2. Become computer literate, as you will need this skill in your work.
3. As a summer job during high school, work in a machine or tool shop to become familiar with such equipment (including their designs, uses, repair, and maintenance techniques).

WELDER

CAREER PROFILE

Duties: Use hand-welding or flame-cutting equipment to weld or join metal components or to fill holes, indentations, or seams of fabricated metal products

Alternate Title(s): Combination Welder; Fabricator; Finishing Technician; Fitter-Welder; Maintenance Welder; Spot Welder; Sub Arc Operator

Salary Range: $20,000 to $50,000 or more

Employment Prospects: Good to Excellent

Advancement Prospects: Fair to Good

Prerequisites:

Education or Training—High school diploma required; vocational training or apprenticeship recommended

Experience—Some machine shop experience is valuable.

Special Skills and Personality Traits—Detail-oriented and physically fit; excellent reading ability; good eyesight, eye-hand coordination, and manual dexterity

Special Requirements—Certification is usually required

CAREER LADDER

```
┌─────────────────────────────────┐
│   Lead or Job-Shop Supervisor;   │
│      Independent Contractor      │
└─────────────────────────────────┘

┌─────────────────────────────────┐
│             Welder               │
└─────────────────────────────────┘

┌─────────────────────────────────┐
│        Apprentice Welder         │
└─────────────────────────────────┘
```

Position Description

Welding is a fabrication process that joins materials, usually metals or thermoplastics, by causing coalescence (the growing together of parts). This is most often accomplished by melting the workpieces and adding a filler material to form a pool of molten material that cools to become a strong joint. Sometimes, however, pressure is used in conjunction with heat, or by itself, to produce the weld. This process is different from soldering and brazing, which melts a lower-melting point material between the workpieces to form a bond between them *without* melting the workpieces. Soldering commonly is employed to join electrical, electronic, and other small metal parts. Brazing produces a stronger joint than does soldering and often is used to join metals other than steel, such as brass. Brazing is also utilized to apply coatings to parts to reduce wear and protect against corrosion. Welding is employed to join beams when constructing buildings, bridges, and other structures and to join pipes in pipelines, power plants, and refineries.

Welders use many types of welding equipment set up in a variety of positions, such as flat, vertical, and overhead. They may perform manual welding, in which the work is entirely controlled by the Welder, or semiautomatic welding, in which the Welder uses machinery (such as a wire feeder) to perform the task.

There are about 100 different types of welding. Arc welding is the most common type. In arc welding, heat to meld the two workpieces is produced by an electric current. Arc welding is used for large jobs, such as fabricated work with heavy plates of metal and large shapes. It is also employed in production line and general assembly operations where speed is necessary. Gas welding is accomplished with a flame combining oxygen and acetylene or oxygen and hydrogen gases and is used for small repairs or delicate jobs on light metals or tubing.

Welders who do both arc and gas welding are commonly referred to as combination welders. Journey level combination welders perform a variety of welding tasks using manual, semiautomatic, and automatic arc and gas equipment.

They work from blueprints, layouts, and work orders, and use their knowledge of fluxes and base metals to analyze the parts to be joined. They select the appropriate welding equipment, execute the planned welds, and examine them (even as they are welding) to ensure they meet standards/ specifications. Highly skilled Welders often are trained to work with a wide variety of materials in addition to steel, such as titanium, aluminum, or plastics.

Arc-cutting Welders trim and cut metal objects. Using a hand-guided torch, they direct the electric arc onto an area of metal. As the metal begins to melt, they cut it along pre-marked lines with arc torches or with a stream of gas flame from thermal torches. Thermal-cutting machine Welders set up and operate machines that cut/shape metal, directing flames from machine-mounted oxygen torches to melt the metal area to be cut. A stream of oxygen or gas is then released from the torch, which cuts the metal along previously marked lines.

Welders often work outdoors and may work high off the ground on a scaffold or platform. They are exposed to certain work hazards, including damage to their eyes resulting from exposure to the intense light created by welding arcs, and can get skin burns from the hot flying metal flecks set off by the welding process. To protect themselves against such hazards, Welders wear goggles and welding hoods with special lenses, heavy gloves, and other protective clothing. Blowers are often installed in their work area to carry away fumes and gases.

Welders are crucial in the construction of wind plants, solar energy power plants, bioenergy facilities, hydroelectric power plants, and geothermal drilling operations and power plants.

Salaries

According to the U.S. Department of Labor's Bureau of Labor Statistics in their *Occupational Outlook Handbook, 2006–07 Edition*, median annual salaries for Welders in May 2004 were $30,594. The middle 50 percent earned between $24,733 and $37,515. The lowest 10 percent had incomes of less than $20,348, while the top 10 percent earned over $46,141.

Employment Prospects

The U.S. Department of Labor's Bureau of Labor Statistics, in their *Occupational Outlook Handbook, 2006–07 Edition* states that employment of welding workers is expected to grow more slowly than average for all occupations through 2014. Nevertheless, job prospects should be excellent, as employers report difficulty finding enough qualified individuals. In addition, the average age of Welders in today's U.S. workforce is 54. Many of these people will retire within the next decade, creating a tremendous need for seasoned workers to replace them.

The major factor affecting employment of Welders is the health of the industries in which they labor. The manufacturing sector is expected to continue to decline as more manufacturing moves overseas. Because almost every manufacturing industry uses welding at some stage or in the repair and maintenance of equipment, this overall decline will affect the demand for Welders. Additionally, pressures to improve productivity and hold down labor costs are leading many companies to invest more in automation, especially computer-controlled and robotically controlled welding machinery. This will reduce the demand for some Welders in manufacturing. However, Welders working on construction projects or in equipment repair will not be affected by technology change to the same extent, because their jobs are not as easily automated.

Advancement Prospects

Routes to advancement vary with the employer, location, and type of work. Generally, Welders can progress to more skilled welding jobs with additional training and experience. The most common step upward is from journey-level worker to lead or job-shop supervisor. Some experienced Welders who have the necessary capital and some business experience may open their own job or repair shops.

Education and Training

Most Welders learn their skills through formal training. High schools, professional technical schools, and two-year colleges all offer welding programs. There are also private welding schools and training programs sponsored by unions. The U.S. Armed Forces also operate welding schools. Training can last a few weeks for low-skilled work, but it takes several years of combined school and on-the-job training for highly skilled work. Some Welders undergo apprenticeship training, which requires them to have a high school diploma. The military is an excellent source of training for Welders. Brazing and welding techniques, as well as safety procedures, can be learned, and credit can be earned for previous work experience when, later, entering a civilian apprenticeship program.

While some employers provide basic training, most prefer to hire Welders with experience or more formal training. Courses in blueprint reading, mathematics, mechanical drawing, physics, chemistry, and metallurgy are helpful. An understanding of electricity is key, and a thorough knowledge of computers is becoming more important, especially for welding machine operators, who are becoming more responsible for the programming of computer-controlled machines.

Special Requirements

Most employers require Welders to be certified. Certification can be gained by programs organized by the Certified Welding Technologies, Inc. (CWT).

Experience, Skills, and Personality Traits

Some machine shop experience is a valuable background for Welders. Welders need good eyesight, excellent hand-eye coordination, and manual dexterity. They should be able to concentrate on detailed work for long periods and be able to bend, stoop, and work in awkward positions. They must be physically fit, as they may be required to lift heavy objects and equipment. In addition, they need to be very safety-oriented.

Unions and Associations

Many Welders belong to unions. Among these are the International Association of Bridge, Structural Ornamental, and Reinforcing Iron Workers; the International Association of Machinists and Aerospace Workers; the International Brotherhood of Boilermakers, Iron Ship Builders, Blacksmiths, Forgers and Helpers; the International Union, United Automobile, Aerospace and Agricultural Implement Workers of America (commonly referred to as the United Workers, or UAW), the United Association of Journeymen and Apprentices of the Plumbing and Pipefitting Industry of the United States and Canada; and the United Electrical, Radio, and Machine Workers of America.

Professional Associations of specific interest for Welders include the American Welding Society (AWS), the Edison Welding Institute (EWI), the Fabricators & Manufacturers Association International (FMA), The Welding Institute (TWI), and the Welding Research Council (WRC).

Tips for Entry

1. While in high school, consider a summer job (or an internship) in a machine shop environment to gain experience with using machine equipment and tools.
2. For information on training opportunities and jobs for welding, contact local employers, the local office of your state employment service, or the American Welding Society (AWS).
3. To gain background on welding as a profession, study the *Welding Journal*, which focuses on what is innovative and what is important to the welding profession.

APPENDIXES

APPENDIX I
EDUCATIONAL INSTITUTIONS

For those job candidates entering one of the energy industries (especially in senior level and/or highly technical posts), a college degree (whether from a two- or four-year program) is generally preferred and, often, a requirement. Many institutions offer degrees in such relevant majors as atmospheric science, biochemistry, construction technology, geology/earth science, materials science, mining and mineral engineering, nuclear engineering technology, petroleum technology, physics, and statistics. A good place to start looking for such institutions is to look online at http://edonline.com, at http://degrees.education.yahoo.com/sub2-engineering_and_technology.htm, at http://www.mapping-your-future.org/features/careership, or at http://www.jets.org (for careers in engineering technology), or for specific energy careers at individual industry professional association Web sites.

The following is a selected list of many of the U.S. four-year colleges/universities that offer undergraduate degrees applicable to the various areas of the energy industries.

(Many of these establishments also offer master's and other higher degrees which are not detailed herein.)

For these undergraduate schools included in this appendix, the listings below provide addresses, telephone numbers, fax numbers, and e-mail addresses, as well as Web sites. Also provided (in alphabetical order) are each school's majors/specialties allied to the energy industries. For further information about courses offered and admission requirements as well as such topics as scholarships, campus housing, and academic calendar, contact the institution(s) of choice. Since the e-mail addresses of college admissions offices frequently change, it is advised to check the institution's Web site. (Increasingly, colleges now provide a link/form on their Web site for directly contacting school departments.)

For a listing of those institutions offering primarily two-year programs dealing with majors appropriate to the energy industries, please check such directories as *Peterson's Two-Year Colleges* published annually by Thomson Peterson.

ALABAMA

Alabama A&M University
P.O. Box 908
Normal, AL 35762
Phone: (256) 851-5245
Fax: (256) 851-5249
E-mail: aboyle@asnaam.aamu.edu
http://www.aamu.edu
Civil engineering, civil engineering technology, mechanical engineering, physics.

Alabama State University
915 South Jackson Street
Montgomery, AL 36104
Phone: (334) 229-4291
Fax: (324) 229-4984
E-mail: dlamar@asunet.alasu.edu
http://www.alasu.edu
Physics.

Athens State University
300 North Beaty Street
Athens, AL 35611
Phone: (205) 233-8220

Fax: (205) 233-6565
E-mail: At Web site
http://www.athens.edu
Instrumentation technology, physics.

Auburn University—Auburn
202 Mary Martin Hall
Auburn, AL 36849
Phone: (334) 844-4080
Fax: (334) 844-6179
E-mail: admissions@auburn.edu
http://www.auburn.edu
Applied mathematics, biochemistry, chemical engineering, civil engineering, environmental science, geography, geology/earth science, materials engineering, mechanical engineering, physics, soil science.

Auburn University—Montgomery
P.O. Box 244023
Montgomery, AL 36124
Phone: (334) 244-3611
Fax: (334) 244-3795
E-mail: mmoore@mail.aum.edu
http://www.aum.edu

Agricultural and biological engineering, biochemistry, civil engineering, mechanical engineering, physics.

Birmingham-Southern College
900 Arkadelphia Road
Birmingham, AL 35254
Phone: (205) 226-4696
Fax: (205) 226-3074
E-mail: admission@bsc.edu
http://www.bsc.edu
Physics.

Faulkner University
5345 Atlanta Highway
Montgomery, AL 36109
Phone: (334) 386-7200
Fax: (334) 386-7137
E-mail: admissions@faulkner.edu
http://www.faulkner.edu
Biological/physical sciences.

Jacksonville State University
700 Pelham Road North
Jacksonville, AL 36265
Phone: (256) 782-5268

Fax: (256) 782-5953
E-mail: info@jsucc.jsu.edu
http://www.jsu.edu
Electrical engineering technology,
geography, physics.

Oakwood College
7000 Adventist Boulevard
Huntsville, AL 35896
Phone: (800) 824-5312
Fax: (256) 726-7154
E-mail: admission@oakwood.edu
http://www.oakwood.edu
Applied mathematics, biochemistry.

Samford University
800 Lakeshore Drive
Birmingham, AL 35299
Phone: (205) 726-3673
Fax: (205) 726-2171
E-mail: admiss@samford.edu
http://www.samford.edu
Biochemistry, engineering physics,
environmental science, geography,
physics.

Spring Hill College
4000 Dauphin Street
Mobile, AL 36608
Phone: (251) 380-3030
Fax: (251) 460-2186
E-mail: admit@shc.edu
http://www.shc.edu
Biochemistry.

Talladega College
627 West Battle Street
Talladega, AL 35160
Phone: (205) 761-6235
Fax: (205) 362-0274
E-mail: admissions@talladega.edu
http://www.talladega.edu
Physics.

Troy University
111 Adams Administration
Troy, AL 36082
Phone: (334) 670-3179
Fax: (334) 670-3733
E-mail: admit@troy.edu
http://www.troy.edu
Electrical engineering technology,
environmental science, surveying
technology.

Tuskegee University
Old Administration Building, Suite 101
Tuskegee, AL 36086
Phone: (334) 727-8500

Fax: (334) 727-5750
E-mail: adm@tuskegee.edu
http://www.tuskegee.edu
Chemical engineering, clinical laboratory
science, construction technology,
mechanical engineering, physics, soil
science.

University of Alabama—Birmingham
HUC 260
1530 Third Avenue South
Birmingham, AL 35294
Phone: (205) 934-8221
Fax: (205) 975-7114
E-mail: undergradadmit@uab.edu
http://www.uab.edu
Biological/physical sciences, civil
engineering, clinical laboratory
science, environmental science,
geography, geology/earth science,
industrial engineering, materials
engineering, mechanical engineering,
metallurgical engineering, physics.

University of Alabama—Huntsville
301 Sparkman Drive
Huntsville, AL 35899
Phone: (256) 824-6070
Fax: (256) 824-6073
E-mail: admitme@email.uah.edu
http://www.uah.edu
Biological/physical sciences, chemical
engineering, civil engineering,
environmental science, geography,
geology/earth science, mechanical
engineering, metallurgical
engineering, physics.

University of North Alabama
UNA Box 5011
Florence, AL 35632
Phone: (256) 765-4318
Fax: (256) 765-4329
E-mail: admissions@una.edu
http://www.una.edu
Geography, geology/earth science,
metallurgical engineering, physics.

University of South Alabama
182 Administration Building
Mobile, AL 36688
Phone: (334) 460-6141
Fax: (334) 460-7023
E-mail: admiss@jaguari.usouthal.edu
http://www.usouthal.edu
Atmospheric science, chemical
engineering, civil engineering, clinical
laboratory science, geography,

geology/earth science, mechanical
engineering, physics, statistics.

ALASKA

University of Alaska—Anchorage
3211 Providence Drive
Anchorage, AK 99508
Phone: (907) 786-1480
Fax: (907) 786-4888
E-mail: At Web site
http://www.uaa.alaska.edu
Biological/physical sciences, civil
engineering, electrical engineering
technology, surveying technology.

University of Alaska—Fairbanks
P.O. Box 757480
Fairbanks, AK 99775
Phone: (907) 474-7500
Fax: (907) 474-5379
E-mail: fyapply@uaf.edu
http://www.uaf.edu
Applied mathematics, biological/physical
sciences, civil engineering, geography,
geological engineering, geology/earth
science, geotechnical engineering,
industrial engineering, mechanical
engineering, mining and mineral
engineering, petroleum engineering,
physics, statistics.

ARIZONA

Arizona State University East
P.O. Box 870112
Tempe, AZ 85387
Phone: (480) 965-7788
Fax: (480) 727-1008
E-mail: Stacie.dana@asu.edu
http://www.east.asu.edu
Applied mathematics, biochemistry,
chemical engineering, civil
engineering, geography, geology/
earth science, industrial engineering,
mechanical engineering, physics.

Arizona State University West
P.O. Box 37100
Phoenix, AZ 85069
Phone: (602) 543-8203
Fax: (602) 543-8312
E-mail: At Web site
http://www.west.asu.edu
Applied mathematics, biochemistry,
chemical engineering, civil
engineering, geography, geology/
earth science, industrial engineering,
mechanical engineering, physics.

**Embry-Riddle Aeronautical
    University—Prescott Campus**
3700 Willow Creek Road
Prescott, AZ 86301
Phone: (928) 777-6600
Fax: (928) 777-6606
E-mail: pradmitt@erau.edu
http://www.erau.edu
Atmospheric science, engineering—
    general, physics.

Grand Canyon University
3300 West Camelback Road
Phoenix, AZ 85061
Phone: (602) 589-2855
Fax: (602) 589-2580
E-mail: admissions@grand-canyon.edu
http://www.grand-canyon.edu
Biochemistry.

Northern Arizona University
P.O. Box 4080
Flagstaff, AZ 86011
Phone: (926) 523-5511
Fax: (928) 523-0226
E-mail: undergraduate.admissions@
    nau.edu
http://www.nau.edu
Biological/physical sciences, civil
    engineering, construction technology,
    engineering physics, environmental
    engineering, environmental science,
    geography, geology/earth science,
    hydrology/water resources science,
    mathematical statistics/probability,
    mechanical engineering, physics.

Prescott College
220 Grove Avenue
Prescott, AZ 86301
Phone: (928) 350-2100
Fax: (928) 776-5242
E-mail: admissions@prescott.edu
http://www.prescott.edu
Biological/physical sciences, geology/
    earth science, soil science.

University of Arizona
P.O. Box 210040
Tucson, AZ 85721
Phone: (520) 621-3237
Fax: (520) 621-9799
E-mail: appinfo@arizona.edu
http://www.arizona.edu
Agricultural and biological engineering,
    atmospheric science, chemical
    engineering, civil engineering,
    engineering—general, engineering
    physics, geography, geological

engineering, geology/earth science,
hydrology/water resources science,
materials science, mechanical
engineering, mining and mineral
engineering, physics.

ARKANSAS

Arkansas State University
P.O. Box 1630
State University, AR 72467
Phone: (870) 972-3024
Fax: (870) 910-8094
E-mail: admissions@astate.edu
http://www.astate.edu
Clinical laboratory science, electrical
    engineering technology, engineering—
    general, engineering technology—
    general, geography, physics,

Arkansas Tech University
Doc Bryan #141
Russellville, AR 72801
Phone: (479) 968-0343
Fax: (479) 964-0522
E-mail: tech.enroll@mai.atu.edu
http://www.atu.edu
Clinical laboratory science, electrical
    engineering technology, engineering
    physics, geology/earth science,
    mechanical engineering, nuclear
    engineering.

Harding University
P.O. Box 12255
Searcy, AR 72149
Phone: (501) 279-4407
Fax: (501) 279-4865
E-mail: admissions@harding.edu
http://www.harding.edu
Biochemistry, mechanical engineering,
    physics.

Henderson State University
1100 Henderson Street
HSU P.O. Box 7560
Arkadelphia, AR 71999
Phone: (870) 230-5028
Fax: (870) 230-5066
E-mail: hardwrv@hsus.edu
http://www.hsu.edu
Clinical laboratory science, physics.

John Brown University
2000 West University Street
Siloam Springs, AR 72761
Phone: (800) 634-6969
Fax: (479) 524-4196
E-mail: jbuinfo@jbu.edu

http://www.jub.edu
Biochemistry, engineering—general.

Ouachita Baptist University
410 Ouachita Street
Arkadelphia, AR 71998
Phone: (870) 245-5110
Fax: (870) 245-5500
E-mail: admissions@alpha.obu.edu
http://www.obu.edu
Engineering physics, physics.

Southern Arkansas University
P.O. Box 9382
Magnolia, AR 71754
Phone: (870) 235-4040
Fax: (870) 235-5072
E-mail: muleriders@saumag.edu
http://www.saumag.edu
Biological/physical sciences.

University of Arkansas—Fayetteville
232 Silas Hunt Hall
Fayetteville, AR 72701
Phone: (479) 575-5346
Fax: (479) 575-7515
E-mail: uofa@uark.edu
http://www.uark.edu
Agricultural and biological engineering,
    chemical engineering, civil
    engineering, geography, geology/earth
    science, mechanical engineering,
    physics.

University of Arkansas—Fort Smith
5210 Grand Avenue
P.O. Box 3649
Fort Smith, AR 72913
Phone: (888) 512-LION
Fax: NA
E-mail: information@uafortsmith.edu
http://www.uafortsmith.edu
Agricultural and biological engineering,
    chemical engineering, civil engineering,
    geography, geology/earth science,
    mechanical engineering, physics.

University of Arkansas—Little Rock
2801 South University Avenue
Little Rock, AR 72204
Phone: (501) 569-3127
Fax: (501) 569-8915
E-mail: admissions@ualr.edu
http://www.ualr.edu
Agricultural and biological engineering,
    applied mathematics, biological/
    physical sciences, chemical
    engineering, civil engineering, civil
    engineering technology, electrical

engineering technology, geography, geology/earth science, mechanical engineering, physics.

University of Arkansas—Monticello
UAM P.O. Box 3600
Monticello, AR 71656
Phone: (870) 460-1034
Fax: (870) 460-1035
E-mail: whitingm@uamont.edu
http://www.uamont.edu
Surveying technology.

University of Arkansas—Pine Bluff
1200 North University Drive, Mail Slot 4981
Pine Bluff, AR 71601
Phone: (870) 575-8000
Fax: (870) 543-8014
E-mail: fulton_E@uapb.edu
http://www.uapb.edu
Agricultural and biological engineering, applied mathematics, geography, geology/earth science, mechanical engineering, physics.

University of Central Arkansas
201 Donaghey Avenue
Conway, AR 72035
Phone: (501) 450-3128
Fax: (501) 450-5228
E-mail: admissions@mail.uca.edu
http://www.uca.edu
Biological/physical sciences, geography, physics.

University of the Ozarks
415 College Avenue
Clarksville, AR 72830
Phone: (479) 979-1227
Fax: (479) 979-1355
E-mail: jdecker@ozarks.edu
http://www.ozarks.edu
Physics.

CALIFORNIA

Azusa Pacific University
901 East Alosta Avenue
Azusa, CA 91702
Phone: (626) 812-3016
Fax: (626) 812-3096
E-mail: admissions@apu.edu
http://www.apu.edu
Biochemistry, physics.

California Institute of Technology
Caltech Office of Undergraduate Admissions
Mail Code 1-94
Pasadena, CA 91125
Phone: (626) 395-6341
Fax: (626) 683-3026
E-mail: ugadmissions@caltech.edu
http://www.caltech.edu
Applied mathematics, chemical engineering, civil engineering, engineering—general, engineering physics, geology/earth science, geophysics/seismology, mechanical engineering, physics.

California Lutheran University
60 West Olsen Road, 1350
Thousand Oaks, CA 91300
Phone: (805) 493-3135
Fax: (805) 493-3114
E-mail: cluadm@clunet.edu
http://www.clunet.edu
Biochemistry, biological/physical sciences, environmental science, geology/earth science, physics.

California Maritime Academy of California State University
200 Maritime Academy Drive
Vallejo, CA 94590
Phone: (707) 654-1330
Fax: (707) 654-1336
E-mail: admission@csum.edu
http://www.csum.edu
Engineering technology—general, mechanical engineering.

California Polytechnic State University—San Luis Obispo
Admissions Office
Cal Poly
San Luis Obispo, CA 93407
Phone: (805) 756-2311
Fax: (805) 756-5400
E-mail: admissions@calpoly.edu
http://www.calpoly.edu
Biochemistry, civil engineering, engineering technology—general, materials engineering, mechanical engineering, metallurgical engineering, physics, soil science, statistics.

California State Polytechnic University—Pomona
3801 West Temple Avenue
Pomona, CA 91768
Phone: (909) 468-5020
Fax: (909) 869-5020
E-mail: cppadmit@csupomona.edu
http://www.csu.pomona.edu

Biotechnology, chemical engineering, civil engineering, construction technology, engineering—general, engineering technology—general, geography, geology/earth science, industrial engineering, materials engineering, mechanical engineering, physics, soil science.

California State University—Bakersfield
9001 Stockdale Highway
Bakersfield, CA 93311
Phone: (661) 664-3036
Fax: (661) 664-3389
E-mail: swatkin@csub.edu
http://www.csub.edu
Geology/earth science, physics.

California State University—Chico
400 West First Street
Chico, CA 95929
Phone: (530) 898-4428
Fax: (530) 898-6456
E-mail: info@csuchico.edu
http://www.csuchico.edu
Applied mathematics, biochemistry, civil engineering, clinical laboratory science, construction technology, geography, geology/earth science, hydrology/water resources science, mechanical engineering, physics, statistics.

California State University—Dominguez Hills
100 East Victoria Street
Carson, CA 90741
Phone: (310) 243-3600
Fax: (310) 516-3609
E-mail: lwise@csudh.edu
http://www.csudh.edu
Geography, geology/earth science, physics.

California State University—East Bay
25800 Carlos Bee Boulevard
Hayward, CA 94542
Phone: (510) 885-2624
Fax: (510) 885-4059
E-mail: askes@csuhayward.edu
http://www.csueastbay.edu
Applied mathematics, biochemistry, geography, geology/earth science, physics, statistics.

California State University—Fresno
5150 North Maple Avenue M/S JA 57
Fresno, CA 93740

Phone: (559) 278-2261
Fax: (559) 278-4812
E-mail: vivian_franco@csufresno.edu
http://www.csufresno.edu
Applied mathematics, civil engineering, civil engineering technology, construction technology, electrical engineering technology, geography, geology/earth science, mechanical engineering, physics, surveying technology.

California State University—Fullerton
800 North State College Boulevard
Fullerton, CA 92834
Phone: (714) 773-2370
Fax: (714) 278-2356
E-mail: admissions@fullerton.edu
http://www.fullerton.edu
Biochemistry, civil engineering, geography, geology/earth science, mechanical engineering, physics, statistics.

California State University—Long Beach
1250 Bellflower Boulevard
Long Beach, CA 90840
Phone: (562) 985-5471
Fax: (562) 985-4973
E-mail: eslb@csulb.edu
http://www.csulb.edu
Applied mathematics, biochemistry, chemical engineering, electrical engineering technology, civil engineering, civil engineering technology, construction technology, geography, geology/earth science, materials engineering, mechanical engineering, physics, statistics.

California State University—Los Angeles
5151 State University Drive
Los Angeles, CA 90032
Phone: (323) 343-3901
Fax: (323) 343-6306
E-mail: admission@calstatela.edu
http://www.calstatela.edu
Biochemistry, civil engineering, geography, geology/earth science, industrial technology, mechanical engineering, physics.

California State University—Northridge
P.O. Box 1286
Northridge, CA 91328
Phone: (818) 677-3773

Fax: (818) 677-4665
E-mail: lorraine.newlon@csun.edu
http://www.csun.edu
Applied mathematics, biochemistry, chemical engineering, civil engineering, engineering mechanics, geography, geology/earth science, materials engineering, mechanical engineering, physics, statistics.

California State University—Sacramento
6000 J Street
Lassen Hall
Sacramento, CA 95819
Phone: (916) 278-3901
Fax: (916) 279-5603
E-mail: admissions@csus.edu
http://www.admissions@csus.edu
Civil engineering, engineering technology—general, geography, geology/earth science, mechanical engineering, mechanical engineering technology, physics.

California State University—San Bernardino
CSUSB-IR, 5500 University Parkway
San Bernardino, CA 92407
Phone: (909) 537-5188
Fax: (909) 537-7034
E-mail: moreinfo@mail.csusb.edu
http://www.csusb.edu
Biochemistry, geography, geology/earth science, physics.

California State University—Stanislaus
801 West Monte Vista Avenue
Turlock, CA 95382
Phone: (209) 667-3070
Fax: (209) 667-3788
E-mail: outreach_help_desk@csustan.edu
http://www.csutan.edu
Geography, geology/earth science, physics.

Chapman University
One University Drive
Orange, CA 92866
Phone: (714) 997-6711
Fax: (714) 997-6713
E-mail: admit@chapman.edu
http://www.chapman.edu
Biochemistry,

Claremont McKenna College
890 Columbia Avenue
Claremont, CA 91711

Phone: (909) 621-8088
Fax: (909) 621-8516
E-mail: admissions@claremontmckenna.edu
http://www.claremontmckenna.edu
Biochemistry, engineering—general, environmental science, physics.

DeVry University—Fremont
6600 Dumbarton Circle
Fremont, CA 94555
Phone: (510) 574-1200
Fax: (510) 742-0868
E-mail: info@devry.edu
http://www.fre.devry.edu
Electrical engineering technology.

DeVry University—Long Beach
3880 Kilroy Airport Way
Long Beach, CA 90806
Phone: (562) 427-4162
Fax: (562) 997-5371
E-mail: cblas@socal.devry.edu
http://www.devry.edu
Electrical engineering technology.

DeVry University—Pomona
901 Corporate Center Drive
Pomona, CA 91768
Phone: (909) 622-9800
Fax: (909) 868-4165
E-mail: bchung@admin.pom.devry.edu
http://www.pom.devry.edu
Electrical engineering technology.

DeVry University—West Hills
22801 Roscoe Boulevard
West Hills, CA 91304
Phone: (818) 932-3001
Fax: (909) 868-4165
E-mail: admissions@devry.com
http://www.devry.edu
Electrical engineering technology.

Dominican University of California
Office of Admissions
50 Acacia Avenue
San Rafael, CA 94901
Phone: (415) 485-3214
Fax: (415) 485-3214
E-mail: enroll@dominican.edu
http://www.dominican.edu
Environmental science.

Fresno Pacific University
1717 South Chestnut Avenue
Fresno, CA 93702
Phone: (559) 453-2039
Fax: (559) 453-2007

E-mail: ugadmis@fresno.edu
http://www.fresno.edu
Applied mathematics, environmental
    science.

Harvey Mudd College
301 East Twelfth Street
Claremont, CA 91711
Phone: (909) 621-8011
Fax: (909) 621-8360
E-mail: admission@hmc.edu
http://www.hmc.edu
Applied mathematics, biological/physical
    sciences, engineering—general.

Humboldt State University
1 Harpst Street
Arcata, CA 95521
Phone: (707) 826-4402
Fax: (707) 826-6190
E-mail: hsuinfo@humboldt.edu
http://www.humboldt.edu
Geography, geology/earth science.

La Sierra University
4700 Pierce Street
Riverside, CA 92515
Phone: (909) 785-2176
Fax: (909) 785-2447
E-mail: ivy@lasierra.edu
http://www.lasierra.edu
Biochemistry, biophysics.

Loma Linda University
Office of Admissions
Loma Linda, CA 92350
Phone: (909) 824-4599
Fax: (909) 824-4291
E-mail: admissions.app@llu.edu
http://www.llu.edu
Clinical laboratory science, geology/earth
    science.

Loyola Marymount University
One LMU Drive, Suite 100
Los Angeles, CA 90045
Phone: (310) 338-2750
Fax: (310) 338-2797
E-mail: admissions@lmu.edu
http://www.lmu.edu
Biochemistry, civil engineering,
    engineering—general, engineering
    physics, mechanical engineering,
    physics.

Master's College and Seminary
21726 Placenta Canyon Road
Santa Clarita, CA 91321
Phone: (661) 259-3540

Fax: (661) 288-1037
E-mail: enrollment@masters.edu
http://www.masters.edu
Biological/physical sciences.

Mills College
5000 MacArthur Boulevard
Oakland, CA 94613
Phone: (510) 430-2135
Fax: (510) 430-3314
E-mail: admission@mills.edu
http://www.mills.edu
Biochemistry.

Mount St. Mary's College
12001 Chalon Road
Los Angeles, CA 90049
Phone: (845) 569-3248
Fax: (845) 562-6762
E-mail: mtstmary@msmc.edu
http://www.msmc.edu
Applied mathematics, biochemistry.

National University
11255 North Torrey Pinos Road
La Jolla, CA 92037
Phone: (858) 642-8180
Fax: (858) 642-8710
E-mail: advisor@nu.edu
http://www.nu.edu
Biological/physical sciences, civil
    engineering drafting/CAD/CADD,
    construction engineering, geology/
    earth science.

Notre Dame de Namur University
1500 Ralston Avenue
Belmont, CA 94002
Phone: (650) 508-3600
Fax: (650) 508-3426
E-mail: admiss@ndnu.edu
http://www.ndnu.edu
Biochemistry.

Occidental College
Office of Admission
1600 Campus Road
Los Angeles, CA 90041
Phone: (323) 259-2700
Fax: (323) 341-4875
E-mail: admission@oxy.edu
http://www.oxy.edu
Biochemistry, geology/earth science,
    geophysics/seismology, physics.

Pacific Union College
Enrollment Services
One Angwin Avenue
Angwin, CA 94508

Phone: (800) 862-7080
Fax: (707) 965-6432
E-mail: enroll@puc.edu
http://www.puc.edu
Biochemistry, biophysics, physics.

Pepperdine University
24255 Pacific Coast Highway
Malibu, CA 90263
Phone: (310) 456-4861
Fax: (310) 506-4861
E-mail: admission-seaver@pepperdine.edu
http://www.pepperdine.edu
Biochemistry, engineering—general.

Pitzer College
1050 North Mills Avenue
Claremont. CA 91711
Phone: (909) 621-8129
Fax: (909) 621-8770
E-mail: admissions@pitzer.edu
http://www.pitzer.edu
Biochemistry, biological/physical
    sciences, biophysics, environmental
    science, physics.

Point Loma Nazarene University
3900 Lomaland Drive
San Diego, CA 92106
Phone: (619) 849-2273
Fax: (619) 849-2601
E-mail: admissions@ptloma.edu
http://www.ptloma.edu
Biochemistry, engineering physics,
    physics,

Pomona College
333 North College Way
Claremont, CA 91711
Phone: (909) 621-8134
Fax: (909) 621-8952
E-mail: admissions@pomona.edu
http://www.pomona.edu
Geology/earth science, physics.

Saint Mary's College of California
P.O. Box 4800
Moraga, CA 94575-4800
Phone: (925) 631-4224
Fax: (925) 376-7193
E-mail: smcadmit@stmarys-ca.edu
http://www.stmarys-ca.edu
Biochemistry, physics.

San Diego State University
5500 Campanile Drive
San Diego, CA 92182
Phone: (619) 594-7800
Fax: (619) 594-1250

E-mail: At Web site
http://www.sdu.edu
Applied mathematics, atomic/molecular
   physics, civil engineering, geography,
   geology/earth science, geophysics/
   seismology, mechanical engineering,
   physics, statistics.

San Francisco State University
1600 Holloway Avenue
San Francisco, CA 94132
Phone: (415) 338-6486
Fax: (415) 338-7196
E-mail: ugadmit@sfsu.edu
http://www.sfsu.edu
Applied mathematics, biochemistry,
   biotechnology, civil engineering,
   clinical laboratory science, geography,
   geology/earth science, geophysics/
   seismology, mechanical engineering,
   physics, statistics.

San Jose State University
1 Washington Square
San Jose, CA 95112
Phone: (408) 283-7500
Fax: (408) 924-2050
E-mail: contact@sjsu.edu
http://www.sjsu.edu
Biochemistry, chemical engineering, civil
   engineering, engineering—general,
   geography, geology/earth science,
   industrial engineering, materials
   engineering, physics.

Santa Clara University
500 El Camino Real
Santa Clara, CA 95053
Phone: (408) 554-4700
Fax: (408) 554-5255
E-mail: none@scu.edu
http://www.scu.edu
Applied mathematics, civil engineering,
   electrical engineering technology,
   engineering—general, environmental
   science, mechanical engineering,
   physics.

Scripps College
1030 Columbia Avenue
Claremont, CA 91711
Phone: (909) 621-8149
Fax: (909) 607-7508
E-mail: admission@scrippscollege.edu
http://www.scrippscollege.edu
Biochemistry, biological/physical
   sciences, engineering—general,
   environmental science, geology/earth
   science, physics.

Sonoma State University
1801 East Cotati Avenue
Rohnert Park, CA 94928
Phone: (707) 664-2778
Fax: (707) 664-2060
E-mail: admitme@sonoma.edu
http://www.sonoma.edu
Geography, geology/earth science,
   physics.

Stanford University
Undergraduate Admission
Old Union 232
Stanford, CA 94305
Phone: (650) 723-2091
Fax: (650) 723-6050
E-mail: admissions@stanford.edu
http://www.stanford.edu
Civil engineering, engineering—general,
   environmental engineering, environmental science, geology/earth science,
   geophysics/seismology, materials engineering, materials science, mechanical
   engineering, petroleum engineering,
   physics, statistics.

University of California—Berkeley
110 Sproul Hall
Berkeley, CA 94720
Phone: (510) 642-3175
Fax: (510) 642-7333
E-mail: ouars@uclink.berkeley.edu
http://www.berkeley.edu
Applied mathematics, atmospheric science, chemical engineering, civil
   engineering, engineering physics,
   environmental engineering, environmental science, geography, geological
   engineering, geology/earth science,
   geophysics/seismology, materials science, mechanical engineering, nuclear
   engineering, physics, statistics.

University of California—Davis
178 Mrak Hall
1 Shields Avenue
Davis, CA 95616
Phone: (530) 752-2971
Fax: (530) 752-1280
E-mail: undergraduateadmissions@
   ucdavis.edu
http://www.ucdavis.edu
Agricultural and biological engineering,
   atmospheric science, biotechnology,
   chemical engineering, civil engineering, geology/earth science, hydrol-
   ogy/water resources science, materials
   engineering, mechanical engineering,
   physics, soil science, statistics.

University of California—Irvine
204 Administration Building
Irvine, CA 92697
Phone: (949) 824-6703
Fax: (949) 824-2711
E-mail: admissions@uci.edu
http://www.uci.edu
Biochemistry, chemical engineering,
   civil engineering, engineering—
   general, environmental engineering,
   geology/earth science, materials
   engineering, mechanical engineering,
   physics.

University of California—Los Angeles
405 Hilgard Avenue
P.O. Box 951436
Los Angeles, CA 90095
Phone: (310) 825-3101
Fax: (310) 206-1206
E-mail: ugadm@saonet.ucla.edu
http://www.ucla.edu
Agricultural and biological engineering,
   applied mathematics, atmospheric
   science, biochemistry, biophysics,
   biotechnology, chemical engineering,
   civil engineering, environmental
   engineering, environmental science,
   geography, geological engineering,
   geology/earth science, geophysics/
   seismology, materials engineering,
   mechanical engineering, physics,
   statistics.

University of California—Merced
P.O. Box 2039
Merced, CA 95344
Phone: (866) 270-7301
Fax: NA
E-mail: admissions@ucmerced.edu
http://www.ucmerced.edu
Environmental engineering, geology/earth
   science, mechanical engineering.

University of California—Riverside
1138 Hinderaker Hall
Riverside, CA 92521
Phone: (909) 787-3411
Fax: (909) 787-6344
E-mail: ugadmiss@pop.ucr.edu
http://www.ucr.edu
Applied mathematics, biochemistry,
   chemical engineering, engineering—
   general, environmental engineering,
   environmental science, geography,
   geology/earth science, geophysics/
   seismology, mechanical engineering,
   physics, soil science, statistics.

University of California—San Diego
9500 Gilman Drive, 0021
La Jolla, CA 92093
Phone: (858) 534-4831
Fax: (858) 534-5723
E-mail: admissionsinfo.ucsd.edu
http://www.ucsd.edu
Applied mathematics, atomic/molecular
  physics, biochemistry, biophysics,
  biotechnology, chemical engineering,
  chemical physics, engineering
  mechanics, engineering physics,
  environmental science, mechanical
  engineering, physics, structural
  engineering.

**University of California—Santa
  Barbara**
Office of Admissions
1210 Cheadle Hall
Santa Barbara, CA 93106
Phone: (805) 893-2881
Fax: (805) 893-2676
E-mail: appinfo@sa.ucsb.edu
http://www.ucsb.edu
Applied mathematics, biochemistry,
  biological/physical sciences, chemical
  engineering, engineering—general,
  geography, geology/earth science,
  geophysics/seismology, mechanical
  engineering, physics, statistics.

University of California—Santa Cruz
Office of Admissions, Cook House
1156 High Street
Santa Cruz, CA 95064
Phone: (831) 459-4008
Fax: (831) 459-4452
E-mail: admissions@ucsc.edu
http://www.admissions.ucsc.edu
Applied mathematics, biochemistry,
  electromechanical technology,
  geology/earth science, geophysics/
  seismology, physics.

University of La Verne
1950 Third Street
La Verne, CA 91750
Phone: (909) 392-2800
Fax: (909) 392-2714
E-mail: admissions@ulv.edu
http://www.ulv.edu
Biological/physical sciences,
  environmental science, physics.

University of Redlands
1200 East Colton Avenue
Redlands, CA 92373
Phone: (909) 335-4074
Fax: (909) 335-4089
E-mail: admissions@redlands.edu
http://www.redlands.edu
Biochemistry, environmental science,
  physics.

University of San Diego
5998 Alcala Park
San Diego, CA 92110
Phone: (619) 260-4506
Fax: (619) 260-6836
E-mail: admissions@sandiego.edu
http://www.sandiego.edu
Industrial engineering, mechanical
  engineering, physics.

University of San Francisco
2130 Fulton Street
San Francisco, CA 94117
Phone: (415) 422-6563
Fax: (415) 422-2217
E-mail: admission@usfca.edu
http://www.usfca.edu
Environmental science, physics.

University of Southern California
700 Childs Way
Los Angeles, CA 90089
Phone: (213) 740-1111
Fax: (213) 740-6364
E-mail: admitusc@usc.edu
http://www.usc.edu
Biophysics, chemical engineering, construction engineering, environmental
  engineering, environmental science,
  geology/earth science, industrial
  engineering, mechanical engineering, petroleum engineering, physics,
  structural engineering, water resource
  engineering.

University of the Pacific
3601 Pacific Avenue
Stockton, CA 95211
Phone: (209) 946-2211
Fax: (209) 946-2413
E-mail: admissions@pacific.edu
http://www.pacific.edu
Applied mathematics, biochemistry,
  biological/physical sciences, civil
  engineering, engineering—general,
  engineering physics, geology/earth
  science, mechanical engineering,
  physics.

**Vanguard University of Southern
  California**
55 Fair Drive
Costa Mesa, CA 92626
Phone: (714) 556-3601
Fax: (714) 966-5471
E-mail: admissions@vanguard.edu
http://www.vanguard.edu
Biological/physical sciences.

Westmont College
955 La Paz Road
Santa Barbara, CA 93108
Phone: (805) 565-6200
Fax: (805) 565-6234
E-mail: admissions@westmont.edu
http://www.westmont.edu
Engineering physics, physics.

Whittier College
13406 Philadelphia Street
P.O. Box 634
Whittier, CA 90608
Phone: (562) 907-4298
Fax: (562) 907-4870
E-mail: admission@whittier.edu
http://www.whittier.edu
Physics.

COLORADO

Adams State College
Office of Admissions
Alamosa, CO 81102
Phone: (719) 587-7712
Fax: (719) 587-7522
E-mail: ascadmit@adams.edu
http://www.adams.edu
Chemical physics, geology/earth science,
  physics.

Colorado Christian University
8787 West Alameda Avenue
Lakewood, CO 80226
Phone: (303) 963-3200
Fax: (303) 963-3201
E-mail: ccuadmissions@ccu.edu
http://www.ccu.edu
Biological/physical sciences, physics.

Colorado College
14 East Cache la Poudre Street
Colorado Springs, CO 80903
Phone: (719) 389-6344
Fax: (719) 389-6816
E-mail: admission@coloradocollege.edu
http://www.coloradocollege.edu
Biochemistry, environmental science,
  geology/earth science, physics.

Colorado School of Mines
Weaver Towers, 1811 Elm Street
Golden, CO 80401
Phone: (303) 273-3220

Fax: (303) 273-3509
E-mail: admit@mines.edu
http://www.mines.edu
Applied mathematics, chemical
    engineering, engineering—general,
    engineering physics, geology/earth
    science, metallurgical engineering,
    mining and mineral engineering,
    petroleum engineering.

Colorado State University—Pueblo
Office of Admissions and Records
2200 Bonforte Boulevard
Pueblo, CO 81001
Phone: (719) 549-2461
Fax: (719) 549-2419
E-mail: info@colostate-pueblo.edu
http://www.colostate-pueblo.edu
Biochemistry, chemical engineering,
    electrical engineering technology, civil
    engineering, civil engineering technol-
    ogy, construction technology, geology/
    earth science, industrial engineering,
    mechanical engineering, mechanical
    engineering technology, physics.

Colorado Technical University
4435 North Chestnut Street
Colorado Springs, CO 80907
Phone: (719) 598-0200
Fax: (719) 598-3740
E-mail: cosadmissions@coloradotech.edu
http://www.coloradotech.edu
Electrical engineering, electronics
    technology.

DeVry University—Colorado Springs
225 South Union Boulevard
Colorado Springs, CO 80910
Phone: (719) 632-3000
Fax: (719) 632-1909
E-mail: admitcs@cs.devry.edu
http://www.devry.edu
Electrical engineering technology.

DeVry University—Denver
1870 West 122nd Avenue
Westminster, CO 90234
Phone: (303) 280-7600
Fax: (303) 280-7606
E-mail: info@devry.edu
http://www.devry.edu
Electrical engineering technology.

Fort Lewis College
1000 Rim Drive
Durango, CO 91301
Phone: (970) 247-7184
Fax: (970) 247-7179

E-mail: admission@fortlewis.edu
http://www.fortlewis.edu
Applied mathematics, biochemistry,
    engineering physics, geology/earth
    science, physics, statistics.

Metropolitan State College of Denver
Campus Box 16, P.O. Box 173362
Denver, CO 80217
Phone: (303) 556-3058
Fax: (303) 556-6345
E-mail: askmetro@mscd.edu
http://www.mscd.edu
Atmospheric science, civil engineering
    technology, physics, surveying
    technology.

Regis University
3333 Regis Boulevard, A-12
Denver, CO 80221
Phone: (303) 458-4900
Fax: (303) 964-5534
E-mail: regisadm@regis.edu/college/asp
http://www.regis.edu
Biochemistry.

United States Air Force Academy
HQ USAFA/RRS
2304 Cadet Drive, Suite 2000
USAF Academy, CO 80840
Phone: (719) 333-2520
Fax: (719) 333-3012
E-mail: webmail@usafa.af.mil
http://www.academyadmissions.com
Atmospheric science, civil engineering,
    engineering—general, engineering
    mechanics, environmental engineering,
    geography, mechanical engineering,
    physics.

University of Colorado—Boulder
Campus Box 30
Boulder, CO 90309
Phone: (303) 492-6301
Fax: (303) 492-7115
E-mail: apply@colorado.edu
http://www.colorado.edu
Applied mathematics, biochemistry,
    chemical engineering, chemical
    physics, civil engineering, engineering
    physics, environmental engineering,
    geography, geology/earth science,
    mechanical engineering, physics.

**University of Colorado—Colorado
    Springs**
Admissions Office
P.O. Box 7150
Colorado Springs, CO 80933
Phone: (719) 262-3383

Fax: (719) 262-3116
E-mail: admrec@mail.uccs.edu
http://www.uccs.edu
Applied mathematics, engineering—
    general, geography, mechanical
    engineering, physics.

**University of Colorado—Denver and
    Health Sciences Center**
P.O. Box 173364, Campus Box 167
Denver, CO 80217
Phone: (303) 556-2704
Fax: (303) 556-4838
E-mail: admission@cudenver.edu
http://www.cudenver.edu
Applied mathematics, biochemistry, civil
    engineering, geography, mechanical
    engineering, physics.

University of Denver
University Hall, Room 110
2197 South University Boulevard
Denver, CO 80208
Phone: (303) 871-2036
Fax: (303) 871-3301
E-mail: admission@du.edu
http://www.du.edu
Biochemistry, biological/physical
    sciences, engineering—general,
    environmental science, geography,
    mechanical engineering, physics.

University of Northern Colorado
UNC Admissions Office
Campus Box 10
Greeley, CO 80639
Phone: (970) 351-2881
Fax: (970) 351-2984
E-mail: admissions.help@unco.edu
http://www.unco.edu
Geography, geology/earth science, physics.

Western State College of Colorado
600 North Adams Street
Gunnison, CO 81231
Phone: (970) 943-2119
Fax: (970) 943-2212
E-mail: discover@western.edu
http://www.western.edu
Geology/earth science.

Westwood College of Technology
7350 North Broadway
Denver, CO 80221
Phone: (303) 426-7000
Fax: (303) 426-1832
E-mail: bsimms@westwood.edu
http://www.westwood.edu
Electrical engineering technology,
    electronics/electrical equipment repair.

CONNECTICUT

Central Connecticut State College
1615 Stanley Street
New Britain, CT 06050
Phone: (860) 832-2278
Fax: (860) 832-2295
E-mail: admissions@ccsu.edu
http://www.ccsu.edu
Civil engineering technology, geography, geology/earth science, industrial technology, mechanical engineering technology, physics.

Connecticut College
270 Mohegan Avenue
New London, CT 06320
Phone: (860) 439-2200
Fax: (860) 439-4301
E-mail: admission@conncoll.edu
http://www.conncoll.edu
Biochemistry, engineering physics, physics.

Eastern Connecticut State University
83 Windham Street
Willimantic, CT 06226
Phone: (860) 465-5286
Fax: (860) 465-5544
E-mail: admissions@easternct.edu
http://www.easternct.edu
Biochemistry, environmental science.

Fairfield University
1073 North Benson Road
Fairfield, CT 06824
Phone: (203) 254-4100
Fax: (203) 254-4199
E-mail: admis@mail.fairfield.edu
http://www.fairfield.edu
Chemical engineering, engineering—general, mechanical engineering, physics.

Quinnipiac University
275 Mount Carmel Avenue
Hamden, CT 06518
Phone: (203) 582-8600
Fax: (203) 582-8906
E-mail: admissions@quinnipiac.edu
http://www.quinnipiac.edu
Biochemistry, biotechnology.

Sacred Heart University
5151 Park Avenue
Fairfield, CT 06432
Phone: (203) 371-7880
Fax: (203) 365-7607
E-mail: enroll@sacredheart.edu
http://www.sacredheart.edu
Biochemistry, environmental science.

Saint Joseph College
1678 Asylum Avenue
West Hartford, CT 06117
Phone: (860) 231-5216
Fax: (860) 231-5744
E-mail: admission@sjc.edu
http://www.sjc.edu
Biochemistry.

Southern Connecticut State University
SCSU-Admissions House
131 Farmham Avenue
New Haven, CT 06515
Phone: (203) 392-5656
Fax: (203) 392-5727
E-mail: adminfo@scsu.ctstateu.edu
http://www.southernct.edu
Geography, physics.

Trinity College
300 Summit Street
Hartford, CT 06016
Phone: (860) 297-2180
Fax: (860) 297-2287
E-mail: admissions.office@trincoll.edu
http://www.trincoll.edu
Biochemistry, engineering—general, environmental science, mechanical engineering, physics.

United States Coast Guard Academy
31 Mohegan Avenue
New London, CT 06320
Phone: (800) 833-8724
Fax: (860) 701-6700
E-mail: admissions@cga.uscg.mil
http://www.cga.edu
Civil engineering, mechanical engineering.

University of Connecticut
2131 Hillside Road, Unit 3088
Storrs, CT 06286
Phone: (860) 486-3137
Fax: (860) 486-1476
E-mail: beahusky@uconn.edu
http://www.uconn.edu
Applied mathematics, biophysics, chemical engineering, civil engineering, clinical laboratory science, engineering physics, environmental science, geography, geology/earth science, industrial engineering, materials engineering, materials science, mechanical engineering, physics, statistics.

University of Hartford
200 Bloomfield Avenue
West Hartford, CT 06117
Phone: (860) 768-4296
Fax: (860) 768-4961
E-mail: admissions@mail.hartford.edu
http://www.hartford.edu
Civil engineering, clinical laboratory science, electrical engineering technology, engineering—general, engineering technology—general, environmental engineering technology, mechanical engineering, mechanical engineering technology, physics.

University of New Haven
300 Orange Avenue
West Haven, CT 06516
Phone: (203) 932-7319
Fax: (203) 931-6093
E-mail: adminfo@newhaven.edu
http://www.newhaven.edu
Chemical engineering, civil engineering, engineering—general, mechanical engineering.

Wesleyan University
Stewart M. Reid House
70 Wyllys Avenue
Middletown, CT 06459
Phone: (860) 685-3000
Fax: (860) 685-3001
E-mail: admiss@wesleyan.edu
http://www.wesleyan.edu
Biochemistry, geology/earth science, physics.

Western Connecticut State University
Undergraduate Admissions Office
181 White Street
Danbury, CT 06810
Phone: (203) 837-9000
Fax: NA
E-mail: At Web site
http://www.wcsu.edu
Atmospheric science, clinical laboratory science.

Yale University
P.O. Box 208234
New Haven, CT 06520
Phone: (203) 432-9316
Fax: (203) 432-9392
E-mail: undergraduate_admissions@yale.edu
http://www.yale.edu
Applied mathematics, biochemistry, chemical engineering, engineering physics, environmental science, mechanical engineering, physics, statistics.

DELAWARE

Delaware State University
1200 North DuPont Highway
Dover, DE 19901
Phone: (302) 857-6361
Fax: (302) 857-6362
E-mail: admissions@dsu.edu
http://www.dsu/edu
Biotechnology, civil engineering
technology, electrical engineering
technology, physics, soil science.

University of Delaware
Admissions Office
116 Hullihen Hall
Newark, DE 19716
Phone: (302) 831-8123
Fax: (302) 931-6095
E-mail: admissions@udel.edu
http://www.udel.edu
Agricultural and biological engineering,
atmospheric science, biochemistry,
biotechnology, chemical engineering,
civil engineering, clinical laboratory
science, environmental engineering,
geography, geology/earth science,
geophysics/seismology, mechanical
engineering, physics, soil science,
statistics.

Wesley College
120 North State Street
Dover, DE 19901
Phone: (302) 736-2400
Fax: (302) 736-2301
E-mail: admissions@wesley.edu
http://www.wesley.edu
Clinical laboratory science.

DISTRICT OF COLUMBIA

American University
4400 Massachusetts Avenue NW
Washington, DC 20016
Phone: (202) 885-6000
Fax: (202) 885-1025
E-mail: afa@american.edu
http://www.american.edu
Applied mathematics, biochemistry, biolog-
ical/physical sciences, physics, statistics.

Catholic University of America
Office Enrollment Services
Washington, DC 20064
Phone: (202) 319-6305
Fax: (202) 319-6533
E-mail: cua-admissions@cua.edu
http://www.cua.edu

Atomic/molecular physics, biochemistry,
civil engineering, clinical laboratory
science, mechanical engineering,
physics.

Gallaudet University
800 Florida Avenue NE
Washington, DC 20002
Phone: (202) 651-5750
Fax: (202) 651-5744
E-mail: admissions@gallaudet.edu
http://www.gallaudet.edu
Physics.

Georgetown University
37th and O Streets NW
103 White-Gravenor
Washington, DC 20057
Phone: (202) 687-3600
Fax: (202) 687-5084
E-mail: guadmiss@georgetown.edu
http://www.georgetown.edu
Biochemistry, physics.

George Washington University
2121 I Street NW, Suite 201
Washington, DC 20052
Phone: (202) 994-6040
Fax: (202) 994-0325
E-mail: gwadm@gwu.edu
http://www.gwu.edu
Applied mathematics, biophysics, civil
engineering, engineering—general,
geography, geology/earth science,
mechanical engineering, physics,
statistics.

Howard University
2400 Sixth Street NW
Washington, DC 20059
Phone: (202) 806-2700
Fax: (202) 806-4462
E-mail: admission@howard.edu
Chemical engineering, civil engineering,
clinical laboratory science, mechanical
engineering, physics.

Trinity University
125 Michigan Avenue NE
Washington, DC 20017
Phone: (202) 884-9400
Fax: (202) 884-9403
E-mail: admissions@trinitydc.edu
http://www.trinitydc.edu
Biochemistry, biological/physical
sciences.

University of the District of Columbia
4200 Connecticut Avenue NW

Washington, DC 20008
Phone: (202) 274-6110
Fax: (202) 274-5552
E-mail: lflannagna@udc.edu
http://www.udc.edu
Civil engineering, electrical engineering
technology, geography, mechanical
engineering, physics.

FLORIDA

Barry University
11300 North East Second Avenue
Miami Shores, FL 33161
Phone: (305) 899-3100
Fax: (305) 899-2971
E-mail: Des-forms@mail.barry.edu
http://www.barry.edu
Clinical laboratory science, engineering—
general, environmental science.

Bethune-Cookman College
640 Dr. Mary McLeod Bethune
Boulevard
Daytona Beach, FL 32114
Phone: (386) 481-2600
Fax: (386) 481-2601
E-mail: admissions@cookman.edu
http://www.bethune.cookman.edu
Clinical laboratory science, physics.

DeVry University—Miramar
2300 Southwest 145th Avenue
Miramar, FL 33027
Phone: (954) 499-9700
Fax: (954) 499-9723
E-mail: openhouse@mir.devry.edu
http://www.devry.edu
Electrical engineering technology.

DeVry University—Orlando
4000 Millenia Boulevard
Orlando, FL 32839
Phone: (407) 370-3131
Fax: (407) 370-3198
E-mail: krochford@orl.devry.edu
http://www.devry.edu
Electrical engineering technology.

Eckerd College
4200 54th Avenue South
St. Petersburg, FL 33711
Phone: (727) 864-8331
Fax: (727) 866-2304
E-mail: admissions@eckerd.edu
http://www.eckerd.edu
Biochemistry, physics.

Embry-Riddle Aeronautical University
600 South Clyde Morris Boulevard
Daytona Beach, FL 32114
Phone: (386) 226-6100
Fax: (386) 226-7070
E-mail: dbadmit@erau.edu
http://www.embryriddle.edu
Civil engineering, electrical engineering
    technology, engineering—general,
    engineering physics, mechanical
    engineering, physics.

Florida A&M University
Suite G-9, Foote-Hilyer Administration
    Center
Tallahassee, FL 32307
Phone: (850) 599-3796
Fax: (950) 599-3069
E-mail: adm@famu.edu
http://www.famu.edu
Agricultural and biological engineering,
    chemical engineering, civil
    engineering, civil engineering
    technology, construction technology,
    electrical engineering technology,
    environmental science, mechanical
    engineering, physics.

Florida Atlantic University
777 Glades Road
P.O. Box 3091
Boca Raton, FL 33431
Phone: (561) 297-3040
Fax: (561) 297-3758
E-mail: admisweb@fau.edu
http://www.fau.edu
Geography, geology/earth science,
    mechanical engineering, physics.

Florida Gulf Coast University
10501 FGCU Boulevard South
Fort Myers, FL 33965
Phone: (239) 590-7878
Fax: (239) 590-7894
E-mail: admissions@fgcu.edu
http://www.fgcu.edu
Agricultural and biological engineering,
    biological/physical sciences,
    biotechnology, civil engineering,
    environmental engineering,
    environmental science.

Florida Institute of Technology
150 West University Boulevard
Melbourne, FL 32901-6975
Phone: (321) 674-8030
Fax: (321) 723-9468
E-mail: admissions@fit.edu
http://www.fit.edu

Analytical chemistry, applied
    mathematics, biochemistry, biological/
    physical sciences, biotechnology,
    chemical engineering, civil
    engineering, engineering—general,
    environmental science, mechanical
    engineering, meteorology, physics.

Florida International University
University Park, PC 140
Miami, FL 33119
Phone: (305) 348-2363
Fax: (305) 348-3648
E-mail: admiss@flu.edu
http://www.flu.edu
Applied mathematics, chemical
    engineering, civil engineering,
    construction technology, geography,
    geology/earth science, mechanical
    engineering, physics, statistics.

Florida Southern College
111 Lake Hollingworth Drive
Lakeland, FL 33801
Phone: (863) 680-4131
Fax: (863) 680-4120
E-mail: fscadm@flsouthern.edu
http://www.flsouthern.edu
Biological/physical sciences.

Florida State University
2500 University Center
Tallahassee, FL 32306
Phone: (850) 644-6200
Fax: (850) 644-0197
E-mail: admissions@admin.fsu.edu
http://www.fsu.edu
Analytical chemistry, atmospheric sci-
    ence, biochemistry, biophysics, chemi-
    cal engineering, civil engineering,
    environmental engineering, environ-
    mental science, geography, geology/
    earth science, industrial engineering,
    materials engineering, mechanical
    engineering, physics, statistics.

Jacksonville University
700 Pelham Road North
Jacksonville, FL 36252
Phone: (904) 256-7000
Fax: (904) 256-7012
E-mail: admissions@ju.edu
http://www.jacksonville.edu
Engineering physics, geography,
    mechanical engineering, physics.

New College of Florida
5700 North Tamiami Trail
Sarasota, FL 34243

Phone: (941) 359-4269
Fax: (941) 359-4435
E-mail: admissions@ncf.edu
http://www.ncf.edu
Physics.

Rollins College
Campus Box 2720
Winter Park, FL 32789
Phone: (407) 646-2161
Fax: (407) 646-1502
E-mail: admission@rollins.edu
http://www.rollins.edu
Physics.

Saint Leo University
Office of Admission
MC 2008, P.O. Box 6665
Saint Leo, FL 33574
Phone: (352) 588-8283
Fax: (352) 588-8257
E-mail: admission@saintleo.edu
http://www.saintleo.edu
Clinical laboratory science.

Stetson University
421 North Woodland Boulevard,
    Unit 8378
DeLand, FL 32723
Phone: (386) 822-7100
Fax: (386) 822-7112
E-mail: admissions@stetson.edu
http://www.stetson.edu
Biochemistry, clinical laboratory science,
    environmental science, geography,
    physics.

University of Central Florida
P.O. Box 160111
Orlando, FL 32816
Phone: (407) 823-3000
Fax: (407) 823-5625
E-mail: admission@mail.ucf.edu
http://www.ucf.edu
Civil engineering, clinical laboratory
    science, electrical engineering tech-
    nology, engineering technology—
    general, environmental engineering,
    industrial engineering, mechanical
    engineering, physics, statistics.

University of Florida
201 Criser Hall, P.O. Box 11400
Gainesville, FL 32611-4000
Phone: (352) 392-1365
Fax: (352) 392-3987
E-mail: At Web site
http://www.ufl.edu

Agricultural and biological engineering, biochemistry, civil engineering, construction technology, engineering mechanics, environmental engineering, geography, geology/earth science, materials engineering, mechanical engineering, nuclear engineering, physics, soil science, statistics, surveying technology.

University of Miami
P.O. Box 248025
Coral Gables, FL 33124
Phone: (305) 284-4323
Fax: (305) 284-2507
E-mail: admission@miami.edu
http://www.miami.edu/admissions
Atmospheric science, biochemistry, biophysics, civil engineering, environmental engineering, geography, geology/earth science, industrial engineering, mathematical statistics/probability, mechanical engineering, meteorology, physics.

University of North Florida
4567 St. Johns Bluff Road, South
Jacksonville, FL 32224
Phone: (904) 620-2624
Fax: (904) 620-2414
E-mail: osprey@unf.edu
http://www.unf.edu
Biological/physical sciences, civil engineering, construction technology, mechanical engineering, physics, statistics.

University of South Florida—St. Petersburg
140 Seventh Avenue South
St. Petersburg, FL 33701
Phone: (727) 553-4USF
Fax: (727) 553-553-2592
E-mail: admissions@stpt.usf.edu
http://www.stpt.usf.edu
Biological/physical sciences, chemical engineering, civil engineering, clinical laboratory science, engineering—general, environmental engineering, geography, geology/earth science, mechanical engineering, physics.

University of South Florida—Tampa
4202 East Fowler Avenue SVC-1036
Tampa, FL 33620-9951
Phone: (813) 874-3350
Fax: (813) 974-9689
E-mail: jglassma@admin.usf.edu
http://www.usf.edu

Biological/physical sciences, chemical engineering, civil engineering, clinical laboratory science, environmental engineering, geography, geology/earth science, mechanical engineering, physics.

University of Tampa
401 West Kennedy Boulevard
Tampa, FL 33606
Phone: (813) 253-6211
Fax: (813) 258-7398
E-mail: admissions@ut.edu
http://www.ut.edu
Biochemistry, environmental science.

University of West Florida
11000 University Parkway
Pensacola, FL 32514
Phone: (850) 474-2230
Fax: (850) 474-3360
E-mail: admissions@uwf.edu
http://uwf.edu
Applied mathematics, biological/physical sciences, electrical engineering technology, engineering technology—general, environmental science, physics.

GEORGIA

Agnes Scott College
141 East College Avenue
Decatur, GA 30030
Phone: (404) 471-6285
Fax: (404) 471-6414
E-mail: admission@agnesscott.edu
http://www.agnesscott.edu
Biochemistry, physics.

Armstrong Atlantic State University
11935 Abecorn Street
Savannah, GA 31419
Phone: (912) 927-5277
Fax: (912) 927-5462
E-mail: adm-info@mail.armstrong.edu
http://www.armstrong.edu
Applied mathematics, clinical laboratory science, physics.

Augusta State University
2500 Walton Way
Augusta, GA 3094
Phone: (706) 737-1632
Fax: (706) 667-4355
E-mail: admission@aug.edu
http://www.aug.edu
Clinical laboratory science, physics.

Berry College
P.O. Box 490159
Mount Berry, GA 30149
Phone: (706) 236-2215
Fax: (706) 236-2248
E-mail: admissions@berry.edu
http://www.berry.edu
Biochemistry, engineering technology—general, environmental science, physics.

Brenau University Women's College
1 Centennial Circle
Gainesville, GA 30501
Phone: (770) 534-6100
Fax: (770) 538-4306
E-mail: wcadmissions@lib.brenau.edu
http://www.brenau.edu
Applied mathematics.

Clark Atlanta University
223 James P. Brawley Drive
Atlanta, GA 30314
Phone: (404) 880-8000
Fax: (404) 880-6174
E-mail: admissions@panthernet.cau.edu
http://www.cau.edu
Engineering—general, physics.

Columbus State University
4225 University Avenue
Columbus, GA 31907
Phone: (866) 264-2035
Fax: NA
E-mail: At Web site
http://www. colstate.edu
Applied mathematics, geology/earth science.

Covenant College
14049 Scenic Highway
Lookout Mountain GA 30750
Phone: (706) 820-2398
Fax: (706) 820-0893
E-mail: admissions@covenant.edu
http://www.covenant.edu
Physics.

DeVry University—Alpharetta
2555 Northwinds Parkway
Alpharetta, GA 30005
Phone: (770) 664-9520
Fax: (770) 664-8824
E-mail: info@devry.edu
http://www.devry.edu
Electrical engineering technology.

DeVry University—Atlanta
3575 Piedmont Road NE, # P100

Atlanta, GA 30305
Phone: (770) 671-1744
Fax: NA
E-mail: info@devry.edu
http://www.devry.edu
Electrical engineering technology.

Emory University
Boisfeuillet Jones Center
201 Dowman Drive NE
Atlanta, GA 30322
Phone: (404) 727-6036
Fax: (404) 727-4303
E-mail: admiss@emory.edu
http://www.emory.edu
Physics.

Fort Valley State University
1005 State University Drive
Fort Valley, GA 31030
Phone: (912) 825-6307
Fax: (912) 875-6394
E-mail: fordd@fvsu.edu
http://www. www.fvsu.edu
Agricultural and biological engineering, electrical engineering technology.

Georgia Institute of Technology
219 Uncle Heine Way
Atlanta, GA 30332
Phone: (404) 894-4154
Fax: (404) 894-9511
E-mail: admissions@gatech.edu
http://www.gatech.edu
Chemical engineering, civil engineering, geology/earth science, industrial engineering, materials engineering, mechanical engineering, nuclear engineering, physics.

Georgia Southern University
P.O. Box 8024
Statesboro, GA 30460
Phone: (912) 681-5391
Fax: (912) 486-7240
E-mail: admissions@georgiasouthern.edu
http://www.georgiasouthern.edu
Civil engineering technology, construction technology, electrical engineering technology, geography, geology/earth science, industrial technology, mechanical engineering technology, physics.

Georgia Southwestern State University
800 Wheatley Street
Americus, GA 31709
Phone: (912) 928-1273
Fax: (912) 931-2983

E-mail: gswapps@canes.gsw.edu
http://www.gsw.edu
Geology/earth science.

Georgia State University
P.O. Box 4009
Atlanta, GA 30302
Phone: (404) 651-2365
Fax: (404) 651-4811
E-mail: admissions@gsu.edu
http://www.gsu.edu
Applied mathematics, geology/earth science, physics.

Kennesaw State University
1000 Chastain Road, Campus Box 0115
Kennesaw, GA 30144
Phone: (770) 423-6000
Fax: (770) 423-6541
E-mail: ksuadmit@kennesaw.edu
http://www.kennesaw.edu
Biochemistry, biotechnology.

Mercer University—Macon
Admissions Office
1400 Coleman Avenue
Macon, GA 31207
Phone: (478) 301-2650
Fax: (478) 301-2828
E-mail: admissions@mercer.edu
http://www.mercer.edu
Biochemistry, engineering—general, environmental science, physics.

Morehouse College
830 Westview Drive Southwest
Atlanta, GA 30314
Phone: (404) 215-2632
Fax: (404) 524-5635
E-mail: janderso@morehouse.edu
http://www.morehouse.edu
Engineering—general, physics.

Oglethorpe University
4484 Peachtree Road Northeast
Atlanta, GA 30319
Phone: (404) 364-8307
Fax: (404) 364-8491
E-mail: admission@oglethorpe.edu
http://www.oglethorpe.edu
Clinical laboratory science, physics.

Piedmont College
P.O. Box 10
Demorest, GA 30535
Phone: (706) 776-0103
Fax: (706) 776-6635
E-mail: ugrad@piedmont.edu
http://www.piedmont.edu
Environmental science.

Savannah State University
College Station, P.O. Box 20209
Savannah, GA 31404
Phone: (912) 356-2181
Fax: (912) 356-2256
E-mail: SSUAdmission@savstate.edu
http://www.savstate.edu
Civil engineering technology, clinical laboratory science, electrical engineering technology.

Southern Polytechnic State University
1100 South Marietta Parkway
Marietta, GA 30060
Phone: (678) 915-4188
Fax: (678) 915-7292
E-mail: admissions@spsu.edu
http://www.spsu.edu
Civil engineering technology, electrical engineering technology, industrial technology, mechanical engineering technology, physics, surveying technology.

Spelman College
350 Spelman Lane
Atlanta, GA 30314
Phone: (404) 270-5193
Fax: (404) 270-5201
E-mail: admiss@spelman.edu
http://www.spelman.edu
Biochemistry, biological/physical sciences, engineering—general, environmental science, physics.

University of Georgia
Terrell Hall
Athens, GA 30602
Phone: (706) 542-8776
Fax: (706) 542-1466
E-mail: undergrad@admissions.uga.edu
http://www.uga.edu
Agricultural and biological engineering, biochemistry, biological/physical sciences, biotechnology, chemical engineering, engineering—general, environmental engineering, geography, geology/earth science, physics.

University of West Georgia
1601 Maple Street
Carrollton, GA 30118
Phone: (678) 839-4000
Fax: (678) 839-4747
E-mail: admiss@westga.edu
http://www.westga.edu
Environmental science, geography, geology/earth science, physics.

Valdosta State University
1500 North Patterson Street

Valdosta, GA 31698
Phone: (229) 333-5791
Fax: (229) 333-5482
E-mail: admissions@valdosta.edu
http://www.valdosta.edu
Applied mathematics, engineering
  technology—general, environmental
  science, physics.

HAWAII

Brigham Young University—Hawaii
BYU-Hawaii #1973
55-220 Kulanui Street
Laie, HI 96762
Phone: (808) 293-3738
Fax: (808) 293-3457
E-mail: admissions@byuh.edu
http://www.byuh.edu
Biochemistry.

Hawaii Pacific University
1164 Bishop Street
Honolulu, HI 96813
Phone: (808) 544-0238
Fax: (808) 544-1136
E-mail: admissions@hpu.edu
http://www.hpu.edu
Applied mathematics, environmental
  science.

University of Hawaii—Hilo
200 West Kawili Street
Hilo, HI 96720
Phone: (808) 974-7414
Fax: (808) 933-0861
E-mail: uhhadm@hawaii.edu
http://www.uhh.hawaii.edu
Geography, geology/earth science,
  physics, soil science.

University of Hawaii—Manoa
2600 Campus Road, QLCSS Room 001
Honolulu, HI 96822
Phone: (808) 956-8975
Fax: (808) 956-4148
E-mail: ar-info@hawaii.edu
http://www.uhm.hawaii.edu
Agricultural and biological engineering,
  civil engineering, clinical laboratory
  science, environmental science, geography, geology/earth science, mechanical
  engineering, meteorology, physics.

IDAHO

Albertson College of Idaho
2112 Cleveland Boulevard
Caldwell, ID 83605

Phone: (208) 459-5305
Fax: (208) 459-5116
E-mail: admission@alberton.edu
http://www.albertson.edu
Engineering—general, geological
  engineering, metallurgical
  engineering.

Boise State University
1910 University Drive
Boise, ID 83725
Phone: (208) 426-1156
Fax: (208) 426-3765
E-mail: bsuinfo@boisestate.edu
http://www.boisestate.edu
Civil engineering, construction
  technology, geology/earth science,
  geophysics/seismology, mechanical
  engineering, physics.

Brigham Young University
Admissions Office
KIM 120
Rexburg, ID 83460
Phone: (208) 496-1020
Fax: (208) 496-1220
E-mail: admissions@byui.edu
http://www.byui.edu
Electrical engineering technology,
  geology/earth science, mechanical
  engineering, physics.

Idaho State University
Admissions Office
Campus P.O. Box 8270
Pocatello, ID 93208
Phone: (208) 282-2475
Fax: (208) 282-4231
E-mail: info@isu.edu
http://www.isu.edu
Biochemistry, civil engineering, clinical
  laboratory science, electrical
  engineering technology, geology/earth
  science, geophysics/seismology,
  mechanical engineering, nuclear
  engineering, physics, surveying
  technology.

Lewis-Clark State College
500 Eighth Avenue
Lewiston, ID 83501
Phone: (208) 792-2210
Fax: (208) 792-2876
E-mail: admissions@lcsc.edu
http://www.lcsc.edu
Electronics/electrical equipment repair,
  industrial electronics technology,
  mechanics/repairers general, welding
  technology.

Northwest Nazarene University
623 Holly Street
Nampa, ID 83686
Phone: (208) 467-8000
Fax: (208) 467-8645
E-mail: admissions@nnu.edu
http://www.nnu.edu
Biological/physical sciences, engineering
  physics, physics.

University of Idaho
UI Admissions Office
P.O. Box 44264
Moscow, ID 83844
Phone: (308) 885-6326
Fax: (308) 885-9119
E-mail: admappl@uidaho.edu
http://www.uidaho.edu
Agricultural and biological engineering,
  applied mathematics, chemical
  engineering, civil engineering,
  geography, geology/earth science,
  geophysics/seismology, mechanical
  engineering, mining and mineral
  engineering, physics, soil science.

ILLINOIS

Augustana College
639 38th Street
Rock Island, IL 61201
Phone: (309) 794-7341
Fax: (309) 794-7422
E-mail: admissions@augustana.edu
http://www.augustana.edu
Engineering physics, geography, geology/
  earth science, physics.

Aurora University
347 South Gladstone Avenue
Aurora, IL 60506
Phone: (630) 844-5533
Fax: (630) 844-5535
E-mail: admission@aurora.edu
http://www.aurora.edu
Clinical laboratory science.

Benedictine University
5700 College Road
Lisle, IL 60532
Phone: (630) 829-6300
Fax: (630) 829-6301
E-mail: admissions@ben.edu
http://www.ben.edu
Biochemistry, clinical laboratory science,
  physics.

Bradley University
1501 West Bradley Avenue

Peoria, IL 61625
Phone: (309) 677-1000
Fax: (309) 677-2797
E-mail: admissions@bradley.edu
http://www.bradley.edu
Biochemistry, civil engineering, clinical laboratory science, construction engineering, electrical engineering technology, engineering physics, environmental engineering, environmental science, geology/earth science, industrial engineering, mechanical engineering, physics.

Chicago State University
9501 South King Drive, ADM-200
Chicago, IL 60628
Phone: (773) 995-2513
Fax: (773) 995-3820
E-mail: ug-admissions@csu.edu
http://www.csu.edu
Biochemistry, geography, physics.

Concordia University
7400 Augusta Street
River Forest, IL 60305
Phone: (708) 209-3100
Fax: (708) 209-3473
E-mail: crfadmis@curf.edu
http://www.curf.edu
Geography.

DePaul University
1 East Jackson Boulevard
Chicago, IL 60604
Phone: (312) 362-8300
Fax: (312) 362-5749
E-mail: admitdpu@depaul.edu
http://www.depaul.edu
Clinical laboratory science, environmental science, geography, physics.

DeVry University—Addison
1221 North Swift Road
Addison, IL 60101
Phone: (630) 953-2000
Fax: (630) 953-1236
E-mail: info@devry.edu
http://www.devry.edu
Electrical engineering technology.

DeVry University—Chicago
3300 North Cambell Avenue
Chicago, IL 60618
Phone: (773) 697-2155
Fax: (773) 697-2710
E-mail: keaster@chi.devry.edu
http://www.devry.edu
Electrical engineering technology.

DeVry University—Tinley Park
18624 West Creek Drive
Tinley Park, IL 60477
Phone: (708) 342-3100
Fax: (708) 342-3505
E-mail: imccauley@tp.devry.edu
http://www.tp.devry.edu
Electrical engineering technology.

Dominican University
7900 West Division
River Forest, IL 60305
Phone: (708) 524-6800
Fax: (708) 524-5990
E-mail: domadmis@dom.edu
http://www.dom.edu
Biochemistry, chemical engineering, civil engineering, environmental science, mechanical engineering.

Eastern Illinois University
600 Lincoln Avenue
Charleston, IL 61920
Phone: (217) 581-2223
Fax: (217) 581-7060
E-mail: cdadmit@www.eiu.edu
http://www.eiu.edu
Clinical laboratory science, geography, geology/earth science, industrial technology, physics.

East-West University
816 South Michigan Avenue
Chicago, IL 60605
Phone: (312) 939-0111
Fax: (312) 939-0083
E-mail: admissions@eastwest.edu
http://www.eastwest.edu
Electrical engineering technology.

Elmhurst College
190 South Prospect Avenue
Elmhurst, IL 60126
Phone: (630) 617-3400
Fax: (630) 617-5501
E-mail: admit@elmhurst.edu
http://www.elmhurst.edu
Geography, physics.

Eureka College
300 East College Avenue
Eureka, IL 61530
Phone: (309) 467-6350
Fax: (309) 467-6576
E-mail: admissions@eureka.edu
http://www.eureka.edu
Engineering—general.

Illinois College
1101 West College

Jacksonville, IL 62650
Phone: (217) 245-3030
Fax: (217) 245-3034
E-mail: admissions@hilltop.ic.edu
http://www.ic.edu
Clinical laboratory science, engineering—general, environmental science, physics.

Illinois Institute of Technology
10 West 33rd Street
Chicago, IL 60616
Phone: (312) 567-3025
Fax: (312) 567-6939
E-mail: admission@iit.edu
http://www.iit.edu
Biophysics, chemical engineering, civil engineering, environmental engineering, materials engineering, mechanical engineering, physics.

Illinois State University
Admissions Office
Campus P.O. Box 2200
Normal, IL 61790
Phone: (309) 438-2181
Fax: (309) 438-3932
E-mail: ugradadm@ilstu.edu
http://www.ilstu.edu
Biochemistry, clinical laboratory science, geography, geology/earth science, industrial technology, physics.

Judson College
1151 North State Street
Elgin, IL 60123
Phone: (847) 628-2510
Fax: (847) 628-2526
E-mail: admission@judsoncollege.edu
http://www.judsoncollege.edu
Physics.

Knox College
Box K-148
Galesburg, IL 61401
Phone: (309) 341-7100
Fax: (309) 341-7070
E-mail: admission@knox.edu
http://www.knox.edu
Biochemistry, physics.

Lewis University
One University Parkway
P.O. Box 297
Romeoville, IL 60446
Phone: (815) 836-5250
Fax: (815) 836-5002
E-mail: admissions@lewisu.edu
http://www.lewisu.edu
Biochemistry, physics.

MacMurray College
447 East College Avenue
Jacksonville, IL 62650
Phone: (217) 479-7056
Fax: (217) 291-0702
E-mail: admissions@mac.edu
http://www.mac.edu
Engineering—general, physics.

McKendree College
701 College Road
Lebanon, IL 62254
Phone: (618) 537-6831
Fax: (618) 537-6496
E-mail: inquiry@mckendree.edu
http://www.mckendree.edu
Clinical laboratory science.

Millikin University
1184 West Main Street
Decatur, IL 62522
Phone: (217) 424-6210
Fax: (217) 425-4669
E-mail: admis@mail.millikin.edu
http://www.millikin.edu
Applied mathematics, physics.

Monmouth College
700 East Broadway
Monmouth, IL 61462
Phone: (309) 457-2131
Fax: (309) 457-2141
E-mail: admit@monm.edu
http://www.monm.edu
Biochemistry, engineering—general,
    environmental science, physics.

National-Louis University
2840 Sheridan Road
Evanston, IL 60201
Phone: (847) 465-0575
Fax: NA
E-mail: ninuinfo@wheeling1.nl.edu
http://www.nl.edu
Applied mathematics, biological/
    physical sciences, clinical laboratory
    science.

North Central College
30 North Brainard Street
P.O. Box 3063
Naperville, IL 60506
Phone: (630) 637-5800
Fax: (630) 637-5819
E-mail: ncadm@noctrl.edu
http://www.northcentralcollege.edu
Applied mathematics, biochemistry,
    biological/physical sciences,
    physics.

Northeastern Illinois University
5500 North St. Louis Avenue
Chicago, IL 60625
Phone: (773) 442-4000
Fax: (773) 442-4020
E-mail: admrec@neiu.edu
http://www.neiu.edu
Geography, geology/earth science,
    physics.

Northern Illinois University
Office of Admissions
Williston Hall 1010, NIU
DeKalb, IL 60115
Phone: (815) 753-0446
Fax: (815) 753-1783
E-mail: admissions-info@niu.edu
http://www.reg.niu.edu
Applied mathematics, atmospheric
    science, clinical laboratory science,
    geography, geology/earth science,
    industrial engineering, industrial
    technology, mathematical statistics/
    probability, mechanical engineering,
    physics.

North Park University
3225 West Foster Avenue
Chicago, IL 60625
Phone: (773) 244-5500
Fax: (773) 244-4953
E-mail: admission@northpark.edu
http://www.northpark.edu
Applied mathematics, clinical laboratory
    science, physics.

Northwestern University
P.O. Box 3060
1801 Hinman Avenue
Evanston, IL 60208
Phone: (847) 491-7271
Fax: (847) 491-5565
E-mail: ug-admission@northwestern.edu
http://www.northwestern.edu
Applied mathematics, biological/physical
    sciences, chemical engineering,
    civil engineering, engineering—
    general, environmental engineering,
    environmental science, geology/earth
    science, geophysics/seismology,
    industrial engineering, materials
    engineering, materials science,
    mechanical engineering, physics.

Olivet Nazarene University
1 University Avenue
Bourbonnais, IL 60914
Phone: (815) 939-5603
Fax: (815) 935-4998

E-mail: admissions@olivet.edu
http://www.olivet.edu
Biological/physical sciences,
    engineering—general, geology/earth
    science.

Quincy University
1800 College Avenue
Quincy, IL 62301
Phone: (217) 228-5215
Fax: (217) 228-5479
E-mail: admissions@quincy.edu
http://www.quincy.edu
Clinical laboratory science.

Rockford College
Office of Undergraduate Admission
5050 East State Street
Rockford, IL 61108
Phone: (815) 226-4050
Fax: (815) 226-226-2822
E-mail: admission@rockford.edu
http://www.rockford.edu
Biochemistry.

Roosevelt University
430 South Michigan Avenue
Chicago, IL 60605
Phone: (312) 341-3515
Fax: (312) 341-3523
E-mail: applyRU@roosevelt.edu
http://www.roosevelt.edu
Electrical engineering technology,
    geography, physics, statistics.

Rush University
600 South Paulina Street, Suite 440
Chicago, IL 60612
Phone: (312) 942-7100
Fax: (312) 942-2219
E-mail: Rush_admissions@rush.edu
http://www.rushu.rush.edu
Clinical laboratory science.

**Southern Illinois University—
    Carbondale**
Admissions & Records, MC 4710
Carbondale, IL 62901
Phone: (618) 453-4405
Fax: (618) 453-3250
E-mail: joinsiuc@siuc.edu
http://www.siuc.edu
Civil engineering, engineering
    technology—general, geography,
    geological engineering, geology/
    earth science, industrial technology,
    mechanical engineering, mining and
    mineral engineering, physics.

Southern Illinois University—Edwardsville
P.O. Box 1600
Edwardsville, IL 62026
Phone: (618) 650-3705
Fax: (618) 650-5013
E-mail: admis@siue.edu
http://www.siue.edu
Civil engineering, construction technology, geography, industrial engineering, mechanical engineering, physics.

University of Chicago
1116 East 59th Street
Chicago, IL 60637
Phone: (773) 702-8650
Fax: (773) 702-4199
E-mail: toneill@uchicago.edu
http://www.uchicago.edu
Applied mathematics, biochemistry, geography, geophysics/seismology, physics, statistics.

University of Illinois—Chicago
P.O. Box 5220
Chicago, IL 60680
Phone: (312) 996-4350
Fax: (312) 413-7628
E-mail: uicAdmit@uic.edu
http://www.uic.edu
Biochemistry, chemical engineering, civil engineering, clinical laboratory science, engineering physics, geology/earth science, geological engineering, materials engineering, mechanical engineering, physics, statistics.

University of Illinois—Springfield
One University Place, MS UHB 1080
Springfield, IL 62703
Phone: (217) 206-4847
Fax: (217) 206-6620
E-mail: admissions@uls.edu
http://www.uls.edu
Clinical laboratory science, environmental science.

University of Illinois—Urbana-Champaign
901 West Illinois Street
Urbana, IL 61801
Phone: (217) 333-0302
Fax: (217) 333-9758
E-mail: admissions@oar.uiuc.edu
http://www.uiuc.edu
Agricultural and biological engineering, biochemistry, biophysics, biotechnology, chemical engineering, civil engineering, engineering—general, engineering mechanics, engineering physics, environmental science, geography, geology/earth science, geotechnical engineering, industrial engineering, materials engineering, materials science, mechanical engineering, physics, statistics, structural engineering.

University of Saint Francis
500 Wilcox Street
Joliet, IL 60435
Phone: (815) 740-5037
Fax: (815) 740-5032
E-mail: admissions@stfrancis.edu
http://www.stfrancis.edu
Clinical laboratory science, environmental science.

Western Illinois University
1 University Circle
115 Sherman Hall
Macomb, IL 61455
Phone: (309) 298-3157
Fax: (309) 298-3111
E-mail: wiuadm@wiu.edu
http://www.wiu.edu
Clinical laboratory science, geography, geology/earth science, industrial technology, meteorology, physics.

Wheaton College
501 College Avenue
Wheaton, IL 60187
Phone: (630) 752-5005
Fax: (630) 752-5285
E-mail: admissions@wheaton.edu
http://www.wheaton.edu
Engineering—general, geology/earth science, physics.

INDIANA

Anderson University
1100 East Fifth Street
Anderson, IN 46012
Phone: (765) 641-4080
Fax: (765) 641-4091
E-mail: info@anderson.edu
http://www.anderson.edu
Biochemistry, physics.

Ball State University
Office of Admissions
2000 West University Avenue
Muncie, IN 47306
Phone: (765) 285-8300
Fax: (765) 285-1632
E-mail: askus@bsu.edu
http://www.bsu.edu
Clinical laboratory science, engineering—general, geography, geology/earth science, industrial technology, physics.

Bethel College
1001 West McKinley Avenue
Mishawaka, IN 46545
Phone: (574) 257-3339
Fax: (574) 257-3335
E-mail: admissions@bethelcollege.edu
http://www.bethel.college.edu
Engineering—general.

Butler University
4600 Sunset Avenue
Indianapolis, IN 46208
Phone: (317) 940-8100
Fax: (317) 940-8150
E-mail: admission@butler.edu
http://www.butler.edu
Engineering physics, physics.

DePauw University
101 East Seminary Street
Greencastle, IN 46135
Phone: (765) 658-4006
Fax: (765) 658-4007
E-mail: admission@depauw.edu
http://www.depauw.edu
Biochemistry, environmental science, geology/earth science, physics.

Earlham College
801 National Road West
Richmond, IN 47374
Phone: (765) 983-1600
Fax: (765) 983-1560
E-mail: admission@earlham.edu
http://www.earlham.edu
Biochemistry, geology/earth science, physics.

Goshen College
1700 South Main Street
Goshen, IN 46526
Phone: (574) 535-7535
Fax: (574) 535-7609
E-mail: admissions@goshen.edu
http://www.goshen.edu
Applied mathematics, physics.

Hanover College
P.O. Box 108
Hanover, IN 47243
Phone: (812) 866-7021
Fax: (812) 866-7098
E-mail: admission@hanover.edu

http://www.hanover.edu
Geology/earth science, physics.

Indiana Institute of Technology
1600 East Washington Boulevard
Fort Wayne, IN 46803
Phone: (260) 422-5561
Fax: (260) 422-7696
E-mail: admissions@indtech.edu
http://www.indtech.edu
Industrial engineering, mechanical
  engineering.

Indiana State University
Office of Admissions
Trey Hall 134
Terra Haute, IN 47809
Phone: (812) 237-2121
Fax: (812) 237-8023
E-mail: admissions@indstate.edu
http://www.indstate.edu
Clinical laboratory science, electrical
  engineering technology, geography,
  geology/earth science, industrial
  technology, mechanical engineering
  technology, physics.

Indiana University—Bloomington
300 North Jordan Avenue
Bloomington, IN 47405
Phone: (812) 855-0661
Fax: (812) 855-5102
E-mail: iuadmit@indiana.edu
http://www.indiana.edu
Biochemistry, geography, geology/earth
  science, physics.

Indiana University—East
2325 Chester Boulevard, WZ 116
Richmond, IN 47374
Phone: (765) 973-8208
Fax: (765) 973-8288
E-mail: eaadmit@indiana.edu
http://www.indiana.edu
Biological/physical sciences, mechanical
  engineering.

Indiana University—Kokomo
Office of Admissions
P.O. Box 9003, KC 230A
Kokomo, IN 46904
Phone: (765) 455-9217
Fax: (765) 455-9537
E-mail: iuadmis@iuk.edu
http://www.iuk.edu
Biological/physical sciences.

Indiana University—Northwest
3400 Broadway

Hawthorn 100
Gary, IN 46408
Phone: (219) 980-6991
Fax: (291) 981-4219
E-mail: admit@iun.edu
http://www.iun.edu
Geology/earth science.

**Indiana University—Purdue University
  Fort Wayne**
2101 East Coliseum Boulevard
Fort Wayne, IN 46805
Phone: (260) 481-6812
Fax: (260) 481-6880
E-mail: ipfwadms@ipfw.edu
http://www.ipfw.edu
Biochemistry, civil engineering, clinical
  laboratory science, construction
  technology, electrical engineering
  technology, geology/earth science,
  industrial technology, mechanical
  engineering, mechanical engineering
  technology, physics, statistics.

**Indiana University—Purdue University
  Indianapolis**
425 North University Boulevard
Cavanaugh Hall, Room 129
Indianapolis, IN 46202
Phone: (317) 274-4591
Fax: (317) 278-1862
E-mail: apply@iupui.edu
http://www.iu.edu
Clinical laboratory science, construction
  technology, electrical engineering
  technology, engineering—general,
  environmental science, geography,
  geology/earth science, mechanical
  engineering, mechanical engineering
  technology, physics.

Indiana University South Bend
1700 Mishawaka Avenue
P.O. Box 7111, A169
South Bend, IN 46634
Phone: (574) 237-4840
Fax: (219) 237-4834
E-mail: admission@iusb.edu
http://www.iusb.edu
Applied mathematics, physics.

Indiana University Southeast
4201 Grant Line Road, UC-100
New Albany, IN 47150
Phone: (812) 941-2212
Fax: (812) 941-2595
E-mail: admissions@ius.edu
http://www.ius.edu
Clinical laboratory science, physics.

Manchester College
604 College Avenue, North
Manchester, IN 46962
Phone: (260) 982-5055
Fax: (260) 982-5239
E-mail: admitinfo@manchester.edu
http://www.manchester.edu
Biochemistry, clinical laboratory science,
  physics.

Oakland City University
143 North Lucretia Street
Oakland City, IN 47660
Phone: (812) 749-4781
Fax: (812) 749-1233
E-mail: ocuadmit@oak.edu
http://www.oak.edu
Applied mathematics.

Purdue University—Calumet
Office of Admissions
2200 169th Street
Hammond, IN 46323
Phone: (219) 989-2213
Fax: (219) 989-2775
E-mail: adms@calumet.purdue.edu
http://www.calumet.purdue.edu
Agricultural and biological engineering,
  applied mathematics, biochemistry,
  biological/physical sciences, chemical
  engineering, clinical laboratory
  science, construction engineering,
  construction technology, electrical
  engineering technology, engineering—
  general, engineering mechanics,
  geology/earth science, industrial
  engineering, materials engineering,
  mechanical engineering, nuclear
  engineering, physics, statistics,
  surveying technology.

**Purdue University—North Central
  Campus**
1401 South U.S. Highway 421
Westville, IN 46391
Phone: (219) 785-5458
Fax: (219) 785-5538
E-mail: admissions@purduenc.edu
http://www.pnc.edu
Agricultural and biological engineering,
  biochemistry, biological/physical
  sciences, chemical engineering,
  clinical laboratory science,
  construction engineering, electrical
  engineering technology, geology/
  earth science, materials engineering,
  mechanical engineering, nuclear
  engineering, physics, statistics,
  surveying technology.

Purdue University—West Lafayette
1080 Schleman Hall
West Lafayette, IN 47907
Phone: (765) 494-1776
Fax: (765) 494-0544
E-mail: admissions@purdue.edu
http://www.purdue.edu
Agricultural and biological engineering, biochemistry, biological/physical sciences, chemical engineering, clinical laboratory science, construction engineering, electrical engineering technology, geology/earth science, materials engineering, mechanical engineering, nuclear engineering, physics, statistics, surveying technology.

Rose-Hulman Institute of Technology
5500 Wabash Avenue
Terre Haute, IN 47803
Phone: (812) 877-8213
Fax: (812) 877-8941
E-mail: admis.ofc@rose-hulman.edu
http://www.rose-hulman.edu
Civil engineering, engineering physics, mechanical engineering, physics.

Saint Joseph's College
P.O. Box 890
Rensselaer, IN 47978
Phone: (219) 866-6170
Fax: (219) 866-6122
E-mail: admissions@saintjoe.edu
http://www.saintjoe.edu
Biochemistry, clinical laboratory science, environmental science.

Saint Mary-of-the-Woods College
Office of Admissions
Guerin Hall
Saint Mary-of-the-Woods, IN 47876
Phone: (812) 535-5106
Fax: (812) 535-4900
E-mail: smwcadms@smwc.edu
http://www.smwc.edu
Biological/physical sciences.

Saint Mary's College
Admission Office
Notre Dame, IN 46556
Phone: (219) 284-4587
Fax: (219) 284-4841
E-mail: admission@saintmarys.edu
http://www.saintmarys.edu
Applied mathematics, statistics.

Taylor University—Fort Wayne Campus
1025 West Rudisill Boulevard
Fort Wayne, IN 46807
Phone: (800) 233-3922
Fax: (260) 744-8660
E-mail: admissions_f@tayloru.edu
http://www.tayloru.edu/fw
Biological/physical sciences, engineering physics, environmental engineering, geography, physics.

Taylor University—Upland
236 West Reade Avenue
Upland, IN 46989
Phone: (765) 998-5134
Fax: (765) 998-4925
E-mail: admissions_U@tayloru.edu
http://www.tayloru.edu
Biological/physical sciences, engineering physics, environmental engineering, environmental science, geography, physics.

Tri-State University
1 University Avenue
Angola, IN 46703
Phone: (260) 665-4132
Fax: (260) 665-4578
E-mail: admit@tristate.edu
http://www.tristate.edu
Civil engineering, mechanical engineering.

University of Evansville
1800 Lincoln Avenue
Evansville, IN 47722
Phone: (812) 479-2468
Fax: (812) 474-4076
E-mail: admission@evansville.edu
http://www.evansville.edu
Applied mathematics, biochemistry, civil engineering, environmental science, mechanical engineering, physics.

University of Indianapolis
1400 East Hanna Avenue
Indianapolis, IN 46227
Phone: (317) 788-3216
Fax: (317) 788-3300
E-mail: admissions@uindy.edu
http://www.indy.edu
Geology/earth science.

University of Notre Dame
230 Main Building
Notre Dame, IN 46556
Phone: (574) 631-7505
Fax: (574) 631-8865
E-mail: admissio.1@nd.edu
http://www.nd.edu
Biochemistry, civil engineering, environmental engineering, environmental science, geology/earth science, mechanical engineering, physics.

University of Saint Francis
2701 Spring Street
Fort Wayne, IN 46808
Phone: (260) 434-3279
Fax: (260) 434-7590
E-mail: admis@sf.edu
http://www.sf.edu
Clinical laboratory science.

University of Southern Indiana
8600 University Boulevard
Evansville, IN 47712
Phone: (812) 464-1765
Fax: (812) 465-7154
E-mail: enroll@usi.edu
http://www.usi.edu
Biological/physical sciences, biophysics, engineering—general, geology/earth science, physics.

Valparaiso University
Office of Admissions, Kretzman Hall
1700 Chapel Drive
Valparaiso, IN 46383-4520
Phone: (219) 464-5011
Fax: (219) 464-6898
E-mail: undergrad.admissions@valpo.edu
http://www.valpo.edu
Atmospheric science, biochemistry, civil engineering, geography, environmental science, geology/earth science, mechanical engineering.

Wabash College
P.O. Box 352
301 West Walnut Avenue
Crawfordsville, IN 47933
Phone: (765) 361-6225
Fax: (765) 361-6437
E-mail: admissions@wabash.edu
http://www.wabash.edu
Physics.

IOWA

Briar Cliff University
Admissions Office
P.O. Box 100
Sioux City, IA 51104
Phone: (712) 279-5200
Fax: (712) 279-1632
E-mail: admissions@briarcliff.edu
http://www.briarcliff.edu
Biological/physical sciences, clinical laboratory science, environmental science.

Buena Vista University
610 West Fourth Street
Storm Lake, IA 50588
Phone: (712) 749-2235
Fax: (712) 749-1459
E-mail: admissions@bvu.edu
http://www.bvu.edu
Biological/physical sciences, physics.

Clarke College
1550 Clarke Drive
Dubuque, IA 52001
Phone: (563) 588-6316
Fax: (563) 588-6789
E-mail: admissions@clarke.edu
http://www.clarke.edu
Biological/physical sciences.

Coe College
1220 First Avenue NE
Cedar Rapids, IA 52402
Phone: (319) 399-8500
Fax: (319) 399-8816
E-mail: admission@coe.edu
http://www.coe.edu
Biochemistry, biological/physical
  sciences, environmental science,
  physics.

Cornell College
600 First Street West
Mount Vernon, IA 52314
Phone: (319) 895-4477
Fax: (319) 895-4451
E-mail: admission@cornellcollege.edu
http://www.cornellcollege.edu
Geology/earth science, physics.

Dordt College
498 Fourth Avenue Northeast
Sioux Center, IA 51250
Phone: (712) 722-6080
Fax: (712) 722-1987
E-mail: admissions@dordt.edu
http://www.dordt.edu
Agricultural and biological engineering,
  civil engineering, clinical laboratory
  science, engineering—general,
  mechanical engineering, physics.

Drake University
2507 University Avenue
Des Moines, IA 50311
Phone: (515) 271-3181
Fax: (515) 271-2831
E-mail: admission@drake.edu
http://www.choose.drake.edu
Biochemistry, environmental science,
  physics.

Graceland University
1 University Place
Lamoni, IA 50140
Phone: (641) 784-5196
Fax: (641) 784-5480
E-mail: admissions@graceland.edu
http://www.graceland.edu
Clinical laboratory science, physics.

Grand View College
1200 Grandview Avenue
Des Moines, IA 50316
Phone: (515) 263-2810
Fax: (515) 263-2974
E-mail: admiss@gvc.edu
http://www.gvc.edu
Applied mathematics.

Grinnell College
Office of Admission
1103 Park Street, Second floor
Grinnell, IA 50112
Phone: (641) 269-3600
Fax: (641) 269-4800
E-mail: askgrin@grinnell.edu
http://www.grinnell.edu
Biochemistry, biological/physical
  sciences, physics.

Hamilton Technical College
1011 East 53rd Street
Davenport, IA 52807
Phone: (563) 386-3570
Fax: NA
E-mail: admissions@
  hamiltontechcollege.com
http://www.hamiltontechcollege.com
Electrical engineering technology.

Iowa State University
100 Alumni Hall
Ames, IA 50011
Phone: (515) 294-5836
Fax: (515) 294-2592
E-mail: admissions@iastate.edu
http://www.iastate.edu
Agricultural and biological engineering,
  biochemistry, biophysics, chemical engineering, civil engineering,
  construction engineering, engineering—general, environmental science,
  geology/earth science, industrial engineering, materials engineering, materials science, mechanical engineering,
  physics, statistics.

Iowa Wesleyan College
601 North Main Street
Mt. Pleasant, IA 52641

Phone: (319) 385-6231
Fax: (319) 385-6296
E-mail: admitrwl@iwc.edu
http://www.iwc.edu
Engineering—general.

Loras College
1450 Alta Vista
Dubuque, IA 52004
Phone: (800) 245-6727
Fax: (563) 588-7119
E-mail: admissions@loras.edu
http://www.loras.edu
Biochemistry, clinical laboratory science,
  engineering physics, physics.

Morningside College
1501 Morningside Avenue
Sioux City, IA 51106
Phone: (712) 274-5111
Fax: (712) 274-5101
E-mail: mscadm@morningside.edu
http://www.morningside.edu
Engineering physics, physics.

Saint Ambrose University
518 West Locust Street
Davenport, IA 52803
Phone: (563) 444-6300
Fax: (563) 333-6297
E-mail: admit@sau.edu
http://www.sau.edu
Biological/physical sciences, engineering
  physics, industrial engineering.

Simpson College
701 North C Street
Indianola, IA 50125
Phone: (515) 961-1624
Fax: (515) 961-1870
E-mail: admiss@simpson.edu
http://www.simpson.edu
Biochemistry, environmental science,
  physics.

University of Iowa
107 Calvin Hall
Iowa City, IA 52242
Phone: (319) 335-3847
Fax: (319) 335-1535
E-mail: admissions@uiowa.edu
http://www.uiowa.edu
Applied mathematics, biochemistry,
  chemical engineering, civil engineering, clinical laboratory science,
  engineering—general, environmental
  science, geography, geology/earth science, industrial engineering, mechanical engineering, physics, statistics.

University of Northern Iowa
1227 West 27th Street
Cedar Falls, IA 50614
Phone: (319) 273-2281
Fax: (319) 273-2885
E-mail: admissions@uni.edu
http://www.uni.edu
Biochemistry, biological/physical sciences, biotechnology, electromechanical technology, engineering physics, environmental science, geography, geology/earth science, industrial technology, physics.

Wartburg College
100 Wartburg Boulevard, P.O. Box 1003
Waverly, IA 50677
Phone: (319) 352-8264
Fax: (319) 352-8579
E-mail: admission@wartburg.edu
http://www.wartburg.edu
Biochemistry, clinical laboratory science, physics.

William Penn University
201 Trueblood Avenue
Oskaloosa, IA 52577
Phone: (641) 673-1012
Fax: (641) 673-2113
E-mail: admissions@wmpenn.edu
http://www.wmpenn.edu
Biological/physical sciences, mechanical engineering.

KANSAS

Benedictine College
1020 North Second Street
Atchinson, KS 66002
Phone: (913) 360-7476
Fax: (913) 367-5462
E-mail: bcadiss@benedictine.edu
http://www.benedictine.edu
Biochemistry, physics.

Emporia State University
1200 Commercial Street
Emporia, KS 66801
Phone: (620) 341-5465
Fax: (620) 341-6599
E-mail: goto@emporia.edu
http://www.emporia.edu
Biochemistry, geology/earth science, physics.

Fort Hays State University
600 Park Street
Hays, KS 67601
Phone: (785) 628-5666
Fax: (785) 628-4187
E-mail: tigers@fhsu.edu
http://www.fhsu.edu
Biological/physical sciences, geology/earth science, physics.

Kansas State University
119 Anderson Hall
Manhattan, KS 66506
Phone: (785) 532-6250
Fax: (785) 532-6393
E-mail: kstate@ksu.edu
http://www.consider.k-state.edu
Agricultural and biological engineering, biochemistry, chemical engineering, civil engineering, engineering technology—general, geography, geology/earth science, industrial engineering, mechanical engineering, physics, statistics.

Kansas Wesleyan University
100 East Claflin Avenue
Salina, KS 67401
Phone: (785) 827-5541
Fax: (785) 827-0927
E-mail: admissions@kwu.edu
http://www.kwu.edu
Physics.

Pittsburg State University
1701 South Broadway
Pittsburg, KS 66762
Phone: (620) 235-4251
Fax: (620) 235-6003
E-mail: psuadmit@pittstate.edu
http://www.pittstate.edu
Biochemistry, clinical laboratory science, construction technology, electrical engineering technology, engineering technology—general, geography, mechanical engineering technology, physics.

Southwestern College
100 College Street
Winfield, KS 67156
Phone: (620) 229-6236
Fax: (620) 229-6344
E-mail: scadmit@sckans.edu
http://www.sckans.edu
Biochemistry, engineering physics, physics.

Tabor College
400 South Jefferson Street
Hillsboro, KS 67063
Phone: (620) 947-3121
Fax: (620) 947-6276
E-mail: admissions@tabor.edu
http://www.tabor.edu
Biochemistry, biological/physical sciences.

University of Kansas
Office of Admissions and Scholarships
1502 Iowa Street
Lawrence, KS 66045
Phone: (785) 864-3911
Fax: (785) 864-5017
E-mail: adm@ku.edu
http://www.ku.edu
Atmospheric science, chemical engineering, civil engineering, engineering physics, geography, geology/earth science, mechanical engineering, petroleum engineering, physics.

Washburn University
1700 Southwest College Avenue
Topeka, KS 66621
Phone: (785) 231-1030
Fax: (785) 296-7933
E-mail: zzdpadm@washburn.edu
http://www.washburn.edu
Electrical engineering technology, physics.

Wichita State University
1845 Fairmount Street
Wichita, KS 67260
Phone: (316) 978-3085
Fax: (316) 978-3174
E-mail: admissions@wichita.edu
http://www.wichita.edu
Electrical engineering technology, geology/earth science, industrial engineering, mechanical engineering, physics.

KENTUCKY

Alice Lloyd College
100 Purpose Road
Pippa Passes, KY 41844
Phone: (606) 368-6036
Fax: (606) 368-6215
E-mail: admissions@alc.edu
http://www.alc.edu
Biological/physical sciences.

Asbury College
1 Macklem Drive
Wilmore, KY 40390
Phone: (859) 858-3511
Fax: (859) 858-3921
E-mail: admissions@asbury.edu
http://www.asbury.edu
Biochemistry.

Bellarmine University
2001 Newburg Road
Louisville, KY 40205
Phone: (502) 452-8131
Fax: (502) 452-8002
E-mail: admissions@bellarmine.edu
http://www.bellarmine.edu
Clinical laboratory science.

Brescia University
717 Frederica Street
Owensboro, KY 42301
Phone: (270) 686-4241
Fax: (270) 686-4314
E-mail: admissions@brescia.edu
http://www.brescia.edu
Biological/physical sciences, clinical laboratory science.

Centre College
600 West Walnut Street
Danville, KY 40422
Phone: (859) 238-5350
Fax: (859) 238-5373
E-mail: admission@centre.edu
http://www.centre.edu
Biochemistry, chemical physics, physics.

Eastern Kentucky University
Coates, P.O. Box 2A
Richmond, KY 40475
Phone: (859) 622-2106
Fax: (606) 622-8024
E-mail: stephen.byn@eku.edu
http://www.eku.edu
Clinical laboratory science, geography, geology/earth science, physics, statistics.

Kentucky State University
400 East Main Street, Third floor
Frankfort, KY 40601
Phone: (502) 597-6813
Fax: (502) 597-5814
E-mail: jburrell@gwmail.kysu.edu
http://www.kysu.edu
Clinical laboratory science, electrical engineering technology.

Kentucky Wesleyan College
3000 Frederica Street
P.O. Box 1039
Owensboro, KY 42302
Phone: (270) 852-3120
Fax: (270) 852-3133
E-mail: admitme@kwc.edu
http://www.kwc.edu
Physics.

Morehead State University
Admissions Center
Morehead, KY 40351
Phone: (606) 783-2000
Fax: (606) 783-5038
E-mail: admissions@morehead-st.edu
http://www.moreheadstate.edu
Geography, geology/earth science, physics.

Murray State University
P.O. Box 9
Murray, KY 42071
Phone: (270) 762-3741
Fax: (270) 762-3780
E-mail: admissions@murraystate.edu
http://www.murraystate.edu
Civil engineering technology, electric engineering technology, electromechanical technology, engineering physics, geology/earth science, physics.

Northern Kentucky University
Administrative Center 400
Nunn Drive
Highland Heights, KY 41099
Phone: (859) 572-5220
Fax: (859) 572-6665
E-mail: admitnku@nku.edu
http://www.nku.edu
Electrical engineering technology, environmental science, geography, geology/earth science, industrial technology, physics.

Thomas More College
333 Thomas More Parkway
Crestview Hill, KY 40107
Phone: (859) 344-3332
Fax: (859) 344-3444
E-mail: admissions@thomasmore.edu
http://www.thomasmore.edu
Clinical laboratory science, physics.

Transylvania University
300 North Broadway
Lexington, KY 40508
Phone: (859) 233-8242
Fax: (859) 233-8797
E-mail: admissions@transy.edu
http://www.transy.edu
Physics.

University of Kentucky
100 Funkhuser Building
Lexington, KY 40506
Phone: (859) 257-2000
Fax: (859) 257-2000
E-mail: admission@uky.edu

http://www.uky.edu
Agricultural and biological engineering, civil engineering, clinical laboratory science, geology/earth science, materials engineering, mechanical engineering, mining and mineral engineering, physics.

University of Louisville
Admissions Office
Louisville, KY 40292
Phone: (502) 852-6531
Fax: (502) 852-4776
E-mail: admitme@louisville.edu
http://www.louisville.edu
Applied mathematics, civil engineering, engineering—general, geography, industrial engineering, mechanical engineering, physics.

University of the Cumberlands
6178 College Station Drive
Williamsburg, KY 40769
Phone: (606) 539-4241
Fax: (606) 539-4303
E-mail: admiss@ucumberlands.edu
http://www.ucumberlands.edu
Physics.

Western Kentucky University
Potter Hall 117
1 Big Red Way
Bowling Green, KY 42101
Phone: (270) 745-2551
Fax: (270) 745-6133
E-mail: admission@wku.edu
http://www.wku.edu
Biochemistry, civil engineering, civil engineering technology, clinical laboratory science, electric engineering technology, environmental engineering technology, geography, geology/earth science, industrial technology, mechanical engineering, physics.

LOUISIANA

Centenary College of Louisiana
P.O. Box 41188
Shreveport, LA 71134
Phone: (318) 869-5131
Fax: (318) 869-5005
E-mail: admissions@centenary.edu
http://www.centenary.edu
Biochemistry, biophysics, environmental science, geology/earth science, physics.

Grambling State University
P.O. Box 864
Grambling, LA 71245
Phone: (318) 274-6423
Fax: (318) 274-3292
E-mail: taylorn@gram.edu
http://www.gram.edu
Construction technology, electrical
    engineering technology, physics.

Grantham University
34641 Grantham College Road
Slidell, LA 70460
Phone: (985) 649-4191
Fax: (985) 649-4183
E-mail: admissions@grantham.edu
http://www.grantham.edu
Electrical engineering technology.

Louisiana State University—Baton Rouge
110 Thomas Boyd Hall
Baton Rouge, LA 70803
Phone: (225) 578-1175
Fax: (225) 578-4433
E-mail: admissions@lsu.edu
http://www.lsu.edu
Chemical engineering, civil engineering,
    environmental engineering, environ-
    mental science, geography, geology/
    earth science, mechanical engineering,
    petroleum engineering.

**Louisiana State University—
    Shreveport**
1 University Place
Shreveport, LA 71115
Phone: (318) 797-5061
Fax: (318) 797-5204
E-mail: admissions@pilot.lsus.edu
http://www.lsus.edu
Biochemistry, chemical engineering,
    civil engineering, environmental
    engineering, environmental science,
    geography, geology/earth science,
    mechanical engineering, petroleum
    engineering, physics.

Louisiana Tech University
P.O. Box 3178
Ruston, LA 71272
Phone: (318) 257-3036
Fax: (318) 257-2499
E-mail: bulldog@latech.edu
http://www.latech.edu
Chemical engineering, civil engineering,
    civil engineering technology,
    clinical laboratory science, electrical
    engineering technology, geography,
    geology/earth science, mechanical
    engineering, physics.

Nicholls State University
P.O. Box 2004
Thibodaux, LA 70310
Phone: (985) 448-4507
Fax: (985) 448-4929
E-mail: nicholls@nicholls.edu
http://www.nicholls.edu
Petroleum technology.

Northwestern State University
209 Roy Hall
Natchitoches, LA 71497
Phone: (318) 357-4078
Fax: (318) 357-4660
E-mail: admissions@nsula.edu
http://www.nsula.edu
Electrical engineering technology,
    industrial technology, physics.

Our Lady of Holy Cross College
4123 Woodland Drive
New Orleans, LA 70131
Phone: (504) 398-2175
Fax: (504) 391-2421
E-mail: kkopecky@olhcc.edu
http://www.olhcc.edu
Biological/physical sciences.

Southeastern Louisiana University
SLU 10752
Hammond, LA 70402
Phone: (985) 549-2066
Fax: (985) 549-5632
E-mail: admissions@selu.edu
http://www.selu.edu
Industrial technology, physics.

**Southern University and A and M
    College**
Office of Admissions
P.O. Box 9901
Baton Rouge, LA 70813
Phone: (225) 771-2430
Fax: (225) 771-2500
E-mail: admit@subr.edu
http://www.subr.edu
Civil engineering, mechanical engineering.

Southern University—Shreveport
3050 Martin Luther King Jr. Drive
Shreveport, LA 71107
Phone: (318) 674-3342
Fax: (318) 674-3338
E-mail: admissions@susla.edu
http://www.susla.edu
Electrical engineering technology.

Tulane University
6823 St. Charles Avenue

New Orleans, LA 70118
Phone: (504) 865-5731
Fax: (504) 862-8715
E-mail: undergrad.admission@tulane.edu
http://www.tulane.edu
Biochemistry, chemical engineering,
    environmental science, geology/earth
    science, physics.

University of Louisiana—Lafayette
P.O. Drawer 41210
Lafayette, LA 70504
Phone: (337) 482-6457
Fax: (337) 482-6195
E-mail: admissions@louisiana.edu
http://www.louisiana.edu
Chemical engineering, civil engineering,
    geology/earth science, industrial
    technology, mechanical engineering,
    petroleum engineering, physics.

University of Louisiana—Monroe
700 University Avenue
Monroe, LA 71209
Phone: (318) 342-5252
Fax: (318) 342-5274
E-mail: rehood@ulm.edu
http://www.ulm.edu
Atmospheric science, clinical laboratory
    science, construction technology,
    mechanical engineering.

University of New Orleans
Admissions Office
AD-103 Lakefront
New Orleans, LA 70148
Phone: (504) 280-6595
Fax: (504) 280-5522
E-mail: admissions@uno.edu
http://www.uno.edu
Civil engineering, clinical laboratory
    science, geography, geology/earth
    science, geophysics/seismology.

Xavier University of Louisiana
One Drexel Drive
Attn: Admissions Office
New Orleans, LA 70125
Phone: (504) 483-7388
Fax: (504) 485-7941
E-mail: apply@xula.edu
http://www.xula.edu
Biochemistry, physics, statistics.

MAINE

Bates College
23 Campus Avenue, Lindholm House
Lewiston, ME 04240

Phone: (207) 786-6000
Fax: (207) 786-6025
E-mail: admissions@bates.edu
http://www.bates.edu
Biochemistry, engineering—general,
    geology/earth science, physics.

Bowdoin College
5000 College Station, Bowdoin College
Brunswick, ME 04111
Phone: (207) 725-3100
Fax: (207) 725-3101
E-mail: admissions@bowdoin.edu
http://www.bowdoin.edu
Biochemistry, chemical physics, geology/
    earth science, geophysics/seismology,
    physics.

Colby College
4000 Mayflower Hill
Waterville, ME 04091
Phone: (207) 872-3168
Fax: (207) 872-3474
E-mail: admissions@colby.edu
http://www.colby.edu
Biochemistry, biological/physical sciences,
    environmental science, geology/earth
    science, physics.

University of Maine—Augusta
46 University Drive
Augusta, ME 04330
Phone: (207) 621-3185
Fax: (207) 621-3116
E-mail: umaar@maine.edu
http://www.uma.maine.edu
Agricultural and biological engineering,
    biochemistry, biological/physical sci-
    ences, chemical engineering, civil engi-
    neering, civil engineering technology,
    clinical laboratory science, electrical
    engineering technology engineering—
    general, engineering physics, mechani-
    cal engineering, physics, soil science.

University of Maine—Farmington
246 Main Street
Farmington, ME 04938
Phone: (207) 778-7050
Fax: (207) 778-8182
E-mail: umfadmit@maine.edu
http://www.umf.maine.edu
Agricultural and biological engineering,
    biological/physical sciences, chemical
    engineering, civil engineering, civil
    engineering technology, engineering—
    general, environmental science,
    geography, mechanical engineering,
    physics, soil science.

University of Maine—Fort Kent
23 University Drive
Fort Kent, ME 04743
Phone: (207) 834-7500
Fax: (207) 834-7609
E-mail: umfkadm@maine.edu
http://www.umfk.maine.edu
Agricultural and biological engineering,
    biological/physical sciences, chemical
    engineering, civil engineering,
    civil engineering technology,
    electrical engineering technology,
    engineering—general, environmental
    science, geology/earth science,
    mechanical engineering, physics, soil
    science.

University of Maine—Orono
5713 Chadbourne Hall
Orono, ME 04469
Phone: (207) 581-1561
Fax: (207) 581-1213
E-mail: um-admit@maine.edu
http://www.maine.edu
Agricultural and biological engineering,
    biological/physical sciences,
    chemical engineering, civil
    engineering, civil engineering
    technology, electrical engineering
    technology, engineering—general,
    geology/earth science, mechanical
    engineering, physics, soil science.

University of Maine—Presque Isle
Office of Admissions
181 Main Street
Presque Isle, ME 04769
Phone: (207) 768-9532
Fax: (207) 768-9777
E-mail: adventure@umpi.maine.edu
http://www.umpi.maine.edu
Geology/earth science, mechanical
    engineering, physics, soil science.

University of New England
11 Hills Beach Road
Biddeford, ME 04005
Phone: (207) 602-2297
Fax: (207) 602-5900
E-mail: admissions@une.edu
http://www.une.edu
Biochemistry, environmental science.

University of Southern Maine
37 College Avenue
Gorham, ME 04038
Phone: (207) 780-5670
Fax: (207) 780-5640
E-mail: usmadm@usm.maine.edu

http://usm.maine.edu
Biotechnology, electrical engineering
    technology, environmental engineering,
    environmental science, geography,
    geology/earth science, physics.

MARYLAND

Capitol College
11301 Springfield Road
Laurel, MD 20708
Phone: (800) 950-1992
Fax: (301) 953-1442
E-mail: admissions@capitol-college.edu
http://www.capitol-college.edu
Electrical engineering technology.

College of Notre Dame of Maryland
4170 North Charles Street
Baltimore, MD 21210
Phone: (410) 532-5330
Fax: (410) 532-6287
E-mail: admiss@ndm.edu
http://www.ndm.edu
Engineering—general, physics.

Columbia Union College
7600 Flower Avenue
Takoma Park, MD 20912
Phone: (301) 891-4080
Fax: (301) 891-4230
E-mail: enroll@cuc.edu
http://www.cuc.edu
Biochemistry.

Frostburg State University
101 Braddock Road
Frostburg, MD 21532
Phone: (301) 687-4201
Fax: (301) 687-7074
E-mail: fsuadmissions@frostburg.edu
http://www.frostburg.edu
Geography, physics.

Hood College
401 Rosemont Avenue
Frederick, MD 21701
Phone: (301) 696-3400
Fax: (301) 696-3819
E-mail: admissions@hood.edu
http://www.hood.edu
Biochemistry.

Johns Hopkins University
3400 North Charles Street
140 Garland Hall
Baltimore, MD 21218
Phone: (410) 516-8171
Fax: (410) 516-6025

E-mail: gotojhu@jhu.edu
http://www.jhu.edu
Applied mathematics, biophysics, chemical engineering, civil engineering, engineering—general, engineering mechanics, environmental engineering, geography, geology/earth science, materials engineering, materials science, mechanical engineering, physics.

Loyola College in Maryland
4501 North Charles Street
Baltimore, MD 21210
Phone: (800) 221-9107
Fax: (410) 617-2176
E-mail: admissions@loyola.edu
http://www.loyola.edu
Applied mathematics, engineering—general, physics.

McDaniel College
2 College Hill
Westminster, MD 21157
Phone: (410) 857-2230
Fax: (410) 857-2757
E-mail: admissions@mcdaniel.edu
http://www.mcdaniel.edu
Biochemistry, environmental science, physics.

Morgan State University
1700 East Cold Spring Lane
Baltimore, MD 21251
Phone: (800) 332-6674
Fax: (410) 319-3684
E-mail: tjenness@moac.morgan.edu
http://www.morgan.edu
Civil engineering, engineering physics, industrial engineering, physics.

Mount St. Mary's University
16300 Old Emmitsburg Road
Emmitsburg, MD 21727
Phone: (301) 447-5214
Fax: (301) 447-5860
E-mail: admissions@msmary.edu
http://www.msmary.edu
Biochemistry.

St. Mary's College of Maryland
Admissions Office
18952 East Fisher Road
St. Mary's City, MD 20686
Phone: (240) 895-5000
Fax: (240) 895-5001
E-mail: admissions@smcm.edu
http://www.smcm.edu
Biochemistry, biological/physical sciences, physics.

Salisbury University
Admissions Office
1101 Camden Avenue
Salisbury, MD 21801
Phone: (410) 543-6161
Fax: (410) 546-6016
E-mail: admissions@salisbury.edu
http://www.salisbury.edu
Clinical laboratory science, geography, geology/earth science, physics.

Towson University
8000 York Road
Towson, MD 21252
Phone: (410) 704-2113
Fax: (410) 704-3030
E-mail: admissions@towson.edu
http://www.towson.edu
Biological/physical sciences, geography, geology/earth science, physics.

United States Naval Academy
117 Decatur Road
Annapolis, MD 21402
Phone: (410) 293-4361
Fax: (410) 295-1815
E-mail: webmail@usna.com
http://www.usna.edu
Engineering—general, mechanical engineering, physics.

University of Maryland—Baltimore County
1000 Hilltop Circle
Baltimore, MD 21250
Phone: (410) 455-2291
Fax: (410) 455-1094
E-mail: admissions@umbc.edu
http://www.umbc.edu
Chemical engineering, civil engineering, engineering—general, environmental science, geography, mechanical engineering, physics, statistics.

University of Maryland—College Park
Mitchell Building
College Park, MD 20742
Phone: (301) 314-8385
Fax: (301) 314-9693
E-mail: um-admit@uga.umd.edu
http://www.umd.edu
Agricultural and biological engineering, biochemistry, chemical engineering, civil engineering, engineering—general, geography, geology/earth science, materials engineering, mechanical engineering, physics.

University of Maryland—Eastern Shore
Office of Admissions
Backbone Road
Princess Anne, MD 21853
Phone: (410) 651-6410
Fax: (410) 651-7922
E-mail: ccmills@mail.umes.edu
http://www.umes.edu
Clinical laboratory science, electrical engineering technology, engineering—general, engineering technology—general.

Villa Julia College
1525 Greenspring Valley Road
Stevenson, MD 21153
Phone: (410) 486-7001
Fax: (410) 602-6600
E-mail: admissions@vjc.edu
http://www.vjc.edu
Biological/physical sciences.

Washington College
300 Washington Avenue
Chestertown, MD 21620
Phone: (410) 778-7700
Fax: (410) 778-7287
E-mail: adm.off@washcoll.edu
http://www.washcoll.edu
Biological/physical sciences, physics.

MASSACHUSETTS

American International College
1000 State Street
Springfield, MA 01109
Phone: (413) 205-3201
Fax: (413) 205-3051
E-mail: inquiry@www.aic.edu
http://www.aic.edu
Biochemistry, biological/physical sciences.

Amherst College
Campus Box 2231, P.O. Box 5000
Amherst, MA 01002
Phone: (413) 542-2328
Fax: (413) 542-2040
E-mail: admission@amherst.edu
http://www.amherst.edu
Geology/earth science, physics.

Anna Marie College
50 Sunset Lane, Box O
Paxton, MA 01612
Phone: (508) 849-3260
Fax: (508) 849-3362
E-mail: admission@annamaria.edu
http://www.annamaria.edu
Biological/physical sciences.

Assumption College
500 Salisbury Street
Worcester, MA 01609
Phone: (508) 767-7285
Fax: (509) 799-4412
E-mail: admiss@assumption.edu
http://www.assumption.edu
Environmental science.

Bay Path College
588 Longmeadow Street
Longmeadow, MA 01106
Phone: (413) 565-1331
Fax: (413) 565-1105
E-mail: admiss@baypath.edu
http://www.baypath.edu
Biotechnology.

Boston College
140 Commonwealth Avenue,
Devlin Hall 208
Chestnut Hill, MA 02467
Phone: (617) 552-3100
Fax: (617) 552-0798
E-mail: ugadmis@bc.edu
http://www.bc.edu
Biochemistry, geology/earth science,
   geophysics/seismology, physics.

Boston University
121 Bay State Road
Boston, MA 02215
Phone: (617) 353-2300
Fax: (617) 353-9695
E-mail: admissions@bu.edu
http://www.bu.edu
Engineering—general, environmental
   science, geography, geology/earth
   science, geophysics/seismology,
   mechanical engineering, physics.

Brandeis University
415 South Street, MS003
Waltham, MA 02454
Phone: (781) 736-3500
Fax: (781) 736-3536
E-mail: admissions@brandeis.edu
http://www.brandeis.edu
Biochemistry, physics.

Bridgewater State College
Gates House
Bridgewater, MA 02325
Phone: (508) 531-1237
Fax: (508) 531-1746
E-mail: admission@bridgew.edu
http://www.bridgew.edu
Biochemistry, geography, geology/earth
   science, physics.

Clark University
950 Main Street
Worcester, MA 01610
Phone: (508) 793-7431
Fax: (508) 793-8821
E-mail: admissions@clarku.edu
http://www.clarku.edu
Biochemistry, environmental science,
   geography, physics.

College of the Holy Cross
Admissions Office
1 College Street
Worcester, MA 01610
Phone: (508) 793-2443
Fax: (508) 793-3888
E-mail: admissions@holycross.edu
http://www.holycross.edu
Physics.

Eastern Nazarene College
23 East Elm Avenue
Quincy, MA 02170
Phone: (617) 745-3000
Fax: (617) 745-3490
E-mail: admissions@enc.edu
http://www.enc.edu
Biochemistry, biological/physical
   sciences, chemical engineering,
   engineering—general, engineering
   physics, physics.

Elms College
291 Springfield Street
Chicopee, MA 01013
Phone: (413) 592-3189
Fax: (413) 594-2781
E-mail: admissions@elms.edu
http://www.elms.edu
Biological/physical sciences.

Emmanuel College
400 the Fenway
Boston, MA 02115
Phone: (617) 735-9715
Fax: (617) 735-9801
E-mail: enroll@emmanuel.edu
http://www.emmanuel.edu
Biochemistry.

Fitchburg State College
160 Pearl Street
Fitchburg, MA 01420
Phone: (978) 665-3144
Fax: (978) 665-4540
E-mail: admissions@fsc.edu
http://www.fsc.edu
Construction technology, electrical
   engineering technology, geography.

Franklin W. Olin College of Engineering
Olin Way
Needham, MA 02492
Phone: (781) 292-2222
Fax: (781) 292-2210
E-mail: info@olin.edu
http://www.olin.edu
Engineering—general, mechanical
   engineering.

Hampshire College
Admissions Office
893 West Street
Amherst, MA 01002
Phone: (413) 559-5471
Fax: (413) 559-5631
E-mail: admissions@hampshire.edu
http://www.hampshire.edu
Applied mathematics, biological/physical
   sciences, geology/earth science,
   physics.

Harvard College
Byerly Hall
8 Garden Street
Cambridge, MA 02138
Phone: (617) 495-1551
Fax: (617) 495-8821
E-mail: college@fas.harvard.edu
http://www.fas.harvard.edu
Applied mathematics, atomic/molecular
   physics, biochemistry, biophysics,
   environmental science, geology/earth
   science, geophysics/seismology,
   physics, statistics.

Massachusetts Institute of Technology
MIT Admissions Office Room 3108
77 Massachusetts Avenue
Cambridge, MA 02139
Phone: (617) 253-4791
Fax: (617) 258-8304
E-mail: admissions@mit.edu
http://www.mit.edu
Chemical engineering, civil engineering,
   environmental engineering, geology/
   earth science, geophysics/seismology,
   materials engineering, mechanical
   engineering, nuclear engineering,
   physics.

Massachusetts Maritime Academy
101 Academy Drive
Buzzards Bay, MA 02532
Phone: (800) 544-3411
Fax: (508) 830-5077
E-mail: admissions@maritime.edu
http://www.maritime.edu
Engineering—general.

Merrimack College
Office of Admission
Austin Hall
North Andover, MA 01845
Phone: (978) 837-5100
Fax: (978) 837-5133
E-mail: admission@merrimack.edu
http://www.merrimack.edu
Biochemistry, civil engineering,
engineering—general, environmental
science, physics.

Mount Holyoke College
Office of Admissions
Newhall Center
South Hadley, MA 01075
Phone: (413) 538-2023
Fax: (413) 538-2409
E-mail: admission@mtholyoke.edu
http://www.mtholyoke.edu
Biochemistry, geography, geology/earth
science, physics, statistics.

Northeastern University
260 Huntington Avenue,
150 Richards Hall
Boston, MA 02115
Phone: (617) 373-2200
Fax: (617) 373-8780
E-mail: admissions@neu.edu
http://www.neu.edu
Biochemistry, chemical engineering, civil
engineering, clinical laboratory science, electrical engineering technology,
engineering—general, geology/earth
science, mechanical engineering,
mechanical engineering technology,
physics.

Regis College
235 Wellesley Street
Weston, MA 02493
Phone: (781) 768-7100
Fax: (781) 768-7071
E-mail: admission@regiscollege.edu
http://www.regiscollege.edu
Biochemistry.

Salem State College
352 Lafayette Street
Salem, MA 01970
Phone: (978) 542-6200
Fax: (978) 542-6893
E-mail: admissions@salemstate.edu
http://www.salemstate.edu
Biochemistry, clinical laboratory science,
geography, geology/earth science.

Simmons College
300 The Fenway

Boston, MA 02115
Phone: (617) 521-2051
Fax: (617) 521-3190
E-mail: ugadm@simmons.edu
http://www.simmons.edu
Biochemistry, environmental science,
physics.

Simon's Rock College of Bard
84 Alford Road
Great Barrington, MA 01230
Phone: (413) 528-7312
Fax: (413) 528-7334
E-mail: admit@simons-rock.edu
http://www.simons-rock.edu
Engineering—general, physics, statistics.

Smith College
17 College Lane
Northampton, MA 01063
Phone: (413) 585-2500
Fax: (413) 585-2527
E-mail: admission@smith.edu
http://www.smith.edu
Biochemistry, chemical engineering,
civil engineering, engineering—
general, engineering mechanics,
environmental engineering,
geology/earth science, mechanical
engineering, physics.

Springfield College
263 Alden Street
Springfield, MA 01109
Phone: (413) 748-3136
Fax: (413) 748-3694
E-mail: admissions@spfldcol.edu
http://www.spfldcol.edu
Biological/physical sciences, clinical
laboratory science.

Stonehill College
320 Washington Street
Easton, MA 02357
Phone: (508) 565-1373
Fax: (508) 565-1545
E-mail: admissions@stonehill.edu
http://www.stonehill.edu
Biochemistry.

Suffolk University
8 Ashburton Place
Boston, MA 02108
Phone: (617) 573-8460
Fax: (617) 742-4291
E-mail: admission@suffolk.edu
http://www.suffolk.edu
Biochemistry, biophysics, environmental
engineering, environmental science,
physics.

Tufts University
Bendetson Hall
Medford, MA 02156
Phone: (617) 627-3170
Fax: (617) 627-3860
E-mail: inquiry@ase.tufts.edu
http://www.tufts.edu
Applied mathematics, chemical
engineering, civil engineering,
engineering—general, engineering
physics, environmental engineering,
geology/earth science, mechanical
engineering, physics.

University of Massachusetts—Amherst
University Admissions Center
Amherst, MA 01003
Phone: (413) 545-0222
Fax: (413) 545-4312
E-mail: mail@admissions.umass.edu
http://www.umass.edu
Biological/physical sciences, chemical
engineering, civil engineering, clinical
laboratory science, environmental
engineering, environmental science,
geography, geology/earth science,
industrial engineering, mechanical
engineering, physics.

University of Massachusetts—Boston
100 Morrissey Boulevard
Boston, MA 02125
Phone: (617) 287-6000
Fax: (617) 287-5999
E-mail: undergrad@umb.edu
http://www.umb.edu
Applied mathematics, biochemistry,
clinical laboratory science,
engineering physics, environmental
science, geography, physics.

**University of Massachusetts—
Dartmouth**
285 Old Westport Road
North Dartmouth, MA 02747
Phone: (508) 999-9605
Fax: (508) 999-8755
E-mail: admissions@umassd.edu
http://www.umassd.edu
Biological/physical sciences, civil engi-
neering, clinical laboratory science,
electrical engineering technology,
mechanical engineering, physics.

University of Massachusetts—Lowell
Office of Undergrad Admissions
883 Broadway Street, Room 110
Lowell, MA 01854
Phone: (978) 934-3931

Fax: (978) 934-3086
E-mail: admissions@uml.edu
http://www.uml.edu
Applied mathematics, chemical engineering, civil engineering, civil engineering technology, clinical laboratory science, electrical engineering technology, environmental science, industrial technology, mechanical engineering, physics.

Wellesley College
Board of Admission
106 Central Street
Wellesley, MA 02481
Phone: (781) 283-2270
Fax: (781) 283-3678
E-mail: admission@wellesley.edu
http://www.wellesley.edu
Biochemistry, biological/physical sciences, geology/earth science, physics.

Wentworth Institute of Technology
555 Huntington Avenue
Boston, MA 02115
Phone: (800) 556-0610
Fax: (617) 989-4591
E-mail: admissions@wit.edu
http://www.wit.edu
Civil engineering technology, electrical engineering technology, mechanical engineering, mechanical engineering technology.

Western New England College
Admissions Office
1215 Wilbraham Road
Springfield, MA 01119
Phone: (413) 782-1321
Fax: (413) 782-1777
E-mail: ugradmis@wnec.edu
http://www.wnec.edu
Industrial engineering, mechanical engineering.

Wheaton College
Office of Admission
Norton, MA 02766
Phone: (508) 286-8251
Fax: (508) 286-8271
E-mail: admission@wheatoncollege.edu
http://www.wheatoncollege.edu
Biochemistry, biological/physical sciences, physics.

Williams College
33 Stetson Court
Williamstown, MA 01267
Phone: (413) 597-2211
Fax: (413) 597-4052

E-mail: admission@william.edu
http://www.william.edu
Geology/earth science, physics.

Worcester Polytechnic Institute
100 Institute Road
Worcester, MA 01609
Phone: (508) 831-5286
Fax: (508) 831-5875
E-mail: admissions@wpi.edu
http://www.wpi.edu
Applied mathematics, biochemistry, biological/physical sciences, biotechnology, chemical engineering, civil engineering, engineering physics, environmental engineering, industrial engineering, mechanical engineering, physics.

Worcester State College
Department of Admissions
486 Chandler Street
Worcester, MA 01602
Phone: (508) 929-8040
Fax: (508) 929-8183
E-mail: admissions@worcester.edu
http://www.worcester.edu
Biological/physical sciences, biotechnology, geography.

MICHIGAN

Albion College
611 East Porter Street
Albion, MI 49224
Phone: (517) 629-0321
Fax: (517) 629-0569
E-mail: admissions@albion.edu
http://www.albion.edu
Biochemistry, biological/physical sciences, environmental science, geology/earth science, physics.

Alma College
614 West Superior Street
Alma, MI 48801
Phone: (989) 463-7139
Fax: (989) 463-7057
E-mail: admissions@alma.edu
http://www.alma.edu
Biochemistry, biological/physical sciences, physics.

Andrews University
Office of Admissions
Berien Springs, MI 49104
Phone: (800) 253-2874
Fax: (616) 471-3228
E-mail: enroll@andrews.edu

http://www.andrews.edu
Biochemistry, biological/physical sciences, biophysics, clinical laboratory science, electrical engineering technology, engineering—general, environmental science, industrial engineering, mechanical engineering, physics.

Baker College of Flint
1050 West Bristol Road
Flint, MI 48507-5508
Phone: (800) 964-4299
Fax: (810) 766-4293
E-mail: adm-fl@baker.edu
http://www.baker.edu
Electrical engineering technology, mechanical engineering.

Baker College of Muskegon
1903 Marquette Avenue
Muskegon, MI 49442
Phone: (231) 777-5200
Fax: (231) 777-5201
E-mail: Kathy.jacobson@baker.edu
http://www.baker.edu
Electrical engineering technology.

Baker College of Owosso
1020 South Washington Street
Owosso, MI 48867
Phone: (989) 729-3350
Fax: (989) 723-3355
E-mail: mike.konopacke.@baker.edu
http://www.baker.edu
Electrical engineering technology.

Baker College of Port Huron
3403 Lapeer Road
Port Huron, MI 48060
Phone: (810) 985-7000
Fax: (810) 985-7066
E-mail: Kenny_d@porthuron.baker.edu
http://www.baker.edu
Electrical engineering technology.

Calvin College
3201 Burton Street Southeast
Grand Rapids, MI 49546
Phone: (616) 526-6106
Fax: (616) 526-6777
E-mail: admissions@calvin.edu
http://www.calvin.edu
Biochemistry, biological/physical sciences, biotechnology, chemical engineering, civil engineering, engineering—general, environmental science, geography, geology/earth science, mechanical engineering, physics.

Central Michigan University
205 Warriner Hall
Mount Pleasant, MI 48859
Phone: (989) 774-3076
Fax: (989) 774-7267
E-mail: cmuadmit@cmich.edu
http://www.cmich.edu
Clinical laboratory science, construction technology, electrical engineering technology, environmental science, geography, geology/earth science, mechanical engineering, meteorology, physics, statistics.

Concordia University
4090 Geddes Road
Ann Arbor, MI 48105
Phone: (888) 734-4237
Fax: NA
E-mail: admissions@cuaa.edu
http://www.cuaa.edu
Biological/physical sciences, physics.

Eastern Michigan University
400 Pierce Hall
Ypsilanti, MI 48197
Phone: (734) 487-3060
Fax: (734) 487-1484
E-mail: admissions@emich.edu
http://www.emich.edu
Biochemistry, biological/physical sciences, clinical laboratory science, electrical engineering technology, geography, geology/earth science, geophysics/seismology, industrial technology, physics, statistics.

Ferris State University
1201 South State Street
Center for Student Services
Big Rapids, MI 49307
Phone: (231) 591-2100
Fax: (231) 591-3944
E-mail: admissions@ferris.edu
http://www.ferris.edu
Applied mathematics, biochemistry, biotechnology, clinical laboratory science, electrical engineering technology, environmental engineering technology, heavy equipment maintenance, statistics, surveying technology, welding technology.

Grand Valley State University
1 Campus Drive
Allendale, MI 49401
Phone: (616) 331-5000
Fax: (616) 331-2000
E-mail: go@gvsu@gvsu.edu
http://www.gvsu.edu
Biochemistry, biological/physical sciences, clinical laboratory science, geography, geology/earth science, mechanical engineering, physics, statistics.

Hope College
69 East Tenth Street, P.O. Box 9000
Holland, MI 49422
Phone: (616) 395-7850
Fax: (616) 395-7130
E-mail: admissions@hope.edu
http://www.hope.edu
Biochemistry, biological/physical sciences, engineering—general, engineering physics, environmental science, geology/earth science, geophysics/seismology, physics.

Kalamazoo College
1200 Academy Street
Kalamazoo, MI 49006
Phone: (616) 337-7166
Fax: (616) 337-7390
E-mail: admission@kzoo.edu
http://www.kzoo.edu
Physics.

Kettering University
1700 West Third Avenue
Flint, MI 48504
Phone: (810) 762-7865
Fax: (810) 762-9837
E-mail: admissions@kettering.edu
http://www.kettering.edu
Applied mathematics, biochemistry, engineering—general, industrial engineering, mechanical engineering, statistics.

Lake Superior State University
650 West Easterday Avenue
Sault Ste. Marie, MI 49783
Phone: (906) 635-2231
Fax: (906) 635-6669
E-mail: admissions@lssu.edu
http://www.lssu.edu
Clinical laboratory science, environmental engineering technology, geology/earth science, mechanical engineering.

Lawrence Technological University
21000 West Ten Mile Road
Southfield, MI 48075
Phone: (248) 204-3160
Fax: (248) 204-3188
E-mail: admissions@ltu.edu
http://www.ltu.edu

Biochemistry, civil engineering, engineering technology—general, industrial technology, mechanical engineering, physics.

Madonna University
36600 Schoolcraft Road
Livonia, MI 48150
Phone: (734) 432-5339
Fax: (734) 432-5393
E-mail: muinfo@smtp.munet.edu
http://www.munet.edu
Biochemistry, biological/physical sciences, chemical engineering, clinical laboratory science.

Michigan State University
250 Administration Building
East Lansing, MI 48824-1046
Phone: (517) 355-8332
Fax: (517) 353-1647
E-mail: adis@msu.edu
http://www.msu.edu
Agricultural and biological engineering, applied mathematics, biochemistry, biological/physical sciences, chemical physics, civil engineering, clinical laboratory science, engineering—general, environmental science, geography, geology/earth science, geophysics/seismology, materials science, mechanical engineering, physics, soil science, statistics.

Michigan Technological University
1400 Townsend Drive
Houghton, MI 49931
Phone: (906) 487-2335
Fax: (906) 487-2125
E-mail: mtu4u@mtu.edu
http://www.mtu.edu
Chemical engineering, clinical laboratory science, electrical engineering technology, engineering—general, environmental science, geological engineering, geology/earth science, geophysics/seismology, materials engineering, mechanical engineering, physics, surveying engineering.

Northern Michigan University
1401 Presque Isle Avenue
304 Cohodas
Marquette, MI 49855
Phone: (906) 227-2650
Fax: (906) 227-1747
E-mail: admiss@nmu.edu
http://www.nmu.edu

Applied mathematics, biochemistry, biological/physical sciences, clinical laboratory science, construction technology, electrical engineering technology, engineering mechanics, geography, hydrology/water resources science, industrial engineering, mechanical engineering, physics.

Oakland University
Office of Admissions
101 North Foundation Hall
Rochester, MI 48309
Phone: (248) 370-3360
Fax: (248) 370-4462
E-mail: ouinfo@oakland.edu
http://www.oakland.edu
Biochemistry, biophysics, engineering physics, mechanical engineering, physics, statistics.

Olivet College
320 South Main Street
Olivet, MI 49076
Phone: (269) 749-7635
Fax: (269) 749-3821
E-mail: admissions@olivetcollege.edu
http://www.olivetcollege.edu
Biological/physical sciences, environmental science, geography.

Saginaw Valley State University
7400 Bay Road
University Center, MI 48710
Phone: (989) 964-4200
Fax: (989) 790-0180
E-mail: admissions@svsu.edu
http://www.svsu.edu
Biochemistry, chemical physics, mechanical engineering, physics.

Spring Arbor University
106 East Main Street
Spring Arbor, MI 49283
Phone: (517) 750-6458
Fax: (517) 750-6458
E-mail: admissions@admin.arbor.edu
http://www.arbor.edu
Biochemistry, engineering technology—general.

University of Detroit—Mercy
P.O. Box 19900
Detroit, MI 48219
Phone: (313) 993-1245
Fax: (313) 993-3326
E-mail: admissions@udmercy.edu
http://www.udmercy.edu

Applied mathematics, biochemistry, civil engineering, engineering—general, mechanical engineering.

University of Michigan—Ann Arbor
1220 Student Activities Building
Ann Arbor, MI 48109
Phone: (734) 764-7433
Fax: (734) 936-0740
E-mail: ugadmiss@umich.edu
http://www.umich.edu
Applied mathematics, atmospheric science, biochemistry, biophysics, chemical engineering, civil engineering, engineering—general, geography, geology/earth science, industrial engineering, materials engineering, materials science, mechanical engineering, metallurgical engineering, nuclear engineering, physics, statistics.

University of Michigan—Dearborn
4901 Evergreen Road
Dearborn, MI 48128
Phone: (313) 593-5100
Fax: (313) 436-9167
E-mail: admissions@umd.umich.edu
http://www.umd.umich.edu
Atmospheric science, biochemistry, biophysics, chemical engineering, civil engineering, clinical laboratory science, engineering—general, engineering physics, geography, geology/earth science, industrial engineering, materials engineering, mechanical engineering, metallurgical engineering, nuclear engineering, physics, statistics.

University of Michigan—Flint
303 East Kearsley Street
245 UPAV
Flint, MI 48502
Phone: (810) 762-3300
Fax: (810) 762-3272
E-mail: admissions@umflint.edu
http://www.umflint.edu
Atmospheric science, biochemistry, biophysics, chemical engineering, civil engineering, clinical laboratory science, clinical laboratory science, engineering—general, engineering physics, environmental science, geography, geological engineering, geology/earth science, industrial engineering, materials engineering, mechanical engineering, metallurgical engineering, nuclear engineering, physics, statistics.

Wayne State University
656 West Kirby Street
Detroit, MI 48202
Phone: (313) 577-3577
Fax: (313) 577-7536
E-mail: admissions@wayne.edu
http://www.wayne.edu
Chemical engineering, civil engineering, electrical engineering technology, electromechanical technology, environmental science, geography, geological engineering, industrial engineering, materials engineering, materials science, mechanical engineering, physics.

Western Michigan University
1903 West Michigan Avenue
Kalamazoo, MI 49008
Phone: (269) 387-2000
Fax: (269) 387-2096
E-mail: ask-wmu@umich.edu
http://www.wmich.edu
Applied mathematics, biochemistry, chemical engineering, civil engineering, construction technology, engineering—general, environmental science, geography, geology/earth science, geophysics/seismology, hydrology/water resources science, industrial engineering, industrial technology, mechanical engineering, physics, statistics, structural engineering.

MINNESOTA

Augsburg College
2211 Riverside Avenue South
Minneapolis, MN 55454
Phone: (612) 330-1001
Fax: (612) 330-1590
E-mail: admissions@augsburg.edu
http://www.augsburg.edu
Clinical laboratory science, engineering—general, physics.

Bemidji State University
1500 Birchmont Drive NE, Deputy Hall
Bemidji, MN 56601
Phone: (218) 755-2040
Fax: (218) 755-2074
E-mail: admissions@bemidjistate.edu
http://www.bemidjistate.edu
Clinical laboratory science, engineering physics, geography, geology/earth science, physics.

Carleton College
100 South College Street
Northfield, MN 55057

Phone: (507) 646-4190
Fax: (507) 646-4526
E-mail: admission@acs.carleton.edu
http://www.carleton.edu
Geology/earth science, physics.

College of St. Benedict
P.O. Box 7155
Collegeville, MN 56321
Phone: (320) 363-2196
Fax: (320) 363-2750
E-mail: admission@csbsju.edu
http://www.csbsju.edu
Biochemistry, biological/physical
    sciences, physics.

College of St. Catherine
Office of Admission, #F-02
2004 Randolph Avenue
St. Paul, MN 55105
Phone: (800) 656-5283
Fax: NA
E-mail: admissions@stkate.edu
http://www.stkate.edu
Biochemistry, clinical laboratory science,
    physics.

College of St. Scholastica
1200 Kenwood Avenue
 Duluth, MN 55811
Phone: (218) 723-6000
Fax: (218) 723-5991
E-mail: admissions@css.edu
http://www.css.edu
Biochemistry.

Concordia College—Moorhead
901 Eighth Street South
Moorhead, MN 56562
Phone: (218) 299-3004
Fax: (218) 299-4720
E-mail: admissions@cord.edu
http://www.goconcordia.com
Applied mathematics, clinical laboratory
    science, physics.

Concordia University—St. Paul
275 Syndicate Street North
Saint Paul, MN 55104
Phone: (651) 641-8230
Fax: (651) 603-6320
E-mail: admiss@csp.edu
http://www.csp.edu
Biological/physical sciences,
    environmental science.

Gustavus Adolphus College
800 West College Avenue
Saint Peter, MN 56082

Phone: (507) 933-7676
Fax: (507) 933-7474
E-mail: admission@gustavus.edu
http://www.gustavus.edu
Biochemistry, geography, geology/earth
    science, physics.

Hamline University
1536 Hewitt Avenue, MS-C 1930
Saint Paul, MN 55104
Phone: (651) 523-2207
Fax: (651) 523-2458
E-mail: CLA-admis@hamline.edu
http://www.hamline.edu
Biochemistry, physics.

Macalester College
1600 Grand Avenue
St. Paul, MN 55105
Phone: (651) 696-6357
Fax: (651) 696-6724
E-mail: admissions@macalester.edu
http://www.macalester.edu
Geology/earth science, physics.

Metropolitan State University
1501 Hennepin Avenue
Minneapolis, MN 55403
Phone: (612) 659-6000
Fax: NA
E-mail: At Web site
http://www. metrostate.edu
Applied mathematics.

Minnesota State University—Mankato
Mankato, TC 122
Mankato, MN 56001
Phone: (507) 389-1822
Fax: (507) 389-1511   ·
E-mail: admissions@mnsu.edu
http://www.mnsu.edu
Biochemistry, biological/physical sciences,
    biotechnology, civil engineering,
    clinical laboratory science, electrical
    engineering technology, engineering—
    general, geography, mechanical
    engineering, mechanical engineering
    technology, physics.

Minnesota State University—Moorhead
Owens Hall
Moorhead, MN 56563
Phone: (218) 477-2161
Fax: (218) 477-4374
E-mail: dragon@mnstate.edu
http://www.mnstate.edu
Clinical laboratory science, construction
    technology, industrial technology,
    physics.

Saint Cloud State University
720 South Fourth Avenue
Saint Cloud, MN 56301
Phone: (320) 308-2244
Fax: (320) 308-2243
E-mail: scsu4u@stcloudstate.edu
http://www.stcloudstate.edu
Atmospheric science, electrical
    engineering technology,
    biotechnology, chemical engineering,
    civil engineering, clinical laboratory
    science, engineering—general,
    engineering technology—general,
    geography, geology/earth science,
    hydrology/water resources science,
    industrial engineering, mechanical
    engineering, mechanical engineering
    technology, physics, statistics,
    surveying technology.

St. John's University
P.O. Box 7155
Collegeville, MN 56321
Phone: (320) 363-2196
Fax: (320) 363-2750
E-mail: admission@csbsju.edu
http://www.csbsju.edu
Biochemistry, biological/physical sciences,
    environmental science, physics.

Saint Mary's University of Minnesota
700 Terrace Heights #2
Winona, MN 55987
Phone: (507) 457-1600
Fax: (507) 457-1722
E-mail: admissions@smumn.edu
http://www.smumn.edu
Atomic/molecular physics, biophysics,
    clinical laboratory science,
    engineering physics, physics.

University of Minnesota—Crookston
170 Owen Hall
2900 University Avenue
Crookston, MN 56716
Phone: (218) 281-8569
Fax: (218) 281-8575
E-mail: info@umcrookston.edu
http://www.umcrookston.edu
Soil science.

University of Minnesota—Duluth
23 Solon Campus Center
1117 University Drive
Duluth, MN 55812
Phone: (218) 726-7171
Fax: (218) 726-7040
E-mail: undadmis@d.umn.edu
http://www.d.umn.edu

Biochemistry, geography, geology/earth science, mechanical engineering, physics, statistics.

University of Minnesota—Morris
600 East Fourth Street
Morris, MN 56267
Phone: (320) 589-6035
Fax: (320) 589-1673
E-mail: admissions@morris.umn.edu
http://www.morris.umn.edu
Geology/earth science, physics, statistics.

University of Minnesota—Twin Cities
240 Williamson Hall
231 Pillsbury Drive SE
Minneapolis, MN 55455
Phone: (612) 625-2008
Fax: (612) 626-1693
E-mail: admissions@tc.umn.edu
http://www1.umn.edu/twincities
Agricultural and biological engineering, biochemistry, biological/physical sciences, chemical engineering, civil engineering, geography, geological engineering, geology/earth science, geophysics/seismology, materials engineering, materials science, mechanical engineering, physics, soil science, statistics.

University of Saint Thomas
2115 Summit Avenue, Mail #32-F1
St. Paul, MN 55105
Phone: (651) 962-6150
Fax: (651) 962-6160
E-mail: admissions@stthomas.edu
http://www.stthomas.edu
Biochemistry, geography, physics.

Winona State University
Office of Admissions
P.O. Box 5838
Winona. MN 55987
Phone: (507) 457-5100
Fax: (507) 457-5620
E-mail: admissions@winona.edu
http://www.winona.edu
Applied mathematics, biological/physical sciences, chemical engineering, engineering—general, engineering mechanics, materials science, mechanical engineering, physics.

MISSISSIPPI

Alcorn State University
1000 ASU Drive #300
Alcorn State, MS 39096

Phone: (601) 877-6147
Fax: (601) 977-6347
E-mail: ebarnes@alcorn.edu
http://www.alcorn.edu
Clinical laboratory science, industrial technology.

Delta State University
Highway 8 West
Cleveland, MS 38733
Phone: (662) 846-4018
Fax: (662) 846-4683
E-mail: dheslep@deltastate.edu
http://www.deltastate.edu
Biological/physical sciences.

Jackson State University
1400 Lynch Street
P.O. Box 17330
Jackson, MS 39217
Phone: (601) 979-2100
Fax: (601) 979-3445
E-mail: schatman@ccaix,jsums.edu
http://www.jsums.edu
Atmospheric science, civil engineering, industrial technology, physics.

Mississippi College
P.O. Box 4026
Clinton, MS 39058
Phone: (601) 925-3800
Fax: (601) 925-3950
E-mail: enrollment-services@mc.edu
http://www.mc.edu
Atomic/molecular physics, biochemistry, engineering physics, physics.

Mississippi State University
P.O. Box 6305
Mississippi State, MS 39762
Phone: (662) 325-2224
Fax: (662) 325-7360
E-mail: admit@admissions.msstate.edu
http://www.msstate.edu
Agricultural and biological engineering, biochemistry, biological/physical sciences, chemical engineering, civil engineering, clinical laboratory science, industrial engineering, mechanical engineering, physics.

Mississippi Valley State University
14000 Highway 82 West
Itta Bena, MS 38941
Phone: (662) 254-3344
Fax: (662) 254-3655
E-mail: nbtaylor@mvsu.edu
http://www.mvsu.edu
Engineering—general.

Tougaloo College
500 West Country Line Road
Tougaloo, MS 39174
Phone: (888) 424-2566
Fax: (601) 977-6185
E-mail: slaterJa@mail.tougaloo.edu
http://www.tougaloo.edu
Physics.

University of Mississippi
145 Martindale
University, MS 38677
Phone: (662) 915-7226
Fax: (662) 915-5869
E-mail: admissions@olemiss.edu
http://www.olemiss.edu
Chemical engineering, civil engineering, clinical laboratory science, engineering—general, mechanical engineering, physics.

University of Southern Mississippi
P.O. Box 5166
Southern Station
Hattiesburg, MS 38406
Phone: (601) 266-5000
Fax: (601) 266-5148
E-mail: admissions@usm.edu
http://www.usm.edu
Clinical laboratory science, electrical engineering technology, geography, physics.

MISSOURI

Avila University
11901 Wornall Road
Kansas City, MO 64145
Phone: (816) 942-8400
Fax: (816) 942-3362
E-mail: admissions@mail.avila.edu
http://www.avila.edu
Biological/physical sciences.

Central Methodist College
411 CMC Square
Fayette, MO 65248
Phone: (660) 248-6251
Fax: (660) 248-1872
E-mail: admissions@cmc.edu
http://www.cmc.edu
Applied mathematics, physics.

Central Missouri State University
Office of Admissions
WDE 1401
Warrensburg, MO 64093
Phone: (660) 543-4290
Fax: (660) 543-8517

E-mail: admit@cmsuvmb.cmsu.edu
http://www.cmsu.edu
Construction technology, electrical
  engineering technology, geography,
  industrial technology, physics.

DeVry University—Kansas City
11224 Homes Street
Kansas City, MO 64131
Phone: (816) 941-2810
Fax: (816) 941-0896
E-mail: ssmeed@kc.devry.edu
http://www.devry.edu
Electrical engineering technology.

Fontbonne University
6800 Wydown Boulevard
St. Louis, MO 63105
Phone: (314) 889-1478
Fax: (314) 889-1451
E-mail: fcadmis@fontbonne.edu
http://www.fontbonne.edu
Biotechnology.

Lincoln University
Admissions Office, P.O. Box 29
Jefferson City, MO 65102
Phone: (573) 681-5599
Fax: (573) 681-5889
E-mail: enroll@lincolnu.edu
http://www.lincolnu.edu
Civil engineering technology, clinical
  laboratory science, mechanical
  engineering technology, physics.

Lindenwood University
309 South Kingshighway
St. Charles, MO 63301
Phone: (314) 949-4949
Fax: (314) 949-4989
E-mail: admissions@lindenwood.edu
http://www.lindenwood.edu
Clinical laboratory science,
  environmental science.

Maryville University of Saint Louis
13550 Conway Road
St. Louis, MO 63141
Phone: (314) 529-9350
Fax: (314) 529-9927
E-mail: admissions@maryville.edu
http://www.maryville.edu
Applied mathematics, biological/physical
  sciences, clinical laboratory science,
  environmental science.

Missouri Southern State University
3950 East Newman Road
Joplin, MO 64801

Phone: (417) 625-9378
Fax: (417) 659-4429
E-mail: admissions@mssu.edu
http://www.mssu.edu
Biochemistry, biotechnology, industrial
  engineering, physics.

Missouri State University
901 South National Avenue
Springfield, MO 65897
Phone: (800) 492-7900
Fax: (417) 836-6334
E-mail: info@missouristate.edu
http://www.missouristate.edu
Clinical laboratory science, construction
  technology, electrical engineering
  technology, engineering physics,
  geography, physics.

Missouri Technical School
1167 Corporate Lake Drive
St. Louis, MO 63132
Phone: (800) 960-TECH
Fax: NA
E-mail: At Web site
http://www.motech.edu
Electrical engineering technology.

Missouri Valley College
500 East College Street
Marshall, MO 65340
Phone: (660) 831-4114
Fax: (660) 831-4233
E-mail: admissions@moval.edu
http://www.moval.edu
Biological/physical sciences.

Missouri Western State University
4525 Downs Drive
Saint Joseph, MO 64507
Phone: (816) 271-4266
Fax: (816) 271-5833
E-mail: admissn@mwsc.edu
http://www.mwsc.edu
Biochemistry, construction technology,
  electrical engineering technology.

Northwest Missouri State University
800 University Drive
Maryville, MO 64468
Phone: (800) 633-1175
Fax: (660) 562-1121
E-mail: admissions@mall.nwmissouri.edu
http://www.nwmissouri.edu
Clinical laboratory science, physics,
  statistics.

Park University
8700 River Park Drive, Campus Box 1

Parkville, MO 64152
Phone: (816) 741-2000
Fax: (816) 741-4462
E-mail: admissions@mail.park.edu
http://www.park.edu
Geography.

Rockhurst University
1100 Rockhurst Road
Kansas City, MO 64110
Phone: (816) 501-4100
Fax: (816) 501-4241
E-mail: admission@rockhurst.edu
http://www.rockhurst.edu
Biochemistry, clinical laboratory science,
  physics.

St. Louis University
221 North Grand Boulevard
Saint Louis, MO 63103
Phone: (314) 977-2500
Fax: (314) 977-7136
E-mail: admitme@slu.edu
http://www.slu.edu
Applied mathematics, atmospheric
  science, biochemistry, environmental
  science, geophysics/seismology,
  mechanical engineering, physics.

Southeast Missouri State University
One University Plaza
Mail Stop 3550
Cape Girardeau, MO 63701
Phone: (573) 651-2590
Fax: (573) 651-5936
E-mail: admissions@semo.edu
http://www.semo.edu
Clinical laboratory science, clinical
  laboratory science, construction
  technology, electrical engineering
  technology, engineering physics,
  geography, industrial technology,
  physics.

Southwest Baptist University
160 University Avenue
Bolivar, MO 65613
Phone: (417) 328-1810
Fax: (417) 328-1808
E-mail: admitme@sbuniv.edu
http://www.sbuniv.edu
Clinical laboratory science.

Truman State University
McClain Hall 205
100 East Normal Street
Kirksville, MO 63501
Phone: (660) 785-4114
Fax: (660) 785-7456

E-mail: admissions@truman.edu
http://www.admissions.truman.edu
Applied mathematics, physics.

University of Missouri—Columbia
230 Jesse Hall
Columbia, MO 65211
Phone: (573) 882-7786
Fax: (573) 882-7887
E-mail: admissions@missouri.edu
http://www.missouri.edu
Agricultural and biological engineering, atmospheric science, biochemistry, chemical engineering, civil engineering, geography, industrial engineering, mechanical engineering, physics, soil science, statistics.

University of Missouri—Kansas City
5100 Rockhill Road, 101 AC
Kansas City, MO 64114
Phone: (816) 235-1111
Fax: (816) 235-5544
E-mail: admit@umkc.edu
http://www.umkc.edu
Civil engineering, clinical laboratory science, geography, mechanical engineering, physics, statistics.

University of Missouri—Rolla
106 Parker Hall
Rolla, MO 65409
Phone: (573) 341-4165
Fax: (573) 341-4082
E-mail: admissions@umr.edu
http://www.umr.edu
Applied mathematics, biochemistry, biophysics, chemical engineering, civil engineering, environmental engineering, geological engineering, geology/earth science, geophysics/ seismology, mechanical engineering, metallurgical engineering, mining and mineral engineering, nuclear engineering, petroleum engineering, physics, statistics.

University of Missouri—Saint Louis
351 Millennium Student Center
9001 Natural Bridge Road
Saint Louis, MO 63121
Phone: (314) 516-8675
Fax: (314) 516-5310
E-mail: admissions@umsl.edu
http://www.umsl.edu
Applied mathematics, civil engineering, mechanical engineering, physics.

Washington University in St. Louis
Campus Box 1089
One Brookings Drive
St. Louis, MO 63130
Phone: (314) 935-6000
Fax: (314) 935-4290
E-mail: admissions@wustl.edu
http://www.wustl.edu
Applied mathematics, biochemistry, biological/physical sciences, biophysics, chemical engineering, civil engineering, civil engineering technology, engineering—general, geology/earth science, mechanical engineering, physics, statistics.

William Jewell College
500 College Hill
Liberty, MO 64068
Phone: (816) 781-7700
Fax: (816) 415-5040
E-mail: admission@william.jewell.edu
http://www.jewell.edu
Biochemistry, clinical laboratory science, physics.

MONTANA

Carroll College
1601 North Benton Avenue
Helena, MT 59625
Phone: (406) 447-4384
Fax: (406) 447-4533
E-mail: enroll@carroll.edu
http://www.carroll.edu
Biological/physical sciences, civil engineering, physics.

Montana State University—Billings
1500 University Drive
Billings, MT 59101
Phone: (406) 657-2158
Fax: (406) 657-2051
E-mail: keverett@msubillings.edu
http://www.msubillings.edu
Physics.

Montana State University—Bozeman
New Student Services
P.O. Box 172190
Bozeman, MT 59717
Phone: (406) 994-2452
Fax: (406) 994-1923
E-mail: admissions@montana.edu
http://www.montana.edu
Biochemistry, biotechnology, chemical engineering, civil engineering, construction technology, mechanical engineering, physics.

Montana State University—Northern
P.O. Box 7751
Havre, MT 59501
Phone: (406) 265-3704
Fax: (406) 265-3777
E-mail: msuadmit@msun.edu
http://www.msun.edu
Electrical engineering technology.

Montana Tech of the University of Montana
1300 West Park Street
Butte, MT 59701
Phone: (406) 496-4178
Fax: (406) 496-4710
E-mail: admissions@mtech.edu
http://www.mtech.edu
Applied mathematics, biological/ physical sciences, civil engineering, engineering—general, environmental engineering, geological engineering, geology/earth science, geophysics/ seismology, materials engineering, materials science, mechanical engineering, metallurgical engineering, mining and mineral engineering, petroleum engineering, statistics, welding technology.

Rocky Mountain College
1511 Poly Drive
Billings, MT 59102
Phone: (406) 657-1026
Fax: (406) 657-1189
E-mail: admissions@rocky.edu
http://www.rocky.edu
Environmental science, geology/earth science.

University of Montana—Missoula
103 Lodge Building
Missoula, MT 59812
Phone: (406) 243-6266
Fax: (406) 243-5711
E-mail: admiss@selway.umt.edu
http://www.umt.edu
Clinical laboratory science, electrical engineering technology, geography, geology/earth science, physics.

University of Montana—Western
710 South Atlantic
Dillon, MT 59725
Phone: (406) 683-7331
Fax: (406) 683-7493
E-mail: admissions@umwestern.edu
http://www.umwestern.edu
Applied mathematics.

NEBRASKA

Bellevue University
1000 Galvin Road South
Bellevue, NE 68005
Phone: (402) 293-2000
Fax: (402) 293-3730
E-mail: info@bellevue.edu
http://www.bellevue.edu
Environmental science.

Concordia University
800 North Columbia Avenue
Seward, NE 68434
Phone: (800) 535-5494
Fax: (402) 643-4073
E-mail: admiss@cune.edu
http://www.cune.edu
Geography.

Creighton University
2500 California Plaza
Omaha, NE 68178
Phone: (402) 280-2703
Fax: (402) 280-2685
E-mail: admissions@creighton.edu
http://www.creighton.edu
Applied mathematics, atmospheric
    science, environmental science.

Hastings College
710 North Turner Avenue
Hastings, NE 68901
Phone: (402) 461-7403
Fax: (402) 461-7490
E-mail: mmolliconi@hastings.edu
http://www.hastings.edu
Physics.

Nebraska Wesleyan University
Admissions Office
5000 Saint Paul Avenue
Lincoln, NE 68504
Phone: (402) 465-2218
Fax: (402) 465-2177
E-mail: admissions@nebrwesleyan.edu
http://www.nebrwesleyan.edu
Biochemistry, physics.

Union College
3800 South 48th Street
Lincoln, NE 68506
Phone: (402) 486-2504
Fax: (402) 486-2566
E-mail: ucenroll@ucollege.edu
http://www.ucollege.edu
Biochemistry, physics.

University of Nebraska—Kearney
905 West 25th Street

Kearney, NE 68849
Phone: (800) 532-7639
Fax: (308) 865-7639
E-mail: admissionsug@unk.edu
http://www.unk.edu
Geography, physics, statistics.

University of Nebraska—Lincoln
1410 Q Street
Lincoln, NE 68588
Phone: (402) 472-2023
Fax: (402) 472-0670
E-mail: nuhusker@unl.edu
http://www.unl.edu
Agricultural and biological engineering,
    atmospheric science, biochemistry,
    chemical engineering, civil
    engineering, construction technology,
    electrical engineering technology,
    geography, geology/earth science,
    hydrology/water resources science,
    industrial engineering, industrial
    technology, mechanical engineering,
    physics, soil science.

University of Nebraska—Omaha
Office of Admissions
6001 Dodge Street, EAB Room 103
Omaha, NE 68182
Phone: (402) 554-2393
Fax: (402) 554-3472
E-mail: unoadm@unomaha.edu
http://www.unomaha.edu
Biotechnology, chemical engineering,
    civil engineering, construction
    technology, engineering physics,
    geography, geology/earth science,
    industrial technology, physics.

Wayne State College
1111 Main Street
Wayne, NE 68787
Phone: (402) 375-7234
Fax: (402) 375-7204
E-mail: admit1@wsc.edu
http://www.wsc.edu
Engineering technology—general,
    geography.

NEVADA

Great Basin College
1500 College Parkway
Elko, NV 89801
Phone: (775) 738-8493
Fax: NA
E-mail: advisor@gwmail.gbcnv.edu
http://www.gbcnv.edu
Surveying engineering.

Sierra Nevada College
999 Tahoe Boulevard
Incline Village, NV 89451
Phone: (775) 831-1314
Fax: (702) 831-1347
E-mail: admissions@sierranevada.edu
http://www.sierranevada.edu
Environmental science.

University of Nevada—Las Vegas
4505 Maryland Parkway
P.O. Box 451021
Las Vegas, NV 89154
Phone: (702) 774-8658
Fax: (702) 774-8008
E-mail: undergraduate.recruitment@
    ccmail.nevada.edu
http://www.unlv.edu
Applied mathematics, civil engineering,
    clinical laboratory science, geological
    engineering, geology/earth science,
    mechanical engineering, physics.

University of Nevada—Reno
1664 North Virginia Street
Reno, NV 89557
Phone: (775) 784-4700
Fax: (775) 784-4283
E-mail: asknevada@unr.edu
http://www.unr.edu
Biochemistry, biotechnology, chemical
    engineering, civil engineering,
    construction technology, engineering
    physics, environmental engineering,
    environmental science, geography,
    geological engineering, geology/earth
    science, geophysics/seismology,
    hydrology/water resources science,
    materials engineering, mechanical
    engineering, metallurgical engineering,
    mining and mineral engineering,
    physics, water resource engineering.

NEW HAMPSHIRE

Daniel Webster College
20 University Drive
Nashua, NH 03063
Phone: (603) 577-6600
Fax: (603) 577-6001
E-mail: admissions@dwc.edu
http://www.dwc.edu
Mechanical engineering.

Dartmouth College
6016 McNutt Hall
Hanover, NH 03755
Phone: (603) 646-2875
Fax: (603) 646-1216

E-mail: admissions.office@dartmouth.edu
http://www.dartmouth.edu
Biochemistry, engineering physics,
  geography, geology/earth science,
  physics.

Franklin Pierce College
Admissions Office
P.O. Box 60
20 College Road
Rindge, NH 03461
Phone: (603) 899-4050
Fax: (603) 889-4394
E-mail: admissions@fpc.edu
http://www.fpc.edu
Environmental science.

Keene State College
229 Main Street
Keene, NH 03435
Phone: (603) 358-2276
Fax: (603) 358-2767
E-mail: admissions@keene.edu
http://www.keene.edu
Applied mathematics, biological/physical
  sciences, chemical physics, electrical
  engineering technology, environmental
  science, geography, geology/earth
  science.

New England College
26 Bridge Street
Henniker, NH 03242
Phone: (603) 428-2223
Fax: (603) 428-3155
E-mail: admission@nec.edu
http://www.nec.edu
Civil engineering, environmental science.

Plymouth State University
17 High Street, MSC 52
Plymouth, NH 03264
Phone: (603) 535-2237
Fax: (603) 535-2714
E-mail: plymouthadmit@plymouth.edu
http://www.plymouth.edu
Atmospheric science, biotechnology,
  geography.

Saint Anselm College
100 Saint Anselm Drive
Manchester, NH 03102
Phone: (603) 641-7500
Fax: (603) 641-7550
E-mail: admission@anselm.edu
http://www.anselm.edu
Biochemistry, biological/physical
  sciences, engineering—general,
  engineering physics, environmental
  science, physics.

**University of New Hampshire—
  Durham**
4 Garrison Avenue
Durham, NH 03024
Phone: (603) 862-1360
Fax: (603) 862-0077
E-mail: admissions@unh.edu
http://www.unh.edu
Biochemistry, civil engineering, clinical
  laboratory science, engineering—
  general, environmental engineering,
  environmental science, geography,
  geology/earth science, materials
  engineering, materials science,
  mechanical engineering, natural
  resource economics, physics.

**University of New Hampshire—
  Manchester**
400 Commercial Street
Manchester, NH 03101
Phone: (603) 629-4150
Fax: (603) 629-2745
E-mail: unhm.admissions@unh.edu
http://www.unh.edu/unhm
Biochemistry, civil engineering,
  clinical laboratory science,
  electrical engineering technology,
  engineering—general, environmental
  engineering, environmental science,
  geography, geology/earth science,
  materials engineering, materials
  science, mechanical engineering,
  physics.

NEW JERSEY

Bloomfield College
1 Park Place
Bloomfield, NJ 07003
Phone: (973) 748-9000
Fax: (973) 748-0916
E-mail: admission@bloomfield.edu
http://www.bloomfield.edu
Clinical laboratory science.

The College of New Jersey
P.O. Box 7718
Ewing, NJ 08628
Phone: (609) 771-2131
Fax: (609) 637-5174
E-mail: admiss@vm.tcj.edu
http://www.tcnj.edu
Engineering—general, mechanical
  engineering, physics, statistics.

College of Saint Elizabeth
Admissions Office
2 Convent Road

Morristown, NJ 07960
Phone: (973) 290-4700
Fax: (973) 290-4710
E-mail: apply@cse.edu
http://www.cse.edu
Biochemistry, clinical laboratory science.

Drew University
Office of College Admissions
Madison, NJ 07940
Phone: (973) 408-3739
Fax: (973) 408-3068
E-mail: cadm@drew.edu
http://www.drew.edu
Biochemistry, physics.

**Fairleigh Dickinson University—
  College at Florham**
285 Madison Avenue
Madison, NJ 07940
Phone: (800) 338-8803
Fax: (973) 443-8088
E-mail: globaleducation@fdu.edu
http://www.fdu.edu
Clinical laboratory science, construction
  technology.

**Fairleigh Dickinson University—
  Metropolitan Campus**
1000 River Road
Teaneck, NJ 07666
Phone: (201) 692-2553
Fax: (201) 692-7319
E-mail: globaleducation@fdu.edu
http://www.fdu.edu
Biochemistry, biological/physical
  sciences, civil engineering technology,
  clinical laboratory science, electrical
  engineering technology, mechanical
  engineering technology.

Georgian Court University
900 Lakewood Avenue
Lakewood, NJ 08701
Phone: (732) 364-2200
Fax: (736) 987-2200
E-mail: admissions@georgian.edu
http://www.georgian.edu
Biochemistry, physics.

Kean University
P.O. Box 411
Union, NJ 07083
Phone: (908) 737-7100
Fax: (908) 737-7105
E-mail: admitme@kean.edu
http://www.kean.edu
Clinical laboratory science, geology/earth
  science.

Monmouth University
Admission
400 Cedar Avenue West
Long Branch, NJ 07764
Phone: (732) 571-3456
Fax: (732) 263-5166
E-mail: admission@monmouth.edu
http://www.monmouth.edu
Clinical laboratory science.

Montclair State University
1 Normal Avenue
Montclair, NJ 07043
Phone: (973) 655-4444
Fax: (973) 655-7700
E-mail: undergraduate.admissions@
montclair.edu
http://www.montclair.edu
Biochemistry, geography, geology/earth
science, physics.

New Jersey City University
2039 Kennedy Boulevard
Jersey City, NJ 07305
Phone: (888) 441-6528
Fax: (201) 200-2044
E-mail: admissions@njcu.edu
http://www.njcu.edu
Geology/earth science, physics.

New Jersey Institute of Technology
University Heights
Newark, NJ 07102
Phone: (973) 596-3300
Fax: (973) 596-3461
E-mail: admissions@njit.edu
http://www.njit.edu
Applied mathematics, chemical
engineering, civil engineering,
engineering technology—general,
environmental engineering,
environmental science, geological
engineering, industrial engineering,
mechanical engineering, physics.

Princeton University
P.O. Box 430, Admission Office
Princeton, NJ 08544
Phone: (609) 258-3060
Fax: (609) 258-6743
E-mail: uaoffice@princeton.edu
http://www.princeton.edu
Chemical engineering, civil engineering,
geology/earth science, mechanical
engineering, physics.

Ramapo College of New Jersey
505 Ramapo Valley Road
Mahwah, NJ 07430

Phone: (201) 684-7300
Fax: (201) 684-7964
E-mail: admissions@ramapo.edu
http://www.ramapo.edu
Biochemistry, biological/physical
sciences, clinical laboratory science,
environmental science, physics.

Richard Stockton College of New Jersey
Jim Leeds Road, P.O. Box 195
Pomona, NJ 08240
Phone: (609) 652-4261
Fax: (609) 748-5541
E-mail: admissions@stockton.edu
http://www.stockton.edu
Biochemistry, geology/earth science,
physics.

Rider University
2083 Lawrenceville Road
Lawrenceville, NJ 08648
Phone: (609) 896-5042
Fax: (609) 895-6645
E-mail: admissions@rider.edu
http://www.rider.edu
Biochemistry, environmental science,
physics.

Rowan University
201 Mullica Hill Road
Glassboro, NJ 08028
Phone: (856) 256-4200
Fax: (856) 256-4430
E-mail: admissions@rowan.edu
http://www.rowan.edu
Biochemistry, chemical engineering, civil
engineering, engineering—general,
geography, materials engineering,
mechanical engineering, physics.

**Rutgers, The State University of New
Jersey—Camden**
406 Penn Street
Camden, NJ 08102
Phone: (856) 225-6498
Fax: (856) 225-6498
E-mail: admissions@ugadm.rutgers.edu
http://www.rutgers.edu
Biological/physical sciences, chemical
engineering, civil engineering,
mechanical engineering, physics.

**Rutgers, The State University of New
Jersey—Newark**
249 University Avenue
Newark, NJ 07102
Phone: (973) 353-5205
Fax: (973) 353-1440
E-mail: newarkadmission@ugadm.
rutgers.edu

http://www.rutgers.edu
Applied mathematics, atmospheric
science, chemical engineering, civil
engineering, clinical laboratory
science, geology/earth science,
mechanical engineering, physics.

**Rutgers, The State University of New
Jersey—New Brunswick/Piscataway**
65 Davidson Road
Piscataway, NJ 08854
Phone: (732) 932-4636
Fax: (732) 445-0237
E-mail: admissions@ugadm.rutgers.edu
http://www.rutgers.edu
Atmospheric science, biochemistry,
chemical engineering, civil
engineering, environmental
engineering, geography, geology/earth
science, mechanical engineering,
physics, statistics.

Saint Peter's College
2641 Kennedy Boulevard
Jersey City, NJ 07306
Phone: (201) 915-9213
Fax: (201) 432-5860
E-mail: admissions@spc.edu
http://www.spc.edu
Biochemistry, biological/physical sciences,
clinical laboratory science, physics.

Seton Hall University
Enrollment Services
400 South Orange Avenue
South Orange, NJ 07079
Phone: (973) 761-9332
Fax: (973) 275-2040
E-mail: thehall@shu.edu
http://www.shu.edu
Biochemistry, physics.

Stevens Institute of Technology
Castle Point on Hudson
Hoboken, NJ 07030
Phone: (201) 216-5194
Fax: (201) 216-8348
E-mail: admissions@stevens.edu
http://www.stevens.edu
Applied mathematics, biochemistry,
chemical engineering, civil
engineering, engineering—general,
environmental engineering, materials
engineering, materials science,
mechanical engineering, physics.

Thomas Edison State College
101 West State Street
Trenton, NJ 08608

Phone: (609) 984-1150
Fax: (609) 984-8447
E-mail: info@tesc.edu
http://www.tesc.edu
Civil engineering technology, clinical laboratory science, construction technology, environmental science, mechanical engineering technology, nuclear engineering technology, physics, radiation protection/health physics technology, surveying technology.

William Paterson University of New Jersey
Admissions Hall
300 Pompton Road
Wayne. NJ 07470
Phone: (973) 720-2125
Fax: (973) 720-2910
E-mail: admissions@wpunj.edu
http://www.wpunj.edu
Biotechnology, environmental science, geography.

NEW MEXICO

Eastern New Mexico University
Station #7, ENMU
Portales, NM 88130
Phone: (505) 562-2178
Fax: (505) 562-2118
E-mail: admissions@enmu.edu
http://www.enmu.edu
Clinical laboratory science, engineering technology—general, geology/earth science, physics.

New Mexico Highlands University
NMHU Office of Student Recruitment
P.O. Box 900
Las Vegas, NM 87701
Phone: (505) 454-3593
Fax: (505) 454-3511
E-mail: recruitment@nmhu.edu
http://www.nmhu.edu
Engineering—general, geology/earth science, physics.

New Mexico Institute of Mining and Technology
Campus Station
801 Leroy Place
Socorro, NM 87801
Phone: (505) 835-5424
Fax: (505) 835-5989
E-mail: admission@admin.nmt.edu
http://www.nmt.edu
Applied mathematics, atmospheric physics/dynamics, biochemistry, chemical engineering, civil engineering, engineering—general, environmental engineering, geology/earth science, geophysics/seismology, materials engineering, mechanical engineering, metallurgical engineering, mining and mineral engineering, petroleum engineering, physics.

New Mexico State University
P.O. Box 30001, MSC 3A
Las Cruces, NM 88003
Phone: (505) 646-3121
Fax: (505) 646-6330
E-mail: admissions@nmsu.edu
http://www.nmsu.edu
Biochemistry, electrical engineering technology, chemical engineering, engineering physics, engineering technology—general, geography, geology/earth science, industrial engineering, mechanical engineering, physics, soil science, surveying technology.

University of New Mexico
Office of Admissions
Student Services Center 150
Albuquerque, NM 87131
Phone: (505) 277-2446
Fax: (505) 277-6686
E-mail: apply@unm.edu
http://www.unm.edu
Biochemistry, chemical engineering, civil engineering, environmental science, geography, geology/earth science, mechanical engineering, nuclear engineering, physics, statistics.

NEW YORK

Adelphi University
Levermore Hall 114
1 South Avenue
Garden City, NY 11530
Phone: (516) 877-3050
Fax: (516) 877-3039
E-mail: admissions@adelphi.edu
http://www.adelphi.edu
Biochemistry, physics.

Alfred University
Alumni Hall
1 Saxon Drive
Alfred, NY 14802
Phone: (607) 871-2115
Fax: (607) 871-2198
E-mail: admwww@alfred.edu
http://www.alfred.edu
Biological/physical sciences, geology/earth science, materials engineering, mechanical engineering, physics.

Bard College
Office of Admissions
Annandale-on-Hudson, NY 12504
Phone: (845) 758-7472
Fax: (845) 758-5208
E-mail: admissions@bard.edu
http://www.bard.edu
Biochemistry, physics.

Barnard College
3090 Broadway
New York, NY 10027
Phone: (212) 854-2014
Fax: (212) 854-6220
E-mail: admissions@barnard.edu
http://www.barnard.edu
Applied mathematics, biochemistry, biophysics, chemical physics, engineering physics, environmental science, geography, physics, statistics.

Canisius College
2001 Main Street
Buffalo, NY 14208
Phone: (716) 888-2200
Fax: (716) 888-3230
E-mail: inquiry@canisius.edu
http://www.canisius.edu
Biochemistry, clinical laboratory science, environmental science, physics, structural engineering.

City University of New York—Baruch College
Undergraduate Admissions
1 Bernard Baruch Way
P.O. Box H-0720
New York, NY 10010
Phone: (646) 312-1400
Fax: (646) 312-1361
E-mail: admissions@baruch.cuny.edu
http://www.baruch.cuny.edu
Biological/physical sciences, statistics.

City University of New York— Brooklyn College
3000 Bedford Avenue
Brooklyn, NY 11210
Phone: (718) 951-5001
Fax: (718) 951-4506
E-mail: adminqry@brooklyn,cuny.edu
http://www.brooklyn.cuny.edu
Biological/physical sciences, geology/earth science, physics.

City University of New York—City College
Convent Avenue at 138th Street
New York, NY 10031
Phone: (212) 650-6977
Fax: (212) 650-6417
E-mail: admissions@ccny.cuny.edu
http://www.ccny.cuny.edu
Biochemistry, chemical engineering, civil engineering, geology/earth science, mechanical engineering, physics.

City University of New York—College of Staten Island
2800 Victory Boulevard, Bldg 2A, Room 104
Staten Island, NY 10314
Phone: (718) 982-2010
Fax: (718) 982-2500
E-mail: recruitment@postbox.csi.cuny.edu
http://www.csi.cuny.edu
Biochemistry, engineering—general, physics.

City University of New York—Hunter College
695 Park Avenue
New York, NY 10021
Phone: (212) 772-4490
Fax: (212) 650-3336
E-mail: admissions@hunter.cuny.edu
http://www.hunter.cuny.edu
Biochemistry, clinical laboratory science, geography, physics, statistics.

City University of New York—Lehman College
350 Bedford Park Boulevard West
Bronx, NY 10468
Phone: (718) 960-8000
Fax: (718) 960-8712
E-mail: wilkes@alpha.lehman.cuny.edu
http://www.lehman.cuny.edu
Biochemistry, biological/physical sciences, geography, geology/earth science, physics.

City University of New York—Queens College
65-30 Kissena Boulevard
Flushing, NY 11367
Phone: (718) 997-5600
Fax: (718) 997-5617
E-mail: admissions@qc.edu
http://www.qc.edu
Biochemistry, environmental science, geology/earth science, physics.

City University of New York—York College
94-20 Guy R. Brewer Boulevard
Jamaica, NY 11451
Phone: (718) 262-2165
Fax: (718) 262-2601
E-mail: admissions@york.cuny.edu
http://www.york.cuny.edu
Biotechnology, geology/earth science, physics.

Clarkson University
P.O. Box 5605
Potsdam, NY 13699
Phone: (315) 268-6479
Fax: (315) 268-7647
E-mail: admission@clarkson.edu
http://www.clarkson.edu
Applied mathematics, chemical engineering, civil engineering, engineering—general, environmental engineering, mechanical engineering, physics, statistics.

Colgate University
13 Oak Drive
Hamilton, NY 13346
Phone: (315) 228-7401
Fax: (315) 228-7544
E-mail: admission@mail.colgate.edu
http://www.colgate.edu
Biochemistry, biological/physical sciences, geography, geology/earth science, physics.

College of Mount St. Vincent
6301 Riverdale Avenue
Riverdale, NY 10471
Phone: (718) 405-3267
Fax: (718) 549-7945
E-mail: admissns@mountsaintvincent.edu
http://www.mountsaintvincent.edu
Biochemistry, physics.

The College of New Rochelle
29 Castle Place
New Rochelle, NY 10805
Phone: (914) 654-5452
Fax: (914) 654-5464
E-mail: admission@cnr.edu
http://www.cnr.edu
Biological/physical sciences.

College of Saint Rose
432 Western Avenue
Albany, NY 12203
Phone: (518) 454-5150
Fax: (518) 454-2013
E-mail: admit@mail.strose.edu
http://www.strose.edu
Biochemistry, clinical laboratory science.

Columbia University—Columbia College
212 Hamilton Hall MC 2807
1130 Amsterdam Avenue
New York, NY 10027
Phone: (212) 854-2521
Fax: (212) 894-1209
E-mail: At Web site
http://www.college.columbia.edu
Applied mathematics, biochemistry, biophysics, chemical physics, environmental science, geology/earth science, geophysics/seismology, physics, statistics.

Columbia University—Fu Foundation School of Engineering and Applied Science
212 Hamilton Hall, MC 2807
1130 Amsterdam Avenue
New York, NY 10027
Phone: (212) 854-2521
Fax: (212) 894-1209
E-mail: ugrad-ask@columbia.edu
http://www.engineering.columbia.edu
Applied mathematics, chemical engineering, civil engineering, engineering mechanics, environmental engineering, geological engineering, materials engineering, materials science, mechanical engineering, metallurgical engineering, mining and mineral engineering.

Concordia College
171 White Plains Road
Bronxville, NY 10708
Phone: (914) 337-9300
Fax: (914) 395-4636
E-mail: admission@concordia-ny.edu
http://www.concordia-ny.edu
Geology/earth science.

Cooper Union for the Advancement of Science and Art
Office of Admissions and Records
30 Cooper Square
New York, NY 10003
Phone: (212) 353-4120
Fax: (212) 353-4242
E-mail: admissions@cooper.edu
http://www.cooper.edu
Civil engineering, mechanical engineering.

Cornell University
Undergraduate Admissions
410 Thurston Avenue
Ithaca, NY 14850
Phone: (607) 255-5241
Fax: (607) 255-0659
E-mail: admissions@cornell.edu
http://www.cornell.edu
Agricultural and biological engineering, applied mathematics, atmospheric science, biochemistry, chemical engineering, civil engineering, engineering—general, engineering mechanics, engineering physics, environmental engineering, environmental science, geology/earth science, materials engineering, materials science, mechanical engineering, meteorology, nuclear engineering, physics, soil science, statistics.

Daemen College
4380 Main Street
Amherst, NY 14226
Phone: (716) 839-8225
Fax: (716) 839-8229
E-mail: admissions@daemen.edu
http://www.daemen.edu
Biochemistry.

DeVry Institute of Technology
3020 Thomson Avenue
Long Island City, NY 11101
Phone: (718) 472-2728
Fax: (718) 361-0004
E-mail: leads@ny.devry.edu
http://www.devry.edu
Electrical engineering technology.

Elmira College
1 Park Place
Elmira, NY 14901
Phone: (607) 735-1724
Fax: (607) 735-1718
E-mail: admissions@elmira.edu
http://www.elmira.edu
Biochemistry, clinical laboratory science.

Excelsior College
7 Columbia Circle
Albany, NY 12203
Phone: (518) 464-8500
Fax: (518) 464-8777
E-mail: admissions@excelsior.edu
http://www.excelsior.edu
Engineering technology—general, geography, geology/earth science, instrumentation technology, nuclear engineering technology, physics.

Hamilton College
Office of Admissions
198 College Hill Road
Clinton, NY 13323
Phone: (315) 859-4421
Fax: (315) 859-4457
E-mail: admission@hamilton.edu
http://www.hamilton.edu
Biochemistry, geology/earth science, physics.

Hartwick College
P.O. Box 4020
Oneonta, NY 13820
Phone: (607) 431-4154
Fax: (607) 431-4102
E-mail: admissions@hartwick.edu
http://www.hartwick.edu
Clinical laboratory science, geology/earth science, physics.

Hobart and William Smith College
629 South Main Street
Geneva, NY 14456
Phone: (315) 781-3472
Fax: (315) 781-3471
E-mail: admissions@hws.edu
http://www.hws.edu
Biochemistry, geology/earth science, physics.

Hofstra University
Admission Center
Bernon Hall
1000 Fulton Avenue
Hempstead, NY 11549
Phone: (516) 463-6700
Fax: (516) 463-5100
E-mail: admitme@hofstra.edu
http://www.hofstra.edu
Applied mathematics, biochemistry, civil engineering, environmental engineering, geography, geology/earth science, industrial engineering, mechanical engineering, physics.

Iona College
715 North Avenue
New Rochelle, NY 10801
Phone: (914) 633-2502
Fax: (914) 633-2642
E-mail: icad@iona.edu
http://www.iona.edu
Applied mathematics, biochemistry, clinical laboratory science, physics.

Ithaca College
100 Job Hall
Ithaca, NY 14850
Phone: (607) 274-3124
Fax: (607) 274-1900
E-mail: admission@ithaca.edu
http://www.ithaca.edu
Biochemistry, physics.

Keuka College
Office of Admissions
Keuka Park, NY 14478
Phone: (315) 279-5254
Fax: (315) 536-5386
E-mail: admissions@mail.keuka.edu
http://www.keuka.edu
Biochemistry, clinical laboratory science.

Le Moyne College
1419 Salt Springs Road
Syracuse, NY 13214
Phone: (315) 445-4300
Fax: (315) 445-4711
E-mail: admission@lemoyne.edu
http://www.lemoyne.edu
Biochemistry, biological/physical sciences, physics.

Long Island University—Brooklyn Campus
1 University Plaza
Brooklyn, NY 11201
Phone: (800) 548-7526
Fax: (718) 797-2399
E-mail: admissions@brooklyn.liu.edu
http://www.liunet.edu
Biochemistry, clinical laboratory science.

Long Island University—C. W. Post Campus
720 Northern Boulevard
Brookville, NY 11548
Phone: (516) 299-2900
Fax: (519) 299-2137
E-mail: enroll@cwpost.liu.edu
http://www.liu.edu
Applied mathematics, geography, geology/earth science, physics.

Manhattan College
Manhattan College Parkway
Riverdale, NY 10471
Phone: (718) 862-7200
Fax: (718) 862-8019
E-mail: admit@manhattan.edu
http://www.manhattan.edu
Biochemistry, chemical engineering, civil engineering, environmental engineering, mechanical engineering, physics.

Marist College
3399 North Road

Poughkeepsie, NY 12601
Phone: (845) 575-3226
Fax: (845) 575-3215
E-mail: admissions@marist.edu
http://www.marist.edu
Biochemistry, clinical laboratory science, environmental science.

Mercy College
555 Broadway
Dobbs Ferry, NY 10522
Phone: (914) 674-7324
Fax: (914) 674-7382
E-mail: admissions@mercy.edu
http://www.mercy.edu
Clinical laboratory science.

Mount Saint Mary College
330 Powell Avenue
Newburgh, NY 12550
Phone: (845) 569-3248
Fax: (845) 562-6762
E-mail: mtstmary@msmc.edu
http://www.msmc.edu
Clinical laboratory science.

Nazareth College of Rochester
4245 East Avenue
Rochester, NY 14618
Phone: (585) 389-2860
Fax: (585) 389-2826
E-mail: admissions@naz.edu
http://www.naz.edu
Biochemistry.

New York Institute of Technology
P.O. Box 8000
Northern Boulevard
Old Westbury, NY 11568
Phone: (516) 686-7520
Fax: (516) 686-7613
E-mail: admissions@nyit.edu
http://www.nyit.edu
Environmental engineering technology, mechanical engineering, physics.

New York University
22 Washington Square North
New York, NY 10011
Phone: (212) 998-4500
Fax: (212) 995-4902
E-mail: admissions@nyu.edu
http://www.nyu.edu
Biochemistry, physics, statistics.

Pace University
1 Pace Plaza
New York, NY 10038
Phone: (212) 346-1323

Fax: (212) 346-1040
E-mail: infoctr@pace.edu
http://www.pace.edu
Biochemistry, clinical laboratory science, geology/earth science, physics.

Paul Smith's College
Sporck Admissions Building
P.O. Box 265, Route 86 & 30
Paul Smiths, NY 12970
Phone: (800) 421-2605
Fax: (518) 327-6016
E-mail: At Web site
http://www.paulsmiths.edu
Biological/physical sciences, environmental science.

Polytechnic University
6 Metrotech Center
Brooklyn, NY 11201
Phone: (718) 260-3100
Fax: (718) 260-3446
E-mail: admitme@poly.edu
http://www.poly.edu
Civil engineering, mechanical engineering, physics.

Rensselaer Polytechnic Institute
110 Eighth Street
Troy, NY 12180
Phone: (518) 276-6216
Fax: (518) 276-4072
E-mail: arpi.edu
http://www.rpi.edu
Biochemistry, biological/physical sciences, biophysics, chemical engineering, civil engineering, engineering—general, engineering mechanics, engineering physics, environmental engineering, environmental science, geology/earth science, industrial engineering, materials engineering, mechanical engineering, nuclear engineering, physics.

Roberts Wesleyan College
2301 Westside Drive
Rochester, NY 14624
Phone: (585) 594-6400
Fax: (585) 594-6371
E-mail: admissions@roberts.edu
http://www.roberts.edu
Biochemistry, biological/physical sciences, physics.

Rochester Institute of Technology
60 Lomb Memorial Drive
Rochester, NY 14623
Phone: (585) 475-6631
Fax: (585) 475-7424

E-mail: admissions@rit.edu
http://www.rit.edu
Applied mathematics, biochemistry, biotechnology, civil engineering technology, electrical engineering technology, environmental engineering technology, industrial engineering, materials engineering, mathematical statistics/probability, mechanical engineering, mechanical engineering technology, physics, statistics.

Russell Sage College
Office of Admissions
45 Ferry Street
Troy, NY 12180
Phone: (518) 244-2217
Fax: (518) 244-6880
E-mail: rscadm@sage.edu
http://www.sage.edu
Biochemistry.

St. Bonaventure University
P.O. Box D
St. Bonaventure, NY 14778
Phone: (716) 375-2400
Fax: (716) 375-4005
E-mail: admissions@sbu.edu
http://www.sbu.edu
Biochemistry, physics.

Saint Francis College
180 Remsen Street
Brooklyn Heights, NY 11201
Phone: (718) 489-5200
Fax: (718) 802-0453
E-mail: admissions@stfranciscollege.edu
http://www.stfranciscollege.edu
Clinical laboratory science.

St. John's University
8000 Utopia Parkway
Jamaica, NY 11439
Phone: (718) 990-2000
Fax: (718) 990-5728
E-mail: admissions@stjohns.edu
http://www.stjohns.edu
Clinical laboratory science, physics.

St. Lawrence University
23 Romoda Drive
Canton, NY 13617
Phone: (800) 285-1856
Fax: NA
E-mail: admissions@stlawu.edu
http://www.stlawu.edu
Biochemistry, biophysics, geology/earth science, geophysics/seismology.

Saint Thomas Aquinas College
125 Route 340
Sparkill, NY 10976
Phone: (845) 398-4100
Fax: (845) 398-4224
E-mail: admissions@stac.edu
http://www.stac.edu
Applied mathematics, biological/physical
  sciences, engineering—general,
  physics.

Sarah Lawrence College
One Mead Way
Bronxville, NY 10708
Phone: (914) 395-2510
Fax: (914) 395-2676
E-mail: slcadmit@slc.edu
http://www.slc.edu
Analytical chemistry, biochemistry,
  biological/physical sciences, geology/
  earth science, physics.

Siena College
515 Loudon Road
Loudonville, NY 12211
Phone: (518) 783-2423
Fax: (518) 783-2436
E-mail: admit@siena.edu
http://www.siena.edu
Applied mathematics, biochemistry,
  physics.

Skidmore College
815 North Broadway
Saratoga Springs, NY 12866
Phone: (518) 580-5570
Fax: (518) 580-5584
E-mail: admissions@skidmore.edu
http://www.skidmore.edu
Biochemistry, environmental science,
  geology/earth science, physics.

State University of New York at Albany
Office of Undergraduate Admissions
1400 Washington Avenue
Albany, NY 12222
Phone: (518) 442-5435
Fax: (518) 442-5383
E-mail: ugadmissions@albany.edu
http://www.albany.edu
Applied mathematics, atmospheric
  science, biochemistry, geography,
  geology/earth science, physics.

**State University of New York at
  Binghamton**
P.O. Box 6001
Binghamton, NY 13902
Phone: (607) 777-2171

Fax: (607) 777-4445
E-mail: admit@binghamton.edu
http://www.binghamton.edu
Biochemistry, geography, geology/earth
  science, industrial engineering,
  materials engineering, mechanical
  engineering, physics.

**State University of New York at
  Brockport**
350 New Campus Drive
Brockport, NY 14420
Phone: (585) 395-2751
Fax: (585) 395-5452
E-mail: admit@brockport.edu
http://www.brockport.edu
Atmospheric science, biochemistry,
  biotechnology, environmental science,
  geology/earth science, hydrology/
  water resources science, meteorology,
  physics.

**State University of New York at
  Cortland**
P.O. Box 2000
Cortland, NY 13045
Phone: (607) 753-4712
Fax: (607) 753-5998
E-mail: admissions@cortland.edu
http://www.cortland.edu
Geography, geology/earth science,
  physics.

**State University of New York at
  Farmingdale**
2350 Broadhollow Road
Farmingdale, NY 11735
Phone: (631) 420-2000
Fax: (631) 420-2633
E-mail: admissions@farmingdale.edu
http://www.farmingdale.edu
Industrial technology, mechanical
  engineering technology.

**State University of New York at
  Fredonia**
178 Central Avenue
Fredonia, NY 14063
Phone: (716) 673-3251
Fax: (716) 673-3249
E-mail: admissions.office@fredonia.edu
http://www.fredonia.edu
Biochemistry, biotechnology, geology/
  earth science, geophysics/seismology,
  physics.

State University of New York at Geneseo
1 College Circle
Geneseo, NY 14454

Phone: (716) 245-5571
Fax: (716) 245-5550
E-mail: admissions@geneseo.edu
http://www.geneseo.edu
Biochemistry, biophysics, geography,
  geology/earth science, geophysics/
  seismology, physics.

**State University of New York at
  New Paltz**
75 South Manheim Boulevard, Suite 1
New Paltz, NY 12561
Phone: (845) 257-3200
Fax: (914) 257-3209
E-mail: admissions@newpaltz.edu
http://www.newpaltz.edu
Geography, geology/earth science,
  physics.

**State University of New York at
  Oswego**
211 Culkin Hall
Oswego, NY 13126
Phone: (315) 312-2250
Fax: (315) 312-3260
E-mail: admiss@oswego.edu
http://www.oswego.edu
Applied mathematics, meteorology,
  physics.

**State University of New York at
  Plattsburgh**
1001 Kehoe Building
Plattsburgh, NY 12091
Phone: (518) 564-2040
Fax: (518) 564-2045
E-mail: admissions@plattsburgh.edu
http://www.plattsburgh.edu
Biochemistry, biotechnology, clinical
  laboratory science, geography,
  geology/earth science, physics.

**State University of New York at
  Potsdam**
44 Pierrepont Avenue
Potsdam, NY 13676
Phone: (315) 267-2180
Fax: (315) 267-2163
E-mail: admissions@potsdam.edu
http://www.potsdam.edu
Biochemistry, biological/physical sciences,
  geology/earth science, physics.

**State University of New York at Stony
  Brook**
Office of Admissions
Stony Brook, NY 11794
Phone: (631) 632-6868
Fax: (631) 632-9898

E-mail: enroll@stonybrook.edu
http://www.stonybrook.edu
Applied mathematics, biochemistry, clinical laboratory science, engineering—general, geology/earth science, materials engineering, mechanical engineering, physics.

State University of New York College at Old Westbury
P.O. Box 210
Old Westbury, NY 11568
Phone: (516) 876-3000
Fax: (516) 876-3307
E-mail: enroll@oldwestbury.edu
http://www.oldwestbury.edu
Biochemistry.

State University of New York College at Oneonta
Alumni Hall 116
State University College
Oneonta, NY 13820
Phone: (607) 436-2524
Fax: (607) 436-3074
E-mail: admissions@oneonta.edu
http://www.oneonta.edu
Atmospheric science, environmental science, geography, geology/earth science, hydrology/water resources science, physics, statistics.

State University of New York College— Buffalo State College
1300 Elmwood Avenue
Buffalo, NY 14222
Phone: (716) 878-4017
Fax: (716) 878-6100
E-mail: admissions@buffalostate.edu
http://www.buffalostate.edu
Biotechnology, chemical engineering, civil engineering, clinical laboratory science, electrical engineering technology, electromechanical technology, engineering—general, engineering physics, environmental engineering, geography, geology/earth science, industrial engineering, mechanical engineering, mechanical engineering technology, physics.

State University of New York College of Agriculture and Technology at Cobleskill
Office of Admissions
Cobleskill, NY 12043
Phone: (518) 255-5525
Fax: (518) 255-6769
E-mail: admissions@cobleskill.edu

http://www.cobleskill.edu
Agricultural and biological engineering, electrical engineering technology, soil science,

State University of New York College of Environmental Science and Forestry
106 Bray Hall
State University of New York-ESF
Syracuse, NY 13210
Phone: (315) 470-6600
Fax: (315) 470-6933
E-mail: esfinfo@esf.edu
http://www.esf.edu
Biochemistry, biological/physical sciences, biotechnology, chemical engineering, civil engineering, construction technology, engineering—general, environmental engineering, environmental science, geography, materials engineering, mechanical engineering, soil science.

State University of New York College of Technology at Alfred
Huntington Administration Building
Alfred, NY 14802
Phone: (800) 425-3733
Fax: (607) 587-4299
E-mail: admissions@alfredstate.edu
http://www.alfredstate.edu
Construction technology, mechanical engineering, surveying engineering, surveying technology.

State University of New York—Empire State College
111 West Avenue
Saratoga, NY 12866
Phone: (518) 587-2100
Fax: (518) 587-9759
E-mail: admissions@esc.edu
http://www.esc.edu
Biological/physical sciences.

State University of New York— Institute of Technology at Utica/ Rome
P.O. Box 3050
Utica, NY 13504
Phone: (315) 792-7500
Fax: (315) 792-7837
E-mail: At website
http://web2.sunyit.edu
Civil engineering technology, electrical engineering technology, industrial technology, mechanical engineering technology.

State University of New York— Maritime College
6 Pennyfield Avenue
Throggs Neck, NY 10465
Phone: (800) 642-1874
Fax: (718) 409-7765
E-mail: admissions@sunymaritime.edu
http://www.sunymaritime.edu
Atmospheric science, engineering— general, mechanical engineering.

Syracuse University
Office of Admissions
200 Crouse-Hinds Hall
Syracuse, NY 13244
Phone: (315) 443-3611
Fax: (315) 443-4226
E-mail: orange@syr.edu
http://www.syracuse.edu
Biochemistry, chemical engineering, civil engineering, engineering physics, environmental engineering, geology/ earth science, materials engineering, mechanical engineering, physics.

Touro College
1602 Avenue J
Brooklyn, NY 14230
Phone: (718) 252-7800
Fax: (718) 253-6479
E-mail: lasAdmit@touro.edu
http://www.touro.edu
Biological/physical sciences.

Union College
Grant Hall, Union College
Schenectady, NY 12308
Phone: (518) 388-6112
Fax: (518) 388-6986
E-mail: admissions@union.edu
http://www.union.edu
Biochemistry, biological/physical sciences, geology/earth science, physics.

United States Military Academy
646 Swift Road
West Point, NY 10996
Phone: (845) 938-4041
Fax: (845) 938-3021
E-mail: admissions@usma.edu
http://www.usma.edu
Chemical engineering, civil engineering, engineering physics, geography, mechanical engineering, nuclear engineering, physics.

University of Rochester
300 Wilson Boulevard
P.O. Box 270251

Rochester, NY 14627
Phone: (585) 275-3221
Fax: (585) 461-4595
E-mail: admit@admissions.rochester.edu
http://www.rochester.edu
Applied mathematics, biochemistry, biological/physical sciences, chemical engineering, engineering—general, environmental science, geology/earth science, mechanical engineering, physics, statistics.

Utica College
1600 Burnside Road
Utica, NY 13052
Phone: (315) 792-3006
Fax: (315) 792-3003
E-mail: admiss@utica.edu
http://www.utica.edu
Physics.

Vassar College
124 Raymond Avenue
Poughkeepsie, NY 12604
Phone: (845) 437-7300
Fax: (845) 437-7063
E-mail: admissions@vassar.edu
http://www.vassar.edu
Biochemistry, geology/earth science, physics.

Wells College
Route 90
Aurora, NY 13026
Phone: (315) 364-3264
Fax: (315) 364-3227
E-mail: admissions@wells.edu
http://www.wells.edu
Biochemistry, environmental science, physics.

Yeshiva University
500 West 18th Street
New York, NY 10033
Phone: (212) 960-5277
Fax: (212) 960-0866
E-mail: yuadmitt@yu.edu
http://www.yu.edu
Engineering—general, physics.

NORTH CAROLINA

Appalachian State University
Office of Admissions
P.O. Box 32004
Boone, NC 28608
Phone: (828) 262-2120
Fax: (828) 262-3296
E-mail: admissions@appstate.edu

http://www.appstate.edu
Clinical laboratory science, electrical engineering technology, geography, geology/earth science, industrial technology, physics, statistics.

Brevard College
400 North Broad Street
Brevard, NC 28712
Phone: (828) 884-8300
Fax: (828) 884-3790
E-mail: admissions@brevard.edu
http://www.brevard,edu
Biological/physical sciences, environmental science.

Campbell University
P.O. Box 546
Buies Creek, NC 27506
Phone: (910) 893-1320
Fax: (910) 893-1288
E-mail: adm@mailcenter.campbell.edu
http://www.campbell.edu
Biochemistry.

Duke University
2138 Campus Drive
Durham, NC 27708
Phone: (919) 684-3214
Fax: (919) 681-8941
E-mail: undergrad.admissions@duke.edu
http://www.duke.edu
Civil engineering, geology/earth science, mechanical engineering, physics.

East Carolina University
Office of Undergraduate Admissions
106 Whichard Building
Greenville, NC 27858
Phone: (252) 328-6640
Fax: (252) 328-6945
E-mail: admis@mail.ecu.edu
http://www.ecu.edu
Biochemistry, clinical laboratory science, construction technology, environmental engineering technology, geography, geology/earth science, industrial technology, physics.

Elizabeth City State University
1704 Weeksville Road
Elizabeth City, NC 27909
Phone: (252) 335-3305
Fax: (252) 335-3537
E-mail: admissions@mail.ecsu.edu
http://www.ecsu.edu
Geology/earth science, industrial technology, physics.

Elon University
2700 Campus Box
Elon, NC 27244
Phone: (336) 278-3566
Fax: (336) 278-7699
E-mail: admissions@elon.edu
http://www.elon.edu
Chemical engineering, engineering—general, engineering physics, environmental engineering technology, physics.

Fayetteville State University
Newbold Station
Fayetteville, NC 28301
Phone: (910) 672-1371
Fax: (910) 672-1414
E-mail: admissions@Uncfsu.edu
http://www.Uncfsu.edu
Geography.

Guilford College
5800 West Friendly Avenue
Greensboro, NC 27410
Phone: (336) 316-2100
Fax: (336) 316-2954
E-mail: admission@guilford.edu
http://www.guilford.edu
Geology/earth science, physics.

High Point University
University Station 3598
High Point, NC 27262
Phone: (336) 841-9216
Fax: (336) 888-6382
E-mail: admiss@highpoint.edu
http://www.highpoint.edu
Clinical laboratory science.

Johnson C. Smith University
100 Beatties Ford Road
Charlotte, NC 28216
Phone: (704) 378-1011
Fax: (704) 378-01242
E-mail: admissions@jcsu.edu
http://www.jcsu.edu
Applied mathematics, biological/physical sciences, engineering—general.

Livingstone College
701 West Monroe Street
Salisbury, NC 28144
Phone: (704) 216-6001
Fax: (704) 216-6215
E-mail: admissions@livingstone.edu
http://www.livingstone.edu
Engineering—general.

Mars Hill College
P.O. Box 370

Mars Hill, NC 28754
Phone: (828) 689-1201
Fax: (828) 689-1473
E-mail: admissions@mhc.edu
http://www.mhc.edu
Biological/physical sciences.

North Carolina A &T University
1601 East Market Street
Greensboro, NC 27411
Phone: (336) 334-7946
Fax: (336) 334-7478
E-mail: uadmit@ncat.edu
http://www.ncat.edu
Agricultural and biological engineering, chemical engineering, civil engineering, materials engineering, mechanical engineering, physics.

North Carolina Central University
Fayetteville Street
Durham, NC 27707
Phone: (919) 560-6298
Fax: (919) 530-7625
E-mail: ebridges@wpo.nccu.edu
http://www.nccu.edu
Environmental science, geography, geology/earth science, physics.

North Carolina State University
P.O. Box 7103
Raleigh, NC 27695
Phone: (919) 515-2434
Fax: (919) 515-5039
E-mail: undergrad_admissions@ncsu.edu
http://www.ncsu.edu
Agricultural and biological engineering, applied mathematics, atmospheric science, biochemistry, chemical engineering, civil engineering, construction engineering, engineering—general, environmental engineering, environmental engineering technology, environmental science, geography, geology/earth science, industrial engineering, materials engineering, mechanical engineering, nuclear engineering, physics, statistics.

Pfeiffer College
P.O. Box 960
Misenheimer, NC 28109
Phone: (800) 338-2060
Fax: (704) 463-1363
E-mail: admissions@pfeiffer.edu
http://www.pfeiffer.edu
Engineering—general.

Queens University of Charlotte
1900 Selwyn Avenue
Charlotte, NC 28274
Phone: (704) 337-2212
Fax: (704) 337-2403
E-mail: admissions@queens.edu
http://www.queens.edu
Biochemistry, statistics.

Saint Augustine's College
1315 Oakwood Avenue
Raleigh, NC 27610
Phone: (919) 516-4016
Fax: (919) 516-5805
E-mail: admissions@st-aug.edu
http://www.st-aug.edu
Applied mathematics, engineering—general.

Shaw University
118 East South Street
Raleigh, NC 27601
Phone: (919) 546-8275
Fax: (919) 546-8271
E-mail: admission@shawu.edu
http://www.shawu.edu
Physics.

University of North Carolina—Asheville
CPO #2210, 117 Lipinsky Hall
Asheville, NC 28804
Phone: (828) 251-6481
Fax: (818) 251-6482
E-mail: admissions@unca.edu
http://www.unca.edu
Atmospheric science, engineering—general, physics.

University of North Carolina—Chapel Hill
Office of Undergraduate Admissions
Jackson Hall 153A
Campus P.O. Box 2220
Chapel Hill, NC 27599
Phone: (919) 966-3621
Fax: (919) 962-3045
E-mail: uadm@email.unc.edu
http://www.unc.edu
Applied mathematics, clinical laboratory science, environmental science, geography, geology/earth science, physics.

University of North Carolina—Charlotte
9201 University City Boulevard
Charlotte, NC 28223
Phone: (704) 687-2213
Fax: (704) 687-6483

E-mail: uncadm@email.uncc.edu
http://www.uncc.edu
Civil engineering, civil engineering technology, clinical laboratory science, electrical engineering technology, geography, geology/earth science, mechanical engineering, mechanical engineering technology, meteorology, physics.

University of North Carolina—Greensboro
123 Mossman Building
Greensboro, NC 27402
Phone: (336) 334-5243
Fax: (336) 334-4180
E-mail: undergrad_admissions@uncg.edu
http://www.uncg.edu
Biochemistry, clinical laboratory science, geography, physics.

University of North Carolina—Pembroke
One University Drive
P.O. Box 1510
Pembroke, NC 28372
Phone: (910) 521-6262
Fax: (910) 521-6407
E-mail: admissions@papa.uncp.edu
http://www.uncp.edu
Environmental science, physics.

University of North Carolina—Wilmington
601 South College Road
Wilmington, NC 28403
Phone: (910) 962-3243
Fax: (910) 962-3038
E-mail: admissions@uncw.edu
http://www.uncw.edu
Clinical laboratory science, environmental science, geography, geology/earth science, physics, statistics.

Wake Forest University
P.O. Box 7305, Reynolds Station
Winston-Salem, NC 27109
Phone: (336) 758-5201
Fax: (336) 758-4324
E-mail: admissions@wfu.edu
http://www.wfu.edu
Clinical laboratory science, physics.

Western Carolina University
232 HFR Administration
Cullowhee, NC 28723
Phone: (828) 227-7317

Fax: (828) 227-7319
E-mail: cauley@email.wcu.edu
http://www.wcu.edu
Construction technology, electrical
engineering technology, environmental
science.

Winston-Salem State University
601 Martin Luther King Jr. Drive
Winston-Salem, NC 27100
Phone: (336) 750-2070
Fax: (336) 750-2079
E-mail: admissions@wssu.edu
http://www.wssu.edu
Biotechnology, clinical laboratory
science.

NORTH DAKOTA

Jamestown College
6081 College Lane
Jamestown, ND 58405
Phone: (701) 252-3467
Fax: (701) 253-4318
E-mail: admissions@jc.edu
http://www.jc.edu
Applied mathematics, biochemistry,
clinical laboratory science.

Minot State University—Minot
500 University Avenue
West Minot, ND 58707
Phone: (701) 858-3350
Fax: (701) 858-3386
E-mail: msu@minotstateu.edu
http://www.minotstateu.edu
Clinical laboratory science, geography,
geology/earth science, physics.

North Dakota State University
P.O. Box 5454
Fargo, ND 58105
Phone: (701) 231-8643
Fax: (701) 231-8802
E-mail: ndsu.admission@ndsu.nodak.edu
http://www.ndsu.edu
Agricultural and biological engineering,
biotechnology, civil engineering,
clinical laboratory science,
construction engineering, engineering
physics, geology/earth science,
industrial engineering, mechanical
engineering, physics, soil science,
statistics.

University of Mary
7500 University Drive
Bismarck, ND 58504
Phone: (701) 255-7500

Fax: (701) 255-7687
E-mail: suerood@umary.edu
http://www.umary.edu
Clinical laboratory science.

University of North Dakota
Enrollment Services
Carnegie Building
Box 8135
Grand Forks, ND 58202
Phone: (800) CALL-UND
Fax: (701) 777-2696
E-mail: enrollment_services@mail.und.
nodak.edu
http://www.und.edu
Atmospheric science, chemical engineer-
ing, civil engineering, clinical labora-
tory science, environmental engineer-
ing, geography, geology/earth science,
mechanical engineering, physics.

OHIO

Ashland University
401 College Avenue
Ashland, OH 44805
Phone: (419) 289-5052
Fax: (419) 289-5999
E-mail: enrollme@ashland.edu
http://www.ashland.edu
Environmental science, geology/earth
science, physics.

Baldwin-Wallace College
275 Eastland Road
Berea, OH 44017
Phone: (440) 826-2222
Fax: (440) 826-3830
E-mail: admission@bw.edu
http://www.bw.edu
Engineering—general, physics.

Bowling Green State University
110 McFall Center
Bowling Green, OH 43403
Phone: (419) 372-2478
Fax: (419) 372-6955
E-mail: admissions@bgnet.bgsu.edu
http://www.bgsu.edu
Clinical laboratory science, construction
technology, electrical engineering
technology, geography, geology/
earth science, industrial technology,
mechanical engineering technology,
physics, statistics.

Capital University
2199 East Main Street
Columbus, OH 43209

Phone: (614) 236-6101
Fax: (614) 236-6926
E-mail: admissions@capital.edu
http://www.capital.edu
Biochemistry.

Case Western Reserve University
103 Tomlinson Hall
10900 Euclid Avenue
Cleveland, OH 44106
Phone: (216) 368-4450
Fax: (216) 368-5111
E-mail: admission@case.edu
http://www.case.edu
Applied mathematics, biochemistry, chemical engineering, civil engineering, engineering—general, engineering physics,
geology/earth science, materials engineering, materials science, mechanical
engineering, physics, statistics.

Cedarville University
251 North Main Street
Cedarville, OH 45314
Phone: (937) 766-7700
Fax: (937) 766-7575
E-mail: admissions@cedarville.edu
http://www.cedarville.edu
Clinical laboratory science, mechanical
engineering, physics.

Central State University
P.O. Box 1004
Wilberforce, OH 45384
Phone: (937) 376-6348
Fax: (937) 376-6648
E-mail: admissions@centralstate.edu
http://www.centralstate.edu
Geology/earth science, industrial
technology.

Cleveland State University
East 24 and Euclid Avenue
Cleveland, OH 44114
Phone: (216) 687-2100
Fax: (216) 687-9210
E-mail: admissions@csuohio.edu
http://www.csuohio.edu
Chemical engineering, civil engineering,
electrical engineering technology,
geology/earth science, mechanical
engineering, physics.

College of Mount Saint Joseph
5701 Delhi Road
Cincinnati, OH 45233
Phone: (513) 244-4531
Fax: (513) 244-4629
E-mail: peggy_minnich@mail.msj.edu

http://www.msj.edu
Biochemistry.

The College of Wooster
847 College Avenue
Wooster, OH 44091
Phone: (330) 263-2322
Fax: (330) 263-2621
E-mail: admissions@wooster.edu
http://www.wooster.edu
Atomic/molecular physics, biochemistry,
    chemical physics, geology/earth
    science, physics.

Defiance College
701 North Clinton Street
Defiance, OH 43612
Phone: (419) 783-2359
Fax: (419) 783-2468
E-mail: admissions@defiance.edu
http://www.defiance.edu
Biological/physical sciences.

Denison University
P.O. Box H
Granville, OH 43023
Phone: (740) 587-6276
Fax: (740) 587-6306
E-mail: admissions@denison.edu
http://www.denison.edu
Biochemistry, geology/earth science,
    physics.

DeVry University—Columbus
1350 Alum Creek Drive
Columbus, OH 43209
Phone: (614) 253-1525
Fax: (614) 253-0843
E-mail: admissions@devry.edu
http://www.devry.edu
Electrical engineering technology.

Heidelberg College
310 East Market Street
Tiffin, OH 44883
Phone: (419) 448-2330
Fax: (419) 448-2334
E-mail: adminfo@heidelberg.edu
http://www.heidelberg.edu
Biological/physical sciences, physics.

Hiram College
P.O. Box 96
Hiram, OH 44234
Phone: (330) 569-5169
Fax: (330) 569-5944
E-mail: admission@hiram.edu
http://www.hiram.edu
Biochemistry, physics.

John Carroll University
20700 North Park Boulevard
University Heights, OH 44118
Phone: (216) 397-4294
Fax: (216) 397-3098
E-mail: admission@jcu.edu
http://www.jcu.edu
Engineering physics, physics.

Kent State University
161 Michael Schwartz
Kent, OH 44242
Phone: (330) 672-2444
Fax: (330) 672-2499
E-mail: kentadm@admissions.kent.edu
http://www.kent.edu
Applied mathematics, electrical engineer-
    ing technology, biotechnology, clinical
    laboratory science, geography, geology/
    earth science, industrial engineering,
    physics.

Kenyon College
Admissions Office, Ransom Hall
Gambier, OH 43002
Phone: (740) 427-5776
Fax: (740) 427-5770
E-mail: admissions@kenyon.edu
http://www.kenyon.edu
Biochemistry, physics.

Malone College
515 25th Street NW
Canton, OH 44709
Phone: (330) 471-8145
Fax: (330) 471-8149
E-mail: admissions@malone.edu
http://www.malone.edu
Clinical laboratory science.

Marietta College
215 Fifth Street
Marietta, OH 45750
Phone: (740) 376-4600
Fax: (740) 376-8888
E-mail: admit@marietta.edu
http://www.marietta.edu
Biochemistry, environmental science,
    geology/earth science, petroleum
    engineering, physics.

Miami University—Hamilton Campus
1601 University Boulevard
Hamilton, OH 45011
Phone: (513) 785-3111
Fax: NA
E-mail: At Web site
http://www.ham.muohio.edu
Engineering technology—general.

**Miami University—Middletown
    Campus**
4200 East University Boulevard
Middletown, OH 45042
Phone: (513) 727-3200
Fax: NA
E-mail: mumadmission@muohio.edu
http://www.mid.muohio.edu
Electrical engineering technology.

Miami University—Oxford Campus
301 South Campus Avenue
Oxford, OH 45056
Phone: (513) 529-2531
Fax: (513) 529-1550
E-mail: admissions@muohio.edu
http://www.muohio.edu
Biochemistry, chemical engineering,
    clinical laboratory science, engineer-
    ing—general, engineering physics,
    engineering technology—general,
    environmental science, geography,
    geology/earth science, mechanical
    engineering, physics, statistics.

Mount Union College
1972 Clark Avenue
Alliance, OH 44601
Phone: (800) 334-6682
Fax: (330) 823-3457
E-mail: admissn@muc.edu
http://www.muc.edu
Biochemistry, geology/earth science,
    physics.

Muskingum College
163 Stormont Drive
New Concord, OH 43762
Phone: (614) 826-8137
Fax: (614) 826-8100
E-mail: adminfo@muskingum.edu
http://www.muskingum.edu
Engineering—general, engineering
    mechanics, geology/earth science.

Oberlin College
101 North Professor Street
Oberlin, OH 44074
Phone: (440) 775-8411
Fax: (440) 775-6905
E-mail: college.admissions@oberlin.edu
http://www.oberlin.edu
Biochemistry, geology/earth science,
    physics.

Ohio Northern University
525 South Main Street
Ada, OH 45810
Phone: (419) 772-2260

Fax: (419) 772-2313
E-mail: admissions-ug@onu.edu
http://www.onu.edu
Biochemistry, civil engineering, engineering—general, industrial technology, mechanical engineering, physics, statistics.

Ohio State University—Columbus
Third Floor Lincoln Tower
1800 Cannon Drive
Columbus, OH 43210
Phone: (614) 292-3980
Fax: (614) 292-4818
E-mail: askabuckeye@osu.edu
http://www.osu.edu
Agricultural and biological engineering, biochemistry, chemical engineering, civil engineering, clinical laboratory science, construction technology, geography, geology/earth science, geophysics/seismology, industrial engineering, materials engineering, materials science, mechanical engineering, metallurgical engineering, physics, statistics, surveying technology, welding technology.

Ohio University—Athens
120 Chubb Hall
Athens, OH 45701
Phone: (740) 593-4100
Fax: (740) 593-0560
E-mail: admissions.freshmen@ohiou.edu
http://www.ohiou.edu
Applied mathematics, atmospheric science, chemical engineering, industrial technology, mechanical engineering, physics.

Ohio University—Chillicothe Campus
101 University Drive
Chillicothe, OH 45601
Phone: (740) 774-7200
Fax: NA
E-mail: At Web site
http://www.chillicothe.ohiou.edu
Environmental engineering technology, industrial technology, mechanical engineering, physics.

Ohio University—Southern
Office of Enrollment Services
1804 Liberty Avenue
Ironton, OH 45638
Phone: (740) 533-3600
Fax: (740) 533-4632
E-mail: askousc.@mail_southern.ohiou.edu

http://www.southern.ohiou.edu
Applied mathematics, atmospheric science, chemical engineering, civil engineering, industrial technology, mechanical engineering, physics.

Ohio University—Zanesville
Office of Admissions
1425 Newark Road
Zanesville, OH 43701
Phone: (740) 588-1439
Fax: (740) 588-1444
E-mail: tumbling@ohiou.edu
http://www.zanesville.ohiou.edu
Atmospheric science, chemical engineering, civil engineering, industrial technology, mechanical engineering, physics.

Ohio Wesleyan University
Admissions Office
61 South Sandusky Street
Delaware, OH 43015
Phone: (740) 368-3020
Fax: (740) 368-3314
E-mail: owuadmit@owu.edu
http://www.owu.edu
Biochemistry, geography, geology/earth science, physics, statistics.

Otterbein College
Office of Admission
1 Otterbein College
Westerville, OH 43081
Phone: (614) 823-1500
Fax: (614) 823-1200
E-mail: uotterb@otterbein.edu
http://www.otterbein.edu
Biochemistry, physics.

Shawnee State University
940 Second Street
Portsmouth, OH 45662
Phone: (740) 351-4SSU
Fax: (740) 351-3111
E-mail: to_ssu@shawnee.edu
http://www.shawnee.edu
Atmospheric science, environmental engineering technology.

University of Akron
381 Buchtel Common
Akron, OH 44325
Phone: (330) 972-7100
Fax: (330) 972-7022
E-mail: admissions@uakron.edu
http://www.uakron.edu
Applied mathematics, chemical engineering, civil engineering,

construction technology, electrical engineering technology, engineering—general, geography, geology/earth science, geophysics/seismology, industrial technology, mechanical engineering, mechanical engineering technology, physics, statistics.

University of Cincinnati
P.O. Box 210091
Cincinnati, OH 45221
Phone: (513) 556-1100
Fax: (513) 556-1105
E-mail: admissions@uc.edu
http://www.uc.edu
Chemical engineering, civil engineering, clinical laboratory science, engineering mechanics, geography, geology/earth science, metallurgical engineering, nuclear engineering, physics.

University of Dayton
300 College Park
Dayton, OH 45469
Phone: (937) 229-4411
Fax: (937) 229-4729
E-mail: admission@udayton.edu
http://www.udayton.edu
Biochemistry, chemical engineering, civil engineering, electrical engineering technology, engineering technology—general, environmental science, geology/earth science, industrial technology, mechanical engineering, mechanical engineering technology, physics.

The University of Findlay
1000 North Main Street
Findlay, OH 45840
Phone: (419) 424-4732
Fax: (419) 434-4898
E-mail: admissions@findlay.edu
http://www.findlay.edu
Hazardous materials technology.

University of Rio Grande
218 North College Avenue, Admissions
Rio Grande, OH 45774
Phone: (740) 245-7206
Fax: (740) 245-7260
E-mail: mabell@urgrgcc.edu
http://www.urgrgcc.edu
Clinical laboratory science, physics.

University of Toledo
2801 West Bancroft Street

Toledo, OH 43606
Phone: (419) 530-8700
Fax: (419) 530-5713
E-mail: enroll@utnet.utoledo.edu
http://www.utoledo.edu
Chemical engineering, civil engineering, electrical engineering technology, electromechanical technology, engineering—general, geography, geology/earth science, industrial engineering, mechanical engineering, mechanical engineering technology, physics.

Urbana University
579 College Way
Urbana, OH 43076
Phone: (937) 484-1356
Fax: (937) 484-1389
E-mail: admiss@urbana.edu
http://www.urbana.edu
Biological/physical sciences.

Ursuline College
2550 Lander Road
Pepper Pike, OH 44124
Phone: (440) 449-4203
Fax: (440) 684-6138
E-mail: admission@ursuline.edu
http://www.ursuline.edu
Biotechnology.

Walsh University
2020 East Maple Street
North Canton, OH 44720
Phone: (800) 362-9846
Fax: (330) 490-7165
E-mail: admissions@walsh.edu
http://www.walsh.edu
Biological/physical sciences, clinical laboratory science.

Wilmington College
Pyle Center, Box 1325
251 Ludovic Street
Wilmington, OH 45117
Phone: (937) 382-6661
Fax: (937) 382-7077
E-mail: admission@wilmington.edu
http://www.wilmington.edu
Biochemistry, geology/earth science.

Wittenberg University
P.O. Box 720
Springfield, OH 45501
Phone: (800) 677-7558
Fax: (937) 327-6379
E-mail: admission@wittenberg.edu
http://www.wittenberg.edu

Biochemistry, biological/physical sciences, geography, geology/earth science, physics.

Wright State University
3640 Colonel Glenn Highway
Dayton, OH 54435
Phone: (937) 775-5700
Fax: (937) 775-5795
E-mail: admissions@wright.edu
http://www.wright.edu
Applied mathematics, biochemistry, electrical engineering technology, engineering—general, engineering physics, environmental engineering technology, geography, geology/earth science, geophysics/seismology, materials engineering, mechanical engineering, physics, statistics.

Xavier University
3800 Victory Parkway
Cincinnati, OH 45207
Phone: (513) 745-3301
Fax: (513) 745-4319
E-mail:xuadmit@xavier.edu
http://www.xavier.edu
Clinical laboratory science, physics.

Youngstown State University
One University Plaza
Youngstown, OH 44555
Phone: (330) 941-2000
Fax: (330) 941-3674
E-mail: enroll@ysu.edu
http://www.ysu.edu
Chemical engineering, civil engineering, civil engineering technology, clinical laboratory science, electrical engineering technology, engineering—general, engineering technology—general, environmental science, geography, geology/earth science, industrial engineering, materials engineering, mechanical engineering, mechanical engineering technology, physics, structural engineering.

OKLAHOMA

Cameron University
2800 West Gore Boulevard
Lawton, OK 73505
Phone: (580) 581-2230
Fax: (580) 581-5514
E-mail: admiss@cua.cameron.edu
http://www.cameron.edu
Biological/physical sciences, physics.

East Central University
Office of Admissions & Records
1100 E 14 PMB J8
Ada, OK 74820
Phone: (580) 332-8000
Fax: (580) 436-5495
E-mail: pdenny@mailclerk.ecok.edu
http://www.ecok.edu
Applied mathematics, physics.

Northeastern State University
Office of Admissions and Records
600 North Grand Avenue
Tahlequah. OK 74464
Phone: (918) 456-5511
Fax: (918) 458-2342
E-mail: nsuadmis@cherkoee.nsuok.edu
http://www.nsuok.edu
Engineering physics, environmental engineering, environmental science, geography, industrial engineering.

Oklahoma Baptist University
500 West University
Shawnee, OK 74804
Phone: (800) 654-3285
E-mail: admissions@okbu.edu
http://www.okbu.edu
Biochemistry, physics.

Oklahoma Christian University
P.O. Box 11000
Oklahoma City, OK 73136
Phone: (405) 425-5050
Fax: (405) 425-5269
E-mail: ifo@oc.edu
http://www.oc.edu
Biochemistry, clinical laboratory science, engineering physics, mechanical engineering, mechanical engineering technology.

Oklahoma City University
2501 North Blackwelder Avenue
Oklahoma City, OK 73106
Phone: (405) 521-5050
Fax: (405) 521-5264
E-mail: uadmission@okcu.edu
http://www.okcu.edu
Biochemistry, biological/physical sciences, biophysics, physics.

Oklahoma Panhandle State University
P.O. Box 430
Goodwell, OK 73939
Phone: (580) 349-1312
Fax: (580) 349-2302
E-mail: opsu@opsu.edu
http://www.opsu.edu
Biological/physical sciences, clinical laboratory science.

Oklahoma State University
323 Student Union
Stillwater, OK 74078
Phone: (405) 744-6858
Fax: (405) 744-5285
E-mail: admit@okstate.edu
http://www.okstate.edu
Agricultural and biological engineering, biochemistry, chemical engineering, civil engineering, clinical laboratory science, construction technology, electrical engineering technology, environmental science, geography, geology/earth science, industrial engineering, mechanical engineering, mechanical engineering technology, physics, soil science, statistics.

Oral Roberts University
7777 South Lewis Avenue
Tulsa, OK 74171
Phone: (918) 495-0518
Fax: (918) 495-6222
E-mail: admissions@oru.edu
http://www.oru.edu
Biochemistry, clinical laboratory science, engineering—general, engineering physics, mechanical engineering, physics.

Southeastern Oklahoma State University
1405 North Fourth Avenue, PMB 4225
Durant, OK 74701
Phone: (580) 745-2060
Fax: (580) 745-7502
E-mail: admissions@sosu.edu
http://www.sosu.edu
Biophysics, biotechnology, electrical engineering technology, engineering technology—general.

Southern Nazarene University
6729 Northwest 39th Expressway
Bethany, OK 73008
Phone: (800) 648-9899
Fax: (405) 491-6320
E-mail: meek@snu.edu
http://www.snu.edu
Biochemistry, physics.

Southwestern Oklahoma State University
100 Campus Drive
Weatherford, OK 73096
Phone: (580) 774-3795
Fax: (580) 774-2795
E-mail: admissions@swosu.edu

http://www.swosu.edu
Engineering—general, engineering physics, physics.

University of Central Oklahoma
100 North University Drive
Edmond, OK 73034
Phone: (405) 974-2338
Fax: (405) 341-4964
E-mail: admituco@ucok.edu
http://www.ucok.edu
Applied mathematics, clinical laboratory science, engineering physics, engineering technology—general, geography, physics, statistics.

University of Oklahoma
1000 Asp Avenue
Norman, OK 73019
Phone: (405) 325-2252
Fax: (405) 325-7124
E-mail: admrec@ou.edu
http://www.ou.edu
Biochemistry, chemical engineering, civil engineering, engineering physics, environmental engineering, environmental science, geography, geological engineering, geology/earth science, geophysics/seismology, industrial engineering, mechanical engineering, meteorology, petroleum engineering, physics.

University of Tulsa
500 South College Avenue
Tulsa, OK 741045
Phone: (918) 631-2307
Fax: (918) 631-5003
E-mail: admission@utulsa.edu
http://www.utulsa.edu
Applied mathematics, biochemistry, chemical engineering, engineering physics, geology/earth science, geophysics/seismology, mechanical engineering, petroleum engineering, physics.

OREGON

Eastern Oregon University
1 University Boulevard
LaGrande, OR 97850
Phone: (541) 962-3393
Fax: (541) 962-3418
E-mail: admissions@eou.edu
http://www.eou.edu
Physics, soil science.

George Fox University
414 North Meridian Street

Newberg, OR 97132
Phone: (503) 554-2240
Fax: (503) 554-3110
E-mail: admissions@georgefox.edu
http://www.georgefox.edu
Engineering—general, mechanical engineering.

Lewis & Clark College
0615 SW Palatine Hill Road
Portland, OR 97219
Phone: (503) 768-7040
Fax: (503) 768-7055
E-mail: admissions@lclark.edu
http://www.lclark.edu
Biochemistry, physics.

Oregon Institute of Technology
3201 Campus Drive
Klamath Falls, OR 97601
Phone: (541) 885-1150
Fax: (541) 885-1115
E-mail: oit@oit.edu
http://www.oit.edu
Clinical laboratory science, electrical engineering technology, mechanical engineering technology, surveying technology.

Oregon State University
104 Kerr Administration Building
Corvallis, OR 97331
Phone: (541) 737-4411
Fax: (541) 737-2482
E-mail: osuadit@orst.edu
http://www.oregonstate.edu
Agricultural and biological engineering, biochemistry, biological/physical sciences, biophysics, biotechnology, chemical engineering, civil engineering, construction engineering, engineering physics, environmental engineering, environmental science, geography, geology/earth science, geophysics/seismology, mechanical engineering, mining and mineral engineering, nuclear engineering, physics.

Pacific University
2043 College Way
Forest Grove, OR 97116
Phone: (503) 352-2218
Fax: (503) 352-2975
E-mail: admissions@pacificu.edu
http://www.pacificu.edu
Physics.

Portland State University
P.O. Box 751

Portland, OR 97207
Phone: (503) 725-3511
Fax: (503) 725-5525
E-mail: admissions@pdx.edu
http://www.pdx.edu
Biochemistry, biological/physical sciences, civil engineering, geology/earth science, mechanical engineering, physics.

Reed College
3203 South East Woodstock Boulevard
Portland, OR 97202
Phone: (503) 777-7511
Fax: (503) 777-7553
E-mail: admission@reed.edu
http://www.reed.edu
Biochemistry, biological/physical sciences, physics.

Southern Oregon University
Office of Admissions
1250 Siskiyou Boulevard
Ashland, OR 97520
Phone: (541) 552-6411
Fax: (541) 552-6614
E-mail: admissions@sou.edu
http://www.sou.edu
Biological/physical sciences, geography, geology/earth science, physics.

University of Oregon
1217 University of Oregon
Eugene, OR 97403
Phone: (541) 346-3201
Fax: (541) 346-5815
E-mail: uoadmit@oregon.uoregon.edu
http://www.uoregon.edu
Biochemistry, biological/physical sciences, environmental science, geography, geology/earth science, physics.

University of Portland
5000 North Willamette Boulevard
Portland, OR 97203
Phone: (503) 943-7147
Fax: (503) 283-7315
E-mail: admission@up.edu
http://www.up.edu
Civil engineering, environmental engineering, environmental science, mechanical engineering, physics.

Western Oregon University
345 North Monmouth Avenue
Monmouth, OR 97361
Phone: (503) 838-8211
Fax: (503) 838-8067
E-mail: wolfgram@wou.edu

http://www.wou.edu
Biological/physical sciences, geography, geology/earth science.

PENNSYLVANIA

Albright College
P.O. Box 15234
13th and Bern Streets
Reading, PA 19612
Phone: (610) 921-7512
Fax: (610) 921-7294
E-mail: admissions@albright.edu
http://www.albright.edu
Biochemistry, physics.

Allegheny College
Office of Admissions
Meadville, PA 16335
Phone: (814) 332-4351
Fax: (814) 337-0431
E-mail: admissions@allegheny.edu
http://www.allegheny.edu
Biochemistry, environmental science, geology/earth science, physics.

Alvernia College
400 South Bernardine Street
Reading, PA 19607
Phone: (610) 796-8220
Fax: (610) 796-8336
E-mail: admissions@alvernia.edu
http://www.alvernia.edu
Biochemistry, clinical laboratory science.

Arcadia University
450 South Easton Road
Glenside, PA 19038
Phone: (215) 572-2910
Fax: (215) 572-4049
E-mail: admiss@arcadia.edu
http://www.arcadia.edu
Biological/physical sciences, engineering—general.

Bloomsburg University of Pennsylvania
104 Student Services Center
400 East Second Street
Bloomsburg, PA 17815
Phone: (570) 389-4316
Fax: (570) 389-4741
E-mail: buadmiss@bloomu.edu
http://www.bloomu.edu
Clinical laboratory science, geography, geology/earth science, physics.

Bryn Mawr College
101 North Merion Avenue
Bryn Mawr, PA 19010

Phone: (610) 526-5152
Fax: (610) 526-7471
E-mail: admissions@brynmawr.edu
http://www.brynmawr.edu
Geology/earth science, physics.

Bucknell University
Freas Hall
Bucknell University
Lewisburg, PA 17837
Phone: (570) 577-1101
Fax: (570) 577-3538
E-mail: admissions@bucknell.edu
http://www.bucknell.edu
Chemical engineering, civil engineering, geography, geology/earth science, mechanical engineering, physics.

Cabrini College
610 King of Prussia Road
Radnor, PA 19087
Phone: (610) 902-8552
Fax: (610) 902-8552
E-mail: admit@cabrini.edu
http://www.cabrini.edu
Biotechnology, clinical laboratory science.

California University of Pennsylvania
250 University Avenue
California, PA 15419
Phone: (724) 938-4404
Fax: (724) 938-4564
E-mail: inquiry@cup.edu
http://www.cup.edu
Applied mathematics, electrical engineering technology, engineering technology—general, environmental science, geography, geology/earth science, physics.

Carnegie Mellon University
5000 Forbes Avenue
Pittsburgh, PA 15213
Phone: (412) 268-2082
Fax: (412) 268-7838
E-mail: undergraduateadmissions@andrew.cmu.edu
http://www.cmu.edu
Biophysics, chemical engineering, chemical physics, civil engineering, materials science, mathematical statistics/probability, mechanical engineering, physics, statistics.

Cedar Crest College
100 College Drive
Allentown, PA 18104
Phone: (610) 740-3780

Fax: (610) 606-4647
E-mail: cccadmis@cedarcrest.edu
http://www.cedarcrest.edu
Biochemistry.

Chatham College
Woodland Road
Pittsburgh, PA 15232
Phone: (412) 365-1290
Fax: (412) 365-1609
E-mail: admissions@chatham.edu
http://www.chatham.edu
Biochemistry, engineering—general,
    physics.

Chestnut Hill College
9601 Germantown Avenue
Philadelphia, PA 19118
Phone: (215) 248-7001
Fax: (215) 248-7082
E-mail: chcapply@chc.edu
http://www.chc.edu
Biochemistry, environmental science.

Cheyney University of Pennsylvania
Cheyney and Creek Roads
Cheyney, PA 19319
Phone: (610) 399-2275
Fax: (610) 399-2099
E-mail: jbrowne@cheyney.edu
http://www.cheyney.edu
Biological/physical sciences, clinical
    laboratory science, geography.

Clarion University of Pennsylvania
Admissions Office
840 Wood Street
Clarion, PA 16214
Phone: (814) 393-2306
Fax: (814) 393-2030
E-mail: admissions@clarion.edu
http://www.clarion.edu
Biological/physical sciences, geography,
    geology/earth science, physics.

College Misericordia
301 Lake Street
Dallas, PA 18612
Phone: (866) 262-6363
Fax: NA
E-mail: info@misericordia.edu
http://www.misericordia.edu
Biochemistry, clinical laboratory science.

DeSales University
2755 Station Avenue
Center Valley, PA 18034
Phone: (610) 282-4443
Fax: (610) 282-0131

E-mail: admiss@desales.edu
http://www.desales.edu
Clinical laboratory science,
    environmental science.

DeVry University—Ft. Washington
1140 Virginia Drive
Ft. Washington, PA 19034
Phone: (866) 338-7934
Fax: NA
E-mail: info.devry.edu
http://www.devry.edu
Electrical engineering technology.

Dickinson College
P.O. Box 1773
Carlisle, PA 17013
Phone: (717) 245-1231
Fax: (717) 245-1443
E-mail: admit@dickinson.edu
http://www.dickinson.edu
Biochemistry, engineering—general,
    environmental science, geology/earth
    science, physics.

Drexel University
3141 Chestnut Street
Philadelphia, PA 19104
Phone: (215) 895-2400
Fax: (215) 895-5939
E-mail: enroll@drexel.edu
http://www.drexel.edu
Atmospheric physics/dynamics,
    biological/physical sciences,
    chemical engineering, civil
    engineering, clinical laboratory
    science, engineering technology—
    general, environmental engineering,
    materials engineering, mechanical
    engineering, physics.

Duquesne University
600 Forbes Avenue
Pittsburgh, PA 15282
Phone: (412) 396-5000
Fax: (412) 396-5644
E-mail: admissions@duq.edu
http://www.duq.edu
Biochemistry, environmental science,
    physics.

Eastern University
1300 Eagle Road
St. Davids, PA 19087
Phone: (610) 341-5967
Fax: (610) 341-1723
E-mail: ugadm@eastern.edu
http://www.eastern.edu
Biochemistry.

**East Stroudsburg University of
    Pennsylvania**
200 Prospect Street
East Stroudsburg, PA 18301
Phone: (570) 422-3542
Fax: (570) 422-3933
E-mail: undergrads@po-box.esu.edu
http://www.esu.edu
Biochemistry, biological/physical
    sciences, biotechnology, clinical
    laboratory science, geography,
    geology/earth science, physics.

Edinboro University of Pennsylvania
Biggers House
Edinboro, PA 16444
Phone: (814) 732-2761
Fax: (814) 732-2420
E-mail: eup_admissions@edinboro.edu
http://www.edinboro.edu
Biological/physical sciences,
    environmental science, geography,
    geology/earth science, physics.

Elizabethtown College
Leffler House
One Alpha Drive
Elizabethtown, PA 17022
Phone: (717) 361-1400
Fax: (717) 361-1365
E-mail: admissions@etown.edu
http://www.etown.edu
Biochemistry, biotechnology, clinical
    laboratory science, engineering—
    general, engineering mechanics,
    engineering physics, environmental
    science, industrial engineering, physics.

Franklin & Marshall College
P.O. Box 3003
Lancaster, PA 17604
Phone: (717) 291-3953
Fax: (717) 291-4389
E-mail: admission@fandm.edu
http://www.fandm.edu
Biochemistry, environmental science,
    geology/earth science, physics.

Gannon University
University Square
Erie, PA 16541
Phone: (814) 871-7240
Fax: (814) 871-5803
E-mail: admissions@gannon.edu
http://www.gannon.edu
Chemical engineering, clinical laboratory
    science, environmental engineering,
    environmental science, industrial
    engineering, mechanical engineering.

Geneva College
3200 College Avenue
Beaver Falls, PA 15010
Phone: (724) 847-6500
Fax: (724) 847-6776
E-mail: admissions@geneva.edu
http://www.geneva.edu
Applied mathematics, chemical
engineering, engineering—general,
physics.

Gettysburg College
300 North Washington Street
Gettysburg, PA 17325
Phone: (717) 337-6100
Fax: (717) 337-6145
E-mail: admiss@gettysburg.edu
http://www.gettysburg.edu
Biochemistry, biological/physical sciences,
chemical engineering, civil engineering, engineering—general, engineering
mechanics, engineering physics, environmental engineering, environmental
science, mechanical engineering,
nuclear engineering, physics.

Grove City College
100 Campus Drive
Grove City, PA 16127
Phone: (724) 458-2100
Fax: (724) 458-3395
E-mail: admissions@gcc.edu
http://www.gcc.edu
Biochemistry, mechanical engineering,
physics.

Gwynedd-Mercy College
1325 Sumneytown Pike
P.O. Box 901
Gwynedd Valley, PA 19437
Phone: (215) 641-5510
Fax: (215) 641-5556
E-mail: admissions@gmc.edu
http://www.gmc.edu
Clinical laboratory science.

Haverford College
370 West Lancaster Avenue
Haverford, PA 19041
Phone: (610) 896-1350
Fax: (610) 896-1338
E-mail: admitme@haverford.edu
http://www.haverford.edu
Geology/earth science, physics.

Holy Family University
Grant and Frankford Avenue
Philadelphia, PA 19114
Phone: (215) 637-3050

Fax: (215) 281-1022
E-mail: undergrad@hfu.edu
http://www.holyfamily.edu
Biochemistry.

Immaculata University
1145 King Road
P.O. Box 642
Immaculata, PA 19345
Phone: (610) 647-4400
Fax: (610) 647-0836
E-mail: admiss@immaculata.edu
http://www.immaculata.edu
Biological/physical sciences.

Indiana University of Pennsylvania
216 Pratt Hall
Indiana, PA 15075
Phone: (724) 357-2230
Fax: (724) 357-6281
E-mail: admissions-inquiry@iup.edu
http://www.iup.edu
Applied mathematics, biochemistry,
biological/physical sciences, clinical
laboratory science, geography,
geology/earth science, physics.

Juniata College
1700 Moore Street
Huntington, PA 16652
Phone: (814) 641-3420
Fax: (814) 641-3100
E-mail: admissions@juniata.edu
http://www.juniata.edu
Biochemistry, engineering—general,
engineering physics, environmental
science, geology/earth science, physics.

Keystone College
1 College Green
La Plume, PA 18440
Phone: (570) 945-8111
Fax: (570) 945-7916
E-mail: admissions@keystone.edu
http://www.keystone.edu
Biochemistry, biological/physical
sciences, clinical laboratory science,
environmental science.

King's College
133 North River Street
Wilkes-Barre, PA 18711
Phone: (570) 208-5858
Fax: (570) 208-5971
E-mail: admissions@kings.edu
http://www.kings.edu
Biological/physical sciences, clinical
laboratory science, environmental
science.

Kutztown University of Pennsylvania
Admission Office
P.O. Box 730
Kutztown, PA 19530
Phone: (610) 683-4060
Fax: (610) 683-1375
E-mail: admission@kutztown.edu
http://www.kutztown.edu
Biological/physical sciences, clinical
laboratory science, environmental
science, geology/earth science, physics.

Lafayette College
118 Markle Hall
Easton, PA 18042
Phone: (610) 330-5100
Fax: (610) 330-5355
E-mail: admissions@lafayette.edu
http://www.lafayette.edu
Biochemistry, chemical engineering, civil
engineering, engineering—general,
geology/earth science, mechanical
engineering, physics.

La Roche College
9000 Babcock Boulevard
Pittsburgh, PA 15237
Phone: (412) 536-1271
Fax: (412) 536-1048
E-mail: admissions@laroche.edu
http://www.laroche.edu
Applied mathematics.

La Salle University
1900 West Olney Avenue
Philadelphia, PA 19141
Phone: (215) 951-1500
Fax: (215) 951-1656
E-mail: admiss@lasalle.edu
http://www.lasalle.edu
Biochemistry, biological/physical
sciences, environmental science,
geology/earth science, statistics.

Lebanon Valley College
101 North College Avenue
Annville, PA 17003
Phone: (717) 867-6181
Fax: (717) 867-6026
E-mail: admissioin@lvc.edu
http://www.lvc.edu
Biochemistry, physics.

Lehigh University
27 Memorial Drive West
Bethlehem, PA 18015
Phone: (610) 758-3000
Fax: (610) 758-4361
E-mail: admissions@lehigh.edu

http://www.lehigh.edu
Biochemistry, biological/physical sciences, chemical engineering, civil engineering, engineering mechanics, engineering physics, environmental engineering, environmental science, geology/earth science, industrial engineering, materials engineering, mechanical engineering, physics, statistics, structural engineering.

Lincoln University
1570 Baltimore Pike, P.O. Box 179
Lincoln University, PA 19352
Phone: (610) 932-8300
Fax: (610) 932-1209
E-mail: admiss@lincoln.edu
http://www.lincoln.edu
Engineering—general, environmental science, physics.

Lock Haven University of Pennsylvania
Lock Haven University
Akeley Hall
Lock Haven, PA 17745
Phone: (570) 893-2027
Fax: (570) 893-2201
E-mail: admissions@lhup.edu
http://www.lhup.edu
Biological/physical sciences, electrical engineering technology, geography, geology/earth science, physics.

Mansfield University of Pennsylvania
Office of Admissions, Alumni Hall
Mansfield, PA 16933
Phone: (570) 662-4243
Fax: (570) 662-4121
E-mail: admissions@mansfield.edu
http://www.mansfield.edu
Biochemistry, clinical laboratory science, geography, geology/earth science, physics.

Marywood University
2300 Adams Avenue
Scranton, PA 18509
Phone: (570) 348-6234
Fax: (570) 961-4763
E-mail: ugadm@ac.marywood.edu
http://www.marywood.edu
Biotechnology, clinical laboratory science, environmental science.

Mercyhurst College
Admissions
501 East 38th Street
Erie, PA 16546
Phone: (800) 825-1926

Fax: (814) 824-2071
E-mail: admug@mercyhurst.edu
http://www.mercyhurst.edu
Biochemistry.

Messiah College
P.O. Box 3005
1 College Avenue
Grantham, PA 17027
Phone: (717) 691-6000
Fax: (717) 796-5374
E-mail: admiss@messiah.edu
http://www.messiah.edu
Biochemistry, engineering—general, environmental science, physics.

Millersville University of Pennsylvania
P.O. Box 1002
Millersville, PA 17551
Phone: (717) 872-3371
Fax: (717) 871-2147
E-mail: admissions@millersville.edu
http://www.millersville.edu
Atmospheric science, geography, geology/earth science, industrial technology, physics.

Moravian College
1200 Main Street
Bethlehem, PA 18018
Phone: (610) 861-1320
Fax: (610) 625-7930
E-mail: admissions@moravian.edu
http://www.moravian.edu
Biochemistry, environmental science, physics.

Muhlenberg College
2400 West Chew Street
Allentown, PA 18104
Phone: (484) 664-3200
Fax: (484) 664-3234
E-mail: admission@muhlenberg.edu
http://www.muhlenberg.edu
Biochemistry, environmental science, physics.

Pennsylvania College of Technology
One College Avenue
Williamsport, PA 17701
Phone: (800) 367-9222
Fax: (570) 321-5551
E-mail: admissions@pct.edu
http://www.pct.edu
Construction technology, electronics/electrical equipment repair, environmental engineering technology, industrial electronics technology, mechanical engineering technology.

Pennsylvania State University— Abington
106 Sutherland
Abington, PA 19001
Phone: (215) 881-7600
Fax: (215) 881-7317
E-mail: abingtonadmissions@psu.edu
http://www.abington.psu.edu
Agricultural and biological engineering, biochemistry, biological/physical sciences, chemical engineering, civil engineering, environmental engineering, geography, geology/earth science, industrial engineering, materials engineering, mechanical engineering, nuclear engineering, petroleum engineering, physics, soil science, statistics.

Pennsylvania State University— Altoona
Office of Admissions
E108 Raymond Smith Building
Altoona, PA 16601
Phone: (800) 848-9843
Fax: (814) 949-5564
E-mail: aaadmit@psu.edu
http://www.aa.psu.edu
Agricultural and biological engineering, atmospheric science, biochemistry, biological/physical sciences, chemical engineering, civil engineering, electrical engineering technology, environmental engineering, geography, geology/earth science, industrial engineering, materials engineering, mechanical engineering, nuclear engineering, petroleum engineering, physics, soil science, statistics.

Pennsylvania State University—Beaver
100 University Drive
Monaca, PA 15061
Phone: (724) 773-3800
Fax: (724) 773-3658
E-mail: br-admissions@psu.edu
http://www.br.psu-edu
Agricultural and biological engineering, atmospheric science, biochemistry, biological/physical sciences, chemical engineering, civil engineering, electrical engineering technology, environmental engineering, geography, industrial engineering, materials engineering, mechanical engineering, nuclear engineering, petroleum engineering, physics, soil science, statistics.

Pennsylvania State University—Berks
14 Perkins Student Center
Reading, PA 19610
Phone: (610) 396-6060
Fax: (610) 396-6077
E-mail: admissions@psu.edu
http://www.bk.psu.edu
Agricultural and biological engineering, atmospheric science, biochemistry, biological/physical sciences, chemical engineering, civil engineering, electrical engineering technology, environmental engineering, geography, geology/earth science, industrial engineering, materials engineering, mechanical engineering, mining and mineral engineering, nuclear engineering, petroleum engineering, physics, soil science, statistics.

Pennsylvania State University—Delaware County
25 Yearsley Mill Road
Media, PA 19083
Phone: (610) 892-1200
Fax: (610) 892-1357
E-mail: admissions-delco@psu.edu
http://www.de.psu.edu
Agricultural and biological engineering, biochemistry, biological/physical sciences, chemical engineering, civil engineering, environmental engineering, geography, geology/earth science, industrial engineering, materials engineering, mechanical engineering, mining and mineral engineering, nuclear engineering, petroleum engineering, physics, soil science, statistics.

Pennsylvania State University—Dubois
108 Hiller
Dubois, PA 15801
Phone: (814) 375-4720
Fax: (814) 375-4784
E-mail: mabl@psu.edu
http://www.ds.psu.edu
Agricultural and biological engineering, atmospheric science, biochemistry, biological/physical sciences, chemical engineering, civil engineering, electrical engineering technology, environmental engineering, geography, geology/earth science, industrial engineering, materials engineering, mechanical engineering, mining and mineral engineering, nuclear engineering, petroleum engineering, physics, soil science, statistics.

Pennsylvania State University—Erie, The Behrend College
5091 Station Road
Erie, PA 16563
Phone: (814) 898-6100
Fax: (814) 898-6044
E-mail: behrend.admissions@psu.edu
http://www.pserie.psu.edu
Agricultural and biological engineering, atmospheric science, electrical engineering technology, mechanical engineering, physics, soil science.

Pennsylvania State University—Fayette
P.O. Box 519
Route 119 North
108 Williams Building
Uniontown, PA 15041
Phone: (724) 430-4130
Fax: (724) 430-4175
E-mail: feadm@psu.edu
http://www.fe.psu.edu
Agricultural and biological engineering, atmospheric science, biochemistry, biological/physical sciences, chemical engineering, civil engineering, electrical engineering technology, geography, geology/earth science, industrial engineering, materials engineering, mechanical engineering, mining and mineral engineering, nuclear engineering, petroleum engineering, physics, soil science, statistics.

Pennsylvania State University—Harrisburg
Swatara Building
777 West Harrisburg Pike
Middletown, PA 17057
Phone: (717) 948-6250
Fax: (717) 948-6325
E-mail: hbgadmit@psu.edu
http://www.hbg.psu.edu
Agricultural and biological engineering, applied mathematics, atmospheric science, civil engineering technology, electrical engineering technology, environmental engineering, mechanical engineering, structural engineering.

Pennsylvania State University—Hazelton
110 Administrative Building
76 University Drive
Hazelton, PA 18202
Phone: (570) 450-3142
Fax: (570) 450-3182
E-mail: admissions-hn@psu.edu

http://www.hn.psu.edu
Agricultural and biological engineering, atmospheric science, biochemistry, biological/physical sciences, chemical engineering, civil engineering, electrical engineering technology, environmental engineering, geography, geology/earth science, industrial engineering, materials engineering, mechanical engineering, nuclear engineering, petroleum engineering, physics, soil science, statistics.

Pennsylvania State University—Lehigh Valley
8380 Mohr Lane
Academic Building
Fogelsville, PA 19051
Phone: (610) 285-5035
Fax: (610) 285-5220
E-mail: admissions-lv@psu.edu
http://www.lv.psu.edu
Agricultural and biological engineering, atmospheric science, biochemistry, biological/physical sciences, chemical engineering, civil engineering, environmental engineering, geography, geology/earth science, industrial engineering, materials engineering, mechanical engineering, mining and mineral engineering, nuclear engineering, petroleum engineering, physics, soil science, statistics.

Pennsylvania State University—McKeesport
100 Frable Building
4000 University Drive
McKeesport, PA 15132
Phone: (412) 675-9010
Fax: (412) 675-9056
E-mail: psumk@psu.edu
http://www.mk.psu.edu
Agricultural and biological engineering, atmospheric science, biochemistry, biological/physical sciences, chemical engineering, civil engineering, geography, geology/earth science, industrial engineering, materials engineering, mechanical engineering, mining and mineral engineering, nuclear engineering, petroleum engineering, physics, soil science, statistics.

Pennsylvania State University—Mont Alto
1 Campus Drive
Mont Alto, PA 17237

Phone: (717) 749-6130
Fax: (717) 749-6132
E-mail: psuma@psu.edu
http://www.ma.psu.edu
Agricultural and biological engineering, atmospheric science, biochemistry, biological/physical sciences, chemical engineering, civil engineering, environmental engineering, geography, geology/earth science, industrial engineering, materials engineering, mechanical engineering, mining and mineral engineering, nuclear engineering, petroleum engineering, physics, soil science, statistics.

Pennsylvania State University—New Kensington
3550 Seventh Street Road, Route 780
Upper Barrell, PA 15068
Phone: (724) 334-5466
Fax: (724) 334-6111
E-mail: nkadmissions@psu.edu
http://www.nk.psu.edu
Agricultural and biological engineering, atmospheric science, biochemistry, biological/physical sciences, chemical engineering, civil engineering, electrical engineering technology, environmental engineering, geography, geology/earth science, industrial engineering, materials engineering, mechanical engineering, mining and mineral engineering, nuclear engineering, petroleum engineering, soil science, statistics.

Pennsylvania State University— Schuylkill—Capital College
200 University Drive
A102 Administrative Building
Schuylkill Haven, PA 17072
Phone: (570) 385-6252
Fax: (570) 385-6272
E-mail: sl-admissions@psu.edu
http://www.sl.psu.edu
Agricultural and biological engineering, biochemistry, biological/physical sciences, chemical engineering, civil engineering, electrical engineering technology, environmental engineering, geology/earth science, industrial engineering, mechanical engineering, metallurgical engineering, meteorology, mining and mineral engineering, nuclear engineering, petroleum engineering, physics, soil science, statistics.

Pennsylvania State University— Shenango
147 Shenango Avenue
Sharon, PA 16146
Phone: (724) 983-2803
Fax: (724) 983-2820
E-mail: psushenango.psu.edu
http://www.shenango.psu.edu
Agricultural and biological engineering, atmospheric science, biochemistry, biological/physical sciences, chemical engineering, civil engineering, geography, geology/earth science, industrial engineering, materials engineering, mechanical engineering, mining and mineral engineering, nuclear engineering, petroleum engineering, physics, soil science, statistics.

Pennsylvania State University— University Park
201 Shields Building
P.O. Box 3000
University Park, PA 16802
Phone: (814) 865-5471
Fax: (814) 863-7590
E-mail: admissions@psu.edu
http://www.psu.edu
Agricultural and biological engineering, atmospheric science, biochemistry, biological/physical sciences, chemical engineering, civil engineering, electrical engineering technology, environmental engineering, geography, geology/earth science, materials engineering, mechanical engineering, meteorology, mining and mineral engineering, natural resource economics, nuclear engineering, petroleum engineering, physics, soil science, statistics, surveying technology.

Pennsylvania State University— Wilkes-Barre
P.O. Box PSU
Lehman, PA 18627
Phone: (570) 675-9238
Fax: (570) 675-9113
E-mail: wbadmissions@psu.edu
http://www.psu.edu
Biochemistry, biological/physical sciences, chemical engineering, civil engineering, environmental engineering, geography, industrial engineering, materials engineering, mechanical engineering, meteorology, mining and mineral engineering,

nuclear engineering, petroleum engineering, physics, soil science, surveying technology.

Pennsylvania State University— Worthington Scranton
120 Ridge View Drive
Dunmore, PA 18512
Phone: (570) 963-2500
Fax: (570) 963-2524
E-mail: wsadmissions@psu.edu
http://www.sn.psu.edu
Agricultural and biological engineering, atmospheric science, biochemistry, biological/physical sciences, chemical engineering, civil engineering, environmental engineering, geography, geology/earth science, industrial engineering, materials engineering, mechanical engineering, mining and mineral engineering, nuclear engineering, petroleum engineering, physics, soil science, statistics.

Pennsylvania State University—York
1031 Edgecomb Avenue
York, PA 17403
Phone: (717) 771-4040
Fax: (717) 771-4005
E-mail: ykadmission@psu.edu
http://www.yk.psu.edu
Agricultural and biological engineering, atmospheric science, biochemistry, biological/physical sciences, chemical engineering, civil engineering, environmental engineering, geology/earth science, industrial engineering, materials engineering, mechanical engineering, mining and mineral engineering, nuclear engineering, petroleum engineering, physics, soil science, statistics.

Philadelphia University
School House Lane & Henry Avenue
Philadelphia, PA 19144
Phone: (215) 951-2800
Fax: (215) 951-2907
E-mail: admissions@PhilaU.edu
http://www.PhilaU.edu
Biochemistry, engineering—general, industrial engineering.

Point Park University
201 Wood Street
Pittsburgh, PA 15222
Phone: (412) 392-3430
Fax: (412) 391-1980
E-mail: enroll@ppc.edu

http://www.ppc.edu
Biotechnology, civil engineering
technology, environmental science,
mechanical engineering technology.

Robert Morris University
6001 University Boulevard
Moon Township, PA 15108
Phone: (412) 262-8206
Fax: (412) 299-2425
E-mail: enrollmentoffice@rmu.edu
http://www.rmu.edu
Applied mathematics, environmental
science.

Rosemont College
1400 Montgomery Avenue
Rosemont, PA 19010
Phone: (610) 526-2966
Fax: (610) 520-4399
E-mail: admissions@rosemont.edu
http://www.rosemont.edu
Biochemistry, environmental science.

Saint Francis University
P.O. Box 600
Loretto, PA 15940
Phone: (814) 472-3000
Fax: (814) 472-3335
E-mail: admissions@francis.edu
http://www.francis.edu
Engineering—general, environmental
science.

Saint Joseph's University
5600 City Avenue
Philadelphia, PA 19131
Phone: (610) 660-1300
Fax: (610) 660-1314
E-mail: admit@sju.edu
http://www.sju.edu
Biochemistry, physics.

Saint Vincent College
3000 Fraser Purchase Road
Latrobe, PA 10650
Phone: (724) 537-4540
Fax: (724) 532-5069
E-mail: admission@stvincent.edu
http://www.stvincent.edu
Biochemistry, engineering—general,
physics.

Seton Hill University
1 Seton Hill Drive
Greensburg, PA 15601
Phone: (724) 838-4255
Fax: (724) 830-1294
E-mail: admit@setonhill.edu

http://www.setonhill.edu
Biochemistry, clinical laboratory science,
engineering—general, physics.

**Shippensburg University of
Pennsylvania**
Old Main 105
1871 Old Main Drive
Shippensburg, PA 17257
Phone: (717) 477-1231
Fax: (717) 477-4016
E-mail: admiss@ship.edu
http://www.ship.edu
Geography, geology/earth science, physics.

**Slippery Rock University of
Pennsylvania**
Office of Admissions
146 North Hall Welcome Center
Slippery Rock, PA 16057
Phone: (724) 738-2015
Fax: (724) 738-2913
E-mail: apply@sru.edu
http://www.sru.edu
Geography, geology/earth science, physics.

Susquehanna University
514 University Avenue
Susquehanna, PA 17870
Phone: (570) 372-4260
Fax: (570) 372-2722
E-mail: suadmiss@susque.edu
http://www.susque.edu
Biochemistry, environmental science,
physics.

Swarthmore College
500 College Avenue
Swarthmore, PA 19081
Phone: (610) 328-8300
Fax: (610) 328-8580
E-mail: admissions@swarthmore.edu
http://www.swarthmore.edu
Biochemistry, chemical physics,
engineering—general, physics.

Temple University
1801 North Broad Street
Philadelphia, PA 19122
Phone: (215) 204-7200
Fax: (215) 204-5694
E-mail: tuadm@mail.temple.edu
http://www.temple.edu
Biochemistry, biophysics, civil engineering,
civil engineering technology,
engineering technology—general,
environmental engineering technology,
geography, geology/earth science,
mechanical engineering, physics.

Thiel College
75 College Avenue
Greenville, PA 16125
Phone: (724) 589-2345
Fax: (724) 589-2013
E-mail: admission@thiel.edu
http://www.thiel.edu
Engineering—general, physics.

University of Pennsylvania
1 College Hall
Philadelphia, PA 19104
Phone: (215) 898-7507
Fax: (215) 898-9670
E-mail: info@admissions.ugao.upenn.edu
http://www.upenn.edu
Biochemistry, biophysics, chemical
engineering, environmental
engineering, geology/earth science,
materials engineering, materials
science, mechanical engineering,
physics, statistics.

University of Pittsburgh—Bradford
Office of Admissions—Hanley Library
300 Campus Drive
Bradford, PA 16701
Phone: (814) 362-7555
Fax: (814) 362-7578
E-mail: admissions@www.upb.pitt.edu
http://www.upb.pitt.edu
Applied mathematics, chemical
engineering, civil engineering,
engineering physics, geography,
geology/earth science, industrial
engineering, materials engineering,
mechanical engineering, petroleum
engineering, physics, statistics.

University of Pittsburgh—Greensburg
1150 Mount Pleasant Road
Greensburg, PA 15601
Phone: (724) 836-9880
Fax: (724) 836-7160
E-mail: upgadmit@pitt.edu
http://www.upg.pitt.edu
Applied mathematics, chemical
engineering, civil engineering,
engineering—general, geography,
geology/earth science, industrial
engineering, materials engineering,
mechanical engineering, petroleum
engineering, physics, statistics.

University of Pittsburgh—Johnstown
157 Blackington Hall
450 Schoolhouse Road
Johnstown, PA 15904

Phone: (814) 269-7050
Fax: (814) 269-7044
E-mail: upjadmit@pitt.edu
http://www.upj.pitt.edu
Chemical engineering, civil engineering, civil engineering technology, engineering physics, geography, geology/earth science, industrial engineering, materials engineering, mechanical engineering, mechanical engineering technology, petroleum engineering, physics, statistics.

University of Pittsburgh—Pittsburgh
4227 Fifth Avenue
First Floor Alumni Hall
Pittsburgh, PA 15260
Phone: (412) 624-7488
Fax: (412) 648-8815
E-mail: oafa@pitt.edu
http://www.pitt.edu
Chemical engineering, civil engineering, engineering physics, geography, geology/earth science, industrial engineering, materials engineering, mechanical engineering, petroleum engineering, physics, statistics.

The University of Scranton
800 Linden Street
Scranton, PA 18501
Phone: (570) 941-7540
Fax: (570) 941-5928
E-mail: admissions@scranton.edu
http://www.scranton.edu
Biochemistry, clinical laboratory science, physics.

University of the Sciences in Philadelphia
Admissions Office
600 South 43rd Street
Philadelphia, PA 19104
Phone: (215) 596-8810
Fax: (215) 596-8821
E-mail: admit@usip.edu
http://www.usip.edu
Biochemistry, environmental science.

Villanova University
800 Lancaster Avenue
Villanova, PA 19085
Phone: (610) 519-4000
Fax: (610) 519-6450
E-mail: gotovu@villanova.edu
http://www.villanova.edu
Chemical engineering, civil engineering, geography, mechanical engineering, physics.

Washington and Jefferson College
60 South Lincoln Street
Washington, PA 15301
Phone: (724) 223-6025
Fax: (724) 223-6534
E-mail: admission@washjeff.edu
http://www.washjeff.edu
Biochemistry, physics.

West Chester University of Pennsylvania
Messikomer Hall
100 West Rosedale Avenue
West Chester, PA 19383
Phone: (610) 436-3411
Fax: (610) 436-2907
E-mail: ugadmiss@wcupa.edu
http://www.wcupa.edu
Analytical chemistry, biochemistry, geography, geology/earth science, physics.

Westminster College
319 South Market Street
New Wilmington, PA 16172
Phone: (724) 946-7100
Fax: (724) 946-7171
E-mail: admis@westminster.edu
http://www.westminster.edu
Biochemistry, biophysics, engineering—general, physics.

Widener University
One University Place
Chester, PA 19013
Phone: (610) 499-4126
Fax: (610) 499-4676
E-mail: admissions.office@widener.edu
http://www.widener.edu
Biochemistry, chemical engineering, civil engineering, engineering—general, mechanical engineering, physics.

Wilkes University
84 West South Street
Wilkes-Barre, PA 18766
Phone: (570) 408-4400
Fax: (570) 408-4904
E-mail: admissions@wilkes.edu
http://www.wilkes.edu
Biochemistry, clinical laboratory science, environmental engineering, geology/earth science, mechanical engineering.

York College of Pennsylvania
Country Club Road
York, PA 17405
Phone: (800) 455-8018
Fax: (717) 849-1607
E-mail: admissions@ycp.edu
http://www.ycp.edu
Mechanical engineering, physics.

RHODE ISLAND

Brown University
P.O. Box 1876
45 Prospect Street
Providence, RI 02912
Phone: (401) 863-2378
Fax: (401) 863-9300
E-mail: admission_undergraduate@brown.edu
http://www.brown.edu
Applied mathematics, biochemistry, biological/physical sciences, biophysics, chemical engineering, chemical physics, civil engineering, engineering physics, environmental science, geology/earth science, materials engineering, geophysics/seismology, mechanical engineering, physics, statistics.

Johnson & Wales University—Providence
8 Abbott Park Place
Providence, RI 02903
Phone: (401) 598-2310
Fax: (401) 598-2948
E-mail: admissions@jwu.edu
http://www.jwu.edu
Electrical engineering technology.

New England Institute of Technology
2500 Post Road
Warwick, RI 02886
Phone: (800) 736-7744
Fax: NA
E-mail: At Web site
http://www.neit.edu
Mechanical engineering.

Providence College
549 River Avenue and Eaton Street
Providence, RI 02918
Phone: (401) 865-2535
Fax: (401) 865-2826
E-mail: pcadmiss@providence.edu
http://www.providence.edu
Biochemistry, engineering physics.

Rhode Island College
Office of Undergraduate Admissions
600 Mount Pleasant Avenue
Providence, RI 02908
Phone: (401) 456-8234
Fax: (401) 456-8817
E-mail: admissions@ric.edu

http://www.ric.edu
Clinical laboratory science, geography,
    physics.

Roger Williams University
One Old Ferry Road
Bristol, RI 02809
Phone: (401) 254-3500
Fax: (401) 254-3557
E-mail: admit@rwu.edu
http://www.rwu.edu
Engineering—general.

Salve Regina University
100 Ochre Point Avenue
Newport, RI 02840
Phone: (401) 341-2908
Fax: (401) 848-2823
E-mail: sruadmis@salve.edu
http://www.salve.edu
Clinical laboratory science.

University of Rhode Island
Undergraduate Admissions Office
14 Upper College Road
Kingston, RI 02881
Phone: (401) 874-7100
Fax: (401) 874-5523
E-mail: uriadmit@etal.uri.edu
http://www.uri.edu
Biochemistry, chemical engineering,
    civil engineering, clinical laboratory
    science, geology/earth science,
    industrial engineering, mechanical
    engineering, physics, soil science.

SOUTH CAROLINA

Benedict College
Harden and Blanding Streets
Columbia, SC 29204
Phone: (803) 253-5143
Fax: (803) 253-5167
E-mail: admission@benedict.edu
http://www.benedict.edu
Electrical engineering technology,
    environmental science, physics.

Charleston Southern University
Enrollment Services
P.O. Box 118087
Charleston, SC 29433
Phone: (843) 863-7050
Fax: (843) 863-7070
E-mail: enroll@csuniv.edu
http://www.charlestonsouthern.edu
Applied mathematics, biological/
    physical sciences, geology/earth
    science, physics.

The Citadel
171 Moultrie Street
Charleston, SC 29409
Phone: (843) 953-5230
Fax: (843) 953-7036
E-mail: admissions@citadel.edu
http://www.citadel.edu
Civil engineering, physics.

Claflin University
400 Magnolia Street
Orangeburg, SC 29115
Phone: (803) 535-5340
Fax: (803) 535-5387
E-mail: mzeigler@claflin.edu
http://www.claflin.edu
Applied mathematics, biochemistry,
    biotechnology, environmental science.

Clemson University
106 Sikes Hall, Box 345124
Clemson, SC 29634
Phone: (864) 656-2987
Fax: (864) 656-2464
E-mail: cuadmissions@clemson.edu
http://www.clemson.edu
Agricultural and biological engineering,
    biochemistry, chemical engineering,
    civil engineering, clinical laboratory
    science, geology/earth science,
    mechanical engineering, physics, soil
    science.

Coastal Carolina University
P.O. Box 261954
Conway, SC 29528
Phone: (843) 349-2026
Fax: (843) 349-2127
E-mail: admissions@coastal.edu
http://www.coastal.edu
Applied mathematics, physics.

Coker College
300 East College Avenue
Hartsville, SC 29550
Phone: (843) 383-8050
Fax: (843) 383-8056
E-mail: admissions@coker.edu
http://www.coker.edu
Clinical laboratory science.

College of Charleston
66 George Street
Charleston, SC 29424
Phone: (843) 953-5670
Fax: (843) 953-6322
E-mail: admissions@cofc.edu
http://www.cofc.edu
Biochemistry, geology/earth science,
    physics.

Converse College
580 East Main Street
Spartanburg, SC 29302
Phone: (864) 596-9040
Fax: (864) 596-9225
E-mail: admissions@converse.edu
http://www.converse.edu
Biochemistry.

Francis Marion University
Office of Admissions
P.O. Box 100547
Florence, SC 29501
Phone: (843) 661-1231
Fax: (843) 661-4635
E-mail: admissions@marion.edu
http://www.marion.edu
Electrical engineering technology, physics.

Furman University
3300 Poinsett Highway
Greenville, SC 29613
Phone: (864) 294-2034
Fax: (864) 294-3127
E-mail: admissions@furman.edu
http://www.furman.edu
Geology/earth science, physics.

Limestone College
1115 College Drive
Gaffey, SC 29340
Phone: (864) 488-4549
Fax: (864) 487-8706
E-mail: admiss@limestone.edu
http://www.limestone.edu
Applied mathematics.

Presbyterian College
503 South Broad Street
Clinton, SC 29325
Phone: (864) 833-8230
Fax: (864) 833-8481
E-mail: admissions@presby.edu
http://www.presby.edu
Physics.

South Carolina State University
300 College Street Northeast
Orangeburg, SC 29117
Phone: (800) 260-5956
Fax: (803) 536-8990
E-mail: admissions@scsu.edu
http://www.scsu.edu
Civil engineering technology, electrical
    engineering technology, nuclear
    engineering, physics.

University of South Carolina—Aiken
471 University Parkway

Aiken, SC 29801
Phone: (803) 641-3366
Fax: (803) 641-3727
E-mail: admit@sc.edu
http://www.usca.edu
Applied mathematics, chemical
    engineering, civil engineering,
    geography, geophysics/seismology,
    mechanical engineering, physics,
    statistics.

University of South Carolina—
    Columbia
Office of Undergraduate Admissions
Columbia, SC 29208
Phone: (803) 777-7000
Fax: (803) 777-0101
E-mail: admissions-ugrad@sc.edu
http://www.sc.edu
Chemical engineering, civil engineer-
    ing, geography, geology/earth
    science, geophysics/seismology,
    mechanical engineering, physics,
    statistics.

University of South Carolina—
    Spartanburg
800 University Way
Spartanburg, SC 29303
Phone: (864) 503-5246
Fax: (864) 503-5727
E-mail: dstewart@uscs.edu
http://www.uscs.edu
Applied mathematics, chemical
    engineering, civil engineering,
    geography, geology/earth science,
    geophysics/seismology, mechanical
    engineering, physics, statistics.

Winthrop University
701 Oakland Avenue
Rock Hill, SC 29733
Phone: (803) 323-2137
Fax: (803) 323-2137
E-mail: admissions@winthrop.edu
http://www.winthrop.edu
Clinical laboratory science.

SOUTH DAKOTA

Augustana College
2001 South Summit Avenue
Sioux Falls, SD 57197
Phone: (605) 274-5516
Fax: (605) 274-5518
E-mail: admission@augie.edu
http://www.augie.edu
Clinical laboratory science, engineering
    physics, physics.

Black Hills State University
1200 University Street, Unit 9502
Spearfish, SD 57799
Phone: (605) 642-6343
Fax: (605) 642-6254
E-mail: admissions@bhsu.edu
http://www.bhsu.edu
Industrial technology.

Mount Mary College
1105 West Eighth Street
Yankton, SD 57078
Phone: (605) 668-1545
Fax: (605) 668-1607
E-mail: mmcadmit@mtmc.edu
http://www.mtmc.edu
Clinical laboratory science.

Northern State University
1200 South Jay Street
Aberdeen, SD 57401
Phone: (605) 626-2544
Fax: (605) 626-2431
E-mail: admissions@northern.edu
http://www.northern.edu
Clinical laboratory science.

South Dakota School of Mines and
    Technology
501 East Saint Joseph Street
Rapid City, SD 57701
Phone: (605) 394-2414
Fax: (605) 394-6131
E-mail: admissions@sdsmt.edu
http://www.sdsmt.edu
Chemical engineering, civil engineering,
    geological engineering, geology/
    earth science, industrial engineering,
    mechanical engineering, metallurgical
    engineering, physics.

South Dakota State University
P.O. Box 2201
Brookings, SD 57007
Phone: (605) 688-4121
Fax: (605) 688-6891
E-mail: admissions@sdstate.edu
http://www.sdstate.edu
Agricultural and biological engineering,
    civil engineering, clinical laboratory
    science, construction technology,
    electrical engineering technology,
    engineering physics, geography,
    mechanical engineering, statistics.

University of Sioux Falls
1101 West 22nd Street
Sioux Falls, SD 57105
Phone: (605) 331-6600

Fax: (605) 331-6615
E-mail: admissions@usiouxfalls.edu
http://www.usiouxfalls.edu
Applied mathematics.

The University of South Dakota
414 East Clark Street
Vermillion, SD 57069
Phone: (605) 677-5434
Fax: (605) 677-6323
E-mail: admiss@usd.edu
http://www.usd.edu
Geology/earth science, physics.

TENNESSEE

Austin Peay State University
P.O. Box 4548
Clarksville, TN 37044
Phone: (931) 221-7661
Fax: (931) 221-6168
E-mail: admissions@apsu.edu
http://www.apsu.edu
Clinical laboratory science, engineering
    technology—general, geology/earth
    science, physics.

Bethel College
325 Cherry Avenue
McKenzie, TN 38201
Phone: (731) 352-4030
Fax: (731) 352-4069
E-mail: admissons@bethel-college.edu
http://www.bethel-college.edu
Applied mathematics, biological/physical
    sciences.

Carson-Newman College
1646 Russell Avenue
Jefferson City, TN 37760
Phone: (865) 471-3223
Fax: (865) 471-3502
E-mail: admitme@cn.edu
http://www.cn.edu
Clinical laboratory science.

Christian Brothers University
Admissions
P.O. Box T-6
650 East Parkway South
Memphis, TN 38104
Phone: (901) 321-3205
Fax: (901) 321-3202
E-mail: admissions@chu.edu
http://www.chu.edu
Biological/physical sciences, chemical
    engineering, civil engineering, engi-
    neering physics, mechanical engineer-
    ing, physics.

East Tennessee State University
P.O. Box 70731
Johnson City, TN 37614
Phone: (423) 439-4213
Fax: (423) 439-4630
E-mail: go2etsu.etsu.edu
http://www.etsu.edu
Geography, physics, surveying
technology.

Fisk University
1000 17th Avenue North
Nashville, TN 37208
Phone: (615) 329-8665
Fax: (615) 329-8774
E-mail: admissions@fisk.edu
http://www.fisk.edu
Physics.

Freed-Hardeman University
158 East Main Street
Henderson, TN 38340
Phone: (731) 989-6651
Fax: (731) 989-6047
E-mail: admissions@fhu.edu
http://www.fhu.edu
Biochemistry.

King College
1350 King College Road
Bristol, TN 37620
Phone: (423) 652-4861
Fax: (423) 652-4727
E-mail: admissions@king.edu
http://www.king.edu
Biochemistry, biophysics, clinical
laboratory science, physics.

Lambuth University
705 Lambuth Boulevard
Jackson, TN 38301
Phone: (731) 425-3223
Fax: (731) 425-3496
E-mail: admit@lambuth.edu
http://www.lambuth.edu
Environmental science.

Lee University
P.O. Box 3450
Cleveland, TN 37320
Phone: (423) 614-8500
Fax: (423) 614-8533
E-mail: admissions@leeuniversity.edu
http://www.leeuniversity.edu
Biochemistry.

Lincoln Memorial University
Cumberland Gap Parkway
Harrogate, TN 37752

Phone: (423) 869-6280
Fax: (423) 869-6250
E-mail: admissions@inetlmu@lmunet.edu
http://www.lmunet.edu
Clinical laboratory science.

Lipscomb University
3901 Granny White Pike
Nashville, TN 37204
Phone: (615) 269-1776
Fax: (615) 269-1804
E-mail: admissions@lipscomb.edu
http://www.lipscomb.edu
Biochemistry, engineering mechanics,
environmental science, physics.

Maryville College
502 East Lamar Alexander Parkway
Maryville, TN 37804
Phone: (865) 981-8092
Fax: (865) 981-8005
E-mail: admissions@maryvillecollege.edu
http://www.maryvillecollege.edu
Biochemistry, chemical physics, civil
engineering, engineering—general,
environmental engineering, industrial
engineering.

Middle Tennessee State University
Office of Admissions
1301 East Main Street
Murfreesboro, TN 37132
Phone: (800) 433-6878
Fax: (615) 898-5478
E-mail: admissions@mtsu.edu
http://www.mtsu.edu
Biological/physical sciences, environmen-
tal engineering technology, geology/
earth science, industrial technology,
physics, soil science.

Southern Adventist University
P.O. Box 370
Collegedale, TN 37315
Phone: (423) 238-2844
Fax: (423) 238-3005
E-mail: admissions@southern.edu
http://www.southern.edu
Biochemistry, biophysics, clinical
laboratory science, physics.

Tennessee State University
P.O. Box 5006
Cookeville, TN 38505
Phone: (931) 372-3888
Fax: (931) 372-6250
E-mail: jcade@tnstate.edu
http://www.tnstate.edu

Biochemistry, biological/physical
sciences, civil engineering,
engineering—general, physics.

Tennessee Technological University
P.O. Box 5006
Cookeville, TN 38505
Phone: (931) 372-3888
Fax: (931) 372-6250
E-mail: admissions@tntech.edu
http://www.tntech.edu
Chemical engineering, civil engineering,
geology/earth science, mechanical
engineering, physics, soil science.

Trevecca Nazarene University
333 Murfreesboro Road
Nashville, TN 37210
Phone: (888) 210-4868
Fax: NA
E-mail: At Web site
http://www.trevecca.edu
Clinical laboratory science.

Tusculum College
P.O. Box 5051
Greenville, TN 37743
Phone: (423) 636-7300
Fax: (423) 638-7166
E-mail: admissions@tusculum.edu
http://www.tusculum.edu
Clinical laboratory science.

Union University
1050 Union University Drive
Jackson, TN 38305
Phone: (731) 661-5000
Fax: (731) 661-5017
E-mail: cgriffin@uu.edu
http://www.uu.edu
Chemical physics, mechanical
engineering, physics.

University of Memphis
229 Administration Building
Memphis, TN 38152
Phone: (901) 678-2111
Fax: (901) 678-3053
E-mail: recruitment@memphis.edu
http://www.memphis.edu
Civil engineering, electrical engineering
technology, geography, geology/earth
science, geophysics/seismology,
mechanical engineering, physics.

University of Tennessee—Chattanooga
615 McCallie Avenue
131 Hooper Hall
Chattanooga, TN 37403

Phone: (423) 425-4662
Fax: (423) 425-4157
E-mail: yancy-freeman@utc.edu
http://www.utc.edu
Applied mathematics, engineering—general, geology/earth science, physics.

University of Tennessee—Knoxville
320 Science Building
Circle Park Drive
Knoxville, TN 37996
Phone: (865) 974-2184
Fax: (865) 974-6341
E-mail: admissions@tennessee.edu
http://www.utk.edu
Agricultural and biological engineering, biochemistry, chemical engineering, civil engineering, clinical laboratory science, engineering physics, geography, geology/earth science, materials science, mechanical engineering, nuclear engineering, physics, soil science.

University of Tennessee—Martin
200 Hall-Moody Administrative Building
Martin, TN 38238
Phone: (731) 881-7020
Fax: (731) 881-7029
E-mail: admitme@utm.edu
http://www.utm.edu
Engineering—general, geology/earth science.

University of the South
735 University Avenue
Sewanee, TN 37383
Phone: (800) 522-2234
Fax: NA
E-mail: admiss@sewanee.edu
http://www.admission.sewanee.edu
Geology/earth science, physics.

Vanderbilt University
2305 West End Avenue
Nashville, TN 37203
Phone: (615) 322-2561
Fax: (615) 343-7765
E-mail: admissions@vanderbilt.edu
http://www.vanderbilt.edu
Chemical engineering, civil engineering, geology/earth science, mechanical engineering, physics.

TEXAS

Abilene Christian University
ACU P.O. Box 29000
Abilene, TX 79699
Phone: (325) 674-2650
Fax: (325) 674-2130
E-mail: info@admissions.acu.edu
http://www.acu.edu
Biochemistry, clinical laboratory science, engineering—general, engineering physics, environmental science, physics.

Angelo State University
2601 West Avenue
San Angelo, TX 76909
Phone: (325) 942-2041
Fax: (325) 942-2078
E-mail: admissions@angelo.edu
http://www.angelo.edu
Biochemistry, clinical laboratory science, physics.

Austin College
90 North Grand Avenue, Suite 6N
Sherman, TX 75090
Phone: (903) 813-3000
Fax: (903) 813-3198
E-mail: admissions@austincollege.edu
http://www.austincollege.edu
Biochemistry, physics.

Baylor University
P.O. Box 97056
Waco, TX 76798
Phone: (254) 710-3435
Fax: (254) 710-3436
E-mail: admissions_serv_office@baylor.edu
http://www.baylor.edu
Applied mathematics, biochemistry, clinical laboratory science, engineering—general, environmental science, geography, geology/earth science, geophysics/seismology, mechanical engineering, physics, statistics.

DeVry University—Irving
4800 Regent Boulevard
Irving, TX 75063
Phone: (972) 929-5777
Fax: (972) 929-2860
E-mail: cwilliams@mail.dal.devry.edu
http://www.devry.edu
Electrical engineering technology.

East Texas Baptist University
1209 North Grove Street
Marshall, TX 75670
Phone: (903) 923-2000
Fax: (903) 923-2001
E-mail: admissions@etbu.edu
http://www.etbu.edu
Clinical laboratory science.

Hardin-Simmons University
P.O. Box 16050
Abilene, TX 79698
Phone: (325) 670-1206
Fax: (325) 671-2115
E-mail: enroll@hsutx.edu
http://www.hsutx.edu
Environmental science, geology/earth science, physics.

Lamar University
P.O. Box 10009
Beaumont, TX 77710
Phone: (409) 880-8888
Fax: (409) 880-8463
E-mail: admissions@hal.lamar.edu
http://www.lamar.edu
Applied mathematics, chemical engineering, civil engineering, clinical laboratory science, engineering—general, geology/earth science, industrial technology, mechanical engineering, physics.

LeTourneau University
P.O. Box 7001
Longview, TX 75607
Phone: (903) 233-3400
Fax: (903) 233-3411
E-mail: admissions@letu.edu
http://www.letu.edu
Clinical laboratory science, electrical engineering technology, engineering—general, mechanical engineering, mechanical engineering technology.

Lubbock Christian University
5601 19th Street
Lubbock, TX 79407
Phone: (800) 720-7151
Fax: (806) 720-7162
E-mail: admissions@lcu.edu
http://www.lcu.edu
Engineering—general.

McMurry University
South 14th and Sayles Boulevard
Abilene, TX 79697
Phone: (915) 793-4700
Fax: (915) 793-4718
E-mail: admissions@mcm.edu
http://www.mcm.edu
Biochemistry, biological/physical sciences, environmental science, physics.

Midwestern State University
3410 Taft Boulevard
Wichita Falls, TX 76308
Phone: (940) 397-4334

Fax: (940) 397-4672
E-mail: admissions@mwsu.edu
http://www.mwsu.edu
Clinical laboratory science, engineering—
general, environmental science,
geology/earth science, mechanical
engineering, physics.

Prairie View A&M University
P.O. Box 3089
University Drive
Prairie View, TX 77446
Phone: (936) 857-2626
Fax: (936) 857-2699
E-mail: admissions@pvamu.edu
http://www.pvamu.edu
Chemical engineering, civil engineering,
clinical laboratory science, construction
technology, electrical engineering
technology, industrial technology,
mechanical engineering, physics.

Rice University
P.O. Box 1892
Houston, TX 77251
Phone: (713) 348-7423
Fax: (713) 348-5952
E-mail: admission@rice.edu
http://www.rice.edu
Applied mathematics, biochemistry,
chemical engineering, chemical
physics, civil engineering,
environmental engineering, geology/
earth science, geophysics/seismology,
materials engineering, mechanical
engineering, physics, statistics.

St. Edward's University
3001 South Congress Avenue
Austin, TX 78704
Phone: (512) 448-8400
Fax: NA
E-mail: infostedwards.edu
http://www.stedwards.edu
Biochemistry.

St. Mary's University
One Camino Santa Maria
San Antonio, TX 78228
Phone: (210) 436-3126
Fax: (210) 431-6742
E-mail: uadm@stmarytx.edu
http://www.stmarytx.edu
Biochemistry, biophysics, geology/earth
science, physics.

Sam Houston State University
P.O. Box 2418, SHSU
Huntsville, TX 77341

Phone: (936) 294-1828
Fax: (936) 294-3758
E-mail: admissions@shsu.edu
http://www.shsu.edu
Clinical laboratory science, construction
technology, electrical engineering
technology, environmental science,
geography, geology/earth science,
physics.

Schreiner University
2100 Memorial Boulevard
Kenville, TX 78028
Phone: (830) 792-7217
Fax: (830) 792-7226
E-mail: admissions@schreiner.edu
http://www.schreiner.edu
Biochemistry, engineering—general.

Southern Methodist University
P.O. Box 750296
Dallas, TX 75275
Phone: (214) 768-2058
Fax: (214) 768-2507
E-mail: enroll_serv@mail.smu.edu
http://www.smu.edu
Biochemistry, civil engineering,
environmental engineering,
environmental science, geology/earth
science, geophysics/seismology,
mechanical engineering, physics,
statistics.

Southwestern Adventist University
P.O. Box 567
Keene, TX 76059
Phone: (800) 433-2240
Fax: (817) 645-3921
E-mail: illingworth@swau.edu
http://www.swau.edu
Applied mathematics, physics.

Southwestern University
Admissions Office
P.O. Box 770
Georgetown, TX 78627
Phone: (512) 863-1200
Fax: (512) 863-9601
E-mail: admission@southwestern.edu
http://www.southwestern.edu
Physics.

Stephen F. Austin State University
P.O. Box 13051, SFA Station
Nacogdoches, TX 75962
Phone: (936) 468-2504
Fax: (936) 468-3849
E-mail: admissions@sfasu.edu
http://www.sfasu.edu

Clinical laboratory science,
environmental science, geography,
geology/earth science, physics.

Sul Ross State University
P.O. Box C-2
Alpine, TX 79832
Phone: (915) 837-8050
Fax: (915) 837-8431
E-mail: admissions@sulross.edu
http://www.sulross.edu
Geology/earth science.

Tarleton State University
P.O. Box T-0030
Tarleton Station
Stephenville, TX 76402
Phone: (254) 968-9125
Fax: (254) 968-9951
E-mail: uadm@tarleton.edu
http://www.tarleton.edu
Clinical laboratory science, engineering
physics, engineering technology—
general, environmental engineering,
hydrology/water resources science,
industrial technology, physics.

Texas A&M University—Commerce
P.O. Box 3011
Commerce, TX 75429
Phone: (903) 886-5106
Fax: (903) 886-5888
E-mail: admissions@tamu-commerce.
edu
http://www.tamu-commerce.edu
Agricultural and biological engineering,
applied mathematics, atmospheric
science, biochemistry, biological/
physical sciences, chemical
engineering, construction technology,
electrical engineering technology,
engineering technology—general,
environmental science, geography,
geology/earth science, geophysics/
seismology, industrial engineering,
mechanical engineering, nuclear
engineering, petroleum engineering,
physics, soil science.

**Texas A&M University—Corpus
Christi**
6300 Ocean Drive
Corpus Christi, TX 78412
Phone: (361) 825-2624
Fax: (361) 825-5887
E-mail: judith.perales@mail.tamucc.edu
http://www.tamucc.edu
Agricultural and biological engineering,
applied mathematics, atmospheric

science, biochemistry, chemical engineering, construction technology, electrical engineering technology, engineering physics, engineering technology—general, environmental science, geology/earth science, geophysics/seismology, industrial engineering, mechanical engineering, nuclear engineering, petroleum engineering, physics, soil science.

Texas A&M University—Galveston
Admissions Office
P.O. Box 1675
Galveston, TX 77553
Phone: (409) 740-4414
Fax: (409) 740-4731
E-mail: seaaggie@tamug.edu
http://www.tamug.edu
Biological/physical sciences, chemical engineering, construction technology, engineering physics, engineering technology—general, environmental science, geology/earth science, geophysics/seismology, hydrology/water resources science, industrial engineering, mechanical engineering, nuclear engineering, petroleum engineering, physics, soil science.

Texas A&M University—Kingsville
700 University Boulevard, MSC 128
Kingsville, TX 78363
Phone: (361) 593-2315
Fax: (361) 593-2195
E-mail: ksossrx@tamuk.edu
http://www.tamuk.edu
Agricultural and biological engineering, applied mathematics, atmospheric science, biochemistry, chemical engineering, civil engineering, construction technology, electrical engineering technology, engineering physics, engineering technology—general, environmental science, geology/earth science, geophysics/seismology, industrial engineering, mechanical engineering, nuclear engineering, petroleum engineering, physics, soil science.

Texas Christian University
Office of Admissions
TCU, P.O. Box 297013
Fort Worth, TX 76129
Phone: (817) 257-7490
Fax: (817) 257-7268
E-mail: frogmail@tcu.edu
http://www.tcu.edu

Biochemistry, engineering—general, engineering physics, environmental science, geology/earth science, physics.

Texas Southern University
3100 Cleburne Street
Houston, TX 77004
Phone: (713) 313-7420
Fax: (713) 313-4317
E-mail: admissions@tsu.edu
http://www.tsu.edu
Civil engineering technology, clinical laboratory science, electrical engineering technology, mechanics/repair—general.

Texas State University—San Marcos
429 North Guadalupe Street
San Marcos, TX 78666
Phone: (512) 245-2364
Fax: (512) 245-9020
E-mail: admissions@txstate.edu
http://www.txstate.edu
Biochemistry, clinical laboratory science, construction technology, environmental science, geography, industrial engineering, industrial technology, physics.

Texas Tech University
P.O. Box 45005
Lubbock, TX 79409
Phone: (806) 742-1480
Fax: (806) 742-0062
E-mail: admissions@ttu.edu
http://www.ttu.edu
Biochemistry, biological/physical sciences, civil engineering, clinical laboratory science, electrical engineering technology, engineering—general, engineering technology—general, environmental engineering, geology/earth science, geophysics/seismology, industrial engineering, mechanical engineering, mechanical engineering technology, petroleum engineering, physics, soil science.

Texas Wesleyan University
1201 Wesleyan Street
Fort Worth, TX 76105
Phone: (817) 531-4422
Fax: (817) 531-7515
E-mail: info@txwesleyan.edu
http://www.txwesleyan.edu
Biochemistry.

Texas Woman's University
P.O. Box 425589

Denton, TX 76204
Phone: (940) 898-3188
Fax: (940) 898-3081
E-mail: admissions@twu.edu
http://www.twu.edu
Clinical laboratory science.

Trinity University
One Trinity Place
San Antonio, TX 78212
Phone: (210) 999-7207
Fax: (210) 999-8164
E-mail: admissions@trinity.edu
http://www.trinity.edu
Biochemistry, geology/earth science, physics.

University of Dallas
1845 East Northgate Drive
Irving, TX 75062
Phone: (972) 721-5266
Fax: (972) 721-5017
E-mail: ugadmis@udallas.edu
http://www.udallas.edu
Biochemistry, physics.

University of Houston—Clear Lake
2700 Bay Area Boulevard
Houston, TX 77058
Phone: (281) 283-7600
Fax: (281) 283-2530
E-mail: admissions@cl.uh.edu
http://www.uhcl.edu
Biochemistry, biophysics, civil engineering, civil engineering technology, clinical laboratory science, construction technology, electrical engineering technology, environmental science, geography, geophysics/seismology, industrial technology, mechanical engineering, physics.

University of Houston—Downtown
Admission Office
One Main Street
Houston, TX 77002
Phone: (713) 221-8522
Fax: (713) 221-8157
E-mail: uhdadmit@uhd.edu
http://www.uhd.edu
Applied mathematics, biochemistry, biological/physical sciences, biophysics, chemical engineering, civil engineering, civil engineering technology, clinical laboratory science, construction technology, electrical engineering technology, geology/earth science, geophysics/

seismology, industrial technology, mechanical engineering, mechanical engineering technology, physics.

University of Houston—Houston
Office of Admissions
122 East Cullen Building
Houston, TX 77204
Phone: (713) 743-1010
Fax: (713) 743-9633
E-mail: admissions@uh.edu
http://www.uh.edu
Applied mathematics, biochemistry, biophysics, chemical engineering, civil engineering, civil engineering technology, clinical laboratory science, construction technology, geology/earth science, geophysics/seismology, industrial technology, mechanical engineering, physics.

University of Houston—Victoria Campus
Enrollment Management Office, UHV
Victoria, TX 77901
Phone: (361) 788-6222
Fax: (361) 572-9377
E-mail: urbanom@jade.vic.uh.edu
http://www.vic.uh.edu
Biochemistry, biophysics, chemical engineering, civil engineering, civil engineering technology, clinical laboratory science, construction technology, electrical engineering technology, geology/earth science, geophysics/seismology, industrial technology, mechanical engineering, physics.

University of Mary Hardin—Baylor
UMHB Box 8004
900 College Street
Belton, TX 76513
Phone: (254) 295-4520
Fax: (254) 295-5049
E-mail: admission@umhb.edu
http://www.umhb.edu
Clinical laboratory science.

University of North Texas
P.O. Box 311277
Denton, TX 76203
Phone: (940) 565-2681
Fax: (940) 565-2408
E-mail: undergrad@unt.edu
http://www.unt.edu
Clinical laboratory science, construction technology, electrical engineering technology, geography, physics.

University of Texas—Arlington
Office of Admissions
P.O. Box 19111
Arlington, TX 76019
Phone: (817) 272-6287
Fax: (817) 272-3435
E-mail: admissions@uta.edu
http://www.uta.edu
Biochemistry, civil engineering, clinical laboratory science, environmental engineering, environmental science, geology/earth science, industrial engineering, mechanical engineering, physics.

University of Texas—Austin
P.O. Box 8058
Austin, TX 78713
Phone: (512) 475-7440
Fax: (512) 475-7475
E-mail: frmn@uts.cc.utexas.edu
http://www.utexas.edu
Biochemistry, chemical engineering, civil engineering, clinical laboratory science, geography, geology/earth science, geophysics/seismology, hydrology/water resources science, industrial engineering, mechanical engineering, petroleum engineering, physics.

University of Texas—Brownsville
80 Fort Brown Street
Brownsville, TX 78520
Phone: (956) 544-8295
Fax: (956) 983-7810
E-mail: admissions@utb.edu
http://www.utb.edu
Engineering physics, environmental engineering, industrial technology, mechanical engineering technology, physics.

University of Texas—Dallas
P.O. Box 830688, MC 11
Richardson, TX 75083
Phone: (972) 883-2342
Fax: (972) 883-6803
E-mail: admissions-status@utdallas.edu
http://www.utdallas.edu
Applied mathematics, biochemistry, geography, geology/earth science, physics, statistics.

University of Texas—El Paso
500 West University Avenue
El Paso, TX 79968
Phone: (915) 747-5576
Fax: (915) 747-8893

E-mail: admission@utep.edu
http://www.utep.edu
Applied mathematics, biological/physical sciences, civil engineering, clinical laboratory science, engineering—general, environmental engineering, environmental science, geology/earth science, geophysics/seismology, industrial engineering, mechanical engineering, metallurgical engineering, physics, statistics.

University of Texas of the Permian Basin
4901 East University Boulevard
Odessa, TX 79762
Phone: (915) 552-2605
Fax: (915) 552-3605
E-mail: admissions@utpb.edu
http://www.utpb.edu
Geology/earth science.

University of Texas—Pan American
Office of Admissions and Records
1201 West University Drive
Edinburgh, TX 78541
Phone: (956) 381-2201
Fax: (956) 381-2212
E-mail: admissions@panam.edu
http://www.panam.edu
Biological/physical sciences, clinical laboratory science, mechanical engineering, physics.

University of Texas—San Antonio
6900 North Loop 1604 West
San Antonio, TX 78249
Phone: (210) 458-4530
Fax: (210) 458-7716
E-mail: prospects@utsa.edu
http://www.utsa.edu
Biological/physical sciences, civil engineering, clinical laboratory science, environmental engineering, environmental science, geography, geology/earth science, mechanical engineering, physics, statistics.

University of Texas—Tyler
3900 University Boulevard
Tyler, TX 75799
Phone: (903) 566-7202
Fax: (903) 566-7068
E-mail: admissions@mail.uttyl.edu
http://www.uttyler.edu
Civil engineering, clinical laboratory science, engineering—general, engineering technology—general, industrial technology, mechanical engineering.

West Texas A&M University
P.O. Box 60907
Canyon, TX 79016
Phone: (806) 651-2020
Fax: (806) 651-5268
E-mail: admissions@mail.wtamu.edu
http://www.wtamu.edu
Biotechnology, clinical laboratory
science, environmental science,
geography, geology/earth science,
industrial technology, mechanical
engineering, physics.

UTAH

Brigham Young University
A-153 ASB
Provo, UT 84602
Phone: (801) 422-2507
Fax: (801) 422-0005
E-mail: admissions@byu.edu
http://www.byu.edu
Biochemistry, biological/physical sciences,
biophysics, biotechnology, chemical
engineering, civil engineering, clinical
laboratory science, geography,
geology/earth science, hydrology/
water resources science, mechanical
engineering, physics, soil science,
statistics.

Southern Utah University
Admissions Office
351 West Center
Cedar City, UT 84720
Phone: (435) 586-7740
Fax: (435) 865-8223
E-mail: Adminfo@suu.edu
http://www.suu.edu
Engineering—general, geology/earth
science, statistics.

University of Utah
210 South 1460 East, Room 250 South
Salt Lake City, UT 84112
Phone: (801) 581-7281
Fax: (801) 585-7864
E-mail: admiss@sa.utah.edu
http://www.utah.edu
Atomic/molecular physics, biochemistry,
chemical engineering, civil
engineering, clinical laboratory
science, engineering—general,
environmental engineering,
environmental science, geography,
geological engineering, geology/earth
science, geophysics/seismology,
materials engineering, mechanical
engineering, metallurgical

engineering, meteorology, mining
and mineral engineering, nuclear
engineering, petroleum engineering,
physics.

Utah State University
0160 Old Main Hill
Logan, UT 84322
Phone: (435) 797-1079
Fax: (435) 797-3708
E-mail: admit@cc.usu.edu
http://www.usu.edu
Agricultural and biological engineering,
civil engineering, clinical laboratory
science, electrical engineering
technology, engineering—general,
environmental engineering,
geography, geology/earth science,
hydrology/water resources science,
mechanical engineering, physics, soil
science, statistics.

Utah Valley State College
800 West University Parkway
Orem, UT 84058
Phone: (801) 863-INFO
Fax: (801) 863-7305
E-mail: uvstart@uvsc.edu
http://www.uvsc.edu
Physics.

Weber State University
1137 University Circle
Ogden, UT 84408
Phone: (801) 626-6744
Fax: (801) 626-6747
E-mail: admissions@weber.edu
http://www.weber.edu
Applied mathematics, clinical laboratory
science, electrical engineering
technology, engineering physics,
geography, geology/earth science,
physics.

VERMONT

Bennington College
Office of Admissions and Financial Aid
Bennington, VT 05201
Phone: (802) 440-4312
Fax: (802) 440-4320
E-mail: admissions@bennington.edu
http://www.bennington.edu
Applied mathematics, environmental
science, physics.

Castleton State College
Office of Admissions
Castleton, VT 05735

Phone: (802) 468-1213
Fax: (802) 468-1476
E-mail: info@castleton.edu
http://www.castleton.edu
Biological/physical sciences,
environmental science, geology/earth
science, statistics.

Lyndon State College
1001 College Road
Lyndonville, VT 05851
Phone: (802) 626-6200
Fax: (802) 626-6335
E-mail: admissions@lyndonstate.edu
http://www.lyndonstate.edu
Atmospheric science, biological/physical
sciences.

Marlboro College
P.O. Box A, South Road
Marlboro, VT 05344
Phone: (802) 258-9236
Fax: (802) 451-7555
E-mail: admissions@marlboro.edu
http://www.marlboro.edu
Biochemistry, biological/physical
sciences, physics.

Middlebury College
Emma Willard House
Middlebury, VT 05763
Phone: (802) 443-3000
Fax: (802) 443-2056
E-mail: admissions@middlebury.edu
http://www.middlebury.edu
Biochemistry, geography, geology/earth
science, physics.

Norwich University
Admissions Office
158 Harmon Drive
Northfield, VT 05663
Phone: (802) 485-2001
Fax: (802) 485-2032
E-mail: nuadm@norwich.edu
http://www.norwich.edu
Biochemistry, civil engineering, geology/
earth science, mechanical engineering,
physics.

Saint Michael's College
1 Winooski Park
Colchester, VT 05439
Phone: (802) 654-3000
Fax: (802) 654-2906
E-mail: admission@smcvt.edu
http://www.smcvt.edu
Biochemistry, engineering—general,
environmental science.

Sterling College
P.O. Box 72
Craftsbury Common, VT 05827
Phone: (802) 586-7711
Fax: (802) 586-2596
E-mail: admissions@sterlingcollege.
edu
http://www.sterlingcollege.edu
Biological/physical sciences, environmental engineering technology, physics,
soil science.

University of Vermont
Admissions Office
194 South Prospect Street
Burlington, VT 05401
Phone: (802) 656-3370
Fax: (802) 656-8611
E-mail: admissions@uvm.edu
http://www.uvm.edu
Biochemistry, civil engineering, clinical
laboratory science, engineering—
general, environmental engineering,
environmental science, geography,
geology/earth science, mechanical
engineering, physics, soil science,
statistics.

VIRGINIA

Averett University
420 West Main Street
Danville, VA 24541
Phone: (434) 791-4996
Fax: (434) 797-2784
E-mail: admit@averett.edu
http://www.averett.edu
Applied mathematics, biological/physical
sciences, clinical laboratory science,
environmental science.

Bridgewater College
402 East College Street
Bridgewater, VA 22812
Phone: (540) 828-5375
Fax: (540) 828-5481
E-mail: admissions@bridgewater.edu
http://www.bridgewater.edu
Clinical laboratory science,
environmental science, physics.

College of William and Mary
P.O. Box 8795
Williamsburg, VA
Phone: (757) 221-4223
Fax: (757) 221-1242
E-mail: admiss@wm.edu
http://www.wm.edu
Geology/earth science, physics.

DeVry University—Crystal City
2341 Jefferson Davis Highway
Arlington, VA 22202
Phone: (703) 414-4100
Fax: (703) 414-4040
E-mail: admissions@devry.edu
http://www.devry.edu
Electrical engineering technology.

Eastern Mennonite University
1200 Park Road
Harrisonburg, VA 22802
Phone: (540) 432-4118
Fax: (540) 432-4444
E-mail: admiss@emu.edu
http://www.emu.edu
Biochemistry, clinical laboratory science,
environmental science.

Ferrum College
P.O. Box 1000
Ferrum, VA 24088
Phone: (540) 365-4290
Fax: (540) 365-4366
E-mail: admissions@ferrum.edu
http://www.ferrum.edu
Clinical laboratory science,
environmental science.

George Mason University
Undergraduate Admissions Office
400 University Drive, MSN 3A4
Fairfax, VA 22030
Phone: (703) 993-2400
Fax: (703) 993-2392
E-mail: admissions@gmu.edu
http://www.gmu.edu
Civil engineering, clinical laboratory
science, geography, geology/earth
science, physics.

Hampden-Sydney College
P.O. Box 667
Hampden-Sydney, VA 23943
Phone: (434) 223-6120
Fax: (434) 223-6346
E-mail: hsapp@hsc.edu
http://www.hsc.edu
Applied mathematics, biochemistry, bio-
physics, engineering—general, physics.

Hampton University
Office of Admissions
Hampton, VA 23668
Phone: (757) 727-5328
Fax: (757) 727-5095
E-mail: admissions@hamptonu.edu
http://www.hamptonu.edu
Chemical engineering, environmental
science, physics.

James Madison University
Sonner Hall, MSC 0101
Harrisonburg, VA 22807
Phone: (540) 568-5681
Fax: (540) 568-3332
E-mail: gotojmu@jmu.edu
http://www.jum.edu
Biotechnology, geography, geology/earth
science, physics.

Jefferson College of Health Sciences
P.O. Box 13186
Roanoke, VA 24031
Phone: (888) 985-8483
Fax: NA
E-mail: admissions@mail.jchs.edu
http://www.jchs.edu
Biological/physical sciences.

Liberty University
1971 University Boulevard
Lynchburg, VA 24502
Phone: (434) 582-5985
Fax: (800) 542-2311
E-mail: admissions@liberty.edu
http://www.liberty.edu
Biochemistry.

Longwood University
Admissions Office
201 High Street
Farmville, VA 23909
Phone: (434) 395-2060
Fax: (434) 395-2332
E-mail: admissions@longwood.edu
http://www.longwood.edu
Physics.

Mary Baldwin College
P.O. Box 1500
Staunton, VA 24402
Phone: (540) 887-7019
Fax: (540) 887-7279
E-mail: admit@mbc.edu
http://www.mbc.edu
Applied mathematics, biochemistry,
clinical laboratory science, physics.

Norfolk State University
700 Park Avenue
Norfolk, VA 23504
Phone: (757) 823-8396
Fax: (757) 823-2078
E-mail: admissions@nsu.edu
http://www.nsu.edu
Clinical laboratory science, construction
technology, electrical engineering
technology, physics.

Old Dominion University
108 Rollins Hall
5215 Hampton Boulevard
Norfolk, VA 23529
Phone: (757) 683-3685
Fax: (757) 683-3255
E-mail: admit@odu.edu
http://www.odu.edu
Biochemistry, civil engineering, civil engineering technology, clinical laboratory science, electrical engineering technology, engineering technology—general, environmental engineering, geography, geology/earth science, mechanical engineering, mechanical engineering technology, nuclear engineering technology, physics.

Radford University
P.O. Box 6903
RU Station
Radford, VA 24142
Phone: (540) 831-5371
Fax: (540) 831-5038
E-mail: ruadmiss@radford.edu
http://www.radford.edu
Clinical laboratory science, geography, geology/earth science.

Randolph-Macon College
P.O. Box 5005
Ashland, VA 23005
Phone: (804) 752-7305
Fax: (804) 752-4707
E-mail: admissions@rmc.edu
http://www.rmc.edu
Physics.

Randolph-Macon Woman's College
2500 Rivermont Avenue
Lynchburg, VA 24503
Phone: (434) 947-8100
Fax: (434) 947-8996
E-mail: admissions@rmwc.edu
http://www.rmwc.edu
Engineering physics, physics.

Roanoke College
221 College Lane
Salem, VA 24153
Phone: (540) 375-2270
Fax: (540) 375-2267
E-mail: admissions@roanoke.edu
http://www.roanoke.edu
Biochemistry, clinical laboratory science, environmental science, physics.

Sweet Briar College
P.O. Box B
Sweet Briar, VA 24505
Phone: (434) 381-6142
Fax: (434) 381-6152
E-mail: admissions@sbc.edu
http://www.sbc.edu
Biochemistry, environmental science, physics.

University of Mary Washington
1301 College Avenue
Fredericksburg, VA 22401
Phone: (540) 654-2000
Fax: (540) 654-1857
E-mail: admit@umw.edu
http://www.umw.edu
Geography, geology/earth science, physics.

University of Richmond
28 Westhampton Way
Richmond, VA 23173
Phone: (804) 289-8640
Fax: (804) 287-6003
E-mail: admissions@richmond.edu
http://www.richmond.edu
Biochemistry, physics.

University of Virginia
Office of Admission
P.O. Box 400160
Charlottesville, VA 22906
Phone: (434) 982-3200
Fax: (434) 924-3587
E-mail: undergradadmission@virginia.edu
http://www.virginia.edu
Applied mathematics, chemical engineering, civil engineering, engineering—general, engineering physics, environmental science, mechanical engineering, physics.

University of Virginia's College—Wise
1 College Avenue
Wise, VA 24293
Phone: (276) 328-0102
Fax: (276) 328-0251
E-mail: admissions@uvwise.edu
http://www.uvwise.edu
Clinical laboratory science.

Virginia Commonwealth University
821 West Franklin Street
P.O. Box 842526
Richmond, VA 23284
Phone: (804) 828-1222
Fax: (804) 828-1899
E-mail: vcuinfo@vcu.edu
http://www.vcu.edu
Biological/physical sciences, chemical engineering, clinical laboratory science, mechanical engineering, physics.

Virginia Military Institute
VMI Office of Admissions
Lexington, VA 24450
Phone: (540) 464-7211
Fax: (540) 464-7746
E-mail: admissions@mail.vmi.edu
http://www.vmi.edu
Civil engineering, mechanical engineering, physics.

Virginia Polytechnic Institute and State University
201 Burruss Hall
Blacksburg, VA 24061
Phone: (540) 231-6267
Fax: NA
E-mail: vtadmiss@vt.edu
http://www.vt.edu
Biochemistry, chemical engineering, civil engineering, engineering mechanics, environmental science, geography, geology/earth science, industrial engineering, materials engineering, mechanical engineering, mining and mineral engineering, physics, statistics.

Virginia State University
One Hayden Street
P.O. Box 9018
Petersburg, VA 23806
Phone: (804) 524-5902
Fax: (804) 524-5056
E-mail: admiss@vsu.edu
http://www.vsu.edu
Engineering technology—general, mechanical engineering technology, physics.

Virginia Wesleyan College
1584 Wesleyan Drive
Norfolk, VA 23502
Phone: (757) 455-3208
Fax: (757) 461-5238
E-mail: admissions@vwc.edu
http://www.vwc.edu
Geology/earth science.

Washington and Lee University
204 West Washington Street
Lexington, VA 24450
Phone: (540) 458-8710
Fax: (540) 458-8062
E-mail: admissions@wlu.edu
http://www.wlu.edu

Chemical engineering, engineering
physics, geology/earth science,
physics.

WASHINGTON

Central Washington University
Admissions Office
400 East Eighth Avenue
Ellensburg, WA 98926
Phone: (509) 963-1211
Fax: (509) 963-3022
E-mail: cwuadmis@cwu.edu
http://www.cwu.edu
Electrical engineering technology,
geography, geology/earth science,
industrial technology, mechanical
engineering technology, physics.

DeVry University—Seattle
3600 South 344th Way
Federal Way, WA 98001
Phone: (253) 943-2800
Fax: (253) 943-3291
E-mail: admissions@sea.devry.edu
http://www.devry.edu
Electrical engineering technology.

Eastern Washington University
526 Fifth Street
Cheney, WA 99004
Phone: (509) 359-2397
Fax: (509) 359-6692
E-mail: admissions@mail.ewu.edu
http://www.ewu.edu
Biochemistry, electrical engineering
technology, geography, geology/earth
science, physics.

The Evergreen State College
2700 Evergreen Parkway NW
Office of Admissions
Olympia, WA 98505
Phone: (360) 867-6170
Fax: (360) 867-6576
E-mail: admissions@evergreen.edu
http://www.evergreen.edu
Biological/physical sciences.

Gonzaga University
502 East Boone Avenue
Spokane, WA 99258
Phone: (509) 323-6572
Fax: (509) 324-5780
E-mail: admissions@gonzaga.edu
http://www.gonzaga.edu
Biochemistry, civil engineering,
engineering—general, mechanical
engineering, physics.

Henry Cogswell College
3002 Colby Avenue
Everett, WA 98021
Phone: (425) 258-3351
Fax: (425) 257-0405
E-mail: admissions@henrycogswell.edu
http://www.henrycogswell.edu
Mechanical engineering.

Pacific Lutheran University
Office of Admissions
12180 Park Street South
Tacoma, WA 98447
Phone: (253) 535-7151
Fax: (253) 536-5136
E-mail: admissions@plu.edu
http://www.plu.edu
Geology/earth science, environmental
science, physics.

Saint Martin's University
5300 Pacific Avenue Southeast
Lacey, WA 98503
Phone: (360) 438-4311
Fax: (360) 412-6189
E-mail: admissions@stmartin.edu
http://www.stmartin.edu
Civil engineering, mechanical
engineering.

Seattle Pacific University
3307 Third Avenue West
Seattle, WA 98119
Phone: (206) 281-2021
Fax: (206) 281-2669
E-mail: admissions@spu.edu
http://www.spu.edu
Biochemistry, physics.

Seattle University
Admissions Office
900 Broadway
Seattle, WA 98122
Phone: (206) 296-2000
Fax: (206) 296-5656
E-mail: admissions@seattleu.edu
http://www.seattleu.edu
Applied mathematics, civil engineering,
clinical laboratory science, mechanical
engineering, physics.

University of Puget Sound
1500 North Warner Street
Tacoma, WA 98416
Phone: (253) 879-3211
Fax: (253) 879-3993
E-mail: admission@ups.edu
http://www.ups.edu
Geology/earth science, physics.

University of Washington
1410 Northeast Campus Parkway
320 Schmitz, P.O. Box 355840
Seattle, WA 98195
Phone: (206) 543-9686
Fax: (206) 685-3655
E-mail: askuwadm@u.washington.edu
http://www.washington.edu
Applied mathematics, atmospheric science,
biochemistry, civil engineering, clinical
laboratory science, engineering—general,
environmental engineering, geography,
geology/earth science, geophysics/
seismology, industrial engineering,
materials engineering, materials science,
mechanical engineering, metallurgical
engineering, nuclear engineering,
physics, surveying technology.

Walla Walla College
Office of Admissions
204 South College Avenue
College Place, WA 99324
Phone: (509) 527-2327
Fax: (509) 527-2397
E-mail: info@wwc.edu
http://www.wwc.edu
Biochemistry, biophysics, civil
engineering, engineering—general,
mechanical engineering, physics.

Washington State University
370 Lighty Student Services
Pullman, WA 99164
Phone: (509) 335-5586
Fax: (509) 335-4902
E-mail: admiss2@wsu.edu
http://www.wsu.edu
Agricultural and biological engineering,
applied mathematics, biochemistry,
biological/physical sciences, biotechnology, civil engineering, environmental science, geology/earth science,
materials engineering, mechanical
engineering, physics, soil science.

Western Washington University
Mail Stop 9009
Bellingham, WA 98225
Phone: (360) 650-3440
Fax: (360) 650-7369
E-mail: admit@cc.wwu.edu
http://www.wwu.edu
Biochemistry, biological/physical
sciences, electrical engineering
technology, environmental science,
geography, geology/earth science,
geophysics/seismology, industrial
technology, physics.

Whitman College
345 Boyer Avenue
Walla Walla, WA 99362
Phone: (509) 527-5176
Fax: (509) 527-4967
E-mail: admission@whitman.edu
http://www.whitman.edu
Physics.

Whitworth College
300 West Hawthorne Road
Spokane, WA 99251
Phone: (509) 777-4786
Fax: (509) 777-3758
E-mail: admission@whitworth.edu
http://www.whitworth.edu
Applied mathematics, engineering—
general, physics.

WEST VIRGINIA

Alderson-Broddus College
P.O. Box 2003
Philippi, WV 26416
Phone: (800) 263-1549
Fax: (304) 457-6239
E-mail: admissions@ab.edu
http://www.ab.edu
Applied mathematics.

Bethany College
Office of Admissions
Bethany, WV 26032
Phone: (304) 829-7611
Fax: (304) 829-7142
E-mail: admission@bethanywv.edu
http://www.bethanywv.edu
Biochemistry, physics.

Bluefield State College
219 Rock Street
Bluefield, WV 24701
Phone: (304) 327-4065
Fax: (304) 325-7747
E-mail: bscadmit@bluefieldstate.edu
http://www.bluefieldstate.edu
Biological/physical sciences, civil
engineering technology.

Concord University—Athens
1000 Vermillion Street
P.O. Box 1000
Athens, WV 24712
Phone: (304) 384-5248
Fax: (304) 384-9044
E-mail: admissions@concord.edu
http://www.concord.edu
Clinical laboratory science, geography,
geology/earth science.

Fairmont State University
1201 Locust Avenue
Fairmont, WV 26554
Phone: (800) 641-5678
Fax: NA
E-mail: At Web site
http://www.fairmontstate.edu
Electrical engineering technology.

Marshall University
1 John Marshall Drive
Huntington, WV 35755
Phone: (304) 696-3160
Fax: (304) 696-3135
E-mail: admissions@marshall.edu
http://www.marshall.edu
Clinical laboratory science,
environmental science, geography,
geology/earth science, physics.

Mountain State University
609 South Kanawha Street
Beckley, WV 25801
Phone: (304) 929-1433
Fax: (304) 253-3463
E-mail: gomsu@mountainstate.edu
http://www.mountainstate.edu
Biological/physical sciences, electrical
engineering technology.

Shepherd College
Office of Admissions
P.O. Box 3210
Shepherdstown, WV 25443
Phone: (304) 876-5212
Fax: (304) 876-5165
E-mail: admoff@shepherd.edu
http://www.shepherd.edu
Electrical engineering technology.

West Liberty State College
P.O. Box 295
West Liberty, WV 26074
Phone: (304) 336-8076
Fax: (304) 336-8403
E-mail: wladmsn1@westliberty.edu
http://www.westliberty.edu
Biotechnology, clinical laboratory
science.

West Virginia State University
P.O. Box 1000
Institute, WV 25112
Phone: (800) 987-2112
Fax: NA
E-mail: At Web site
http://www. wvstateu.edu
Applied mathematics, electrical
engineering technology, physics.

West Virginia University
Admissions Office
P.O. Box 6009
Morgantown, WV 26506
Phone: (304) 293-2121
Fax: (304) 293-3080
E-mail: wvuadmissions@arc.wvu.edu
http://www.wvu.edu
Biochemistry, chemical engineering,
civil engineering, clinical laboratory science, geography, geol-
ogy/earth science, industrial engineering, mechanical engineering,
mining and mineral engineering,
petroleum engineering, physics,
soil science.

**West Virginia University Institute of
Technology**
Box 10, Old Main
Montgomery, WV 25136
Phone: (304) 442-3167
Fax: (304) 442-3097
E-mail: admissions@wvutech.edu
http://www.wvutech.edu
Civil engineering, electrical engineering
technology, mechanical engineering.

West Virginia Wesleyan College
59 College Avenue
Buckhannon, WV 26201
Phone: (304) 473-8510
Fax: (304) 473-8108
E-mail: admission@wvwc.edu
http://www.wvwc.edu
Environmental science, physics.

WISCONSIN

Beloit College
700 College Street
Beloit, WI 53511
Phone: (608) 363-2500
Fax: (608) 363-2075
E-mail: admiss@beloit.edu
http://www.beloit.edu
Biochemistry, engineering—general,
geology/earth science, physics.

Carroll College
100 North East Avenue
Waukesha, WI 53186
Phone: (262) 524-7220
Fax: (262) 951-3037
E-mail: ccinfo@ccadmin.cc.edu
http://www.cc.edu
Applied mathematics, biochemistry,
clinical laboratory science.

Lakeland College
P.O. Box 359
Sheboygan, WI 53082
Phone: (920) 565-2111
Fax: (920) 565-1206
E-mail: admissions@lakeland.edu
http://www.lakeland.edu
Biochemistry.

Lawrence University
P.O. Box 599
Appleton, WI 54912
Phone: (920) 832-6500
Fax: (920) 832-6782
E-mail: excel@lawrence.edu
http://www.lawrence.edu
Biochemistry, biological/physical
    sciences, geology/earth science,
    geophysics/seismology, physics.

Marquette University
P.O. Box 1881
Milwaukee, WI 53201
Phone: (414) 288-7302
Fax: (414) 288-3764
E-mail: admissions@marquette.edu
http://www.marquette.edu
Biochemistry, chemical physics, civil
    engineering, engineering—general,
    environmental engineering, mechanical
    engineering, physics, statistics.

Milwaukee School of Engineering
1025 North Broadway
Milwaukee, WI 53202
Phone: (414) 277-6763
Fax: (414) 277-7475
E-mail: explore@msoe.edu
http://www.msoe.edu
Electrical engineering technology,
    industrial engineering, mechanical
    engineering, mechanical engineering
    technology.

Mount Mary College
2900 North Menomonee River Parkway
Milwaukee, WI 53222
Phone: (414) 256-1219
Fax: (414) 256-0180
E-mail: admiss@mtmary.edu
http://www.mtmary.edu
Biological/physical sciences.

Northland College
1411 Ellis Avenue
Ashland, WI 54806
Phone: (715) 682-1224
Fax: (715) 682-1258
E-mail: admit@northland.edu

http://www.northland.edu
Biological/physical sciences, geology/
    earth science, physics.

Ripon College
300 Seward Street
P.O. Box 248
Ripon, WI 54971
Phone: (920) 748-8114
Fax: (920) 748-8335
E-mail: adminfo@ripon.edu
http://www.ripon.edu
Biochemistry, physics.

St. Norbert College
100 Grant Street
De Pere, WI 54115
Phone: (920) 403-3005
Fax: (920) 403-4072
E-mail: admit@snc.edu
http://www.snc.edu
Biological/physical sciences, environ-
    mental science, physics.

University of Wisconsin—Eau Claire
105 Garfield Avenue
Eau Claire, WI 54701
Phone: (715) 836-5415
Fax: (715) 836-2409
E-mail: admissions@uwec.edu
http://www.uwec.edu
Geography, geology/earth science, physics.

University of Wisconsin—Green Bay
2420 Nicolet Drive
Green Bay, WI 53411
Phone: (920) 465-2111
Fax: (920) 465-5754
E-mail: uwgb@uwgb.edu
http://www.uwgb.edu
Biological/physical sciences,
    environmental science, physics.

University of Wisconsin—La Crosse
1725 State Street
La Crosse, WI 54601
Phone: (608) 785-8939
Fax: (608) 785-8940
E-mail: admissions@uwlax.edu
http://www.uwlax.edu
Biochemistry, clinical laboratory science,
    geography, physics.

University of Wisconsin—Madison
Red Gym and Armory
716 Langdon Street
Madison, WI 53706
Phone: (608) 262-3961
Fax: (608) 262-7706

E-mail: onwisconsin@admissions.wisc.
    edu
http://www.wisc.edu
Agricultural and biological engineering,
    biochemistry, biological/physical
    sciences, chemical engineering,
    civil engineering, clinical laboratory
    science, engineering mechanics,
    engineering physics, geography,
    geological engineering, geology/earth
    science, geophysics/seismology,
    industrial engineering, materials
    engineering, mechanical engineering,
    nuclear engineering, physics, soil
    science, statistics.

University of Wisconsin—Milwaukee
P.O. Box 749
Milwaukee, WI 53201
Phone: (414) 229-3800
Fax: (414) 229-6940
E-mail: uwmlook@uwm.edu
http://www.uwm.edu
Applied mathematics, civil engineering,
    clinical laboratory science, geography,
    geology/earth science, materials
    engineering, mechanical engineering,
    physics.

University of Wisconsin—Oshkosh
Dempsey Hall 135
800 Algoma Boulevard
Oshkosh, WI 54901
Phone: (920) 424-0202
Fax: (920) 424-1098
E-mail: oshadmuw@uwosh.edu
http://www.uwosh.edu
Geography, geology/earth science,
    physics.

University of Wisconsin—Parkside
P.O. Box 2000
Kenosha, WI 53141
Phone: (262) 595-2355
Fax: (262) 595-2008
E-mail: matthew.jensen@uwp.edu
http://www.uwp.edu
Geography, geology/earth science,
    physics.

University of Wisconsin—Platteville
1 University Plaza
Platteville, WI 53818
Phone: (608) 342-1125
Fax: (608) 342-1122
E-mail: schumacr@uwplatt.edu
http://www.uwplatt.edu
Civil engineering, engineering physics,
    geography, mechanical engineering.

University of Wisconsin—River Falls
410 South Third Street
112 South Hall
River Falls, WI 54022
Phone: (715) 425-3500
Fax: (715) 425-0676
E-mail: admit@uwrf.edu
http://www.uwrf.edu
Biological/physical sciences,
    biotechnology, geography, geology/
    earth science, physics, soil science.

University of Wisconsin—Stevens Point
Student Services Center
Stevens Point, WI 54481
Phone: (715) 346-2441
Fax: (715) 346-3957
E-mail: admiss@uwsp.edu
http://www.uwsp.edu
Biological/physical sciences, clinical
    laboratory science, geography,
    physics, soil science.

University of Wisconsin—Stout
Admissions, UW—Stout
Menomonie, WI 54751
Phone: (715) 232-1411
Fax: (715) 232-1667
E-mail: admissions@uwstout.edu

http://www.uwstout.edu
Applied mathematics, construction
    technology, engineering technology—
    general.

University of Wisconsin—Superior
Belknap and Catlin
P.O. Box 2000
Superior, WI 54880
Phone: (715) 394-8230
Fax: (715) 394-8107
E-mail: admissions@uwsuper.edu
http://www.uwsuper.edu
Biological/physical sciences.

University of Wisconsin—Whitewater
800 West Main Street
Baker Hall
Whitewater, WI 53190
Phone: (414) 472-1234
Fax: (414) 472-1515
E-mail: uwwadmit@uww.edu
http://www.uww.edu
Geography, physics.

Viterbo University
900 Viterbo Drive
La Crosse, WI 54601
Phone: (608) 796-3010

Fax: (608) 796-3020
E-mail: admission@viterbo.edu
http://www.viterbo.edu
Biochemistry.

Wisconsin Lutheran College
8800 West Bluemound Road
Milwaukee, WI 53226
Phone: (414) 443-8811
Fax: (414) 443-8514
E-mail: admissions@wlc.edu
http://www.wlc.edu
Biochemistry.

WYOMING

University of Wyoming
Admissions Office
P.O. Box 3435
Laramie, WY 82071
Phone: (307) 766-5160
Fax: (307) 766-4042
E-mail: why-wyo@uwyo.edu
http://www.uwyo.edu
Chemical engineering, geography,
    geology/earth science, geophysics/
    seismology, physics, statistics.

APPENDIX II
MAJOR TRADE PERIODICALS
AND OTHER PUBLICATIONS

Most professional associations, organizations, and unions publish their own newsletters and journals, some of which are listed below, while some are listed in Appendix IV.

Check the Web sites of associations or unions of interest for the availability of other such publications.

DIRECTORIES AND YEARBOOKS

Oil and Gas Directory. Houston, Tex.: Geophysical Directory, Inc., 2006.

Plunkett's Energy Industry Almanac 2007: Energy Industry Market Research, Statistics, Trends & Leading Companies. Houston, Tex.: Plunkett Research, Ltd., 2006.

Plunkett's Renewable, Alternative & Hydrogen Energy Industry Almanac 2007: Renewable, Alternative & Hydrogen Energy Industry Market Research, Statistics, Trends & Leading Companies. Houston, Tex.: Plunkett Research, Ltd., 2007.

Synerjy—A Directory of Renewable Energy. New York: Synerjy, 2007.

Who's Who in Natural Gas & Electric Power. Rockville, Md.: United Communications Group, 2006.

Worldwide Offshore Petroleum Directory. Houston, Tex.: Pennwell Corporation—Petroleum Division, 2006.

PERIODICALS

AAPG (American Association of Petroleum Geologists) Bulletin
1444 South Boulder Avenue
Tulsa, OK 74119
Phone: (800) 364-2274
Fax: (918) 560-2694

E-mail: At Web site
http://aapgbull.geoscienceworld.org

American Gas: The Monthly Magazine of the American Gas Association
American Gas Association
400 North Capitol Street NW, Suite 460
Washington, DC 20001
Phone: (202) 824-7000
Fax: NA
E-mail: shamm@aga.org
http://www.aga.org

Biomass & Bioenergy
Elsevier—HQ
360 Park Avenue South
New York, NY 10010
Phone: (888) 437-4636
Fax: (212) 633-3913
E-mail: a.mcguire@elsevier.com
http://www.elsevier.com

Coal Age
Mining Media
13544 Eads Road
Prairieville, LA 70769
Phone: (225) 673-9400
Fax: (225) 677-8277
E-mail: At Web site
http://www.mining-media.com

Coal Power
Trade Fair Group
11000 Richmond, Suite 500
Houston, TX 77042
Phone: (832) 242-1969
Fax: (832) 242-1971
E-mail: NA
http://www.poweronline.com

Electric Light and Power
PennWell Corporation
1421 South Sheridan Road
Tulsa, OK 74112
Phone: (800) 331-4463
Fax: (918) 831-9804
E-mail: headquarters@pennwell.com
http://www.pennwell.com

The Electricity Journal
Elsevier—HQ
300 Park Avenue South
New York, NY 10010
Phone: (888) 437-4636
Fax: (212) 663-3913
E-mail: a.mcguire@elsevier.com
http://www.elesevier.com

Energy
U.S. National Technical Information Service
5285 Port Royal Road
Springfield, VA 22161
Phone: (800) 553-6847
Fax: (703) 487-4639
E-mail: info@ntis.gov
http://www.ntis.gov

Energy-Tech
Magellan Publishing
801 Bluff Street
Dubuque, IA 52001
Phone: (563) 588-3850
Fax: (563) 588-3848
E-mail: sales@magellanpubs.com
http://www.magellanpubs.com

EPRI (Electric Power Research Institute) Journal
P.O. Box 10412

Palo Alto, CA 94303
Phone: (650) 855-2000
Fax: (650) 855-2900
E-mail: askepri@epri.com
http://www.epri.com

Fuel Cell Technology News
Business Communications Company, Inc.
40 Washington Street, Suite 110
Wellesley, MA 02981
Phone: (781) 489-7304
Fax: (781) 489-7308
E-mail: sales@bccresearch.com
http://www.bccresearch.com

Geotimes
American Geological Institute
4220 King Street
Alexandria, VA 22302
Phone: (703) 379-2480
Fax: (703) 379-7563
E-mail: geotimes@agiweb.org
http://www.geotimes.org

Home Power Magazine
P.O. Box 520
Ashland, CA 97520
Phone: (800) 707-6585
Fax: NA
E-mail: hp@homepower.org
http://www.homepower.org

Journal of Energy Resources
Technology
American Society of Mechanical
Engineers
3 Park Avenue
New York, NY 10016
Phone: (800) 843-2763
Fax: (212) 591-7841
E-mail: infocentral@asme.org
http://www.asme.org

Journal of Engineering for Gas
Turbines and Power
American Society of Mechanical
Engineers
3 Park Avenue
New York, NY 10016
Phone: (800) 843-2763
Fax: (973) 882-1717
E-mail: infocentral@asme.org
http://www.asme.org

Journal of Petroleum Science &
Engineering
Elsevier Science Publisher
Customer Service Department
6277 Sea Harbor Drive

Orlando, FL 32887
Phone: (877) 839-7126
Fax: (407) 363-1354
E-mail: usjcs@elsevier.com
http://www.elsevier.com

Journal of Petroleum Technology
Society of Petroleum Engineers
9555 West Sam Houston Parkway,
Suite 360
Houston, TX 77036
Phone: (730) 779-9595
Fax: (713) 779-4216
E-mail: jpt@spe.org
http://www.spe.org

Journal of Wind Engineering
AMSET Centre
Horninghold, Leicestershire LE16 8DH
United Kingdom
Phone: 44 1858 555 204
Fax: 44 1858 555 504
E-mail: At Web site
http://www.multi-science.co.uk/windeng.
htm

The Landman Magazine
American Association of Professional
Landmen
4100 Fossil Creek Boulevard
Forth Worth, TX 76133
Phone: (817) 847-7700
Fax: (817) 847-7704
E-mail: aapl@landman.org
http://www.landman.org

Monthly Energy Review
U.S. Government Printing Office and
Superintendent of Documents
P.O. Box 371954
Pittsburgh, PA 15250
Phone: (202) 512-1800
Fax: (202) 512-2250
E-mail: InfoCtr@eia.doe.gov
http://www.eia.doe.gov/emeu/mer/
contents.html

National Driller Magazine
BNP Media
Energy and Power Management
1050 IL Route 83, Suite 200
Bensenville, IL 60106
Phone: (630) 694-4331
Fax: (248) 786-1358
E-mail: bombardd@bnpmedia.com
http://www.bnpmedia.com

North American Wind Power
Zackin Publications, Inc.
P.O. Box 2180

70 Edwin Avenue
Waterbury, CT 06722
Phone: (800) 325-6745
Fax: (203) 262-9680
E-mail: info@cmi-online.com
http://www.cmi-online.com

Nuclear News
American Nuclear Society
555 North Kensington Avenue
La Grange Park, IL 60526
Phone: (800) 323-3044
Fax: (708) 352-0499
E-mail: nucnews@ans.org
http://www.ans.org

Nuclear Plant Journal
799 Roosevelt Road, Building 6,
Suite 208
Glen Ellyn, IL 60137
Phone: (630) 858-6161
Fax: (630) 858-8787
E-mail: NPJ@goinfo.com
http://npj.goinfo.com

Nuclear Power Today
EIN Publishing Inc.
119 South Fairfax Street
Alexandria, VA 22314
Phone: (800) 726-6898
Fax: (703) 683-3893
E-mail: sakes@eintoday.com
http://www.eintoday.com

Power
TradeFair Group Publications, Ltd.
11000 Richmond Avenue, Suite 500
Houston, TX 77042
Phone: (832) 242-1969
Fax: (832) 242-1971
E-mail: powermag@halldata.com
http://www.powermag.com

Power & Gas Marketing
Oildom Publishing Company of Texas, Inc.
1160 Dairy Ashford, Suite 610
Houston, TX 77029
Phone: (281) 558-6930
Fax: (281) 558-7029
E-mail: oklinger@oildompublishing.com
http://www.oildompublishing.com

Power Engineering
PennWell Corporation
1421 South Sheridan Road
Tulsa, OK 74112
Phone: (800) 331-4463
Fax: (918) 831-9497
E-mail: pe@pennwell.com
http://www.pennwell.com

Refocus Magazine
Elsevier Advanced Technology
360 Park Avenue South
New York, NY 10010
Phone: (212) 633-3199
Fax: (212) 633-3140
E-mail: info@elsevier.com
http://www.elsevier.com

Renewable Energy Today
EIN Publishing Inc.
119 South Fairfax Street
Alexandria, VA 22314
Phone: (800) 726-6898
Fax: (703) 683-3893
E-mail: sakes@eintoday.com
http://www.eintoday.com

Renewable Energy World
35-37 William Road
London NW1 3ER
United Kingdom
Phone: 44 171 387 8558
Fax: 44 171 387 8998
E-mail: james@jxj.com
http://www.jxj.com

Retail Energy Monthly
Association of Energy Engineers
4025 Pleasantdale Road, Suite 420
Atlanta, GA 30340
Phone: (770) 447-5083
Fax: (770) 447-4354
E-mail: whit@aeecenter.org
http://www.aeecenter.org

RSO Magazine
Radiation Safety Association Publishers
19 Pendleton Drive
P.O. Box 19
Hebron, CT 06248
Phone: (860) 228-0487
Fax: (860) 228-4402
E-mail: publish@radpro.com
http://www.radpro.com

Solar Today Magazine
American Solar Society
2400 Central Avenue, Suite G-1
Boulder, CO 80301
Phone: (303) 443-3130
Fax: (303) 443-3212
E-mail: ases@ases.org
http://www.ases.org

Wind Energy (Journal)
John Wiley & Sons, Inc.
Attn: Subscription Department
111 River Street
Hoboken, NJ 07030-5774
Phone: (800) 825-7550
Fax: (201) 748-6021
E-mail: subinfo@wiley.com
http://www.wiley.com/WileyCDA/
    WileyTitle/productCd-WE.html

Windpower Monthly
P.O. Box 100
DK-8420 Knebel
Denmark
Phone: 45 86 36 5900
Fax: 45 86 36 5626
E-mail: mail@windpower-monthly.com
http://www.windpower-monthly.com

World Energy Magazine
3300 South Gessner Street, Suite 200
Houston, TX 77003
Phone: (800) 860-3483
Fax: (713) 627-1638
E-mail: info@ipscorp.com
http://www.ipscorp.com

APPENDIX III
PROFESSIONAL, INDUSTRY, AND TRADE ASSOCIATIONS, GUILDS, AND UNIONS

Since many of these organizations operate on limited budgets, be sure to enclose a self-addressed, stamped envelope when querying any of them for data not available online. Not all of these groups maintain full-time offices, so some cannot be reached via phone, fax, or e-mail. In addition, contact information for some of these organizations may change when a new president or director is selected.

A. GUILDS AND UNIONS

Associated Builders and Contractors (ABC)
4250 North Fairfax Drive, Ninth Floor
Arlington, VA 22203
Phone: (703) 812-2000
Fax: NA
E-mail: At Web site
http://www.abc.org

Atlantic Independent Union (AIU)
520 Cinnaminson Avenue
Palmyra, NJ 08065
Phone: (856) 303-4731
Fax: (856) 346-0803
E-mail: president@aiaunion.org
http://www.aiaunion.org

Communication Workers of America (CWA)
501 Third Avenue NW
Washington, DC 20001
Phone: (202) 434-1100
Fax: (202) 434-1279
E-mail: cwaweb@cwa-union.org
http://www.cwa-union.org

Distribution Contractors Association (DCA)
101 West Renner Street, Suite 460
Richardson, TX 75082
Phone: (972) 680-0261
Fax: (972) 680-0461
E-mail: dca@dca-online.org
http://www.dca-online.org

Independent Electrical Contractors (IECI)
4401 Ford Avenue, Suite 1100
Alexandria, VA 22302
Phone: (800) 456-4324
Fax: (703) 540-7448
E-mail: info@ieci.org
http://www.ieci.org

International Association of Bridge, Structural, Ornamental, and Reinforcing Iron Workers
1750 New York Avenue NW, Suite 400
Washington, DC 20006
Phone: (202) 383-4000
Fax: (202) 638-4856
E-mail: At Web site
http://www.ironworkers.org

International Association of Machinists and Aerospace Workers (IAMAW)
9000 Machinists Place
Upper Marlboro, MD 20772
Phone: (301) 967-4500
Fax: NA
E-mail: websteward@goiam.org
http://www.iamaw.org

International Brotherhood of Boilermakers, Iron Ship Builders, Blacksmiths, Forgers, and Helpers
753 State Avenue, Suite 570
Kansas City, KS 66101
Phone: (913) 371-2640
Fax: (913) 281-8197
E-mail: NA
http://www.boilermakers.org

International Brotherhood of Electrical Workers (IBEW)
1125 15th Street NW
Washington, DC 20005
Phone: (202) 833-7000
Fax: (202) 467-6316
E-mail: At Web site
http://www.ibew.org

International Union, United Automobile, Aerospace and Agricultural Implement Workers of America, also known as United Auto Workers (UAW)
Solidarity House
8000 East Jefferson
Detroit, MI 48214
Phone: (313) 926-5000
Fax: NA
E-mail: At Web site
http://www.uaw.org

International Union of Bricklayers and Allied Craftworkers, International Masonry Institute (IMI)
42 East Street
Annapolis, MD 21401
Phone: (800) 803-0295
Fax: (301) 261-2855
E-mail: www.imiweb.org
http://www.imiweb.org

International Union of Electronic, Electrical, Salaried, Machine, and Furniture Workers (IUE)
501 Third Street NW
Washington, DC 20001
Phone: (202) 513-6300
Fax: (202) 513-6357
E-mail: jdclark@cwa-union.org
http://www.iueacwa.org

International Union of Operating Engineers (IUOE)
1125 17th Street NW
Washington, DC 20036
Phone: (202) 429-9100
Fax: NA
E-mail: At Web site
http://www.iuoe.org

International Union of Petroleum and Industrial Workers (IUPIW)
8131 East Rosecrans Avenue
Paramount, CA 90723
Phone: (800) 624-5842
Fax: (562) 408-1073
E-mail: petroleumworkers@aol.com
http://www.iupiw.org

National Association of Reinforcing Steel Contractors (NARSC)
P.O. Box 280
Fairfax, VA 22038
Phone: (703) 591-1870
Fax: (703) 591-1895
E-mail: info@narsc.com
http://www.narsc.com

National Electrical Contractors Association (NECA)
3 Metro Center, Suite 1100
Bethesda, MD 20814
Phone: (301) 657-3110
Fax: (301) 215-4500
E-mail: At Web site
http://www.necanet.org

Sheet Metal and Air-Conditioning Contractors' National Association (SMACNA)
4201 Lafayette Center Drive
Chantilly, VA 20151
Phone: (703) 803-2980
Fax: (703) 803-3732
E-mail: info@smacna.org
http://www.smacna.org

Sheet Metal Workers' International Association (SMWIA)
1750 New York Avenue NW
Washington, DC 20006
Phone: (202) 783-5880
Fax: NA
E-mail: info@smwia.org
http://www.smwia.org

United Association of Journeymen and Apprentices of the Plumbing and Pipefitting Industry (UA)
901 Massachusetts Avenue NW
Washington, DC 20001
Phone: (202) 628-5823
Fax: (202) 628-5024
E-mail: At Web site
http://www.ua.org

United Brotherhood of Carpenters and Joiners of America (UBCJA)
c/o UBC Insignia Products Department

14110-D Sullyfield Circle
Chantilly, VA 20151
Phone: (703) 378-9000
Fax: (703) 378-9777
E-mail: At Web site
http://www.carpenters.org

United Electrical, Radio and Machine Workers of America (UE)
One Gateway Center, Suite 400
Pittsburgh, PA 15222
Phone: (412) 471-8919
Fax: (412) 471-8999
E-mail: ue@rankandfile-ue.org
http://www.ueinternational.org

United Mine Workers of America (UMWA)
8315 Lee Highway
Fairfax, VA 22031
Phone: (703) 208-7200
Fax: (703) 208-7200
E-mail: At Web site
http://www.umwa.org

United Steelworkers of America (USWA)
Five Gateway Center
Pittsburgh, PA 15222
Phone: (412) 562-2400
Fax: NA
E-mail: webmaster@uswa.org
http://www.uswa.org

Utility Workers Union of America AFL-CIO (UWUA)
815 16th Street NW
Washington, DC 20006
Phone: (888) 843-8982
Fax: (202) 974-8201
E-mail: rfarley@aflcio.org
http://www.uwua.net

B. ASSOCIATIONS

Accreditation Board for Engineering and Technology, Inc. (ABET)
111 Market Place, Suite 1050
Baltimore, MD 21202
Phone: (410) 347-7700
Fax: (410) 625-2238
E-mail: accreditation@abet.org
http://www.abet.org

Air and Waste Management Association (AWMA)
One Gateway Center, 3rd floor
420 Fort Duquesne Boulevard
Pittsburgh, PA 15222
Phone: (800) 270-3444

Fax: (412) 232-3450
E-mail: info@awma.org
http://www.awma.org

Air and Water Management Association (AWMA)
One Gateway Center, 3rd floor
420 Fort Duquesne Boulevard
Pittsburgh, PA 15222
Phone: (800) 270-3444
Fax: (412) 232-3450
E-mail: info@awma.org
http://www.awma.org

American Academy of Environmental Engineers (AAEE)
130 Holiday Court, Suite 100
Annapolis, MD 21401
Phone: (410) 266-3311
Fax: (410) 266-7653
E-mail: At Web site
http://www.aaee.net

American Academy of Health Physicists (AAHP)
1313 Dolly Madison Boulevard, Suite 402
McLean, VA 22101
Phone: (703) 790-1745
Fax: (703) 790-2672
E-mail: aahp@BurtInc.com
http://www.hps1.org/aahp

American Association of Drilling Engineers (AADE)
P.O. Box 940069
Houston, TX 77094
Phone: (281) 293-2800
Fax: (281) 293-2800
E-mail: info@aade.org
http://www.aade.org

American Association of Petroleum Geologists (AAPG)
1444 South Boulder Avenue
Tulsa, OK 74101
Phone: (918) 584-2555
Fax: (918) 560-2665
E-mail: At Web site
http://www.aapg.org

American Association of Professional Landmen (AAPL)
4100 Fossil Creek Boulevard
Fort Worth, TX 76137
Phone: (817) 847-7700
Fax: (817) 847-7704
E-mail: aapl@landman.org
http://www.landman.org

American Chemical Society (ACS)
1155 16th Street NW
Washington, DC 20036
Phone: (800) 227-5558
Fax: (202) 776-8258
E-mail: help@acs.org
http://www.acs.org

American Coal Ash Association (ACAA)
15200 East Girard Avenue, Suite 3050
Aurora, CO 80014
Phone: (720) 870-7897
Fax: (720) 870-7889
E-mail: info@acaa-usa.org
http://www.acaa.org

American Coal Foundation (ACF)
101 Constitution Avenue NW,
    Suite 525 East
Washington, DC 20001
Phone: (202) 463-9785
Fax: (202) 463-9786
E-mail: info@teachcoal.org
http://www.teachcoal.org

American Congress on Surveying and Mapping (ACSM)
6 Montgomery Village Avenue, Suite 403
Gaithersburg, MD 20879
Phone: (240) 632-9716
Fax: (240) 632-1321
E-mail: info@acsm.net
http://www.acsm.net

American Gas Association (AGA)
P.O. Box 79226
Baltimore, MD 21279
Phone: (202) 824-7000
Fax: (202) 824-7115
E-mail: dparker@aga.org
http://www.aga.org

American Geological Institute (AGI)
4220 King Street
Alexandria, VA 22302
Phone: (703) 379-2480
Fax: (703) 379-7563
E-mail: pleahy@agiweb.org
http://www.agiweb.org

American Geophysical Union (AGU)
2000 Florida Avenue NW
Washington, DC 20009
Phone: (800) 966-2481
Fax: (202) 328-0566
E-mail: service@agu.org
http://www.agu.org

American Institute of Chemical Engineers (AICHE)
3 Park Avenue
New York, NY 10016
Phone: (800) 242-4363
Fax: (212) 591-8888
E-mail: At Web site
http://www.aiche.org

American Institute of Hydrology (AIH)
300 Village Green Circle, Suite 201
Smyrna, GA 30080
Phone: (770) 384-1634
Fax: (770) 438-6172
E-mail: aihydro@aol.com
http://www.aihydro.org

American Institute of Mining, Metallurgical and Petroleum Engineers (AIME)
P.O. Box 270728
Littleton, CO 80127
Phone: (303) 948-4255
Fax: (303) 949-4260
E-mail: aime@aimehq.org
http://www.aimeny.org

American Institute of Physics (AIP)
One Physics Ellipse
College Park, MD 20740
Phone: (301) 209-3100
Fax: NA
E-mail: At Web site
http://www.aip.org

American Institute of Professional Geologists (AIPG)
1400 West 122nd Avenue, Suite 250
Westminster, CO 80234
Phone: (303) 412-6205
Fax: (303) 253-9220
E-mail: aipg@aipg.org
http://www.aipg.org

American Marketing Association (AMA)
311 South Wacker Drive, Suite 5800
Chicago, IL 60606
Phone: (800) 262-1150
Fax: (312) 542-9000
E-mail: At Web site
http://www.marketingpower.com

American Meteorological Society (AMS)
45 Beacon Street
Boston, MA 02108
Phone: (617) 227-2425
Fax: (617) 742-8718

E-mail: ckassas@ametsoc.org
http://www.ametsoc.org

American Nuclear Society (ANS)
555 North Kensington Avenue
La Grange Park, IL 60526
Phone: (800) 323-3044
Fax: (708) 352-0499
E-mail: At Web site
http://www.ans.org

American Petroleum Institute (API)
1200 L Street NW
Washington, DC 20003
Phone: (202) 662-8000
Fax: N/A
E-mail: At Web site
http://www.api.org

American Public Gas Association (APGA)
201 Massachusetts Avenue NE, Suite C-4
Washington, DC 20002
Phone: (800) 927-4204
Fax: (202) 464-0246
E-mail: At Web site
http://www.apga.org

American Public Power Association (APPA)
2301 M Street NW
Washington, DC 20037
Phone: (202) 467-2900
Fax: (202) 467-2910
E-mail: mrufe@appanet.org
http://www.appanet.org

American Society for Engineering Education (ASEE)
1818 N Street NW, Suite 600
Washington, DC 20036
Phone: (202) 331-3500
Fax: (202) 265-8504
E-mail: membership@asee.org
http://www.asee.org

American Society for Mining and Reclamation (ASMR)
3134 Montavesta Road
Lexington, KY 40502
Phone: (859) 351-9032
Fax: (859) 335-6529
E-mail: asmr@insightbb.com
http://ces.ca.uky.edu

American Society for Quality (ASQ)
600 North Plankinton Avenue
Milwaukee, WI 53203
Phone: (800) 248-1946

Fax: (414) 272-1734
E-mail: Hepburn@asq.org
http://www.asq.org

**American Society for Testing and
  Materials (ASTM) International**
100 Barr Harbor Drive
P.O. Box C700
West Conshohocken, PA 19428
Phone: (610) 832-9585
Fax: (610) 832-9555
E-mail: service@astm.org
http://www.astm.org

**American Society of Certified
  Engineering Technicians (ASCET)**
P.O. Box 1536
Brandon, MS 39043
Phone: (601) 824-8991
Fax: NA
E-mail: general-manager@ascet.org
http://www.ascet.org

**American Society of Civil Engineers
  (ASCE)**
1801 Alexander Bell Drive
Reston, VA 20191
Phone: (800) 548-2723
Fax: (703) 295-6222
E-mail: member@asce.org
http://www.asce.org

**American Society of Heating,
  Refrigerating and Air-Conditioning
  Engineers, Inc. (ASHRAE)**
1791 Tullie Circle NE
Atlanta, GA 30329
Phone: (800) 527-4723
Fax: (404) 321-5478
E-mail: ashrae@ashrae.org
http://www.ashrae.org

**American Society of Mechanical
  Engineers (ASME)**
3 Park Avenue
New York, NY 10016
Phone: (800) 843-2763
Fax: NA
E-mail: infocentral@asme.org
http://www.asme.org

**American Society of Safety Engineers
  (ASSE)**
1800 East Oakton Street
Des Plaines, IL 60018
Phone: (847) 699-2929
Fax: (847) 768-3434
E-mail: customerservice@asse.org
http://www.asse.org

American Solar Energy Society (ASES)
2400 Central Avenue, Suite A
Boulder, CO 80301
Phone: (303) 443-3130
Fax: (303) 443-3212
E-mail: ases@ases.org
http://www.ases.org

**American Teleservices Association
  (ATA)**
3815 River Crossing Parkway, Suite 20
Indianapolis, IN 46290
Phone: (317) 816-9336
Fax: NA
E-mail: At Web site
http://www.ataconnect.org

**American Underground Contractor
  Association (AUCA)**
3001 Hennepin Avenue, South, Suite
  D202
Minneapolis, MN 55408
Phone: (212) 465-5591
Fax: (212) 631-3787
E-mail: underground@AUCA.org
http://www.AUCA.org

American Welding Society (AWS)
550 Northwest Lejeune Road
Miami, FL 33126
Phone: (305) 443-9353
Fax: (305) 443-7359
E-mail: rhenda@aws.org
http://www.aws.org

**American Wind Energy Association
  (AWEA)**
1101 14th Street NW, 12th floor
Washington, DC 20005
Phone: (202) 383-2500
Fax: (202) 383-2505
E-mail: windmail@awea.org
http://www.awea.org

**ASM International [formerly American
  Society of Metals]**
9639 Kinsman Road
Materials Park, OH 44073
Phone: (440) 338-5151
Fax: (440) 338-4634
E-mail: info@asminternational.org
http://www.asminternational.org

**Associated General Contractors of
  America (AGC)**
2300 Wilson Boulevard, Suite 400
Arlington, VA 22201
Phone: (703) 548-3118
Fax: (703) 548-3119

E-mail: info@agc.org
http://www.agc.org

**Association of American Geographers
  (AAG)**
1710 16th Street NW
Washington, DC 20009
Phone: (202) 239-1450
Fax: (202) 239-2744
E-mail: info@aag.org
http://www.aag.org

**Association of Energy Engineers
  (AEE)**
4025 Pleasantdale Road, Suite 420
Atlanta, GA 30340
Phone: (770) 447-5083
Fax: (770) 446-3969
E-mail: At Web site
http://www.aee.org

**Association of Environmental and
  Engineering Geologists (AEEG)**
P.O. Box 460518
Denver, CO 80296
Phone: (303) 757-2926
Fax: (303) 757-2969
E-mail: aeg@aegweb.org
http://www.aegweb.org

**Association of Professional Energy
  Managers (APEM)**
3916 West Oak Street, Suite D
Burbank, CA 91505
Phone: (818) 972-2159
Fax: (818) 972-2863
E-mail: At Web site
http://www.apem.org

**Board of Certified Safety Professionals
  (BCSP)**
208 Burwash Avenue
Savoy, IL 61874
Phone: (217) 359-9263
Fax: (217) 359-0055
E-mail: At Web site
http://www.bcsp.org

Brick Industry Association (BIA)
1850 Centennial Park Drive, Suite 301
Reston, VA 20191
Phone: (703) 620-0010
Fax: (703) 620-3928
E-mail: brickinfo@bia.org
http://www.brickinfo.org

**Center for Energy and Economic
  Development (CEED)**
333 John Carlyle Street

Alexandria, VA 22314
Phone: (703) 684-6292
Fax: (703) 684-6297
E-mail: webmaster@ceednet.org
http://www.ceednet.org

Certified Welding Technologies, Inc. (CWT)
4602 Hampton Court
Jeffersonville, IN 47130
Phone: (502) 396-8686
Fax: (812) 284-3238
E-mail: jwest@weldingcertification.com
http://www.weldingcertification.com

Council of Petroleum Accountants Societies, Inc. (COPAS)
3900 East Mexico Avenue, Suite 602
Denver, CO 80210
Phone: (303) 300-1131
Fax: (303) 300-3733
E-mail: At Web site
http://www.copas.org

Dangerous Goods Advisory Council (DGAC)
1100 H Street NW, Suite 740
Washington, DC 20005
Phone: (202) 289-4550
Fax: (202) 289-4034
E-mail: info@dgac.org
http://www.dgac.org

Edison Welding Institute (EWI)
1250 Arthur E. Adams Drive
Columbus, OH 43221
Phone: (614) 688-5000
Fax: (614) 688-5001
E-mail: info@ewi.org
http://www.ewi.org

Electrical Generating Systems Association (EGSA)
1650 South Dixie Highway, Suite 500
Boca Raton, FL 33432
Phone: (561) 750-5575
Fax: (561) 395-8557
E-mail: e-mail@egsa.org
http://www.egsa.org

Electric Power Research Institute (EPRI)
3420 Hillview Avenue
Palo Alto, CA 94304
Phone: (800) 313-3744
Fax: N/A
E-mail: At Web site
http://www.my.epri.com

Electric Power Supply Association (EPSA)
1401 New York Avenue NW, 11th floor
Washington, DC 20005
Phone: (202) 628-8200
Fax: (202) 628-8260
E-mail: At Web site
http://www.epsa.org

Electronics Technicians Association (ETA)
5 Depot Street
Greencastle, IN 46135
Phone: (765) 653-8262
Fax: (765) 653-4287
E-mail: eta@eta-i.org
http://www.eta-i.org

Energy Providers Coalition for Education (EPCE)
c/o CAEL
6021 South Syracuse Way, Suite 213
Greenwood Village, CO 80111
Phone: (303) 804-4672
Fax: (303) 773-0026
E-mail: info@epceonline.com
http://www.epceonline.org

Environmental Careers Organization (ECO)
179 South Street
Boston, MA 02111
Phone: (617) 426-4375
Fax: NA
E-mail: At Web site
http://www.eco.org

Fabricators & Manufacturers Association International (FMA)
833 Featherstone Road
Rockford, IL 61107
Phone: (815) 399-8775
Fax: (815) 484-7701
E-mail: info@fmanet.org
http://www.fmanet.org

Gas Processors Association (GPA)
6526 East Sixtieth Street
Tulsa, OK 74145
Phone: (918) 493-3872
Fax: (918) 493-3875
E-mail: gpa@gasprocessors.com
http://www.gasprocessors.com

Gas Technology Institute (GTI)
1700 South Mt. Prospect Road
Des Plaines, IL 60016
Phone: (847) 768-0500
Fax: (847) 768-0501

E-mail: businessdevelopmentinfo@gastechnology.org
http://www.gastechnology.org

Geological Society of America (GSA)
P.O. Box 9140
Boulder, CO 80301
Phone: (888) 443-4472
Fax: (303) 357-1071
E-mail: gsaservice@geosociety.org
http://www.geosociety.org

Geothermal Energy Association (GEA)
209 Pennsylvania Avenue SE
Washington, DC 20003
Phone: (202) 454-5261
Fax: (202) 454-5256
E-mail: geo@geo-energy.org
http://www.geo-energy.org

Geothermal Resources Council (GRC)
P.O. Box 1350
2001 Second Street, Suite 5
Davis, CA 95617
Phone: (530) 758-2360
Fax: (530) 758-2839
E-mail: grc@geothermal.org
http://www.geothermal.org

Health Physics Society (HPS)
1313 Dolly Madison Boulevard
Suite 402
McLean, VA 22101
Phone: (730) 790-1745
Fax: (703) 790-2672
E-mail: hps@burkinc.com
http://www.hps.org

Home Builders Institute (HBI)
1201 15th Street NW, Sixth Floor
Washington, DC 20005
Phone: (800) 795-7955
Fax: (202) 266-8999
E-mail: postmaster@hbi.org
http://www.hbi.org

Independent Electrical Contractors, Inc. (IECI)
4401 Ford Avenue, Suite 1100
Alexandria, VA 22302
Phone: (703) 549-7351
Fax: (703) 549-7448
E-mail: info@ieci.org
http://www.ieci.org

Independent Petroleum Association of America (IPAA)
1201 15th Street NW, Suite 300
Washington, DC 20005

Phone: (202) 857-4722
Fax: (202) 8 57-4799
E-mail: info@ipaa.org
http://www.ipaa.org

Institute of Electrical and Electronics Engineers (IEEE)
445 Hoes Lane
Piscataway, NJ 08855
Phone: (732) 981-0060
Fax: (732) 981-1721
E-mail: At Web site
http://www.ieee.org

Institute of Industrial Engineers (IIE)
3577 Parkway Lane, Suite 200
Norcross, GA 30092
Phone: (770) 449-0461
Fax: NA
E-mail: cs@iienet.org
http://www.iienet.org

Institute of Petroleum Accounting (IPA)
University of Texas—Marquis Hall, Room 315
P.O. Box 305460
Denton, TX 76205
Phone: (940) 565-3170
Fax: (940) 369-8839
E-mail: ipa@unt.edu
http://www.unt.edu/ipa/contact.htm

Institute of Shaft Drilling Technology (ISDT)
1352 Southwest 175th Street
Seattle, WA 98166
Phone: (202) 243-2558
Fax: (202) 244-7994
E-mail: At Web site
http://www.isdt.org

Instrument Society of America (ISA)
67 Alexander Drive
P.O. Box 12277
Research Triangle Park, NC 27709
Phone: (919) 549-8411
Fax: (919) 549-8288
E-mail: info@isa.org
http://www.isa.org

International Association for Environmental Hydrology (IAEH)
2607 Hopeton Drive
San Antonio, TX 78230
Phone: (201) 984-7583
Fax: (201) 564-8581
E-mail: hydroweb@gmail.com
http://www.hydroweb.com

International Association of Administrative Professionals (IAAP)
10502 NW Ambassador Drive
P.O. Box 20404
Kansas City, MO 64195
Phone: (816) 891-6660
Fax: (816) 891-9118
E-mail: service@iaap-hq.org
http://www.iaap-hq.org

International Association of Business Communicators (IABC)
One Hallidie Plaza, Suite 600
San Francisco, CA 94102
Phone: (800) 776-4222
Fax: (415) 544-4747
E-mail: N/A
http://www.iabc.com

International Association of Electrical Inspectors (IAEI)
P.O. Box 830848
Richardson, TX 75083
Phone: (800) 780-4234
Fax: (972) 235-3855
E-mail: iaei@iaei.org
http://www.iaei.org

International Electrical Testing Association (NETA)
P.O. Box 687
Morrison, CO 80465
Phone: (888) 300-6382
Fax: (303) 697-8431
E-mail: neta@netaworld.org
http://www.netaworld.org

International Erosion Control Association (IECA)
3001 South Lincoln Avenue, Suite A
Steamboat Springs, CO 80487
Phone: (800) 455-4322
Fax: (970) 879-8563
E-mail: At Web site
http://www.ieca.org

International League of Electrical Associations (ILEA)
12165 West Center Road, Suite 59
Omaha, NE 68144
Phone: (402) 330-7227
Fax: (402) 330-7283
E-mail: niec2005@aol.com
http://www.ileaweb.org

International Research Center for Energy and Economic Development (ICEED)
850 Willowbrook Road

Boulder, CO 80302
Phone: (303) 442-4014
Fax: (303) 442-5042
E-mail: At Web site
http://www.iceed.org

International Society of Certified Electronics Technicians (ISCET)
3608 Pershing Avenue
Fort Worth, TX 76107
Phone: (800) 946-0201
Fax: (817) 921-3741
E-mail: info@iscet.org
http://www.iscet.org

International Society of Explosives Engineers (ISEE)
30325 Bainbridge Road
Cleveland, OH 44139
Phone: (440) 349-4400
Fax: (440) 349-3788
E-mail: At Web site
http://www.isee.org

Interstate Natural Gas Association of America (INGAA)
10 G Street NE
Washington, DC 20002
Phone: (202) 216-5900
Fax: (202) 216-0870
E-mail: NA
http://www.ingaa.org

Junior Engineering Technical Society (JETS)
1420 King Street, Suite 405
Alexandria, VA 22314
Phone: (703) 548-5387
Fax: (703) 548-0769
E-mail: info@jets.org
http://www.jets.org

Materials Research Society (MRS)
506 Keystone Drive
Warrendale, PA 15086
Phone: (724) 779-3003
Fax: (724) 779-8313
E-mail: info@mrs.org
http://www.mrs.org

Mining and Metallurgical Society of America (MMSA)
476 Wilson Avenue
Novato, CA 94947
Phone: (415) 897-1380
Fax: NA
E-mail: info@mmsa.net
http://www.mmsa.net

Millwright Group (MG)
c/o Specialized Carriers and Rigging
  Association
2750 Prosperity Avenue, Suite 620
Fairfax, VA 22031
Phone: (703) 698-0291
Fax: (703) 698-0297
E-mail: info@scrannat.org
http://www.scrannat.org

**The Minerals, Metals, & Materials
  Society (TMS)**
184 Thorn Hill Road
Warrendale, PA 15086
Phone: (724) 776-9000
Fax: (724) 776-3770
E-mail: members@tms.org
http://www.tms.org

**Mine Safety and Health Administration
  (MSHA)**
1100 Wilson Boulevard
Arlington, VA 22209
Phone: (202) 693-9400
Fax: (202) 693-9401
E-mail: At Web site
http://www.msha.gov

**Mining and Metallurgical Society of
  America (MMSA)**
476 Wilson Avenue
Novato, CA 94947
Phone: (415) 897-1380
Fax: N/A
E-mail: info@mmsa.net
http://www.mmsa.net

**National Association of Power
  Engineers (NAPE)**
1 Springfield Street
Chicopee, MA 01013
Phone: (413) 592-6273
Fax: NA
E-mail: NAPENATL@verizon.net
http://www.powerengineers.com

**National Center for Construction
  Education and Research**
3600 NW 43rd Street, Building G
Gainesville, FL 32606
Phone: (888) 622-3720
Fax: (352) 334-0932
http://www.nccer.org

**National Concrete Masonry
  Association (NCMA)**
13750 Sunrise Valley Drive
Herndon, VA 20171-4662
Phone: (703) 713-1900

Fax: (703) 713-1910
E-mail: ncma@ncma.org
http://www.ncma.org

**National Council for Examiners
  for Engineering and Surveying
  (NCEES)**
P.O. Box 1686
Clemson, SC 29633
Phone: (800) 250-3196
Fax: (864) 654-6033
E-mail: infor@ncees.org
http://www.ncees.org

**National Council of Structural
  Engineers Association (NCSEA)**
645 North Michigan Avenue, Suite 540
Chicago, IL 60611
Phone: (312) 649-4600
Fax: (312) 649-5840
E-mail: At Web site
http://www.ncsea.com

**National Credentialing Agency for
  Laboratory Personnel (NCA)**
P.O. Box 15945-289
Lenexa, KS 66285
Phone: (913) 895-4613
Fax: (913) 895-4652
E-mail: nca-info@goamp.com
http://www.nca-info.org

**National Electrical Contractors
  Association (NECA)**
3 Bethesda Metro Center, Suite 1100
Bethesda, MD 20814
Phone: (301) 657-3110
Fax: (301) 215-4500
E-mail: N/A
http://www.necanet.org

**National Electrical Manufacturers
  Association (NEMA)**
1300 North 17th Street, Suite 1752
Rosslyn, VA 22209
Phone: (703) 841-3200
Fax: (703) 841-5900
E-mail: communications@nema.org
http://www.nema.org

**National Gas Supply Association
  (NGSA)**
805 15th Street NW, Suite 510
Washington, DC 20005
Phone: (202) 326-9300
Fax: (202) 326-9330
E-mail: skip.horvat@ngsa.org
http://www.ngsa.org

National Hydropower Association (NHA)
1 Massachusetts Avenue NW, Suite 850
Washington, DC 20001
Phone: (202) 682-1700
Fax: (202) 682-9478
E-mail: info@hydro.org
http://www.hydro.org

**National Institute for Certification in
  Engineering Technologies (NICET)**
1420 King Street
Alexandria, VA 22314
Phone: (888) 476-4238
Fax: N/A
E-mail: tech@nicet.org
http://www.nicet.org

**National Management Association
  (NMA)**
2210 Arbor Boulevard
Dayton, OH 45439
Phone: (937) 294-0421
Fax: NA
E-mail: nma@nma1.org
http://www.nma1.org

National Mining Association (NMA)
101 Constitution Avenue NW,
  Suite 500 East
Washington, DC 20001
Phone: (202) 463-2600
Fax: (202) 463-2666
E-mail: craulston@nma.org
http://www.nma.org

**National Society of Professional
  Engineers (NSPE)**
1420 King Street
Alexandria, VA 22314
Phone: (703) 684-2800
Fax: (703) 836-4875
E-mail: memserv@nspe.org
http://www.nspe.org

**National Society of Professional
  Surveyors (NSPS)**
6 Montgomery Village Avenue, Suite 403
Gaithersburg, MD 20879
Phone: (240) 632-9716
Fax: (240) 632-1321
E-mail: trisha.milburn@acsm.net
http://www.nspsmo.org

**National Tooling and Machining
  Association (NTMA)**
9300 Livingston Road
Fort Washington, MD 20744
Phone: (800) 248-6862
Fax: (301) 248-7104

E-mail: At Web site
http://www.ntma.org

**North American Electric Reliability
   Corporation (NERC)**
116-390 Village Boulevard
Princeton, NJ 08540
Phone: (609) 452-8060
Fax: (609) 452-9550
E-mail: info@nerc.com
http://soc.nerc.net

**North American Young Generation in
   Nuclear (NA-YGN)**
P.O. Box 10014
La Grange, IL 60525
Phone: (877) 526-2946
Fax: NA
E-mail: At Web site
http://www.na-ygn.org

Nuclear Energy Institute (NEI)
1776 I Street NW, Suite 400
Washington, DC 20006
Phone: (202) 739-8000
Fax: (202) 739-4019
E-mail: At Web site
http://www.nei.org

**Petroleum Equipment Suppliers
   Association (PESA)**
9225 Katy Freeway, Suite 310
Houston, TX 77024
Phone: (713) 932-0168
Fax: (713) 932-0497
E-mail: NA
http://www.pesa.org

**Petroleum Technology Transfer
   Council (PTTC)**
623 Arrowhead Street
P.O. Box 246
Sand Springs, CO 74063
Phone: (918) 241-5801
Fax: (918) 241-5728
E-mail: info@pttc.org
http://www.pttc.org

**Professional Reactor Operator
   Society (PROS)**
P.O. Box 484

Byron, IL 61010
Phone: (815) 234-8140
Fax: (815) 234-8140
E-mail: At Web site
http://nucpros.com

**Public Relations Society of America
   (PRSA)**
33 Maiden Lane, 11th floor
New York, NY 10038
Phone: (212) 460-1400
Fax: (212) 995-0757
E-mail: info@prsa.org
http://www.prsa.org

Renewable Fuels Association (RFA)
1 Massachusetts Avenue NW,
   Suite 820
Washington, DC 20001
Phone: (202) 289-3835
Fax: (202) 289-7519
E-mail: info@ethanolrfa.org
http://www.ethanolrfa.org

**Society for Mining, Metallurgy, and
   Exploration, Inc. (SME)**
8307 Shaffer Parkway
Littleton, CO 80127
Phone: (800) 763-3132
Fax: (303) 973-3845
E-mail: cs@smenet.org
http://www.smenet.org

**Society of Exploration Geophysicists
   (SEG)**
8801 South Yale
Tulsa, OK 74137
Phone: (918) 497-5500
Fax: (918) 497-5557
E-mail: At Web site
http://seg.org

**Society of Manufacturing Engineers
   (SME)**
One SME Drive
Dearborn, MI 49121
Phone: (800) 733-4763
Fax: (313) 425-3400
E-mail: service@sme.org
http://www.sme.org

Society of Petroleum Engineers (SPE)
P.O. Box 833836
Richardson, TX 75083
Phone: (972) 952-9393
Fax: NA
E-mail: service@spe.org
http://www.spe.org

Solar Electric Power Association
1341 Connecticut Avenue NW, Suite 3.2
Washington, DC 20036
Phone: (202) 857-0898
Fax: (480) 393-5631
E-mail: info@solarelectricpower.org
http://www.solarelectricpower.org

**Solar Energy Industries Association
   (SEIA)**
805 15th Street NW, Suite 510
Washington, DC 20005
Phone: (202) 682-0556
Fax: (202) 682-7779
E-mail: info@seia.org
http://www.seia.org

**Water Environment Federation
   (WEF)**
601 Wythe Street
Alexandria, VA 23314
Phone: (800) 666-0206
Fax: (703) 684-2492
E-mail: csc@wef.org
http://www.wef.org

Welding Research Council (WRC)
P.O. Box 1942
New York, NY 10156
Phone: (216) 658-3847
Fax: (216) 658-3854
E-mail: At Web site
http://www.forengineers.org

**Women's International Network of
   Utility Professionals (WINUP)**
P.O. Box 1197
Gallatin, TN 37066
Phone: (615) 452-5152
Fax: (615) 452-6060
E-mail: rsimpson@gallatinelectric.com
http://www.winup.org

APPENDIX IV
USEFUL WEB SITES FOR THE
ENERGY INDUSTRIES

INTRODUCTION

For anyone involved in any aspect of the energy industries as a vocation, the Internet has become an increasingly valuable resource in today's high-tech electronic age.

The following are a selection of useful Web sites to help in your industry researching, such as job searching, trade news, career research, and networking. (Web sites that do not have self-explanatory names are annotated with a brief explanation situated between the site name and its URL.)

These listed URLs may well be ones you wish to bookmark and/or list in your Favorites folder. In addition, by utilizing one or more of the search engines listed below—or using one of your own preferred search engines—you can fairly easily lay the foundation for researching most any organization, individual, or topic. Naturally, the information offered on any Web site is only as good as the source itself and needs to be constantly reevaluated by you for its

track record of providing consistently reliable data. As has always been true, the Internet is in a constant state of flux; even well-established Web sites often change their Web address. Typically, if you click on a link that has recently changed its URL, you will be switched automatically to its new Web address (which you can then bookmark and/or list in your Favorites). If your link proves to be cold/dead, use a search engine to provide hits for the Web site in question. Most times, this step will lead you to the new home page of the desired site. (As always, when using a search engine, if your query is more than one word, place the name/term in quotes to narrow and target the search.)

While the Internet and e-mail are great tools to employ in starting/furthering your career in energy, do not ignore traditional person-to-person contact with colleagues, mentors, family, friends, and others within your support network. They are equally vital in keeping you on track in your work and life.

SEARCH ENGINES

HOW TO USE SEARCH ENGINES

Bare Bones 101
http://www.sc.edu/beaufort/library/pages/
     bones/bones.shtml

Organic SEO Wiki
http://www.organicseo.org

Search.com
http://www.search.com

SearchEngineWatch
http://searchenginewatch.com

Spider's Apprentice
http://www.monash.com/spidap4.html

WebRef
http://webreference.com/content/search

SEARCH ENGINES (BY COUNTRY)

http://www.philb.com/countryse.htm

SEARCH ENGINES (GENERAL)

Alltheweb
http://alltheweb.com

Alta Vista
http://www.altavista.com

A9
http://a9.com

Answers.com
http://www.answers.com

AOL
http://www.aol.com

Ask.com
http://www.ask.com

AT1
http://www.at1.com

Blogs – Search Engines
an increasingly important venue for industry news and trends; note that many

general search engines now provide a subcategory targeted for locating blogs by subject matter

Blogdigger
http://www.blogdigger.com

Blogflux
http://dir.blogflux.com

Bloggernity
http://www.bloggernity.com

BlogSearchEngine
http://www.blogsearchengine.com

Bloogz: World Wide Blog
http://www.bloogz.com

Daypop
http://www.daypop.com

Feedster
http://www.feedster.com

Gigablast
http://www.gigablast.com

Google Blog Search
http://blogsearch.google.com

IceRocket.com
http://blogs.icerocket.com

LS Blog
http://www.lsblogs.com

QuackTrack
http://quacktrack.com

Technorati
http://www.technorati.com

Yahoo Blog Search
http://ysearchblog.com

Clusty
http://clusty.com

Copernic
Free and paid versions of special download
    software available at site; generally
    does not work with Macintosh system
http://copernic.com

CrossEngine
http://www.crossengine.com

Ditto
http://www.ditto.com

Dogpile
http://www.dogpile.com

Excite
http://www.excite.com

Factbites
http://www.factbites.com

Findspot
http://www.findspot.com

The Front Page
http://www.thefrontpage.com

Galaxy
http://www.galaxy.com

Gigablast
http://www.gigablast.com

GoFish
http://www.gofish.com

Google
http://www.google.com

Google Scholar
http://scholar.google.com

HotBot
http://www.hotbot.com

HotSheet
http://www.hotsheet.com

Itool
http://www.itools.com

KartOO
http://www.kartoo.com

LookSmart
http://search.looksmart.com

Lycos
http://www.lycos.com

Metacrawler
http://metacrawler.com

MSN
http://www.msn.com

Omgili
Search engine for discussion forums
http://omgili.com

Singingfish
http://www.singingfish.com

Soople
http://www.soople.com

Starting Page
http://www.startingpage.com

Starting Point
http://www.stpt.com

Teoma
http://www.directhit.com

WebCrawler
http://webcrawler.com

Wikipedia
http://en.wikipedia.org

WiseNut
http://www.wisenut.com

Yahoo
http://www.yahoo.com

EDUCATION WEB SITES

Academic Info—Educational
    Resources
http://www.academicinfo.net

American Universities
http://www.clas.ufl.edu/CLAS/american-
    universities.html

Best Sites for Financial Aid
http://www.cslr.org

College and University Home Pages
http://www.mit.edu:8001/people/
    cdemello/univ.html

CollegeNet
Guide to colleges, universities, and
    scholarships
http://www.collegenet.com

College Search
http://www.utexas.edu/world/univ

College Xpress
http://www.collegeexpress.com

Education Index
http://www.educationindex.com

Education Web Sites
An extensive listing of education Web
    sites, including search engines
http://ejw.18.com/educweb.htm

Google Directory—Education
http://www.google.com/Top/Reference/
    Education

LearnNet
http://www.chemsoc.org/networks/learnnet

National Center for Education Statistics
http://nces.ed.gov

Petersons.com
http://www.petersons.com

The Princeton Review
http://www.princetonreview.com/
college/research/majors/majorBasics.
asp?majorID=174

Trade Schools and Career Education
http://educhoices.org

Worldwide Learn
http://www.worldwidelearn.com/online-
education-guide

Yahoo! Education
Guide to courses and degrees in
Engineering and Technology,
Networking, and Security
http://degrees.education.yahoo.com/sub2-
engineering_and_technology

Yahoo's Colleges and Universities by States
http://dir.yahoo.com/Education/Higher_
Education

ENERGY RESOURCES

American Oil Chemist's Society
http://www.aocs.org

American Petroleum Institute
http://www.api.org

CHEMINDUSTRY.COM
Chemical/oil/gas industries resource
links
http://www.chemindustry.com

EDA Inc.
http://www.edasolutions.com

The Electricity Forum
http://www.electricityforum.com

E-mail newsletters
Some are free, others are subscription-based.
Sign-up is at the publication's Web site

EarthToys
http://www.earthtoys.com/emagazine.
php

Electric Light & Power E-Newsletter
http://www.pennwell.com

Electric Power Daily
http://www.platts.com

Energy (U.S. National Technical Information Service Newsletter)
http://www.ntis.gov

Energy Compass
http://www.energyintel.com/Publication
HomePage.asp?publication_id=1

Energy Intelligence Briefing
http://www.energyintel.com/
Publication
HomePage.asp?publication_id=2

Gas Market Reconnaissance
http://www.energyintel.com
PublicationHomePage.asp?
publication_id=17

The Hydrogen and Fuel Cell Letter
http://www.hfcletter.com

Hydrogen Association News
http://www.hydrogenassociation.org/
newsletter

International Oil Daily
http://www.energyintel.com/
Publication
HomePage.asp?publication_id=31

International Petroleum Finance
http://www.energyintel.com/
Publication
HomePage.asp?publication_id=8

National Conference of State Legislatures Newsletter
http://www.ncsl.org/programs/energy/
ENewsMenu.htm

Natural Gas Week
http://www.energyintel.com

Newsletter Access
Links to various energy (production)
newsletters
http://www.newsletteraccess.com/
search.php?a=cat&s=0&l=25&cat_
id=60

Offshore Weekly Report
http://www.omeda.com/cgi-winos.cgi?
newsletter

Oil and Gas Journal
http://www.omeda.com/cgi-win/ogjo.
cgi?NEWSLETTER

Oil Daily
http://www.energyintel.com/
Publication
HomePage.asp?publication_id=5

Oil Market Intelligence
http://www.energyintel.com/
PublicationHomePage.
asp?publication_id=6

Petroleum Intelligence Weekly
http://www.energyintel.com/
Publication
HomePage.asp?publication_id=4

Power Market Today Newsletters
http://intelligencepress.com/
subscribers/ngi/ng20070514.html

Renewable Energy News
http://www.renewableenergyaccess.
com

Small Wind Energy
http://www.irecusa.org/index.
php?id=40

Solar & Renewable Energy Outlook
http://www.iaquality.com

Sustainable Energy News
http://www.inforse.org/s_e_news.php3

Wind Energy Weekly
http://www.awea.org

World Energy Monthly Review
http://www.ipscorp.com

World Gas Intelligence
http://www.energyintel.com/
Publication
HomePage.asp?publication_id=10

Worldwide Energy
http://www.wvpubs.com

Energy Industry CBT Alliance
http://www.eicaonline.com

Energy Industry Today
http://energy.einnews.com

Energy Online
http://www.energyonline.com

Hydrocarbon Online
http://www.hydrocarbononline.com/
content/homepage/default.asp?
VNETCOOKIE=NO

Nuclear Energy Institute
http://www.nei.org

Oil Online
http://www.oilonline.com/info/calendar.
asp

Renewable Energy Access
http://www.renewableenergyaccess.com/
rea/home

Research Reports International
Portal to energy industry
http://www.researchreportsintl.com

Rigzone
Portal to oil and gas industry
http://www.rigzone.com

ScienceResearch.com
A portal allowing access to numerous
scientific journals and public science
databases, plus links to other free science portals
http://www.scienceresearch.com

**Solstice (Center for Renewable Energy
and Sustainable Technology) (CREST)**
http://solstice.crest.org

World Meteorological Organization
http://www.wmo.ch/pages/index_en.html

World Coal Institute
http://www.worldcoal.org

GOVERNMENT WEB SITES

Energy Information Agency
http://www.eia.doe.gov

Federal Energy Regulatory Commission
http://www.ferc.gov

**International Atomic Energy Agency
(United Nations)**
http://www.iaea.org

U.S. Department of Energy
http://www.energy.gov

**U.S. Department of Energy: Energy
Efficiency and Renewable Energy**
http://www.eere.energy.gov

**U.S. Department of Labor,
Occupational Safety and Health
Administration (OSHA)**
http://www.osha.gov

**U.S. Department of Labor, Office of
Apprenticeship Training, Employer
and Labor Services (OATELS)**
http://www.dol.gov/dol/topic/training/
apprenticeship.htm

**U.S. Department of Labor, State
Apprenticeship Information**
http://www.doleta.gov/atels_bat

U.S. Energy Information Agency
http://www.eia.doe.gov

U.S. Environmental Protection Agency
http://www.epa.gov

**U.S. Nuclear Regulatory Commission
(NRC)**
http//www.nrc.gov

JOB SEARCH/SALARY SURVEY/CAREER INFORMATION WEB SITES

Some of these Web sites require a
subscription fee for their use.

America's CareerInfoNet
http://www.careerinfonet.org

America's Service Locator
http://www.servicelocator.org

B2B Jobs
http://www.b2byellowpages.com/jobs/
index.cgi

CareerOneStop
http://www.careeronestop.org

Dev Bistro
http://www.devbistro.com

Dice
http://seeker.dice.com/jobsearch/genthree/
index.jsp

Employnow
http://www.employnow.com

Energy and Power Career Guide
http://www.khake.com/page49.html

**Environmental Careers Organization
(ECO)**
http://www.eco.org

Google
http://directory.google.com/Top/Regional/
North_America/United_States/
Business_and_Economy/Employment

Hot Jobs
http://www.hotjobs.com

Job Hunt
http://www.job-hunt.org

Job Profiles
http://www.jobprofiles.org

Jobs.aol.com
http://jobs.aol.com/?sem=1&ncid=
AOLCAR00170000000004

Job Search
http://jobsearch.monster.com

JobSmart Salary Info
http://jobsmart.org/tools/salary/sal-prof.
htm

Jobs.net
http://jobs.net

Jobs Search
http://jobs.ea.com

JobStar Central
http://jobstar.org/tools/salary/sal-prof.php

Monster
http://www.monster.com

MSN Careerbuilder
http://jobs.msn.careerbuilder.com/
    Custom/MSN/FindJobs.aspx

OILCAREERS.com
http://www.oilcareers.com/knowmore.asp

PayScale
http://www.payscale.com

The Real Rate Survey
http://www.realrates.com/survey.htm

Roadtechs.com
http://www.roadtechs.com

Salary.com
http://www.salary.com

Salary Wizard
http://swz-hoovers.salary.com

Sloan Career Corner
http://www.careercornerstone.org/
    engother/metallurgical.htm

TheLadders
Job site for $100K+ job listings
http://www.theladders.com

Think Energy Group
http://www.thinkenergygroup.com/think.
    nsf/EnergyJobs?OpenForm

TopUSAjobs.com
http://topusajobs.com

True Careers
General career information
http://www.truecareers.com/jobseeker/
    careerresources/default.shtml

USAJobs
Career information on government jobs
http://www.usajobs.opm.gov

Vault
http://www.vault.com

Wageweb Salary Survey Data Online
http://www.wageweb.com/index.htlm

Wetfeet
http://www.wetfeet.com

Yahoo
http://careers.yahoo.com/employment/
    carrer_resources/salaries_and_benefits

GLOSSARY OF ENERGY TERMS

[Words in full uppercase within a definition have their own separate entry in the glossary.]

Abandoned well   A well that is permanently shut down because it has ceased to produce crude oil or natural gas or because it was a dry hole. It is converted to a condition whereby it can be left indefinitely without further attention and will not damage freshwater supplies, potential petroleum or gas RESERVOIRs or the environment.

Acidizing   A method of improving POROSITY and PERMEABILITY of a RESERVOIR by injecting acid under pressure to dissolve reservoir rock.

Amperes   A measure (amperage) of the volume of electric current flow (as opposed to the "pressure" of a flow, which is measured in volts). The product of volts times amperes is equal to power, which is measured in WATTs. Amperes are commonly referred to simply as "amps."

Anemometer   An instrument for measuring and displaying wind speed or velocity.

Anthracite   The hardest, most organically mature coal, having the highest carbon content and lowest water content.

Aquifer   A water-bearing stratum of permeable sand, rock, or gravel.

Array   A group of PHOTOVOLTAIC (PV) modules connected together in a power system.

Auger   A rotary drill employed in mining/excavation that uses a screw-shaped device to penetrate, break up, and transport the drilled material without the use of drilling fluids.

Augmentor   Device that increases the air flow through a wind turbine rotor. Called CONCENTRATORS when used on the upwind side of a wind turbine and diffusers when used on the downwind side.

Barrel   The common unit for measuring petroleum. One barrel contains approximately 159 litres.

Biofuels   Liquid fuels, such as ETHANOL and biodiesel, made from BIOMASS. These fuels can be in their pure state or blended with gasolines.

Biomass   Organic materials containing stored chemical energy that can be utilized as an energy source. These include tree and plant residues, agricultural crops and wastes, wood and wood wastes, animal wastes, and municipal and industrial wastes.

Bitumen   Solid or semi-solid petroleum that cannot be pumped without being heated or diluted.

Bituminous coal   The second hardest, most organically mature coal.

Blowout   An uncontrolled flow of gas, oil, or other fluids from a drilling well.

Boiler   A large furnace that burns fuel to produce steam for power, processing, or heating. Also a device to burn BIOMASS fuel to heat water for generating steam.

British thermal unit (BTU)   The quantity of heat required to raise the temperature of one pound of water by one degree Fahrenheit.

CAD (computer-aided design)   A combination of hardware and software that enables architects and engineers in their design work. CAD systems allow an engineer to view a design from any angle and to zoom in or out for close-up and long-distance views. In addition, the computer keeps track of design dependencies so that when the engineer changes one value, all other values that depend on it are automatically changed accordingly.

CAM (computer-aided manufacturing)   The process of using specialized computers to control, monitor, and adjust tools and machinery employed in manufacturing.

Casing   A series of tubular steel pipes joined by threads and couplings that line the WELLBORE of a drilling well to prevent water and rock from entering.

Chlorofluorocarbons (CFCs)   Chemical compounds that are used as aerosol propellants, solvents, and refrigerants, which contribute to the depletion of the ozone layer and to the build-up of GREENHOUSE GASES.

Coking   The process of heating coal in a coke oven in the absence of air to high temperatures (between 1000° and 1100° Centigrade) for 16 to 20 hours to produce an extremely pure form of carbon.

Collector   A device that concentrates the Sun's power into a contained area and converts it to heat and electricity.

Compressed natural gas (CNG)   Natural gas that has been greatly compressed and is stored in high-pressure surface containers. CNG is used as a transportation fuel for vehicles.

Compressor stations   Permanent facilities containing machines (compressors) that supply the energy needed to move natural gas at increased pressures.

Concentrator   A tool that employs lenses and/or mirrors to focus and enhance the Sun's rays onto a PHOTOVOLTAIC surface. Also a device that concentrates the wind stream striking a wind TURBINE rotor.

Coolant   A fluid phase in a nuclear REACTOR that, in cooling the reactor core, creates steam to drive TURBINEs to generate electricity.

Core   A cylindrical sample of rock cut by a special bit during the drilling process.

Crude oil   Naturally occurring liquid petroleum.

Current   The flow of electrons in an electrical CONDUCTOR. Current is measured in AMPERES.

Decommissioning   Removal of a facility (such as a nuclear REACTOR) from service, including actions taken to safely dismantle buildings, reclaim land, and restore the site to other uses.

Deregulation   The process of changing natural gas (or petroleum, or electricity) market regulations to allow a greater role for market forces to balance supply and demand and set prices. It does *not* imply the absence of regulation.

Derrick   A load-bearing tower-like structure over a natural gas or crude oil well that holds the hoisting and lowering equipment for drilling, testing, and working of wells.

Direct current (DC)   Electrical energy that flows in one direction. This type of electric power typically comes from PHOTOVOLTAIC (PV) cells and batteries.

Directional (deviated) well   A well drilled at an angle from the vertical by using a slanted drilling rig or by deflecting the drill bit; directional wells are utilized to drill multiple wells from a common drilling pad or to reach a subsurface location beneath land or water where regular drilling cannot be done.

Distribution lines   Low-VOLTAGE power lines used to transport small amounts of power from a DISTRIBUTION STATION or a regional supply center to the customer's local transformer.

Distribution station   An electrical component that receives electrical power at a high VOLTAGE and then transforms that high voltage to a lower voltage, suitable for distribution of electric power to local customers.

Downstream   The refining and marketing sector of the petroleum industry.

Drilling mud   Specialized mud (clay in water or oil with chemical additives) mixed at the drill site and pumped down the drill string to remove drill cuttings, cool and lubricate the drill bit, and maintain the required pressure at the bottom of the well.

Drilling rig   The surface equipment used to drill for oil or gas consisting chiefly of a DERRICK, a winch for lifting and lowering drill pipe, a rotary table to turn the drill pipe, and engines to drive the winch and rotary table.

Ethanol   Colorless, flammable liquid produced as a petrochemical through the hydration of ethylene and, biologically, by the fermentation of sugars with yeast. Currently, the main FEEDSTOCK in the United States for the production of ethanol is corn.

Fault   A displacement of subsurface layers of earth or rock that sometimes seals an oil-bearing formation by placing it next to a nonporous formation.

Feedstock   Any material converted to another form or product.

FERC   Stands for Federal Energy Regulatory Commission, the agency that regulates interstate movement of electrical power and natural gas within the United States.

Fission   The splitting of an atom in two, releasing energy; induced fission occurs when a free neutron collides with a nucleus, causing it to split, unlike spontaneous fission, which occurs without external influence.

Flaring   Controlled burning of natural gas that cannot be processed for sale because of technical or economic reasons. Flaring contributes to the emission of sulphur dioxide and GREENHOUSE GASES. Depending on the combustion efficiency of the flare, there may be other compounds produced in very small quantities, some of which are considered toxic.

Fly ash   PARTICULATE MATTER from coal ash that exits boilers along with hot gases. Pollution control equipment removes more than 90 percent of the fly ash before it can be released into the atmosphere.

Fossil fuels   Fuels formed by decayed plants and animals that have undergone transformation through heat and pressure. Oil, coal, and natural gas are examples.

Fracturing   Pumping special fluids down a well at high pressure to create cracks in the rock formation that will allow RESERVOIR fluids (or gas) to flow more easily into the WELLBORE.

Gasification   The process of turning LIQUEFIED NATURAL GAS into a vaporous or gaseous state by increasing the temperature and decreasing the pressure.

Geothermal energy   Energy available in the ground and rocks beneath the Earth's crust, such as molten rock or hot-water geysers.

Greenhouse gases   Gases that trap heat near the Earth's surface, including carbon dioxide, methane, nitrous oxide, and water vapor. These gases occur through natural processes (such as ocean currents, cloud cover, volcanoes) and human activities (such as the burning of FOSSIL FUELS).

Grid   Network of high-VOLTAGE TRANSMISSION LINES for distributing electric power to customers.

High-level waste   Used nuclear fuel that is highly radioactive and requires long-term management and storage in shielded facilities.

Hydropower   The use of water power to generate electricity, which is produced by utilizing the kinetic energy available in flowing water.

In-situ   Phrase meaning in its original plate; in-situ recovery refers to various methods employed to recover deeply buried oil BITUMEN deposits.

Inverter   An appliance used to convert DC electric power (as from a PHOTOVOLTAIC cell) into standard AC electric current.

Joint implementation   A means of reducing global GREENHOUSE GAS emissions whereby a country receives credit for supporting emissions reductions elsewhere—

for example, planting trees, or replacing inefficient power generation facilities in a developing country.

Joule   The international unit of energy, defined as the energy produced by a power of one WATT for one second.

Kilowatt-hour (kWh)   A measure of electric energy. Customers are usually charged for electricity based on a rate of cents per kilowatt-hour.

Lignite   The lowest rank of coal, often referred to as brown coal, used almost exclusively as fuel for steam-electric power generation.

Liquefaction   The process by which natural gas is converted into LIQUEFIED NATURAL GAS.

Liquefied natural gas (LNG)   Natural gas that has been cooled and at which point it is condensed into a liquid that is colorless, odorless, non-corrosive, and non-toxic.

Liquefied petroleum gases (LPG)   Hydrocarbon materials lighter than gasoline, such as ethane, propane, and butane, which are kept in a liquid state through compression and/or refrigeration and are marketed for various industrial and domestic gas uses. Commonly referred to as bottled gas.

Local distribution company (LDCs)   Companies that own and operate electricity distribution systems, or natural gas distribution systems, also known as distributors.

Longwall mining   An underground mining method wherein hydraulic supports are used to brace the mine roof while large machines cut and remove the coal from the coal face; once a seam is mined out, the hydraulic supports are removed and the roof is allowed to collapse.

Low-level waste   Consists of industrial clothing, tools, and equipment, which have become slightly contaminated by radioactivity. These wastes comprise most of the nuclear power industry's waste volume, and they are stored at the REACTOR site or at dedicated waste management facilities.

Measurement-while-drilling (MWD) tool   Technology that transmits information from measuring devices within the well to the surface while drilling is ongoing.

Megawatt   A measure of bulk electric power; the unit is generally used to describe the output of an electric generator.

Midstream   The processing, storage, and transportation sector of the petroleum industry.

NERC   Stands for North American Electric Reliability Counci, which publishes standards designed to maintain reliable electric service in North America.

Non-renewable resources   Natural resources that cannot be replaced after they have been consumed. The term applies particularly to FOSSIL FUELS such as coal, oil, and natural gas, but also refers to other mineral resources.

Nuclear Regulatory Commission (NRC)   Licenses operators of nuclear power plants.

Ocean energy systems   Energy conversion technologies that harness the energy in ocean waves, tides, and the thermal gradients (heat) in the oceans.

Octane   A performance rating of gasoline; the higher the octane number, the greater the anti-knock quality of the gasoline.

Offshore platform   A fixed structure from which wells are drilled offshore for the production of oil and natural gas.

OPEC   The Organization of Petroleum Exporting Counties, an international oil cartel that includes Saudi Arabia, Kuwait, Iran, Iraq, Venezuela, Qatar, Libya, Indonesia, United Arab Emirates, Algeria, Nigeria, Ecuador, and Gabon.

Open pit   A method of SURFACE MINING where the coal seams are too deep for STRIP MINING but accessible through deep excavations.

Particulate matter   Dust, ash, soot, metals, and other tiny bits of solid or liquid particles that can cause health problems released into the air. Particulate matter derive from natural sources (such as forest fires and volcanoes) and human sources (such as burning of FOSSIL FUELS, dust from mining operations, road dust, and wood burning in stoves and chimneys).

Permeability   The capacity of a substance (such as rock) to transmit a fluid. The degree of permeability depends on the number, size, and shape of the pores and/or fractures in the substance and their interconnections.

Petrochemicals   Chemicals derived from petroleum that are used as FEEDSTOCKS for the manufacture of a variety of plastics and other products, such as synthetic rubber.

Photovoltaics   Thin silicone wafers that convert any light, not only sunlight, directly into electricity.

Polychlorinated biphenyls (PCBs)   A group of synthetic organic compounds containing chlorine, formerly used as insulating fluids in electrical equipment.

Porosity   The ratio of the aggregate volume of pore spaces in rock or soil to its total volume, usually stated as a percent.

Power tower   Type of concentrating solar power system that employs a field of mirrors to track the Sun and focus its light onto a single point on a tower. At this focal point, a fluid is heated and passed through a steam TURBINE to generate electricity.

Radon   Clear, odorless, radioactive gas that occurs naturally in the environment and is produced by the radioactive decay of uranium. Radon is not dangerous in open air, but in confined spaces, where it accumulates, it can be a health hazard.

Reactor   Vessel in which nuclear fission is controlled and harnessed.

Regasification   The process by which LIQUEFIED NATURAL GAS is heated, converting it into its gaseous state.

Renewable energy Naturally-occurring energy sources that are continually replenished. Examples include wind, solar light, and water.

Reservoir A natural underground container of liquids, such as water or steam (or, in the petroleum context, oil or gas).

Room and pillar mining A mining method wherein sizeable volumes of coal are removed (the "rooms") leaving large pillars of coal to support the mine roof.

Rotary drilling A method of drilling wells using a cutting tool bit attached to the lower end of a revolving drill pipe.

Rotor The assembly of blades and hub on a wind TURBINE.

Seismic surveys Studies using sound waves to create detailed models of underlying geological formations and to find oil and natural gas RESERVOIRs.

Service rig A truck-mounted rig, usually smaller than a drilling rig, that is brought in to complete a well or to perform maintenance, replace equipment, or improve production.

Solar dish system A system that uses mirrors clustered in the general shape of a parabolic (curved) dish to focus SOLAR ENERGY onto a heat engine positioned at the focal point of the mirrors. The heat engine converts solar energy into electricity.

Solar energy Radiant energy produced and transmitted to the Earth's surface by the Sun.

Solar farm Facility where many PHOTOVOLTAIC modules are interconnected in arrays to generate power. These are usually one MEGAWATT or more in generating capacity.

Solar thermal energy systems Systems that use concentrating COLLECTORs to focus the Sun's radiant energy onto or into receivers to produce heat.

Strip mining A method of SURFACE MINING used where the coal seams are very shallow and extensive.

Sub-bituminous coal Black coal softer than BITUMINOUS.

Substation An electrical facility where the VOLTAGE of incoming and outgoing circuits is changed and controlled.

Surface mining The process of removing soil and rock to expose and remove coal.

Tailings Waste products from the mining, extraction, and upgrading process.

Thermal plants Power plants that burn fuels such as coal, oil, or natural gas to produce steam to generate electricity.

Transformer An electromagnetic device for changing alternating current (AC) electricity to higher or lower VOLTAGES.

Transmission line Structures and CONDUCTORS that carry bulk supplies of electrical energy from power-generating units.

Turbine A bladed, rotating engine activated by the reaction or impulse, or both, of a directed current of fluid. In electric power applications, such as geothermal plants, the turbine is attached to and spins a generator to produce electricity.

Upstream The exploration and production sector of the petroleum industry.

Voltage A measure of the electric pressure that pushes electric current through a circuit (just as pressure causes water to flow in a pipe).

Watt A common measure of electrical power, which equals the power used when one AMPERE of current flows through an electric circuit with a potential (electrical pressure) of one volt. Commonly quoted as kW (kilowatts or 1,000 watts) or mW (MEGAWATTS or 1,000,000 watts).

Wellbore A hole drilled or bored into the earth, usually cased with metal pipe, for the production of gas or oil.

Wellhead The equipment used to maintain surface control of a well.

Well logging Assessing the geologic, engineering, and physical properties and characteristics of geothermal RESERVOIRs with instruments placed in the WELLBORE.

Wind energy Energy from moving air which is converted to electricity by using wind to turn electricity generators.

Wind farm Cluster of wind TURBINEs for generating electricity. These are set up in areas where there are steady and prevalent winds.

Wind tower Tubular tower, made of steel, to support a TURBINE. Because wind speed increases with height, taller towers help turbines to capture more WIND ENERGY and generate more electricity.

Wireline logging tools Special tools or equipment, such as logging tools, packers, or measuring devices (to gauge PERMEABILITY, POROSITY, and electrical properties of RESERVOIR fluids), designed to be lowered into a drilling well on a wireline (small-diameter steel cable).

BIBLIOGRAPHY

Ackerman, Thomas (ed.). *Wind Power in Power Systems.* Hoboken, N.J.: John Wiley & Sons, 2005.

Aubrecht, Gordon J. *Energy: Physical, Environmental, and Social Impact.* 3d ed. Upper Saddle River, N.J.: Pearson/Prentice Hall, 2006.

Beaty, H. Wayne. *Electric Power Distribution Systems: A Nontechnical Guide.* Tulsa, Okla.: PennWell Group, 1998.

Bevelacqua, Joseph John. *Basic Health Physics: Problems and Solutions.* Hoboken, N.J.: Wiley-Interscience, 1999.

Blanchard, Roger D. *The Future of Global Oil Production: Facts, Figures, Trends and Projections, by Region.* Jefferson, N.C.: McFarland, 2005

Bradfer, T. *Solar Revolution: The Economic Transformation of the Global Energy Industry.* Cambridge, Mass.: MIT Press, 2006.

Breeze, Paul. *Power Generation Technologies.* Philadelphia, Pa.: Elsevier Science & Technology Books, 2005.

Bureau of Labor Statistics, U.S. Department of Labor. *Career Guide to Industries, 2006–07 Edition.* Oil and Gas Extraction. Available online at http://www.bls.gov/oco/cg/cgs005.htm.

———. *National Industry-Specific Occupational Employment and Wage Estimates, May 2005.* Electric Power Generation, Transmission and Distribution. Available online at http://www.bls.gov/oes/current/oessrci.htm.

———. *Occupational Outlook Handbook, 2006–07 Edition.* Accountants and Auditors. Available online at http://www.bls.gov/oco/ocos001.htm.

———. *Occupational Outlook Handbook, 2006–07 Edition.* Assemblers and Fabricators. Available online at http://www.bls.gov/oco/ocos217.htm.

———. *Occupational Outlook Handbook, 2006–07 Edition.* Atmospheric Scientists. Available online at http://www.bls.gov/oco/ocos051.htm.

———. *Occupational Outlook Handbook, 2006–07 Edition.* Brickmasons, Blockmasons, and Stonemasons. Available online at http://www.bls.gov/oco/ocos201.htm.

———. *Occupational Outlook Handbook, 2006–07 Edition.* Carpenters. Available online at http://www.bls.gov/oco/ocos202.htm.

———. *Occupational Outlook Handbook, 2006–07 Edition.* Chemists and Materials Scientists. Available online at http://www.bls.gov/oco/ocos049.htm.

———. *Occupational Outlook Handbook, 2006–07 Edition.* Construction and Extraction Occupations. Available online at http://www.bls.gov/oco/oco20057.htm.

———. *Occupational Outlook Handbook, 2006–07 Edition.* Customer Service Representatives. Available online at http://www.bls.gov/oco/ocos280.htm.

———. *Occupational Outlook Handbook, 2006–07 Edition.* Electrical and Electronics Installers and Repairers. Available online at http://www.bls.gov/oco/ocos184.htm.

———. *Occupational Outlook Handbook, 2006–07 Edition.* Engineering and Natural Sciences Managers. Available online at http://www.bls.gov/oco/ocos009.htm.

———. *Occupational Outlook Handbook, 2006–07 Edition.* Engineering Technicians. Available online at http://www.bls.gov/oco/ocos112.htm.

———. *Occupational Outlook Handbook, 2006–07 Edition.* Engineers. Available online at http://www.bls.gov/oco/ocos027.htm.

———. *Occupational Outlook Handbook, 2006–07 Edition.* Environmental Scientists and Hydrologists. Available online at http://www.bls.gov/oco/ocos050.htm.

———. *Occupational Outlook Handbook, 2006–07 Edition.* Geoscientists. Available online at http://www.bls.gov/oco/ocos288.htm.

———. *Occupational Outlook Handbook, 2006–07 Edition.* Industrial Machinery Mechanics and Maintenance Workers. Available online at http://www.bls.gov/oco/ocos191.htm.

———. *Occupational Outlook Handbook, 2006–07 Edition.* Line Installers and Repairers. Available online at http://www.bls.gov/oco/ocos195.htm.

———. *Occupational Outlook Handbook, 2006–07 Edition.* Maintenance and Repair Workers, General. Available online at http://www.bls.gov/oco/ocos194.htm.

———. *Occupational Outlook Handbook, 2006–07 Edition.* Market and Survey Researchers. Available online at http://www.bls.gov/oco/ocos013.htm.

———. *Occupational Outlook Handbook, 2006–07 Edition.* Material Moving Occupations. Available online at http://www.bls.gov/oco/ocos243.htm.

———. *Occupational Outlook Handbook, 2006–07 Edition.* Millwrights. Available online at http://www/.bls/gov/oco/ocos190.htm.

———. *Occupational Outlook Handbook, 2006–07 Edition.* Occupational Health and Safety Specialists and Technicians. Available online at heep://www.bls.gov/oco/ocos017.htm.

———. *Occupational Outlook Handbook, 2006–07 Edition.* Physicists and Astronomers. Available online at http://www.bls.gov/oco/ocos052.htm.

————. *Occupational Outlook Handbook, 2006–07 Edition*. Pipelayers, Plumbers, Pipefitters, and Steamfitters. Available online at http://www.bls.gov/oco/ocos211.htm.

————. *Occupational Outlook Handbook, 2006–07 Edition*. Power Plant Operators, Distributors, and Dispatchers. Available online at http://www.bls.gov/oco/ocos227.htm.

————. *Occupational Outlook Handbook, 2006–07 Edition*. Production Occupations. Available online at http://www.bls.gov/oco/oco20059.htm.

————. *Occupational Outlook Handbook, 2006–07 Edition*. Public Relations Specialists. Available online at http://www.bls.gov/oco/ocos086.htm.

————. *Occupational Outlook Handbook, 2006–07 Edition*. Science Technicians. Available online at http://www.bls.gov/oco/ocos115.htm.

————. *Occupational Outlook Handbook, 2006–07 Edition*. Sheet Metal Workers. Available online at http://www/.bls.gov.oco/ocos214.htm.

————. *Occupational Outlook Handbook, 2006–07 Edition*. Structural and Reinforcing Iron and Metal Workers. Available online at http://www.bls.gov/oco/ocos215.htm.

————. *Occupational Outlook Handbook, 2006–07 Edition*. Surveyors, Cartographers, Photogrammetrists, and Surveying Technicians. Available online at http://www.bls.gov/oco/ocos040.htm.

————. *Occupational Outlook Handbook, 2006–07 Edition*. Welding, Soldering, and Brazing Workers. Available online at http://www.bls.gov/oco/ocos226.htm.

Chung, Laura Walker, and the Staff of Vault. *Vault Career Guide to the Energy Industry*. New York: Vault, 2005.

Cohen, Bernard. *The Nuclear Energy Option*. London: Plenum Publishing, 1990.

Conaway, Charles F. *The Petroleum Industry: A Nontechnical Guide*. Tulsa, Okla.: PennWell Publishing, 1999.

DeGalan, Julie, and Bryon Middlekauff. *Great Jobs for Environmental Studies Majors*. New York: VGM Career Books/McGraw-Hill, 2002.

Dickson, Mary H., and Mario Fanelli (eds.). *Geothermal Energy: Utilization and Technology*. Ridley Park, Pa.: Stylus Publisher, 2005.

Duffy, Robert J. *Nuclear Politics in America: A History and Theory of Government Regulation*. Laurence, Kans.: University Press of Kansas, 1997.

Estill, Lyle. *Biodiesel Power: The Passion, the People, and the Politics of the Next Renewable Fuel*. British Columbia, Canada: New Society Publishers, 2005.

Ewing, Rex A. *Power with Nature: Solar and Wind Energy Demystified*. Masonville, Colo.: PixyJack Press, 2004.

Fentiman, Audeen W., and James H. Saling. *Radioactive Waste Management*. 2d ed. New York: Taylor & Francis, 2003.

Finck, Dr. Phillip J. *Statement, as Deputy Associate Laboratory Director Applied Science and Technology and National Security at Argonne National Laboratory, before the U.S. House of Representatives Committee on Science, Energy Subcommittee, during the Hearing on Nuclear Fuel Reprocessing, June 16, 2005*. Available online at http://www.agiweb.org/gap/legis109/yucca_hearings_cont.html#june16.

Gipe, Paul. *Wind Power: Renewable Energy for Home, Farm, and Business*. rev and expanded ed. White River Junction, Vt.: Chelsea Green, 2004.

Goode, James B. *The Cutting Edge: Mining in the 21st Century*. Ashland, Ky.: The Jesse Stuart Foundation, 2000.

Goodell, Jeff. *Big Coal: The Dirty Secret Behind America's Energy Future*. New York: Houghton Mifflin, 2006.

Hala, Jiri, and James E. Navratil. *Radioactivity, Ionizing Radiation, and Nuclear Energy*. Brno, Czech Republic: Knovoj, 2003.

Hayes, Geoffrey. *Coal Mining*. Buckinghamshire, England: Shire Publications, 2004.

Hoffmann, Peter. *Tomorrow's Energy: Hydrogen, Fuel Cells, and the Prospects for a Cleaner Planet*. Cambridge, Mass.: MIT Press, 2001.

Humphries, Marc, ed. *U.S. Coal: A Primer on the Major Issues*. New York: Novinka Books, 2004.

Hyne, Norman J. *Nontechnical Guide to Petroleum Geology, Exploration, Drilling, and Production*. 2d ed. Tulsa, Okla.: PennWell Publishing, 2001.

Jones, David, and Peter Pujado, eds. *Handbook of Petroleum Processing*. New York: Springer, 2006.

Kernot, Charles. *The Coal Industry*. Abington, Cambridge, England: Woodhead Publishing, 2000.

Krueger, Gretchen Dewailly. *Opportunities in Petroleum Careers*. Lincolnwood, Ill.: VGM/NTC Publishing, 1999.

Laird, Frank N. *Solar Energy, Technology Policy and Institutional Values*. New York: Cambridge University Press, 2001.

Langenkamp, R. D. *Handbook of Oil Industry Terms and Phrases*. 5th ed. Tulsa, Okla.: PennWell Publishing, 1994.

Lillington, John. *The Future of Nuclear Power*. Philadelphia, Pa.: Elsevier, 2004.

Manwell, James, et al. *Wind Energy Explained: Theory, Design and Application*. Hoboken, N.J.: John Wiley & Sons, 2002.

McCarthy, John. *Frequently Asked Questions About Nuclear Energy*. Available online at http://www-formal.stanford.edu/jmc/progress/nuclear-faq.html.

McIntyre, Maureen, ed. *Solar Energy: Today's Technologies for a Sustainable Future*. Boulder, Colo.: American Solar Energy Society, 1997.

Meyers, Robert A. *Handbook of Petroleum Refinery Processes*. 3d ed. New York: McGraw-Hill, 2007.

Miller, A., and M. Joyce. *Accelerator Operators and Software Development*. Available online at http://arxiv.org/ftp/physics/papers/0111/0111076.pdf.

Miller, Bruce G. *Coal Energy Systems*. New York: Academic Press, 2004.

Miura, Takatoshi, ed. *Advanced Coal Combustion*. Huntington, N.Y.: Nova Science Publishers, 2001.

Muray, Raymond. *Nuclear Energy: An Introduction to the Concepts, Systems, & Applications of Nuclear Resources*. 6th rev. ed. Philadelphia, Pa.: Elsevier, 2008.

Ocic, Ozren and Bozana Perisic. *Oil Refineries in the 21st Century: Energy Efficient, Cost Effective, Environmentally Benign*. Hoboken, N.J.: John Wiley & Sons, 2005.

Pabla, A. S. *Electric Power Distribution*. New York: McGraw-Hill, 2004.

Pansini, Anthony J. *Guide to Electric Power Distribution Systems*. 6th ed. Kansas City, Mo.: CRC Press, 2005.

Passero, Barbara, ed. *Energy Alternatives*. Farmington Hills, Mich.: Greenhaven Press, 2006.

Patel, Mukind R. *Wind and Solar Power Systems: Design Analysis and Operations*. 2d ed. Kansas City, Mo.: CRC Press, 2005.

Perlin, John. *From Space to Earth: The Story of Solar Electricity*. Boston, Mass.: Harvard University Press, 2002.

Rifkin, Jeremy. *The Hydrogen Economy: The Creation of the Worldwide Energy Web and the Redistribution of Power on Earth*. New York: Tarcher/Putnam, 2002.

Risoluti, Piero, ed. *Nuclear Waste: A Technological and Political Challenge*. New York: Springer, 2004.

Seltzer, Curtis. *Fire in the Hole: Miners and Managers in the American Coal Industry*. Lexington, Ky.: University Press of Kentucky, 1985.

Roberts, Paul. *The End of Oil: On the Edge of a Perilous New World*. Boston, Mass.: Houghton Mifflin, 2004.

Rottenberg, Dan. *In the Kingdom of Coal*. New York: Routledge, 2003.

Shively, Bob, and John Ferrare. *Understanding Today's Electricity Business*. San Francisco, Calif.: Enerdynamics, 2005.

_____. *Understanding Today's Natural Gas Business*. San Francisco, Calif.: Enerdynamics, 2005.

Suppes, Galen J., and Truman Storvich. *Sustainable Nuclear Power*. Philadelphia, Pa.: Elsevier, 2006.

Telles, Marco A. *Wind Energy: Technology, Commercial Projects, and Laws*. Hauppauge, N.Y.: Nova Science Publishers, 2006.

Vaitheeswaran, Vijay V. *Power to the People: How the Coming Energy Revolution Will Transform an Industry, Change Our Lives, and Maybe Even Save the Planet*. New York: Farrar, Straus & Giroux, 2003.

Van Krevelen, D. W. *Coal*. 3d ed. Philadelphia, Pa.: Elsevier Science, 1993.

Warkentin-Glenn, Denise. *Electric Power Industry in Nontechnical Language*. 2d ed. Tulsa, Okla.: PennWell Publishing, 2006.

Woodburn, John H. *Opportunities in Energy Careers*. Lincolnwood, Ill.: VGM/NTC Publishing, 1992.

INDEX

ABOUT THE AUTHORS

ALLAN TAYLOR, a freelance author, editor, indexer, and researcher, comes from a family long involved in the publishing and newspaper industries, and, as a production manager, has participated in the computerization of bibliographic and scientific/technical databases. He is the coauthor of *Career Opportunities in Writing, Career Opportunities in Television and Cable, Career Opportunities in the Internet, Video Games, and Multimedia,* and *The Encyclopedia of Ethnic Groups in Hollywood* (all Facts On File), and a freelance editor and indexer for such publishers as Aurum Press, Belle Publishing, Contemporary Books, Hoover Institution Press, John Wiley & Sons, Kensington Books, McFarland & Company, Routledge, St. Martin's Press, Scarecrow Press, Seven Locks Press, and Thunder's Mouth Press. In addition, he has created special bibliographic indexes for such volumes as *The Great Spy Pictures, Hollywood Songsters, 101 Things I Don't Know About Art, Questions and Answers About Community Associations,* and *Women Doctors Guide to Health and Healing.*

Mr. Taylor's publishing industry posts include tenures at the R. R. Bowker Company (Bibliographic Services), Engineering Information, Inc. (Production Manager), and Graphic Typesetting Services (Proofreading/Technical Specifications Department Manager). He resides in Los Angeles, California. His Web site is at http://www.tataylor.net.

JAMES ROBERT PARISH, a former entertainment reporter, publicist, and book series editor, is the author of many published biographies and reference books about the entertainment industry including *The Hollywood Book of Extravagance, It's Good to Be the King: The Seriously Funny Life of Mel Brooks, The Hollywood Book of Breakups, Fiasco: Hollywood's Iconic Flops, The American Movies Reference Book, The Complete Actors TV Credits, The Hollywood Songsters, The Hollywood Book of Scandals, The Hollywood Book of Death, The RKO Gals, Katharine Hepburn, Whitney Houston, Gus Van Sant,* and *Whoopi Goldberg.* With Allan Taylor he coauthored *Career Opportunities in Writing, Career Opportunities in Television and Cable, Career Opportunities in the Internet, Video Games, and Multimedia,* and *The Encyclopedia of Ethnic Groups in Hollywood* (all Facts On File) and has written several entries in the Ferguson Young Adult biography series (including Gloria Estefan, Jim Henson, Twyla Tharp, Denzel Washington, Katie Couric, Stan Lee, Halle Berry, Steven Spielberg, Tom Hanks, and Stephen King).

Mr. Parish is a frequent on-camera interviewee on cable and network TV for documentaries on the performing arts both in the United States and in the United Kingdom. He resides in Studio City, California. His Web site is at http://www.jamesrobertparish.com.